3e > Readings in
Developmental Psychology

Amy E. Scrima
Judy Buchalski
Lake Michigan College

 Learning Solutions

Boston Burr Ridge, IL Dubuque, IA New York San Francisco St. Louis
Bangkok Bogotá Caracas Lisbon London Madrid
Mexico City Milan New Delhi Seoul Singapore Sydney Taipei Toronto

READINGS IN DEVELOPMENTAL PSYCHOLOGY

4 5 6 7 8 9 0   KNG KNG 14 13

ISBN-13: 978-0-07-804016-0
ISBN-10: 0-07-804016-7

Learning Solutions Representative: Ann Hayes
Production Editor: Nichole Birkenholz
Cover Design: Aivo Kivi
Printer/Binder: King Printing

TABLE OF CONTENTS

Preface

Welcome to the third edition of Readings in Developmental Psychology!

Regardless of your major, Human Development is one of the most important topics you will ever study. No matter who you are, you will have many opportunities to apply the ideas in these readings in both your personal and professional life. The main goal of this new edition is to help you learn to identify those opportunities and use your new found knowledge in a meaningful way.

Why a customized book of readings instead of a traditional textbook?

Good question – and there are actually many reasons. First of all, this book is an edited compilation of many text selections and articles, carefully chosen and arranged from many different sources. This allows us much greater flexibility in the content we present and in the way it is presented. The readings in this book should correspond directly to lecture, saving the student time and effort by focusing only on the most relevant information.

We also have included some of our own writings and summaries in an effort to increase understanding of each individual topic as well as how it all fits together. This further allows us to highlight the topics and issues that are of most relevance in the field today. Creating a customized text is also a faster process than that required of a standardized text, which enables us to include the most up to date research developments.

How are the readings organized?

The format for this book is chronological, starting with life's beginnings in utero and ending with a discussion of death and dying. This format was chosen for ease of navigation and accessibility of content. That is not to say that these topics must or should be presented in this order. There are many different approaches to covering content and all should be accommodated with the flexible functionality of this book.

These readings were revised to reflect the most up to date findings in the most relevant topics of developmental psychology today. Presenting these topics in the context of the most recent research is important because the study of human development includes many scientific endeavors (neuroscience, behavioral science, medical science, etc.) of which our understanding is constantly evolving.

About the Editors

Amy Scrima has taught at Lake Michigan College for 8 years and has loved every minute of it. She earned her B.A. at Purdue University and worked with children as a social worker for several years until going to graduate school at Western Michigan University. There she received her M.A. and Ph.D. in applied behavioral science with a focus on instructional design and organizational management. She then worked in the corporate sector developing instructional training programs and systems. She started teaching in graduate school and ended up loving it, which is why she's looking forward to a long and rewarding teaching career, learning and growing with her students. She also loves living in Michigan and being outdoors, especially with her husband and kids.

Judy Buchalski has retired from the classroom after 37 years of teaching psychology and human development classes. That's funny because being a college instructor was something she only intended to do "for awhile". Her undergraduate (Michigan State) and graduate (University of Toledo) training prepared her for a life in research. Since community college teaching offers few chances for empirical research, over the years she sublimated her research urges by teaching research to her students and publishing their work in *The Lake Michigan College Journal of Psychology*. In the future she plans to use her background in developmental psychology to better understand her grandchildren.

This edition is dedicated to our families.

Amy's husband, Brian; her children, Jessi and Parker and her parents, Joe and Kay.

Judy's husband, Spike; her children, Mike and Ellen; her son in law, John; her grandchildren, Phoebe and Matthew and her mom and dad.

Introduction
Understanding Change

Welcome to the study of human development. **Developmental psychology** is the branch of psychology which is devoted to the scientific investigation of the growth and change of human beings through the lifespan. This investigation has been ongoing for about 100 years and in that time the field has acquired its own, unique set of terminology. This terminology must be understood if we are to comprehend the fascinating phenomena involved in the process of human development. In recognition of the importance of a growing psychological vocabulary, readers will often find key words and phrases in bold throughout the text.

Opportunities for Change

All development involves change of some sort. Indeed, for our purposes, development is nearly synonymous with change. Most of the changes an organism undergoes take place during specific periods of time. These periods of development have a beginning and an end, so it is appropriate to refer to them as time frames. Most aspects of physical development are governed by critical periods. **A critical period is a time frame during which some aspect of development must happen.** If maturation does not occur within this space of time, it will never take place. For example, a healthy human embryo develops arm buds approximately 30 days after fertilization. By day 33, these arm buds should begin segmenting into shoulder, arm, and hand regions. If an embryo does not develop arm buds during this time period, functional arms will never form. It is not possible to reattempt arm bud formation once this short critical period has passed.

By contrast, other developmental phenomena are said to take place within sensitive periods. **A sensitive period is a time frame during which some aspect of development can occur most easily and most efficiently.** Therefore, it might be said that a sensitive period is the *ideal time* for some aspect of development to occur. Development can happen later as well, though probably not as easily or quickly. For example, the minutes and hours immediately following birth are a sensitive period for bonding between a newborn and its primary and secondary caregivers. If for some reason bonding cannot begin immediately, it can occur later, but because this is an ideal time to establish emotional connection, parents are strongly encouraged to begin forming those powerful attachment relationships right away. In another developmental arena, it is easier for toddlers to learn two languages at once than it is for adults to later take on a second language. This is because the first few years of life function as a sensitive period for the acquisition of language. In general, we see that sensitive periods constitute optimal opportunities for development. However, some latitude is available if these opportunities are delayed. Notice, too, that sensitive periods are a bit less sharply delineated than critical periods.

Types of Change

When we are asked to consider development, we almost always think first of growth. For example, it is obvious that you have many more cells in your body today than you did when you were small. You are taller now, and you most certainly weigh more. These are all evidences that your body has grown. Your knowledge base has grown as well. You can spell and define more words that you were able to master when you were in grade school. In general, your knowledge of the world has expanded. You simply know more. Therefore, for purposes of this discussion, **growth is synonymous with quantitative change, an increase in the amount of something.**

But if quantitative change were all that you had experienced since birth, you would simply look like a five to six-foot tall baby—massively round head and all—rather than having the characteristic appearance of an adult. Obviously, something more than simple growth has occurred in the years since your birth. Your body has not just increased in size; you have matured as well. The term **maturation refers to qualitative change, a change in the specific properties and overall functionality of an organism.** Maturation is not just more of the same thing; maturation is transformation. Caterpillars do not simply grow into bigger caterpillars; over time they transform into butterflies and moths. By the same token, if all you had done was quantitatively increase your knowledge over the years, you would certainly know *more than you did as a child,* but you would still "know" or experience the world as a child...simply, directly, concretely. Instead you are able to think and problem-solve like an adult, using analogies and abstractions, in your search for meaning.

Gesell's Trends of Physical Development

As head of the Yale Child Guidance Clinic for years, researcher Arnold Gesell contributed greatly to the current knowledge base of infant and child behavior. He is known widely for his landmark normative studies, and he is credited with identifying four major trends that govern physical development.

The first of these four trends, the **cephalocaudal trend dictates that development proceeds longitudinally, beginning in the head region of the body and gradually working downward toward the tail region.** This means that changes take place first in the body's upper half. This is the reason that the head of a growing embryo is identifiable long before any other embryonic body parts. Gesell's trends describe how our bodies come into being, but they also describe the pattern of emergence of our physical behaviors as well. Therefore, another example of the cephalocaudal trend would be the observation that infants and toddlers are able to successfully coordinate arm movements before leg movements.

The **proximal-distal trend predicts that all development begins at the midpoint of the body and then spreads out to the extremities.** As mentioned above, human embryos develop arm buds before hands form. Hands, in turn, develop before finger segments or finger outlines can form. This is an example of proximal-distal development at work.

But, as Gesell discovered, developmental trends are not merely directional. In fact, the **bilateral trend demonstrates a preservation of body symmetry through simultaneous growth of limb or organ pairs.** For example, both legs develop at the same time, as do both kidneys. This maintains relative latitudinal equality between the left and right sides of the body.

The last of Gesell's developmental trends is differentiation. **Differentiation is the trend toward ever-increasing functional specialization.** The starkest example of this occurs in the first week of prenatal development. After fertilization of the ovum, the resulting zygote multiplies into a mass of undifferentiated cells, each cell exactly like every other. From this point, the cells begin to change or *specialize* into three tissue layers, which then further specialize into body organs and organ systems.

Differentiation is a very useful concept. Developmental psychologists note that the concept of differentiation is not limited to physical development. Indeed, it can also be used to better understand the *qualitative change* of psychological aspects of development. For example, differentiation can be used to describe the development of emotional expression and experience. Emotion begins with a general state of excitement in the newborn and then becomes increasingly more specific, as many different forms of positive and negative emotions emerge throughout the first five years of childhood.

Another application of differentiation is language development. Each baby starts with a very basic preverbal repertoire of sounds which he shares with infants all over the world. Over time we each come to speak a very different native tongue. As years pass, we add more words to our vocabularies (quantitative change), but we also change the ways we use those words. For example, we develop the ability to communicate with others when they are not physically present by using written language (qualitative change). You will find many examples of these concepts, throughout the stages of development, in the readings to follow.

Chapter 1
Prenatal Development

Our first chapter focuses on a period of development many take for granted – development in utero. New research continues to confirm the impacts of the internal and external environment on the developing zygote, embryo and fetus. We will examine the physical and functional changes that occur during pregnancy and the many possible effects on this process by the outside environment as well as the internal conditions of the mother. Be thinking about the many complex variables that can occur during these nine months and what a physiologically amazing process reproduction actually is. And this is just the beginning!

What are the three stages of prenatal development, and what happens during each stage?

gestation Period of development between conception and birth.

gestational age Age of an unborn baby, usually dated from the first day of an expectant mother's last menstrual cycle.

Prenatal Development: Three Stages

For many women, the first clear (though not necessarily reliable) sign of pregnancy is a missed menstrual period. But even before that first missed period, a pregnant woman's body undergoes subtle but noticeable changes. Table 4-1 lists early signs and symptoms of pregnancy. Although these signs are not unique to pregnancy, a woman who experiences one or more of them may wish to take a home pregnancy test or to seek medical confirmation that she is pregnant.

During **gestation,** the period between conception and birth, an unborn child undergoes dramatic processes of development. The normal range of gestation is between 37 and 41 weeks (Martin et al., 2009). **Gestational age** is usually dated from the first day of an expectant mother's last menstrual cycle.

Prenatal (prebirth) development takes place in three stages: *germinal, embryonic,* and *fetal.* (Table 4-2 gives a month-by-month description.) During these three stages of gestation, the fertilized ovum, or *zygote,* grows into an *embryo* and then a *fetus.*

Table 4-1 Early Signs and Symptoms of Pregnancy	
Physical Change	**Causes and Timing**
Tender, swollen breasts or nipples	Increased production of the female hormones estrogen and progesterone stimulates breast growth to prepare for producing milk (most noticeable in a first pregnancy).
Fatigue; need to take extra naps	Woman's heart is pumping harder and faster to produce extra blood to carry nutrients to the unborn baby. Stepped-up production of hormones takes extra effort. Progesterone depresses central nervous system and may cause sleepiness. Concerns about pregnancy may sap energy.
Slight bleeding or cramping	*Implantation bleeding* may occur about 10 to 14 days after fertilization when fertilized ovum attaches to lining of uterus. Many women also have cramps (similar to menstrual cramps) as the uterus begins to enlarge.
Nausea with or without vomiting	Rising levels of estrogen produced by placenta and fetus cause stomach to empty more slowly. Also, heightened sense of smell may trigger nausea in response to certain odors, such as coffee, meat, dairy products, or spicy foods. *Morning sickness* may begin as early as 2 weeks after conception, but usually around 4 to 8 weeks, and may occur at any time of day.
Food cravings	Hormonal changes may alter food preferences, especially during first trimester, when hormones have greatest impact.
Frequent urination	Enlarging uterus during first trimester exerts pressure on the bladder.
Frequent, mild headaches	Increased blood circulation caused by hormonal changes may bring on headaches.
Constipation	Increase in progesterone may slow digestion, food passes more slowly through intestinal tract.
Mood swings	Flood of hormones early in pregnancy can produce emotional highs and lows.
Faintness and dizziness	Lightheaded feeling may be triggered by blood vessel dilation and low blood pressure; also may be triggered by low blood sugar.
Raised basal body temperature	Basal body temperature (taken first thing in the morning) normally rises soon after ovulation each month and then drops during menstruation. When menstruation ceases, temperature remains elevated.

Source: Mayo Clinic, 2005.

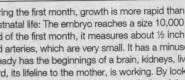

Month	Description

1 month

During the first month, growth is more rapid than at any other time during prenatal or postnatal life: The embryo reaches a size 10,000 times greater than the zygote. By the end of the first month, it measures about ½ inch in length. Blood flows through its veins and arteries, which are very small. It has a minuscule heart, beating 65 times a minute. It already has the beginnings of a brain, kidneys, liver, and digestive tract. The umbilical cord, its lifeline to the mother, is working. By looking very closely through a microscope, it is possible to see the swellings on the head that will eventually become eyes, ears, mouth, and nose. Its sex cannot yet be detected.

7 weeks

By the end of the second month, the fetus is less than 1 inch long and weighs only ⅓ ounce. Its head is half its total body length. Facial parts are clearly developed, with tongue and teeth buds. The arms have hands, fingers, and thumbs, and the legs have knees, ankles, and toes. The fetus has a thin covering of skin and can make handprints and footprints. Bone cells appear at about 8 weeks. Brain impulses coordinate the function of the organ system. Sex organs are developing; the heartbeat is steady. The stomach produces digestive juices; the liver, blood cells. The kidneys remove uric acid from the blood. The skin is now sensitive enough to react to tactile stimulation. If an aborted 8-week-old fetus is stroked, it reacts by flexing its trunk, extending its head, and moving back its arms.

3 months

By the end of the third month, the fetus weighs about 1 ounce and measures about 3 inches in length. It has fingernails, toenails, eyelids (still closed), vocal cords, lips, and a prominent nose. Its head is still large—about one-third its total length—and its forehead is high. Sex can easily be detected. The organ systems are functioning, and so the fetus may now breathe, swallow amniotic fluid into the lungs and expel it, and occasionally urinate. Its ribs and vertebrae have turned into cartilage. The fetus can now make a variety of specialized responses: It can move its legs, feet, thumbs, and head; its mouth can open and close and swallow. If its eyelids are touched, it squints; if its palm is touched, it makes a partial fist; if its lip is touched, it will suck; and if the sole of the foot is stroked, the toes will fan out. These reflexes will be present at birth but will disappear during the first months of life.

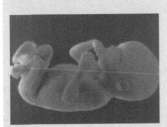

4 months

The body is catching up to the head, which is now only one-fourth the total body length, the same proportion it will be at birth. The fetus now measures 8 to 10 inches and weighs about 6 ounces. The umbilical cord is as long as the fetus and will continue to grow with it. The placenta is now fully developed. The mother may be able to feel the fetus kicking, a movement known as *quickening,* which some societies and religious groups consider the beginning of human life. The reflex activities that appeared in the third month are now brisker because of increased muscular development.

5 months

The fetus, now weighing about 12 ounces to 1 pound and measuring about 1 foot, begins to show signs of an individual personality. It has definite sleep-wake patterns, has a favorite position in the uterus (called its *lie*), and becomes more active—kicking, stretching, squirming, and even hiccuping. By putting an ear to the mother's abdomen, it is possible to hear the fetal heartbeat. The sweat and sebaceous glands are functioning. The respiratory system is not yet adequate to sustain life outside the womb; a baby born at this time does not usually survive. Coarse hair has begun to grow for eyebrows and eyelashes, fine hair is on the head, and a woolly hair called *lanugo* covers the body.

(continue)

Table 4-2	Prenatal Development (*continued*)

Month	Description
 6 months	The rate of fetal growth has slowed down a little—by the end of the sixth month, the fetus is about 14 inches long and weighs 1¼ pounds. It has fat pads under the skin; the eyes are complete, opening, closing, and looking in all directions. It can hear, and it can make a fist with a strong grip. A fetus born during the sixth month still has only a slight chance of survival because the breathing apparatus has not matured. However, medical advances have made survival increasingly likely.
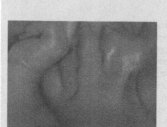 7 months	By the end of the seventh month, the fetus, about 16 inches long and weighing 3 to 5 pounds, has fully developed reflex patterns. It cries, breathes, and swallows, and it may suck its thumb. The lanugo may disappear at about this time, or it may remain until shortly after birth. Head hair may continue to grow. The chances that a fetus weighing at least 3½ pounds will survive are good, provided it receives intensive medical attention. It will probably need to be kept in an isolette until a weight of 5 pounds is attained.
 8 months	The 8-month-old fetus is 18 to 20 inches long and weighs between 5 and 7 pounds. It living quarters are becoming cramped, and so its movements are curtailed. During this month and the next, a layer of fat develops over the fetus's entire body, which will enable it to adjust to varying temperatures outside the womb.
 9 months—newborn	About a week before birth, the fetus stops growing, having reached an average weight of about 7½ pounds and a length of about 20 inches, with boys tending to be a little longer and heavier than girls. Fat pads continue to form, the organ systems are operating more efficiently, the heart rate increases, and more wastes are expelled through the umbilical cord. The reddish color of the skin is fading. At birth, the fetus will have been in the womb for about 266 days, although gestational age is usually estimated at 280 days because most doctors date the pregnancy from the mother's last menstrual period.

Note: Even in these early stages, individuals differ. The figures and descriptions given here represent averages.

What turns a single-celled zygote into a creature with a specific shape and pattern? Research suggests that an identifiable group of genes is responsible for this transformation in vertebrates, presumably including human beings. These genes produce molecules called *morphogens,* which are switched on after fertilization and begin sculpting arms, hands, fingers, vertebrae, ribs, a brain, and other body parts (Echeland et al., 1993; Krauss, Concordet, & Ingham, 1993; Riddle, Johnson, Laufer, & Tabin, 1993).

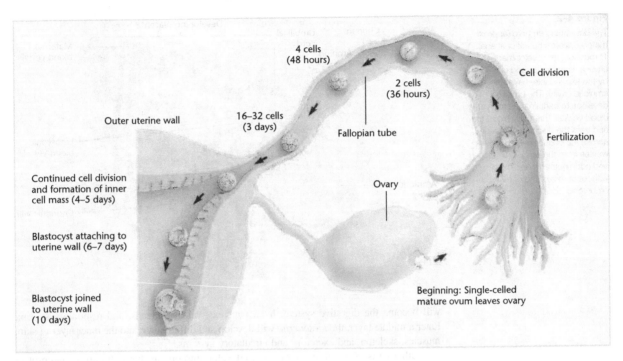

Figure 4-1

Early development of a human embryo. This simplified diagram shows the progress of the ovum as it leaves the ovary, is fertilized in the fallopian tube, and then divides while traveling to the lining of the uterus. Now a blastocyst, it is implanted in the uterus, where it will grow larger and more complex until it is ready to be born.

Both before and after birth, development proceeds according to two fundamental principles: Growth and motor development occur from the top down and from the center of the body outward.

The **cephalocaudal principle** (from Latin, meaning "head to tail") dictates that development proceeds from the head to the lower part of the trunk. An embryo's head, brain, and eyes develop earliest and are disproportionately large until the other parts catch up. At 2 months of gestation, the embryo's head is half the length of the body. By the time of birth, the head is only one-fourth the length of the body but is still disproportionately large. According to the **proximodistal principle** (from Latin, "near to far"), development proceeds from parts near the center of the body to outer ones. The embryo's head and trunk develop before the limbs, and the arms and legs before the fingers and toes.

The Germinal Stage (Fertilization to 2 Weeks)

During the **germinal stage,** the first 2 weeks after fertilization, the zygote divides, becomes more complex, and is implanted in the wall of the uterus (Figure 4-1).

Within 36 hours after fertilization, the zygote enters a period of rapid cell division and duplication, or *mitosis*. Some 72 hours after fertilization, it has divided into 16 to 32 cells; 24 hours later it has 64 cells.

While the fertilized ovum is dividing, it is also making its way down the fallopian tube to the uterus, a journey of 3 or 4 days. Its form changes into a *blastocyst*, a fluid-filled sphere, which floats freely in the uterus until the 6th day after fertilization, when it begins to implant itself in the uterine wall. Only about 10 to 20 percent of fertilized ova complete the task of implantation and continue to develop.

Before implantation, as cell differentiation begins, some cells around the edge of the blastocyst cluster on one side to form the *embryonic disk*, a thickened cell mass from which the embryo begins to develop. This mass is already differentiating into two layers. The upper layer, the *ectoderm*, will become the outer layer of skin, the nails, hair, teeth, sensory organs, and the nervous system, including the brain and spinal cord. The lower layer, the *endoderm,*

cephalocaudal principle Principle that development proceeds in a head-to-tail direction; that is, that upper parts of the body develop before lower parts of the trunk.

proximodistal principle Principle that development proceeds from within to without; that is, that parts of the body near the center develop before the extremities.

germinal stage First 2 weeks of prenatal development, characterized by rapid cell division, increasing complexity and differentiation, and implantation in the wall of the uterus.

Figure 4-2

The developing embryo (approximately 6 weeks gestational age). Throughout its development, the embryo is enclosed and cushioned by the expandable, fluid-filled amniotic cavity. The umbilical cord develops to cantain the embryonic blood vessels that carry blood to and from the placenta. Diffusion across the chorionic villi removes wastes from the embryonic blood and adds nutrients and oxygen without commingling of maternal of embryonic blood.

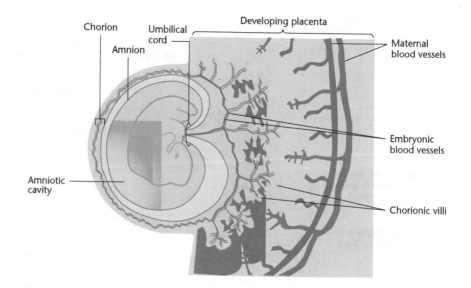

will become the digestive system, liver, pancreas, salivary glands, and respiratory system. Later a middle layer, the *mesoderm,* will develop and differentiate into the inner layer of skin, muscles, skeleton, and excretory and circulatory systems.

Other parts of the blastocyst begin to develop into organs that will nurture and protect the embryo: the *amniotic cavity,* or *amniotic sac,* with its outer layers, the *amnion* and *chorion,* the *placenta,* and the *umbilical cord* (Figure 4-2). The *amniotic sac* is a fluid-filled membrane that encases the developing embryo, giving it room to move. The *placenta,* which contains both maternal and embryonic tissue, develops in the uterus to allow oxygen, nourishment, and wastes to pass between mother and embryo. It is connected to the embryo by the *umbilical cord.* Nutrients from the mother pass from her blood to the embryonic blood vessels and are then carried, via the umbilical cord, to the embryo. In turn, embryonic blood vessels in the umbilical cord carry embryonic wastes to the placenta, where they can be eliminated by maternal blood vessels. The mother's and embryo's circulatory systems are not directly linked; instead, this exchange occurs by diffusion across the blood vessel walls. The placenta also helps to combat internal infection and gives the unborn child immunity to various diseases. It produces the hormones that support pregnancy, prepare the mother's breasts for lactation, and eventually stimulate the uterine contractions that will expel the baby from the mother's body. In short, it is a complex life support system for the developing child.

The Embryonic Stage (2 to 8 Weeks)

embryonic stage Second stage of prenatal development (2 to 8 weeks), characterized by rapid growth and development of major body systems and organs.

During the **embryonic stage,** from about 2 to 8 weeks, the organs and major body systems—respiratory, digestive, and nervous—develop rapidly. This is a critical period when the embryo is most vulnerable to destructive influences in the prenatal environment (Figure 4-3). Any organ system or structure that is developing at the time of exposure is most likely to be affected. Because of this, defects that occur later in pregnancy are likely to be less serious as the major organ systems and physical structures of the body are complete.

spontaneous abortion Natural expulsion from the uterus of a embryo that cannot survive outside the womb; also called *miscarriage.*

The most severely defective embryos usually do not survive beyond the first *trimester,* or 3-month period, of pregnancy. A **spontaneous abortion,** commonly called a *miscarriage,* is the expulsion from the uterus of an embryo or fetus that is unable to survive outside the womb. As many as 1 in 4 recognized pregnancies end in miscarriage, and the actual figure may be as high as 1 in 2 because many spontaneous abortions take place before the woman realizes she is pregnant. About 3 out of 4 miscarriages occur during the first trimester (Neville, n.d.).

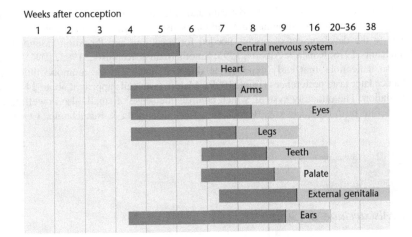

Weeks after conception

Figure 4-3
When birth defects occur. Body parts and systems are most vulnerable to damage when they are developing most rapidly (*darkly shaded areas*), generally within the first trimester of pregnancy.
Note: Intervals of time are not all equal.
Source: J. E. Brody, 1995; data from March of Dimes.

The Puritans in colonial New England believed that miscarriages could be brought on by violent passion, such as grief or anger, or by violent movements, as in dancing, running, or horseback riding (Reese, 2000). We now know that most miscarriages result from abnormal pregnancies; about 50 to 70 percent involve chromosomal abnormalities (Hogge, 2003) and result in miscarriages mainly in early stages of pregnancy. Smoking, drinking alcohol, and drug use increase the risks of miscarriage later in pregnancy (American College of Obstetricians and Gynecologists, 2002). Losing an unborn baby can be extremely painful, as we discuss in Box 4-1.

Males are more likely than females to be spontaneously aborted or to be *stillborn* (dead at or after the 20th week of gestation). Thus, although about 125 males are concieved for every 100 females, only about 105 boys are born for every 100 girls. Males' greater vulnerability continues after birth: more of them die early in life, and at every age they are more susceptible to many disorders. As a result, there are only 96 males for every 100 females in the United States (Martin et al., 2009; U.S. Department of Health and Human Services [USDHHS] 1996a).

The Fetal Stage (8 Weeks to Birth)

The appearance of the first bone cells at about 8 weeks signals the **fetal stage,** the final stage of gestation. During this period, the fetus grows rapidly to about 20 times its previous length, organs and body systems become more complex, and the fetus puts on a layer of fat in preparation for birth. Right up to that moment, "finishing touches" such as fingernails, toenails, and eyelids continue to develop.

Fetuses are not passive passengers in their mothers' wombs. They breathe, kick, turn, flex their bodies, do somersaults, squint, swallow, make fists, hiccup, and suck their thumbs. The flexible membranes of the uterine walls and amniotic sac, which surround the protective buffer of amniotic fluid, permit and stimulate limited movement. Fetuses also can feel pain, but it is unlikely that they do so before the third trimester (Lee, Ralston, Drey, Partridge, & Rosen, 2005).

Scientists can observe fetal movement through **ultrasound,** the use of high-frequency sound waves to detect the outline of the fetus. Other instruments can monitor heart rate, changes in activity level, states of sleep and wakefulness, and cardiac reactivity.

The movements and activity level of fetuses show marked individual differences, and their heart rates vary in regularity and speed. There also are differences between males and females. Male fetuses, regardless of size, are more active and tend to move more vigorously than female fetuses throughout gestation. Thus infant boys' tendency to be more active than girls may be at least partly inborn (DiPietro, Hodgson, Costigan, Hilton, & Johnson, 1996).

Beginning at about the 12th week of gestation, the fetus swallows and inhales some of the amniotic fluid in which it floats. The amniotic fluid contains substances that cross

fetal stage Final stage of prenatal development (from 8 weeks to birth), characterized by increased differentiation of body parts and greatly enlarged body size.

ultrasound Prenatal medical procedure using high-frequency sound waves to detect the outline of a fetus and its movements, used to determine whether a pregnancy is progressing normally.

the placenta from the mother's bloodstream and enter the fetus's bloodstream. Partaking of these substances may stimulate the budding senses of taste and smell and may contribute to the development of organs needed for breathing and digestion (Mennella & Beauchamp, 1996; Ronca & Alberts, 1995; Smotherman & Robinson, 1995, 1996). There are also indications that early exposure to different flavors in the amniotic fluid may influence later taste preferences (Eliot, 1999). Mature taste cells appear at about 14 weeks of gestation. The olfactory system, which controls the sense of smell, also is well developed before birth (Bartoshuk & Beauchamp, 1994; Mennella & Beauchamp, 1996).

Around the World

Box 4-1 *Mourning a Miscarriage or Stillbirth*

At a Buddhist temple in Tokyo, small statues of infants accompanied by toys and gifts are left as offerings to Jizo, an enlightened being who is believed to watch over miscarried and aborted fetuses and eventually, through reincarnation, to guide them into a new life. The ritual of *mizuko kuyo,* a rite of apology and remembrance, is observed as a means of making amends to the lost life (Orenstein, 2002).

The Japanese word *mizuko* means "water child." Japanese Buddhists believe that life flows into an organism gradually, like water, and a mizuko is somewhere on the continuum between life and death (Orenstein, 2002). In English, in contrast, there is no word for a miscarried, aborted, or stillborn fetus, nor any ritual of mourning. Families, friends, and health professionals tend to avoid talking about such losses, which may seem insignificant compared with the loss of a living child (Van, 2001). Or people make unhelpful comments such as, "It was better this way" or "This happens all the time." (See table for advice on what to say to someone who has suffered a pregnancy loss.) Grief can be more wrenching without social support, and "the silence our society casts over the topic makes it hard for women and families to get the information and help they need" (Grady, 2002, p. 1).

How do prospective parents cope with the loss of a child they never knew? Each person's or couple's experience of loss is unique (Van, 2001). A woman may feel a sense of inadequacy or failure. She may feel anger (at herself or others for not being able to prevent the miscarriage or stillbirth, or at her partner for not being supportive enough), guilt (if the woman had mixed feelings about becoming a mother, or if she thinks the loss of the baby may have resulted from something she did), or anxiety ("Will I be able to have another child?"). Children in the family may blame themselves, especially if they had some negative feelings about the expected birth. The parents may mourn not only for what is now lost but for what the lost child might have become. Feelings of pain and grief may recur, often on the expected due date or on the anniversary of the loss (Neville, n.d.).

Differences in the ways men and women grieve may be a source of tension and divisiveness in a couple's relationship (Caelli, Downie, & Letendre, 2002). The man may have been less focused on the pregnancy, and his body does not give him physical reminders of the loss (Grady, 2002). In one small study, 11 men whose child had died in utero reported being overcome with frustration and helplessness during and after the delivery, but several found relief in supporting their partners (Samuelsson, Radestad, & Segesten, 2001). In another study, grieving parents perceived their spouses and extended families as most helpful and their doctors as least helpful. Some bereaved parents benefited from a support group, and some did not (DiMarco,

Talking to Someone Who Has Had a Miscarriage or Stillbirth

When Speaking to a Friend Who Has Experienced Pregnancy Loss

Do . . .	Bring up the subject; Ignoring the loss can be painful.
	Listen with empathy and compassion.
	Express sadness and regret.
	Let your friend grieve, cry, and take the time necessary to heal.
Don't . . .	Minimize or trivialize the loss or pain.
	Ask why it happened—often there is no real answer.
	Expect your friend to move on before she is ready.

Source: Grady, 2002.

Menke, & McNamara, 2001). Couples who have gone through pregnancy loss may need extra-compassionate care during a later pregnancy (Caelli et al., 2002).

Grief counselors suggest that adjustment to a pregnancy loss may be eased if the parents are allowed to see and hold their deceased baby—something that is often not possible. Here are some other suggestions (Brin, 2004; Grady, 2002; Neville, n.d.):

- Set aside time to talk about the loss.
- Create and hold a memorial ceremony or ritual; online resources may help.
- Name the miscarried or stillborn baby.
- Plant a tree or flowering bush in the lost baby's name.
- Write poetry or keep a journal.
- Put items such as an ultrasound photo, a lock of hair, or a mold of the baby's hands or feet in a memory box.
- Create a special certificate.
- Seek private counseling or a support group. In one study of women who had experienced stillbirth, those who attended support groups had fewer symptoms of traumatic stress than those who did not attend support groups (Cacciatore, 2007).

What's your view ❓

- Have you ever had a spontaneous abortion (miscarriage) or stillbirth, or do you know anyone who has? If so, how did you or your acquaintance cope with the loss? How did others react to it?
- Do you think recognition of such losses through ceremonies or rituals would be helpful?

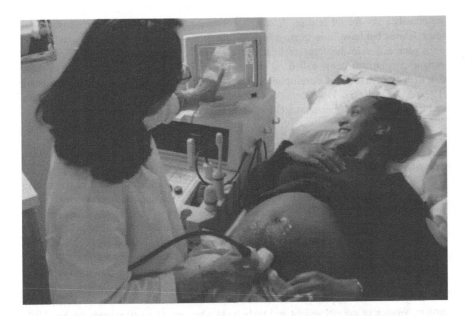

The most effective way to prevent birth complications is early prenatal care, which may include ultrasound checkups, such as this woman is having, to follow the fetus's development. Ultrasound is a diagnostic tool that presents an immediate image of the fetus in the womb.

Fetuses respond to the mother's voice and heartbeat and the vibrations of her body, suggesting that they can hear and feel. Hungry infants, no matter on which side they are held, turn toward the breast in the direction from which they hear the mother's voice (Noirot & Algeria, 1983, cited in Rovee-Collier, 1996). Thus familiarity with the mother's voice may have an evolutionary survival function: to help newborns locate the source of food. Responses to sound and vibration seem to begin at 26 weeks of gestation, rise, and then reach a plateau at about 32 weeks (Kisilevsky, Muir, & Low, 1992).

Fetuses seem to learn and remember. In one experiment, 3-day-old infants sucked more on a nipple that activated a recording of a story their mother had frequently read aloud during the last 6 weeks of pregnancy than they did on nipples that activated recordings of two other stories. Apparently, the infants recognized the pattern of sound they had heard in the womb. A control group, whose mothers had not recited a story before birth, responded equally to all three recordings (DeCasper & Spence, 1986). Similar experiments have found that newborns age 2 to 4 days prefer musical and speech sequences heard before birth. They also prefer their mother's voice to those of other women, female voices to male voices, and their mother's native language to another language (DeCasper & Fifer, 1980; DeCasper & Spence, 1986; Fifer & Moon, 1995; Lecanuet, Granier-Deferre, & Busnel, 1995; Moon, Cooper, & Fifer, 1993). They also seem to show recognition of smell (Varendi, Porter & Wineberg, 1997).

Prenatal Development: Environmental Influences

Maternal Factors

In traditional societies, pregnancy is recognized as a dangerous time for both a woman and her unborn baby. Among the Beng people of West Africa's Ivory Coast, for example, a woman who has "taken a belly" is warned to stay away from corpses, lest her baby be born diseased; not to offend someone who might curse her pregnancy; and not to eat certain foods, such as pureed yams, lest her labor be difficult (Gottlieb, 2000). Such unscientific beliefs have a basis in fact: because the prenatal environment is the mother's body, virtually everything that affects her well-being, from her diet to her moods, may alter her unborn child's environment and influence its growth and health.

A **teratogen** is an environmental agent, such as a virus, a drug, or radiation, that can interfere with normal prenatal development. However, not all environmental hazards

Checkpoint ✔

Can you . . .

✔ Identify two principles that govern physical development and give examples of their application during the prenatal period?

✔ Explain why defects and miscarriages are most likely to occur during the embryonic stage?

✔ Summarize findings about fetal activity, sensory development, and memory?

Guidepost 2

What environmental influences can affect prenatal development?

teratogen Environmental agent, such as a virus, a drug, or radiation, that can interfere with normal prenatal development and cause developmental abnormalities.

are equally risky for all fetuses. An event, substance, or process may be teratogenic for some fetuses but have little or no effect on others. Sometimes vulnerability may depend on a gene either in the fetus or in the mother. For example, fetuses with a particular variant of a growth gene, called *transforming growth factor alpha,* have 6 times more risk than other fetuses of developing a cleft palate if the mother smokes while pregnant (Hwang et al., 1995). The timing of exposure (refer to Figure 4-3), the dose, duration, and interaction with other teratogenic factors also may make a difference.

Nutrition and Maternal Weight

According to the evolutionary biologist David Haig (1993), pregnancy creates an unconscious conflict between a prospective mother and her fetus over the nutrients the mother provides. From an evolutionary perspective, it is adaptive for the fetus to obtain maximum amounts of nutrients from the mother, whereas it is adaptive for the mother to limit the transfer of nutrients to the fetus to maintain her own health and her ability to bear future children. Yet because the fetus has direct access to the maternal blood supply through the placenta, the mother does not have much control over the amount of nutrients she "loses" to her fetus. It is important, then, for an expectant mother to take in enough nutrients to adequately feed both herself and her fetus.

Pregnant women typically need 300 to 500 additional calories a day, including extra protein. Women of normal weight and body build who gain 16 to 40 pounds are less likely to have birth complications or to bear babies whose weight at birth is dangerously low or overly high. Yet about 1 in 3 mothers gain more or less than the recommended amounts (Martin et al., 2009). Either too much or too little weight gain can be risky. If a woman does not gain enough, her baby is likely to suffer growth retardation in the womb, to be born prematurely, to experience distress during labor and delivery, or to die at or near birth. Some research has shown that maternal calorie restriction during pregnancy might put children at risk for later obesity, perhaps by setting their metabolism to be thrifty (Caballero, 2006).

A woman who gains too much weight risks having a large baby that needs to be delivered by induced labor or cesarean section (Chu et al., 2008; Martin et al., 2009). Among 41,540 pregnant U.S. women, those who gained more than 40 pounds doubled their chances of bearing a baby weighing 9 pounds or more. A fetus that large poses serious risks to both mother and baby during delivery and is likely to become overweight or obese later in life (Hillier et al., 2008).

Desirable weight gain depends on body mass index (BMI) before pregnancy. Women who are overweight or obese before becoming pregnant or in the early months of pregnancy tend to have longer deliveries, to need more health care services (Chu et al., 2008), and to bear infants with birth defects (Stothard, Tennant, Bell, & Rankin, 2009; Watkins, Rasmussen, Honein, Botto, & Moore, 2003). A recent study conducted by the U.S. Centers for Disease Control and Prevention of over 12,000 infants found that women who were overweight or obese before pregnancy were about 18 percent more likely than normal weight women to have a baby with certain kinds of heart defects (Gilboa et al., 2009). Obesity also increases the risk of other complications of pregnancy, including miscarriage, difficulty inducing labor, and a greater likelihood of cesarean delivery (Brousseau, 2006; Chu et al., 2008; Cnattingius, Bergstrom, Lipworth, & Kramer, 1998).

What an expectant mother eats is also important. For example, newborns whose mothers ate fish high in DHA, an omega-3 fatty acid found in certain fish, such as Atlantic salmon and tuna, showed more mature sleep patterns (a sign of advanced brain development) than infants whose mothers' blood had lower levels of DHA (Cheruku, Montgomery-Downs, Farkas, Thoman, & Lammi-Keefe, 2002; Colombo et al., 2004) and also were more attentive at 12 and 18 months of age (Colombo et al., 2004).

Only fairly recently have we learned of the critical importance of folic acid, or folate (a B vitamin), in a pregnant woman's diet. For some time, scientists have known that China has the highest incidence in the world of babies born with anencephaly and spina bifida, but it was not until the 1980s that researchers linked that fact with the timing of the babies' conception. Traditionally, Chinese couples marry in January or February and try to conceive as soon as possible. Thus their pregnancies often begin in the winter, when rural women have little access to fresh fruits and vegetables, important sources of folic acid.

After medical detective work established the lack of folic acid as a cause of anencephaly and spina bifida, China embarked on a massive program to give folic acid supplements to prospective mothers. The result was a large reduction in the prevalence of these defects (Berry et al., 1999). Addition of folic acid to enriched grain products has been mandatory since 1998 in the United States, where the incidence of these defects also has fallen (Honein, Paulozzi, Mathews, Erickson, & Wong, 2001). Women of childbearing age are urged to take folate supplements and to include this vitamin in their diets by eating plenty of fresh fruits and vegetables even before becoming pregnant, as damage from folic acid deficiency can occur during the early weeks of gestation (American Academy of Pediatrics [AAP] Committee on Genetics, 1999; Mills & England, 2001). If all women took 5 milligrams of folic acid each day before pregnancy and during the first trimester, an estimated 85 percent of neural-tube defects could be prevented (Wald, 2004).

Vitamin D deficiency during pregnancy in women with a gene variant called DRB1*1501 may increase the risk of a child's developing multiple sclerosis later in life. This gene–environment interaction is most common in northern European regions that get little sunshine, an important source of Vitamin D (Ramagopalan et al., 2009).

Malnutrition

Prenatal malnutrition may have long-range effects. In rural Gambia, in western Africa, people born during the *hungry season,* when foods from the previous harvest are depleted, are 10 times more likely to die in early adulthood than people born during other parts of the year (Moore et al., 1997). In a study done in the United Kingdom, children whose mothers had had low vitamin D levels late in pregnancy showed low bone mineral content at age 9, potentially increasing their risk of osteoporosis in later life (Javaid et al., 2006). And, as we reported in Chapter 3, studies have revealed a link between fetal undernutrition and schizophrenia.

It is important to identify malnutrition early in pregnancy so that it can be treated. Malnourished women who take dietary supplements while pregnant tend to have bigger, healthier, more active, and more visually alert infants (J. L. Brown, 1987; Vuori et al., 1979); and women with low zinc levels who take daily zinc supplements are less likely to have babies with low birth weight and small head circumference (Goldenberg et al., 1995). In a large-scale randomized study of low-income households in 347 Mexican communities, women who took nutrient-fortified dietary supplements while pregnant or lactating tended to have infants who grew more rapidly and were less likely to be anemic (Rivera, Sotres-Alvarez, Habicht, Shamah, & Villalpando, 2004).

Physical Activity and Strenuous Work

Among the Ifaluk people of the Western Caroline Islands, women are advised to refrain from harvesting crops during the first 7 months of pregnancy, when the developing fetus is thought to be weak, but resume manual labor during the last 2 months to encourage a speedy delivery (Le, 2000). Actually, moderate exercise any time during pregnancy does not seem to endanger the fetuses of healthy women (Committee on Obstetric Practice, 2002; Riemann & Kanstrup Hansen, 2000). Regular exercise prevents constipation and improves respiration, circulation, muscle tone, and skin elasticity, all of which contribute to a more comfortable pregnancy and an easier, safer delivery (Committee on Obstetric Practice, 2002). Employment during pregnancy generally entails no special hazards. However, strenuous working conditions, occupational fatigue, and long working hours may be associated with a greater risk of premature birth (Luke et al., 1995).

The American College of Obstetrics and Gynecology (1994) recommends that women in low-risk pregnancies be guided by their own abilities and stamina. The safest course seems to be for pregnant women to exercise moderately, not pushing themselves and not raising their heart rate above 150, and, as with any exercise, to taper off at the end of each session rather than stop abruptly.

Moderate, regular exercise is beneficial for pregnant women and does not seem to endanger the fetus.

Checkpoint

Can you . . .

✔ Summarize recommendations concerning an expectant mother's diet and physical activity?

Drug Intake

Practically everything an expectant mother takes in makes its way to the uterus. Drugs may cross the placenta, just as oxygen, carbon dioxide, and water do. Vulnerability is greatest in the first few months of gestation during the formation of the major systems and structures of the body. What are the effects of the use of specific drugs during pregnancy? Let's look first at medical drugs; then at alcohol, nicotine, and caffeine; and finally at some illegal drugs: marijuana, cocaine, and methamphetamine.

Medical Drugs It once was thought that the placenta protected the fetus against drugs the mother took during pregnancy—until the early 1960s, when a tranquilizer called *thalidomide* was banned after it was found to have caused stunted or missing limbs, severe facial deformities, and defective organs in some 12,000 babies. The thalidomide disaster sensitized medical professionals and the public to the potential dangers of taking drugs while pregnant.

Among the medicinal drugs that may be harmful are the antibiotic tetracycline; certain barbiturates, opiates, and other central nervous system depressants; several hormones, including diethylstilbestrol (DES) and androgens; certain anticancer drugs, such as methotrexate; and Accutane, a drug often prescribed for severe acne (Koren, Pastuszak, & Ito, 1998). Angiotensin-converting enzyme (ACE) inhibitors and nonsteroidal anti-inflammatory drugs (NSAIDs), such as naproxen and ibuprofen, have been linked to birth defects when taken anytime from the first trimester on (Cooper et al., 2006; Ofori, Oraichi, Blais, Rey, & Berard, 2006).

The AAP Committee on Drugs (1994) recommends that *no* medication be prescribed for a pregnant or breast-feeding woman unless it is essential for her health or her child's. When practical and consistent with the essentiality of controlling her symptoms, a woman should be withdrawn from psychotropic medication prior to conception. Infants whose mothers took antidepressants such as Prozac during pregnancy tend to show signs of disrupted neurobehavioral activity (Zeskind & Stephens, 2004) and are at increased risk of severe respiratory failure (Chambers et al., 2006). Certain antipsychotic drugs used to manage severe psychiatric disorders, like lithium, may have serious potential effects on the fetus, including withdrawal symptoms at birth (AAP Committee on Drugs, 2000). If medication is utilized, the most effective drug with the fewest side effects should be selected. Pregnant women should not take over-the-counter drugs without consulting a doctor (Koren et al., 1998).

Research has shown that most psychotropic drugs administered to a lactating woman can be found in her breast milk. The concentration tends to be low, and, therefore, there is little likelihood of an effect on the infant. Thus there appears to be no concrete evidence at the present time with which to recommend that a woman requiring psychotropic medication avoid breast-feeding. However, it must be emphasized that if a mother chooses to breast-feed while receiving medications, the infant should be observed for signs of drug effects (AAP Committee on Drugs, 1982).

Alcohol As many as 5 infants in 1,000 born in the United States suffer from **fetal alcohol syndrome (FAS),** a combination of retarded growth, facial and bodily malformations, and disorders of the central nervous system. FAS and other, less severe, alcohol-related conditions are estimated to occur in nearly 1 in every 100 births (Sokol, Delaney-Black, & Nordstrom, 2003).

Prenatal alcohol exposure is the most common cause of mental retardation and the leading preventable cause of birth defects in the United States (Sokol et al., 2003) and is a risk factor for development of drinking problems and alcohol disorders in young adulthood (Alati et al., 2006; Baer, Sampson, Barr, Connor, & Streissguth, 2003).

The more the mother drinks, the greater are the effects. Moderate or heavy drinking during pregnancy seems to disturb an infant's neurological and behavioral functioning, and this may affect early social interaction with the mother, which is vital to emotional development (Nugent, Lester, Greene, Wieczorek-Deering, & Mahony, 1996). Heavy drinkers who continue to drink after becoming pregnant are likely to have babies with reduced skull and brain growth as compared with babies of nondrinking women or expectant mothers who stop drinking (Handmaker et al., 2006).

FAS-related problems can include, in infancy, reduced responsiveness to stimuli, slow reaction time, and reduced visual acuity (sharpness of vision) (Carter et al., 2005; Sokol

fetal alcohol syndrome (FAS)
Combination of mental, motor, and developmental abnormalities affecting the offspring of some women who drink heavily during pregnancy.

et al., 2003); and, throughout childhood, short attention span, distractibility, restlessness, hyperactivity, learning disabilities, memory deficits, and mood disorders (Sokol et al., 2003) as well as aggressiveness and problem behavior (Sood et al., 2001). Some FAS problems recede after birth; but others, such as retardation, behavioral and learning problems, and hyperactivity, tend to persist. Enriching these children's education or general environment does not seem to enhance their cognitive development (Kerns, Don, Mateer, & Streissguth, 1997; Spohr, Willms, & Steinhausen, 1993; Streissguth et al., 1991; Strömland & Hellström, 1996), but they may be less likely to develop behavioral and mental health problems if they are diagnosed early and are reared in stable, nurturing environments (Streissguth et al., 2004).

Breast-feeding mothers should avoid alcoholic beverages because alcohol has been shown to become concentrated in breast milk, and its use can inhibit milk production. An occasional, small alcoholic drink is acceptable, but breast-feeding should be avoided for 2 hours after the drink (Anderson, 1995).

A woman who drinks and smokes while pregnant is taking grave risks with her future child's health.

Nicotine Maternal smoking has been identified as the single most important factor in low birth weight in developed countries (DiFranza, Aligne, & Weitzman, 2004). Women who smoke during pregnancy are more than 1½ times as likely as non-smokers to bear low-birth-weight babies (weighing less than 5½ pounds at birth). Even light smoking (fewer than five cigarettes a day) is associated with a greater risk of low birth weight (Hoyert, Mathews, Menacker, Strobino, & Guyer, 2006; Martin et al., 2007; Shankaran et al., 2004).

Tobacco use during pregnancy also brings increased risks of miscarriage, growth retardation, stillbirth, small head circumference, sudden infant death, colic (uncontrollable, extended crying for no apparent reason) in early infancy, hyperkinetic disorder (excessive movement), and long-term respiratory, neurological, cognitive, and behavioral problems (AAP Committee on Substance Abuse, 2001; DiFranza et al., 2004; Hoyert, Mathews, et al., 2006; Linnet et al., 2005; Martin et al., 2007; Pendlebury et al., 2008; Shah, Sullivan, & Carter, 2006; Shankaran et al., 2004; Smith et al., 2006; Sondergaard, Henriksen, Obel, & Wisborg, 2001). The effects of prenatal exposure to secondhand smoke on cognitive development tend to be worse when the child also experiences socioeconomic hardships, such as substandard housing, malnutrition, and inadequate clothing during the first 2 years of life (Rauh et al., 2004).

Caffeine Can the caffeine a pregnant woman consumes in coffee, tea, cola, or chocolate cause trouble for her fetus? For the most part, results have been mixed. It does seem clear that caffeine is *not* a teratogen for human babies (Christian & Brent, 2001). A controlled study of 1,205 new mothers and their babies showed no effect of reported caffeine use on low birth weight, premature birth, or retarded fetal growth (Santos, Victora, Huttly, & Carvalhal, 1998). On the other hand, in a controlled study of 1,063 pregnant women, those who consumed at least two cups of regular coffee or five cans of caffeinated soda daily had twice the risk of miscarriage as those who consumed no caffeine (Weng, Odouli, & Li, 2008). Four or more cups of coffee a day during pregnancy is related to increased risk of sudden death in infancy (Ford et al., 1998).

Marijuana, Cocaine, and Methamphetamine Studies of marijuana use by pregnant women are sparse and the results inconsistent. However, some evidence suggests that heavy marijuana use can lead to birth defects, low birth weight, withdrawal-like symptoms (excessive crying and tremors) at birth, and increased risk of attention disorders and learning problems later in life (March of Dimes Birth Defects Foundation, 2004b). In two longitudinal studies, prenatal use of marijuana was associated with impaired attention, impulsivity, and difficulty in use of visual and perceptual skills after age 3, suggesting that the drug may affect functioning of the brain's frontal lobes (Fried & Smith, 2001).

Cocaine use during pregnancy has been associated with spontaneous abortion, delayed growth, premature labor, low birth weight, small head size, birth defects, impaired neurological development, and mild cognitive deficits into preadolescence (Bennett, Bendersky, & Lewis, 2008; Bunikowski et al., 1998; Chiriboga, Brust, Bateman, & Hauser, 1999; Macmillan et al., 2001; March of Dimes Birth Defects Foundation, 2004a; Scher,

Richardson, & Day, 2000; Shankaran et al., 2004). In some studies, cocaine-exposed newborns show acute withdrawal symptoms and sleep disturbances (O'Brien & Jeffery, 2002). In a more recent study, high prenatal cocaine exposure was associated with childhood behavior problems, independent of the effects of alcohol and tobacco exposure (Bada et al., 2007). So great has been the concern about "crack babies" that some states have taken criminal action against expectant mothers suspected of using cocaine.

Other studies, however, have found no specific connection between prenatal cocaine exposure and physical, motor, cognitive, emotional, or behavioral deficits that could not also be attributed to other risk factors, such as low birth weight; exposure to tobacco, alcohol, or marijuana; or a poor home environment (Frank, Augustyn, Knight, Pell, & Zuckerman, 2001; Messinger et al., 2004; Singer et al., 2004). Many of the effects associated with prenatal cocaine exposure may be due to indirect effects such as these rather than stemming directly from the drug itself.

Methamphetamine use among pregnant women is an increasing concern in the United States. In a study of 1,618 infants, 84 were found to have been exposed to methamphetamine. The methamphetamine-exposed infants were more likely to have low birth weight and to be small for their gestational age than the remainder of the sample. This finding suggests that prenatal methamphetamine exposure is associated with fetal growth restriction (Smith et al., 2006).

Early treatment for alcohol, nicotine, and other substance abuse can greatly improve health outcomes. Among 2,073 women enrolled in an early prenatal care program, risks of stillbirth, preterm delivery, low birth weight, and placental separation from the uterus were no higher than for a control group of 46,553 women with no evidence of substance abuse, whereas risks for 156 untreated substance abusers were dramatically higher (Goler, Armstrong, Taillac, & Osejo, 2008).

Maternal Illnesses

Both prospective parents should try to prevent all infections—common colds, flu, urinary tract and vaginal infections, as well as sexually transmitted diseases. If the mother does contract an infection, she should have it treated promptly.

acquired immune deficiency syndrome (AIDS) Viral disease that undermines effective functioning of the immune system.

Acquired immune deficiency syndrome (AIDS) is a disease caused by the human immunodeficiency virus (HIV), which undermines functioning of the immune system. If an expectant mother has the virus in her blood, *perinatal transmission* may occur: The virus may cross over to the fetus's bloodstream through the placenta during pregnancy, labor, or delivery or, after birth, through breast milk.

The biggest risk factor for perinatal HIV transmission is a mother who is unaware she has HIV. In the United States, new pediatric AIDS cases have declined steadily since 1992 due to routine testing and treatment of pregnant women and newborn babies and to advances in the prevention, detection, and treatment of HIV infection in infants. The risk of transmission also can be reduced by choosing cesarean delivery, especially when an infected woman has not received antiretroviral therapy, and by promotion of alternatives to breast-feeding among high-risk women (CDC, 2006a).

Rubella (German measles), if contracted by a woman before her 11th week of pregnancy, is almost certain to cause deafness and heart defects in her baby. Chances of catching rubella during pregnancy have been greatly reduced in Europe and the United States since the late 1960s, when a vaccine was developed that is now routinely administered to infants and children. However, rubella is still a serious problem in developing countries where immunizations are not routine (Plotkin, Katz, & Cordero, 1999).

An infection called *toxoplasmosis,* caused by a parasite harbored in the bodies of cattle, sheep, and pigs and in the intestinal tracts of cats, typically produces either no symptoms or symptoms like those of the common cold. In an expectant woman, however, especially in the second and third trimesters of pregnancy, it can cause fetal brain damage, severely impaired eyesight or blindness, seizures, miscarriage, stillbirth, or death of the baby. If the baby survives, there may be later problems, including eye infections, hearing loss, and learning disabilities. Treatment with antiparasitic drugs during the first year of life can reduce brain and eye damage (McLeod et al., 2006). To avoid infection, expectant mothers should not eat raw or very rare meat, should wash hands and all work surfaces after touching raw meat, should peel or thoroughly wash raw fruits and vegetables, and should not dig in a garden where cat feces may be buried. Women who have a cat should have it checked for the disease, should not feed it raw meat, and, if possible, should have someone else empty the litter box (March of Dimes Foundation, 2002).

Offspring of mothers with diabetes are 3 to 4 times more likely than offspring of other women to develop a wide range of birth defects (Correa et al., 2008). Research on mice suggests why: High blood glucose levels, typical in diabetics, deprive an embryo of oxygen, with resultant cell damage, during the first 8 weeks of pregnancy when its organs are forming. Women with diabetes need to be sure their blood glucose levels are under control *before* becoming pregnant (Li, Chase, Jung, Smith, & Loeken, 2005). Use of multivitamin supplements during the 3 months before conception and the first 3 months of pregnancy can help reduce the risk of diabetes-associated birth defects (Correa, Botto, Liu, Mulinare, & Erickson, 2003).

Maternal Anxiety and Stress

Some tension and worry during pregnancy are normal and do not necessarily increase risks of birth complications such as low birth weight (Littleton, Breitkopf, & Berenson, 2006). Moderate maternal anxiety may even spur organization of the developing brain. In a series of studies, 2-year-olds whose mothers had shown moderate anxiety midway through pregnancy scored higher on measures of motor and mental development than did age-mates whose mothers had not shown anxiety during pregnancy (DiPietro, 2004; DiPietro, Novak, Costigan, Atella, & Reusing, 2006).

On the other hand, a mother's self-reported anxiety during pregnancy has been associated with an 8-month-old's inattentiveness during a developmental assessment (Huizink, Robles de Medina, Mulder, Visser, & Buitelaar, 2002) and a preschooler's negative emotionality or behavioral disorders in early childhood (Martin, Noyes, Wisenbaker, & Huttunen, 2000; O'Connor, Heron, Golding, Beveridge, & Glover, 2002).

Unusual maternal stress during pregnancy may have harmful effects on the unborn child (Dingfelder, 2004; Huizink, Mulder, & Buitelaar, 2004). In one study, pregnant women whose partners or children died or were hospitalized for cancer or heart attacks were at elevated risk of giving birth to children with malformations, such as cleft lip, cleft palate, and heart malformations (Hansen, Lou, & Olsen, 2000). Even stress *before conception* may have injurious long-term effects. In one experiment, when female rats were subjected to ongoing, unpredictable stressors, such as 24-hour isolation, food and water deprivation, constant light, crowding, and electric shocks, for 7 days before being mated, their adult offspring engaged in less social interaction than the offspring of a control group, and the female offspring of the stressed mothers were more fearful. These findings suggest that a child born to a woman who has suffered from early physical, emotional, or sexual abuse may bear permanent scars (Shachar-Dadon, Schulkin, & Leshem, 2009).

Maternal Age

On December 30, 2006, in Barcelona, Spain, Maria del Carmen Bousada became the oldest woman on record to give birth. She had become pregnant after in vitro fertilization and delivered twins by cesarean section about a week before her 67th birthday. In August and November, 2008, two Indian women who claimed to be 70, Omkari Panwar and Rajo Devi, apparently topped that record, also giving birth after IVF. However, these women's ages could not be confirmed because they had no birth certificates.

Birthrates of U.S. women in their 30s and 40s are at their highest levels since the 1960s, in part due to multiple births associated with fertility treatments—an example of a history-graded influence. The number of births to women in their early 40s more than doubled between 1990 and 2006, and the number of births to women in their late 40s nearly quadrupled (Figure 4-4). Births to women ages 50 to 54 have increased an average of 15 percent each year since 1997 (Martin et al., 2009).

Although most risks to the baby's health are not much greater than for babies born to younger mothers, the chance of miscarriage or stillbirth rises with maternal age, reaching 90 percent for women age 45 or older (Heffner, 2004). Women over 30 to 35 are more likely to experience complications due to diabetes, high blood pressure, or severe bleeding and are at higher risk of premature delivery. Their babies are more likely to show retarded fetal growth, birth defects, and chromosomal abnormalities, such as Down

Figure 4-4

From 1970 to 2006 the proportion of first births to women aged 35 years and over increased nearly 8 times. In 2006, about 1 out of 12 first births were to women aged 35 years and over compared with 1 out of 100 in 1970.

Source: CDC/NCHS. National Vital Statistics System.

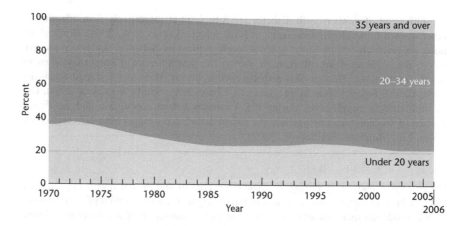

syndrome. However, due to widespread screening among older expectant mothers, fewer malformed infants are born nowadays (Berkowitz, Skovron, Lapinski, & Berkowitz, 1990; P. Brown, 1993; Cunningham & Leveno, 1995; Heffner, 2004).

Adolescents also tend to have premature or underweight babies (Fraser, Brockert, & Ward, 1995; Martin et al., 2007). These newborns are at heightened risk of death in the 1st month, disabilities, or health problems.

Outside Environmental Hazards

Air pollution, chemicals, radiation, extremes of heat and humidity, and other hazards of modern life can affect prenatal development. Pregnant women who regularly breathe air that contains high levels of fine combustion-related particles are more likely to bear infants who are premature or undersized (Parker, Woodruff, Basu, & Schoendorf, 2005) or have chromosomal abnormalities (Bocskay et al., 2005). Exposure to high concentrations of disinfection by-products is associated with low birth weight and slowed fetal growth (Hinckley, Bachand, & Reif, 2005). Women who work with chemicals used in manufacturing semiconductor chips have about twice the rate of miscarriage as other female workers (Markoff, 1992), and women exposed to DDT tend to have more preterm births (Longnecker, Klebanoff, Zhou, & Brock, 2001). Two common insecticides, chlorpyrifos and diazinon, apparently have caused stunting of prenatal growth (Whyatt et al., 2004). Research in the United Kingdom found a 33 percent increase in risk of nongenetic birth defects among families living within 2 miles of hazardous waste sites (Vrijheld et al., 2002).

Fetal exposure to low levels of environmental toxins, such as lead, mercury, and dioxin, as well as nicotine and ethanol, may help explain the sharp rise in asthma, allergies, and autoimmune disorders such as lupus (Dietert, 2005). In a longitudinal study of a birth cohort of children born in high-traffic areas of Manhattan and the Bronx, where asthma prevalence (more than 25 percent) is among the highest in the United States, children exposed prenatally to polycyclic aromatic hydrocarbons emitted by carbon-containing fuels were at heightened risk of developing asthma symptoms by age 5. Both maternal exposure to the hydrocarbons and the children's asthma symptoms were associated with epigenetic changes in the gene ACSL3, which affects the lungs (Perera et al., 2009). Childhood cancers, including leukemia, have been linked to pregnant mothers' drinking chemically contaminated groundwater (Boyles, 2002) and use of home pesticides (Menegaux et al., 2006). Infants exposed prenatally even to low levels of lead, especially during the third trimester, tend to show IQ deficits during childhood (Schnaas et al., 2006).

Women who have routine dental X-rays during pregnancy triple their risk of having full-term, low-birth-weight babies (Hujoel, Bollen, Noonan, & del Aguila, 2004). In utero exposure to radiation 8 through 15 weeks after fertilization has been linked to mental retardation, small head size, chromosomal malformations, Down syndrome, seizures, and poor performance on IQ tests and in school (Yamazaki & Schull, 1990).

Checkpoint ✔

Can you . . .

✔ Discuss the short- and long-term effects on the developing fetus of a mother's use of medical and recreational drugs during pregnancy?

✔ Summarize the risks of maternal illnesses and stress, delayed childbearing, and exposure to chemicals and radiation?

Paternal Factors

A man's exposure to lead, marijuana or tobacco smoke, large amounts of alcohol or radiation, DES, pesticides, or high ozone levels may result in abnormal or poor quality sperm (Sokol et al., 2006; Swan et al., 2003). Offspring of male workers at a British nuclear processing plant were at elevated risk of being born dead (Parker, Pearce, Dickinson, Aitkin, & Craft, 1999). Babies whose fathers had diagnostic X-rays within the year prior to conception or had high lead exposure at work tended to have low birth weight and slowed fetal growth (Lin, Hwang, Marshall, & Marion, 1998; Shea, Little, & ALSPAC Study Team, 1997).

Men who smoke have an increased likelihood of transmitting genetic abnormalities (AAP Committee on Substance Abuse, 2001). A pregnant woman's exposure to the father's secondhand smoke has been linked with low birth weight, infant respiratory infections, sudden infant death, and cancer in childhood and adulthood (Ji et al., 1997; Rubin, Krasilnikoff, Leventhal, Weile, & Berget, 1986; Sandler, Everson, Wilcox, & Browder, 1985; Wakefield, Reid, Roberts, Mullins, & Gillies, 1998). In a study of 214 nonsmoking mothers in New York City, exposure to *both* paternal smoking and urban air pollution resulted in a 7 percent reduction in birth weight and a 3 percent reduction in head circumference (Perera et al., 2004).

Older fathers may be a significant source of birth defects due to damaged or deteriorated sperm. Birthrates for fathers ages 30 to 49 have risen substantially since 1980 (Martin et al., 2009). Advancing paternal age is associated with increases in the risk of several rare conditions, including dwarfism (Wyrobek et al., 2006). Advanced age of the father also may be a factor in a disproportionate number of cases of schizophrenia (Byrne et al., 2003; Malaspina et al., 2001), bipolar disorder (Frans et al., 2008), and autism and related disorders (Reichenberg et al., 2006; Tsuchiya et al., 2008).

What's your view

- Because tobacco can produce genetic abnormalities in a man's sperm, should men of childbearing age be forced to abstain from them? How could such a prohibition be enforced?

Checkpoint ✓

Can you . . .

✔ Identify several ways in which environmentally caused defects can be influenced by the father?

Chapter 2
Infancy

In this chapter we'll look at the first stage of "postnatal" life. Physical development, especially of the brain, is occurring exponentially fast during this time, as are developmental advancements in motor skills, cognitive skills and language development. We will look at all of these burgeoning changes in turn and introduce some very important life stage theories from Jean Piaget, Lev Vygotsky and Erik Erikson.

PHYSICAL DEVELOPMENT IN INFANCY

Infancy is a time of rapid physical and nervous system development, accomplishments that ensure an infant's survival and ability to cope with its world. The typical newborn weighs about 7½ pounds and is about 20 inches in length. In one year after its birth, an infant's length increases by one-half and its weight almost triples. Infancy sees exciting changes in psychomotor development as well as potential danger. For example, the number of U.S. babies dying shortly after birth increased for the first time in 50 years. The infant mortality rate climbed from 6.8 deaths per 1,000 live births in 2001 to 7.0 deaths in 2002. The cause of this increase remains unclear (Martin, 2004).

Developmental Milestones of Infancy

In his careful analysis of physical growth and development, Tanner (1990) described growth as like the weaving of a cloth whose design never repeats itself. The underlying threads, each coming from the reel at its own rhythm, interact with one another continuously, in a manner always highly regulated and controlled. To help you visualize the rapid growth that occurs during infancy, consider Table 8.1.

As their baby's growing physical competence becomes observable, parents begin to treat their child differently, recognizing greater individuality and maturity. Different parenting practices now spring into action and these varied practices reflect the culture into which a child is born. The manner in which Balinese mothers carry their children affects children's motor development; infants in Ghana show superior motor abilities due to their considerable physical freedom; the expectations of Jamaican mothers help their infants to sit and walk relatively early (Bornstein, 1995). In other words, different families in different cultures go about parenting in different ways.

Growing children experience changes in shape and body composition, in the distribution of tissues, and in their developing motor skills, and these changes then influence cognitive, psychosocial, and emotional development. For example, the infant's head at birth is about a quarter of the body's total length, but in the adult it is about one-seventh of body length. Different tissues (muscles, nerves) also grow at different rates, and total growth represents a complex series of changes. Underlying this rapidly unfolding and complex process is, of course, proper nutrition.

Brain Development

From the beginnings of the nervous system, which we discussed in chapter 4, a picture of the brain appears with which you're familiar. The top of the neural tube leads to the formation of the two cerebral hemispheres and the four lobes of the cerebral cortex. The rest of the tube turns into the spinal cord. Figure 8.1 illustrates these features and suggests the functions of each.

Shown here are the brain's lobes and functional areas.

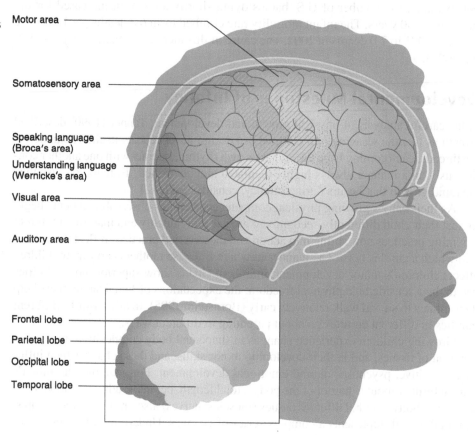

FIGURE 8.1
The human brain.

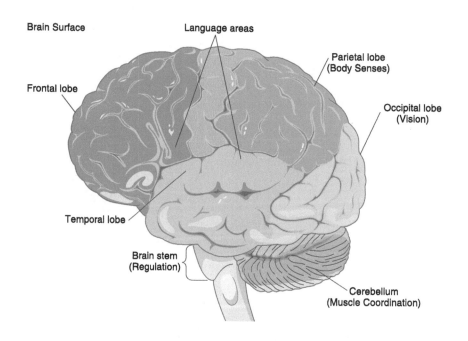

AN INFORMED VIEW: Building the Brain Structures

Tracing the evolutionary pathway of the brain leads to the conclusion that our brains developed in a bottom to top direction, starting with the brain stem and steadily moving to the more recent appearance of the cortical areas. The older areas of the brain (brain stem, hypothalamus) are closely linked to the urges and expression of rage, passion, and fear, whereas the cortical areas, devoted to thinking and problem solving, act as a brake on the limbic system. Figure 8.2 illustrates the appearance of several important brain structures that influence a child's life, from crying, regulating body temperature, eating habits, impulses, and thought processes.

- Starting in the lower regions of the brain (the cerebrum seems to sit on the spinal area), you can see the *brain stem*, which controls critical bodily functions such as breathing, states of sleep and wakefulness, and automatic muscular activities such as standing.

- Figure 8.2 shows an area called the *limbic system*, which includes the amygdala, hippocampus, and hypothalamus. The limbic system is deeply involved in emotional behavior and memory.

- The *amygdala*, which sits just above the brain stem, is a center for emotional learning and remembering. Studies of individuals with damaged amygdalas testify to the inability of these individuals to judge the emotional significance of events. In his popular book *Emotional Intelligence*, Daniel Goleman notes that life without the amygdala is a life stripped of personal meanings.

- The *hypothalamus*, often called the "brain center," connects with many of the other brain areas and is particularly concerned with maintaining the body's internal conditions. For example, the hypothalamus seems to control thirst, hunger, body temperature, sex, and emotions, a full-time job by any standards!

- The *thalamus* acts as the main coordinator of information coming into the body. For example, as a child looks around, listens to sounds, and reacts emotionally, the thalamus acts to send this information to the proper brain areas.

- In Figure 8.2, you can see that attached to the brain stem is the *cerebellum* whose major duty is to coordinate muscular movements. For example, if a person's cerebellum is damaged, control of fine movement is lost so that the person cannot reach out and pick up an object.

- Finally, the *hippocampus* acts as a storage space for shortterm memory until it can transmit its content to the frontal cortex.

With these brain functions in mind, we can now turn our attention to the unfolding story of how we're continuing to build our knowledge of brain development.

You may also wish to learn more about it by going to our Web site at http://www.mhhe.com/dacey6.

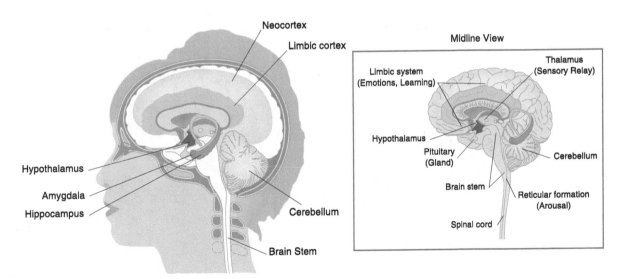

FIGURE 8.2
The human brain—side and midline views.

What can we make of all this remarkable activity? Nature has taken breathtaking steps to ensure that a baby will be able to adapt to its challenging environment at birth. Then, if you stop and think about it, you'll come to the conclusion that this tremendous potential can't be wasted. What a shame if a baby's environment doesn't present vital stimulation, and brain cells and connections are lost through disuse, for example, the situation of a child whose parents rarely speak to or read to their child.

The adult human brain weighs about 3 to 4 pounds and contains about 100 billion neurons (Gopnik, Meltzoff, & Kuhl, 2000). As we have seen, nervous system development begins during the embryonic period when neurons reproduce at the rate of about 250,000 per minute. During infancy, connections among the neurons begin to increase notably (as much as 100 to 1,000 connections for each of the billions of neurons). This amazing complexity provides the biological basis for cognitive development. Estimates are that the baby's brain at birth is about a quarter of its adult size. At 6 months it's about 50 percent of its adult weight; 60 percent at 1 year; 75 percent at 2 1/2 years; 90 percent at 6 years; and 95 percent at 10 years. About 75 percent of the human brain develops outside of the womb in direct relationship with its environment (Shore, 1996). The developmental pattern is seen in Figure 8.3.

How We're Learning about the Brain

Today's brain researchers rely heavily on tools such as the following (Gazzaniga, Ivry, & Mangun, 1998; Bear, Connors, & Paradiso, 2001; Restak, 2001).

- *Electroencephalogram.* The nerve impulse is electrical and when large numbers of neurons are active they produce enough electrical signals to be measured by plac-

FIGURE 8.3
Brain development.

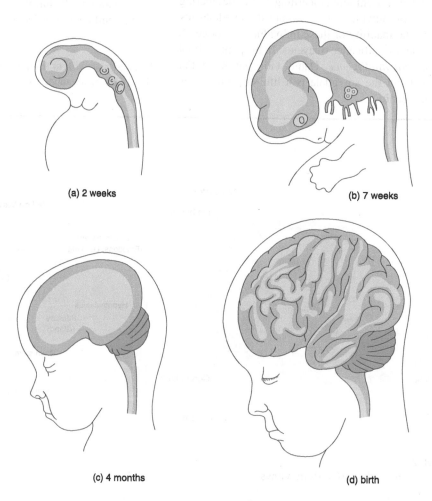

(a) 2 weeks

(b) 7 weeks

(c) 4 months

(d) birth

ing electrodes on the scalp identifying different behavioral states, for example, deep sleep.

- *Computed axial tomography* (*CAT*). The frequently used CAT scan is an advanced version of X-ray techniques, which presents three-dimensional pictures of the brain.
- *Positron emission tomography* (*PET*). PET scans measure the amount of blood-flow associated with brain activity. Tiny radioactive elements (about the same amount of radioactivity you would receive from a chest X-ray) are injected into the bloodstream and become tracers that the PET scan can detect.
- *Magnetic resonance imaging* (*MRI*). The increasingly popular MRI depends on the magnetic quality of blood to measure internal structures.

Another example of startling new breakthroughs in brain research is the ability to grow new brain cells to replace damaged brain cells (in mice). It was long thought that brain cells, once damaged, could never be replaced. However, recent research (Saltus, 2000) has discovered that neural brain cells migrate through the brain, attach to damaged nerves, and transform themselves into the appropriate nerves cells. As a result, the future looks brighter for sufferers of such diseases as Parkinson's and Lou Gehrig's disease.

An Infant's Brain, Neurons, and Communication

From your previous reading about neurons, you probably recall their importance in understanding brain action. As a refresher, Figure 8.4 illustrates what they look like.

Examining Figure 8.4 you can see that the communication process in the nervous system consists of the following steps (Fields, 2004).

- The messages (called *nerve impulses*) that travel along the neurons are electrical.
- For neurons to communicate with each other, the dendrites of one cell receive a message from the axon of another cell.
- To cross the space (called a *synapse*) between the axon and dendrite, the nerve impulse needs the help of a chemical transmitter (called a *neurotransmitter*).
- Once the message has crossed the synapse, it resumes its journey as an electrical signal.

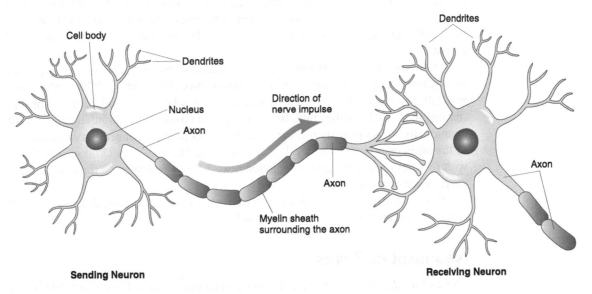

FIGURE 8.4
How neurons connect.

TABLE 8.1   Rethinking the Brain

Old Thinking	New Thinking
A brain's development depends solely on genes.	Brain development depends on the interactions between genes and experience.
Experiences before 3 years are relatively insignificant.	Experiences during infancy are critical for the structure of the brain and its potential.
A good relationship between a child and parents facilitates development and learning.	A secure relationship not only aids development, but it also affects the way the brain is wired.
Brain development proceeds steadily—that is, in a linear fashion.	Brain development is essentially nonlinear—that is, there are ideal times for different kinds of experiences.
The brain is less active during the early years.	During these years, an infant's brain may be twice as active as an adolescent's or adult's.

Adapted from R. Shore. (1997). Rethinking the brain: New insights into early development. New York: Families and Work Institute.

You'll recall that nature has manufactured billions of brain cells more than will be needed to ensure that the brain will be able to form enough connections for all the needed abilities and skills that demand new connections. Those neurons that *don't* make connections simply die. And—this may startle you—this exercise in survival (some connections die, some connections survive) continues throughout our lives, giving new and critical meaning to the expression "use it or lose it." You may also recall Darwin's famous belief in the survival of the fittest: the fittest of our neurons are those that make connections and survive. So the lesson here is not only for our children, but for all of us: Keep busy, seek challenges, stay alert.

Making Connections Thanks to the prodigious research of the neuroscientists for the past two decades, we now know that infants absorb their experiences and use them to continually shape their brains. It happens this way: An infant gobbles up information from the outside world through its eyes, ears, nose, hands, and so forth, and translates it into nerve impulses that travel along neurons (axon of one cell to dendrites of another), making connection with the dendrites of other neurons along its pathway. The brain cells that receive this information survive; those that don't, perish. It's as simple as that.

Environmental stimulation, including teachers, parents, and other people and events, affect all parts of the brain. We'll stress throughout our work how important it is to talk *to* a baby. The language areas of the baby's brain respond, resulting in superior language skills for the child. It's also important to surround an infant with a warm, emotionally supportive environment, which results in more connections in those parts of the brain responsible for developing emotions. The result? A child who is blessed with feelings of security and an emotional well-being that spreads throughout all aspects of her or his life.

Consequently, these new findings have forced us to change our thinking about the brain and its functions, as seen in Table 8.1.

Neonatal Reflexes

Reflex   When a stimulus repeatedly elicits the same response.

Think of a *reflex* as an automatic response to certain stimuli (Greenfield, 1997). Popular examples include the eye blink and the knee jerk. All of the activities needed to sustain life's functions are present at birth (breathing, sucking, swallowing, elimina-

TABLE 8.2 Neonatal Reflexes

Name of Reflex	How Elicited	Description of Response
Plantar grasp	Press thumbs against the balls of the infant's foot	Toes tend to curl
Babinski	Gently stroke lateral side of sole of foot	Toes spread in an outward and upward manner
Babkin	Press palm of hand while infant lies on back	Mouth opens; eyes close
Rooting	Gently touch cheek of infant with light finger pressure	Head turns toward finger in effort to suck
Sucking	Mouth contacts nipple of breast or bottle	Mouth and tongue used to manipulate (suck) nipple
Moro	Loud noise or sudden dropping of infant	Stretches arms and legs and then hugs self; cries
Grasping	Object or finger is placed in infant's palm	Fingers curl around object
Tonic neck	Place infant flat on back	Infant assumes fencer position: turns head and extends arm and leg in same direction as head
Stepping	Support infant in upright position; soles of feet brush surface	Infant attempts regular progression of steps

Adapted from R. Shore. (1997). Rethinking the brain: New insights into early development. New York: Families and Work Institute.

tion). These reflexes serve a definite purpose: The gag reflex enables infants to spit up mucus; the eye blink protects the eyes from excessive light; an antismothering reflex facilitates breathing.

In an attempt to rank an infant's reflexes in order of importance, Harris and Liebert (1992) note that the most crucial reflexes are those associated with breathing. Breathing patterns are not fully established at birth, and sometimes infants briefly stop breathing. These periods are called *apnea*, and although there is some concern that apnea may be associated with sudden infant death, these periods are quite common in all infants. Usually they last for about 2 to 5 seconds; episodes that extend from about 10 to 20 seconds may suggest the possibility of a problem. Sneezing and coughing are both reflexes that help to clear air passages.

Apnea Brief periods when breathing is suspended.

Next in importance are those reflexes associated with feeding. Infants suck and swallow during the prenatal period and continue at birth. They also demonstrate the rooting reflex, in which they'll turn toward a nipple or a finger placed on the cheek and attempt to get it into the mouth. Table 8.2 describes some of the more important neonatal reflexes.

Newborn Abilities

In the days immediately following birth until about 2 weeks to 1 month, the infant is called a *neonate*. During this period, babies immediately begin to use their abilities to adapt to their environment. Among the most significant of these are the following:

Neonate Term for an infant in the first days and weeks after birth.

- *Infants display clear signs of imitative behavior at 7 to 10 days.* (Try this: Stick out your tongue at a baby who is about 10 days old. What happens? The baby will stick its tongue out at you!) Here neonates are telling us that they have the ability to imitate almost immediately after birth, an ability that should alert parents to immediately demonstrate desirable behavior for their children to learn and imitate. Infants' imitation of such tongue movements as just described is well established in babies as young as a few hours to more than 6 weeks of age (Gopnik, Meltzoff, & Kuhl, 1999; Jones, 1996).
- *Infants can see at birth* and, if you capture their attention with an appropriate object (such as a small, red rubber ball held at about 10 inches from the face), they will track it as you move the ball from side to side. Infants react to color at between

Sample photographs of a model's happy, surprised, and sad expressions, and an infant's corresponding expressions. How would you classify the effects on development that a mother's facial expressions have on a child?

Courtesy of Dr. Tiffany Field and *Science.* From Field, et al., Model and Infant Expressions from "Discrimination and Imitation of Facial Express by Neonates" in Science, fig. 2, Vol. 218, pp. 179–181, October 8, 1982. Reprinted by permission of the American Association for the Advancement of Science.

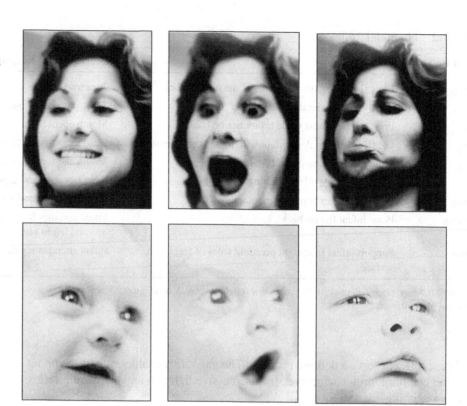

2 and 4 months; depth perception appears at about 4 to 5 months (Brazelton & Nugent, 1995).

- *Infants not only can hear at birth* (*and prenatally*) but also can perceive the direction of the sound. In a famous yet simple experiment, Michael Wertheimer (1962) sounded a clicker (similar to those children play with) from different sides of a delivery room only 10 minutes after an infant's birth. The infant not only reacted to the noise but also attempted to turn in the direction of the sound, indicating that children immediately tune into their environment (Olds, London, & Ladewig, 1996).

- *Infants are active seekers of stimulation.* Infants want—actually need—people, sounds, and physical contact to stimulate their cognitive development and to give them a feeling of security in their world. Remember that infants are engaged in a subtle, though powerful battle to establish control over their bodies. For example, they are struggling to regulate their bodily functions such as eating, breathing, and heart rate. But for brief moments, perhaps for only 15 or 20 seconds, they stop these efforts and pay close attention to the environment in a search for stimulation. This happens even when they are hungry.

  One of the authors takes students to Boston's Children's Hospital for observation visits and attempts to find a nurse bottle feeding an infant. Watching what happens when someone moves into the baby's field of vision, observers are surprised at the baby's reaction. *The baby stops sucking and stares intently at that person's face*—not for long, but long enough to interrupt feeding. You may not be too impressed with this but think about it. An infant's hunger drive is extremely powerful, yet, momentarily, the need for stimulation is even stronger, indicating that infants show a willingness, even a need, to interact with other human beings.

- *Infants, using these abilities, begin their efforts to master the developmental tasks of the first two years*: learning to take solid foods, learning to talk, learning to walk.

Motor Development

Parents are fascinated by their child's motor development: Is she sitting up on time? Shouldn't she be crawling by now? I wonder if she'll ever walk. Why can't she hold her head steady? Motor development occurs in both the head-to-feet direction (called *cephalocaudal*) and a *proximodistal* direction (from the center of the body to the extremities).

For many years, research into infant locomotion has been at a standstill, mainly because of the belief that neuromuscular maturation was the primary agent of motor development. Recently, however, modern investigators using high-speed film, computerized video recordings, and infrared emitting diodes, have provided new insights into changes in coordination, balance, and strength in infants' locomotion.

Studies have shown that continuity of walking movements in the first year may be masked by underlying changes in the infant's muscle distribution and body fat and the differential effect of gravity. For example, newborns with chubby legs step less than slender-legged infants. But when slender-legged infants were weighted with an amount usually gained over the first months of life, they stopped stepping (Adolph, 1997).

Following are several important characteristics of motor control.

Head Control

The most obvious initial head movements are from side to side, although the 1- month-old infant occasionally lifts its head when in a prone position. Four-month-old infants can hold their head steady while sitting and will lift their head and shoulders to a 90 degree angle when on their abdomen. By the age of 6 months, most youngsters can balance their head quite well.

Locomotion: Crawling and Creeping

Crawling and creeping are two distinct developmental phases. In *crawling*, the infant's abdomen touches the floor and the weight of the head and shoulders rests on the elbows. Locomotion is mainly by arm action. The legs usually drag, although some youngsters push with their legs. Most youngsters can crawl after age 7 months.

Creeping is more advanced than crawling, since movement is on the hands and knees and the trunk does not touch the ground. After age 9 months, most youngsters can creep.

Most descriptions of crawling and creeping are quite uniform. The progression is from propulsion on the abdomen to quick, accurate movements on the hands and knees, but the sequence is endlessly varied. Youngsters adopt a bewildering diversity of positions and movements that can only loosely be grouped together.

Locomotion: Standing and Walking

After about age 7 months, infants when held will support most of their weight on their legs. Coordination of arm and leg movements enables babies to pull themselves up and grope toward control of leg movements. The first steps are a propulsive, lunging forward. Gradually a smooth, speedy, and versatile gait emerges. The world now belongs to the infant.

Once babies begin to walk, their attention darts from one thing to another, thus quickening their perceptual development (our next topic). Tremendous energy and mobility, coupled with a growing curiosity, push infants to search for the boundaries of their world. It is an exciting time for youngsters but a watchful time for parents, since they must draw the line between encouraging curiosity and initiative and protecting the child from personal injury. The task is not easy. It is, however, a problem for all aspects of development: What separates unreasonable restraint from reasonable freedom?

Note the steady development of body control in this picture, especially the head and upper body. Control of the lower body and legs follows by several months. Why is it important that control of the upper body appears early in development?

Crawling Locomotion in which the infant's abdomen touches the floor and the weight of the head and shoulders rests on the elbows.

Creeping Movement is on hands and knees and the trunk does not touch the ground; creeping appears from 9 months in most youngsters.

Most youngsters somewhere in the 7 to 9 month period begin to pull themselves up to a standing position. Their legs are now strong enough to support them while standing. Explain how locomotion contributes to other forms of development.

Finally, we want to call your attention to changes in theorizing about and research into motor development. Reflecting current thinking about development (see chapters 1 and 2), recent studies have incorporated a multicausal explanation of motor development (Lockman & Thelen, 1993; Thelen, 1995). For example, in analyzing the stepping reflex previously discussed (see p. 120), Thelen (1995) commented on the disappearance of this behavior by 2 or 3 months, yet kicking, which has the same movement pattern as stepping, is *not* lost. How can these differences be explained? Thelen (1995) pointed to a change of posture, plus weight gain (the legs get heavier) and the pull of gravity as the multicausal answer.

Table 8.3 summarizes milestones in motor development.

TABLE 8.3   Milestones in Motor Development

Age	Head Control	Grasping	Sitting	Creeping, Crawling	Standing, Walking
1–3 months	Can lift head and chest while prone	Grasps objects, briefly holds objects, carries objects to mouth	Sits awkwardly with support		
4–8 months	Holds head steady while sitting, balances head	Develops skillful use of thumb	Transition from sitting with slight support to brief periods without support	Crawling movements appear at about 7 months (trunk touches floor)	
8–12 months	Has established head control	Coordinates hand activities, handedness begins to appear	Good trunk control, sits alone steadily	Creeping (trunk raised from floor) begins at 9–10 months and continues until steady walking	Can stand and take steps holding on to something; by 12 months will pull self up
12–14 months		Handedness pronounced, holds crayon, marks line	Can sit from standing position		Stands alone; begins to walk alone
18 months					Begins to run

Adapted from R. Shore. (1997). Rethinking the brain: New insights into early development. New York: Families and Work Institute.

PIAGET'S THEORY OF COGNITIVE DEVELOPMENT

Piaget thought that, just as our physical bodies have structures that enable us to adapt to the world, we build mental structures that help us to adapt to the world. Adaptation involves adjusting to new environmental demands. Piaget also stressed that children actively construct their own cognitive worlds; information is not just poured into their minds from the environment. He sought to discover how children at different points in their development think about the world and how these systematic changes occur.

Processes of Development

Poet Nora Perry asked, "Who knows the thoughts of the child?" As much as anyone, Piaget knew. Through careful observations of his own three children—Laurent, Lucienne, and Jacqueline—and inquisitive interviews of other children, Piaget changed our perceptions of the way children think about the world.

What processes do children use as they construct their knowledge of the world? Piaget argued that these processes are especially important in this regard: schemes, assimilation, accommodation, organization, equilibrium, and equilibration.

Piaget with his wife and three children; he often used his observations of his children to provide examples of his theory.

One term that cognitive theorists like Piaget use a lot is the word **schema**. According to Piaget, a schema is a way of gathering and processing information about your world. As such it is also a way of storing information in memory. Schemas can be many things:

A big of information in words
or
A mental image
or
A pattern of action

As adults we are familiar with the "bit of information in words" type schema. We use this one most of the time to share information with one another. During a lecture, this kind of schema is being shared by the professor with the student. Likewise, when you read a book, schemas of this sort are passing fro the author to the reader.

But, long before you had facility with this type of schema, you were already storing information about your world using "mental image" schemas. By making pictures of your world, accompanied by sounds and feelings (perhaps even tastes and smells,) you could understand your world and store information about it.

Even more primitive are the "pattern of action" schemas. Available to us in a rudimentary form from birth on, these schemas are body movements that the baby performs that allow the little one to interact with, understand and store memories about its world.

As we mature, we do not lose the ability to use our more primitive (in the sense that they are available earlier) schemas. If I ask you to remember the most beautiful sunset you have ever seen, you will be retrieving a mental image schema. Likewise when you learn a new sport or skill, or master a new dance, you are using pattern of action schemas.

Piaget's theory of cognitive development could best be described as an interaction theory. That is, Piaget believes that cognitive development occurs because of an interplay of genetic and environmental factors. One of the most common mistakes that students make when interpreting his theory is to assume that since Piaget posits that we have a genetic "timetable" of sorts that governs cognitive development, that our mental maturation will take place "no matter what." Nothing could be further from the truth. For example, raise a child in a closet (as some disturbed parents have done) and that child will not go through the predicted stages on schedule. Case histories of children who were abused in this way reveal that these children emerge from these experiences developmentally disabled (retarded). Piaget's point is this: a child must have environmental experiences that fall within the parameters of "normal" if cognitive development is to proceed normally. How can normal environmental experiences bring about cognitive maturation? Consider the following flow chart:

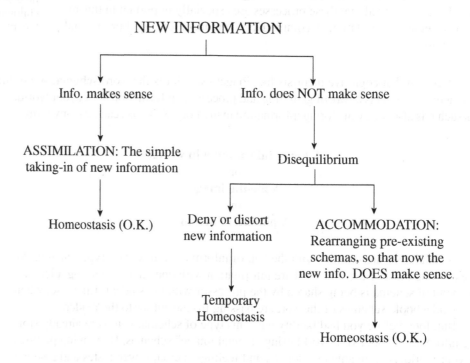

NEW INFORMATION

Info. makes sense   Info. does NOT make sense

ASSIMILATION: The simple taking-in of new information   Disequilibrium

Homeostasis (O.K.)   Deny or distort new information   ACCOMMODATION: Rearranging pre-existing schemas, so that now the new info. DOES make sense.

Temporary Homeostasis   Homeostasis (O.K.)

This flowchart illustrates what happens when we encounter new information. If the information makes sense, we simply take it in. It is understood and perhaps stored in the memory. This process is what Piaget calls **assimilation**. The new information does not conflict with our version of reality, so accepting that information (assimilating it) leaves us in a state of cognitive equilibrium or, to use a word with which you have more familiarity, homeostasis.

However, if the information in question does NOT make sense, this throws us into a state Piaget describes as disequilibrium. As the name implies, we feel off balance cognitively, or as we would say in common language "confused." Confusion is not a state that humans enjoy; we find confusion (disequilibrium) aversive. Piaget believes that we desperately need to "make sense" of things. So, we are strongly motivated to "do something" to end the confusion. A choice that is always available to human beings is the choice to employ a defense mechanism. In this case we would most likely deny or distort the new information that conflicts with how we believe reality to be. We all know people who "see only what they want to see" or twist facts to fit with their version of the truth or operate under the philosophy, "My mind's made up; don't confuse me with the facts." While this approach temporarily may leave the person in a state of homeostasis, this "comfort" will last only as long as the defense mechanism is in place. If the information is persistent or pervasive, the effort required to maintain the defense is persistent or pervasive, the effort required to maintain the defense mechanism may be costly to the individual. But, more importantly for our discussion, this is NOT the road to further cognitive development. If some kind of cognitive maturity is our goal, then this path is a dead end street. This is what I am referring to in my Introductory Psychology lectures, when I tell my classes that utilizing massive defense mechanisms leave us "less bright" than we could be.

Obviously, a better "choice" would be the path that Piaget describes as **accommodation**. When faced with information that does not make sense, it is possible to alter one's version of reality…Piaget describes this as "rearranging pre-existing schemas"…so that the new information can now "fit in." Accommodation requires of us that we stretch and grow cognitively, thus bringing about a qualitative change in our thinking. In simple parlance, accommodation means changing our thinking, or quite literally, "changing your mind." Once this is done homeostasis is restored.

A couple of observations: Obviously, accommodation is going to be a lot harder than assimilation. Assimilation is mere quantitative change, whereas accommodation is qualitative change. We humans are very impatient with our own confusion. Wouldn't be interesting if, instead of nearly panicking the next time you feel confused, you could instead say to yourself, "Ah, confusion…That's my signal that soon I am about to become wiser!" perhaps then we could be more patient with our confusion.

Piagetian Approach: The Sensorimotor Stage

The first of Piaget's four stages of cognitive development is the **sensorimotor stage.** During this stage, from birth to approximately age 2, infants learn about themselves and their world through their developing sensory and motor activity as they change from creatures who respond primarily through reflexes and random behavior into goal-oriented toddlers.

sensorimotor stage In Piaget's theory, first stage in cognitive development, during which infants learn through senses and motor activity.

schemes Piaget's term for organized patterns of thought and behavior used in particular situations.

Substages of the Sensorimotor Stage

The sensorimotor stage consists of six substages (Table 7-3) that flow from one to another as a baby's **schemes,** organized patterns of thought and behavior, become more elaborate. During the first five substages, babies learn to coordinate input from their senses and organize their activities in relation to their environment. During the sixth substage, they progress from trial-and-error learning to the use of symbols and concepts to solve simple problems.

Table 7-3	Six Substages of Piaget's Sensorimotor Stage of Cognitive Development*		
Substages	**Ages**	**Description**	**Behavior**
1. Use of reflexes	Birth to 1 month	Infants exercise their inborn reflexes and gain some control over them. They do not coordinate information from their senses. They do not grasp an object they are looking at.	Dorri begins sucking when her mother's breast is in her mouth.
2. Primary circular reactions	1 to 4 months	Infants repeat pleasurable behaviors that first occur by chance (such as thumb sucking). Activities focus on the infant's body rather than the effects of the behavior on the environment. Infants make first acquired adaptations; that is, they suck different objects differently. They begin to coordinate sensory information and grasp objects.	When given a bottle, Dylan, who is usually breast-fed, is able to adjust his sucking to the rubber nipple.
3. Secondary circular reactions	4 to 8 months	Infants become more interested in the environment; they repeat actions that bring interesting results (such as shaking a rattle) and prolong interesting experiences. Actions are intentional but not initially goal directed.	Alejandro pushes pieces of dry cereal over the edge of his high chair tray one at a time and watches each piece as it falls to the floor.
4. Coordination of secondary schemes	8 to 12 months	Behavior is more deliberate and purposeful (intentional) as infants coordinate previously learned schemes (such as looking at and grasping a rattle) and use previously learned behaviors to attain their goals (such as crawling across the room to get a desired toy). They can anticipate events.	Anica pushes the button on her musical nursery rhyme book, and "Twinkle, Twinkle, Little Star" plays. She pushes this button over and over again, choosing it instead of the buttons for the other songs.
5. Tertiary circular reactions	12 to 18 months	Toddlers show curiosity and experimentation; they purposefully vary their actions to see results (for example, by shaking different rattles to hear their sounds). They actively explore their world to determine what is novel about an object, event, or situation. They try out new activities and use trial and error in solving problems.	When Bjorn's big sister holds his favorite board book up to his crib bars, he reaches for it. His first efforts to bring the book into his crib fail because the book is too wide. Soon, Bjorn turns the book sideways and hugs it, delighted with his success.
6. Mental combinations	18 to 24 months	Because toddlers can mentally represent events, they are no longer confined to trial and error to solve problems. Symbolic thought enables toddlers to begin to think about events and anticipate their consequences without always resorting to action. Toddlers begin to demonstrate insight. They can use symbols, such as gestures and words, and can pretend.	Jenny plays with her shape box, searching carefully for the right hole for each shape before trying—and succeeding.

*Infants show enormous cognitive growth during Piaget's sensorimotor stage, as they learn about the world through their senses and their motor activities. Note their progress in problem solving and the coordination of sensory information. All ages are approximate.

Much of this early cognitive growth comes about through **circular reactions,** in which an infant learns to reproduce pleasurable or interesting events originally discovered by chance. Initially, an activity produces a sensation so enjoyable that the baby wants to repeat it. The repetition then feeds on itself in a continuous cycle in which cause and effect keep reversing (Figure 7-1). The original chance behavior has been consolidated into a new scheme.

In the *first substage* (birth to about 1 month), neonates begin to exercise some control over their inborn reflexes, engaging in a behavior even when its normal stimulus is not present. For example, newborns suck reflexively when their lips are touched. But they soon learn to find the nipple even when they are not touched, and they suck at times when they are not hungry. These newer behaviors illustrate how infants modify and extend the scheme for sucking.

In the *second substage* (about 1 to 4 months), babies learn to repeat a pleasant bodily sensation first achieved by chance (say, sucking their thumbs, as shown in Figure 7-1a). Piaget called this a *primary circular reaction*. Also, babies begin to turn toward sounds, showing the ability to coordinate different kinds of sensory information (vision and hearing).

circular reactions Piaget's term for processes by which an infant learns to reproduce desired occurrences originally discovered by chance.

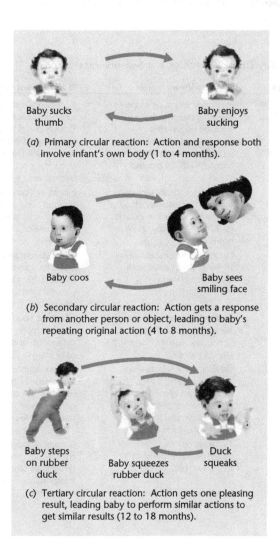

(*a*) Primary circular reaction: Action and response both involve infant's own body (1 to 4 months).

Baby sucks thumb → Baby enjoys sucking

(*b*) Secondary circular reaction: Action gets a response from another person or object, leading to baby's repeating original action (4 to 8 months).

Baby coos → Baby sees smiling face

(*c*) Tertiary circular reaction: Action gets one pleasing result, leading baby to perform similar actions to get similar results (12 to 18 months).

Baby steps on rubber duck → Baby squeezes rubber duck → Duck squeaks

Figure 7-1

Primary, secondary, and tertiary circular reactions.

The *third substage* (about 4 to 8 months) coincides with a new interest in manipulating objects and learning about their properties. Babies engage in *secondary circular reactions:* intentional actions repeated not merely for their own sake, as in the second substage, but to get results *beyond the infant's own body.* For every, a baby this age will repeatedly shake a rattle to hear its noise or (as shown in Figure 7-1b) coo when a friendly face appears, so as to make the face stay longer.

By the time infants reach the *fourth substage, coordination of secondary schemes* (about 8 to 12 months), they have built on the few schemes they were born with. They have learned to generalize from past experience to solve new problems, and they can distinguish means from ends. They will crawl to get something they want, grab it, or push away a barrier to it (such as someone else's hand). They try out, modify, and coordinate previous schemes to find one that works. This substage marks the development of complex, goal-directed behavior.

In the *fifth substage* (about 12 to 18 months), babies begin to experiment with new behavior to see what will happen.

This 8-month-old baby crawling after a ball is in the fourth substage of Piaget's sensorimotor stage, coordination of secondary schemes.

Table 7-4	Key Developments of the Sensorimotor Stage	
Concept or Skill	**Piaget's View**	**More Recent Findings**
Imitation	Invisible imitation develops around 9 months; deferred imitation begins after development of mental representations in the sixth substage (18–24 months).	Controversial studies have found invisible imitation of facial expressions in newborns and deferred imitation as early as 6 weeks. Deferred imitation of complex activities seems to exist as early as 6 months.
Object permanence	Develops gradually between the third and sixth substage. Infants in the fourth substage (8–12 months) make the A-not-B error.	Infants as young as 3½ months (second substage) seem to show object knowledge, though interpretation of findings is in dispute.
Symbolic development	Depends on representational thinking, which develops in the sixth substage (18–24 months).	Understanding that pictures stand for something else occurs at about 19 months. Children under 3 tend to have difficulty interpreting scale models.
Categorization	Depends on representational thinking, which develops during the sixth substage (18–24 months).	Infants as young as 3 months seem to recognize perceptual categories, and 7-month-olds categorize by function.
Causality	Develops slowly between 4–6 months and 1 year, based on an infant's discovery, first of effects of own actions and then of effects of outside forces.	Some evidence suggests early awareness of specific causal events in the physical world, but general understanding of causality may be slower to develop.
Number	Depends on use of symbols, which begins in the sixth substage (18–24 months).	Infants as young as 5 months may recognize and mentally manipulate small numbers, but interpretation of findings is in dispute.

Once they begin to walk, they can more easily explore their environment. They now engage in *tertiary circular reactions,* varying an action to get a similar result, rather than merely repeating pleasing behavior they have accidentally discovered. For example, a toddler may squeeze a rubber duck that squeaked when stepped on, to see whether it will squeak again (as shown in Figure 7-1c). For the first time, children show originality in problem solving. By trial and error, they try out behaviors until they find the best way to attain a goal.

The *sixth substage, mental combinations* (about 18 months to 2 years), is a transition into the preoperational stage of early childhood. **Representational ability**—the ability to mentally represent objects and actions in memory, largely through symbols such as words, numbers, and mental pictures—frees toddlers from immediate experience. They can pretend, and their representational ability affects the sophistication of their pretending (Bornstein, Haynes, O'Reilly, & Painter, 1996). They can think about actions before taking them. They no longer have to go through laborious trial and error to solve problems.

During these six substages, infants develop the abilities to think and remember. They also develop knowledge about aspects of the physical world, such as objects and spatial relationships. Researchers inspired by Piaget have found that some of these developments conform fairly closely to his observations, but other developments, including representational ability, may occur earlier than Piaget claimed. (Table 7-4 compares Piaget's views on these and other topics with more current findings; refer to this table as you read on.)

representational ability Piaget's term for capacity to store mental images or symbols of objects and events.

Checkpoint ✔

Can you . . .

✔ Summarize major developments during the six substages of the sensorimotor stage?

✔ Explain how primary, secondary, and tertiary circular reactions work?

✔ Tell why the development of representational ability is important?

Do Imitative Abilities Develop Earlier Than Piaget Thought?

Imitation is an important way of learning; it becomes especially valuable toward the end of the first year, as babies try out new skills (Nelson, 2005). Piaget maintained that **invisible imitation**—imitation using parts of their body that babies cannot see, such as the mouth—develops at about 9 months, after **visible imitation,** using parts that babies can see, such as the hands or feet. Yet in a series of studies by Andrew Meltzoff and M. Keith Moore (1983, 1989), babies less than 72 hours old appeared to imitate adults by opening their mouths and sticking out their tongues—a response that other research has found to disappear by about 2 months (Bjorklund & Pellegrini, 2000). According to Meltzoff and Gopnik (1993), this early behavior is the result of an evolved "like me" mechanism; the infant seeks to imitate faces that have the same properties (tongues that can stick out) as his or her own. This "like me" mechanism, Meltzoff (2007) suggests, may be the basis for *social cognition*—the ability to understand the goals, actions, and feelings of others. Meltzoff and Moore (1994) further suggest that infants have an inborn predisposition to imitate human faces that may serve the evolutionary (survival) purpose of communication with a caregiver (Rakison, 2005).

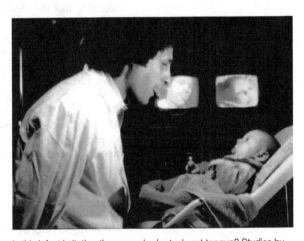

Is this infant imitating the researcher's stuck-out tongue? Studies by Andrew N. Meltzoff suggest that infants as young as 2 weeks are capable of invisible imitation. But other researchers found that only the youngest babies make this response, suggesting that the tongue movement may merely be exploratory behavior.

Other researchers have suggested that the tongue thrust may simply be exploratory behavior aroused by the sight of an adult tongue—or of some other narrow, pointed object approaching an infant's mouth (Bjorklund, 1997; S. S. Jones, 1996; Kagan, 2008). The tongue thrust may serve a different adaptive purpose for a young infant, who may be responding to purely perceptual information, than for an older infant whose response is based on a cognitive representation of another person's behavior (Bjorklund & Pellegrini, 2000; Kagan, 2008). If so, use of the same term *imitation* to describe both types of behavior may be misleading (Kagan, 2008).

invisible imitation Imitation with parts of one's body that one cannot see.

visible imitation Imitation with parts of one's body that one can see.

deferred imitation Piaget's term for reproduction of an observed behavior after the passage of time by calling up a stored symbol of it.

Piaget also held that children under 18 months cannot engage in **deferred imitation** of an act they saw some time before because they have not yet developed the ability to retain mental representations. However, some researchers suggest that Piaget underestimated infants' and toddlers' representational ability because of their limited ability to talk about what they remember. Babies as young as 6 *weeks* have appeared to imitate an adult's facial movements after a 24-hour delay, in the presence of the same adult, who this time was expressionless. This finding, according to Meltzoff and Moore (1994, 1998), suggests that very young babies retain a mental representation of an event. Deferred imitation of novel or complex events seems to begin by 6 to 9 months (Bauer, 2002; Meltzoff & Moore, 1998). Thus the findings on deferred imitation agree with those on operant conditioning (Rovee-Collier, 1999); infants do seem capable of remembering after a delay.

elicited imitation Research method in which infants or toddlers are induced to imitate a specific series of actions they have seen but not necessarily done before.

In **elicited imitation,** researchers induce infants and toddlers to imitate a specific series of actions they have seen but not necessarily done before. The initial demonstration may be accompanied by a simple verbal explanation (Bauer, 1996, 2002; Bauer, Wenner, Dropik, & Wewerka, 2000; Bauer, Wiebe, Carver, Waters, & Nelson, 2003). After a 1-month delay, with no further demonstration or explanation, more than 40 percent of 9-month-olds can reproduce a simple two-step procedure, such as dropping a toy car down a vertical chute and then pushing the car with a rod to make it roll to the end of a track and turn on a light (Bauer, 2002; Bauer et al., 2003). One study reliably predicted individual differences in performance of this task from scans of the infants' brains as they looked at photos of the same procedure a week after first seeing it. The memory traces of infants who could not repeat the procedure in the right order were less robust, indicating that they had failed to consolidate the memory for long-term storage (Bauer et al., 2003).

Elicited imitation is much more reliable during the 2nd year; nearly 8 out of 10 toddlers 13 to 20 months old can repeat an unfamiliar, multistep sequence (such as putting together a metal gong and causing it to ring) a year after seeing it done (Bauer, 1996; Bauer et al., 2000). Prior practice helps to reactivate children's memories, especially if some new items have been substituted for the original ones (Hayne, Barr, & Herbert, 2003). Four factors seem to determine young children's long-term recall: (1) the number of times a sequence of events has been experienced, (2) whether the child actively participated or merely observed, (3) whether the child is given verbal reminders of the experience, and (4) whether the sequence of events occurs in a logical, causal order (Bauer et al., 2000).

Development of Knowledge about Objects and Space

The ability to perceive the size and shape of objects and to discern their movements may be an early evolved mechanism for avoidance of predators (Rakison, 2005). The *object concept*—the idea that objects have independent existence, characteristics, and locations in space—is a later *cognitive* development fundamental to an orderly view of physical reality. The object concept is the basis for children's awareness that they themselves exist apart from objects and other people. It is essential to understanding a world full of objects and events.

When Does Object Permanence Develop?

object permanence Piaget's term for the understanding that a person or object still exists when out of sight.

One aspect of the object concept is **object permanence,** the realization that an object or person continues to exist when out of sight. According to Piaget, object permanence develops gradually during the sensorimotor stage. At first, infants have no such concept. By the third substage, from about 4 to 8 months, they will look for something they have dropped, but if they cannot see it, they act as if it no longer exists. In the fourth substage, about 8 to 12 months, they will look for an object in a place where they first found it after seeing it hidden, even if they later saw it being moved to another place. Piaget called this the **A-not-B error.** In the fifth substage, 12 to 18 months, they no longer make this error; they will search for an object in the last place they saw it hidden. However, they will not search for it in a place where they did not see it hidden. By the sixth substage, 18 to 24 months, object permanence is fully achieved; toddlers will look for an object even if they did not see it hidden.

Esther Thelen's dynamic systems theory proposes that the decision of where to search for a hidden object is not about what babies *know,* but about what they *do,* and why. One factor is how much time has elapsed between the infant's seeing the object hidden in a new place and the infant's reaching for it. If the elapsed time is brief, the infant is more likely to reach for the object in the new location. When the time interval is longer, however, the memory of having previously found the object in the old place inclines the infant to search there again, and that inclination grows stronger the more times the infant has found it there (Smith & Thelen, 2003; Spencer, Smith, & Thelen, 2001; Spencer et al., 2006).

Other research suggests that babies may fail to search for hidden objects because they cannot yet carry out a two-step or two-handed sequence of actions, such as moving a cushion or lifting the cover of a box before grasping the object. When given repeated opportunities, during a period of 1 to 3 months, to explore, manipulate, and learn about such a task, infants at 6 to 12 months can succeed (Bojczyk & Corbetta, 2004).

When object permanence is tested by hiding the object only by darkness, making it retrievable in one motion, infants in the third substage (4 to 8 months) perform surprisingly well (Goubet & Clifton, 1998).

Methods based only on infants' looking behavior eliminate the need for any motor activity and thus can be used at very early ages. As we discuss next, some research using information-processing methodology suggests that infants as young as 3 or 4 months seem not only to have a sense of object permanence but also have some understanding of causality, categorization, number, and other principles governing the physical world.

A-not-B error Tendency for 8- to 12-month-old infants to search for a hidden object in a place where they previously found it rather than in the place where they most recently saw it being hidden.

Symbolic Development, Pictorial Competence, and Understanding of Scale

Much of the knowledge people acquire about their world is gained, not through direct observation or experience but through *symbols,* intentional representations of reality. Learning to interpret symbols is, then, an essential task of childhood. First, however, children must become *symbol-minded:* attentive to symbols and their relationships to the things they represent (DeLoache, 2004). One aspect of symbolic development is the growth of *pictorial competence,* the ability to understand the nature of pictures (DeLoache, Pierroutsakos, & Uttal, 2003).

In studies carried out in both the United States and Africa's Ivory Coast, Judy DeLoache and her colleagues (DeLoache et al., 2003; DeLoache, Pierroutsakos, Uttal, Rosengren, & Gottlieb, 1998; Pierroutsakos & DeLoache, 2003) have observed infants using their hands to explore pictures as if they were objects—feeling, rubbing, patting, or grasping them or attempting to lift a depicted object off the page. This manual exploration of pictures diminishes by 15 months, but not until about 19 months do children point at a picture of a bear or telephone while saying its name ("beh" or "teltone"), showing an understanding that a picture is a symbol of something. By age 2, children understand that a picture is *both* an object and a symbol (Preissler & Bloom, 2007).

Although toddlers may spend a good deal of time watching television, they at first seem unaware that what they are seeing is a representation of reality (Troseth, Saylor, & Archer, 2006). In one series of experiments, 2- and 2½-year-olds watched on a video monitor as an adult hid an object in an adjoining room. When taken to the room, the 2½-year-olds found the hidden object easily, but 2-year-olds could not. Yet the younger children did find the object if they had watched through a window as it was being hidden (Troseth

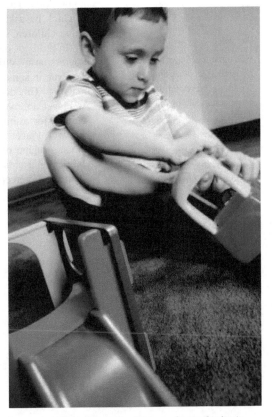

In one study, 18-to 36-month-olds were observed trying to slide down tiny slides, and squeeze into toy cars after similar, but child-sized objects were removed from their playrooms.

dual representation hypothesis
Proposal that children under age 3 have difficulty grasping spatial relationships because of the need to keep more than one mental representation in mind at the same time.

What's your view ?

- On the basis of observations by Piaget and the research they inspired, what factors would you consider in purchasing a toy for an infant or toddler?

Checkpoint ✔

Can you . . .

✔ Summarize Piaget's views on imitation, object permanence, pictorial competence, and understanding of scale?

✔ Explain why Piaget may have underestimated some of infants' cognitive abilities, and discuss the implications of more recent research?

& DeLoache, 1998). Apparently, what the 2-year-olds lacked was representational under-standing of screen images. In a follow-up experiment, 2-year-olds who were told face to face where to find a hidden toy were able to do so, whereas 2-year-olds who received the same information from a person on a video were not (Troseth et al., 2006).

Toddlers often make *scale errors*—momentary misperceptions of the relative sizes of symbolic and real objects. In one study, 18- to 36-month-olds were videotaped trying to slide down tiny slides, sit in dollhouse chairs, and squeeze into miniature cars after similar, but child-sized, objects were removed from their playroom. Such scale errors are clearly distinguishable from pretend play (DeLoache, Uttal, & Rosengren, 2004) and may in part result from lack of impulse control. In addition, the researchers suggested, two different brain systems normally work together during interactions with familiar objects. One system enables the child to recognize and categorize an object ("That's a buggy") and plan what to do with it ("I'm going to lie in it"). A separate system may be involved in perceiving the size of the object and using this information to control actions pertaining to it. Faulty communication between these immature brain systems may help explain young children's frequent scale errors (DeLoache, 2006).

The **dual representation hypothesis** offers yet another proposed explanation of why 2-year-olds have problems interpreting scale models. According to this hypothesis, it is difficult for toddlers to mentally represent both a symbol and the object it stands for at the same time, and so they may confuse the two (DeLoache, 2006; DeLoache et al., 2003).

Evaluating Piaget's Sensorimotor Stage

According to Piaget, the journey from reflex behavior to the beginnings of thought is a long, slow one. For a year and a half or so, babies learn only from their senses and movements; not until the last half of the 2nd year do they make the breakthrough to conceptual thought. Now, as we have seen, research using simplified tasks and modern tools suggests that certain limitations Piaget saw in infants' early cognitive abilities, such as object permanence, may instead have reflected immature linguistic and motor skills. The answers that Piaget received were as much a function of the ways in which he asked the questions as they were a reflection of the actual abilities of young children.

In terms of describing what children do under certain circumstances, and the basic progression of skills, Piaget was correct. He was an astute observer of child behavior. However, in some ways infants and toddlers are more cognitively competent than Piaget imagined. This does not mean that infants come into the world with minds fully formed. As Piaget observed, immature forms of cognition precede more mature forms. We can see this, for example, in the errors young infants make in searching for hidden objects. However, Piaget may have been mistaken in his emphasis on motor experience as the primary engine of cognitive growth. Infants' perceptions are far ahead of their motor abilities, and today's methods enable researchers to make observations and inferences about those perceptions.

Guideposts for Study

1. When and how do emotions develop, and how do babies show them?

2. How do infants show temperament differences, and how enduring are those differences?

3. How do infants gain trust in their world and form attachments, and how do infants and caregivers read each other's nonverbal signals?

4. When and how does the sense of self arise, and how do toddlers exercise autonomy and develop standards for socially acceptable behavior?

5. When and how do gender differences appear?

6. How do infants and toddlers interact with siblings and other children?

7. How do parental employment and early child care affect infants' and toddlers' development?

Foundations of Psychosocial Development

Although babies share common patterns of development, each, from the start, shows a distinct **personality:** the relatively consistent blend of emotions, temperament, thought, and behavior that makes each person unique. One baby may usually be cheerful; another easily upset. One toddler plays happily with other children; another prefers to play alone. Such characteristic ways of feeling, thinking, and acting, which reflect both inborn and environmental influences, affect the way children respond to others and adapt to their world. From infancy on, personality development is intertwined with social relationships (Table 8-1). This combination is called *psychosocial development.*

In our exploration of psychosocial development we first look at emotions, the building blocks of personality; then at temperament, or disposition; and then at an infant's earliest social experiences in the family. Then we discuss how parents shape behavioral differences between boys and girls.

Guidepost 1

When and how do emotions develop, and how do babies show them?

personality The relatively consistent blend of emotions, temperament, thought, and behavior that makes each person unique.

Table 8-1	Highlights of Infants' and Toddlers' Psychosocial Development, Birth to 36 Months
Approximate Age, Months	**Characteristics**
0–3	Infants are open to stimulation. They begin to show interest and curiosity, and they smile readily at people.
3–6	Infants can anticipate what is about to happen and experience disappointment when it does not. They show this by becoming angry or acting warily. They smile, coo, and laugh often. This is a time of social awakening and early reciprocal exchanges between the baby and the caregiver.
6–9	Infants play "social games" and try to get responses from people. They "talk" to, touch, and cajole other babies to get them to respond. They express more differentiated emotions, showing joy, fear, anger, and surprise.
9–12	Infants are intensely preoccupied with their principal caregiver, may become afraid of strangers, and act subdued in new situations. By 1 year, they communicate emotions more clearly, showing moods, ambivalence, and gradations of feeling.
12–18	Toddlers explore their environment, using the people they are most attached to as a secure base. As they master the environment, they become more confident and more eager to assert themselves.
18–36	Toddlers sometimes become anxious because they now realize how much they are separating from their caregiver. They work out their awareness of their limitations in fantasy and in play and by identifying with adults.

Source: Adapted from Sroufe, 1979.

Emotions

emotions Subjective reactions to experience that are associated with physiological and behavioral changes.

Emotions, such as sadness, joy, and fear, are subjective reactions to experience that are associated with physiological and behavioral changes. Fear, for example, is accompanied by a faster heartbeat and, often, by self-protective action. A person's characteristic pattern of emotional reactions begins to develop during infancy and is a basic element of personality. People differ in how often and how strongly they feel a particular emotion, in the kinds of events that may produce it, in the physical manifestations they show, and in how they act as a result. Culture influences the way people feel about a situation and the way they show their emotions. For example, some Asian cultures, which stress social harmony, discourage expressions of anger but place much importance on shame. The opposite is often true in American culture, which stresses self-expression, self-assertion, and self-esteem (Cole, Bruschi, & Tamang, 2002).

First Signs of Emotion

Newborns plainly show when they are unhappy. They let out piercing cries, flail their arms and legs, and stiffen their bodies. It is harder to tell when they are happy. During the 1st month, they become quiet at the sound of a human voice or when they are picked up, and they may smile when their hands are moved together to play pat-a-cake. As time goes by, infants respond more to people—smiling, cooing, reaching out, and eventually going to them.

These early signals or clues to babies' feelings are important indicators of development. When babies want or need something, they cry; when they feel sociable, they smile or laugh. When their messages bring a response, their sense of connection with other people grows. Their sense of control over their world grows too, as they see that their cries bring help and comfort and that their smiles and laughter elicit smiles and laughter in return. They become more able to participate actively in regulating their states of arousal and their emotional life.

Crying Crying is the most powerful way—and sometimes the only way—infants can communicate their needs. Some research has distinguished four patterns of crying (Wolff, 1969): the basic *hunger cry* (a rhythmic cry, which is not always associated with hunger); the *angry cry* (a variation of the rhythmic cry, in which excess air is forced through the vocal cords); the *pain cry* (a sudden onset of loud crying without preliminary moaning, sometimes followed by holding the breath); and the *frustration cry* (two or three drawn-out cries, with no prolonged breath-holding) (Wood & Gustafson, 2001).

Some parents worry that picking up a crying baby will spoil the infant. However, if parents wait until cries of distress escalate to shrieks of rage, it may become more difficult to soothe the baby; and such a pattern, if experienced repeatedly, may interfere with an infant's developing ability to regulate, or manage, his or her emotional state (R. A. Thompson, 1991). Ideally, the most developmentally sound approach may be to *prevent* distress, making soothing unnecessary.

Smiling and Laughing The earliest faint smiles occur spontaneously soon after birth, apparently as a result of subcortical nervous system activity. These involuntary smiles frequently appear during periods of REM sleep (refer to Chapter 5). Through 1 month of age, smiles are often elicited by high-pitched tones when an infant is drowsy. During the 2nd month, as visual recognition develops, babies smile more at visual stimuli, such as faces they know (Sroufe, 1997; Wolff, 1963).

Social smiling, when newborn infants gaze at their parents and smile at them, does not develop until the 2nd month of life. Social smiling signals the infant's active, positive participation in the relationship. The development of smiling involves both changes in the timing of smiles and in the form of the smiles themselves. Laughter is a smile-linked vocalization that becomes more common between 4 and 12 months when it may signify the most intense positive emotion (Salkind, 2005).

Crying enables this baby to communicate his needs. Parents generally learn to recognize whether their baby is crying because of hunger, anger, frustration, or pain.

Through 6 months of age, infant smiles reflect an emotional exchange with a partner. As babies grow older, they become more actively engaged in mirthful exchanges. A 6-month-old may giggle in response to the mother making unusual sounds or appearing with a towel over her face; a 10-month-old may laughingly try to put the towel back on her face when it falls off. This change reflects cognitive development: By laughing at the unexpected, babies show that they know what to expect. By turning the tables, they show awareness that they can make things happen. Laughter also helps babies discharge tension, such as fear of a threatening object (Sroufe, 1997).

By 12 to 15 months, infants are intentionally communicating to the partner about objects. Anticipatory smiling—in which infants smile at an object and then gaze at an adult while continuing to smile—may be the first step. Anticipatory smiling rises sharply between 8 and 10 months and seems to be among the first types of communication in which the infant refers to an object or experience.

Early smiles may help predict later development. Four-month-olds who smile more in response to a mobile show a more exuberant temperament style at 4 years, being more likely to talk and engage. Six-month-old infants who smile at a still face are more likely to be securely attached at 12 months. So the form of infant smiles as well as their timing changes with development. Just as infants exercise more control over when they smile between 3 and 6 months, they also become more capable of using very intense smiles to participate in highly arousing social situations.

An infant's earliest smiles are involuntary, but beginning at 1 month, smiles generally become more frequent and more social. This baby may be smiling at the sight of a parent or caregiver.

When Do Emotions Appear?

Emotional development is an orderly process; complex emotions unfold from simpler ones. According to one model of emotional development (Lewis, 1997; Figure 8-1), babies soon after birth show signs of contentment, interest, and distress. These are diffuse, reflexive, mostly physiological responses to sensory stimulation or internal processes. During the next 6 months or so, these early emotional

Contentment   Interest   Distress

Joy   Surprise   Sadness, disgust

First 6 months

Anger, fear

Consciousness, as in self-referential behavior

From 18 to 24 months

Embarrassment*
Envy
Empathy

Acquisition and retention of standards and rules

From 2½ to 3 years

Embarrassment*
Pride
Shame
Guilt

Figure 8-1

Differentiation of emotions during the first 3 years. The primary, or basic, emotions emerge during the first 6 months or so; the self-conscious emotions develop around 18 to 24 months, as a result of the emergence of self-awareness (consciousness of self) together with accumulation of knowledge about societal standards and rules.

Note: There are two kinds of embarrassment. The earlier kind does not involve evaluation of behavior and may simply be a response to being singled out as the object of attention. The second kind, evaluative embarrassment, which emerges during the 3rd year, is a mild form of shame.

Source: Adapted from Lewis, 1997, Fig. 1, p. 120.

states differentiate into true emotions: joy, surprise, sadness, disgust, and, last, anger and fear—reactions to events that have meaning for the infant. As we discuss in a subsequent section, the emergence of these basic, or primary, emotions is related to the biological clock of neurological maturation.

Self-conscious emotions, such as embarrassment, envy, and empathy (discussed in more detail in a subsequent section) arise only after children have developed **self-awareness:** the cognitive understanding that they have a recognizable identity, separate and different from the rest of their world. This consciousness of self seems to emerge between 15 and 24 months. Self-awareness is necessary before children can be aware of being the focus of attention, identify with what other "selves" are feeling, or wish they had what someone else has. By about age 3, having acquired self-awareness plus a good deal of knowledge about their society's accepted standards, rules, and goals, children become better able to evaluate their thoughts, plans, desires, and behavior against what is considered socially appropriate. Only then can they demonstrate the **self-evaluative emotions** of pride, guilt, and shame (Lewis, 1995, 1997, 1998). In other words, children must understand that they are separate from someone else—and that others might have opinions about the wrongness or rightness of their behavior—before they can understand and feel these social emotions.

Guilt and shame are distinct emotions, even though both may be responses to wrongdoing. Children who fail to live up to behavioral standards may feel guilty (that is, regret their behavior), but they do not necessarily feel a lack of self-worth, as when they feel ashamed. Their focus is on a bad *act,* not a bad *self* (Eisenberg, 2000).

Brain Growth and Emotional Development

The development of the brain after birth is closely connected with changes in emotional life. This is a bidirectional process: emotional experiences not only are affected by brain development but also can have long-lasting effects on the structure of the brain (Mlot, 1998; Sroufe, 1997).

Four major shifts in brain organization correspond roughly to changes in emotional processing (Schore, 1994; Sroufe, 1997; refer to Figure 6-6). During the first 3 months, differentiation of basic emotions begins as the *cerebral cortex* becomes functional, bringing cognitive perceptions into play. REM sleep and reflexive behavior, including the spontaneous neonatal smile, diminish.

The second shift occurs around 9 or 10 months, when the *frontal lobes* begin to interact with the *limbic system,* a seat of emotional reactions. At the same time, limbic structures such as the *hippocampus* become larger and more adultlike. Connections between the frontal cortex and the *hypothalamus* and limbic system, which process sensory information, may facilitate the relationship between the cognitive and emotional spheres. As these connections become denser and more elaborate, an infant can experience and interpret emotions at the same time.

The third shift takes place during the 2nd year, when infants develop self-awareness, self-conscious emotions, and a greater capacity for regulating their emotions and activities. These changes, which may be related to myelination of the frontal lobes, are accompanied by greater physical mobility and exploratory behavior.

The fourth shift occurs around age 3, when hormonal changes in the autonomic (involuntary) nervous system coincide with the emergence of evaluative emotions. Underlying the development of such emotions as shame may be a shift away from dominance by the *sympathetic system,* the part of the autonomic system that prepares the body for action, and the maturation of the *parasympathetic system,* the part of the autonomic system that is involved in excretion and sexual excitation.

Altruistic Helping, Empathy, and Social Cognition

A guest of 18-month-old Alex's father—a person Alex had never seen before—dropped his pen on the floor, and it rolled under a cabinet, where the guest couldn't quite reach it. Alex, being small enough, crawled under the cabinet, retrieved the pen, and gave it to the guest. By acting out of concern for a stranger with no expectation of reward, Alex showed **altruistic behavior** (Warneken & Tomasello, 2006).

Altruistic behavior seems to come naturally to toddlers. Well before the second birthday, children often help others, share belongings and food, and offer comfort (Zahn-Waxler, Radke-Yarrow, Wagner, & Chapman, 1992). However, rewarding such behavior tends to undermine it. In an experiment in Leipzig, Germany, 20-month-olds repeatedly helped an adult by picking up dropped objects, even when doing so required them to stop playing. Children who received a material reward for their help were less likely to help again than children who received only praise or no reward (Warneken & Tomasello, 2008).

In another experiment, 18-month-olds helped in 6 out of 10 situations in which the experimenter was having trouble reaching a goal but did *not* help in similar situations in which the experimenter did *not* seem to be having trouble—for example, when he had dropped a pen deliberately. Such behavior may reflect **empathy,** the ability to imagine how another person might feel in a particular situation (Zahn-Waxler et al., 1992). As we have mentioned, this ability to "put oneself in another person's place" emerges during the 2nd year, and it increases with age (Eisenberg, 2000; Eisenberg & Fabes, 1998).

The roots of empathy, however, can be seen in early infancy. Two- to 3-month-olds react to others' emotional expressions (Tomasello, 2007). Six-month-olds engage in *social evaluation,* valuing someone on the basis of that person's treatment of others. In one series of experiments (Hamlin, Wynn, & Bloom, 2007), 6- and 10-month-old infants saw a wooden character ("the climber") repeatedly attempt to climb a hill. On the third attempt, the infants saw the climber either assisted by a "helper," who pushed up from behind, or pushed down by a "hinderer." When the infants in both age groups were encouraged to reach for either the helper or the hinderer, they overwhelmingly chose the helper. In a follow-up study, the infants saw a neutral character that followed the same route as either the helper or hinderer but did not interact with the climber. When given a choice between the helper and the neutral character, the infants preferred the helper; and between the neutral character and the hinderer, they preferred the neutral character.

Research in neurobiology has recently identified special brain cells called *mirror neurons,* which may underlie empathy and altruism. **Mirror neurons,** located in several parts of the brain, fire when a person does something but also when he or she observes someone else doing the same thing. By "mirroring" the activities and motivations of others, they allow a person to see the world from someone else's point of view. Mirror neurons have been linked to imitative learning as well as to the emergence of self-awareness, of language, and of abstract reasoning. Autism spectrum disorders (refer to Box 6-1 in Chapter 6) may represent a breakdown or suppression of the mirroring system; children with autism and related disorders are less empathic, less emotionally connected to others, and less able to read their emotional states than are other children, and functional MRIs show less mirror neuron activity in their brains (Iacoboni, 2008; Iacoboni & Mazziotta, 2007; Oberman & Ramachandran, 2007).

Empathy depends on **social cognition,** the cognitive ability to understand that others have mental states and to gauge their feelings and intentions. Piaget maintained that **egocentrism** (inability to see another person's point of view) delays the development of this ability until the concrete operational stage of middle childhood, but more recent research suggests that social cognition begins much earlier. In one study, 9-month-olds (but not 6-month-olds) reacted differently to a person who was unwilling to give them a toy than to a person who tried to give them a toy but accidentally dropped it. This finding suggests that the older infants had gained some understanding of another person's intentions (Behne, Carpenter, Call, & Tomasello, 2005).

Shared Intentionality and Collaborative Activity

The motivation to help and share and the ability to understand the intentions of others together contribute to an important development between 9 and 12 months of age, collaboration with caregivers in joint activities, such as a child holding and handing over a pair of socks and a caregiver dressing the child. Such activities require **shared intentionality:** joint attention to a mutual goal (Tomasello, 2007).

Collaborative activities increase during the 2nd year of life as toddlers become more adept at communication—first with gestures, then with words. At 12 months, Jasmine

empathy Ability to put oneself in another person's place and feel what the other person feels.

mirror neurons Neurons that fire when a person does something or observes someone else doing the same thing.

social cognition Ability to understand that other people have mental states and to gauge their feelings and intentions.

egocentrism Piaget's term for inability to consider another person's point of view; a characteristic of young children's thought.

Checkpoint ✔

Can you . . .

✔ Explain the significance of patterns of crying, smiling, and laughing?

✔ Trace a proposed sequence of emergence of the basic, self-conscious, and evaluative emotions and its connection with neurological development?

✔ Discuss the emergence of altruistic behavior, empathy, social cognition, and collaborative activity, and tell how these developments are related?

shared intentionality Joint attention to a mutual goal.

points at a ball to show that she wants to play a game of rolling it back and forth with her father. When the ball rolls under a chair, she points to let her father know where it is. And when her father loses interest in the game, she points to remind him that it is his turn. The vocabulary explosion that frequently occurs during the 2nd year enables more complex and flexible collaborative communication (Tomasello, 2007).

Temperament

Guidepost 2

How do infants show temperament differences, and how enduring are those differences?

temperament Characteristic disposition or style of approaching and reacting to situations.

Temperament is sometimes defined as a person's characteristic, biologically based way of approaching and reacting to people and situations. Temperament has been described as the *how* of behavior: not *what* people do, but *how* they go about doing it (Thomas & Chess, 1977). Two toddlers, for example, may be equally able to dress themselves and may be equally motivated, but one may do it more quickly than the other, be more willing to put on a new outfit, and be less distracted if the cat jumps on the bed. Also, temperament may affect not only the way children approach and react to the outside world but the way they regulate their mental, emotional, and behavioral functioning (Rothbart, Ahadi, & Evans, 2000).

Temperament has an emotional dimension; but unlike emotions such as fear, excitement, and boredom, which come and go, temperament is relatively consistent and enduring. Individual differences in temperament, which are thought to derive from a person's basic biological makeup, form the core of the developing personality.

Studying Temperament Patterns: The New York Longitudinal Study

easy children Children with a generally happy temperament, regular biological rhythms, and a readiness to accept new experiences.

difficult children Children with irritable temperament, irregular biological rhythms, and intense emotional responses.

slow-to-warm-up children Children whose temperament is generally mild but who are hesitant about accepting new experiences.

To better appreciate how temperament affects behavior, let's look at three sisters. Amy, the eldest, was a cheerful, calm baby who ate, slept, and eliminated at regular times. She greeted each day and most people with a smile, and the only sign that she was awake during the night was the tinkle of the musical toy in her crib. When Brooke, the second sister, woke up, she would open her mouth to cry before she even opened her eyes. She slept and ate little and irregularly; she laughed and cried loudly, often bursting into tantrums; and she had to be convinced that new people and new experiences were not threatening before she would have anything to do with them. The youngest sister, Christina, was mild in her responses, both positive and negative. She did not like most new situations, but if allowed to proceed at her own slow pace, she would eventually become interested and involved.

Amy, Brooke, and Christina exemplify the three main types of temperament found by the New York Longitudinal Study (NYLS). In this pioneering study on temperament, researchers followed 133 infants into adulthood. The researchers collected data from parents on how active the children were; how regular they were in hunger, sleep, and bowel habits; how readily they accepted new people and situations; how they adapted to changes in routine; how sensitive they were to noise, bright lights, and other sensory stimuli; how intensely they responded; whether their mood tended to be pleasant, joyful, and friendly or unpleasant, unhappy, and unfriendly; and whether they persisted at tasks or were easily distracted (Thomas, Chess, & Birch, 1968).

The researchers were able to place most of the children in the study into one of three categories (Table 8-2).

Seven-month-old Luisa's ready smile and affable nature are signs of an easy temperament.

- Forty percent were **easy children** like Amy: generally happy, rhythmic in biological functioning, and accepting of new experiences.
- Ten percent were what the researchers called **difficult children** like Brooke: more irritable and harder to please, irregular in biological rhythms, and more intense in expressing emotion.
- Fifteen percent were **slow-to-warm-up children** like Christina: mild but slow to adapt to new people and situations (Thomas & Chess, 1977, 1984).

Many children (including 35 percent of the NYLS sample) do not fit neatly into any of these three categories. A baby may eat and sleep regularly but be afraid

Table 8-2	Three Temperamental Patterns (according to the New York Longitudinal Study)	
Easy Child	**Difficult Child**	**Slow-to-Warm-Up Child**
Has moods of mild to moderate intensity, usually positive.	Displays intense and frequently negative moods; cries often and loudly; also laughs loudly.	Has mildly intense reactions, both positive and negative.
Responds well to novelty and change. Quickly develops regular sleep and feeding schedules.	Responds poorly to novelty and change. Sleeps and eats irregularly.	Responds slowly to novelty and change. Sleeps and eats more regularly than the difficult child, less regularly than the easy child.
Takes to new foods easily.	Accepts new foods slowly.	Shows mildly negative initial response to new stimuli (a first encounter with a new person, place, or situation).
Smiles at strangers.	Is suspicious of strangers.	
Adapts easily to new situations.	Adapts slowly to new situations.	
Accepts most frustrations with little fuss.	Reacts to frustration with tantrums.	
Adapts quickly to new routines and rules of new games.	Adjusts slowly to new routines.	Gradually develops liking for new stimuli after repeated, unpressured exposures.

Source: Adapted from A. Thomas & Chess, Genesis and evolution of behavioral disorders: From infancy to early adult life. *American Journal of Psychiatry,* 141 (1) 1984, pp. 1–9. Copyright © 1984 by the American Psychiatric Association. Reproduced with permission.

of strangers. A child may be easy most of the time, but not always. Another child may warm up slowly to new foods but adapt quickly to new babysitters (Thomas & Chess, 1984). A child may laugh intensely but not show intense frustration, and a child with rhythmic toilet habits may show irregular sleeping patterns (Rothbart et al., 2000). All these variations are normal.

How Is Temperament Measured?

Because the complex interviewing and scoring procedures used in the NYLS are cumbersome, many researchers use short-form questionnaires. A parental self-report instrument, the Rothbart Infant Behavior Questionnaire (IBQ) (Gartstein & Rothbart, 2003; Rothbart et al., 2000) focuses on several dimensions of infant temperament similar to those in the NYLS: activity level, positive emotion (smiling and laughing), fear, frustration, soothability, and duration of orienting (a combination of distractibility and attention span) as well as such additional factors as intensity of pleasure, perceptual sensitivity, and attentional shifting. Parents rate their infants with regard to recent concrete events and behaviors ("How often during the past week did the baby smile or laugh when given a toy?" rather than "Does the baby respond positively to new events?").

Although parental ratings are the most commonly used measures of children's temperament, their validity is in question. For example, studies of twins have found that parents tend to rate a child's temperament by comparison with other children in the family—for example, labeling one child inactive in contrast to a more active sibling (Saudino, 2003a). Still, observations by researchers may reflect biases as well (Seifer, 2003). Parents see their children in a variety of day-to-day situations, whereas a laboratory observer sees only how the child reacts to particular standardized situations. Thus a combination of methods may provide a more accurate picture of how temperament affects child development (Rothbart & Hwang, 2002; Saudino, 2003a, 2003b).

How Stable Is Temperament?

Temperament appears to be largely inborn, probably hereditary (Braungart, Plomin, DeFries, & Fulker, 1992; Emde et al., 1992; Schmitz et al., 1996; Thomas & Chess, 1977, 1984), and fairly stable. Newborn babies show different patterns of sleeping, fussing, and activity, and these differences tend to persist to some degree (Korner, 1996; Korner et al., 1985). Studies using the IBQ have found strong links between infant temperament and childhood personality at age 7 (Rothbart, Ahadi, Hershey, & Fisher, 2001; Rothbart et al., 2000). Other researchers, using temperament types similar to those of the NYLS, have found that temperament at age 3 closely predicts aspects of personality at ages 18 and 21 (Caspi, 2000; Caspi & Silva, 1995; Newman, Caspi, Moffitt, & Silva, 1997).

That does not mean, however, that temperament is fully formed at birth. Temperament develops as various emotions and self-regulatory capacities appear (Rothbart et al., 2000) and can change in response to parental treatment and other life experiences (Belsky, Fish, & Isabella, 1991; Kagan & Snidman, 2004). Temperament may be affected by culturally influenced child-raising practices. Infants in Malaysia, an island group in Southeast Asia, tend to be less adaptable, more wary of new experiences, and more readily responsive to stimuli than U.S. babies. This may be because Malay parents do not often expose young children to situations that require adaptability, and they encourage infants to be acutely aware of sensations, such as the need for a diaper change (Banks, 1989).

Temperament and Adjustment: "Goodness of Fit"

goodness of fit Appropriateness of environmental demands and constraints to a child's temperament.

According to the NYLS, the key to healthy adjustment is **goodness of fit**—the match between a child's temperament and the environmental demands and constraints the child must deal with. We can think of goodness of fit as a descriptor of the child-caregiver relationship, or of the fit between the child and the wider social context. If a very active child is expected to sit still for long periods, if a slow-to-warm-up child is constantly pushed into new situations, or if a persistent child is constantly taken away from absorbing projects, tensions may occur. Infants with difficult temperaments may be more susceptible to the quality of parenting than infants with easy or slow-to-warm-up temperaments and may need more emotional support combined with respect for their autonomy (Belsky, 1997, 2005; Stright, Gallagher, & Kelley, 2008). Caregivers who recognize that a child acts in a certain way, not out of willfulness, laziness, stupidity, or spite but largely because of inborn temperament, may be less likely to feel guilty, anxious, or hostile, to feel a loss of control, or to be rigid or impatient. They can anticipate the child's reactions and help the child adapt—for example, by giving early warnings of the need to stop an activity or by gradually introducing a child to new situations.

Shyness and Boldness: Influences of Biology and Culture

As we have mentioned, temperament seems to have a biological basis. In longitudinal research with about 500 children starting in infancy, Jerome Kagan and his colleagues studied an aspect of temperament called *inhibition to the unfamiliar,* or behavioral inhibition, which has to do with how boldly or cautiously the child approaches unfamiliar objects and situations and is associated with certain biological characteristics.

When presented at 4 months with a series of new stimuli, about 20 percent of the infants became easily aroused and eventually cried, pumped their arms and legs, and sometimes arched their backs; this group were called inhibited or "high-reactive." About 40 percent showed little distress or motor activity and were more likely to smile spontaneously; they were labeled as uninhibited or "low-reactive." The researchers suggested that inhibited children may be born with an unusually excitable amygdala, a part of the brain that detects and reacts to unfamiliar events and is involved in emotional reactions (Kagan & Snidman, 2004).

Infants identified as inhibited or uninhibited seemed to maintain these patterns to some degree during childhood (Kagan, 1997; Kagan & Snidman, 1991a, 1991b, 2004), along with specific differences in physiological characteristics. Inhibited children were more likely to have a thin body build, narrow face, and blue eyes, whereas uninhibited children were taller, heavier, and more often brown-eyed. In addition, inhibited children showed higher and less variable heart rates than uninhibited children, and the pupils of their eyes dilated more (Arcus & Kagan, 1995). It may be that the genes that contribute to reactivity and inhibited or uninhibited behavior also influence these physiological traits (Kagan & Snidman, 2004).

What's your view ?

- In the United States, many people consider shyness undesirable. How should a parent handle a shy child? Do you think it is best to accept the child's temperament or try to change it?

These findings suggest, again, that experience can moderate or accentuate early tendencies. Male toddlers who were inclined to be fearful and shy were more likely to remain so at age 3 if their parents were highly accepting of the child's reactions. If parents did not limit their sons to exposure to new situations that they knew the children could handle, the boys tended to become less inhibited (Park, Belsky, Putnam, & Crnic, 1997). In other research, when mothers responded neutrally to infants who were behaviorally inhibited, the inhibition tended to remain stable or increase. These authors suggested that caregivers' sensitivity may affect the neural systems that underlie reactions to stress and novelty (Fox, Hane, & Pine, 2007). Other environmental influences, such as birth order, race/ethnicity, culture, relationships with teachers and peers, and unpredictable events also can reinforce or soften a child's original temperament bias (Kagan & Snidman, 2004).

Developmental Issues in Infancy

How does a dependent newborn, with a limited emotional repertoire and pressing physical needs, become a child with complex feelings and the abilities to understand and control them? Much of this development revolves around issues regarding relationships with caregivers.

Developing Trust

For a far longer period than the young of other mammals, human babies are dependent on others for food, for protection, and for their very lives. How do they come to trust that their needs will be met? According to Erikson (1950), early experiences are the key.

The first of Erikson's eight stages in psychosocial development (refer to Table 2-2 in Chapter 2) is **basic trust versus basic mistrust.** This stage begins in infancy and continues until about 18 months. In these early months, babies develop a sense of the reliability of the people and objects in their world. They need to develop a balance between trust (which lets them form intimate relationships) and mistrust (which enables them to protect themselves). If trust predominates, as it should, children develop the virtue, or strength, of *hope:* the belief that they can fulfill their needs and obtain their desires (Erikson, 1982). If mistrust predominates, children will view the world as unfriendly and unpredictable and will have trouble forming quality relationships.

basic trust versus basic mistrust Erikson's first stage in psychosocial development, in which infants develop a sense of the reliability of people and objects.

Diane's sensitivity to Anna's needs contributes to the development of Anna's sense of basic trust—her ability to rely on the people and things in her world. Trust is necessary, according to Erikson, for children to form intimate relationships.

Erikson's Eight Stages of Development

Whereas Freud taught that our personalities were formed by around the age of 5 years, Erikson disagreed and felt that important periods of development occurred throughout the life span. For example, Freud called the period from age 6 to puberty the latency period because he believed not much psychologically was going on. However, this is a period when children are starting to go to school; they are learning to work and to gain satisfaction from success and from accomplishments; they are learning to be sociable, to share, and to cooperate with peers; and they are learning about social structures, such as the fact that teachers are in charge and represent authorities. Erikson (1963, 1968)

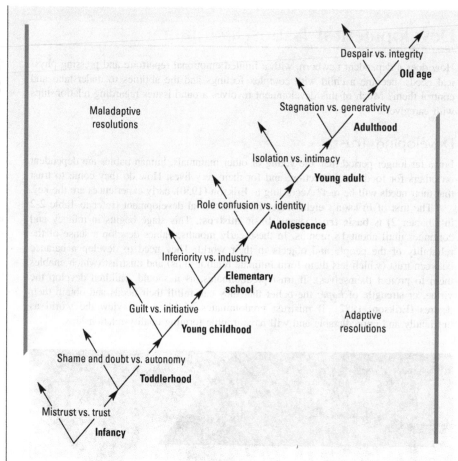

Figure 10.2

Erikson's eight stages of development.

argued that much development occurred during the years that Freud thought were quiet. Indeed, Erikson believed that the development of personality lasted well into adulthood and even old age (Erikson, 1975). He outlined **eight stages of development** through which we all pass (Figure 10.2).

Not only did Erikson disagree with Freud about the time span of development, but he also disagreed with Freud about the conflict, or crisis, that occurs at each stage. Whereas Freud felt that the crises were inherently sexual, Erikson believed that the crises were of a social nature. After all, he argued, the persons with whom we have our first social relationships are our parents. Thus, there could be crises of learning to trust our parents, learning to be autonomous from them, learning from them how to act as an adult. He called these **psychosocial conflicts** rather than the psychosexual conflicts that formed Freud's developmental stages.

Although Erikson disagreed with Freud on these two issues of development, he did agree with Freud on several other points. First, like Freud, Erikson kept a **stage model of development,** implying that people go through the stages in a certain order and that there is a specific issue that characterizes each stage. Second, Erikson believed that each stage represented a conflict, a **developmental crisis,** that needed to be resolved. Third, Erikson maintained the notion of **fixation,** meaning that if the crisis was not successfully and adaptively resolved, then personality development could become arrested and the person would continue to be preoccupied by that crisis in development.

Trust Versus Mistrust

When children are born, they are completely dependent on those around them. Their first questions would most likely be "Who's going to take care of me, and will they do a good job? Can I trust that they will feed me when I am hungry, clothe me when I am cold, comfort me when I cry, and generally take care of me?" If children are well taken care of, if their basic needs are met, then they will develop a sense of trust in their caregivers. This sense of trust, according to Erikson, forms the basis of future relationships, with such children growing up believing that other people are approachable, trustable, and generally good and loving. However, some infants are not well taken care of, for various reasons, and they never receive the love and care they need. Such infants may develop a sense that others are not to be trusted and may develop a lifelong pattern of mistrust in others, suspiciousness, and feelings of estrangement, isolation, or social discomfort when around others.

The critical element in developing trust is sensitive, responsive, consistent caregiving. Erikson saw the feeding situation as the setting for establishing the right mix of trust and mistrust. Can the baby count on being fed when hungry, and can the baby therefore trust the mother as a representative of the world? Trust enables an infant to let the mother out of sight "because she has become an inner certainty as well as an outer predictability" (Erikson, 1950, p. 247).

Checkpoint ✔

Can you . . .

✔ Explain the importance of basic trust, and identify the critical element in its development?

Developing Attachments

When Ahmed's mother is near, he looks at her, smiles at her, babbles to her, and crawls after her. When she leaves, he cries; when she comes back, he squeals with joy. When he is frightened or unhappy, he clings to her. Ahmed has formed his first attachment to another person.

Attachment is a reciprocal, enduring emotional tie between an infant and a caregiver, each of whom contributes to the quality of the relationship. From an evolutionary point of view, attachments have adaptive value for babies, ensuring that their psychosocial as well as physical needs will be met (MacDonald, 1998). According to ethological theory, infants and parents are biologically predisposed to become attached to each other, and attachment promotes a baby's survival.

Studies of functional MRIs of Japanese and U.S. mothers identified neural bases for attachment. In the Japanese study, certain areas of a mother's brain were activated at the sight of her own 16-month-old baby smiling at the mother or crying for her, but not at the sight of other infants showing those behaviors (Noriuchi, Kikuchi, & Senoo, 2008). A U.S. study highlighted the pleasure a new mother gets from seeing her infant's smiling face. In this longitudinal study, researchers videotaped the infants' faces during play at 5 to 10 months of age. At least 3 months later, the mothers saw these images for the first time. Happy-faced images of their own infant—but not of another infant—activated maternal reward-processing brain regions associated with the brain chemical dopamine. For reasons that are not clear, sad facial expressions on their own and other infants did *not* elicit such differing maternal responses (Strathearn, Li, Fonagy, & Montague, 2008).

attachment Reciprocal, enduring tie between two people—especially between infant and caregiver—each of whom contributes to the quality of the relationship.

Studying Patterns of Attachment

The study of attachment owes much to the ethologist John Bowlby (1951), a pioneer in the study of bonding in animals. From his animal studies and from observations of disturbed children in a London psychoanalytic clinic, Bowlby became convinced of the importance of the mother-baby bond and warned against separating mother and baby without providing good substitute care. Mary Ainsworth (1967), a student of Bowlby's in the early 1950s, went on to study attachment in African babies in Uganda through naturalistic observation in their homes. Ainsworth later devised the **Strange Situation,** a now-classic laboratory-based technique designed to assess attachment patterns between an infant and an adult. Typically, the adult is the mother (though other adults have taken part as well), and the infant is 10 to 24 months old.

The Strange Situation consists of a sequence of eight episodes of gradually increasing stress, which takes less than half an hour. The episodes are designed to trigger the emergence of attachment-related behaviors. During that time, the mother twice leaves the baby in an unfamiliar room, the first time with a stranger. The second time she leaves the baby alone, and the stranger comes back before the mother does. The mother then encourages the baby to explore and play again and gives comfort if the baby seems to need it (Ainsworth, Blehar, Waters, & Wall, 1978). Of particular concern is the baby's response each time the mother returns.

When Ainsworth and her colleagues observed 1-year-olds in the Strange Situation and at home, they found three main patterns of attachment. These are *secure* (the most common category, into which about 60 to 75 percent of low-risk North American babies fall) and two forms of anxious, or insecure, attachment: *avoidant* (15 to 25 percent) and *ambivalent,* or *resistant* (10 to 15 percent) (Vondra & Barnett, 1999).

Babies with **secure attachment** might cry or protest when a caregiver leaves but are able to obtain the comfort they need, effectively and quickly demonstrating flexibility and resilience when faced with stressful situations. They are usually cooperative and relatively free of anger. Babies with **avoidant attachment** are unaffected by a caregiver leaving or returning. They show little emotion either positively or negatively. Babies with **ambivalent (resistant) attachment** become anxious even before a caregiver leaves and become increasingly upset when he or she departs. Upon the caregiver's return, ambivalent babies demonstrate their distress and anger by seeking contact while at the same time resisting it by kicking or squirming. Resistant babies can be difficult to comfort as their anger frequently overcomes their ability to gain comfort from a caregiver.

These three attachment *patterns* are universal in all cultures in which they have been studied—cultures as different as those in Africa, China, and Israel—though the percentage of infants in each category varies (van IJzendoorn & Kroonenberg, 1988; van IJzendoorn & Sagi, 1999). Attachment *behaviors,* however, vary across cultures. Among the Gusii of East Africa, on the western edge of Kenya, infants are greeted with handshakes, and Gusii infants reach out for a parent's hand much as Western infants cuddle up for a hug (van IJzendoorn & Sagi, 1999).

Other research (Main & Solomon, 1986) identified a fourth pattern, **disorganized-disoriented attachment,** which is the least secure. Babies with the disorganized pattern seem to lack a cohesive strategy to deal with the stress of the Strange Situation. Instead, they show contradictory, repetitive, or misdirected behaviors (such as seeking closeness to the stranger instead of the mother). They may greet the mother brightly when she returns but then turn away or approach without looking at her. They seem confused and afraid (Carlson, 1998; van IJzendoorn, Schuengel, & Baermans-Kranenburg, 1999).

Disorganized attachment is thought to occur in at least 10 percent of low-risk infants but in much higher proportions in certain at-risk populations, such as premature children and those whose mothers abuse alcohol or drugs (Vondra & Barnett, 1999). It is most prevalent in babies with mothers who are insensitive, intrusive, or abusive; who are fearful or frightening and thus leave the infant with no one to alleviate the fear the mother arouses; or who have suffered unresolved loss or have unresolved feelings about their childhood attachment to their own parents. The natural tendency of infants is to approach the mother when they are frightened. When they are frightened *by* the mother, this puts into place an incompatible motivational system and results in the collapse of strategies. The likelihood of disorganized attachment increases in the presence of multiple risk factors, such as maternal insensitivity plus marital discord plus parenting stress. Disorganized attachment is a reliable predictor of later behav-

Strange Situation Laboratory technique used to study infant attachment.

secure attachment Pattern in which an infant is quickly and effectively able to find comfort from a caregiver when faced with a stressful situation.

avoidant attachment Pattern in which an infant rarely cries when separated from the primary caregiver and avoids contact on his or her return.

ambivalent (resistant) attachment Pattern in which an infant becomes anxious before the primary caregiver leaves, is extremely upset during his or her absence, and both seeks and resists contact on his or her return.

disorganized-disoriented attachment Pattern in which an infant, after separation from the primary caregiver, shows contradictory behaviors on his or her return.

ioral and adjustment problems (Bernier & Meins, 2008; Carlson, 1998; van IJzendoorn et al., 1999).

Some infants seem to be more susceptible to disorganized attachment than others. Some manage to form organized attachments despite atypical parenting, while others who are *not* exposed to atypical parenting form disorganized attachments (Bernier & Meins, 2008). One explanation might be a *gene-environment interaction* (discussed in Chapter 3). Studies have identified a variant of the DRD4 gene as a possible risk factor for disorganized attachment, and the risk increases nearly 19-fold when the mother has an unresolved loss (Gervai et al., 2005; Lakatos et al., 2000, 2002; van IJzendoorn & Bakermans-Kranenburg, 2006). Another explanation might be a *gene-environment correlation* (also discussed in Chapter 3). The infant's inborn characteristics may place unusually stressful demands on a parent and thus elicit parenting behaviors that promote disorganized attachment (Bernier & Meins, 2008).

Contrary to Ainsworth's original findings, babies seem to develop attachments to both parents at about the same time, and security of attachment to father and mother is usually quite similar (Fox, Kimmerly, & Schafer, 1991).

Babies with disorganized-disoriented attachment may seem confused or afraid when faced with the Strange Situation.

How Attachment Is Established

On the basis of a baby's interactions with the mother, proposed Ainsworth and Bowlby, the baby builds a working model of what can be expected from her. A working model is a set of expectations the baby has about how the mother is likely to respond in interactions. As long as the mother continues to act the same way, the model holds up. If her behavior changes—not just once or twice but repeatedly—the baby may revise the model, and security of attachment may change.

A baby's working model of attachment is related to Erikson's concept of basic trust. Secure attachment reflects trust; insecure attachment, mistrust. Securely attached babies have learned to trust not only their caregivers but their own ability to get what they need. Thus babies who cry a lot and whose mothers respond by soothing them tend to be securely attached (Del Carmen, Pedersen, Huffman, & Bryan, 1993). Mothers of securely attached infants and toddlers tend to be sensitive and responsive (Ainsworth et al., 1978; Braungart-Rieker, Garwood, Powers, & Wang, 2001; De Wolff & van IJzendoorn, 1997; Isabella, 1993; NICHD Early Child Care Research Network, 1997). Equally important are mutual interaction, stimulation, a positive attitude, warmth and acceptance, and emotional support (De Wolff & van IJzendoorn, 1997; Lundy, 2003).

Alternative Methods to Study Attachment

Although much research on attachment has been based on the Strange Situation, some investigators have questioned its validity. The Strange Situation *is* strange; it is also artificial. It asks mothers not to initiate interaction, exposes babies to repeated comings and goings of adults, and expects the infants to pay attention to them. Also, the Strange Situation may be less valid in some non-Western cultures. Research on Japanese infants, who are less commonly separated from their mothers than U.S. babies, showed high rates of resistant attachment, which may reflect the extreme stressfulness of the Strange Situation for these babies (Miyake, Chen, & Campos, 1985).

Because attachment influences a wider range of behaviors than are seen in the Strange Situation, some researchers have begun to supplement it with methods that enable them to study children in natural settings. The Waters and Deane (1985) Attachment Q-set (AQS) has mothers or other home observers sort a set of descriptive words or phrases ("cries a lot"; "tends to cling") into categories ranging from most to least characteristic of the child and then compare these descriptions with expert descriptions of the prototypical secure child. An analysis of 139 studies found the observer version (but not the maternal report version) a valid measure of attachment security, correlating well with results from the Strange Situation and with measures of maternal sensitivity. The AQS also seems to have cross-cultural validity (van IJzendoorn, Vereijken, Bakermans-Kranenburg, & Riksen-Walraven, 2004). In a study using the AQS, mothers in China, Colombia, Germany, Israel, Japan, Norway, and the United States described their children as behaving more like than unlike the "most secure child." Furthermore, the mothers' descriptions of "secure-base" behavior were about as similar across cultures as within a culture. These findings suggest that the tendency to use the mother as a secure base is universal, though it may take somewhat varied forms (Posada et al., 1995).

The Role of Temperament

How much influence does temperament exert on attachment and in what ways? Findings vary (Susman-Stillman, Kalkoske, Egeland, & Waldman, 1996; Vaughn et al., 1992). In a study of 6- to 12-month-olds and their families, both a mother's sensitivity and her baby's temperament influenced attachment patterns (Seifer, Schiller, Sameroff, Resnick, & Riordan, 1996). Neurological or physiological conditions may underlie temperament differences in attachment. For example, variability in heart rate is associated with irritability, and heart rate seems to vary more in insecurely attached infants (Izard, Porges, Simons, Haynes, & Cohen, 1991).

A baby's temperament may have not only a direct impact on attachment but also an indirect impact through its effect on the parents. In a series of studies in the Netherlands (Van den Boom, 1989, 1994), 15-day-old infants classified as irritable were much more likely than nonirritable infants to be insecurely (usually avoidantly) attached at 1 year. However, irritable infants whose mothers received home visits, with instruction on how to soothe their babies, were as likely to be rated as securely attached as the nonirritable infants. Thus irritability on an infant's part may prevent the development of secure attachment but not if the mother has the skills to cope with the baby's temperament (Rothbart et al., 2000). Goodness of fit between parent and child may well be a key to understanding security of attachment.

Stranger Anxiety and Separation Anxiety

Chloe used to be a friendly baby, smiling at strangers and going to them, continuing to coo happily as long as someone—anyone—was around. Now, at 8 months, she turns away when a new person approaches and howls when her parents try to leave her with a babysitter. Chloe is experiencing both **stranger anxiety,** wariness of a person she does not know, and **separation anxiety,** distress when a familiar caregiver leaves her.

Stranger anxiety and separation anxiety used to be considered emotional and cognitive milestones of the second half of infancy, reflecting attachment to the mother. However, newer research suggests that although stranger anxiety and separation anxiety are fairly typical, they are not universal. Whether a baby cries when a parent leaves or when someone new approaches may say more about the baby's temperament or life circumstances than about security of attachment (R. J. Davidson & Fox, 1989).

Babies rarely react negatively to strangers before age 6 months, commonly do so by 8 or 9 months, and do so more and more throughout the rest of the 1st year (Sroufe, 1997). This change may reflect cognitive development. Chloe's stranger anxiety involves memory for faces, the ability to compare the stranger's appearance with her mother's, and perhaps the recollection of situations in which she has been left with a stranger. If Chloe were allowed to get used to the stranger gradually in a familiar setting, she might react more positively (Lewis, 1997; Sroufe, 1997).

Separation anxiety may be due not so much to the separation itself as to the quality of substitute care. When substitute caregivers are warm and responsive and play with 9-month-olds *before* they cry, the babies cry less than when they are with less responsive caregivers (Gunnar, Larson, Hertsgaard, Harris, & Brodersen, 1992).

Stability of care is also important. Pioneering work by René Spitz (1945, 1946) on institutionalized children emphasizes the need for substitute care to be as close as possible to good mothering. Research has underlined the value of continuity and consistency in caregiving, so children can form early emotional bonds with their caregivers.

Today, neither intense fear of strangers nor intense protest when the mother leaves is considered to be a sign of secure attachment. Researchers measure attachment more by what happens when the mother returns than by how many tears the baby sheds when she leaves.

Long-Term Effects of Attachment

As attachment theory proposes, security of attachment seems to affect emotional, social, and cognitive competence (van IJzendoorn & Sagi, 1997). The more secure a child's attachment to a nurturing adult, the easier it seems to be for the child to develop good relationships with others. If children, as infants, had a secure base and could count on parents' or caregivers' responsiveness, they are likely to feel confident enough to be

stranger anxiety Wariness of strange people and places, shown by some infants from age 6 to 12 months.

separation anxiety Distress shown by someone, typically an infant, when a familiar caregiver leaves.

actively engaged in their world (Jacobsen & Hofmann, 1997). In a study of seventy 15-month-olds, those who were securely attached to their mothers, as measured by the Strange Situation, showed less stress in adapting to child care than did insecurely attached toddlers (Ahnert, Gunnar, Lamb, & Barthel, 2004).

Securely attached toddlers tend to have larger, more varied vocabularies than those who are insecurely attached (Meins, 1998). They have more positive interactions with peers, and their friendly overtures are more likely to be accepted (Fagot, 1997). Insecurely attached toddlers tend to show more fear, distress, and anger, whereas securely attached children are more joyful (Kochanska, 2001).

Between ages 3 and 5, securely attached children are likely to be more curious, competent, empathic, resilient, and self-confident; to get along better with other children; and to form closer friendships than children who were insecurely attached as infants (Arend, Gove, & Sroufe, 1979; Elicker, Englund, & Sroufe, 1992; J. L. Jacobson & Wille, 1986; Waters, Wippman, & Sroufe, 1979; Youngblade & Belsky, 1992). They interact more positively with parents, preschool teachers, and peers and are better able to resolve conflicts (Elicker et al., 1992). They tend to have a more positive self-image (Elicker et al., 1992; Verschueren, Marcoen, & Schoefs, 1996).

Secure attachment seems to prepare children for the intimacy of friendship (Carlson, Sroufe, & Egeland, 2004). In middle childhood and adolescence, securely attached children (at least in Western cultures, where most studies have been done) tend to have the closest, most stable friendships (Schneider, Atkinson, & Tardif, 2001; Sroufe, Carlson, & Shulman, 1993).

Insecurely attached children, in contrast, often have inhibitions and negative emotions in toddlerhood, hostility toward other children at age 5, and dependency during the school years (Calkins & Fox, 1992; Kochanska, 2001; Lyons-Ruth, Alpern, & Repacholi, 1993; Sroufe et al., 1993). Those with disorganized attachment tend to have behavior problems at all levels of schooling and psychiatric disorders at age 17 (Carlson, 1998).

In a longitudinal study of 1,364 families with 1-month-old infants, children who were avoidantly attached at 15 months tended to be rated by their mothers as less socially competent than secure children and by their teachers as more aggressive or anxious during the preschool and school-age years. However, effects of parenting on the children's behavior during these years were more important than early attachment. Insecure or disorganized children whose parenting had improved were less aggressive in school than those whose parenting did not improve or got worse. Secure children, on the other hand, were relatively immune to parenting that became less sensitive, perhaps because their early working models buoyed them up even under changed conditions. This study suggests that the continuity generally found between attachment and later behavior can be explained by continuity in the home environment (NICHD Early Child Care Research Network, 2006).

Intergenerational Transmission of Attachment Patterns

The *Adult Attachment Interview* (AAI) (George, Kaplan, & Main, 1985; Main, 1995; Main, Kaplan, & Cassidy, 1985) asks adults to recall and interpret feelings and experiences related to their childhood attachments. Studies using the AAI have found that the way adults recall early experiences with parents or caregivers is related to their emotional well-being and may influence the way they respond to their own children (Adam, Gunnar, & Tanaka, 2004; Dozier, Stovall, Albus, & Bates, 2001; Pesonen, Räikkönen, Keltikangas-Järvinen, Strandberg, & Järvenpää, 2003; Slade, Belsky, Aber, & Phelps, 1999). A mother who was securely attached to *her* mother or who understands why she was insecurely attached can accurately recognize her baby's attachment behaviors, respond encouragingly, and help the baby form a secure attachment to her (Bretherton, 1990). Mothers who are preoccupied with their past attachment relationships tend to show anger and intrusiveness in interactions with their children. Their recollections of these relationships may or may not be accurate in terms of the reality of the relationships, but their memories of experiences with caregivers will affect their relationships with children. Depressed mothers who dismiss memories of their past attachments tend to be cold and unresponsive to their children (Adam et al., 2004). Parents' attachment history also influences their perceptions of their baby's temperament, and those perceptions may affect the parent-child relationship (Pesonen et al., 2003).

Fortunately, the cycle of insecure attachment can be broken. In one study, 54 first-time Dutch mothers who were classified by the AAI as insecurely attached received home visits in which they were either given video feedback to enhance sensitive parenting or participated in discussions of their childhood experiences in relation

Checkpoint ✔

Can you . . .

✔ Identify four patterns of attachment?

✔ Discuss how attachment is established, including the role of temperament?

✔ Identify factors affecting stranger anxiety and separation anxiety?

✔ Tell how long-term behavioral differences are influenced by attachment patterns?

to their current caregiving. After the interventions, these mothers were more sensitive than a control group who had not received the visits. Maternal gains in sensitivity were most effective in affecting the security of infants who had negative emotional temperaments (Klein-Velderman, Bakermans-Kranenburg, Juffer, & van IJzendoorn, 2006).

Emotional Communication with Caregivers: Mutual Regulation

At 1 month, Max gazes attentively at his mother's face. At 2 months, when his mother smiles at him and rubs his tummy, he smiles back. By the 3rd month, Max smiles first, inviting his mother to play (Lavelli & Fogel, 2005).

Infants are communicating beings; they have a strong drive to interact with others. The ability of both infant and caregiver to respond appropriately and sensitively to each other's mental and emotional states is known as **mutual regulation.** Infants take an active part in mutual regulation by sending behavioral signals, like Max's smile, that influence the way caregivers behave toward them (Lundy, 2003). Healthy interaction occurs when a caregiver reads a baby's signals accurately and responds appropriately. When a baby's goals are met, the baby is joyful or at least interested (Tronick, 1989). If a caregiver ignores an invitation to play or insists on playing when the baby has signaled "I don't feel like it," the baby may feel frustrated or sad. When babies do not achieve desired results, they keep on sending signals to repair the interaction. Normally, interaction moves back and forth between well-regulated and poorly regulated states, and babies learn from these shifts how to send signals and what to do when their initial signals are not effective. Mutual regulation helps babies learn to read others' behavior and to develop expectations about it. Even very young infants can perceive emotions expressed by others and can adjust their own behavior accordingly (Legerstee & Varghese, 2001; Montague & Walker-Andrews, 2001; Termine & Izard, 1988), but they are disturbed when someone—whether the mother or a stranger, and regardless of the reason—breaks off interpersonal contact (Striano, 2004).

Measuring Mutual Regulation: The "Still-Face" Paradigm

The **still-face paradigm** (Tronick, Als, Adamson, Wise, & Brazelton, 1978) is a research procedure usually used to measure mutual regulation in 2- to 9-month-old infants, though even newborns have shown the still-face response (Nagy, 2008). In the *still-face* episode, which follows a normal face-to-face interaction, the mother suddenly becomes stony-faced, silent, and unresponsive. Then, a few minutes later, she resumes normal interaction, the *reunion* episode. During the still-face episode, infants tend to stop smiling and looking at the mother. They may make faces, sounds, or gestures or may touch themselves, their clothing, or a chair, apparently to comfort themselves or to relieve the emotional stress created by the mother's unexpected behavior (Cohn & Tronick, 1983; E. Z. Tronick, 1989; Weinberg & Tronick, 1996). In essence, they become dysregulated.

How do infants react during the reunion episode? In one study, 6-month-olds showed even more positive behavior during that episode—joyous expressions and utterances and gazes and gestures directed toward the mother—than before the still-face episode. Nonetheless, the persistence of sad or angry facial expressions, "pick-me-up" gestures, distancing, and indications of stress, as well as an increased tendency to fuss and cry, suggested that the negative feelings stirred by a breakdown in mutual regulation were not readily eased (Weinberg & Tronick, 1996).

Social Referencing

When babies look at their caregivers upon encountering a new person or toy, they are engaging in **social referencing,** seeking out emotional information to guide behavior (Hertenstein & Campos, 2004). In social referencing, one person forms an understanding of how to act in an ambiguous, confusing, or unfamiliar situation by seeking out and interpreting another person's perception of it.

Research provides experimental evidence of social referencing at 1 year (Moses, Baldwin, Rosicky, & Tidball, 2001). When exposed to jiggling or vibrating toys fastened to the floor or ceiling, both 12- and 18-month-olds moved closer to or farther from the

mutual regulation Process by which infant and caregiver communicate emotional states to each other and respond appropriately.

still-face paradigm Research procedure used to measure mutual regulation in infants 2 to 9 months old.

What's your view ❓

- Do you see any ethical problems with the still-face paradigm or the Strange Situation? If so, do you think the benefits of these kinds of research are worth any potential risks?

social referencing Understanding an ambiguous situation by seeking out another person's perception of it.

toys depending on the experimenters' expressed emotional reactions ("Yecch!" or "Nice!"). In one pair of studies (Mumme & Fernald, 2003), 12-month-olds (but not 10-month-olds) adjusted their behavior toward certain unfamiliar objects according to nonvocal emotional signals given by an actress on a television screen. In another pair of studies (Hertenstein & Campos, 2004), whether 14-month-olds touched plastic creatures that dropped within their reach was related to the positive or negative emotions they had seen an adult express about the same objects an hour before; 11-month-olds responded to such emotional cues if the delay was very brief (3 minutes).

Social referencing—and the ability to retain information gained from it—may play a role in such key developments of toddlerhood as the rise of self-conscious emotions (embarrassment and pride), the development of a sense of self, and the processes of *socialization* and *internalization*.

Developmental Issues in Toddlerhood

About halfway between their first and second birthdays, babies become toddlers. This transformation can be seen, not only in such physical and cognitive skills as walking and talking but in the ways children express their personalities and interact with others. A toddler becomes a more active, intentional partner in interactions and sometimes initiates them. Caregivers can now more clearly read the child's signals. Such in-sync interactions help toddlers gain communicative skills and social competence and motivate compliance with a parent's wishes (Harrist & Waugh, 2002).

Let's look at three psychological issues that toddlers—and their caregivers—have to deal with: the emerging *sense of self;* the growth of *autonomy,* or self-determination; and *socialization,* or *internalization of behavioral standards.*

The Emerging Sense of Self

The **self-concept** is our image of ourselves—our total picture of our abilities and traits. It describes what we know and feel about ourselves and guides our actions (Harter, 1996, 1998). Children incorporate into their self-image the picture that others reflect back to them.

When and how does the self-concept develop? From a jumble of seemingly isolated experiences (say, from one breast-feeding session to another), infants begin to extract consistent patterns that form rudimentary concepts of self and other. Depending on what kind of care the infant receives and how she or he responds, pleasant or unpleasant emotions become connected with experiences that play an important part in the growing concept of the self (Harter, 1998).

By at least 3 months infants pay attention to their mirror image (Courage & Howe, 2002). Four- to 9-month-olds show more interest in images of others than of themselves (Rochat & Striano, 2002). This early *perceptual* discrimination may be the foundation of the *conceptual* self-concept that develops in the middle of the 2nd year.

Between 4 and 10 months, when infants learn to reach, grasp, and make things happen, they experience a sense of personal *agency,* the realization that they can control external events. At about this time infants develop *self-coherence,* the sense of being a physical whole with boundaries separate from the rest of their world (Harter, 1998). These developments occur in interaction with caregivers in games such as peekaboo, in which the infant becomes increasingly aware of the difference between self and other ("I see you!").

The emergence of *self-representation* ("the idea of the me")—a conscious knowledge of the self as a distinct, identifiable being (Lewis, 2003)—builds on this dawning perceptual discrimination between self and others. Self-representation can be tested by studying whether infants recognize themselves in a mirror (Lewis & Carmody, 2008). In a classic line of research, investigators dabbed rouge on the noses of 6- to 24-month-olds and sat them in front of a mirror. Three-fourths of 18-month-olds and all 24-month-olds touched their red noses more often than before, whereas babies

Checkpoint ✓

Can you . . .

✔ Describe how mutual regulation works and explain its importance?

✔ Give examples of how infants seem to use social referencing?

Guidepost 4

When and how does the sense of self arise, and how do toddlers exercise autonomy and develop standards for socially acceptable behavior?

self-concept Sense of self; descriptive and evaluative mental picture of one's abilities and traits.

younger than 15 months never did. This behavior suggests that these toddlers had self-awareness. They knew they did not normally have red noses and recognized the image in the mirror as their own (Lewis, 1997; Lewis & Brooks, 1974). In a later study, 18- and 24-month-olds were about as likely to touch a sticker on their legs, which was visible only in a mirror, as on their faces (Nielsen, Suddendorf, & Slaughter, 2006). Once children can recognize themselves, they show a preference for looking at their own video image over an image of another child the same age (Nielsen, Dissanayake, & Kashima, 2003).

Pretend play, which typically begins during the last half of the 2nd year, is another measure or sign of self-representation—an early indication of the ability to understand others' mental states as well as the child's own (Lewis & Carmody, 2008). A third measure or sign of self-representation is the use of first-person pronouns, such as *me* and *mine*, usually at 20 to 24 months (Lewis, 1997; Lewis & Carmody, 2008). Between 19 and 30 months, children begin to apply descriptive terms ("big" or "little," "straight hair" or "curly hair") and evaluative ones ("good," "pretty," or "strong") to themselves. The rapid development of language enables children to think and talk about the self and to incorporate parents' verbal descriptions ("You're so smart!" "What a big boy!") into their emerging self-image (Stipek, Gralinski, & Kopp, 1990).

Brain maturation underlies the development of self-representation. Magnetic resonance imaging (MRI) scans of 15- to 30-month-olds showed that signal intensities in a specific brain region (the left temporo-parietal junction) were strongest in children, regardless of age, who recognized their image in a mirror, engaged in pretend play with others, and used personal pronouns (Lewis & Carmody, 2008).

Developing Autonomy

As children mature—physically, cognitively, and emotionally—they are driven to seek independence from the very adults to whom they are attached. "Me do!" is the byword as toddlers use their developing muscles and minds to try to do everything on their own—not only to walk, but to feed and dress themselves and to explore their world.

Erikson (1950) identified the period from about 18 months to 3 years as the second stage in psychosocial development, **autonomy versus shame and doubt,** which is marked by a shift from external control to self-control. Having come through infancy with a sense of basic trust in the world and an awakening self-awareness, toddlers begin to substitute their own judgment for their caregivers'. The virtue, or strength, that emerges during this stage is *will.* Toilet training is an important step toward autonomy and self-control. So is language. As children are better able to make their wishes understood, they become more powerful and independent. Since unlimited freedom is neither safe nor healthy, said Erikson, shame and doubt have a necessary place. Toddlers need adults to set appropriate limits, and shame and doubt help them recognize the need for those limits.

autonomy versus shame and doubt Erikson's second stage in psychosocial development, in which children achieve a balance between self-determination and control by others.

In the United States, the "terrible twos" are a normal sign of the drive for autonomy. Toddlers have to test the notions that they are individuals, that they have some control over their world, and that they have new, exciting powers. They are driven to try out their own ideas, exercise their own preferences, and make their own decisions. This drive typically shows itself in the form of *negativism,* the tendency to shout "No!" just for the sake of resisting authority. Almost all U.S. children show negativism to some degree; it usually begins before age 2, tends to peak at about 3½ to 4, and declines by age 6. Caregivers who view children's expressions of self-will as a normal, healthy striving for independence, not as stubbornness, can help them learn self-control, contribute to their sense of competence, and avoid excessive conflict. (Table 8-3 gives specific, research-based suggestions for dealing with the terrible twos.)

This toddler is showing autonomy—the drive to exert her own power over her environment.

Table 8-3	Dealing with the Terrible Twos

The following research-based guidelines can help parents of toddlers discourage negativism and encourage socially acceptable behavior.

- *Be flexible.* Learn the child's natural rhythms and special likes and dislikes.
- *Think of yourself as a safe harbor,* with safe limits, from which a child can set out and discover the world and to which the child can keep coming back for support.
- *Make your home child-safe.* Make unbreakable objects that are safe to explore available.
- *Avoid physical punishment.* It is often ineffective and may even lead a toddler to do more damage.
- *Offer a choice*—even a limited one—to give the child some control. ("Would you like to have your bath now or after we read a book?")
- *Be consistent* in enforcing necessary requests.
- *Don't interrupt an activity unless absolutely necessary.* Try to wait until the child's attention has shifted.
- *If you must interrupt, give warning.* ("We have to leave the playground soon.")
- *Suggest alternative activities* when behavior becomes objectionable. (When Ashley is throwing sand in Keiko's face, say, "Oh, look! Nobody's on the swings now. Let's go over and I'll give you a good push!")
- *Suggest; don't command.* Accompany requests with smiles or hugs, not criticism, threats, or physical restraint.
- *Link requests with pleasurable activities.* ("It's time to stop playing so that you can go to the store with me.")
- *Remind the child of what you expect* ("When we go to this playground, we *never* go outside the gate.")
- *Wait a few moments before repeating a request* when a child doesn't comply immediately.
- *Use time-outs to end conflicts.* In a nonpunitive way, remove either yourself or the child from a situation.
- *Expect less self-control during times of stress* (illness, divorce, the birth of a sibling, or a move to a new home).
- *Expect it to be harder for toddlers to comply with "dos" than with "don'ts".* "Clean up your room" takes more effort than "Don't write on the furniture."
- *Keep the atmosphere as positive as possible.* Make your child want to cooperate.

Sources: Hasweli, Hock, & Wenar, 1981: Kochanska & Aksan, 1995; Kopp, 1982; Kuczynski & Kochanska 1995; Power & Chapieski, 1986.

Checkpoint ✔

Can you . . .

✔ Trace the early development of the sense of self?

✔ Describe the conflict of autonomy versus shame and doubt?

✔ Explain why the "terrible twos" is considered a normal phenomenon, and suggest reasons this transition may not exist in some cultures?

Many U.S. parents might be surprised to hear that the terrible twos are not universal. In some developing countries, the transition from infancy to early childhood is relatively smooth and harmonious, as we discuss in Box 8-2.

The Roots of Moral Development: Socialization and Internalization

Socialization is the process by which children develop habits, skills, values, and motives that make them responsible, productive members of society. Compliance with parental expectations can be seen as a first step toward compliance with societal standards. Socialization rests on **internalization** of these standards. Children who are successfully socialized no longer merely obey rules or commands to get rewards or avoid punishment; they have made society's standards their own (Grusec & Goodnow, 1994; Kochanska & Aksan, 1995; Kochanska, Tjebkes, & Forman, 1998).

Developing Self-Regulation

Laticia, age 2, is about to poke her finger into an electric outlet. In her child-proofed apartment, the sockets are covered, but not here in her grandmother's home. When Laticia hears her father shout "No!" the toddler pulls her arm back. The next time she goes near an outlet, she starts to point her finger, hesitates, and then says "No." She has stopped herself from doing something she remembers she is not supposed to do. She is beginning to show **self-regulation:** control of her behavior to conform to a caregiver's demands or expectations, even when the caregiver is not present.

socialization Development of habits, skills, values, and motives shared by responsible, productive members of a society.

internalization During socialization, process by which children accept societal standards of conduct as their own.

self-regulation A person's independent control of behavior to conform to understood social expectations.

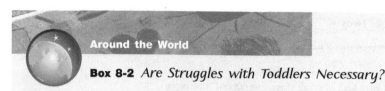

Box 8-2 *Are Struggles with Toddlers Necessary?*

Are the terrible twos a normal phase in child development? Many Western parents and psychologists think so. Actually, though, this transition does not appear to be universal.

In Zinacantan, Mexico, toddlers do not typically become demanding and resistant to parental control. Instead of asserting independence from their mothers, toddlerhood in Zinacantan is a time when children move from being mama's babies to being mother's helpers, responsible children who may tend a new baby and who help with household tasks (Edwards, 1994). A similar developmental pattern seems to occur in Mazahua families in Mexico and among Maya families in San Pedro, Guatemala. San Pedro parents "do not report a particular age when they expect children to become especially contrary or negative" (Mosier & Rogoff, 2003, p. 1058).

One arena in which issues of autonomy and control appear in Western cultures is in sibling conflicts over toys and the way children respond to parental handling of these conflicts. To explore these issues, a cross-cultural study compared 16 San Pedro families with 16 middle-class European American families in Salt Lake City. All of the families had toddlers 14 to 20 months old and older siblings 3 to 5 years old. The researchers interviewed each mother about her child-raising practices. They then handed the mother a series of attractive objects (such as nesting dolls and a jumping-jack puppet) and, in the presence of the older sibling, asked the mother to help the toddler operate them, with no instructions about the older child. Researchers who observed the ensuing interactions found striking differences in the way siblings interacted in the two cultures and in the way the mothers viewed and handled sibling conflict.

The older siblings in Salt Lake City often tried to take and play with the objects, but this generally did not happen in San Pedro. Instead, the older San Pedro children would offer to help their younger siblings work the objects, or the two children would play with them together. When there was a conflict over possession of the objects, mothers in both communities were more likely to endorse the toddler's right to have it first, but this tendency was far more characteristic of San Pedro mothers than of Salt Lake City mothers. San Pedro mothers favored the toddlers 94 percent of the time, even taking an object away from the older child if the younger child wanted it; and the older siblings

tended to go along, willingly handing the objects to the toddlers or letting them have the objects from the start. In contrast, in more than one-third of the interactions in Salt Lake City, the mothers tried to treat both children equally, negotiating with them or suggesting that they take turns or share. These observations were consistent with reports of mothers in both cultures of how they handled such issues at home. San Pedro children are given a privileged position until age 3; then they are expected to willingly cooperate with social expectations.

What explains these cultural contrasts? A clue emerged when the mothers were asked at what age children can be held responsible for their actions. Most of the Salt Lake City mothers maintained that their toddlers already understood the consequences of touching prohibited objects; several said this understanding arises as early as 7 months. Yet all but one of the San Pedro mothers placed the age of understanding social consequences of actions much later—between 2 and 3 years. The Salt Lake City mothers regarded their toddlers as capable of intentional misbehavior and punished their toddlers for it; most San Pedro mothers did not. All of the Salt Lake City preschoolers (toddlers and their siblings) were under direct caregiver supervision; 11 of the 16 San Pedro preschoolers were on their own much of the time and had more mature household responsibilities.

The researchers suggest that the terrible twos may be a phase specific to societies that place individual freedom before the needs of the group. Ethnographic research suggests that in societies that place higher value on group needs freedom of choice does exist, but it goes hand in hand with interdependence, responsibility, and expectations of cooperation. Salt Lake City parents seem to believe that responsible behavior develops gradually from engaging in fair competition and negotiations. San Pedro parents seem to believe that responsible behavior develops rapidly when children are old enough to understand the need to respect others' desires as well as their own.

What's your view ?

From your experience or observation of toddlers, which of the two ways of handling sibling conflict would you expect to be more effective?

Self-regulation is the foundation of socialization, and it links all domains of development —physical, cognitive, social, and emotional. Until Laticia was physically able to get around on her own, electric outlets posed no hazard. To stop herself from poking her finger into an outlet requires that she consciously understand and remember what her father told her. Cognitive awareness, however, is not enough; restraining herself also requires emotional control. By reading their parents' emotional responses to their behavior, children continually absorb information about what conduct their parents approve of. As children process, store, and act on this information, their strong desire to please their parents leads them to do as they know their parents want them to, whether or not the parents are there to see.

Before they can control their behavior, children may need to be able to regulate, or control, their *attentional processes* and to modulate negative emotions (Eisenberg, 2000). Attentional regulation enables children to develop willpower and cope with frustration (Sethi, Mischel, Aber, Shoda, & Rodriguez, 2000).

The growth of self-regulation parallels the development of the self-conscious and evaluative emotions, such as empathy, shame, and guilt (Lewis, 1995, 1997, 1998). It requires the ability to wait for gratification. It is correlated with measures of conscience development, such as resisting temptation and making amends for wrongdoing (Eisenberg, 2000). In most children, the full development of self-regulation takes at least 3 years (Kopp, 1982).

Children of Working Parents

How do parental employment and early child care affect infants' and toddlers' development?

Parents' work determines more than the family's financial resources. Much of adults' time, effort, and emotional involvement go into their occupations. How do their working and their child care arrangements affect young children? Most research on this subject pertains to mothers' work.

Effects of Maternal Employment

More than half (55.1 percent) of mothers of infants in their 1st year of life and 59.2 percent of women with children under 3 were in the labor force in 2007, a dramatic increase since 1975 (U.S. Bureau of Labor Statistics, 2008a; Figure 8-2). However, labor force participation of *married* mothers of infants, which peaked in 1997 at 59.2 percent, fell to 54.6 percent in 2007, and the participation rate for married mothers of children under 3 dropped from about 64 percent in 1997-1998 to just over 60 percent in 2007 (Cohany & Sok, 2007; U.S. Bureau of Labor Statistics, 2008a, 2008b).

How does early maternal employment affect children? Longitudinal data on 900 European American children from the National Institute of Child Health and Human Development (NICHD) Study of Early Child Care, discussed in the next section, showed negative effects on cognitive development at 15 months to 3 years when mothers worked 30 or more hours a week by a child's 9th month. Maternal sensitivity, a high-quality home environment, and high-quality child care lessened but did not eliminate these negative effects (Brooks-Gunn, Han, & Waldfogel, 2002).

Similarly, among 6,114 children from the National Longitudinal Survey of Youth (NLSY), those whose mothers worked full time in the 1st year after giving birth were more likely to show negative cognitive and behavioral outcomes at ages 3 to 8 than children whose mothers worked part time or not at all during their 1st year. Children in disadvantaged families showed fewer negative cognitive effects than children in more advantaged families (Hill, Waldfogel, Brooks-Gunn, & Han, 2005).

On the other hand, a longitudinal study of an ethnically, socioeconomically, and geographically diverse sample of 1,364 children during their first 3 years suggests that the economic and social benefits of maternal employment may outweigh any disadvantages

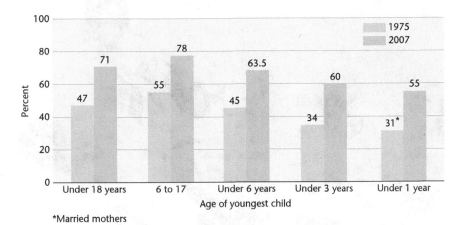

*Married mothers

Figure 8-2

Labor force participation rates of mothers with children, 1975 and 2007. Labor force participation by mothers of children of all ages has increased dramatically in the past three decades. In 1975, fewer than half of all mothers were working or looking for work. In 2007, about 7 out of 10 mothers were labor force participants. Participation rates in 2007 ranged from 55 percent for mothers whose youngest child was under 1 year old to 78 percent for mothers whose youngest child was age 6 to 17.

Sources: Data from Hayghe, 1986; U.S. Bureau of Labor Statistics, 2007, 2008a, 2008b.

resulting from reduced time with a child. Mothers who worked outside the home compensated for some of their work time by reducing time spent on non–child care activities. Differences in time spent with infants were modestly related to maternal sensitivity but did not seem to affect social or cognitive outcomes. Infants whose mothers spent more time with them did have more stimulating home environments, but so did infants whose mothers spent more time at work. It seems, then, that mothers who are temperamentally prone to be sensitive and to provide stimulating, warm home environments may find ways to do so whether or not they are employed (Huston & Aronson, 2005).

Early Child Care

One factor in the impact of a mother's working outside the home is the type of substitute care a child receives. Recent data estimates that about 60 percent of U.S. children not yet in kindergarten are in some type of regular child care (Iruka & Carver, 2006). More than 50 percent of the 11.3 million children whose mothers were employed received care from relatives—30 percent from grandparents, 25 percent from their fathers, 3 percent from siblings, and 8 percent from other relatives. More than 30 percent were in organized day care or preschools. With nonrelative care averaging $129 a week (U.S. Census Bureau, 2008b) and center-based care in 33 states and the District of Columbia costing more than tuition at a public 4-year college (Children's Defense Fund, 2008b), affordability and quality of care are pressing issues.

Factors Affecting Early Child Care

The impact of early child care may depend on the type, amount, quality, and stability of care as well as the family's income and the age at which children start receiving non-maternal care. By 9 months, about 50 percent of U.S. infants are in some kind of regular nonparental child care arrangement, and 86 percent of these infants enter child care before they reach 6 months. More than 50 percent of these babies are in child care more than 30 hours a week (NCES, 2005).

Temperament and gender may make a difference (Crockenberg, 2003). Shy children in child care experience greater stress, as shown by cortisol levels, than sociable children (Watamura, Donzella, Alwin, & Gunnar, 2003), and insecurely attached children undergo greater stress than securely attached children when introduced to full-time child care (Ahnert et al., 2004). Boys are more vulnerable to stress, in child care and elsewhere, than are girls (Crockenberg, 2003).

Caregivers' responsiveness to infants' needs is the most important factor in high-quality day care.

Table 8-4	Checklist for Choosing a Good Child Care Facility

- Is the facility licensed? Does it meet minimum state standards for health, fire, and safety? (Many centers and home care facilities are not licensed or regulated.)
- Is the facility clean and safe? Does it have adequate indoor and outdoor space?
- Does the facility have small groups, a high adult-to-child ratio, and a stable, competent, highly involved staff?
- Are caregivers trained in child development?
- Are caregivers warm, affectionate, accepting, responsive, and sensitive? Are they authoritative but not too restrictive and neither too controlling nor merely custodial?
- Does the program promote good health habits?
- Does it provide a balance between structured activities and free play? Are activities age appropriate?
- Do the children have access to educational toys and materials that stimulate mastery of cognitive and communicative skills at a child's own pace?
- Does the program nurture self-confidence, curiosity, creativity, and self-discipline?
- Does it encourage children to ask questions, solve problems, express feelings and opinions, and make decisions?
- Does it foster self-esteem, respect for others, and social skills?
- Does it help parents improve their child-rearing skills?
- Does it promote cooperation with public and private schools and the community?

Sources: American Academy of Pediatrics [AAP], 1986; Belsky, 1984; K. A. Clarke-Stewart, 1987; NICHD Early Child Care Research Network, 1996; S. W. Olds, 1989: Scarr, 1998.

Quality of care contributes to cognitive and psychosocial competence (Marshall, 2004; de Schipper, Riksen-Walraven, & Geurts, 2006). Quality of care can be measured by *structural characteristics,* such as staff training and the ratio of children to caregivers; and by *process characteristics,* such as the warmth, sensitivity, and responsiveness of caregivers and the developmental appropriateness of activities. Structural quality and process quality may be related; in one study, well-trained caregivers and low child-staff ratios were associated with higher process quality, which, in turn, was associated with better cognitive and social outcomes (Marshall, 2004).

The most important element in quality of care is the caregiver; stimulating interactions with responsive adults are crucial to early cognitive, linguistic, and psychosocial development. Low staff turnover is important; infants need consistent caregiving to develop trust and secure attachments (Burchinal, Roberts, Nabors, & Bryant, 1996; Shonkoff & Phillips, 2000). Stability of care facilitates coordination between parents and child care providers, which may help protect against any negative effects of long hours of care (Ahnert & Lamb, 2003). The Checklist in Table 8-4 provides basic guidelines for selecting a high-quality child care facility.

The NICHD Study: Isolating Child Care Effects

Because child care is an integral part of what Bronfenbrenner calls a child's bioecological system (refer to Chapter 2), it is difficult to measure its influence alone. The most comprehensive attempt to separate child care effects from such other factors as family characteristics, the child's characteristics, and the care the child receives at home is an ongoing study sponsored by the National Institute of Child Health and Human Development (NICHD).

This longitudinal study of 1,364 children and their families began in 1991 in 10 university centers across the United States, shortly after the children's birth. The sample was diverse socioeconomically, educationally, and ethnically; nearly 35 percent of the families were poor or near poor. Most infants entered nonmaternal care before 4 months and received, on average, 33 hours of care each week. Child care arrangements varied widely in type and quality. Researchers measured the children's social, emotional, cognitive, and physical development at frequent intervals starting at the age of 1 month old.

The study showed that the amount and quality of care children received as well as the type and stability of care influenced specific aspects of development. Long days in child care have been associated with stress for 3- and 4-year-olds (Belsky et al., 2007; NICHD Early Child Care Research Network, 2003). And the 15 percent of 2- and 3-year-olds who experience more than one regular child care arrangement are at increased risk of behavior problems and are less likely to help and share (Morrissey, 2009).

On the other hand, children in child care centers with low child-staff ratios, small group sizes, and trained, sensitive, responsive caregivers who provide positive interactions and language stimulation tend to score higher on tests of language comprehension, cognition, and readiness for school than do children in lower-quality care. Their mothers also report fewer behavior problems (NICHD Early Child Care Research Network, 1999a, 2000, 2002). Children who received high-quality care before entering kindergarten are likely to have better vocabulary scores in fifth grade than children who received lower-quality care (Belsky et al., 2007).

However, factors related to child care are less influential than family characteristics, such as income, the home environment, the amount of mental stimulation the mother provides, and the mother's sensitivity to her child. These characteristics strongly predict developmental outcomes, regardless of how much time children spend in outside care (Belsky et al., 2007; Marshall, 2004; NICHD Early Child Care Research Network, 1998a, 1998b, 2000, 2003).

Child care has no direct effect on attachment. However, when unstable, poor-quality, or more-than-minimal amounts of child care (10 or more hours a week) are combined with insensitive, unresponsive mothering, insecure attachment is more likely. On the other hand, high-quality care seems to help offset insensitive mothering (NICHD Early Child Care Research Network, 1997, 2001b).

It should not be surprising that what look like effects of child care often may be related to family characteristics. After all, stable families with favorable home environments are more able and therefore more likely to place their children in high-quality care. One area in which the NICHD study did find independent effects of child care was in interactions with peers. Between ages 2 and 3, children whose caregivers are sensitive and responsive tend to become more positive and competent in play with other children (NICHD Early Child Care Research Network, 2001a).

To sum up, the NICHD findings give high-quality child care good marks overall, especially for its impact on cognitive development and interaction with peers. Some observers say that the areas of concern the study pinpoints—stress levels in infants and toddlers and possible behavior problems related to amounts of care and multiple caregiving arrangements—might be counteracted by activities that enhance children's attachment to caregivers and peers, emphasize child-initiated learning and internalized motivation, and focus on group social development (Maccoby & Lewis, 2003).

What's your view ?

- In the light of findings about effects of early child care, what advice would you give a new mother about the timing of her return to work and the selection of child care?

Checkpoint ✓

Can you . . .

✔ Evaluate the impact of a mother's employment on her baby's well-being?

✔ List at least five criteria for good child care?

✔ Discuss the impact of child care and of family characteristics on emotional, social, and cognitive development?

Language acquisition for this 2-year-old involves learning to sign rather than to speak.

LANGUAGE DEVELOPMENT

Meryl was 16 months old before she finally said her first recognizable word. One day when Karen went into Meryl's room to get her up from her nap, Meryl announced with a serious look, "Mama." Karen was elated. "Mama! Yes, mama! I'm your mama!" she told Meryl, picking her up and giving her a hug that made the little girl squirm. Minutes later Karen was on the phone, sharing the news with her mother at work.

To parents, children's first words are among the most exciting milestones in their development. Language opens up new, more efficient ways to communicate. When parents ask their child a question or give an instruction, they can get a verbal response.

Emerging language is one example of a general capacity for **symbolic representation**—the use of ideas, images, sounds, or other symbols to stand for objects and events. The capacity for symbolic representation appears during a major transition period—the transition from infancy to childhood. This transition is called the *toddler period* because it coincides with the time when children learn to walk. The toddler period lasts from roughly 12 months of age to about 30 months of age.

Language is an abstract, rule-governed system of arbitrary symbols that can be combined in countless ways to communicate information. Language is not synonymous with speech.

The sign language used by deaf people is a genuine language that can express any desired idea. In contrast, a bird mimicking speech is not displaying true language; to the bird, words are simply sounds that do not symbolize anything.

This section begins with a look at the various components of human language to give you some idea of what is involved in mastering a language. Next we examine the course of early language learning, including mastery of sound patterns, word meanings, grammar, and the social use of language. We then consider the relative contributions of the child and the environment to the process of language development. Finally, we discuss three nonlinguistic aspects of toddler cognitive development that are related to the emergence of symbolic representation—the development of gestures, pretend play, and understanding of iconic symbols such as pictures.

Symbolic representation:
The use of ideas, images, or other symbols to stand for objects or events.

Language:
An abstract, rule-governed system of arbitrary symbols that can be combined in countless ways to communicate information.

Questions to Think About As You Read

- How do nature and nurture interact in children's acquisition of language?
- How are cognitive and social development intertwined with language development?

THE COMPONENTS OF LANGUAGE

When 2½-year-old Meryl hands Mrs. Jasper a string of beads and requests, "Tie it, pwease," her simple words reflect a major accomplishment. They show that Meryl is mastering the many conventions of language for combining sounds into meaningful words, and words into meaningful sentences. Meryl knows the sound combination /tai/ means to fasten two pieces of string together. She also knows that, for her sentence to make sense, the object *it* must follow the verb, not precede it. Meryl does not think of speech in terms of such rules, but she follows them nonetheless. She is also starting to follow conventions for how to word sentences in various social contexts, such as using *please* to make a request, especially of an adult. All this Meryl has mastered in the year since she spoke her first word. To understand the size of the task faced by language-learning toddlers, let's look more closely at the various components of language.

Language Development Milestones

Sounds, Structure, Meaning, and Conversational Rules

All languages can be broken down into five major subsystems: *phonology, semantics, morphology, syntax,* and *pragmatics.* Becoming a competent speaker of a language requires learning all five.

Phonology refers to the system of sounds used in a language, the rules for combining those sounds to make words, and the use of stress and intonation in spoken sentences. Every language has its own set of **phonemes**—speech sounds that contrast with one another and can change the meaning of a word. For example, in English the sound /b/ in *bat* is a different phoneme from the sound /p/ in *pat,* which is why you immediately recognize these two words as different. Other languages include phonemes not used in English, such as the tongue-trilled /r/ in Spanish, the German /ch/ sounds, and the clicking sounds used in some African languages.

Semantics consists of the meanings of words and sentences. A sentence might be perfectly correct grammatically but nevertheless be confusing because it breaks semantic rules. For instance, if a preschooler told you "My daddy is having a baby," you would ask for clarification, even though the child's grammar is flawless, because the meaning of the word *daddy* is inconsistent with the meaning of the phrase *having a baby.*

Morphology is the system of rules for combining units of meaning to form words or to modify word meanings. The smallest meaningful units in a language are called **morphemes.** Many words are single morphemes, such as *child, language,* and *speak.* Other words consist of several morphemes. The word *unspeakable* has three morphemes: the prefix *un-* (meaning not), the root word *speak,* and the suffix *-able* (meaning capable of being done).

Syntax refers to the rules for organizing words into phrases and sentences. Following the rules of syntax allows speakers to form grammatical sentences and convey the meanings they intend. *The boy kissed the girl* and *The girl kissed the boy* are both grammatical sentences, but they mean different things because of their word order. *Kissed the*

Phonology:
The system of sounds used in a language, the rules for combining those sounds to make words, and the use of stress and intonation in spoken sentences.

Phonemes:
Speech sounds that contrast with one another in a particular language and can change the meaning of a word.

Semantics:
The meanings of words and sentences.

Morphology:
The system of rules for combining morphemes to form words or to modify word meanings.

Morphemes:
The smallest meaningful units in a language.

Syntax:
The rules for organizing words into phrases and sentences.

Pragmatics:
The rules governing conversation and social use of language.

girl the boy is hard to interpret because it does not follow the usual rules of English syntax.

Pragmatics is the set of rules governing conversation and social use of language. It includes knowing how to use language to accomplish social goals. For example, there are various ways to make requests in English. If you wanted someone to open a window, you could say "Open the window!" or "Would you please open the window?" or "Can you open the window?" or even "It's hot in here." Native speakers of English know these can all be requests, varying in politeness and directness. Pragmatics also includes knowing how to adjust language to fit different social situations. You talk differently to your friends than to your professors, even to convey the same basic information. Similarly, if you were explaining how to play a game to a 5-year-old, your choice of words and sentence structure would be quite different than if you were speaking to an adult. In each case your language is guided by rules of pragmatics.

Productive and Receptive Skills

Another way to view what children master when they learn their native language is in terms of the mental skills required. Children need two sets of skills to be able to communicate effectively: **productive skills,** which are used to put ideas into words, and **receptive skills,** which are used to understand what other people say.

Productive skills:
Language skills used to put ideas into words.

Receptive skills:
Language skills used to understand what other people say.

Many parents believe infants can grasp much of what they are told before they are able to talk. Parents tend to overestimate this ability in their babies, but they are correct that receptive skills emerge sooner than productive ones (Golinkoff et al., 1987). This can be seen in every aspect of language development, including phonology (Jusczyk, 1997). As a toddler Meryl could not pronounce the phoneme /l/. Her *l*'s sounded like *w*'s. One day Karen teasingly said to Meryl, "Wet's go!" Meryl responded, "No. Not wet's. Say *wet's*." Although Meryl mispronounced /l/, she could hear the difference between a correct and an incorrect pronunciation by someone else. Her receptive phonology was more advanced than her productive phonology. Similarly, young children understand words not yet in their active vocabularies, and they understand sentences much longer and more complex than the ones they speak.

MAJOR TASKS IN EARLY LANGUAGE LEARNING

Malcolm was an early talker; even at 8 or 9 months, he was constantly babbling strings of nonsense syllables that sounded startlingly like real speech. "Ah-ma-ka?" he might ask of DeeDee, his voice rising in a question as he jangled a set of car keys above his head. When DeeDee laughed and answered that those were indeed for the car, he bobbed his head, smiling as if he understood: "Ah-ka-ba-ba! Ah-ka-ba!"

To describe how children become able to communicate linguistically, we will look at how development proceeds in each subsystem of language. We will examine how children master the sound system of their native language *(phonology),* how they learn the meanings of individual words *(semantics),* and how they develop sets of rules about the structure of language—rules for modifying word meanings *(morphology)* and for organizing words into sentences *(syntax).* Finally, we consider how they learn to use language in socially appropriate ways *(pragmatics).*

Learning the Sound Patterns of a Language

One difficult aspect of learning a language is mastering its sound patterns. Think about your own experiences listening to foreign languages; the sounds probably blurred together, with no obvious pauses between words. Now imagine the task confronting children who do not even know words exist. Somehow, just by hearing others talk, they learn to recognize and produce the phonemes of their language. Ultimately, they break down the stream of speech sounds they hear into words, and they begin to produce recognizable words themselves.

Much progress toward mastering the sounds of a language occurs in the first year of life, even before babies produce words. During this time, dramatic changes in babies' vocalizations culminate in the production of speech sounds. This early period of **prelinguistic vocalization** can be divided into five stages (Menn and Stoel-Gammon, 1993).

In the first weeks of life, infants' only means of vocal communication is **crying.** Crying is a reflexive vocalization that occurs automatically

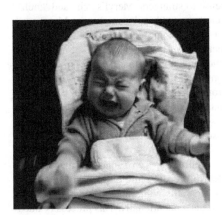

whenever babies are overly aroused, but their cries vary somewhat depending on the nature of their discomfort.

At around 2 months, babies start to make sounds expressing pleasure and contentment. This behavior is called **cooing** because it involves many vowel sounds, especially /u/, and very few consonant sounds. Babies also begin to laugh and chuckle during the cooing stage.

At about 4 months, babies enter the stage of **vocal play.** During this stage, they seem to be trying out the range of their vocal abilities, and they produce sounds that vary greatly in pitch and loudness. They also begin to utter occasional simple syllables consisting of consonant-vowel combinations (*ba, ga, ma,* etc.)

The fourth stage, **canonical babbling,** begins at around 6 months. During this stage, babies' vocalizations sound increasingly like speech. Instead of isolated syllables, they begin to produce strings of syllables. At first, these strings consist mostly of one syllable repeated over and over (e.g., *ma-ma-ma-ma*). Later, strings of different vowel and consonant combinations become more common, with utterances like Malcolm's "Ah-ka-ba-ba."

During the canonical babbling stage, children are not yet imitating the particular phonemes of their native language. When Meryl, Malcolm, Maggie, and Mikey began to babble, they not only made sounds corresponding to English phonemes, they also made some sounds that are phonemes in other languages. Infants around the world initially babble similar sounds, despite being exposed to very different languages. However, they do not produce *all* the phonemes found in human speech, and the most frequent and infrequent sounds are fairly similar across languages (Locke and Pearson, 1992). This suggests that the early development of speech sounds is constrained by infants' physical limitations. Linguistic input from the environment becomes important during this stage, however. Deaf infants engage in vocal play very similar to that of babies who can hear, but they are slow to produce the clear consonant-vowel syllables of canonical babbling (Oller and Eilers, 1988). (The box on page 240 provides more information about language development of deaf infants.)

By 10 months or so, most infants progress to the fifth stage, **conversational babbling** or **jargon,** in which they begin to use adultlike stress and intonation, as Malcolm did when "asking" DeeDee about the car keys. Because of its stress and intonation, jargon sounds like conversational speech. It seems to include questions and statements, but without identifiable words. During this stage, there begin to be differences in the particular sounds babies produce, depending on the language they are acquiring (Boysson-Bardies and Vihman, 1991).

Prelinguistic vocalization:
Sounds produced by infants during the first year of life, before they begin to speak.

Crying:
Reflexive vocalization that occurs automatically whenever an infant is overly aroused.

In the first stage of prelinguistic vocalization, infants can communicate only by crying.

Cooing:
Prelinguistic vocalizations that consist largely of vowel sounds and express pleasure and contentment.

Vocal play:
Prelinguistic vocalizations that vary greatly in pitch and loudness, including occasional simple syllables.

Canonical babbling:
Prelinguistic vocalizations consisting of strings of syllables that sound increasingly like speech.

 Child Development CD
Prelinguistic Vocalization

Early Detection of Hearing Impairment

Conversational babbling or jargon
Prelinguistic vocalizations in which infants use adultlike stress and intonation.

Protowords:
Vocalizations that seem to have consistent meanings for a child and are used in attempts to communicate, but do not closely resemble adult words in sound or meaning.

Between 10 and 12 months, most children start to make the transition from babbling to true speech. A few **protowords** may appear—vocalizations that seem to have consistent meanings for a child and are used in attempts to communicate, but do not closely resemble adult words in sound or meaning. Children's protowords are idiosyncratic; unlike real words, they usually do not make sense to strangers. Meryl's "eh" and "muh" are examples of protowords; Karen and her mother could understand what Meryl was trying to communicate with these sounds, but other people could not. Children's protowords and their first real words are constructed from a limited set of speech sounds appropriate to their native language, usually the same sounds that became predominant during the conversational babbling stage (Bloom, 1998). Interestingly, there is great similarity across languages in children's early pronunciation errors, suggesting continuing physical constraints on children's sound production. For example, English-speaking children frequently substitute a /t/ sound for a /k/ sound, as in saying *tat* for *cat*. The same error has been observed in children learning such disparate languages as German and Hindi (Locke and Pearson, 1992).

The developmental sequence involved in acquiring speech sounds during the first year of life suggests that two things are needed to prepare children to begin speaking. First, they must gain control over their speech apparatus—the mouth, lips, tongue, and vocal cords—enabling them to produce speech sounds intentionally. This process is aided

A CLOSER LOOK

LANGUAGE DEVELOPMENT OF DEAF CHILDREN

About 1 in 1,000 babies is born with a severe hearing impairment (Watkin and Baldwin, 1999). The process of language development for these babies differs in some ways from that experienced by hearing babies, but in other ways it is quite similar. Understanding the similarities and differences is useful not only for determining the most effective ways to foster the development of communication skills in deaf infants, but also for clarifying the roles of biology and the environment in language development.

Early in infancy deaf babies produce sounds very similar to those of hearing babies (Hoff, 2001). During the crying, cooing, and vocal play stages, their vocalizations do not differ from those of hearing infants in quantity or quality, and the timetable for these stages of prelinguistic vocalizations is similar. These early developments seem to depend on biologically built-in factors, rather than environmental input. Around 6 to 9 months, differences in vocalization begin to appear. As already mentioned, deaf infants are slow to produce the consonant-vowel syllables of canonical babbling (Oller and Eilers, 1988). From this point on, environmental input becomes increasingly important in the development of vocalization and eventually of spoken language. Over time, the amount of babbling produced by hearing infants increases, while the amount produced by deaf infants declines.

About 10 percent of deaf infants have deaf parents; usually these babies are exposed to formal sign language from birth (Hoff, 2001). For them, the development of sign language follows a course similar to the development of spoken language in hearing infants (Petitto, 2000). Beginning at 4 to 6 months, they engage in manual babbling, producing fragmentary hand movements that gradually

come to resemble adult signs. At about the same age hearing infants speak their first words, deaf infants start to produce clear single-word signs (Capirci, Montanari, and Volterra, 1998). They also produce two-word combinations of signs, grammatical morphemes, and complex syntax on roughly the same timetable as hearing infants (Hoff, 2001).

Some researchers have argued that deaf infants' first signs emerge earlier than hearing infants' first words because the motor skills needed for manual signing develop earlier than those needed to control the vocal apparatus (Bonvillian and Folven, 1993). However, careful longitudinal observation of deaf and hearing infants with and without exposure to sign language has revealed great similarities in their early manual behavior. What some researchers (and parents) have interpreted as early signs are probably nonlinguistic gestures. Studies in which a distinction is made between true signs and nonlinguistic gestures have found no difference in the timing of first words and first signs (Capirci, Montanari, and Volterra, 1998).

Deaf babies who are not exposed to sign language early in development often create their own sign systems for communication, known as *homesign* (Morford, 1998). Homesign includes both pointing gestures and descriptive gestures, and these gestures are combined and modified in structured ways reminiscent of more formal languages. Homesign commonly includes nouns and verbs, variations in hand shape and motion that serve morphological functions, and ordering preferences similar to syntax. Although they are not as complex as formal spoken and sign languages, homesign systems provide some idea of the human brain's capacity to create a language in the absence of input from the environment.

considerably by brain development and by such physical changes as emergence of teeth and development of muscles in the tongue. Second, children must learn the phonemes of their particular language by paying close attention to the speech sounds they hear and beginning to imitate them. Only when they can recognize and produce appropriate speech sounds are they ready to combine sounds to make words.

Learning Words and Their Meanings

First Words Most children say their first identifiable words around their first birthday, although there is great variation in the exact age. First words usually refer to familiar persons *(mama),* body parts *(nose, feet),* animals *(doggie),* and objects *(shoe, ball).* Many children's early vocabularies are dominated by words referring to objects and people they regularly interact with (Bates, Bretherton, and Snyder, 1988; Dromi, 1999; Nelson, 1973). First words may also express feelings *(naughty, goodboy),* movement *(up, down, allgone, byebye),* and social commands that are not broken down into their component words *(gimmefive!).* For example, as Malcolm watches a car disappear down the street, he might comment "bye" or "allgone"; although *allgone* is two words for adults, many

Toddlers' first words often refer to familiar objects, animals, or people.

toddlers treat it as one. Another common topic during the single-word phase is the concept *no.* Young toddlers often develop several ways to express this concept. In addition to the traditional "no," they might say "me" or "mine," meaning "No, *me* do it" or "No, that's *mine.*"

Children differ in the purposes for which they use their first words. Some initially use words mainly to *refer to objects and events;* their first words are mostly nouns, plus some verbs and adjectives. This is a **referential style** of word use. Other children initially use words mainly to *express social routines;* their first words are primarily pronouns, such as *me* or *mine,* and formulas, such as *stopit.* This is an **expressive style** of word use. These differences in how first words are used are related to other aspects of social and cognitive development (Bates et al., 1988; Goldfield and Snow, 1993). Referential children are more likely to be firstborn and tend to come from more educated families than expressive children (Nelson, 1973). Mothers of referential children often encourage labeling by asking their children many questions, while mothers of expressive children tend to use language more to direct their children's behavior (Olsen-Fulero, 1982). Referential children initially acquire words faster than expressive children do, but there is no difference in how grammatical their speech is (Clark, 1983).

Referential style: A style of early word use in which words primarily refer to objects and events.

Expressive style: A style of early word use in which words primarily express social routines.

Vocabulary Growth   New words are acquired rather slowly during early toddlerhood; by 18 to 19 months, children have an average vocabulary of about fifty words (Bloom, 1998). In most children the rate of vocabulary growth increases dramatically at about 18 months of age, as shown in Figure 7.1. This sudden increase in word acquisition is known as the **vocabulary spurt.** Referential children, who are learning mostly nouns, show a more obvious vocabulary spurt than expressive children, who are adding roughly equal proportions of nouns and other kinds of words to their vocabularies (Goldfield and Reznick, 1990). Around the time of the vocabulary spurt, many English-speaking children also begin producing verbs to name actions and events (Tomasello and Kruger, 1992).

During the preschool years, children's vocabularies continue to increase rapidly, although the exact rate of growth is not certain. An early study suggested that the average

Vocabulary spurt:
A sudden increase in word acquisition at about 18 months of age.

ESTIMATES OF VOCABULARY GROWTH AS A FUNCTION OF AGE
This figure illustrates the slow initial growth of productive vocabulary, followed by a spurt in growth at about 18 months of age. The two scales indicate the uncertainty about the size of toddlers' and preschoolers' vocabularies. *(Source: Based on Carey, 1978; Miller, 1981; and Smith, 1926.)*

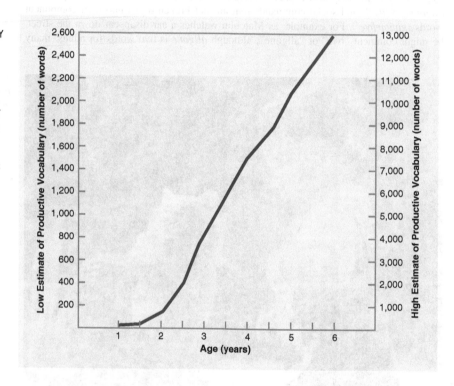

productive vocabulary—the number of words a child actually uses when speaking—was 1,222 for 3½-year-olds and 2,526 for 6-year-olds (Smith, 1926). More recent work has yielded much higher estimates—up to 8,000 to 14,000 words for the average 6-year-old (Carey, 1978). The actual number probably lies somewhere between these extremes. Productive vocabulary size is hard to measure because after the early stages there is no easy way to keep track of all the words a child actually uses.

Children's *receptive* vocabulary (words they can understand, even if they don't use them) is larger than their productive vocabulary. A truly remarkable growth in receptive vocabulary occurs between ages 1 and 6. During the preschool years, children learn on average 5.5 new words per day, resulting in a receptive vocabulary of around 10,000 words by the end of first grade and around 40,000 by the end of fifth grade (Anglin, 1993).

Children differ considerably in timing and rate of vocabulary growth. In one study, first words appeared at ages from 10 to 17 months, and the vocabulary spurt occurred at anywhere from 13 to 25 months (Bloom, 1993). Socioeconomic status has considerable impact on children's vocabulary development; children from low-income and working-class families show slower rates of vocabulary growth than children from middle-class and professional families (Fenson et al., 1994; Hart and Risley, 1995).

Processes of Word Learning Children's earliest words tend to be bound to the particular contexts in which they are learned (Dromi, 1999; Nelson, 1985). It is not until around the time of the vocabulary spurt that children start to use words to refer to *categories* of objects, people, and events. A milestone in language development comes when the child discovers that everything has a name (Gopnik and Meltzoff, 1987; Nelson, 1985). Now vocabulary building speeds up as the toddler begins to ask incessantly, "What that?"

The task of word learning is all the more complex because most of the words children learn are not often spoken separately. Usually children must pick out the critical group of sounds from a longer string. When DeeDee says to Malcolm, "Look at the ball *roll*," Malcolm must extract the new word *roll* from his mother's flow of speech. The ability to do this apparently emerges in infancy; one recent study found that 8-month-olds could group sounds from a continuous flow of speech into words (Saffran, Aslin, and Newport, 1996).

Toddlers sometimes make mistakes in the location of word boundaries, producing sentences like "Readit the book." In this case, the child has incorrectly concluded that the verb is *readit,* rather than *read.* Such mistakes are called **segmentation errors.** They are fairly common, especially where unstressed syllables come at boundaries between words (Gleitman and Wanner, 1982), but children usually correct them quickly.

Once toddlers have identified a string of sounds as a word, they must figure out what that word means. Even before age 2, children seem to be able to use the linguistic and nonlinguistic context in which an unfamiliar word appears to make a quick and reasonably accurate guess as to its meaning (Carey, 1978; Woodward, Markman, and Fitzsimmons, 1994). This process is known as **fast mapping.** In a study by Tracy Heibeck and Ellen Markman (1987), 2- to 4-year-olds received brief exposure to unfamiliar terms for colors *(chartreuse, amaranth, maroon),* shapes *(oval, hexagon, trapezoid),* and textures *(coarse, fibrous, granular).* In each case, the experimenter used the unfamiliar term in contrast to a familiar one, such as *blue, round,* or *fuzzy* ("Bring me the chartreuse one. Not the blue one, the chartreuse one."). When the children were tested a few minutes later, even 2-year-olds showed comprehension of the unfamiliar terms, especially those referring to shapes.

The process of fast mapping is helped along by **joint attention**—the tendency for language-learning children and their adult conversation partners to share a focus of attention. Caregivers often talk about things their babies are already paying attention to, or try to direct the babies' attention to particular objects (Baldwin, 1991; Tomasello, 1988). Babies as young as 16 months are able to use such cues as direction of an adult's gaze to determine what object the adult is labeling (Akhtar and Tomasello, 1996; Baldwin et al., 1996).

Fast mapping can work only if children have built-in assumptions about the most likely meanings of unfamiliar words. Suppose DeeDee points to a large red ball and says the word *ball.* How can Malcolm figure out that *ball* is the name of the thing itself, not one of its qualities (color, shape, size) or DeeDee's action (pointing)? Some theorists suggest that children have an inborn tendency to perceive objects (Spelke and Newport,

Segmentation errors:
Mistakes in detecting boundaries between words in a sentence.

Fast mapping:
A process in which a young child uses context cues to make a quick and reasonably accurate guess about the meaning of an unfamiliar word.

Joint attention
The tendency for language-learning children and their adult conversation partners to share a focus of attention.

Joint attention with caregivers helps toddlers learn word meanings quickly.

Whole-object assumption:
Children's tendency to assume that unfamiliar words are names for objects rather than for attributes or actions.

Lexical contrast:
Children's tendency to assume that no two words have the same meaning.

Underextensions:
Language errors in which the meaning a child attaches to a word is too restricted.

Overextensions:
Language errors in which the meaning a child attaches to a word is too broad.

1998) and to assume unfamiliar words are names for objects rather than attributes or actions (Huttenlocher and Smiley, 1987; Woodward and Markman, 1998). This tendency is known as the **whole-object assumption.**

But what if DeeDee holds up the ball and says, "Look, Malcolm, it's red"? How does Malcolm figure out that *red* is not just another word meaning *ball?* Children also seem to have a built-in tendency to assume that no two words have the same meaning, and thus unfamiliar words must refer to things for which they do not already have labels (Clark, 1988, 1990; Markman, 1987). This assumption is known as **lexical contrast** (*lexical* means "pertaining to words"). When Malcolm hears *red* in reference to this ball, he assumes it contrasts in meaning with the word *ball,* which he already knows. As possible meanings for *red,* he therefore considers features for which he has no labels. When he hears *red* also applied to his toy fire truck, his overalls, and his new winter coat, he concludes that *red* must be the name for a particular color.

Errors in Early Word Learning Once toddlers isolate a word, they very seldom assign entirely the wrong meaning to it. Malcolm is not likely to decide *red* means any round object that bounces and scream "Red!" when he sees his brother's new basketball. Such errors are rare in toddlers' productive language but may be more common in their understanding of what others say.

Toddlers' semantic errors are usually errors of under- and overextension. **Underextensions** occur when a word is used correctly but in too restricted a way. Suppose Mikey is given a toy dump truck and told that it is a *truck.* If he then starts to use the word to refer to toy trucks only and not to full-sized trucks he sees on the road, he has an underextended concept of truck. In **overextensions,** toddlers make the opposite mistake. Because their definition of a certain word is not sufficiently restricted, they sometimes use it when it doesn't really apply. If Mikey initially uses *truck* to refer to *any* wheeled vehicle, he is overextending its meaning.

Underextensions are much less obvious than overextensions. When children overextend the meaning of a word, they use it in clearly inappropriate ways, such as calling a squirrel *kitty.* When they underextend the meaning of a word, they simply fail to use it where it could have been used. Careful observations of toddlers over time show that they do sometimes underextend word meanings. One 8-month-old boy responded to the word *shoes* by crawling to the shoes in a particular closet (Reich, 1976). Gradually he generalized the meaning of *shoes* to shoes in another closet, then to shoes left outside closets, and finally to shoes on people's feet. A similar pattern can be seen in a little girl who at first applied the word *car* only to cars moving on the street outside her living room window (Bloom, 1973). Six months passed before she extended the meaning to cars in other situations.

Overextensions are very common in toddlers' speech. The word *ball,* for example, is often applied to a range of relatively small, round objects, such as apples, melons, and eggs. Most overextensions of nouns refer to objects broadly similar in appearance, especially in shape (Clark, 1983). Children may overextend the same word in a variety of ways. One little boy used the word *Nunu* (the name of the family dog) to refer not only to all dogs but also to other animals, to furry slippers and coats, and even to black olives in a salad, which resembled the dog's nose (de Villiers and de Villiers, 1979). Toddlers also overextend verbs and other parts of speech. One toddler initially used the word *out* to refer to opening or closing a door. Later the child generalized the meaning of *out* to peeling fruit, shelling peas, and undoing shoelaces (Clark, 1973).

One study of language development in six children found that the rate of overextensions was very high in the initial stages of vocabulary building, but dropped dramatically as the toddlers learned more words (Kuczaj, 1982). This pattern makes sense; the more words children know, the more likely they are to know what word to use in a given context.

When children overextend a word, it does not necessarily mean they are unaware of the boundaries of the word's meaning. Suppose Mikey wants to call attention to a bus that just went by. If he knows the word *truck* but not the word *bus,* he might use *truck*

If Maggie knows the words cheese, truck, cookie, mama, kitty, dada, blankie, go, *and* milk, *how would she label the objects shown here? She might well call the first object* truck, *the next two* cookie, *and the third* cheese. *These labels are incorrect, but they represent smart mistakes because she has chosen the best words available. She would not be likely to label any of these objects* kitty *or* blankie.

instead of nothing at all. This example suggests that toddlers may sometimes *knowingly* produce overextensions. They use a word in a wrong context not because they're unaware it doesn't quite fit, but because it is the word in their vocabulary that comes closest to what they want to say. In these cases the child is searching for the right word and is very responsive to corrective feedback from adults ("No, that's not a truck; that's a bus"). Receiving feedback following errors of overextension is one of the most effective ways for children to learn new words (Merriman, 1986).

Studies of *receptive* overextension show that toddlers have more knowledge of word meanings than their rate of productive overextensions suggests. Even if Mikey called a bus *truck,* he could probably pick out the correct objects from a set of toys if asked "Where's the bus? Where's the truck?" (Clark, 1983). This implies that Mikey does have the concept *bus,* even though he doesn't know the word *bus* as well as he knows *truck.* He uses *truck* when he can't remember *bus* because trucks and buses have some features in common.

To summarize, toddlers' under- and overextensions of words follow a common pattern:

- When words are first learned, they tend to be used only in the specific contexts in which they were originally heard, resulting in underextensions (Carey, 1978).

- As children begin to explore the limits of word meanings (Does *ball* mean all round objects? Does *truck* mean anything with wheels?), overextensions occur.

- A toddler may *knowingly* overextend a word because it is the closest one available in his or her vocabulary.

- Finally, as children's vocabularies grow, the rate of overextensions declines.

Learning Morphological Rules

Children's first words are usually single morphemes: *Mommy, Daddy, milk, more, doggie, go, cookie, sock.* Each is a unit of language representing a single object, action, or quality. As language development proceeds, children gradually add **grammatical morphemes** to the words they speak—units of language that carry little meaning by themselves, but that change the meaning of words and sentences in systematic ways. English grammatical morphemes include prefixes, suffixes, auxiliary verbs, articles, and certain prepositions. For instance, an *-s* added to the end of most English nouns changes their meaning from singular to plural and is therefore a grammatical morpheme.

English-speaking children generally do not begin to use grammatical morphemes until after they start to combine words into sentences. However, many languages, such

Grammatical morpheme: A unit of language that carries little meaning by itself, but that changes the meaning of words or sentences in a systematic way.

as Turkish and Russian, have more grammatical morphemes than English does—for example, different endings for nouns depending on whether they are used as subjects or objects in sentences. Children learning these languages add grammatical morphemes to words earlier than children learning English do, often before they begin to combine words into sentences (Hoff, 2001; Peters, 1995).

Order of Acquisition Roger Brown (1973) studied the learning of grammatical morphemes in three children he called Eve, Adam, and Sarah. He found that they acquired these morphemes in a consistent order, although their speed of acquisition varied considerably. The same pattern appeared in a cross-sectional study of a large group of children (de Villiers and de Villiers, 1978). First, children begin to add *-s* to nouns to form plurals and *-ing* to verbs to form present participles (as in *going* or *running*). Somewhat later, children start to use *-ed* to form past tense verbs (as in *jumped*) and *-s* to form the third person singular (as in *she sits*). Among the last grammatical morphemes to appear are those for contractions of the verb *to be* (the *'s* in *it's big,* or the *'re* in *they're playing*).

The order in which toddlers acquire grammatical morphemes has nothing to do with how often they hear each of these morphemes in the language spoken to them. Contrary to what you might expect, the most frequently heard morphemes are not acquired first (Brown, 1973). Instead, three other factors seem to govern the order of acquisition.

First, *grammatical complexity* plays a role. Brown (1973) suggested that morphemes that produce the simplest changes in a word's function in a sentence are learned first. By this he meant forms that are the closest to the active, declarative form of a verb (as *going* is to *go*) or to the base morpheme of a noun (as *socks* is to *sock*).

Second, *semantic complexity* is involved (Brown, 1973). The *-ing* that forms the present participle adds to the verb the quite simple idea of ongoing action. In contrast, adding an *-s* to a verb to form the third person singular (as in *she sits*) is more semantically complex even though it appears structurally simple. This is so because it adds several ideas: that we are talking about someone else, that only one person or object is referred to *(he, she,* or *it,* not *they),* and that the action takes place in the present.

Finally, the *phonological characteristics* of a morpheme—how it sounds—also influence when it is acquired. For example, Turkish children acquire some grammatical morphemes earlier than children learning other languages. Most Turkish grammatical morphemes are full syllables; many are word endings pronounced with considerable stress, which makes them more noticeable (Aksu-Koc and Slobin, 1985).

Productivity and Overregularization The acquisition of grammatical morphemes is of particular interest to developmentalists because it shows that language learning involves discerning rules. For instance, children do not learn the plural forms of nouns word by word. Instead, they learn a general rule about forming plurals: in English, add the suffix *-s* or *-es* and the noun becomes "more than one." In a classic study, Jean Berko (1958) showed how children apply morphological rules even to words they have never heard before. She taught children that an unusual birdlike creature was called a *wug.* Then she showed them a picture of two of these creatures and said: "Now there is another one. There are two____." (See Figure 7.2.) The children's task was to fill in the blank. Those who had acquired the rule of adding *-s* to form the plural readily answered "wugs." Berko's study shows the great *productivity* of

THIS IS A WUG.

NOW THERE IS ANOTHER ONE. THERE ARE TWO OF THEM. THERE ARE TWO _____.

Figure 7.2
AN ITEM FROM BERKO'S WUG STUDY

language—the fact that it allows almost unlimited output because it is governed by general rules. As a result, we can take even an unfamiliar word and modify its meaning in ways others will understand.

Learning Syntactic Rules

Exceptions to morphological rules are potential stumbling blocks for children. Most English nouns become plural by adding -s or -es, but sometimes this rule does not apply (*mouse/mice, foot/feet*). Similarly, the usual way to form the past tense of English verbs is to add the suffix -*ed*, but irregular verbs do not follow this convention (*go/went, come/came*). You might think children would learn regular forms first and tackle the exceptions later, but this is not the usual pattern (Marcus et al., 1992). Instead, correct irregular past tenses and plurals often appear early, with the child saying *came, did, mice, feet*, and so on. Shortly thereafter an odd thing happens. The child starts to impose regular forms on irregular nouns and verbs so that *mice* becomes *mouses, feet* becomes *foots, came* becomes *comed,* and *did* becomes *doed.* These errors are called **overregularizations.** Overregularizations appear about the same time the child begins to use regular past tenses and plurals reliably. Apparently, the child learns the -*ed* and -*s* rules and applies them indiscriminately. Overregularizations do not completely replace the correct irregular forms, however. Most children use overregularized forms only occasionally— about 2.5 percent of the time for verbs (Marcus et al., 1992) and about 8 percent of the time for nouns (Marcus, 1995). By age 6 or 7, children use correct forms almost all the time (Cazden, 1968), although school-age children still occasionally produce incorrect irregular forms, such as "I *brang* my lunch."

Overregularizations:
Language errors in which a child applies a morphological rule to a word that is an exception to the rule.

Overregularization is an example of what developmentalists call a *growth error.* When overregularization appears, the number of mistakes a child makes in forming past tenses and plurals increases, which might seem like a setback in language development. However, the mistakes are due not to regression or loss of ability, but to the emergence of a more advanced way of thinking. Even though children who overregularize temporarily make more mistakes, they are in fact making progress toward understanding the morphological rules of their language.

Overregularization provides insight into the cognitive processes underlying language learning. When learning something complex, such as a language, children seem to search automatically for regularities. To find them, they must first learn a number of examples from which rules can be drawn. At this early stage they learn each regular and irregular form separately. From this pool of examples, they filter out the irregular ones and zero in on the patterns used most. They then begin to apply these rules in other cases, including irregular nouns and verbs. Gradually, they develop an understanding of which verbs and nouns are exceptions to the rules, and overregularizations fade out.

This learning process is clearly very complex, as anyone who has ever tried to master irregular forms in a second language knows. Yet preschoolers seem to accomplish it with little effort, just from hearing spoken language. Long before adulthood, morphological rules and most exceptions to them seem second nature to us, even though we may still be caught off guard when asked what the plural of *moose* is or whether the past tense of *fly* is ever *flied.* (It is, in the sentence "The batter flied out.") Our hesitation in answering such questions reminds us what a remarkable achievement it is for young children to master morphological rules.

Learning to Form Sentences

We noted earlier that *syntax* is a language's rules for organizing words into phrases and sentences. In any system of syntax, individual words each belong to a particular **form class,** such as nouns, verbs, and adjectives. In English, for instance, *dog* and *justice* are classified as nouns, *sit* and *believe* as verbs, and *lazy* and *purple* as adjectives. Syntactic rules specify how words belonging to various form classes can be combined to make phrases, clauses, and sentences.

Form class:
A category of words in a language that can fill similar syntactic roles in forming phrases and sentences.

One set of syntactic rules governs how phrases are formed. For example, an article and a noun make up a noun phrase, such as *the boy* or *a dog.* Other syntactic rules limit the ways in which phrases can be put together to make sentences. For example, *A dog bit the boy* and *The boy bit a dog* are acceptable sentences in English, but *Bit the boy a dog* normally is not.

Form classes, phrases, and sentences are all highly abstract categories. Children cannot learn syntactic rules simply on the basis of noticing how specific words, like *dog* or *boy,* are used in sentences and then figuring out a rule for each individual word. Instead, children somehow extract and use rules involving these abstract categories from the particular, concrete examples of speech they hear. This is *not* to say that young children are consciously aware they are learning and using grammatical rules. It will be years before they are cognitively advanced enough to understand and talk explicitly about grammatical categories and rules.

A very important feature of syntactic rules is their productivity. Just as morphological rules allow for tremendous output in forming and modifying words, so syntactic rules allow for countless possible sentences just by placing different words in various roles. Once children can use the rules of syntax, their ability to create new meaningful sentences becomes virtually unlimited.

The One-Word Stage When children first start saying recognizable words, they use only one word at a time. To an adult, a single word is often just a label for an object, action, or quality. To a toddler, a single word can be an attempt to communicate much more. For example, when Meryl says "mama," she may be simply labeling her mother, or she may be trying to express some idea related to Karen that an older child would express in a phrase or sentence (de Villiers and de Villiers, 1978). How to interpret Meryl's meaning depends on the context in which she says the word. If she says "mama" when Karen enters the room, she might be trying to communicate *Here is mama.* If she says "mama" after Karen leaves the house, she might be trying to express *I want my mama.* If she says "mama" while holding up Karen's purse, she might be trying to tell someone *This belongs to mama.* A word that conveys such extended meaning is called a **holophrase.** When a toddler says a single word, it is not always obvious whether it is just a label or whether it is intended to communicate a more complex meaning. To tell the difference, listeners must pay attention to context, including the child's gestures, facial expression, and tone of voice.

Holophrase:
A single word that conveys the meaning of a phrase or sentence.

Toddlers' early sentences often require considerable interpretation.

First Sentences At 18 to 24 months of age, toddlers usually start to produce two-word sequences. This change typically occurs soon after the vocabulary spurt, but it is even more closely connected to the appearance of verbs in the child's vocabulary (Bloom, 1998). The earliest two-word sequences may not really be sentences. Often they seem to be expressing two separate ideas, one after the other. For example, psychologist Lois Bloom's daughter Allison said "daddy, car" on one occasion when her father left in the car. On another similar occasion, she said "car, daddy" (Bloom, 1973). In both cases, she paused between the two words, as if she were conveying two related, but separate thoughts ("There goes *daddy.* Daddy is in the *car.*"). Such a pause between words is not characteristic of true sentences. And since Allison spoke these two words in both possible orders, word order was apparently unimportant to what she wanted to say. In true English sentences, in contrast, word order *is* important. Thus, the first words toddlers speak in close succession may be a kind of transitional step from one-word statements to true sentences.

Toddlers' earliest true two-word sentences are usually composed of nouns, verbs, and adjectives. Few articles *(a, the)*, conjunctions *(and, or)*, or prepositions *(of, by)* appear, even though these words are common in adult speech. As we have mentioned, English-speaking toddlers at first do not add grammatical morphemes to words. They also ignore most auxiliary verbs, such as *can, may,* or *would.* When Maggie at 18 months wanted to express the idea *I can see the teddy bear,* she said simply: "See teddy." In this phase the child seems to omit words that are not essential to the central meaning of the sentence. This style of talking is called **telegraphic speech** because it sounds somewhat like the terse wording of a telegram. Telegraphic speech has been observed among children learning a wide range of languages, including German, Finnish, and Kaluli (a language spoken in Papua New Guinea) (Hoff, 2001).

Interestingly, young toddlers use telegraphic speech even when adults specifically model longer sentences for them (Brown and Fraser, 1963). When Christine repeatedly encouraged 18-month-old Maggie to say "I love my grandma," Maggie's words came out simply "Love gama." Using more than two words to express a single idea seemed to exceed her current cognitive capacity.

Although a child's earliest sentences are telegraphic, they are not arbitrary groupings of words. Most two-word sentences seem to express a relatively small set of basic meanings, listed in Table 7.1. The categories of meanings expressed at the two-word stage are remarkably similar across languages (Slobin, 1970). Out of context, children's two-word utterances are nearly as ambiguous as their one-word utterances. Adults must still rely heavily on context, gestures, facial expressions, and intonation to interpret what a child means. In our toddler vignette, 2-year-old Mikey greeted his father with a broad smile, outstretched arms, and a joyous "Daddy home!" Clearly, this was meant as a happy announcement that his father had returned. On another occasion, when Christine let Mikey talk to his father on the phone, he said sternly, "Daddy *home!*" with stress on the second word. Here his meaning seemed to be the command "Daddy, come home *now!*"

Telegraphic speech:
A toddler speech style in which words not essential to the meaning of a sentence are omitted.

PRIVATE SPEECH
PIAGET VERSUS VYGOTSKY

private speech Talking aloud to oneself with no intent to communicate.

Anna, age 4, was alone in her room painting. When she finished, she was overheard saying aloud, "Now I have to put the pictures somewhere to dry. I'll put them by the window. They need to get dry now. I'll paint some more dinosaurs."

Private speech—talking aloud to oneself with no intent to communicate with others—is normal and common in childhood, accounting for 20 to 50 percent of what 4- to 10-year-old children say (Berk, 1986a). Two- to 3-year-olds engage in "crib talk," playing with sounds and words. Four- and 5-year-olds use private speech as a way to express fantasies and emotions (Berk, 1992; Small, 1990). Older children "think out loud" or mutter in barely audible tones.

Piaget (1962/1923) saw private speech as a sign of cognitive immaturity. According to Piaget, because young children are egocentric, they are unable to recognize others' viewpoints and therefore are unable to communicate meaningfully. Instead, they simply vocalize whatever is on their own minds. Another reason young children talk while they do things, said Piaget, is that they do not yet distinguish between words and the actions the words stand for, or symbolize. By the end of the preoperational stage, he said, with cognitive maturation and social experience, children become less egocentric and more capable of symbolic thought and so discard private speech.

Like Piaget, Vygotsky (1962/1934) believed that private speech helps young children integrate language with thought. However, Vygotsky did not look upon private speech as egocentric. He saw it as a special form of communication: conversation with the self. As such, he said, it serves a very important function in the transition between early social speech (often experienced in the form of adult commands) and inner speech (thinking in words)—a transition toward the internalization of socially derived control of behavior ("Now I have to put the pictures somewhere to dry"). Vygotsky suggested that private speech follows an inverted U-shaped curve: it increases during the pre-school years and then fades away during the early part of middle childhood as children become more able to guide and master their actions.

Research generally supports Vygotsky as to the functions of private speech. In an observational study of 93 low- to middle-income 3- to 5-year-olds, 86 percent of the children's remarks were *not* egocentric (Berk, 1986a). The most sociable children and those who engage in the most social speech tend to use the most private speech as well, apparently supporting Vygotsky's view that private speech is stimulated by social experience (Berk, 1986a, 1986b, 1992; Berk & Garvin, 1984; Kohlberg, Yaeger, & Hjertholm, 1968). There also is evidence for the role of private speech in self-regulation (Berk & Garvin, 1984; Furrow, 1984). Private speech tends to increase when children are trying to do difficult tasks, especially without adult supervision (Berk, 1992; Berk & Garvin, 1984).

According to one ranking (Bivens & Berk, 1988), children progress through at least three levels of private speech: (1) speech that is purely self-expressive (word play, repetition of syllables, expression of feelings, or talking to dolls or imaginary playmates); (2) vocal statements relevant to a task at hand (commenting on what one is doing or needs to do or has done, asking and then answering one's own questions, or sounding out words); and (3) external signs of task-directed inner speech (inaudible muttering or lip and tongue movements). Preschool girls, who tend to be more verbally advanced than preschool boys, use more mature forms of private speech; and middle-income children use more mature forms than low-income children (Berk, 1986a).

How much do children engage in private speech? The pattern now appears more complex than Vygotsky's U-shaped curve. Some studies have reported no age changes in overall use of private speech; others have found variations in the timing of its decline. The brightest children tend to use it earliest. Whereas Vygotsky considered the need for private speech a universal stage of cognitive development, studies have found a wide range of individual differences, with some children using it very little or not at all (Berk, 1992).

Understanding the significance of private speech has practical implications, especially in school (Berk, 1986a). Talking to oneself or muttering should not be considered misbehavior; a child may be struggling with a problem and may need to think out loud.

Checkpoint

Can you . . .

✓ Trace normal progress in 3- to 6-year-olds' vocabulary, grammar, syntax, and conversational abilities?

✓ Give reasons children of various ages use private speech?

Chapter 3
Early Childhood

Early Childhood is a time of continued rapid development - physical, cognitive, emotional and social changes are all taking place. All of this growth coupled with an increasing expansion of their newfound language skills gives these children the tools necessary to wonder and question and learn. How the people in the child's environment answer those questions, will start to shape their understanding of how the world works.

PHYSICAL AND MOTOR DEVELOPMENT

Growth in childhood proceeds at a less frantic pace than in infancy. Children during this period grow about another 12 inches and continue to gain weight at the rate of about 5 pounds a year. Body proportions are also changing, with the legs growing faster than the rest of the body. By about age 6, the legs make up almost 45 percent of body length. At the beginning of this period, children usually have all their baby teeth; at the end of the period, children begin to lose them. Boys and girls show about the same rate of growth during these years.

Features of Physical Development

Look at Figure 10.1, the human growth curve. (Note that 10 centimeters equal 4 inches.) This curve strikingly illustrates the regularity of physical growth. Most parts of the body (except the brain and the reproductive organs) follow this pattern (Tanner, 1989). With the exception of the two spurts at infancy and adolescence, growth is highly predictable for almost all boys and girls, given satisfactory conditions.

The Sequence of Early Childhood Growth

We know that different cells, tissues, and organs grow at different rates. (Some tissues never lose the ability to grow, such as hair, skin, and nails.) In humans, for example, body length at birth is about four times the length of the face at birth, so the head is relatively large. But the head grows more slowly than the trunk or limbs, so that they gradually become proportional.

Parents and children alike are quite conscious of the appearance and loss of "baby" teeth and the arrival of the first permanent teeth. At about 2½ years all of the primary teeth have come through, which most children begin to lose between 5 and 6 years. At about this time, the first permanent teeth appear. Children continue to lose their primary teeth and gain new permanent teeth at about the same time. The timing can be different for some children, however, so that gaps between teeth may appear or new teeth arrive before the baby teeth have fallen out, causing a space problem that may require professional attention.

Children's rapidly developing motor skills are clearly seen in their drawings from uncontrolled scribbling to controlled "within the lines" attempts to their own creative expressions. Summarize the many developmental benefits of drawing.

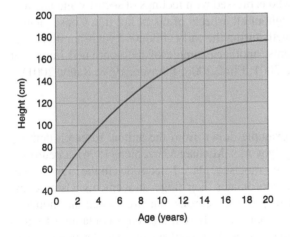

FIGURE 10.1
The human growth curve.

From John F. Travers, *The Growing Child*, Scott, Foresman and Company, Glenview, IL, 1982. Reprinted by permission of the author.

Continuing Brain Development

Kurt Fischer, a cognitive psychologist at the Harvard Graduate School of Education, has spent many years studying the relationship between the appearance of new mental abilities and changes in the rate of brain growth in children (see particularly Dawson & Fischer, 1994). As a result of his research, Fischer believes he has found evidence for at least 12 brain growth spurts between birth and 21 years of age. He reached his conclusions based on studies of the growth of head size and brain activity (using EEG readings and increases in the density of synaptic junctions).

During the early childhood years, three brain growth spurts appear: at ages 2, 4, and 7. At 4 years of age, children understand much more about the world around them. They probably experience some type of preschool world, which they enjoy because they find pleasure in interacting with others. They're beginning to decide which of their playmates they like and which they don't; most importantly, they're learning *why* they like some and dislike others. They can run, jump, chase others, and PLAY! With their steadily growing cognitive abilities, they imagine all kinds of playmates and engage in fantastic activities.

So during these years children experience a slower brain growth pattern. In other words, while it took $2\frac{1}{2}$ years to grow 75 percent, in the next $3\frac{1}{2}$ years brain growth will increase only 15 percent. Figure 10.2 illustrates this process.

The nature of the changes occurring during the early childhood years is interesting to trace. Microscopic examinations have repeatedly shown an increase in dendrites, accompanied by growth in the number of synapses. These changes, while not changes in structure, nevertheless help to explain the growing cognitive ability of 2- to 6-year-olds. The neural foundation is being laid for children to form more connections, providing a network that furthers cognition and learning (Howard, 2000; Johnson, 1998, 1999).

The great task of the early childhood years is to form connections. Children of these years gobble up information from the outside world through their eyes, ears, nose, hands, and so on, and translate it into nerve impulses, which travel along neurons (from the axon of one cell to the dendrites of another). The brain cells that receive this information survive; those that don't, die. It's as simple as that.

For example, there probably is no more important stimulation than parents talking *to* their baby. The language areas of the brain respond, resulting in superior language skills for a child. Children also need a warm, emotionally supportive environment, which results in more connections in those parts of the brain responsible for developing emotions. The result is a child who is blessed with feelings of security and an emotional well-being that spreads throughout all aspects of his or her life. Consequently, we can say that continued brain growth during the early childhood years parallels cognitive and language accomplishments, another example of the continued impact of biopsychosocial forces (Andreasen, 2001; Eliot, 2000; Johnson, 1998; Ratey, 2001).

How the Brain Works

The following is just one example drawn from the animal research demonstrating how the brain actually works. Michael Merzenich (1996), a neuroscientist at the University of San Francisco, placed electrodes in the brains of six monkeys, in the region that coordinates their finger movements. Using computer imaging, he traced a map of the neurons that fired when the monkeys moved their fingers. Next, he put four different-size cups containing food—one at a time—in front of their cages. The monkeys reached through the bars and, by wiggling their fingers, could reach the food, take it into the cage, and eat it. After each monkey was successful with one cup, Merzenich next placed a different-sized cup before the monkey.

Merzenich did this until all of the monkeys were successful with each of the four cups. *The computer images of their brain areas controlling the finger movements had greatly increased in size. But after they had mastered all of the*

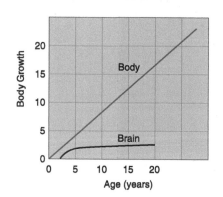

FIGURE 10.2
Slowing growth of the brain.

cups, the responsible brain areas began to shrink! Their brains had pushed the control of this behavior to lower brain areas that didn't require as much involvement of the cerebral cortex. In other words, the finger-moving behavior had become more automatic. This makes sense when you think of how you learned to drive a car. Initially, you concentrated with ferocious attention on what you were doing. Now you drive almost automatically—but carefully.

What does this experiment tell us? First, we know now that the brain is perfectly capable of rewiring itself. Second, if not sufficiently stimulated, once active neurons will fade and perish or will be commandeered by another activity. Thanks to this and similar experiments, we can draw two important conclusions that affect a child's environment.

- Stimulating experiences are essential for the fulfillment of a child's brain development.
- There is a critical period for brain development and, if that period is missed, learning and mastery of tasks become much more difficult.

Although the hemispheres seem to be almost identical, there are important differences between the two. These differences are clues to a brain's organization. If you are right-handed, for example, your left cerebral hemisphere is lateralized for **handedness** and for control of your speech—you are "left lateralized." Figure 10.3 illustrates **lateralization**.

Handedness Children's preference for using one hand over the other.

Lateralization Refers to a preferred side of the brain for a particular activity.

Influences on Physical Development in Early Childhood

In an excellent overview of physical development, Tanner (1989) indicated how the interaction of heredity and environment produces the rate and kinds of physical growth. Among the chief contributing forces are the following:

- *Genetic elements.* Hereditary elements, as we have seen, are of immense importance to the regulation of growth. The genetic growth plan is given at conception and functions throughout the entire growth period.
- *Nutrition.* Active preschoolers need a well-balanced diet—bread, cereal, fruit, vegetables, meat, milk—and they require several wholesome snacks. Parents, for as long as possible, should restrict sweets and soda drinks. Almost as important, preschoolers should begin to develop good eating habits (Lutz & Przytulski, 1997; Tamborlane, 1997a).
- *Disease.* Short-term illnesses cause no permanent retardation of the growth rate, although they may cause some disturbance if the child's diet is consistently inadequate (an abundance of empty calories). Major disease usually causes a slowing of growth, followed by a catch-up period if circumstances become more favorable.

FIGURE 10.3
Lateralization of handedness.

The energy of the early childhood years is seen in the physical activities of the period: constant motion followed by periods of rest and nutrition. Can you propose techniques by which the energy of these years can be safely and positively directed?

- *Psychological disturbance.* Stress can produce decided effects on physical development, beginning with the prenatal period. For example, stress and anxiety are associated with low birth weight and early delivery (Azar, 1999b). During the early childhood years, children experience the trauma of leaving home for preschool and kindergarten, adjusting to new adults and peers. If these events are coupled with any trouble at home (conflict, divorce), the impact on the children can be decidedly negative. There is always the danger that adverse experiences can—not always—cause a negative self-concept (Rutter & Rutter, 1993). (We'll explore this topic at greater length in chapter 10.)
- *Socioeconomic status.* Children from different social classes differ in average body size at all ages. Tanner gives the example of differences in height between British children of the professional class and those of laborers. Children of the professional class are from 1 inch taller at age 3 and 2 inches taller at adolescence. A consistent pattern appears in all such studies, indicating that children in more favorable circumstances are larger than those growing up under less favorable economic conditions. The difference seems to stem from nutrition, sleep, exercise, and recreation.
- *Secular trends.* During the past hundred years the tendency has been for children to become progressively larger at all ages. This is especially true in Europe and America.

This brief overview of physical development again illustrates the importance of the biopsychosocial model. For example, you may be tempted to think that physical growth is essentially biological, mainly determined by heredity. Note, however, the role played by nutrition and socioeconomic status. The interaction among biological, psychological, and social influences testifies to the power of the biopsychosocial model in explaining development.

Growing Motor Skills

When early childhood children reach the age of 6, no one—neither parents nor teachers—is surprised by what they can do physically. Think back to the infancy period and recall how often we referred to what children couldn't do. Stand, walk, run—we tend to take the accomplishments of the 6-year-old for granted, but a great deal of neuromuscular development had to occur before these motor skills became so effortless.

Motor skills Skills (both gross and fine) resulting from physical development enabling children to perform smooth and coordinated physical acts.

We are concerned here with two types of **motor skills**: *gross* (using the large muscles) and *fine* (using the small muscles of the hands and fingers). Thanks to perceptual and motor development, 3- and 4-year-old children can hold crayons, copy triangles, button their clothes, and unlace their shoes. Table 10.1 summarizes the development of motor skills.

TABLE 10.1 The Emergence of Motor Skills

Age	Gross Skills	Fine Skills
2	Runs, climbs stairs, jumps from object (both feet)	Throws ball, kicks ball, turns page, begins to scribble
3	Hops, climbs stairs with alternating feet, jumps from bottom step	Copies circle, opposes thumb to finger, scribbling continues to improve
4	Runs well, skillful jumping, begins to skip, pedals tricycle	Holds pencil, copies square, walks balance beam
5	Hops about 50 feet, balances on one foot, can catch large ball, good skipping	Colors within lines, forms letters, dresses and undresses self with help, eats more neatly
6	Carries bundles, begins to ride bicycle, jumps rope, chins self, can catch a tennis ball	Ties shoes, uses scissors, uses knife and fork, washes self with help

The physical picture of the early childhood youngster is one of energy and growing motor skill. Adequate rest is critical and parents should establish a routine to avoid problems. For example, to reconcile a rambunctious child with the necessity of sleep, parents should minimize stimulation through a consistent, easily recognized program: washing, toothbrushing, storytelling, and gentle but firm pressure to sleep. Careful and thoughtful adult care should prevent undue difficulties.

The Special Case of Drawing

Children love to draw and their artwork has long attracted the attention of scholars as far back as John Ruskin in 1857 with his book *The Elements of Drawing*. In a finely tuned sequence, which no one has to teach them, children move from the pincer movements of infancy to random scribbles to skillful creations. As they do, certain questions arise: Why do children scribble? What are they trying to say in their art? Why do they draw stick figures when they know people don't look that way (Schirrmacher, 1998)?

In analyzing children's art, it's important to remember that their drawings are the expression of *what they are capable of doing*. That is, the early childhood youngster is limited in eye-hand coordination, motor ability, and manual dexterity. But their drawings, as crude as an adult may think they are, tell us much about a child's personality and emotional state.

The early childhood years are a time when children show a great love for drawing. Not only are their drawings a sign of motor development, but they also indicate levels of cognitive development and can be emotionally revealing.

AN INFORMED VIEW: Children and Their Drawings

Children love to draw and are fascinated by the illustrations in the books they read. One reason for the appeal of these illustrations is that many illustrators have adapted the style of children's drawings to their own work. Among them are Lois Ehlert (*Color Zoo, Chica Chica Boom Boom*, etc.), who constantly uses bright, primary colored geometric shapes to create letters and objects of nature. In Todd Parr's *The Feel Good Book*, the illustrations resemble the primitive drawings of small artists. Children's own artwork has long attracted the attention of scholars for many reasons, ranging from artistic to psychological. (For an interesting discussion of this topic, see Milbrath, 1998.)

We have previously mentioned the work of Rhoda Kellogg (1970), who taught preschool children for many years. During this time she collected more than 1 million children's drawings and paintings that were done by thousands of children. You would enjoy reading Kellogg's description of children's art and derive insights from her work, such as her belief that the basic line formation and motifs that are appealing in children's art are *also to be found in the art of adults* (Kellogg, 1970).

Kellogg believed that children's drawing passes through the following four stages, with the first stage of their artistic development consisting of 20 basic scribbles.

1. *Placement*, which refers to where on the paper the child places the drawing (2 to 3 years).

2. *Shape*, which refers to diagrams with different shapes (about 3 years).

3. *Design*, which refers to a combination of forms (about 3 to 4 years).

4. *Pictorial*, which refers to representations of humans, animals, buildings, and more (about 4 to 5 years).

By 2 years of age, children have achieved 17 placement patterns. At 3 years, they're using circles, crosses, squares, and rectangles. By the time children are 4 years old they enter the pictorial stage.

As well-known artist Mitsumasa Anno (in Marcus, 2002) points out, remarkable as it may seem, even children as young as 2 years *understand* when shown a simple drawing with circles for heads and rectangles for bodies and single lines for arms and legs that "this is Father, this is Mother." This is one of a child's first steps toward abstract understanding.

(You may also wish to learn more about children's art by going to our Web site at http:/www.mhhe.com/dacey6.)

Random scribbling Drawing in which children use dots and lines with simple arm movements.

Controlled scribbling Drawing in which children carefully watch what they are doing, when before they looked away.

For example, 2-year-olds grab markers and scribble enthusiastically (using dots and lines) and seem fascinated by their ability to produce lines as a result of their movements. Parents and preschool teachers should encourage this **random scribbling** as a necessary first step in children's creative growth. During this phase of random scribbling, which continues until about age 3, children are free from any evaluation of their drawings; they're simply having fun.

Three-year-olds hold a crayon with their whole hand and then begin to use their wrists, which permits them to draw curves and loops. In this **controlled scribbling**, they become engrossed with geometric figures and are beginning to realize their lines can represent objects. Now their art matches their cognitive development and reflects their growing symbolic power. For example, they'll point to their creation and say, "That's a man." This phase lasts until about age 4.

Four- and 5-year-olds show greater control and attention to what they are doing, deliberately attempting to create representations of objects. For example, they'll use a circle to represent a head or the sun. Young children produce exciting creations, using a combination of symbols that vary widely from child to child (Wachowiak & Clements, 1997). Artistic expression seems to peak by the end of the early childhood period. During these years, children begin to paint and hold the brush with thumb and fingers. They hold the paper in place with the free hand. They give names to their drawings and begin to show representation (using one thing for another—see the cognitive section of the chapter).

Children's drawings not only are good clues to their motor coordination but also, as we'll see, provide insights into their cognitive and emotional lives, another example of how a biopsychosocial perspective helps us to understand development.

Guideposts for Study

1. What are typical cognitive advances and immature aspects of preschool children's thinking?

2. What memory abilities expand in early childhood?

3. How is preschoolers' intelligence measured, and what factors influence it?

4. How does language improve, and what happens when its development is delayed?

5. What purpose does early childhood education serve, and how do children make the transition to kindergarten?

Guidepost 1

What are typical cognitive advances and immature aspects of preschool children's thinking?

preoperational stage In Piaget's theory, the second major stage of cognitive development, in which children become more sophisticated in their use of symbolic thought but are not yet able to use logic.

Piagetian Approach: The Preoperational Child

Jean Piaget called early childhood the **preoperational stage** of cognitive development because children this age are not yet ready to engage in logical mental operations, as they will be in the concrete operational stage in middle childhood. However, the preoperational stage, which lasts from approximately ages 2 to 7, is characterized by a great expansion in the use of symbolic thought, or representational ability, which first emerges near the end of the sensorimotor stage. Let's look at some advances and some immature aspects of preoperational thought (Tables 10-1 and 10-2) and at recent research, some of which challenges Piaget's conclusions.

Table 10-1	Cognitive Advances during Early Childhood	
Advance	**Significance**	**Example**
Use of symbols	Children do not need to be in sensorimotor contact with an object, person, or event in order to think about it.	Simon asks his mother about the elephants they saw on their trip to the circus several months earlier.
	Children can imagine that objects or people have properties other than those they actually have.	Rolf pretends that a slice of apple is a vacuum cleaner "vrooming" across the kitchen table.
Understanding of identities	Children are aware that superficial alterations do not change the nature of things.	Antonio knows that his teacher is dressed up as a pirate but is still his teacher underneath the costume.
Understanding of cause and effect	Children realize that events have causes.	Seeing a ball roll from behind a wall, Aneko looks behind the wall for the person who kicked the ball.
Ability to classify	Children organize objects, people, and events into meaningful categories.	Rosa sorts the pinecones she collected on a nature walk into two piles: "big" and "little."
Understanding of number	Children can count and deal with quantities.	Lindsay shares some candy with her friends, counting to make sure that each girl gets the same amount.
Empathy	Children become more able to imagine how others might feel.	Emilio tries to comfort his friend when he sees that his friend is upset.
Theory of mind	Children become more aware of mental activity and the functioning of the mind.	Bianca wants to save some cookies for herself, so she hides them from her brother in a pasta box. She knows her cookies will be safe there because her brother will not look in a place where he doesn't expect to find cookies.

Advances of Preoperational Thought

Advances in symbolic thought are accompanied by a growing understanding of causality, identities, categorization, and number. Some of these understandings have roots in infancy and toddlerhood; others begin to develop in early childhood but are not fully achieved until middle childhood.

The Symbolic Function

"I want ice cream!" announces Kerstin, age 4, trudging indoors from the hot, dusty backyard. She has not seen anything that triggered this desire—no open freezer door, no television commercial. She no longer needs this kind of sensory cue to think about something. She remembers ice cream and its coldness and taste, and she purposefully seeks it out. This absence of sensory or motor cues characterizes the **symbolic function:** the ability to use symbols, or mental representations—words, numbers, or images to which a person has attached meaning. Without symbols, people could not communicate verbally, make change, read maps, or treasure photos of distant loved ones. Having symbols for things helps children remember and think about them without having them physically present.

Preschool children show the symbolic function through deferred imitation, pretend play, and language. *Deferred imitation* (refer to Chapter 7), which becomes more robust after 18 months, is based on having kept a mental representation of an observed action—as when 3-year-old Bart scolds his little sister, using the same words he heard his father say to the delivery boy who was late bringing the pizza. In **pretend play,** also called *fantasy play, dramatic play,* or *imaginary play,* children may make an object, such as a doll, represent, or symbolize, something else, such as a person. *Language* uses a system

symbolic function Piaget's term for ability to use mental representations (words, numbers, or images) to which a child has attached meaning.

pretend play Play involving imaginary people or situations; also called *fantasy play, dramatic play,* or *imaginary play.*

Table 10-2	Immature Aspects of Preoperational Thought (according to Piaget)	
Limitation	**Description**	**Example**
Centration: Inability to decenter	Children focus on one aspect of a situation and neglect others.	Jacob teases his younger sister that he has more juice than she does because his juice box has been poured into a tall, skinny glass, but hers has been poured into a short, wide glass.
Irreversibility	Children fail to understand that some operations or actions can be reversed, restoring the original situation.	Jacob does not realize that the juice in each glass can be poured back into the juice box from which it came, contradicting his claim that he has more than his sister.
Focus on states rather than on transformations	Children fail to understand the significance of the transformation between states.	In the conservation task, Jacob does not understand that transforming the shape of a liquid (pouring it from one container into another) does not change the amount.
Transductive reasoning	Children do not use deductive or inductive reasoning; instead they jump from one particular to another and see cause where none exists.	Luis was mean to his sister. Then she got sick. Luis concludes that he made his sister sick.
Egocentrism	Children assume everyone else thinks, perceives, and feels as they do.	Kara doesn't realize that she needs to turn a book around so that her father can see the picture she is asking him to explain to her. Instead, she holds the book directly in front of her, so only she can see it.
Animism	Children attribute life to inanimate objects.	Amanda says that spring is trying to come but winter is saying, "I won't go! I won't go!"
Inability to distinguish appearance from reality	Children confuse what is real with outward appearance.	Courtney is confused by a sponge made to look like a rock. She states that it looks like a rock and it really is a rock.

of symbols to communicate; words stand for objects and concepts in our world.

Understanding Objects Space

It is not until at least age 3 that most children reliably grasp the relationships between pictures, maps, or scale models and the larger or smaller objects or spaces they represent. Older preschoolers can use simple maps, and they can transfer the spatial understanding gained from working with models to maps and vice versa (DeLoache, Miller, & Pierroutsakos, 1998). In a series of experiments, preschoolers were asked to use a simple map to find or place an object at the corresponding location in a similarly shaped but much larger space. Some 90 percent of 5-year-olds but only 60 percent of 4-year-olds were able to do so (Vasilyeva & Huttenlocher, 2004).

Understanding Causality

Piaget maintained that preoperational children cannot yet reason logically about cause and effect. Instead, he said, they reason by **transduction.** They mentally link two events, especially events close in time, whether or not there is logically a causal relationship. For example, Luis may think that his "bad" thoughts or behavior caused his own or his sister's illness or his parents' divorce.

As Anna pretends to listen to her father's heart, she is showing a major cognitive achievement, deferred imitation—the ability to repeat an action she observed some time before.

transduction In Piaget's terminology, preoperational child's tendency to mentally link particular experiences, whether or not there is logically a causal relationship.

Yet, when tested on situations they can understand, young children do grasp cause and effect. In naturalistic observations of 2½- to 5-year-olds' everyday conversations with their parents, children showed flexible causal reasoning, appropriate to the subject. Types of explanations ranged from physical ("The scissors have to be clean so I can cut better") to social–conventional ("I have to stop now because you said to") (Hickling & Wellman, 2001). However, preschoolers seem to view all causal relationships as equally and absolutely predictable. In one series of experiments, 3- to 5-year-olds, unlike adults, were just as sure that a person who does not wash his or her hands before eating will get sick as they were that a person who jumps up will come down (Kalish, 1998).

Understanding Identities and Categorization

The world becomes more orderly and predictable as preschool children develop a better understanding of *identities:* the concept that people and many things are basically the same even if they change in form, size, or appearance. This understanding underlies the emerging self-concept.

Categorization, or classification, requires a child to identify similarities and differences. By age 4, many children can classify by two criteria, such as color and shape. Children use this ability to order many aspects of their lives, categorizing people as "good" or "bad," "nice" or "mean," and so forth.

One type of categorization is the ability to distinguish living from nonliving things. When Piaget asked young children whether the wind and the clouds were alive, their answers led him to think they were confused about what is alive and what is not. The tendency to attribute life to objects that are not alive is called **animism.** However, when later researchers questioned 3- and 4-year-olds about something more familiar to them— differences between a rock, a person, and a doll—the children showed they understood that people are alive and rocks and dolls are not. They did not attribute thoughts or emotions to rocks, and they cited the fact that dolls cannot move on their own as evidence that dolls are not alive (Gelman, Spelke, & Meck, 1983).

animism Tendency to attribute life to objects that are not alive.

Understanding Number

Research by Karen Wynn suggests that infants as young as 4½ months have a rudimentary concept of number. They seem to know that if one doll is added to another

Table 10-3	Key Elements of Number Sense in Young Children
Area	**Components**
Counting	Grasping one-to-one correspondence
	Knowing stable order and cardinality principles
	Knowing the count sequence
Number knowledge	Discriminating and coordinating quantities
	Making numerical magnitude comparisons
Number transformation	Simple addition and subtraction
	Calculating in story problems and nonverbal contexts
	Calculating "in the head"
Estimation	Approximating or estimating set sizes
	Using reference points
Number patterns	Copying number patterns
	Extending number patterns
	Discerning numerical relationships

Source: Adapted from Jordan et al., 2006.

doll, there should be two dolls, not just one. Other research has found that *ordinality*—the concept of comparing quantities (*more or less, bigger or smaller*)—seems to begin at around 12 to 18 months and at first is limited to comparisons of very few objects (Siegler, 1998). By age 4, most children have words for comparing quantities. They can say that one tree is *bigger* than another or that one cup holds *more* juice than another. If they have one cookie and then get another cookie, they know they have more cookies than they had before and that if they give one cookie to another child, they have fewer cookies. They also can solve numerical ordinality problems ("Megan picked six apples, and Joshua picked four apples; which child picked more?") with up to nine objects (Byrnes & Fox, 1998).

Not until age 3½ or older do most children consistently apply the *cardinality* principle in counting (Wynn, 1990). That is, when asked to count six items, children younger than 3½ tend to recite the number-names (one through six) but not to say how many items there are altogether (six). However, there is some evidence that children as young as 2½ use cardinality in practical situations, such as checking to make sure which plate has more cookies on it (Gelman, 2006). By age 5, most children can count to 20 or more and know the relative sizes of the numbers 1 through 10 (Siegler, 1998). Children intuitively devise strategies for adding by counting on their fingers or by using other objects (Naito & Miura, 2001).

By the time they enter elementary school, most children have developed basic "number sense" (Jordan, Kaplan, Oláh, & Locunia, 2006). This basic level of number skills (Table 10-3) includes *counting, number knowledge* (ordinality), *number transformations* (simple addition and subtraction), *estimation* ("Is this group of dots more or less than 5?"), and recognition of *number patterns* (2 plus 2 equals 4, and so does 3 plus 1).

SES and preschool experience affect how rapidly children advance in math. By age 4, children from middle-income families have markedly better number skills than low-SES children, and their initial advantage tends to continue. Children whose preschool teachers do a lot of "math talk" (such as asking children to help count days on a calendar) tend to make greater gains (Klibanoff, Levine, Huttenlocher, Vasilyeva, & Hedges, 2006). Also, playing number board games with children enhances their numerical knowledge. In a recent study, children from low-income backgrounds who played number board games demonstrated large, stable gains in numerical knowledge after only four 15- to 20-minute sessions (Ramani & Siegler, 2008).

Checkpoint ✔

Can you . . .

✔ Summarize findings about preschool children's understanding of symbols, causality, identities, categories, and number?

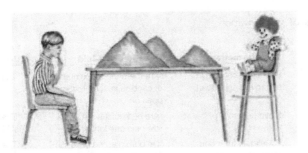

Figure 10-1
Piaget's three-mountain task. A preoperational child is unable to describe the mountains from the doll's point of view—an indication of egocentrism, according to Piaget.

Immature Aspects of Preoperational Thought

According to Piaget, one of the main characteristics of preoperational thought is **centration:** the tendency to focus on one aspect of a situation and neglect others. He said preschoolers come to illogical conclusions because they cannot **decenter**—think about several aspects of a situation at one time. Centration can limit young children's thinking about both physical and social relationships.

Egocentrism

Egocentrism is a form of centration. According to Piaget, young children center so much on their own point of view that they cannot take in another's. Three-year-olds are not as egocentric as newborn babies; but, said Piaget, they still think the universe centers on them. Egocentrism may help explain why young children sometimes have trouble separating reality from what goes on inside their heads and why they may show confusion about what causes what. When Emily believes that her "bad thoughts" have made her brother sick or that she caused her parents' marital troubles, she is thinking egocentrically.

To study egocentrism, Piaget designed the *three-mountain task* (Figure 10-1). A child sits facing a table that holds three large mounds. A doll is placed on a chair at the opposite side of the table. The investigator asks the child how the mountains would look to the doll. Piaget found that young children usually could not answer the question correctly; instead, they described the mountains from their own perspective. Piaget saw this as evidence that preoperational children cannot imagine a point of view different from their own (Piaget & Inhelder, 1967).

However, another experimenter who posed a similar problem in a different way got different results (Hughes, 1975). A child sat in front of a square board divided by "walls" into four sections. A toy police officer stood at the edge of the board; a doll was moved from one section to another. After each move the child was asked, "Can the police officer see the doll?" Then another toy police officer was brought into the action, and the child was told to hide the doll from both officers. Thirty children between ages 3½ and 5 were correct 9 out of 10 times.

Why were these children able to take another person's point of view (the police officer's) when those doing the mountain task were not? It may be because the "police officer" task calls for thinking in more familiar, less abstract, and less complex ways. Most children do not look at mountains and do not think about what other people might see when looking at one, but most preschoolers know something about dolls and police officers and hiding. Thus young children may show egocentrism primarily in situations beyond their immediate experience.

Conservation

Another classic example of centration is the failure to understand **conservation,** the fact that two things that are equal remain so if their appearance is altered, so long as nothing is added or taken away. Piaget found that children do not fully grasp this principle until the stage of concrete operations. (Table 10-4 shows how various dimensions of conservation have been tested.)

centration In Piaget's theory, tendency of preoperational children to focus on one aspect of a situation and neglect others.

decenter In Piaget's terminology, to think simultaneously about several aspects of a situation.

egocentrism Piaget's term for an inability to consider another person's point of view; a characteristic of young children's thought.

conservation Piaget's term for awareness that two objects that are equal according to a certain measure remain equal in the face of perceptual alteration so long as nothing has been added to or taken away from either object.

Table 10-4	Tests of Various Kinds of Conservation			
Conservation Task	**What Child Is Shown***	**Transformation**	**Question for Child**	**Preoperational Child's Usual Answers**
Number	Two equal, parallel rows of candies	Space the candies in one row farther apart.	"Are there the same number of candies in each row or does one row have more?"	"The longer one has more."
Length	Two parallel sticks of the same length	Move one stick to the right.	"Are both sticks the same size or is one longer?"	"The one on the right (or left) is longer."
Liquid	Two identical glasses holding equal amounts of liquid	Pour liquid from one glass into a taller, narrower glass.	"Do both glasses have the same amount of liquid or does one have more?"	"The taller one has more."
Matter (mass)	Two balls of clay of the same size	Roll one ball into a sausage shape.	"Do both pieces have the same amount of clay or does one have more?"	"The sausage has more."
Weight	Two balls of clay of the same weight	Roll one ball into a sausage shape.	"Do both weigh the same or does one weigh more?"	"The sausage weighs more."
Area	Two toy rabbits, two pieces of cardboard (representing grassy fields), with blocks or toys (representing barns on the fields); same number of "barns" on each board	Rearrange the blocks on one piece of cardboard.	"Does each rabbit have the same amount of grass to eat or does one have more?"	"The one with the blocks close together has more to eat."
Volume	Two glasses of water with two equal-sized balls of clay in them	Roll one ball into a sausage shape.	"If we put the sausage back in the glass, will the water be the same height in each glass, or will one be higher?"	"The water in the glass with the sausage will be higher."

*Child then acknowledges that both items are equal.

irreversibility Piaget's term for a preoperational child's failure to understand that an operation can go in two or more directions.

Checkpoint ✔

Can you . . .

✔ Tell how centration limits preoperational thought?

✔ Discuss research that challenges Piaget's views on egocentrism in early childhood?

✔ Give several reasons preoperational children have difficulty with conservation?

theory of mind Awareness and understanding of mental processes.

In one type of conservation task, conservation of liquid, 5-year-old Justin is shown two identical clear glasses, each short and wide and each holding the same amount of water. Justin is asked, "Is the amount of water in the two glasses equal?" When he agrees, the researcher pours the water in one glass into a third glass, a tall, thin one. Justin is now asked, "Do both glasses contain the same amount of water? Or does one contain more? Why?" In early childhood—even after watching the water being poured out of one of the short, fat glasses into a tall, thin glass or even after pouring it himself—Justin will say that either the taller glass or the wider one contains more water. When asked why, he says, "This one is bigger this way," stretching his arms to show the height or width. Preoperational children cannot consider height *and* width at the same time because they cannot *decenter* as described above. Since they center on one aspect, they cannot think logically, said Piaget.

The ability to conserve is also limited by **irreversibility**: failure to understand that an operation or action can go in two or more directions. Once Justin can imagine restoring the original state of the water by pouring it back into the other glass, he will realize that the amount of water in both glasses must be the same.

Preoperational children commonly think as if they were watching a slide show with a series of static frames: they *focus on successive states,* said Piaget, and do not recognize the transformation from one state to another. In the conservation experiment, they focus on the water as it stands in each glass rather than on the water being poured from one glass to another, and so they fail to realize that the amount of water is the same.

Do Young Children Have Theories of Mind?

Theory of mind is the awareness of the broad range of human mental states—beliefs, intents, desires, dreams, and so forth—and the understanding that others have their own distinctive beliefs, desires and intentions. Having a theory of mind allows us to understand and predict the behavior of others and makes the social world understandable.

Different people may have different theories of mind depending upon social experiences. The emerging field of social neuroscience has contributed to understanding the theory of mind by imaging human brains while individuals perform tasks demanding the understanding of an intention, belief, or other mental state.

Piaget (1929) was the first scholar to investigate children's theory of mind. He sought to determine children's understanding of mind by asking them questions such as "Where do dreams come from?" and "What do you think with?" On the basis of their answers, he concluded that children younger than 6 cannot distinguish between thoughts or dreams and real physical entities and therefore have no theory of mind. However, more recent research indicates that between ages 2 and 5, and especially around age 4, children's knowledge about mental processes grows dramatically.

Again, methodology seems to have made the difference. Piaget's questions were abstract, and he expected children to be able to put their understanding into words. Contemporary researchers observe children in everyday activities or give them concrete examples. In this way, we have learned, for example, that 3-year-olds can tell the difference between a boy who has a cookie and a boy who is thinking about a cookie; they know which boy can touch, share, and eat it (Astington, 1993). Let's look at several aspects of theory of mind.

Knowledge about Thinking and Mental States

Between ages 3 and 5, children come to understand that thinking goes on inside the mind; that it can deal with either real or imaginary things; that someone can be thinking of one thing while doing or looking at something else; that a person whose eyes and ears are covered can think about objects; that someone who looks pensive is probably thinking; and that thinking is different from seeing, talking, touching, and knowing (Flavell et al., 1995).

However, preschoolers generally believe that mental activity starts and stops. Not until middle childhood do children know that the mind is continuously active (Flavell, 1993; Flavell et al., 1995). Preschoolers also have little or no awareness that they or other people think in words, or "talk to themselves in their heads," or that they think while they are looking, listening, reading, or talking (Flavell, Green, Flavell, & Grossman, 1997).

Preschoolers tend to believe they can dream about anything they wish. Five-year-olds show a more adultlike understanding, recognizing that physical experiences, emotions, knowledge, and thoughts can affect the content of dreams. Not until age 11, however, do children fully realize that they cannot control their dreams (Woolley & Boerger, 2002).

Social cognition, the recognition that others have mental states, accompanies the decline of egocentrism and the development of empathy. By age 3, children realize that if someone gets what he wants he will be happy, and, if not, he will be sad (Wellman & Woolley, 1990). Four-year-olds begin to understand that people have differing beliefs about the world—true or mistaken—and that these beliefs affect their actions.

The young girl on the right is old enough to know that her cousin needs consoling. Empathy, the ability to understand another person's feelings, begins at an early age.

False Beliefs and Deception

A researcher shows 3-year-old Madeline a candy box and asks what is in it. "Candy," she says. But when Madeline opens the box, she finds crayons, not candy. "What will a child who hasn't opened the box think is in it?" the researcher asks. "Crayons," says Madeline, not understanding that another child would be fooled by the box as she was. And then she says that she originally thought crayons would be in the box (Flavell, 1993; Flavell et al., 1995).

The understanding that people can hold false beliefs flows from the realization that people hold mental representations of reality, which can sometimes be wrong. Three-year-olds, like Madeline, appear to lack such an understanding (Flavell et al., 1995). An analysis of 178 studies in various countries, using a number of variations on false-belief tasks, found this consistent developmental pattern (Wellman & Cross, 2001; Wellman, Cross, & Watson, 2001).

However, when preschoolers were taught to respond to a false-belief task with gestures rather than with words, children near their fourth birthday—but not younger children—did better than on the traditional verbal-response tasks. Thus gestures may help children on the verge of grasping the idea of false beliefs to make that conceptual leap (Carlson, Wong, Lemke, & Cosser, 2005).

Three-year-olds' failure to recognize false beliefs may stem from egocentric thinking. At that age, children tend to believe that everyone else knows what they know and believes what they do, and, like Madeline, they have trouble understanding that their beliefs can be false (Lillard & Curenton, 1999). Four-year-olds understand that people who see or hear different versions of the same event may come away with different beliefs. Not until about age 6, however, do children realize that two people who see or hear the same thing may interpret it differently (Pillow & Henrichon, 1996).

Because deception is a deliberate effort to plant a false belief in someone else's mind, it requires a child to suppress the impulse to be truthful. Some studies have found that children become capable of deception as early as age 2 or 3, and others at 4 or 5. The difference may have to do with the means of deception children are expected to use. In a series of experiments, 3-year-olds were asked whether they would like to play a trick on an experimenter by giving a false clue about which of two boxes a ball was hidden in. The children were better able to carry out the deception when asked to put a picture of the ball on the wrong box or to point to that box with an arrow than when they pointed with their fingers, which children this age are accustomed to doing truthfully (Carlson, Moses, & Hix, 1998).

Piaget maintained that young children regard all falsehoods—intentional or not—as lies. However, when 3- to 6-year-olds were told a story about the danger of eating contaminated food and were given a choice between interpreting a character's action as a lie or a mistake, about three-fourths of the children in all age groups characterized it accurately (Siegal & Peterson, 1998). Apparently, then, even 3-year-olds have some understanding of the role of intent in deception.

Distinguishing between Appearance and Reality

According to Piaget, not until about age 5 or 6 do children understand the distinction between what *seems* to be and what *is*. Much research bears him out, though some studies have found this ability beginning to emerge before age 4 (Friend & Davis, 1993; Rice, Koinis, Sullivan, Tager-Flusberg, & Winner, 1997).

In one classic series of experiments (Flavell, Green, & Flavell, 1986), 3-year-olds apparently confused appearance and reality in a variety of tests. For example, when the children put on special sunglasses that made milk look green, they said the milk *was* green, even though they had just seen white milk. However, 3-year-olds' difficulty distinguishing appearance from reality may itself be more apparent than real. When children were asked questions about the uses of such objects as a candle wrapped like a crayon, only 3 out of 10 answered correctly. But when asked to respond with actions rather than words ("I want a candle to put on a birthday cake"), 9 out of 10 handed the experimenter the crayonlike candle (Sapp, Lee, & Muir, 2000).

Distinguishing between Fantasy and Reality

Sometime between 18 months and 3 years, children learn to distinguish between real and imagined events. Three-year-olds know the difference between a real dog and a dog in a dream, and between something invisible (such as air) and something imaginary. They can pretend and can tell when someone else is pretending (Flavell et al., 1995). By age 3, and, in some cases, by age 2, they know that pretense is intentional; they can tell the difference between trying to do something and pretending to do the same thing (Rakoczy, Tomasello, & Striano, 2004).

Still, the line between fantasy and reality may seem to blur at times. In one study (Harris, Brown, Marriott, Whittall, & Harmer, 1991), 4- to 6-year-olds, left alone in a room, preferred to touch a box holding an imaginary bunny rather than a box holding an imaginary monster, even though most of the children claimed they were just pretending.

The Everyday World

Box 10-1 *Imaginary Companions*

At 3½, Anna had 23 "sisters" with such names as Och, Elmo, Zeni, Aggie, and Ankie. She often talked to them on the telephone because they lived about 100 miles away, in the town where her family used to live. During the next year, most of the sisters disappeared, but Och continued to visit, especially for birthday parties. Och had a cat and a dog (which Anna had begged for in vain), and whenever Anna was denied something she saw advertised on television, she announced that she already had one at her sister's house. But when a live friend came over and Anna's mother happened to mention one of her imaginary companions, Anna quickly changed the subject.

All 23 sisters—and some "boys" and "girls" who have followed them—lived only in Anna's imagination, as she well knew. Like an estimated 25 to 65 percent of children between ages 3 and 10 (Woolley, 1997), she created imaginary companions, with whom she talked and played. This normal phenomenon of childhood is seen most often in firstborn and only children, who lack the close company of siblings. Like Anna, most children who create imaginary companions have many of them (Gleason, Sebanc, & Hartup, 2000). Girls are more likely than boys to have imaginary friends, or at least to acknowledge them; boys are more likely to impersonate imaginary characters (Carlson & Taylor, 2005).

Children who have imaginary companions can distinguish fantasy from reality, but in free-play sessions they are more likely to engage in pretend play than are children without imaginary companions (M. Taylor, Cartwright, & Carlson, 1993). They play more happily and more imaginatively than other children and are more cooperative with other children and adults (D. G. Singer & Singer, 1990; J. L. Singer & Singer, 1981); and they do not lack for friends at preschool (Gleason et al., 2000). They are more fluent with language, watch less television, and show more curiosity, excitement, and persistence during play. In one study of 152 preschoolers, 4-year-olds who reported having imaginary companions did better on theory-of-mind tasks (such as differentiating appearance and reality and recognizing false beliefs) than children who did not create such companions (M. Taylor & Carlson, 1997), and these children showed greater emotional understanding 3 years later. Having imaginary companions remains common in the early school years; almost one-third of the children who reported having had imaginary companions (65 percent of the sample in all) were still playing with them at age 7 (Taylor, Carlson, Maring, Gerow, & Charley, 2004).

Children's relationships with imaginary companions are like peer relationships; they are usually sociable and friendly, in contrast with the way children "take care of" personified objects, such as stuffed animals and dolls (Gleason et al., 2000). Imaginary playmates are good company for an only child like Anna. They provide wish-fulfillment mechanisms ("There was a monster in my room, but Elmo scared it off with magic dust"), scapegoats ("I didn't eat those cookies—-Och must have done it!"), a safe way to express the child's own fears ("Aggie is afraid she's going to be washed down the drain"), and support in difficult situations (When Anna went to a scary movie, she "took" her imaginary companion with her).

What's your view ❓

How should parents respond to children's talk about imaginary companions?

However, in a partial replication of the study, in which the experimenter stayed in the room and clearly ended the pretense, only about 10 percent of the children touched or looked in either of the boxes, and almost all showed a clear understanding that the creatures were imaginary (Golomb & Galasso, 1995). Thus it is difficult to know, when questioning children about pretend objects, whether children are giving serious answers or are keeping up the pretense (M. Taylor, 1997).

Magical thinking in children age 3 and older does not seem to stem from confusion between fantasy and reality. Often, magical thinking is a way to explain events that do not seem to have obvious realistic explanations (usually because children lack knowledge about them) or simply to indulge in the pleasures of pretending—as with the belief in imaginary companions, which we discuss in Box 10-1. Magical thinking tends to decline near the end of the preschool period (Woolley, Phelps, Davis, & Mandell, 1999).

All in all, then, the research on various theory-of-mind topics suggests that young children may have a clearer picture of reality than Piaget believed.

Influences on Individual Differences in Theory-of-Mind Development

Some children develop theory-of-mind abilities earlier than others. In part this development reflects brain maturation and general improvements in cognition. What other influences explain individual differences?

Infant social attention has been closely linked to theory of mind development (Wellman & Liu, 2004). In a recent study, 45 children were evaluated as infants and then again as 4-year-olds. Measures of infant social attention significantly predicted later theory of mind, demonstrating strong support for continuity in social cognition (Wellman, Lopez-Duran, LaBounty, & Hamilton, 2008).

Social competence and language development contribute to an understanding of thoughts and emotions (Cassidy, Werner, Rourke, Zubernis, & Balaraman, 2003). Children whose teachers and peers rate them high on social skills are better able to recognize false beliefs, to distinguish between real and feigned emotion, and to take another person's point of view. These children also tend to have strong language skills (Cassidy et al., 2003; Watson, Nixon, Wilson, & Capage, 1999). The *kind* of talk a young child hears at home may affect the child's understanding of mental states. A mother's reference to others' thoughts and knowledge is a consistent predictor of a child's later mental state language. Children show the most benefit from "mother talk" when it fits the child's current level of understanding. Empathy usually arises earlier in children whose families talk a lot about feelings and causality (Dunn, 1991; Dunn, Brown, Slomkowski, Tesla, & Youngblade, 1991).

Families that encourage pretend play stimulate the development of theory-of-mind skills. As children play roles, they try to assume others' perspectives. Talking with children about how the characters in a story feel helps them develop social understanding (Lillard & Curenton, 1999).

Bilingual children, who speak and hear more than one language at home, do somewhat better than children with only one language on certain theory-of-mind tasks (Bialystok & Senman, 2004; Goetz, 2003). Bilingual children know that an object or idea can be represented linguistically in more than one way, and this knowledge may help them see that different people may have different perspectives. Bilingual children also recognize the need to match their language to that of their partner, and this may make them more aware of others' mental states. Finally, bilingual children tend to have better attentional control, and this may enable them to focus on what is true or real rather than on what only seems to be so (Bialystok & Senman, 2004; Goetz, 2003).

An incomplete or ineffective theory of mind may be a sign of a cognitive or developmental impairment. Individuals with this type of impairment have a hard time understanding things from any other perspective than their own. Thus they have difficulty determining the intentions of others, lack understanding of how their behavior affects others, and have a difficult time with social reciprocity. Research suggests that children with autism do not employ a theory of mind and that these children have particular difficulties with tasks requiring them to understand another person's mental state (Baron-Cohen, Leslie, & Frith, 1985).

Checkpoint ✔

Can you . . .

✔ Give examples of research that challenges Piaget's views on young children's cognitive limitations?

✔ Describe changes between ages 3 and 6 in children's knowledge about the way their minds work?

VYGOTSKY'S THEORY OF COGNITIVE DEVELOPMENT

Piaget's theory is a major developmental theory. Another developmental theory that focuses on children's cognition is Vygotsky's theory. Like Piaget, Vygotsky emphasized that children actively construct their knowledge and understanding. In Piaget's theory, children develop ways of thinking and understanding by their actions and interactions with the physical world. In Vygotsky's theory, children are more often described as social creatures than in Piaget's theory. They develop their ways of thinking and understanding primarily through social interaction (Berninger & others, 2004). Their cognitive development depends on the tools provided by society, and their minds are shaped by the cultural context in which they live (Elkind, 2004; Kozulin & others, 2003; Stetsenko & Arievitch, 2004).

Here we take a look at his ideas about how children learn and his view of the role of language in cognitive development.

The Zone of Proximal Development

zone of proximal development (ZPD) Vygotsky's term for tasks too difficult for children to master alone but that can be mastered with assistance.

Zone of proximal development (ZPD) is Vygotsky's term for the range of tasks that are too difficult for the child to master alone but that can be learned with guidance and assistance of adults or more-skilled children. Thus, the lower limit of the ZPD is the level of skill reached by the child working independently. The upper limit is the level of additional responsibility the child can accept with the assistance of an able instructor (see Figure 2.11). The ZPD captures the child's cognitive skills that are in the process of maturing and can be accomplished only with the assistance of a more-skilled person (Fidalgo & Pereira, 2005; Goos, 2004; Gray & Feldman, 2004; Kinginger, 2002; Kulczewski, 2005). Vygotsky (1962) called these the "buds" or "flowers" of development, to distinguish them from the "fruits" of development, which the child already can accomplish independently. Vygotsky's emphasis on the ZPD underscores his belief in the importance of social influences, especially instruction, on children's cognitive development.

Let's consider an example that reflects the zone of proximal development (Frede, 1995, p. 125):

> A 5-year-old child is pushing a small shopping cart through the house area of his preschool. His teacher notices that he is putting fruit in the small basket and all other groceries in the larger section of the cart. She has watched him sort objects over the past few weeks and thinks that he may now be able to classify along two dimensions at the same time, with some help from her. She goes to the cash register to pretend to be the cashier and says, "We need to be careful how we divide your groceries into bags. We want to use one bag for things that go in the refrigerator, and other bags for things that will go in the cabinet." Together they devise a system with one bag for each of the following categories: food in cartons that will go into the refrigerator, loose vegetables and fruit for the refrigerator, food cartons that go in the cabinet, and food cans for the cabinet. In this example, the child's unassisted level of classification was fairly gross—fruit versus nonfruit. With the teacher's help, he was able to apply a more sophisticated form of classification.

Scaffolding

Closely linked to the idea of the ZPD is the concept of scaffolding. **Scaffolding** means changing the level of support. Over the course of a teaching session, a more-skilled person (a teacher or advanced peer) adjusts the amount of guidance to fit the child's current performance (de Vries, 2005; Donovan & Smolkin, 2002; John-Steiner & Mahn, 2003; Many, 2002). When the student is learning a new task, the skilled person may use direct instruction. As the student's competence increases, less guidance is given.

Dialogue is an important tool of scaffolding in the zone of proximal development (Tappan, 1998). Vygotsky viewed children as having rich but unsystematic, disorganized, and spontaneous concepts. In a dialogue, these concepts meet with the skilled helper's more systematic, logical, and rational concepts. As a result, the child's concepts become more systematic, logical, and rational. For example, a dialogue might take place between a teacher and a child when the teacher uses scaffolding to help a child understand a concept like "transportation."

Language and Thought

The use of dialogue as a tool for scaffolding is only one example of the important role of language in a child's development. According to Vygotsky, children use speech not only for social communication, but also to help them solve tasks. Vygotsky (1962) further believed that young children use language to plan, guide, and monitor their behavior. This use of language for self-regulation is called private speech. For Piaget private speech is egocentric and immature, but for Vygotsky it is an important tool of thought during the early childhood years.

Vygotsky said that language and thought initially develop independently of each other and then merge. He emphasized that all mental functions have external, or social,

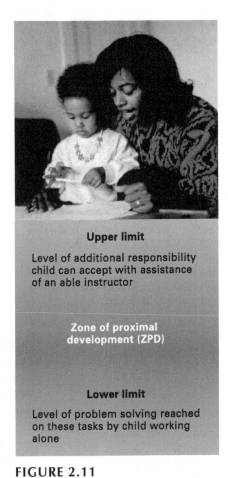

Upper limit
Level of additional responsibility child can accept with assistance of an able instructor

Zone of proximal development (ZPD)

Lower limit
Level of problem solving reached on these tasks by child working alone

FIGURE 2.11
Vygotsky's Zone of Proximal Development. Vygotsky's zone of proximal development has a lower limit and an upper limit. Tasks in the ZPD are too difficult for the child to perform alone. They require assistance from an adult or a skilled child. As children experience the verbal instructions or demonstration, they organize the information in their existing mental structures, so they can eventually perform the skill or task alone.

scaffolding In cognitive development, Vygotsky used this term to describe the changing support over the course of a teaching session, with the more-skilled person adjusting guidance to fit the child's current performance level.

Lev Vygotsky (1896-1934), shown here with his daughter, believed that children's cognitive development is advanced through social interaction with skilled individuals embedded in a sociocultural backdrop.

www.mhhe.com/santrockldt3

Vygotsky's Theory
Vygotsky Resources
Vygotsky Links
Scaffolding

origins. Children must use language to communicate with others before they can focus inward on their own thoughts. Children also must communicate externally and use language for a long period of time before they can make the transition from external to internal speech. This transition period occurs between 3 and 7 years of age and involves talking to oneself. After a while, the self-talk becomes second nature to children, and they can act without verbalizing. When this occurs, children have internalized their egocentric speech in the form of inner speech, which becomes their thoughts.

Vygotsky believed that children who use a lot of private speech are more socially competent than those who don't (Santiago-Delefosse & Delefosse, 2002). He argued that private speech represents an early transition in becoming more socially communicative. For Vygotsky, when young children talk to themselves, they are using language to govern their behavior and guide themselves. For example, a child working on a puzzle might say to herself, "Which pieces should I put together first? I'll try those green ones first. Now I need some blue ones. No, that blue one doesn't fit there. I'll try it over here."

Researchers have found support for Vygotsky's view that private speech plays a positive role in children's development (Winsler, Diaz, & Montero, 1997; Winsler, Carlton, & Barry, 2000). Researchers have found that children use private speech more when tasks are difficult, following errors, and when they are not sure how to proceed (Berk, 1994). They also have revealed that children who use private speech are more attentive and improve their performance more than children who do not use private speech (Berk & Spuhl, 1995).

Teaching Strategies

Vygotsky's theory already has been embraced by many teachers and has been successfully applied to education (Bearison & Dorval, 2002; Bodrova & Leong, 2003; Rogoff, 2003; Rowe & Wertsch, 2004; Tudge & Scrimsher, 2003; Winsler & others, 2002). Here are some ways Vygotsky's theory can be incorporated in classrooms:

1. *Use the child's zone of proximal development.* Teaching should begin toward the zone's upper limit, so that the child can reach the goal with help and move to a higher level of skill and knowledge. Offer just enough assistance. You might ask, "What can I do to help you?" Or simply observe the child's intentions and attempts, smoothly providing support when needed. When the child hesitates, offer encouragement. And encourage the child to practice the skill. You may watch and appreciate the child's practice or offer support when the child forgets what to do.

2. *Use more-skilled peers as teachers.* Remember that it is not just adults that Vygotsky believed are important in helping children learn important skills. Children also benefit from the support and guidance of more-skilled children (John-Steiner & Mahn, 2003).

3. *Monitor and encourage children's use of private speech.* Be aware of the developmental change from externally talking to oneself when solving a problem during the preschool years to privately talking to oneself in the early elementary school years. In the elementary school years, encourage children to internalize and self-regulate their talk to themselves.

4. *Effectively assess the child's ZPD.* Like Piaget, Vygotsky did not believe that formal, standardized tests are the best way to assess children's learning. Rather, Vygotsky argued that assessment should focus on determining the child's zone of proximal development (Camilleri, 2005; Meijer & Elshout, 2001). The skilled helper presents the child with tasks of varying difficulty to determine the best level at which to begin instruction.

5. *Place instruction in a meaningful context.* In education today, there is an increased emphasis on moving away from abstract presentations of material to providing students with opportunities to experience learning in meaningful, real-world settings. Thus, instead of just teaching children to memorize math formulas, students work on math problems with real-world implications (Santrock, 2006).

6. *Transform the classroom with Vygotskian ideas.* What does a Vygotskian classroom look like? The Kamehameha Elementary Education Program (KEEP) is based on Vygotsky's theory (Tharp, 1994). The zone of proximal development is the key element of instruction in this program. Children might read a story and then interpret its meaning. Many of the learning activities take place in small groups. All children spend at least 20 minutes each morning in a setting called "Center One." In this context, scaffolding is used to improve children's literary skills. The instructor asks questions, responds to students' queries, and builds on the ideas that students generate. Thousands of children from low-income families have attended KEEP public schools—in Hawaii, on an Arizona Navajo Indian reservation, and in Los Angeles. Compared with a control group of non- KEEP children, the KEEP children participated more actively in classroom discussion, were more attentive in class, and had higher reading achievement (Tharp & Gallimore, 1988). The Applications in Life-Span Development interlude further explores the education of children.

APPLICATIONS IN LIFE-SPAN DEVELOPMENT

Guided Participation

Vygotsky's concept of the zone of proximal development—that children learn by interacting with more experienced adults and peers, who help them think beyond the "zone" in which they would be able to perform without assistance—has focused primarily on schooling and academic learning. Barbara Rogoff (1990, 1998, 2003; Rogoff, Turkanis, & Bartlett, 2001) argues that many of Vygotsky's ideas, including the zone of proximal development, are important in understanding children's development beyond the classroom in everyday interactions with adults and peers. She proposes that children serve a sort of apprenticeship in thinking through *guided participation* in social and cultural activities. One of the main ways that guided participation occurs is through mutual structuring of participation.

The structuring includes the choice of activities for children and shared activities. In terms of choice of activities, parents can extend or limit children's opportunities by making decisions about how much and when to expose children to books, television, and child care. Structuring also involves children's engagement in routines and play that gives them opportunities to learn about cultural traditions and practices. For example, in the Zambian culture of Chewa, children play numerous games, such as "hide-and-seek, guessing games, complex sand drawing games, imaginative games representing local work and family routines, skill games like jacks and a rule game requiring considerable strategic planning and numerical calculations, and constructing models of wire or clay" (Rogoff, 2003, p. 297). Rogoff (2003) also emphasizes the importance of observational learning, or as she calls it, learning by "osmosis," in which children adopt values, skills, and mannerisms by simply watching and listening to peers and adults.

Rogoff (2003) says that guided participation is widely used around the world. Cultures may differ, though, in the goals of development—what content is to be learned—and the means for providing guided participation. Around the world, caregivers and children arrange children's activities and revise children's responsibilities as they gain skill and knowledge. With guidance, children participate in cultural activities that socialize them into skilled activities. For example, Mayan

At about 7 years of age, Mayan girls in Guatemala are assisted in beginning to learn to weave a simple belt, with the loom already set up for them. The young girl shown here is American developmental psychologist Barbara Rogoff's daughter, being taught to weave by a Mayan woman. *How is Rogoff's idea of a cognitive apprenticeship compatible with Vygotsky's theory?*

mothers in Guatemala help their daughters learn to weave through guided partic-ipation. In the United States and in many other nations, creative thinkers interact with a knowledgeable person rather than by only studying books or by attending classes and exhibits.

Cognitive development occurs as new generations collaborate with older generations in varying forms of interpersonal engagement and institutional practices.

—BARBARA ROGOFF
Contemporary Psychologist, University of California—Santa Cruz

social constructivist approach
An emphasis on the social contexts of learning and the construction of knowledge through social interaction. Vygotsky's theory reflects this approach.

www.mhhe.com/santrockldt3

Barbara Rogoff's Views
The Collaborative
Classroom

Evaluating Vygotsky's Theory

Even though their theories were proposed at about the same time, most of the world learned about Vygotsky's theory later than they learned about Piaget's theory, so Vygot-sky's theory has not yet been evaluated as thoroughly. Vygotsky's view of the importance of sociocultural influences on children's development fits with the current belief that it is important to evaluate the contextual factors in learning (Kozulin & others, 2003).

We already have mentioned several comparisons of Vygotsky's and Piaget's the-ories, collaboration, social interaction, and sociocultural activity (Rogoff, 1998, 2003). The endpoint and Piaget's view that such speech is immature. Although both theories are constructivist, Vygotsky's is a **social constructivist approach**, which emphasizes the social contexts of learning and the construction of knowledge through social interaction.

In moving from Piaget to Vygotsky, the conceptual shift is from the individual to col-laboration, social interaction, and sociocultural activity (Rogoff, 1998, 2003). The end-point of cognitive development for Piaget is formal operational thought. For Vygotsky, the endpoint can differ depending on which skills are considered to be the most impor-tant in a particular culture. For Piaget, children construct knowledge by transforming, or-ganizing, and reorganizing previous knowledge. For Vygotsky, children construct knowledge through social interaction (Hogan & Tudge, 1999). The implication of Pi-aget's theory for teaching is that children need support to explore their world and discover knowledge. The main implication of Vygotsky's theory for teaching is that students need many opportunities to learn with the teacher and more-skilled peers. In both Piaget's and Vygotsky's theories, teachers serve as facilitators and guides, rather than as directors and molders of learning. Figure 2.12 compares Vygotsky's and Piaget's theories.

Criticisms of Vygotsky's theory also have surfaced. Some critics say he overem-phasized the role of language in thinking. Also, his emphasis on collaboration and

	VYGOTSKY		PIAGET	
Sociocultural Context	Strong Emphasis		Little Emphasis	
Constructivism	Social constructivist		Cognitive constructivist	
Stages	No general stages of development proposed		Strong emphasis on stages (sensorimotor, preoper-ational, concrete operational, and formal operational)	
Key Processes	Zone of proximal development, language, dialogue, tools of the culture		Schema, assimilation, accommodation, operations, conservation, classification, hypothetical-deductive reasoning	
Role of Language	A major role; language plays a powerful role in shaping thought		Language has a minimal role; cognition primarily directs language	
View on Education	Education plays a central role, helping children learn the tools of the culture.		Education merely refines the child's cognitive skills that have already emerged.	
Teaching Implications	Teacher is a facilitator and guide, not a director; establish many opportunities for children to learn with the teacher and more-skilled peers		Also views teacher as a facilitator and guide, not a director; provide support for children to explore their world and discover knowledge	

FIGURE 2.12
Comparison of Vygotsky's and Piaget's Theories

The Development Self-concept

Defining Self-concept

Self-concept has been defined in a variety of ways, depending upon the psychological focus being brought to bear. From a developmental and functional perspective, **self-concept** can be thought of as **a set of assumptions believed to be true about oneself.** The utility of this particular definition lies in the implicit reminder that it is possible and even likely that what we believe about ourselves is to some degree in error. Indeed, psychologists estimate that most of us have at least a slightly erroneous self-concept. As we look more closely at the information that goes into establishing a child's self-concept, perhaps we will also gain some insight into why some of our assumptions about ourselves are bound to be inaccurate.

Developing Self-concept through Childhood

INFANCY AND EARLY CHILDHOOD

The earliest source of information, that begins our understanding of who we are, comes from the people who are closest to us when we are infants and toddlers. The **verbal and nonverbal messages we receive from our caregivers** become our earliest knowledge about who we are. *Verbal messages* might include young children simply being told who and how they are. For example, "You are stubborn." "You look like your mommy." "You're so smart!" Other times the *verbal messages* children receive come to them indirectly, as they overhear what others say about them. This sometimes happens because adults tend to underestimate the child's ability to understand what is being said. Hence, they might talk *about* the child as if she/he were not present. For example, "He's just like his father. You can't tell him a thing." "Too bad she looks like her mother."

Interestingly, nonverbal messages are even more likely to be taken to heart than verbal messages. *Nonverbal messages* include how people react to us, how they treat us, their tone of voice and facial expression when addressing us, whether they ignore us or are affectionate to us, to name a few examples. The potency of nonverbal messages seems especially powerful for small children, who are likely to interpret the treatment they receive as a reflection of their own self-worth. Thus, the child who is the beneficiary of loving glances and physical affection is likely to believe herself to be lovable. Unfortunately, the opposite is also the case.

So, we see the potential for inaccurate information to become part of the self-concept has begun. Caregivers who are over-burdened or ill-trained or simply self-absorbed may treat the child in such a way that conveys verbal and nonverbal messages that they never intended to be taken to heart. Nevertheless, that information is now part of the child's self-concept.

MIDDLE CHILDHOOD

As the child enters the larger world of school and extracurricular activities, and her new-found cognitive abilities allow her to develop into a more truly *social* being, she becomes aware of the talents, abilities and characteristics of others. Inevitably, she will compare herself to others, especially her age mates. For better or for worse, she will find that she is faster than some and slower than others; bigger than some but smaller than others; more competent than some but, alas, less able than others. The result of these comparisons is important information which also becomes part of her self-concept.

ADOLESCENCE

In early adolescence the child may begin to reflect on the self-concept she has thus far developed, thanks to her new-found ability to engage in abstract thought. As she begins to wonder how she came to think of herself the way she does, she may make certain revisions in her self-concept. She may also revise her own evaluation of her self-concept. The evaluation of our self-concept is sometimes referred to as *self-esteem*.

From Description to Prediction

If self-concept were merely descriptive, it would be interesting to us in the same way that other descriptors are, such as our height, or our age, or our hometown. But, self-concept is *not* just descriptive; it is also *predictive*. That means it has the power to change our lives. When you say, "I'm lazy," you are not just saying, "at this moment of time I am lazy". You are also saying that you will probably continue to be a lazy person for as far into the future as you can imagine. You have "predicted" how your life will unfold.

How does self-concept go from being merely descriptive to being predictive? One possible explanation includes ideas from several areas of psychological research. For purpose of illustration, let's begin by imagining parents who have a small child. Further, let us imagine that these parents communicate negative messages to the child on a regular basis. Perhaps they say these things to motivate the child to "do better". Perhaps they are not even aware that they say these disparaging things. Examples of this might be as follows:

"You spilled your milk, dummy."

"You'd better tie your shoes before you trip again, dummy."

"Close the door. You're letting flies in the kitchen, dummy."

Perhaps, if questioned about their comments, these parents would explain that they are trying to get the child to take a polarity with regard to this negative message. That is, they want the child to think something like this:

> "Mommy thinks I'm a dummy. Well, I'll show her I'm not a dummy by being smarter and more competent!"

PART 1: THE MESSAGE IS INTERNALIZED

These parents no doubt hope the child will be determined to be more careful, more competent and make better decisions in the future. But, all too often this plan backfires. Since the child is so young, it is highly likely that the child will take that negative message to heart. The message will simply be internalized into the child's self-concept. This happens because, according to **Jean Piaget**, the child is cognitively immature. When children are 2 to 7 years old, they are in what Piaget calls the **preoperational stage** with regard to their cognitive development. Preoperational children have characteristic ways of thinking that include **ludic symbolism**, **artificialism** and **egocentrism.**

Ludic Symbolism: The preoperational child exhibits an aspect of magical thinking called ludic symbolism. According to Piaget, this means that the child believes that names magically make things what they are. For example, the child thinks that a ball is a ball because it's called "ball". To call it anything else would transform it into something other than a ball. *That means that the child also believes that when my parents call me a dummy, they magically turn me into a dummy.*

Artificialism: Preoperational children, in the throes of artificialism, believe that grown-ups (especially their parents) created everything, know everything and control everything. Therefore, *when my all-wise, all-powerful parents say I'm a dummy, I must be a dummy.*

Egocentrism: According to Piaget, preoperational children are naturally and normally egocentric in their thinking. Their cognitive immaturity makes it pretty much impossible for them to think about another person's thought processes or take another person's perspective. By contrast, a cognitively mature adult has some protection from the criticism of others. If an adult were told, "You're stupid," the adult could say to herself, "He *thinks* I'm stupid. Well, that's just *his* opinion, and he's wrong!" But a young child, given the same message, would have no choice but to internalize the message. *Because his egocentrism makes it impossible for him to place this message where it belongs...in the mind of the parent...the message is personalized. "You're a dummy" becomes "I'm a dummy" in the child's self-concept.*

Taken together, we see why a young child is so vulnerable to the messages received from others. This child believes what he is told about himself. He doesn't evaluate the information or decide whether or not he agrees with it; the message simply becomes part of the self-concept.

PART 2: GATHERING EVIDENCE

Psychologists who study sensation and perception tell us that reality is not something that we merely experience. Instead, reality is something we **construct** in our brains. As we construct our own, personal versions of reality, we often employ a **perceptual set.** Perceptual set theory refers to the way our brains can be programmed or "set up" to see what we expect to see and hear what we expect to hear. The result is that often we construct a version of reality that fulfills our expectations. In a way, perceptual set also functions as a **perceptual filter**, in that it allows experiences that correspond to our expected version of reality to be noticed and remembered. Likewise, the perceptual filter can also exclude experiences which are not consistent with our expectations. Thus, our expectations are often fulfilled.

Self-concept functions as a perceptual set and a perceptual filter. This means that we tend to notice and remember experiences which conform to and confirm our self-concept. Specifically, in the example we are using, the child who already believes that he is a dummy will tend to notice and remember the experiences he has that confirm what he already knows about himself: that he is a dummy.

PART 3: REALITY CHANGES

Self-fulfilling prophecy: The predictive aspect of self-concept begins to come into play when the child's life (not just his perception of his life) begins to reflect his beliefs about himself. He doesn't just *think* he is inadequate; he actually begins to fail. This change comes about because the negative messages he has received eventually undermine the child's confidence. He begins to expect to do poorly. This anticipation of failure can inhibit the child from participating whole-heartedly in normal childhood learning activities.

In the case of the child in our example, his **reality change** could happen in a number of ways:

1. Fear of public humiliation could prevent the child from participating in the classroom learning activities.
2. Or, the child's anxiety about his academic performance could directly interfere with his cognitive functioning. This would be similar to **test anxiety**, in which fear associated with an exam causes one's mind to "go blank".
3. Or, the child might decide to avoid both of these negative experiences and simply withdraw and dissociate from the classroom activities entirely. This might be seen by teachers and parents as the child "giving up" or "not trying".

Either way, the child now is a failure. What he believed about himself has come true. This is a classic example of **self-fulfilling prophecy.**

In the example we have just examined, a direct **verbal** message from the parents was used. It is important to remember that the same process would operate if the message were **nonverbal.** For example, the child who is shown no physical affection might come to have "I am unlovable" in her self-concept. This could lead to the child becoming an adult who finds it difficult to be close to others, with all the ensuing relationship problems that is likely to entail. By the time this child becomes an adult, she will have plenty of evidence that she is indeed unlovable.

Clearly, these examples use **negative parental messages**, which in turn lead to negative reality changes. Negative examples are dramatic, and therefore perhaps more memorable. But, we need to remember that **positive parental messages** (both verbal and nonverbal) work the same way. Communicating our love to a child teaches that child that she is both lovable and a person of worth. Obviously, anyone who has control over the information that goes into a small child's self-concept has a great deal of influence on the rest of that child's life.

How to Praise a Child

Praise is important......but it has to be the right *kind* of praise!

We know that children want praise and approval from the people who are most important to them, like their parents. Fortunately, most parents enjoy praising their children, especially if the child has succeeded at a meaningful task. Earning a good grade on a school assignment is a circumstance in which parents would be likely to give a child praise.

After studying how children respond to praise for decades, psychologist Carol Dweck has found evidence that some forms of praise lead children to try harder and feel more self-confident, while other kinds of praise can lead to just the opposite, lack of confidence and poor self-esteem.

Carol Dwek's Mindset Theory

Dweck has found that many adults automatically praise children (and other adults) for their **ability.** These adults are likely to tell a child who has earned an "A" on an assignment, "You're so smart!" But this kind of praise is a double edged sword, in that it leads the child to think, "I got an A because I'm smart. If I get a C does that mean I'm *not* so smart?" Dweck found that children will then avoid challenging tasks, because they fear looking "not smart". Perhaps even more insidiously, if they run into a task that isn't easy for them, they assume that they simply are not capable of doing that task ("I'm just not smart at math.") This way of thinking is what Dweck calls a **Fixed Mindset.**

On the other hand, if children are praised for their **effort,** they come to realize that the harder they work, the more likely they are to succeed at any task. Setbacks are *not* seen as evidence of inferiority or lack of ability; setbacks are simply reminders that one has to work a bit harder or try something new. Under these circumstances, children develop what Dweck calls a **Growth Mindset.**

In the following article, Dweck describes the difference between Fixed Mindset and Growth Mindset, and discusses the fascinating research that lead her to understand how important these concepts can be in shaping a child's life.

The Perils and Promises of Praise

The wrong kind of praise creates self-defeating behavior. The right kind motivates students to learn.

CAROL S. DWECK

We often hear these days that we've produced a generation of young people who can't get through the day without an award. They expect success because they're special, not because they've worked hard.

Is this true? Have we inadvertently done something to hold back our students?

I think educators commonly hold two beliefs that do just that. Many believe that (1) praising students' intelligence builds their confidence and motivation to learn, and (2) students' inherent intelligence is the major cause of their achievement in school. Our research has shown that the first belief is false and that the second can be harmful—even for the most competent students.

As a psychologist, I have studied student motivation for more than 35 years. My graduate students and I have looked at thousands of children, asking why some enjoy learning, even when it's hard, and why they are resilient in the face of obstacles. We have learned a great deal. Research shows us how to praise students in ways that yield motivation and resilience. In addition, specific interventions can reverse a student's slide into failure during the vulnerable period of adolescence.

Fixed or Malleable?

Praise is intricately connected to how students view their intelligence. Some students believe that their intellectual ability is a fixed trait. They have a certain amount of intelligence, and that's that. Students with this fixed mind-set become excessively concerned with how smart they are, seeking tasks that will prove their intelligence and avoiding ones that might not (Dweck, 1999, 2006). The desire to learn takes a backseat.

Other students believe that their intellectual ability is something they can develop through effort and education. They don't necessarily believe that anyone can become an Einstein or a Mozart, but they do understand that even Einstein and Mozart had to put in years of effort to become who they were. When students believe that they can develop their intelligence, they focus on doing just that. Not worrying about how smart they will appear, they take on challenges and stick to them (Dweck, 1999, 2006).

> **When students believe that they can develop their intelligence, they focus on doing just that.**

More and more research in psychology and neuroscience supports the growth mind-set. We are discovering that the brain has more plasticity over time than we ever imagined (Doidge, 2007); that fundamental aspects of intelligence can be enhanced through learning (Sternberg, 2005); and that dedication and persistence in the face of obstacles are key ingredients in outstanding achievement (Ericsson, Charness, Feltovich, & Hoffman, 2006).

Alfred Binet (1909/1973), the inventor of the IQ test, had a strong growth mind-set. He believed that education could transform the basic capacity to learn. Far from intending to measure fixed intelligence, he meant his test to be a tool for identifying students who were not profiting from the public school curriculum so that other courses of study could be devised to foster their intellectual growth.

The Two Faces of Effort

The fixed and growth mind-sets create two different psychological worlds. In the fixed mind-set, students care first and foremost about how they'll be judged: smart or not smart. Repeatedly, students with this mind-set reject opportunities to learn if they might make mistakes (Hong, Chiu, Dweck, Lin, & Wan, 1999; Mueller & Dweck, 1998). When they do make mistakes or reveal deficiencies, rather than correct them, they try to hide them (Nussbaum & Dweck, 2007).

They are also afraid of effort because effort makes them feel dumb. They believe that if you have the ability, you shouldn't need effort (Blackwell, Trzesniewski, & Dweck, 2007), that ability should bring success all by itself. This is one of the worst beliefs that students can hold. It can cause many bright students to stop working in school when the curriculum becomes challenging.

Finally, students in the fixed mind-set don't recover well from setbacks. When they hit a setback in school, they *decrease* their efforts and consider cheating (Blackwell et al., 2007). The idea of fixed intelligence does not offer them viable ways to improve.

Let's get inside the head of a student with a fixed mind-set as he sits in his classroom, confronted with algebra for the first time. Up until then, he has breezed through math. Even when he barely paid attention in class and skimped on his homework, he always got As. But this is different. It's hard. The student feels anxious and thinks, "What if I'm not as good at math as I thought? What if other kids understand it and I don't?" At some level, he realizes that he has two choices: try hard, or turn off. His interest in math begins to wane, and his attention wanders. He tells himself, "Who cares about this stuff? It's for nerds. I could do it if I wanted to, but it's so boring. You don't see CEOs and sports stars solving for x and y."

By contrast, in the growth mind-set, students care about learning. When they make a mistake or exhibit a deficiency, they correct it (Blackwell et al., 2007; Nussbaum & Dweck, 2007). For them, effort is a *positive* thing: It ignites their intelligence and causes it to grow. In the face of failure, these students escalate their efforts and look for new learning strategies.

Let's look at another student—one who has a growth mind-set—having her first encounter with algebra. She finds it new, hard, and confusing, unlike anything else she has ever learned. But she's determined to understand it. She listens to everything the teacher says, asks the teacher questions after class, and takes her textbook home and reads the chapter over twice. As she begins to get it, she feels exhilarated. A new world of math opens up for her.

It is not surprising, then, that when we have followed students over challenging school transitions or courses, we find that those with growth mind-sets outperform their classmates with fixed mind-sets—even when they entered with equal skills and knowledge. A growth mind-set fosters the growth of ability over time (Blackwell et al., 2007; Mangels, Butterfield, Lamb, Good, & Dweck, 2006; see also Grant & Dweck, 2003).

The Effects of Praise

Many educators have hoped to maximize students' confidence in their abilities, their enjoyment of learning, and their ability to thrive in school by praising their intelligence. We've studied the effects of this kind of praise in children as young as 4 years old and as old as adolescence, in students in inner-city and rural settings, and in students of different ethnicities—and we've consistently found the same thing (Cimpian, Arce, Markman, & Dweck, 2007; Kamins & Dweck, 1999; Mueller & Dweck, 1998): Praising students' intelligence gives them a short burst of pride, followed by a long string of negative consequences.

In many of our studies (see Mueller & Dweck, 1998), 5th grade students worked on a task, and after the first set of problems, the teacher praised some of them for their intelligence ("You must be smart at these problems") and others for their effort ("You must have worked hard at these problems"). We then assessed the students' mind-sets. In one study, we asked students to agree or disagree with mind-set statements, such as, "Your intelligence is something basic about you that you

can't really change." Students praised for intelligence agreed with statements like these more than students praised for effort did. In another study, we asked students to define intelligence. Students praised for intelligence made significantly more references to innate, fixed capacity, whereas the students praised for effort made more references to skills, knowledge, and areas they could change through effort and learning. Thus, we found that praise for intelligence tended to put students in a fixed mind-set (intelligence is fixed, and you have it), whereas praise for effort tended to put them in a growth mind-set (you're developing these skills because you're working hard).

We then offered students a chance to work on either a challenging task that they could learn from or an easy one that ensured error-free performance. Most of those praised for intelligence wanted the easy task, whereas most of those praised for effort wanted the challenging task and the opportunity to learn.

Next, the students worked on some challenging problems. As a group, students who had been praised for their intelligence *lost* their confidence in their ability and their enjoyment of the task as soon as they began to struggle with the problem. If success meant they were smart, then struggling meant they were not. The whole point of intelligence praise is to boost confidence and motivation, but both were gone in a flash. Only the effort-praised kids remained, on the whole, confident and eager.

When the problems were made somewhat easier again, students praised for intelligence did poorly, having lost their confidence and motivation. As a group, they did worse than they had done initially on these same types of problems. The students praised for effort showed excellent performance and continued to improve.

Finally, when asked to report their scores (anonymously), almost 40 percent of the intelligence-praised students lied. Apparently, their egos were so wrapped up in their performance that they couldn't admit mistakes. Only about 10 percent of the effort-praised students saw fit to falsify their results.

Praising students for their intelligence, then, hands them not motivation and resilience but a fixed mind-set with all its vulnerability. In contrast, effort or "process" praise (praise for engagement, perseverance, strategies, improvement, and the like) fosters hardy motivation. It tells students what they've done to be successful and what they need to do to be successful again in the future. Process praise sounds like this:

- You really studied for your English test, and your improvement shows it. You read the material over several times, outlined it, and tested yourself on it. That really worked!
- I like the way you tried all kinds of strategies on that math problem until you finally got it.
- It was a long, hard assignment, but you stuck to it and got it done. You stayed at your desk, kept up your concentration, and kept working. That's great!
- I like that you took on that challenging project for your science class. It will take a lot of work—doing the research, designing the machine, buying the parts, and building it. You're going to learn a lot of great things.

What about a student who gets an *A* without trying? I would say, "All right, that was too easy for you. Let's do something more challenging that you can learn from." We don't want to make something done quickly and easily the basis for our admiration.

What about a student who works hard and *doesn't* do well? I would say, "I liked the effort you put in. Let's work together some more and figure out what you don't understand." Process praise keeps students focused, not on something called ability that they may or may not have and that magically creates success or failure, but on processes they can all engage in to learn.

Motivated to Learn

Finding that a growth mind-set creates motivation and resilience—and leads to higher achievement—we sought to develop an intervention that would teach this mind-set to students. We decided to aim our intervention at students who were making the transition to 7th grade because this is a time of great vulnerability. School often gets more difficult in 7th grade, grading becomes more stringent, and the environment becomes more impersonal. Many students take stock of themselves and their intellectual abilities at this time and decide whether they want to be involved with school. Not surprisingly, it is often a time of disengagement and plunging achievement.

We performed our intervention in a New York City junior high school in which many students were struggling with the transition and were showing plummeting grades. If students learned a growth mind-set, we reasoned, they might be able to meet this challenge with increased, rather than decreased, effort. We therefore developed an eight-session workshop in which both the control group and the growth-mind-set group learned study skills, time management techniques, and memory strategies (Blackwell et al., 2007). However, in the growth-mind-set intervention, students also learned about their brains and what they could do to make their intelligence grow.

They learned that the brain is like a muscle—the more they exercise it, the stronger it becomes. They learned that every time they try hard and learn something new, their brain forms new connections that, over time, make them smarter. They learned that intellectual development is not the natural unfolding of intelligence, but rather the formation of new connections brought about through effort and learning.

Students were riveted by this information. The idea that their intellectual growth was largely in their hands fascinated them. In fact, even the most disruptive students suddenly sat still and took notice, with the most unruly boy of the lot looking up at us and saying, "You mean I don't have to be dumb?"

Indeed, the growth-mind-set message appeared to unleash students' motivation. Although both groups had experienced a steep decline in their math grades during their first months of junior high, those receiving the growth-mind-set intervention showed a significant rebound. Their math grades improved. Those in the control group, despite their excellent study skills intervention, continued their decline.

What's more, the teachers—who were unaware that the intervention workshops differed—singled out three times as many students in the growth-mindset intervention as showing marked changes in motivation. These students had a heightened desire to work hard and learn. One striking example was the boy who thought he was dumb. Before this experience, he had never put in any extra effort and often didn't turn his homework in on time. As a result of the training, he worked for hours one evening to finish an assignment early so that his teacher could review it and give him a chance to revise it. He earned a *B+* on the assignment (he had been getting *C*s and lower previously).

Other researchers have obtained similar findings with a growth-mind-set intervention. Working with junior high school students, Good, Aronson, and Inzlicht (2003) found an increase in math and English achievement test scores; working with college students, Aronson, Fried, and Good (2002) found an increase in students' valuing of academics, their enjoyment of schoolwork, and their grade point averages.

To facilitate delivery of the growth-mind-set workshop to students, we developed an interactive computer-based version of the intervention called *Brainology*. Students work through six modules, learning about the brain, visiting virtual brain labs, doing virtual brain experiments, seeing how the brain changes with learning, and learning how they can make their brains work better and grow smarter.

We tested our initial version in 20 New York City schools, with encouraging results. Almost all students (anonymously polled) reported changes in their study habits and motivation to learn resulting directly from their learning of the growth mind-set. One student noted that as a result of the animation she had seen about the brain, she could actually "picture the neurons growing bigger as they make more connections." One student referred to the value of effort: "If you do not give up and you keep studying, you can find your way through."

Adolescents often see school as a place where they perform for teachers who then judge them. The growth mind-set changes that perspective and makes school a place where students vigorously engage in learning for their own benefit.

Going Forward

Our research shows that educators cannot hand students confidence on a silver platter by praising their intelligence. Instead, we can help them gain the tools they need to maintain their confidence in learning by keeping them focused on the *process* of achievement.

Maybe we have produced a generation of students who are more dependent, fragile, and entitled than previous generations. If so, it's time for us to adopt a growth mind-set and learn from our mistakes. It's time to deliver interventions that will truly boost students' motivation, resilience, and learning.

References

Aronson, J., Fried, C., & Good, C. (2002). Reducing the effects of stereotype threat on African American college students by shaping theories of intelligence. *Journal of Experimental Social Psychology, 38,* 113–125.

Binet, A. (1909/1973). *Les idées modernes sur les enfants* [Modern ideas on children]. Paris: Flamarion. (Original work published 1909)

Blackwell, L., Trzesniewski, K., & Dweck, C. S. (2007). Implicit theories of intelligence predict achievement across an adolescent transition: A longitudinal study and an intervention. *Child Development, 78*, 246–263.

Cimpian, A., Arce, H., Markman, E. M., & Dweck, C. S. (2007). Subtle linguistic cues impact children's motivation. *Psychological Science, 18*, 314–316.

Doidge, N. (2007). *The brain that changes itself: Stories of personal triumph from the frontiers of brain science.* New York: Viking.

Dweck, C. S. (1999). *Self-theories: Their role in motivation, personality and development.* Philadelphia: Taylor and Francis/Psychology Press.

Dweck, C. S. (2006). *Mindset: The new psychology of success.* New York: Random House.

Ericsson, K. A., Charness, N., Feltovich, P. J., & Hoffman, R. R. (Eds.). (2006). *The Cambridge handbook of expertise and expert performance.* New York: Cambridge University Press.

Good, C., Aronson, J., & Inzlicht, M. (2003). Improving adolescents' standardized test performance: An intervention to reduce the effects of stereotype threat. *Journal of Applied Developmental Psychology, 24*, 645–662.

Grant, H., & Dweck, C. S. (2003). Clarifying achievement goals and their impact. *Journal of Personality and Social Psychology, 85*, 541–553.

Hong, Y. Y., Chiu, C., Dweck, C. S., Lin, D., & Wan, W. (1999). Implicit theories, attributions, and coping: A meaning system approach. *Journal of Personality and Social Psychology, 77*, 588–599.

Kamins, M., & Dweck, C. S. (1999). Person vs. process praise and criticism: Implications for contingent self-worth and coping. *Developmental Psychology, 35*, 835–847.

Mangels, J. A., Butterfield, B., Lamb, J., Good, C. D., & Dweck, C. S. (2006). Why do beliefs about intelligence influence learning success? A social-cognitive-neuroscience model. *Social, Cognitive, and Affective Neuroscience, 1*, 75–86.

Mueller, C. M., & Dweck, C. S. (1998). Intelligence praise can undermine motivation and performance. *Journal of Personality and Social Psychology, 75*, 33–52.

Nussbaum, A. D., & Dweck, C. S. (2007). Defensiveness vs. remediation: Self-theories and modes of self-esteem maintenance. *Personality and Social Psychology Bulletin.*

Sternberg, R. (2005). Intelligence, competence, and expertise. In A. Elliot & C. S. Dweck (Eds.), *The handbook of competence and motivation* (pp. 15–30). New York: Guilford Press.

Critical Thinking

1. How does praise motivate students to learn?
2. In what ways might praise impair learning?
3. What is the difference between a "fixed mind-set" and a "growth mind-set"?

CAROL S. DWECK is the Lewis and Virginia Eaton Professor of Psychology at Stanford University and the author of *Mindset: The New Psychology of Success* (Random House, 2006).

initiative versus guilt Erikson's third stage in psychosocial development, in which children balance the urge to pursue goals with moral reservations that may prevent carrying them out.

Checkpoint ✔

Can you . . .

✔ Trace self-concept development between ages 3 and 6 and discuss cultural influences on self-definition?

✔ Tell how young children's self-esteem differs from that of school-age children?

✔ Describe how the "helpless" pattern arises and how it can affect children's reactions to failure?

✔ Describe the typical progression in understanding conflicting emotions and emotions directed toward the self?

✔ Discuss the conflict involved in Erikson's third stage of psychosocial development?

Guidepost 2

How do boys and girls become aware of the meaning of gender, and what explains differences in behavior between the sexes?

gender identity Awareness, developed in early childhood, that one is male or female.

Checkpoint ✔

Can you . . .

✔ Summarize the main behavioral and cognitive differences between boys and girls?

Erikson: Initiative versus Guilt

The need to deal with conflicting feelings about the self is at the heart of Erikson's (1950) third stage of psychosocial development: **initiative versus guilt.** The conflict arises from the growing sense of purpose, which spurs a child to plan and carry out activities, and the growing pangs of conscience the child may have about such plans.

Preschool children can do—and want to do—more and more. At the same time, they are learning that some of the things they want to do meet social approval and others do not. How do they reconcile their desire to *do* with their desire for approval? Children who learn how to regulate these opposing drives develop the virtue of *purpose,* the courage to envision and pursue goals without being unduly inhibited by guilt or fear of punishment (Erikson, 1982).

If this conflict is not resolved adequately, said Erikson, a child may grow into an adult who is constantly striving for success or showing off; is inhibited and unspontaneous or self-righteous and intolerant; or suffers from impotence or psychosomatic illness. With ample opportunities to do things on their own—but under guidance and consistent limits—children can attain a healthy balance and avoid the tendency to overdo competition and achievement and the tendency to be repressed and guilt ridden.

Gender

Gender identity, awareness of one's femaleness or maleness and all it implies, is an important aspect of the developing self-concept. How different are young boys and girls? What causes those differences? How do children develop gender identity, and how does it affect their attitudes and behavior?

Gender Differences

Gender differences are psychological or behavioral differences between males and females. As we discussed in Chapter 8, measurable differences between baby boys and girls are few. Although some gender differences become more pronounced after age 3, boys and girls on average remain more alike than different. Extensive evidence from many studies supports this *gender similarities hypothesis* (Hyde, 2005). Fully 78 percent of gender differences are small to negligible, and some differences, such as in self-esteem, change with age.

Physically, among the larger gender differences are boys' higher activity level, superior motor performance, especially after puberty, and their moderately greater propensity for physical aggression (Hyde, 2005) beginning by age 2 (Archer, 2004; Baillargeon et al., 2007; Pellegrini & Archer, 2005). (Aggression is discussed later in this chapter.)

Despite the overlap in behavior between young boys and girls, research involving children aged 2½ to 8 has consistently identified striking differences in playtime preferences and styles. A recent investigation on gender-based behaviors has demonstrated that sex-typed preferences increase between toddlerhood and middle childhood and that the degree of sex-typed behavior exhibited early in life is a strong indicator of later gender-based behavior (Golombok et al., 2008).

Cognitive gender differences are few and small (Spelke, 2005). Overall, intelligence test scores show no gender differences (Keenan & Shaw, 1997), perhaps because the most widely used tests are designed to eliminate gender bias (Neisser et al., 1996). Boys and girls do equally well on tasks involving basic mathematical skills and are equally capable of learning math. However, there are small differences in specific abilities. Girls tend to perform better on tests of verbal fluency, mathematical computation, and memory for locations of objects. Boys tend to perform better in verbal analogies, mathematical word problems, and memory for spatial configurations. In most studies, these differences do not emerge until elementary school or later (Spelke, 2005). Also, boys' mathematical abilities vary more than girls', with more boys at both the highest and lowest ends of the ability range (Halpern et al., 2007.) In early childhood and again during preadolescence and adolescence, girls tend to use more responsive language, such as praise, agreement, acknowledgment, and elaboration on what someone else has said (Leaper & Smith, 2004).

We need to remember, of course, that gender differences are valid for large groups of boys and girls but not necessarily for individuals. By knowing a child's sex, we cannot predict whether that *particular* boy or girl will be faster, stronger, smarter, more obedient, or more assertive than another child.

Perspectives on Gender Development

What accounts for gender differences, and why do some of them emerge as children grow older? Some explanations center on the differing experiences and social expectations that boys and girls meet almost from birth. These experiences and expectations concern three related aspects of gender identity: gender roles, gender-typing, and gender stereotypes.

Table 11-1	Five Perspectives on Gender Development		
Theories	**Major Theorists**	**Key Processes**	**Basic Beliefs**
Biological Approach		Genetic, neurological, and hormonal activity	Many or most behavioral differences between the sexes can be traced to biological differences.
Evolutionary Developmental Approach	Charles Darwin	Natural sexual selection	Children develop gender roles in preparation for adult mating and reproductive behavior.
Psychoanalytic Approach Psychosexual theory	Sigmund Freud	Resolution of unconscious emotional conflict	Gender identity occurs when child identifies with same-sex parent.
Cognitive Approach Cognitive-developmental theory	Lawrence Kohlberg	Self-categorization	Once a child learns she is a girl or he is a boy, child sorts information about behavior by gender and acts accordingly.
Gender-schema theory	Sandra Bem, Carol Lynn Martin & Charles F. Halverson	Self-categorization based on processing of cultural information	Child organizes information about what is considered appropriate for a boy or a girl on the basis of what a particular culture dictates and behaves accordingly. Child sorts by gender because the culture dictates that gender is an important schema.
Social Learning Approach Social cognitive theory	Albert Bandura	Observation of models, reinforcement	Child mentally combines observations of multiple models and creates own behavioral variations.

Gender roles are the behaviors, interests, attitudes, skills, and personality traits that a culture considers appropriate for males or females. All societies have gender roles. Historically, in most cultures, women have been expected to devote most of their time to caring for the household and children, and men have been providers and protectors. Women have been expected to be compliant and nurturant; men, to be active, aggressive, and competitive. Today gender roles in Western cultures have become more diverse and more flexible.

Gender-typing (refer to Chapter 8), the acquisition of a gender role, takes place early in childhood; but children vary greatly in the degree to which they become gender-typed (Iervolino, Hines, Golombok, Rust, & Plomin, 2005). **Gender stereotypes** are overgeneralizations about male or female behavior ("All females are passive and dependent; all males are aggressive and independent"). Gender stereotypes pervade many cultures. They appear to some degree in children as young as 2 or 3, increase during the preschool years, and reach a peak at age 5 (Campbell, Shirley, & Candy, 2004; Ruble & Martin, 1998).

How do children acquire gender roles, and why do they adopt gender stereotypes? Are these purely social constructs, or do they reflect innate differences between males and females? The answers are not either-or. Let's look at five theoretical perspectives on gender development (summarized in Table 11-1): *biological, evolutionary developmental, psychoanalytic, cognitive,* and *social learning.* Each of these perspectives can contribute to our understanding; though, none fully explains why boys and girls differ in some respects but not in others.

Biological Approach

The existence of similar gender roles in many cultures suggests that some gender differences may be biologically based. Investigators are uncovering evidence of genetic, hormonal, and neurological explanations for gender differences.

Scientists have identified more than 50 genes that may explain differences in anatomy and function between the brains of male and female mice. If similar genetic differences exist in humans, then sexual identity may be hardwired into the brain even before sexual organs form and hormonal activity begins (Dewing, Shi, Horvath, & Vilain, 2003).

gender roles Behaviors, interests, attitudes, skills, and traits that a culture considers appropriate for each sex; differs for males and females.

gender-typing Socialization process whereby children, at an early age, learn appropriate gender roles.

gender stereotypes Preconceived generalizations about male or female role behavior.

By age 5, when the brain reaches approximate adult size, boys' brains are about 10 percent larger than girls' brains, mostly because boys have more gray matter in the cerebral cortex, whereas girls have greater neuronal density (Reiss, Abrams, Singer, Ross, & Denckla, 1996).

Hormones in the bloodstream before or about the time of birth affect the developing brain. The male hormone testosterone is related to aggressiveness in adult animals, but the relationship in humans is less clear (Simpson, 2001). For one thing, hormonal influences are hard to disentangle from genetic or later environmental influences (Iervolino et al., 2005). Although testosterone levels do not appear to be related to aggressiveness in children (Constantino et al., 1993), an analysis of fetal testosterone levels and the development of gender-typical play has shown a link between higher testosterone levels and male-typical play in boys (Auyeng et al., 2009).

Some research focuses on children with unusual prenatal hormonal histories. Girls with a disorder called *congenital adrenal hyperplasia* (CAH) have high prenatal levels of *androgens* (male sex hormones). Although raised as girls, they tend to develop into tomboys, showing preferences for "boys' toys," rough play, and male playmates, as well as strong spatial skills. *Estrogens* (female hormones) seem to have less influence on boys' gender-typed behavior. However, these studies are natural experiments and cannot establish cause and effect. Factors other than hormonal differences may play a role (Ruble & Martin, 1998).

Perhaps the most dramatic examples of biologically based research have to do with infants born with ambiguous sexual structures that appear to be part male and part female. John Money and his colleagues (Money, Hampson, & Hampson, 1955) developed guidelines for infants born with such disorders, recommending that the child be assigned as early as possible to the gender that holds the potential for the most nearly normal functioning.

However, studies demonstrate the difficulty of predicting the outcome of sex assignment at birth. In one study, 14 genetically male children born without normal penises but with testes were legally and surgically assigned to female sex during the 1st month of life and were raised as girls. Between ages 5 and 16, eight declared themselves male (though two were living ambiguously). Five declared unwavering female identity but expressed difficulty fitting in with other girls; and one, after learning that she had been born male, refused to discuss the subject with anyone. Meanwhile, two boys whose parents had refused the initial sexual assignment remained male (Reiner & Gearhart, 2004). In another study, 25 of 27 genetically male children born without penises were raised as girls but considered themselves boys and, as children, engaged in rough play (Reiner, 2000). These cases suggest that gender identity may be rooted in chromosomal structure and cannot easily be changed (Diamond & Sigmundson, 1997).

Evolutionary Developmental Approach

The evolutionary developmental approach sees gendered behavior as biologically based—with a purpose. From this controversial perspective, children's gender roles underlie the evolved mating and child-rearing strategies of adult males and females.

According to Darwin's (1871) **theory of sexual selection,** the selection of sexual partners is a response to the differing reproductive pressures that early men and women confronted in the struggle for survival of the species (Wood & Eagly, 2002). The more widely a man can "spread his seed," the greater his chances to pass on his genetic inheritance. Thus men in general tend to seek as many partners as possible. They value physical prowess because it enables them to compete for mates and for control of resources and social status, which women value. Because a woman invests more time and energy in pregnancy and can bear only a limited number of children, each child's survival is of utmost importance to her. Thus she looks for a mate who will remain with her and support their offspring. The need to raise each child to reproductive maturity also explains why women tend to be more caring and nurturant than men (Bjorklund & Pellegrini, 2000; Wood & Eagly, 2002).

According to evolutionary theory, male competitiveness and aggressiveness and female nurturance develop during childhood as preparation for these adult roles. Boys

theory of sexual selection Darwinian theory, which holds that selection of sexual partners is influenced by the differing reproductive pressures that early men and women confronted in the struggle for survival of the species.

play at fighting; girls play at parenting. In caring for children, women often must put a child's needs and feelings ahead of their own. Thus young girls tend to be better able than young boys to control and inhibit their emotions and to refrain from impulsive behavior (Bjorklund & Pellegrini, 2000).

If this theory is correct, gender roles should be universal and resistant to change. Evidence in support of the theory is that in all cultures women tend to be children's primary caregivers, though in some societies this responsibility is shared with the father or others (Wood & Eagly, 2002). Evidence against the theory is men's greater involvement in child raising today than in the past in the United States and in other Western societies (Wood & Eagly, 2002).

Critics of evolutionary theory suggest that society and culture are as important as biology in determining gender roles. Evolutionary theory claims that men's primary role is to provide for subsistence while women's primary role is child care, but in some nonindustrial societies women are the main or equal providers. In an analysis of mating preferences in 37 cultures, women in traditional societies did tend to prefer older men with financial resources, and men to prefer younger women with homemaking skills; but these preferences were less pronounced in more egalitarian societies where women had reproductive freedom and educational opportunities (Wood & Eagly, 2002).

Some evolutionary theorists, therefore, see the evolution of gender roles as a dynamic process. They acknowledge that gender roles (such as men's involvement in child rearing) may change in an environment different from that in which these roles initially evolved (Crawford, 1998).

Psychoanalytic Approach

"Dad, where will you live when I grow up and marry Mommy?" asks Juan, age 4. From the psychoanalytic perspective, Juan's question is part of his acquisition of gender identity. That process, according to Freud, is one of **identification,** the adoption of characteristics, beliefs, attitudes, values, and behaviors of the parent of the same sex. Freud considered identification an important personality development of early childhood; some social learning theorists also have used the term.

According to Freud, identification will occur for Juan when he represses or gives up the wish to possess the parent of the other sex (his mother) and identifies with the parent of the same sex (his father). But although this explanation for gender development has been influential, it has been difficult to test and has little research support (Maccoby, 1992). Despite some evidence that preschoolers tend to act more affectionately toward the other-sex parent and more aggressively toward the same-sex parent (Westen, 1998), the majority of developmental psychologists today favor other explanations.

Cognitive Approaches

Sarah figures out she is a girl because people call her a girl. As she continues to observe and think about her world, she concludes that she will always be female. She comes to understand gender by actively thinking about and constructing her own gender-typing. This is the heart of Lawrence Kohlberg's (1966) cognitive-developmental theory.

Kohlberg's Cognitive-Developmental Theory In Kohlberg's theory, *gender knowledge precedes gendered behavior* ("I am a boy, so I like to do boy things"). Children *actively* search for cues about gender in their social world. As children come to realize which gender they belong to, they adopt behaviors they perceive as consistent with being male or female. Thus 3-year-old Sarah prefers dolls to trucks because she sees girls playing with dolls and therefore views playing with dolls as consistent with her being a girl. And she plays mostly with other girls, whom she assumes will share her interests (Martin & Ruble, 2004; Ruble & Martin, 1998).

The acquisition of gender roles, said Kohlberg, hinges on **gender constancy,** more recently called *sex-category constancy*—a child's realization that his or her sex will always be the same. Once children achieve this realization, they are motivated to adopt behaviors appropriate to their sex. Gender constancy seems to develop in three stages:

identification In Freudian theory, process by which a young child adopts characteristics, beliefs, attitudes, values, and behaviors of the parent of the same sex.

gender constancy Awareness that one will always be male or female. Also called *sex-category constancy*.

gender identity, gender stability, and gender consistency (Martin et al., 2002; Ruble & Martin, 1998; Szkrybalo & Ruble, 1999). *Gender identity* (awareness of one's own gender and that of others) typically occurs between ages 2 and 3. *Gender stability* comes when a girl realizes that she will grow up to be a woman, and a boy that he will grow up to be a man—in other words, that gender does not change. However, children at this stage may base judgments about gender on superficial appearances (clothing or hairstyle) and stereotyped behaviors. Sometime between ages 3 and 7, or even later—comes *gender consistency:* the realization that a girl remains a girl even if she has a short haircut and plays with trucks, and a boy remains a boy even if he has long hair and wears earrings. Once children realize that their behavior or dress will not affect their sex, they may become less rigid in their adherence to gender norms (Martin et al., 2002).

Much research challenges Kohlberg's view that gender-typing depends on gender constancy. Long before children attain the final stage of gender constancy, they show gender-typed preferences (Bussey & Bandura, 1992; Martin & Ruble, 2004; Ruble & Martin, 1998). For example, gender preferences in toys and playmates appear as early as 12 to 24 months. However, these findings do not challenge Kohlberg's basic insight: that gender concepts influence behavior (Martin et al., 2002).

Today, cognitive-developmental theorists no longer claim that gender constancy must precede gender-typing (Martin et al., 2002). Instead, they suggest that gender-typing may be heightened by the more sophisticated understanding that gender constancy brings (Martin & Ruble, 2004). Each stage of gender constancy increases children's receptivity to gender-relevant information. The achievement of gender identity may motivate children to learn more about gender; gender stability and gender consistency may motivate them to be sure they are acting "like a boy" or "like a girl." Studies have found significant links between levels of gender constancy and various aspects of gender development (Martin et al., 2002).

gender-schema theory Theory that children socialize themselves in their gender roles by developing a mentally organized network of information about what it means to be male or female in a particular culture.

Anna's enjoyment of her truck shows that she is not restricted in her play by gender stereotypes. According to Bem's gender-schema theory, parents can help their children avoid such stereotypes by encouraging them to pursue their own interests, even when these interests are unconventional for their sex.

Gender-Schema Theory Another cognitive approach is **gender-schema theory.** Like cognitive-developmental theory, it views children as actively extracting knowledge about gender from their environment *before* engaging in gender-typed behavior. However, gender-schema theory places more emphasis on the influence of culture. Once children know what sex they are, they develop a concept of what it means to be male or female *in their culture.* Children then match their behavior to their culture's view of what boys and girls are "supposed" to be and do. Among the theory's leading proponents are Sandra Bem (1983, 1985, 1993), Carol Lynn Martin, and Charles F. Halverson (Martin & Halverson, 1981; Martin et al., 2002).

According to this theory, gender schemas promote gender stereotypes by influencing judgments about behavior. When a new boy his age moves in next door, 4-year-old Brandon knocks on his door, carrying a toy truck—apparently assuming that the new boy will like the same toys he likes. Bem suggests that children who show such stereotypical behavior may be experiencing pressure for gender conformity that inhibits healthy self-exploration. However, there is little evidence that gender schemas are at the root of stereotyped behavior or that children who are highly gender-typed necessarily feel pressure to conform (Yunger, Carver, & Perry, 2004).

Another problem with both gender-schema theory and Kohlberg's theory is that gender-stereotyping does not always become stronger with increased gender knowledge; in fact, the opposite is often true (Bussey & Bandura, 1999). Another view, which has research support, is that gender-stereotyping rises and then falls in a developmental pattern (Ruble & Martin, 1998; Welch-Ross & Schmidt, 1996). Around ages 4 to 6, when, according to gender-schema theory, children are constructing and then consolidating their gender schemas, they notice and remember only information consistent with these schemas and even exaggerate it. In fact, they tend to *mis*remember information that challenges gender stereotypes, such as photos of a girl sawing wood or a boy cooking, and to insist that the genders in the photos were the other way around. Young children are quick to accept gender labels; when told that an unfamiliar toy is meant for the other sex, they will drop it quickly, and they expect others to do the same (C. L. Martin, Eisenbud, & Rose, 1995; Martin & Ruble, 2004; Ruble & Martin, 1998).

By ages 5 and 6, children develop a repertoire of rigid stereotypes about gender that they apply to themselves and others. A boy will pay more attention to what he considers boys' toys and a girl to girls' toys. A boy will expect to do better at boy things than at girl things, and if he does try, say, to dress a doll, he will be all thumbs. Then, around age 7 or 8, schemas become more complex as children begin to take in and integrate contradictory information, such as the fact that many girls have short hair. Children develop more complex beliefs about gender and become more flexible in their views about gender roles (Martin & Ruble, 2004; Ruble & Martin, 1998; M. G. Taylor, 1996; Trautner et al., 2005).

Cognitive approaches to gender development have made an important contribution by exploring how children think about gender and what they know about it at various ages. However, these approaches may not fully explain the link between knowledge and conduct. There is disagreement about precisely what mechanism prompts children to act out gender roles and why some children become more strongly gender-typed than others (Bussey & Bandura, 1992, 1999; Martin & Ruble, 2004; Ruble & Martin, 1998). Some investigators point to socialization.

Social Learning Approach

According to Walter Mischel (1966), a traditional social learning theorist, children acquire gender roles by imitating models and being rewarded for gender-appropriate behavior—in other words, by responding to environmental stimuli. Children generally choose models they see as powerful or nurturing. Typically, one model is a parent, often of the same sex, but children also pattern their behavior after other adults or after peers. Behavioral feedback, together with direct teaching by parents and other adults, reinforces gender-typing. A boy who models his behavior after his father is commended for acting "like a boy." A girl gets compliments on a pretty dress or hairstyle. In this model, *gendered behavior precedes gender knowledge* ("I am rewarded for doing boy things, so I must be a boy").

Since the 1970s, however, studies have cast doubt on the power of same-sex modeling alone to account for gender differences. As cognitive explanations have come to the fore, traditional social learning theory has lost favor (Martin et al., 2002). Albert Bandura's (1986; Bussey & Bandura, 1999) newer **social cognitive theory,** an expansion of social learning theory, incorporates some cognitive elements.

social cognitive theory Albert Bandura's expansion of social learning theory; holds that children learn gender roles through socialization.

According to social cognitive theory, observation enables children to learn much about gender-typed behaviors before performing them. They can mentally combine observations of multiple models and generate their own behavioral variations. Instead of viewing the environment as a given, social cognitive theory recognizes that children select or even create their environments through their choice of playmates and activities. However, critics say that social cognitive theory does not explain how children differentiate between boys and girls before they have a concept of gender, or what initially motivates children to acquire gender knowledge, or how gender norms become internalized—questions that other cognitive theories attempt to answer (Martin et al., 2002).

For social cognitive theorists, socialization—the way a child interprets and internalizes experiences with parents, teachers, peers, and cultural institutions—plays a central part in gender development. Socialization begins in infancy, long before a conscious understanding of gender begins to form. Gradually, as children begin to regulate their activities, standards of behavior become internalized. A child no longer needs praise, rebukes, or a model's presence to act in socially appropriate ways. Children feel good about themselves when they live up to their internal standards and feel bad when they do not. A substantial part of the shift from socially guided control to self-regulation of gender-related behavior may take place between ages 3 and 4 (Bussey & Bandura, 1992). How do parents, peers, and the media influence this development?

Family Influences When former Louisiana governor Kathleen Blanco's 4-year-old grandson David was asked what he wanted to be when he grew up, he wasn't sure. He shrugged off all his mother's suggestions—firefighter, soldier, policeman, airplane pilot.

Finally, she asked whether he'd like to be governor. "Mom," he replied, "I'm a boy!" (Associated Press, 2004a).

David's response illustrates how strong family influences may be, even fostering counterstereotypical preferences. Usually, though, experience in the family seems to reinforce gender-typical preferences and attitudes. We say "seems" because it is difficult to separate parents' genetic influence from the influence of the environment they create. Also, parents may be responding to rather than encouraging children's gender-typed behavior (Iervolino et al., 2005).

Boys tend to be more strongly gender-socialized concerning play preferences than girls. Parents, especially fathers, generally show more discomfort if a boy plays with a doll than if a girl plays with a truck (Lytton & Romney, 1991; Ruble & Martin, 1998; Sandnabba & Ahlberg, 1999). Girls have more freedom than boys in their clothes, games, and choice of playmates (Miedzian, 1991).

In egalitarian households, the father's role in gender socialization seems especially important (Fagot & Leinbach, 1995). In an observational study of 4-year-olds in British and Hungarian cities, boys and girls whose fathers did more housework and child care were less aware of gender stereotypes and engaged in less gender-typed play than peers in more gender-typical families (Turner & Gervai, 1995).

Siblings also influence gender development, according to a 3-year longitudinal study of 198 first- and secondborn siblings and their parents. Secondborns tend to become more like their older siblings in attitudes, personality, and leisure activities, whereas firstborns are more influenced by their parents and less by their younger siblings (McHale, Updegraff, Helms-Erikson, & Crouter, 2001). Young children with an older sibling of the same sex tend to be more gender-typed than those whose older sibling is of the other sex (Iervolino et al., 2005).

Peer Influences Anna, at age 5, insisted on dressing in a new way. She wanted to wear leggings with a skirt over them, and boots—indoors and out. When her mother asked her why, Anna replied, "Because Katie dresses like this—and Katie's the king of the girls!"

Even in early childhood, the peer group is a major influence on gender-typing. By age 3, preschoolers generally play in sex-segregated groups that reinforce gender-typed behavior, and the influence of the peer group increases with age (Martin et al., 2002; Ruble & Martin, 1998). Children who play in same-sex groups tend to be more gender-typed than children who do not (Maccoby, 2002; Martin & Fabes, 2001). Peer groups show more disapproval of boys who act like girls than of girls who are tomboys (Ruble & Martin, 1998). Indeed, play choices at this age may be more strongly influenced by peers and the media than by the models children see at home (Turner & Gervai, 1995). Generally, however, peer and parental attitudes reinforce each other (Bussey & Bandura, 1999).

Cultural Influences When a young girl in Nepal touched the plow that her brother was using, she was scolded. In this way she learned that as a female she must refrain from acts her brother was expected to perform (D. Skinner, 1989).

In the United States, television is a major format for the transmission of cultural attitudes toward gender. Although women in television programs and commercials are now more likely to be working outside the home and men are sometimes shown caring for children or cooking, for the most part life as portrayed on television continues to be more stereotyped than life in the real world (Coltrane & Adams, 1997; Ruble & Martin, 1998).

Social learning theory predicts that children who watch a lot of television will become more gender-typed by imitating the models they see on the screen. Dramatic supporting evidence emerged from a natural experiment in several Canadian towns with access to television transmission for the first time. Children who had had relatively unstereotyped attitudes showed marked increases in traditional views 2 years later (Kimball, 1986).

Children's books, especially illustrated ones, have long been a source of gender stereotypes. An analysis of 200 top-selling and award-winning children's books uncovered nearly twice as many male as female main characters and strong gender-stereotyping. Female main characters nurtured more, were portrayed in indoor settings, and appeared to have no paid occupations (Hamilton, Anderson, Broaddus, & Young, 2006). Fathers were largely absent, and when they appeared, they were shown as withdrawn and ineffectual (Anderson & Hamilton, 2005).

Major strengths of the socialization approach include the breadth and multiplicity of processes it examines and the scope for individual differences it reveals. But this very complexity makes it difficult to establish clear causal connections between the way children are raised and the way they think and act. Just what aspects of the home environment and the peer culture promote gender-typing? Do parents and peers treat boys and girls differently because they *are* different or because the culture says they *should be* different? Does differential treatment *produce* or *reflect* gender differences? Or, as social cognitive theory suggests, is there a bidirectional relationship? Further research may help us see how socializing agents mesh with children's biological tendencies and cognitive understandings with regard to gender-related attitudes and behavior.

It seems likely that none of the theories we have discussed has the full answer to how gender identity and gender-typing develop. Today "it is widely acknowledged that . . . cognitive, environmental, and biological factors are all important" (Martin et al., 2002, p. 904). A recent *biosocial theory,* for example, holds that psychological aspects of gender arise from interaction between the physical characteristics of the sexes (such as men's greater physical strength and women's reproductive capacity), their developmental experiences, and the character of the societies in which they live (Wood & Eagly, 2002).

Play: The Business of Early Childhood

Carmen, age 3, pretends that the pieces of cereal floating in her bowl are "fishies" swimming in the milk, and she "fishes," spoonful by spoonful. After breakfast, she puts on her mother's hat, picks up a briefcase, and is a "mommy" going to work. She rides her tricycle through the puddles, comes in for an imaginary telephone conversation, turns a wooden block into a truck and says, "Vroom, vroom!" Carmen's day is one round of play after another.

It would be a mistake to dismiss Carmen's activities as "just fun." Although play may not seem to serve any obvious purpose, it has important current and long-term functions (Bjorklund & Pellegrini, 2002; P. K. Smith, 2005b). Play is important to healthy development of body and brain. It enables children to engage with the world around them; to use their imagination; to discover flexible ways to use objects and solve problems; and to prepare for adult roles.

Play contributes to all domains of development. Through play, children stimulate the senses, exercise their muscles, coordinate sight with movement, gain mastery over their bodies, make decisions, and acquire new skills. As they sort blocks of different shapes, count how many they can pile on each other, or announce that "my tower is bigger than yours," they lay the foundation for mathematical concepts. As they cooperate to build sandcastles or tunnels on the beach, they learn skills of negotiation and conflict resolution (Ginsburg & Committee on Communications and Committee on Psychosocial Aspects of Child and Family Health, 2007). Indeed, play is so important to children's development that the United Nations High Commissioner for Human Rights (1989) has recognized it as a right of every child. Unfortunately, the trend to full-day kindergarten has markedly reduced the time for free play (Ginsburg et al., 2007).

Children need plenty of time for free exploratory play. Today, many parents expose young children to enrichment videos and academically oriented toys. These activities may—or may not—be valuable in themselves, but not if they interfere with child-directed play. According to evolutionary theory, any activity that serves so many vital functions at a certain stage of life must have an evolutionary basis, as we discuss in Box 11-1.

Checkpoint

Can you . . .

✔ Distinguish among five basic approaches to the study of gender development?

✔ Assess evidence for biological explanations of gender differences?

✔ Compare how various theories explain the acquisition of gender roles, and assess the support for each theory?

✔ Discuss the role of socialization in gender acquisition?

Guidepost 3

How do preschoolers play, and how does play contribute to and reflect development?

The Research World

Box 11-1 *Does Play Have an Evolutionary Basis?*

Children play for the pure pleasure it brings. Yet from an evolutionary standpoint, play serves a greater purpose. This activity that (1) takes up considerable time and energy, (2) shows a characteristic age progression, peaking in childhood and declining with sexual maturity, (3) is encouraged by parents, and (4) occurs in all cultures seems to have been naturally selected for its significant benefits for children (Bjorklund & Pellegrini, 2000; P. K. Smith, 2005b).

Many psychologists and educators see play as an adaptive activity characteristic of the long period of immaturity and dependence during which children gain the physical attributes and cognitive and social learning necessary for adult life. Play aids bone and muscle development and gives children a chance to master activities and develop a sense of their capabilities (Bjorklund & Pellegrini, 2000). Through play, children practice, in a risk-free environment, behaviors and skills they will need as adults (Hawes, 1996). Animal studies suggest that the evolution of play may be linked to the evolution of intelligence. The most intelligent animals—birds and mammals—play, whereas less intelligent species—fish, reptiles, and amphibians—do not, as far as we can tell (Hawes, 1996). In addition, the type of play animals engage in maps onto the skills they will need as adults: predators engage in predatory play (for example, kittens stalk and pounce on moving things), prey engage in escape/avoidance types of play (for example, gazelles engage in stotting play—jumping with all four feet high in the air).

Parents, according to evolutionary theory, encourage play because the future benefits of children's skill acquisition outweigh any benefits of current productive activity in which children, at their relatively low skill levels, might engage (P. K. Smith, 2005b). Gender differences in children's play enable boys and girls to practice adult behaviors important for reproduction and survival (Bjorklund & Pellegrini, 2002; Geary, 1999).

Different types of play serve different adaptive functions. Early *locomotor play* is common among all mammals and may support

brain development. Later, *exercise play* may help develop muscle strength, endurance, physical skills, and efficiency of movement (P. K. Smith, 2005b). *Play with objects* is found mainly among primates: humans, monkeys, and apes. Object play may have served an evolutionary purpose in the development of tools, by enabling people to learn the properties of objects and what can be done with them (Bjorklund & Pellegrini, 2002). In premodern societies, object play tends to focus on developing useful skills, such as making baskets and pounding grain (P. K. Smith, 2005b). Young mammals, like human children, engage in *social play,* such as wrestling and chasing each other, which strengthens social bonds, facilitates cooperation, and lessens aggression (Hawes, 1996).

Dramatic play seems to be an almost exclusively human activity. It appears to be universal but is less frequent in societies in which children are expected to participate in adult work (P. K. Smith, 2005a). In traditional hunter-gatherer societies, children imitate adult subsistence activities such as hunting, fishing, and preparing food. These highly repetitive routines seem to serve primarily as practice for adult activities (P. K. Smith, 2005b). As humans began to settle in permanent communities, dramatic play may have evolved so as to practice the changing skills needed for new ways of life. In modern urban industrial societies, themes of dramatic play are highly influenced by the mass media. At least in higher-SES families, dramatic play is encouraged by an abundance of toys, the absence of demands on children to help in subsistence activities, heavy parental involvement in play, and play-based preschool curricula (P. K. Smith, 2005a).

Investigators still have much to learn about the functions and benefits of play, but one thing seems clear: the time children spend playing is time well spent.

What's your view

From observations of children's play, what immediate and long-range purposes does it appear to serve?

Children of differing ages have differing styles of play, play with different things, and spend different amounts of time in various types of play (Bjorklund & Pellegrini, 2002). Physical play, for example, begins in infancy with apparently aimless rhythmic movements. As gross motor skills improve, preschoolers exercise their muscles by running, jumping, skipping, hopping, and throwing. Toward the end of this period and into middle childhood, *rough-and-tumble play* involving wrestling, kicking, and chasing becomes more common, especially among boys, as dicussed in Chapter 12.

Researchers categorize children's play in varying ways. One common classification system is by *cognitive complexity.* Another classification is based on the *social dimension* of play.

Cognitive Levels of Play

Courtney, at 3, talked for a doll, using a deeper voice than her own. Miguel, at 4, wore a kitchen towel as a cape and "flew" around as Batman. These children were engaged in pretend play involving make-believe people or situations.

Pretend play is one of four levels of play identified by Smilansky (1968) as showing increasing cognitive complexity: functional play, constructive play, dramatic play, and formal games with rules. Although there is a general developmental progression to the types of play, this is not a stage theory.

The simplest level, which begins during infancy, is **functional play** (sometimes called *locomotor play*). It consists of repeated practice in large muscular movements, such as rolling a ball (Bjorklund & Pellegrini, 2002).

The second level, **constructive play** (also called *object play*), is the use of objects or materials to make something, such as a house of blocks or a crayon drawing. Children spend an estimated 10 to 15 percent of their time playing with objects, such as blocks (Bjorklund & Pellegrini, 2002).

The third level, which Smilansky called **dramatic play** (also called *pretend play, fantasy play,* or *imaginative play*), involves make-believe objects, actions, or roles; it rests on the symbolic function, which emerges during the last part of the 2nd year (Piaget, 1962). Although functional play and constructive play precede dramatic play in Smilanksy's hierarchy, these three types of play often occur at the same ages (Bjorklund & Pellegrini, 2002; Smith, 2005a).

Dramatic play peaks during the preschool years, increasing in frequency and complexity (Bjorklund & Pellegrini, 2002; Smith, 2005a), and then declines as school-age children become more involved in **formal games with rules**—organized games with known procedures and penalties, such as hopscotch and marbles. However, many children continue to engage in pretending well beyond the elementary school years. An estimated 12 to 15 percent of preschoolers' time is spent in pretend play (Bjorklund & Pellegrini, 2002), but the trend toward academically oriented kindergarten programs may limit the amount of time children can spend in such play (Bergen, 2002; Ginsburg et al., 2007).

Dramatic play at age 2 is largely imitative, often initiated by an adult caregiver and following familiar scripts such as feeding a baby doll or taking a stuffed animal's temperature. By age 3 or 4, pretense becomes more imaginative and self-initiated. Children may use a block to represent a cup or just imagine the cup (Smith, 2005a).

Dramatic play involves a combination of cognition, emotion, language, and sensorimotor behavior. It may strengthen the development of dense connections in the brain and strengthen the later capacity for abstract thought. Studies have found the quality of dramatic play to be associated with social and linguistic competence (Bergen, 2002). By making "tickets" for an imaginary train trip or "reading eye charts" in a "doctor's office," children build emergent literacy skills (Christie, 1991, 1998). Pretend play also may further the development of theory-of-mind skills (Smith, 2005b).

The Social Dimension of Play

In a classic study done in the 1920s, Mildred B. Parten (1932) identified six types of play ranging from the least to the most social (Table 11-2). She found that as children get older, their play tends to become more social—that is, more interactive and more cooperative. At first children play alone, then alongside other children, and finally together. Today, however, many researchers view Parten's characterization of children's play development as too simplistic, as children of all ages engage in all of Parten's categories of play (K. H. Rubin, Bukowski, & Parker, 1998).

Parten apparently regarded nonsocial play as less mature than social play. She suggested that young children who continue to play alone may develop social, psychological, or educational problems. However, certain types of nonsocial play, particularly parallel play and solitary independent play, may consist of activities that *foster* cognitive, physical, and social development. In one study of 4-year-olds, *parallel constructive play* (for example, working on puzzles near another child who is also doing so) was most common among children who were good problem solvers, were popular with other children, and were seen by teachers as socially skilled (K. Rubin, 1982).

Researchers now look not only at *whether* a child plays alone but at *why*. Among 567 kindergartners, teachers, observers, and classmates rated almost 2 out of 3 children who played alone as socially and cognitively competent; they simply preferred to play that way (Harrist, Zain, Bates, Dodge, & Pettit, 1997). On the other hand, solitary play sometimes can be a sign of shyness, anxiety, fearfulness, or social rejection

functional play Lowest cognitive level of play, involving repetitive muscular movements; also called *locomotor play.*

constructive play Second cognitive level of play, involving use of objects or materials to make something; also called *object play.*

dramatic play Play involving imaginary people or situations; also called *fantasy play, pretend play,* or *imaginative play.*

formal games with rules Organized games with known procedures and penalties.

Table 11-2	Parten's Categories of Social and Nonsocial Play
Category	**Description**
Unoccupied behavior	The child does not seem to be playing but watches anything of momentary interest.
Onlooker behavior	The child spends most of the time watching other children play. The onlooker talks to them, asking questions or making suggestions, but does not enter into the play. The onlooker is definitely observing particular groups of children rather than anything that happens to be exciting.
Solitary independent play	The child plays alone with toys that are different from those used by nearby children and makes no effort to get close to them.
Parallel play	The child plays independently but among the other children, playing with toys like those used by the other children but not necessarily playing with them in the same way. Playing *beside* rather than *with* the others, the parallel player does not try to influence the other children's play.
Associative play	The child plays with other children. They talk about their play, borrow and lend toys, follow one another, and try to control who may play in the group. All the children play similarly if not identically; there is no division of labor and no organization around any goal. Each child acts as she or he wishes and is interested more in being with the other children than in the activity itself.
Cooperative or organized supplementary play	The child plays in a group organized for some goal—to make something, play a formal game, or dramatize a situation. One or two children control who belongs to the group and direct activities. By a division of labor, children take on different roles and supplement each other's efforts.

Source: Adapted from Parten, 1932, pp. 249–251.

What's your view ❓

- How do you think the growing use of computers for both games and educational activities might affect preschool children's social and cognitive development?

Checkpoint

Can you . . .

✔ Describe four cognitive levels of play, according to Smilansky and others, and six categories of social and nonsocial play, according to Parten?

✔ Explain the connection between the cognitive and social dimensions of play?

✔ Discuss the functions of dramatic play?

(Coplan, Prakash, O'Neil, & Armer, 2004; Henderson, Marshall, Fox, & Rubin, 2004; Spinrad et al., 2004).

Reticent play, a combination of Parten's unoccupied and onlooker categories, is often a manifestation of shyness (Coplan et al., 2004). However, such reticent behaviors as playing near other children, watching what they do, or wandering aimlessly may sometimes be a prelude to joining in others' play (K. H. Rubin et al., 1998; Spinrad et al., 2004). In a short-term longitudinal study, reticent children were well-liked and showed few problem behaviors (Spinrad et al., 2004). Nonsocial play, then, seems to be far more complex than Parten imagined.

One kind of play that becomes more social during the preschool years is dramatic play (K. H. Rubin et al., 1998; Singer & Singer, 1990). Children typically engage in more dramatic play when playing with someone else than when playing alone (Bjorklund & Pellegrini, 2002). As dramatic play becomes more collaborative, story lines become more complex and innovative, offering rich opportunities to practice interpersonal and language skills and to explore social conventions and roles. In pretending together, children develop joint problem-solving, planning, and goal-seeking skills; gain understanding of other people's perspectives; and construct an image of the social world (Bergen, 2002; Bodrova & Leong, 1998; Bjorklund & Pellegrini, 2002; Davidson, 1998; J. E. Johnson, 1998; Nourot, 1998; Smith, 2005a).

How Gender Influences Play

As we have mentioned, sex segregation is common among preschoolers and becomes more prevalent in middle childhood. This tendency seems to be universal across cultures (P. K. Smith, 2005a). Although biology (sex hormones), gender identification, and adult reinforcement all seem to influence gender differences in play, the influence of the peer group may be more powerful (Smith, 2005a). By 3 years of age girls are much more

Preschool boys and girls prefer different types of play. Boys engage in rough-and-tumble play; girls play more quietly and cooperatively.

likely to play with dolls and tea sets whereas boys prefer toy guns and trucks (Dunn & Hughes, 2001; O'Brien & Huston, 1985; Servin, Bohlin, & Berlin, 1999). Girls tend to select other girls as playmates, and boys prefer other boys (Maccoby & Jacklin, 1987), a phenomenon known as **gender segregation.** Boys' tendency to be more active and physically aggressive as compared to girls' more nurturing play styles are likely contributors to gender segregation. Boys play spontaneously on sidewalks, streets, or empty lots; girls tend to choose more structured, adult-supervised activities (Benenson, 1993; Bjorklund & Pellegrini, 2002; Fabes, Martin, & Hanish, 2003; Serbin, Moller, Gulko, Powlishta, & Colburne, 1994; P. K. Smith, 2005a).

Girls engage in more dramatic play than boys. Boys' pretend play often involves danger or discord and competitive, dominant roles, as in mock battles. Girls' pretend stories generally focus on social relationships and nurturing, domestic roles, as in playing house (Bjorklund & Pellegrini, 2002; Pellegrini & Archer, 2005; Smith, 2005a). However, boys' play is more strongly gender-stereotyped than girls' (Bjorklund & Pellegrini, 2002). Thus, in mixed-sex groups, play tends to revolve around traditionally masculine activities (Fabes et al., 2003). See Table 11-3 for a summary of gender differences in play styles.

gender segregation Tendency to select playmates of one's own gender.

Table 11-3	Early Childhood Play Styles	
	Boys	**Girls**
Toys	Toy guns Trucks and cars Trains	Dolls Tea sets Domestic toys
Playmates	Large groups of other boys Friendships founded on shared activities and interests	Small groups of other girls Friendships founded on emotional and physical closeness
Activities	Rough-and-tumble Physically aggressive	Conversational Nurturing
Conflict Resolution	Physical force	Compromise
Communication Style	Talk to give information and commands	Talk to strengthen relationships

Source: Golomobok et al., 2008.

How Culture Influences Play

Cultural values affect the play environments adults set up for children, and these environments in turn affect the frequency of specific forms of play across cultures (Bodrova & Leong, 1998). One observational study compared 48 middle-class Korean American and 48 middle-class Anglo American children in separate preschools (Farver, Kim, & Lee, 1995). The three Anglo American preschools, in keeping with normative U.S. values, encouraged independent thinking and active involvement in learning by letting children select from a wide range of activities. The Korean American preschool, in keeping with traditional Korean values, emphasized developing academic skills and completing tasks. The Anglo American preschools encouraged social interchange among children and collaborative activities with teachers. In the Korean American preschool, children were allowed to talk and play only during outdoor recess.

Not surprisingly, the Anglo American children engaged in more social play, whereas the Korean Americans engaged in more unoccupied or parallel play. At the same time, Korean American children played more cooperatively, often offering toys to other children—very likely a reflection of their culture's emphasis on group harmony. Anglo American children were more aggressive and often responded negatively to other children's suggestions, reflecting the competitiveness of American culture.

Parenting

As children increasingly become their own persons, their upbringing can be a complex challenge. Parents must deal with small people who have minds and wills of their own but who still have a lot to learn about what kinds of behavior work well in society.

Forms of Discipline

The word *discipline* means "instruction" or "training." In the field of child development, **discipline** refers to methods of molding character and of teaching self-control and acceptable behavior. It can be a powerful tool for socialization with the goal of developing self-discipline. What forms of discipline work best? Researchers have looked at a wide range of techniques.

Reinforcement and Punishment

"You're such a wonderful helper, Nick! Thank you so much for putting away your toys." Nick's mother smiles warmly at her son as he plops his dump truck into the toy box. Her words and actions provide gentle discipline for her son and teach him that putting away his toys is a positive behavior that should be repeated.

Parents sometimes punish children to stop undesirable behavior, but children usually learn more from being reinforced for good behavior. *External* reinforcements may be tangible (treats, more playtime) or intangible (a smile, a word of praise, a hug, extra attention, or a special privilege). Whatever the reinforcement, the child must see it as rewarding and must receive it fairly consistently and immediately after showing the desired behavior. Eventually, the behavior should provide an *internal* reinforcement: a sense of pleasure or accomplishment.

Still, at times punishment, such as isolation or denial of privileges, is necessary. Children cannot be permitted to run out into traffic or hit another child. Sometimes a child is willfully defiant. In such situations, punishment, if consistent, immediate, and clearly tied to the offense, may be effective. It should be administered calmly, in private, and aimed at eliciting compliance, not guilt. It is most effective when accompanied by a short, simple explanation (AAP Committee on Psychosocial Aspects of Child and Family Health, 1998; Baumrind, 1996a, 1996b).

Too harsh punishment, on the other hand, can be harmful. Children who are punished harshly and frequently may have trouble interpreting other people's actions and words; they may attribute hostile intentions where none exist (B. Weiss, Dodge, Bates, & Pettit,

Checkpoint ✔

Can you . . .

✔ Tell how gender and culture influence the way children play, and give examples?

 *Guidepost 4*

How do parenting practices influence development?

discipline Methods of molding children's character and of teaching them to exercise self-control and engage in acceptable behavior.

1992). Young children who have been punished harshly may later act aggressively, even though the punishment is intended to stop what a parent sees as purposely aggressive behavior (Nix et al., 1999). Or such children may become passive because they feel helpless. Children may become frightened if parents lose control and may eventually try to avoid a punitive parent, undermining the parent's ability to influence behavior (Grusec & Goodnow, 1994).

Corporal punishment has been defined as "the use of physical force with the intention of causing a child to experience pain, but not injury, for the purpose of correction or control of the child's behavior" (Straus, 1994a, p. 4). It can include spanking, hitting, slapping, pinching, shaking, and other physical acts. Corporal punishment is popularly believed to be more effective than other remedies and to be harmless if done in moderation by loving parents (McLoyd & Smith, 2002), but a growing body of evidence points to serious negative consequences (Straus, 1999; Straus & Stewart, 1999; Box 11-2). An ongoing debate on the appropriateness of the use of corporal punishment in schools rages in the United States. Twenty states permit the use of corporal punishment in schools. In 2007 more than 200,000 students were hit as punishment. Some educators believe it is an effective deterant to harmful misbehaviors, like fighting, but others assert that corporal punishment degrades the educational environment (Human Rights Watch, 2008).

Unlike child abuse, which bears little or no relation to the child's personality or behavior, corporal punishment is more frequently used with children who are aggressive and hard to manage, characteristics that may be genetically based (Jaffee et al., 2004). The line between some forms of punishment and physical or emotional abuse is not always easy to draw, but discipline clearly becomes abusive when it results in injury to a child.

Psychological aggression refers to verbal attacks that may result in psychological harm, such as (1) yelling or screaming, (2) threatening to spank or hit the child, (3) swearing or cursing at the child, (4) threatening to send the child away or kick the child out of the house, and (5) calling the child dumb or lazy. Some psychologists equate the last three categories with emotional abuse. Psychological aggression, like physical aggression (spanking), is almost universal among U.S. parents. In a nationally representative sampling of 991 parents, 98 percent reported using some form of psychological aggression by the time a child was 5, and about 90 percent thereafter (Straus & Field, 2003).

Inductive Reasoning, Power Assertion, and Withdrawal of Love

When Sara took candy from a store, her father did not lecture her on honesty, spank her, or tell her what a bad girl she had been. Instead, he explained how the owner of the store would be harmed by her failure to pay for the candy, asked her how she thought the store owner might feel, and then took her back to the store to return the candy.

Inductive techniques, such as those Sara's father used, are designed to encourage desirable behavior or discourage undesirable behavior by reasoning with a child. They include setting limits, demonstrating logical consequences of an action, explaining, discussing, negotiating, and getting ideas from the child about what is fair. Inductive techniques are usually the most effective method of getting children to accept parental standards (M. L. Hoffman, 1970a, 1970b; Jagers, Bingham, & Hans, 1996; McCord, 1996).

Inductive reasoning tends to arouse empathy for the victim of wrongdoing as well as guilt on the part of the wrongdoer (Krevans & Gibbs, 1996). Kindergartners whose mothers reported using reasoning were more likely to see the moral wrongness of behavior that hurts other people (as opposed to merely breaking rules) than children whose mothers took away privileges (Jagers et al., 1996).

Two other broad categories of discipline are power assertion and temporary withdrawal of love. **Power assertion** is intended to stop or discourage undesirable behavior through physical or verbal enforcement of parental control; it includes demands, threats, withdrawal of privileges, spanking, and other types of punishment. **Withdrawal of love** may include ignoring, isolating, or showing dislike for a child. Neither of these is as effective as inductive reasoning in most circumstances, and both may be harmful (M. L. Hoffman, 1970a, 1970b; Jagers et al., 1996; McCord, 1996).

corporal punishment Use of physical force with the intention of causing pain but not injury so as to correct or control behavior.

psychological aggression Verbal attack that may result in psychological harm.

inductive techniques Disciplinary techniques designed to induce desirable behavior by appealing to a child's sense of reason and fairness.

power assertion Disciplinary strategy designed to discourage undesirable behavior through physical or verbal enforcement of parental control.

withdrawal of love Disciplinary strategy that involves ignoring, isolating, or showing dislike for a child.

Box 11-2 *The Case against Corporal Punishment*

"Spare the rod and spoil the child" may sound old-fashioned, but corporal punishment has become a hot issue. Many people still believe that spanking instills respect for authority, motivates good behavior, and is a necessary part of responsible parenting (Kazdin & Benjet, 2003). Alternatively, some child development professionals view any corporal punishment as verging on child abuse (Straus, 1994b). Other professionals find no harm in corporal punishment in moderation when prudently administered by loving parents (Baumrind, 1996a, 1996b; Baumrind, Larzelere, & Cowan, 2002).

Corporal punishment is banned in many countries, including Austria, Bulgaria, Croatia, Cyprus, Denmark, Finland, Germany, Hungary, Iceland, Israel, Latvia, Norway, Romania, Sweden, and Ukraine. In the United States, all states except Minnesota allow parents to administer corporeal punishment, though some insist that it be reasonable, appropriate, moderate, or necessary, and some recognize that excessive corporal punishment can be abusive (Gershoff, 2002). Corporal punishment is allowed in schools in 20 states, though a bill introduced in 2010 aims to ban corporal punishment in all schools. The Supreme Court of Canada in January 2004 ruled out corporal punishment in schools and also forbade it for infants or teenagers in any setting (Center for Effective Discipline, 2005). The United Nations Convention on the Rights of Children opposes all forms of physical violence against children.

Nevertheless, some form of corporal punishment is widely used on U.S. infants and is near-universal among parents of toddlers. In interviews with a nationally representative sample of 991 parents in 1995, 35 percent reported using corporal punishment—usually hand slapping—on infants and fully 94 percent on 3- and 4-year-olds. About 50 percent of the parents used corporal punishment on 12-year-olds, 30 percent on 14-year-olds, and 13 percent on 17-year-olds (Straus & Stewart, 1999).

Why do parents hit children? No doubt, because hitting gets children to comply (Gershoff, 2002). However, a large body of research has found negative short- and long-term associations with its use. Apart from the risk of injury or abuse, these outcomes may include, in childhood, lack of moral internalization; poor parent-child relationships; increased physical aggressiveness, antisocial behavior, and delinquency; and diminished mental health. Outcomes in adulthood can include aggression, criminal or antisocial behavior, anxiety disorders, depression, alcohol problems, and partner or child abuse (Gershoff, 2002; MacMillan et al., 1999; Strassberg, Dodge, Pettit, & Bates, 1994).

Most of this research was cross-sectional or retrospective or did not consider that the spanked children may have been aggressive in the first place and that their aggressive behavior or some other factor might have led their parents to spank them (Gershoff, 2002). Since 1997, several large, nationally representative landmark studies of children from age 3 through adolescence (Brezina, 1999; Gunnoe & Mariner, 1997; Simons, Lin, & Gordon, 1998; Strauss & Paschall, 1999; Straus, Sugarman, & Giles-Sims, 1997) have controlled for the child's behavior at the time of first measurement. These studies found that the more physical punishment a child receives, the more aggressive the child becomes and the more likely the child is to be antisocial or aggressive as an adult (Straus & Stewart, 1999).

Why the link between corporal punishment and aggressive behavior? As social learning theory would predict, children may imitate the punisher and may come to consider infliction of pain an acceptable response to problems. Corporal punishment also may arouse anger and resentment, causing children to focus on

their own hurts instead of on the wrong they have done to others. Furthermore, as with any punishment, the effectiveness of spanking diminishes with repeated use; children may feel free to misbehave if they are willing to take the consequences. Also, reliance on physical punishment may weaken parents' authority when children become teenagers, too big and strong to spank even if spanking were appropriate (AAP Committee on Psychosocial Aspects of Child and Family Health, 1998; Gershoff, 2002; McCord, 1996). Frequent spanking may even inhibit cognitive development (Straus & Paschall, 1999).

Critics of this research point out that corporal punishment does not occur in isolation; we cannot be sure that the observed outcomes were attributable to it and not to other parental behaviors or family circumstances, such as stressful events, marital discord, lack of parental warmth, or substance abuse (Kazdin & Benjet, 2003). A 6-year study of 1,990 European American, African American, and Hispanic children found that spanking does not predict an increase in problem behavior if it is done in the context of a mother's strong emotional support (McLoyd & Smith, 2002). Also, physical discipline is less likely to cause aggression or anxiety in cultures where it is seen as normal, such as in Kenya (Lansford et al., 2005).

Still, the research strongly suggests that frequent or severe corporal punishment is potentially harmful to children. Furthermore, there is no clear line between mild and harsh spanking, and one often leads to the other (Kazdin & Benjet, 2003). Thus, even though no harm from very mild spanking has been established (Larzelere, 2000), it seems prudent to choose other, less risky means of discipline that have no potentially adverse effects (Kazdin & Benjet, 2003).

The American Academy of Pediatrics Committee on Psychosocial Aspects of Child and Family Health (1998) urges parents to avoid spanking. Instead, the committee suggests teaching children to use words to express feelings, giving them choices and helping them evaluate the consequences, and modeling orderly behavior and cooperative conflict resolution. The committee recommends positive reinforcement to encourage desired behaviors and verbal reprimands, time-outs (brief isolation to give the child a chance to cool down), or removal of privileges to discourage undesired behaviors—all within a positive, supportive, loving parent-child relationship.

A child who is spanked is likely to imitate that behavior. Studies show that children who are spanked tend to become aggressive.

What's your view

Did your parents ever spank you? If so, how often and in what kinds of situations? Would you spank, or have you ever spanked, your own child? Why or why not?

The effectiveness of parental discipline may hinge on how well the child understands and accepts the parent's message, both cognitively and emotionally (Grusec & Goodnow, 1994). For the child to accept the message, the child has to recognize it as appropriate, so parents need to be fair and accurate as well as clear and consistent about their expectations. They need to fit the discipline to the misdeed and to the child's temperament and cognitive and emotional level. A child may be more motivated to accept the message if the parents are normally warm and responsive and if they arouse the child's empathy for someone the child has harmed (Grusec & Goodnow, 1994). How well children accept a disciplinary method also may depend on whether the type of discipline used is accepted in the family's culture (Lansford et al., 2005).

One point on which many experts agree is that a child interprets and responds to discipline in the context of an ongoing relationship with a parent. Some researchers, therefore, look beyond specific parental practices to overall styles, or patterns, of parenting.

Parenting Styles

Why does Stacy hit and bite the nearest person when she cannot finish a jigsaw puzzle? What makes David sit and sulk when he cannot finish the puzzle, even though his teacher offers to help him? Why does Consuelo work on the puzzle for 20 minutes and then shrug and try another? Why are children so different in their responses to the same situation? Temperament is a major factor, of course, but some research suggests that styles of parenting affect children's competence in dealing with their world.

Diana Baumrind and the Effectiveness of Authoritative Parenting

In pioneering research, Diana Baumrind (1971, 1996b; Baumrind & Black, 1967) studied 103 preschool children from 95 families. Through interviews, testing, and home studies, she measured how children were functioning, identified three parenting styles, and described typical behavior patterns of children raised according to each. Baumrind's work and the large body of research it inspired have established strong associations between each parenting style and a particular set of child behaviors (Baumrind, 1989; Darling & Steinberg, 1993; Pettit, Bates, & Dodge, 1997).

Authoritarian parenting, according to Baumrind, emphasizes control and unquestioning obedience. Authoritarian parents try to make children conform rigidly to a set standard of conduct and punish them for violating it, often using power-assertive techniques. They are more detached and less warm than other parents. Their children tend to be more discontented, withdrawn, and distrustful.

Permissive parenting emphasizes self-expression and self-regulation. Permissive parents make few demands and allow children to monitor their own activities as much as possible. They consult with children about policy decisions and rarely punish. They are warm, noncontrolling, and undemanding or even indulgent. Their preschool children tend to be immature—the least self-controlled and the least exploratory.

Authoritative parenting emphasizes a child's individuality but also stress social constraints. Authoritative parents have confidence in their ability to guide children, but they also respect children's independent decisions, interests, opinions, and personalities. They are loving and accepting but also demand good behavior and are firm in maintaining standards. They impose limited, judicious punishment when necessary, within the context of a warm, supportive relationship. They favor inductive discipline, explaining the reasoning behind their stand and encouraging verbal negotiation and give-and-take. Their children apparently feel secure in knowing both that they are loved and what is expected of them. These preschoolers tend to be the most self-reliant, self-controlled, self-assertive, exploratory, and content.

Eleanor Maccoby and John Martin (1983) added a fourth parenting style—*neglectful,* or *uninvolved*—to describe parents who, sometimes because of stress or depression, focus on their own needs rather than on those of the child. Neglectful parenting has been linked with a variety of behavioral disorders in childhood and adolescence (Baumrind, 1991; Parke & Buriel, 1998; R. A. Thompson, 1998).

What's your view

- As a parent, what form of discipline would you favor if your 3-year-old snuck a cookie from the cookie jar? Refused to take a nap? Hit his little sister? Tell why.

Checkpoint

Can you . . .

✔ Compare various forms of discipline, and identify factors that influence their effectiveness?

authoritarian parenting Parenting style emphasizing control and obedience.

permissive parenting Parenting style emphasizing self-expression and self-regulation.

authoritative parenting Parenting style blending warmth and respect for a child's individuality with an effort to instill social values.

Why does authoritative parenting tend to enhance children's social competence? It may be because authoritative parents set sensible expectations and realistic standards. By making clear, consistent rules, they let children know what is expected of them and give them a standard of behavior by which to judge themselves. In authoritarian homes, children are so strictly controlled that often they cannot make independent choices about their behavior; in permissive homes, children receive so little guidance that they may be uncertain and anxious about whether they are doing the right thing. In authoritative homes, children know when they are meeting expectations and can decide whether it is worth risking parental displeasure to pursue a goal. These children are expected to perform well, fulfill commitments, and participate actively in family duties as well as in family fun. They know the satisfaction of accepting responsibilities and achieving success. Parents who make reasonable demands show that they believe their children can meet them—and that they care enough to insist that their children do so.

When conflict arises, an authoritative parent can teach children positive ways to communicate their point of view and negotiate acceptable alternatives ("If you don't want to throw away those rocks you found, where do you think we should keep them?"). Internalization of this broader set of skills, not just of specific behavioral demands, may well be a key to the success of authoritative parenting (Grusec & Goodnow, 1994).

Support and Criticisms of Baumrind's Model

In research based on Baumrind's work, the superiority of authoritative parenting (or similar conceptions of parenting style) has repeatedly been supported. Identifying and promoting positive parenting practices is crucial to preventing early-onset problem behavior (Dishion & Stormshak, 2007). In a longitudinal study of 585 ethnically and socioeconomically diverse families in Tennessee and Indiana with children from prekindergarten through Grade 6, four aspects of early supportive parenting—warmth, use of inductive discipline, interest and involvement in children's contacts with peers, and proactive teaching of social skills—predicted positive behavioral, social, and academic outcomes (Pettit et al., 1997). Families at high-risk for problem behavior in children who participated in a "Family Check Up" program that provided critical parenting support services were able to improve childhood outcomes by an early focus on positive and proactive parenting practices (Dishion et al., 2008).

Still, Baumrind's model has provoked controversy because it seems to suggest that there is one "right" way to raise children. Also, because Baumrind's findings are correlational, they merely establish associations between each parenting style and a particular set of child behaviors. They do not show that different styles of child rearing *cause* children to be more or less competent. It is also impossible to know whether the children Baumrind studied were, in fact, raised in a particular style. It may be that some of the better-adjusted children were raised inconsistently, but by the time of the study their parents had adopted the authoritative pattern (Holden & Miller, 1999). In addition, Baumrind did not consider innate factors, such as temperament, that might have affected children's competence and exerted an influence on the parents. Children may elicit parenting styles based on their own behavior; an easy child might, for example, elicit authoritarian parenting.

Cultural Differences in Parenting Styles

Another concern is that Baumrind's categories reflect the dominant North American view of child development and may not apply to some other cultures or socioeconomic groups. Among Asian Americans, obedience and strictness are not associated with harshness and domination but instead with caring, concern, involvement, and maintenance of family harmony. Traditional Chinese culture, with its emphasis on respect for elders, stresses adults' responsibility to maintain the social order by teaching children socially proper behavior. This obligation is carried out through firm and just control and governance of the child, and even by physical punishment if necessary (Zhao, 2002). Although Asian American parenting is frequently described as authoritarian, the warmth and supportiveness that characterize Chinese American family relationships may more closely resemble Baumrind's authoritative parenting but without the emphasis on the American values of individuality, choice, and freedom (Chao, 1994) and with stricter parental control (Chao, 2001).

Indeed, a dichotomy between the individualistic values of Western parenting and the collectivist values of Asian parenting may be overly simplistic. In interviews with 64 Japanese mothers of 3- to 6-year-olds (Yamada, 2004), the mothers' descriptions of their parenting practices reflected the search for a balance between granting appropriate autonomy and exercising disciplinary control. The mothers let children make their own decisions within what they saw as the child's personal domain, such as play activities, playmates, and clothing, and this domain enlarged with the child's age. When health, safety, moral issues, or conventional social rules were involved, the mothers set limits or exercised control. When conflicts arose, the mothers used reason rather than power-assertive methods or sometimes gave in to the child, apparently on the theory that the issue wasn't worth struggling over—or that the child might be right after all.

Neighborhood Effects on Parenting Styles

Increasing evidence has shown links between children's neighborhoods and their developmental outcomes (Brooks-Gunn, Duncan, Leventhal, & Aber, 1997; Goering & Feins, 2003). A recent longitudinal study of Canadian children found that residence in poor, disorganized neighborhoods led to more maternal depression and family dysfunction, which was linked to less consistent and more punitive parenting styles. The less supportive environment of these types of neighborhoods and the lack of cohesion among residents places higher demands on parents to oversee and protect their children. These neighborhoods have fewer positive role models and fewer institutional resources to support families. (Kohen, Leventhal, Dahinten, & McIntosh, 2008).

Special Behavioral Concerns

Three specific issues of special concern to parents, caregivers, and teachers of preschool children are how to promote altruism, curb aggression, and deal with fears that often arise at this age.

Prosocial Behavior

Alex, at 3½, responded to two preschool classmates' complaints that they did not have enough modeling clay, his favorite plaything, by giving them half of his. Alex was showing **altruism:** motivation to help another person with no expectation of reward. Altruistic acts like Alex's often entail cost, self-sacrifice, or risk. Altruism is at the heart of **prosocial behavior,** voluntary activity intended to benefit another.

Even before the second birthday, children often help others, share belongings and food, and offer comfort. Cooperative behavior analysis has revealed three preferences for sharing resources; a preference to share with close relations, reciprocity (a preference to share with people who have shared with you), and indirect reciprocity (a preference to share with people who share with others). In a set of experiments on 3½-year-old children, researchers were able to demonstrate that these preferences are present and functional in young children (Olson & Spelke, 2008).

Is there a prosocial personality or disposition? A longitudinal study that followed 32 4- and 5-year-olds into early adulthood suggests that there is and that it emerges early and remains somewhat consistent throughout life. Preschoolers who were sympathetic and spontaneously shared with classmates tended to show prosocial understanding and empathic behavior as much as 17 years later. Preschoolers who are shy or withdrawn tend to be less prosocial, perhaps because they hesitate to reach out to others (Coplan et al., 2004).

Genes and environment each contribute to individual differences in prosocial behavior, an example of gene—environment correlation. This finding comes from a study of 9,319 twin pairs whose prosocial behavior was rated by parents and teachers at ages 3, 4, and 7.

Checkpoint ✓

Can you . . .

✔ Describe and evaluate Baumrind's model of parenting styles?

✔ Discuss how parents' ways of resolving conflicts with young children can contribute to the success of authoritative child rearing?

✔ Discuss criticisms of Baumrind's model and cultural variations in parenting styles?

Guidepost 5

Why do young children help or hurt others, and why do they develop fears?

altruism Motivation to help others without expectation of reward; may involve self-denial or self-sacrifice.

prosocial behavior Any voluntary behavior intended to help others.

Children given responsibilities at home tend to develop prosocial qualities, such as cooperation and helpfulness. This 3-year-old boy, who is learning to cook, is likely to have caring relationships with people as well.

What's your view ❓

- In a society in which "good Samaritans" are sometimes blamed for "butting into other people's business" and are sometimes attacked by the very persons they try to help, is it wise to encourage children to offer help to strangers?

instrumental aggression
Aggressive behavior used as a means of achieving a goal.

overt (direct) aggression
Aggression that is openly directed at its target.

relational (indirect or social) aggression Aggression aimed at damaging or interfering with another person's relationships, reputation, or psychological well-being; can be overt or covert.

Parents who showed affection and followed positive (inductive) disciplinary strategies tended to encourage their children's natural tendency to prosocial behavior (Knafo & Plomin, 2006). Parents of prosocial children typically are prosocial themselves. They point out models of prosocial behavior and steer children toward stories, films, and television programs that depict cooperation, sharing, and empathy and encourage sympathy, generosity, and helpfulness (Singer & Singer, 1998). Media exposure to educational and youth-oriented programs has been shown to have prosocial effects by increasing children's altruism, cooperation, and even tolerance for others (Wilson, 2008). Relationships with siblings provide an important laboratory for trying out caring behavior and learning to see another person's point of view. Peers and teachers also can model and reinforce prosocial behavior (Eisenberg, 1992; Eisenberg & Fabes, 1998).

Cultures vary in the degree to which they foster prosocial behavior. Traditional cultures in which people live in extended family groups and share work seem to foster prosocial values more than cultures that stress individual achievement (Eisenberg & Fabes, 1998).

Aggression

When Noah roughly snatches a ball away from Jake, he is interested only in getting the ball, not in hurting or dominating Jake. This is **instrumental aggression,** or aggression used as an instrument to reach a goal—the most common type in early childhood. Between ages 2½ and 5, children commonly struggle over toys and control of space. Instrumental aggression surfaces mostly during social play; children who fight the most also tend to be the most sociable and competent. In fact, the ability to show some instrumental aggression may be a necessary step in psychosocial development.

As children develop more self-control and become better able to express themselves verbally, they typically shift from showing aggression with blows to doing it with words (Coie & Dodge, 1998). However, individual differences remain. In a longitudinal study of 383 preschoolers, 11 percent of the girls and 9 percent of the boys showed high levels of aggression between ages 2 and 5. Boys and girls who were inattentive at age 2, and girls who showed poor emotion regulation at that age, tended to have conduct problems at age 5 (Hill, Degan, Calkins, & Keane, 2006). Children who, as preschoolers, often engage in violent fantasy play may, at age 6, be prone to violent displays of anger (Dunn & Hughes, 2001).

Gender Differences in Aggression

Aggression is an exception to the generalization that boys and girls are more similar than different (Hyde, 2005). In all cultures studied, as among most mammals, boys are more physically and verbally aggressive than girls. This gender difference is apparent by age 2 (Archer, 2004; Baillargeon et al., 2007; Pellegrini & Archer, 2005). Research with genetically engineered mice suggests that the Sry gene on the Y chromosome may play a role (Gatewood et al., 2006).

However, girls may be more aggressive than they seem (McNeilly-Choque, Hart, Robinson, Nelson, & Olsen, 1996; Putallaz & Bierman, 2004). Whereas boys engage in more **overt (direct) aggression**—physical or verbal aggression openly directed at its target—girls, especially as they grow older, are more likely to engage in **relational (indirect or social) aggression.** This more subtle kind of aggression consists of damaging or interfering with relationships, reputation, or psychological well-being, often through teasing, manipulation, ostracism, or bids for control. It may include spreading rumors, name-calling, put-downs, or excluding someone from a group. It can be either overt or covert (indirect)—for example, making mean faces or ignoring someone.

Among preschoolers, it tends to be direct and face-to-face ("You can't come to my party if you don't give me that toy") (Archer, 2004; Brendgen et al., 2005; Crick, Casas, & Nelson, 2002).

From an evolutionary perspective, boys' greater overt aggressiveness, like their greater size and strength, may prepare them to compete for a mate (Archer, 2004). Males produce many sperm; females generally produce only one ovum at a time. Males seek to mate as frequently and widely as possible, and they have less investment in each individual offspring; thus they can afford to take the risks of physical aggression. Females are strongly motivated to protect and nurture the few offspring they have; thus they shy away from direct confrontations that could put them at physical risk (Pellegrini & Archer, 2005).

Influences on Aggression

Why are some children more aggressive than others? Temperament may play a part. Children who are intensely emotional and low in self-control tend to express anger aggressively (Eisenberg, Fabes, Nyman, Bernzweig, & Pinuelas, 1994).

Both physical and social aggression have genetic and environmental sources, but their relative influence differs. Among 234 6-year-old twins, physical aggression was 50 to 60 percent heritable; the remainder of the variance was attributable to nonshared environmental influences (unique experiences). Social aggression was much more environmentally influenced; the variance was only 20 percent genetic, 20 percent explained by shared environmental influences, and 60 percent by unshared experiences (Brendgen et al., 2005).

Parental behaviors strongly influence aggressiveness. In one study, 5-year-old boys who had been exposed prenatally to cocaine and who lived in poor, unstable, or stressful environments with single mothers tended to be high in aggressive behavior, such as fighting and bullying (Bendersky, Bennett, & Lewis, 2006). In several longitudinal studies, insecure attachment and lack of maternal warmth and affection in infancy predicted aggressiveness in early childhood (Coie & Dodge, 1998; MacKinnon-Lewis, Starnes, Volling, & Johnson, 1997). Manipulative behaviors such as withdrawal of love and making a child feel guilty or ashamed may foster social aggression (Brendgen et al., 2005).

Aggressiveness may result from a combination of a stressful and unstimulating home atmosphere, harsh discipline, lack of maternal warmth and social support, exposure to aggressive adults and neighborhood violence, and transient peer groups, which prevent stable friendships (Dodge, Pettit, & Bates, 1994; Grusec & Goodnow, 1994). In a study of 431 Head Start participants in an inner-city neighborhood, parents reported that more than half had witnessed gang activity, drug trafficking, police pursuits and arrests, or people carrying weapons, and some of the children and families had been victimized themselves. These children showed symptoms of distress at home and aggressive behavior at school (Farver, Xu, Eppe, Fernandez, & Schwartz, 2005).

Why does witnessing violence lead to aggression? In a classic social learning experiment (Bandura, Ross, & Ross, 1961), 3- to 6-year-olds individually watched films of adult models playing with toys. Children in one experimental group saw the adult model play quietly. The model for a second experimental group spent most of the 10-minute session punching, throwing, and kicking a life-size inflated doll. A control group did not see any model. After the sessions, the children, who were mildly frustrated by seeing toys they were not allowed to play with, went into another playroom. The children who had seen the aggressive model acted much more aggressively than those in the other groups, imitating many of the same things they had seen the model say and do. The children who had seen the quiet model were less aggressive than the control group. This finding suggests that parents may be able to moderate the effects of frustration by modeling nonaggressive behavior.

In a classic experiment by Albert Bandura, children who had seen a film of an adult hitting and kicking an inflated clown were more likely to imitate the aggressive behavior if they had seen the adult being rewarded or experiencing no consequences than if they had seen the adult being punished.

Electronic media including television, movies, and video games have enormous power for modeling either prosocial behavior or aggression. In Chapter 14 we discuss the influence of media violence on aggressive behavior.

Table 11-4	Childhood Fears
Age	**Fears**
0–6 months	Loss of support; loud noises
7–12 months	Strangers; heights; sudden, unexpected, and looming objects
1 year	Separation from parent; toilet; injury; strangers
2 years	Many stimuli, including loud noises (vacuum cleaners, sirens and alarms, trucks, and thunder), animals, dark rooms, separation from parent, large objects or machines, changes in personal environment, unfamiliar peers
3 years	Masks; dark; animals; separation from parent
4 years	Separation from parent; animals; dark; noises (including noises at night)
5 years	Animals; "bad" people; dark; separation from parent; bodily harm
6 years	Supernatural beings (e.g., ghosts, witches); bodily injury; thunder and lightning; dark; sleeping or staying alone; separation from parent
7–8 years	Supernatural beings; dark; media events (e.g., news reports on the threat of nuclear war or child kidnapping); staying alone; bodily injury
9–12 years	Tests and examinations in school; school performances; bodily injury; physical appearance; thunder and lightning; death; dark

Source: From Morris, R. J. & Kratochwill, T. R. *Treating Children's Fears and Phobias: A Behavioral Approach,* Allyn and Bacon, Boston, MA. Copyright © 1983 by Pearson Education. Reprinted by permission of the publisher.

Culture and Aggression

How much influence does culture have on aggressive behavior? One research team asked closely matched samples of 30 Japanese and 30 U.S. middle- to upper-middle-class preschoolers to choose pictured solutions to hypothetical conflicts or stressful situations (such as having one's block tower knocked down, having to stop playing and go to bed, being hit, hearing parents argue, or fighting on a jungle gym). The children also were asked to act out such situations using dolls and props. The U.S. children showed more anger, more aggressive behavior and language, and less emotional control than the Japanese children (Zahn-Waxler, Friedman, Cole, Mizuta, & Hiruma, 1996).

These results are consistent with child-rearing values in the two cultures. In Japan, anger and aggression contradict the cultural emphasis on harmony. Japanese mothers are more likely than U.S. mothers to use inductive discipline, pointing out how aggressive behavior hurts others. Japanese mothers show strong disappointment when children fail to meet behavioral standards. However, the cross-cultural difference in children's anger and aggressiveness was significant even apart from mothers' behavior, suggesting that temperament differences also may have been at work (Zahn-Waxler et al., 1996).

What's your view ?

• Are there situations in which a child should be encouraged to be aggressive?

Fearfulness

Passing fears are common in early childhood and are tied to cognitive development. Many 2- to 4-year-olds are afraid of the unfamiliar—strangers, animals, and loud noises. By age 6, children are more likely to be afraid of the dark and imaginary creatures (DuPont, 1983; Stevenson-Hinde & Shouldice, 1996). Eventually fears of imaginery things disappear as children grow older.

Young children's fears stem largely from their intense fantasy life and their tendency to confuse appearance with reality. Sometimes their imaginations get carried away, and they worry about being attacked by a lion or being abandoned. Also, they are more likely to be frightened by something that looks scary, such as a cartoon monster, than by something capable of doing great harm, such as a nuclear explosion (Cantor, 1994). For the most part, older children's fears are more realistic and self-evaluative (for example, fear of failing a test) (Stevenson-Hinde & Shouldice, 1996; Table 11-4).

Fears may stem from personal experience or from hearing about other people's experiences (Muris, Merckelbach, & Collaris, 1997). A preschooler whose mother is sick in bed may become upset by a story about a mother's death, even the death of an animal mother. Often fears result from appraisals of danger, such as the likelihood of being bitten by a dog, or are triggered by events, such as when a child who was hit by a car becomes afraid to cross the street. Children who have lived through an earthquake, a kidnapping, or some other frightening event may fear that it will happen again (Kolbert, 1994).

Parents can allay children's fears by instilling a sense of trust and normal caution without being too protective—and also by overcoming their own unrealistic fears. They can reassure a fearful child and encourage open expression of feelings. Ridicule ("Don't be such a baby!"), coercion ("Pat the nice doggie—it won't hurt you"), and logical persuasion ("The closest bear is 20 miles away, locked in a zoo!") are not helpful. Not until elementary school can children tell themselves that what they fear is not real (Cantor, 1994).

Relationships with Other Children

Although the most important people in young children's world are the adults who take care of them, relationships with siblings and playmates become more important in early childhood. Virtually every characteristic activity and personality issue of this age, from gender development to prosocial or aggressive behavior, involves other children.

Let's look first at sibling relationships and then at children who grow up with no siblings. Then we will explore relationships with peers and friends.

Sibling Relationships

"It's mine!"
"No, it's mine!"
"Well, I was playing with it first!"

The earliest, most frequent, and most intense disputes among siblings are over property rights—who owns a toy or who is entitled to play with it. Although exasperated adults may not always see it that way, sibling disputes and their settlement can be viewed as socialization opportunities, in which children learn to stand up for principles and negotiate disagreements (Ross, 1996). Joint dramatic play is another arena for socialization. Siblings who frequently play "let's pretend" develop a history of shared understandings that allow them to more easily resolve issues and build on each other's ideas (Howe, Petrakos, Pinaldi, & LeFebvre, 2005).

Despite the frequency of conflict, sibling rivalry is not the main pattern between brothers and sisters early in life. Although some rivalry exists, so do affection, interest, companionship, and influence. Observations spanning 3½ years that began when younger siblings were about age 1½ and older siblings ranged from 3 to 4½ found prosocial and play-oriented behaviors to be more common than rivalry, hostility, and competition (Abramovitch, Corter, & Lando, 1979; Abramovitch, Corter, Pepler, & Stanhope, 1986; Abramovitch, Pepler, & Corter, 1982). Older siblings initiated more behavior, both friendly and unfriendly; younger siblings tended to imitate the older siblings. As the younger children reached age 5, the siblings became less physical and more verbal, both in showing aggression and in showing care and affection.

At least one finding of this research has been replicated in many studies: Same-sex siblings, particularly girls, are closer and play together more peaceably than boy-girl siblings (Kier & Lewis, 1998). Because older siblings tend to dominate younger siblings, the quality of the relationship is more affected by the emotional and social adjustment of the older child (Pike, Coldwell, & Dunn, 2005).

The quality of sibling relationships tends to carry over to relationships with other children. A child who is aggressive with siblings is likely to be aggressive with friends as well (Abramovitch et al., 1986). Siblings who frequently play amicably together tend to develop prosocial behaviors (Pike et al., 2005).

Likewise, friendships can influence sibling relationships. Older siblings who have experienced a good relationship with a friend before the birth of a new sibling are likely to treat their younger siblings better and are less likely to develop antisocial behavior in adolescence (Kramer & Kowal, 2005). For a young child at risk for behavioral problems,

Checkpoint

Can you . . .

✔ Discuss influences that contribute to altruism, aggression, and fearfulness?

 Guidepost 6

How do young children get along with—or without—siblings, playmates, and friends?

Checkpoint

Can you . . .

✔ Explain how the resolution of sibling disputes contributes to socialization?

✔ Tell how birth order and gender affect typical patterns of sibling interaction?

a positive relationship with *either* a sibling or a friend can buffer the effect of a negative relationship with the other (McElwain & Volling, 2005).

The Only Child

In the United States, 21 percent of children under 18 have no siblings in the home (Kreider & Fields, 2005). Are only children spoiled, selfish, lonely, or maladjusted? An analysis of 115 studies found that "onlies" do comparatively well. In occupational and educational achievement and verbal intelligence, they perform slightly better than children with siblings. Only children tend to be more motivated to achieve and to have slightly higher self-esteem; and they do not differ in emotional adjustment, sociability, or popularity. Perhaps these children do better because, consistent with evolutionary theory, parents, who have limited time and resources to spend, focus more attention on only children, talk to them more, do more with them, and expect more of them than do parents with more than one child (Falbo, 2006; Falbo & Polit, 1986; Polit & Falbo, 1987). And, because most children today spend considerable time in play groups, child care, and preschool, only children do not lack opportunities for social interaction with peers (Falbo, 2006).

Research in China also has produced largely encouraging findings about only children. In 1979, to control an exploding population, the People's Republic of China established a controversial official policy of limiting families to one child. Although the policy has since been relaxed somewhat, most urban families now have only one child, and most rural families no more than two (Hesketh, Lu, & Xing, 2005). Thus, in many Chinese cities, schoolrooms are almost completely filled with children who have no brothers or sisters. This situation offered researchers a natural experiment: an opportunity to study the adjustment of large numbers of only children.

A review of the literature found no significant differences in behavioral problems (Tao, 1998). Indeed, only children seemed to be at a distinct psychological advantage in a society that favors and rewards such a child. Among 731 urban children and adolescents, those with siblings reported higher levels of fear, anxiety, and depression than only children, regardless of sex or age (Yang, Ollendick, Dong, Xia, & Lin, 1995).

Among 4,000 third and sixth graders, personality differences between only children and those with siblings—as rated by parents, teachers, peers, and the children themselves—were few. Only children's academic achievement and physical growth were about the same as, or better than, those with siblings (Falbo & Poston, 1993). In a randomized study in Beijing first-grade classrooms (Jiao, Ji, & Jing, 1996), only children outperformed class-mates with siblings in memory, language, and mathematics skills. This finding may reflect the greater attention, stimulation, hopes, and expectations that parents shower on a child they know will be their first and last.

Most of the studies used urban samples. Further research may reveal whether the findings hold up in rural areas and small towns, where children with siblings are more numerous, and whether only children maintain their cognitive superiority as they move through school.

Checkpoint

Can you . . .

✔ Compare development of only children with that of children with siblings?

Playmates and Friends

Friendships develop as people develop. Toddlers play alongside or near each other, but not until about age 3 do children begin to have what we could consider friends. The ability to relate to peers in groups, as opposed to one-on-one relationships, is a major transition that takes place in the preschool years (Hay, Payne, & Chadwick, 2004). Through friendships and interactions with casual playmates, young children learn how to get along with others. They learn that being a friend is the way to have a friend. They learn how to solve problems in relationships, they learn how to put themselves in another person's place, and they see models of various kinds of behavior. They learn moral values and gender-role norms, and they practice adult roles.

Preschoolers usually like to play with children of their own age and sex, and who are similar to them in observable characteristics. Children who have frequent positive experiences with each other are most likely to become friends (Rubin et al., 1998;

Snyder, West, Stockemer, Gibbons, & Almquist-Parks, 1996). About 3 out of 4 preschoolers have such mutual friendships (Hartup & Stevens, 1999). Friendships are more satisfying—and more likely to last—when children see them as relatively harmonious and as validating their self-worth. Being able to confide in friends and get help from them is less important at this age than when children get older (Ladd, Kochenderfer, & Coleman, 1996).

The traits that young children look for in a playmate are similar to the traits they look for in a friend (Hart, DeWolf, Wozniak, & Burts, 1992). In one study, 4- to 7-year-olds rated the most important features of friendships as doing things together, liking and caring for each other, sharing and helping one another, and, to a lesser degree, living nearby or going to the same school. Younger children rated physical traits, such as appearance and size, higher than did older children, and they rated affection and support lower (Furman & Bierman, 1983).

Young children learn the importance of *being* a friend in order to *have* a friend. One way of being a friend is for a sighted child to help a blind playmate enjoy the feel of the sand and the sound of the surf.

Preschool children prefer prosocial playmates (Hart et al., 1992). They reject disruptive, demanding, intrusive, or aggressive children and tend to ignore those who are withdrawn, or tentative (Ramsey & Lasquade, 1996; Roopnarine & Honig, 1985).

Well-liked preschoolers and kindergartners and those who are rated by parents and teachers as socially competent generally cope well with anger. They respond directly in ways that minimize further conflict and keep relationships going. They avoid insults and threats. Unpopular children tend to hit, hit back, or tattle (Fabes & Eisenberg, 1992).

Peer relationships are affected by children's relationships with parents (Kerns & Barth, 1995), siblings (Herrera & Dunn, 1997), and teachers (Howes, Matheeson, & Hamilton, 1994). Parenting styles and practices can influence peer relationships. Popular children generally have warm, positive relationships with both mother and father. The parents are likely to be authoritative and the children to be both assertive and cooperative (Coplan et al., 2004; Isley, O'Neil, & Parke, 1996; Kochanska, 1992; Roopnarine & Honig, 1985).

Chapter 4
Middle Childhood

Middle Childhood is characterized by a very life changing event – school. As children spend less time with their caregivers and more time with teachers and peers, their world literally changes. We'll look at the many changes taking place in the context of the life stage models we introduced last chapter and discuss the shifting focus from family to friends.

PHYSICAL CHANGES IN MIDDLE CHILDHOOD

Changes in height and weight are not the only noticeable physical differences in middle childhood. Recent research (Bjorklund, 2000; Case, 1998; Dawson & Fischer, 1995) testifies to the advances made in the cognitive neurosciences. For example, Kurt Fischer, a cognitive psychologist at the Harvard Graduate School of Education, believes that he has found evidence of at least 12 brain growth spurts between birth and 21 years of age. Two of these (7 years, 11 years) fall within the middle childhood period (Fischer & Rose, 1994). Whether it's learning to walk, talk, read, or make new friends, the brain is ready to supply a child with all of the neural firepower needed to be successful. Note in Figure 11.1 the increase in working memory.

The task of those adults who are around children during these electrifying times is to provide the appropriate stimulation that will make them want to participate in this enticing world, thereby adding new connections and strengthening those already present. You can see a good example of this in John Fitzgerald's (2000) fascinating children's story "The Great Brain."

Now, we return to those missing 100 million neurons we mentioned in our previous discussion of brain development. Nature has manufactured billions of brain cells more than will be needed to ensure that the brain will be able to form enough connections for all the needed abilities and skills that demand new connections. Those neurons that *don't*

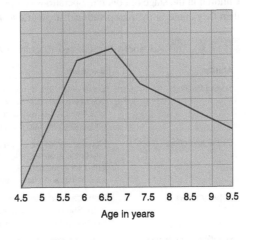

FIGURE 11.1
Increases in working memory.

make connections simply die. Also, and this may surprise some readers, this exercise in survival (some connections die, some connections survive) continues throughout our lives. You may also recall Darwin's famous belief in the survival of the fittest: The fittest of our neurons are those that make connections and survive. So the lesson here is not only for our children, but also for all of us: Keep busy, seek challenges, stay alert.

Body proportion changes in middle childhood also. Head size comes more in line with body size. Whereas an adult's head size is estimated to be about one-seventh of total body size, the preschooler's is about one-fourth. This difference gradually decreases during the middle childhood years. Also, the loss of baby teeth and the emergence of permanent teeth change the shape of the lower jaw. By the end of the middle childhood period, the youngster's body is more in proportion and is more like an adult's.

Changes in arms, legs, and trunk size also occur. The trunk becomes thinner and longer, and the chest becomes broader and flatter. Arms and legs begin to stretch but, as yet, show little sign of muscle development. Hands and feet grow more slowly than arms and legs, which helps to explain some of the awkwardness we see during these years. Children are tremendously active physically and gradually display a steady improvement in motor coordination (Tanner, 1989). Unhappily, all children are not so fortunate.

Guideposts for Study

1. How do school-age children's thinking and moral reasoning differ from those of younger children?
2. What advances in information-processing skills occur during middle childhood?
3. How accurately can schoolchildren's intelligence be measured?
4. How do communicative abilities expand during middle childhood?
5. What factors influence school achievement?
6. How do schools meet special needs?

Guidepost 1

How do school-age children's thinking and moral reasoning differ from those of younger children?

concrete operations The third stage of Piagetian cognitive development (approximately from age 7 to 12), during which children develop logical but not abstract thinking.

Piagetian Approach:
The Concrete Operational Child

At about age 7, according to Piaget, children enter the stage of **concrete operations** and begin to use mental operations to solve concrete (actual) problems. Children now can think logically because they can take multiple aspects of a situation into account. However, their thinking is still limited to real situations in the here and now.

Cognitive Advances

Children in the stage of concrete operations can perform many tasks at a much higher level than they could in the preoperational stage (Table 13-1). They have a better understanding

Table 13-1	Advances in Selected Cognitive Abilities during Middle Childhood
Ability	**Example**
Spatial thinking	Danielle can use a map or model to help her search for a hidden object and can give someone else directions for finding the object. She can find her way to and from school, can estimate distances, and can judge how long it will take her to go from one place to another.
Cause and effect	Douglas knows which physical attributes of objects on each side of a balance scale will affect the result (i.e., number of objects matters but color does not). He does not yet know which spatial factors, such as position and placement of the objects, make a difference.
Categorization	Elena can sort objects into categories, such as shape, color, or both. She knows that a subclass (roses) has fewer members than the class of which it is a part (flowers).
Seriation and transitive inference	Catherine can arrange a group of sticks in order, from the shortest to the longest, and can insert an intermediate-size stick into the proper place. She knows that if one stick is longer than a second stick, and the second stick is longer than a third, then the first stick is longer than the third.
Inductive and deductive reasoning	Dominic can solve both inductive and deductive problems and knows that inductive conclusions (based on particular premises) are less certain than deductive ones (based on general premises).
Conservation	Felipe, at age 7, knows that if a clay ball is rolled into a sausage, it still contains the same amount of clay (conservation of substance). At age 9, he knows that the ball and the sausage weigh the same. Not until early adolescence will he understand that they displace the same amount of liquid if dropped in a glass of water.
Number and mathematics	Kevin can count in his head, can add by counting up from the smaller number, and can do simple story problems.

of spatial concepts, causality, categorization, inductive and deductive reasoning, conservation, and number.

Spatial Relationships and Causality

Why can many 6- or 7-year-olds find their way to and from school, whereas most younger children cannot? One reason is that children in the stage of concrete operations can better understand spatial relationships. They have a clearer idea of how far it is from one place to another and how long it will take to get there, and they can more easily remember the route and the landmarks along the way. Experience plays a role in this development: A child who walks to school becomes more familiar with the neighborhood.

Both the ability to understand maps and models and the ability to communicate spatial information improve with age (Gauvain, 1993). So do judgments about cause and effect. When 5- to 12-year-olds were asked to predict how levers and balance scales would perform under varying conditions, the older children gave more correct answers. Children understood the influence of physical attributes (the number of objects on each side of a scale) earlier than they recognized the influence of spatial factors (the distance of objects from the center of the scale) (Amsel, Goodman, Savoie, & Clark, 1996).

Categorization

The ability to categorize helps children think logically. Categorization includes such relatively sophisticated abilities as *seriation, transitive inference,* and *class inclusion,* which improve gradually between early and middle childhood. Children show that they understand **seriation** when they can arrange objects in a series according to one or more dimensions, such as length (shortest to longest) or color (lightest to darkest). By 7 or 8, children can grasp the relationships among a group of sticks on sight and arrange them in order of size (Piaget, 1952).

seriation Ability to order items along a dimension.

Transitive inference is the ability to infer a relationship between two objects from the relationship between each of them and a third object (for example, if a > b, and b > c, then a > c). Catherine is shown three sticks: a yellow one, a green one, and a blue one. She is shown that the yellow stick is longer than the green one, and the green one is longer than the blue. Without physically comparing the yellow and blue sticks, she immediately says that the yellow one is longer than the blue one (Chapman & Lindenberger, 1988; Piaget & Inhelder, 1967).

transitive inference Understanding the relationship between two objects by knowing the relationship of each to a third object.

Class inclusion is the ability to see the relationship between a whole and its parts. Piaget (1964) showed preoperational children a bunch of 10 flowers—7 roses and 3 carnations—and asked whether there were more roses or more flowers. The children tended to say there were more roses because they were comparing the roses with the carnations rather than with the whole bunch. Not until age 7 or 8, and sometimes not even then, do children consistently reason that roses are a subclass of flowers and that, therefore, there cannot be more roses than flowers (Flavell, 1963; Flavell, Miller, & Miller, 2002). However, even 3-year-olds show a rudimentary awareness of class inclusion, depending on the type of task, the practical cues they receive, and their familiarity with the categories of objects they are tested on (Johnson, Scott, & Mervis, 1997).

class inclusion Understanding the relationship between a whole and its parts.

Inductive and Deductive Reasoning

According to Piaget, children in the stage of concrete operations use only **inductive reasoning.** Starting with observations about particular members of a class of people, animals, objects, or events, they draw general conclusions about the class as a whole. ("My dog barks. So does Terry's dog and Melissa's dog. So it looks as if all dogs bark.") Inductive conclusions must be tentative because it is always possible to come across new information (a dog that does not bark) that does not support the conclusion.

inductive reasoning Type of logical reasoning that moves from particular observations about members of a class to a general conclusion about that class.

Deductive reasoning, which Piaget believed does not develop until adolescence, starts with a general statement (premise) about a class and applies it to particular members of the class. If the premise is true of the whole class and the reasoning is sound, then the conclusion must be true: "All dogs bark. Spot is a dog. Spot barks."

deductive reasoning Type of logical reasoning that moves from a general premise about a class to a conclusion about a particular member or members of the class.

What's your view ?

• How can parents and teachers help children improve their reasoning ability?

Researchers gave 16 inductive and deductive problems to 16 kindergartners, 17 second graders, 16 fourth graders, and 17 sixth graders. The problems were designed so as to not call on knowledge of the real world. For example, one deductive problem was "All poggops wear blue boots. Tombor is a poggop. Does Tombor wear blue boots?" The corresponding inductive problem was "Tombor is a poggop. Tombor wears blue boots. Do all poggops wear blue boots?" Contrary to Piagetian theory, second graders (but not kindergartners) were able to answer both kinds of problems correctly (Galotti, Komatsu, & Voelz, 1997). Given age-appropriate testing methods, evidence of inductive and deductive reasoning is present considerably earlier than Piaget would have predicted.

Conservation

In solving various types of conservation problems, children in the stage of concrete operations can work out the answers in their heads; they do not have to measure or weigh objects. If one of two identical clay balls is rolled or kneaded into a different shape—say, a long, thin snake—Felipe, who is in the stage of concrete operations, will say that the ball and the snake still contain the same amount of clay. Stacy, who is in the preoperational stage, is deceived by appearances. She says the long, thin roll contains more clay because it looks longer.

Felipe, unlike Stacy, understands the principle of *identity:* he knows the clay is still the same clay even though it has a different shape. He also understands the principle of *reversibility:* he knows he can change the snake back into a ball. And he can *decenter:* he can focus on both length and width. He recognizes that although the ball is shorter than the snake, it is also thicker. Stacy centers on one dimension (length) while excluding the other (thickness).

Typically, children can solve problems involving conservation of substance, like this one, by about age 7 or 8. However, in tasks involving conservation of weight—in which they are asked, for example, whether the ball and the snake weigh the same—children typically do not give correct answers until about age 9 or 10. In tasks involving conservation of volume—in which children must judge whether the snake and the ball displace an equal amount of liquid when placed in a glass of water—correct answers are rare before age 12. Piaget's term for this inconsistency in the development of different types of conservation is **horizontal décalage.** Children's thinking at this stage is so concrete, so closely tied to a particular situation, that they cannot readily transfer what they have learned about one type of conservation to another type, even though the underlying principles are the same. Décalage occurs often enough that its implications on Piaget's theory must be considered. If human development truly occurs in stages, then all aspects of a particular domain should occur at the same time once the fundamental underlying skill is achieved. The fact that a child can reverse, decenter, or understand identity but cannot pass conservation tasks undermines the qualitative/stages aspect of Piaget's theory.

horizontal décalage Piaget's term for an inability to transfer learning about one type of conservation to other types, which causes a child to master different types of conservation tasks at different ages.

Number and Mathematics

By age 6 or 7, many children can count in their heads. They also learn to *count on:* to add 5 and 3, they start counting at 5 and then go on to 6, 7, and 8 to add the 3. It may take 2 or 3 more years for them to perform a comparable operation for subtraction, but by age 9 most children can either count up from the smaller number or down from the larger number to get the answer (Resnick, 1989).

Children also become more adept at solving simple story problems, such as "Pedro went to the store with $5 and spent $2 on candy. How much did he have left?" When the original amount is unknown ("Pedro went to the store, spent $2 and had $3 left. How much did he start out with?"), the problem is harder because the operation needed to solve it (addition) is not as clearly indicated. Few children can solve this kind of problem before age 8 or 9 (Resnick, 1989).

Research with minimally schooled people in developing countries suggests that children learn to add and subtract through concrete experience in a cultural context (Guberman, 1996; Resnick, 1989). These intuitive procedures are different from those taught in school. In a study of Brazilian street vendors ages 9 to 15, a researcher acting as a customer said, "I'll take two coconuts." Each one cost 40 cruzeiros; she paid with a 500-cruzeiros bill and asked, "What do I get back?" The child counted up from 80: "Eighty, 90, 100, . . ." and gave the customer 420 cruzeiros. However, when this same child was given a similar problem in the classroom ("What is 500 minus 80?"), he arrived at the wrong answer by incorrectly using a series of steps learned in school (Carraher, Schliemann, & Carraher, 1988). This observation suggests that teaching math through concrete applications may be more effective than teaching abstract rules.

Some intuitive understanding of fractions seems to exist by age 4, as children show when they distribute portions of pizza (Mix, Levine, & Huttenlocher, 1999; Sophian, Garyantes, & Chang, 1997). Young children tend not to think about the quantity a fraction represents; instead, they focus on the numerals that make it up. Thus, they may say that 1/2 plus 1/3 equals 2/5. Also difficult for many children to grasp at first is the fact that 1/2 is bigger than 1/4—that the smaller fraction (1/4) has the larger denominator (Siegler, 1998; Sophian & Wood, 1997).

The ability to estimate progresses with age. When asked to place 24 numbers along a line from 0 to 100, almost all kindergartners exaggerate the distances between low numbers and minimize the distances between high numbers. Most second graders produce number lines that are more evenly spaced (Siegler & Booth, 2004). Second, fourth, and sixth graders show a similar progression in producing number lines from 0 to 1,000 (Siegler & Opfer, 2003), most likely reflecting the experience older children gain in dealing with larger numbers. Besides improving in *number line estimation,* school-age children also improve in three other types of estimation: *computational estimation,* such as estimating the sum in an addition problem; *numerosity estimation,* such as estimating the number of candies in a jar; and *measurement estimation,* such as estimating the length of a line (Booth & Siegler, 2006).

Influences of Neurological Development and Schooling

Piaget maintained that the shift from the rigid, illogical thinking of younger children to the flexible, logical thinking of older children depends on both neurological development and experience in adapting to the environment. Support for a neurological influence comes from scalp measurements of brain activity during a conservation task. Children who had achieved conservation of volume had different brain wave patterns from those who had not yet achieved it, suggesting that they may have been using different brain regions for the task (Stauder, Molenaar, & Van der Molen, 1993).

Abilities such as conservation may depend in part on familiarity with the materials being manipulated; children can think more logically about things they know something about. Thus understanding of conservation may come, not only from new patterns of mental organization but also from culturally defined experience with the physical world.

Today's schoolchildren may not be advancing through Piaget's stages as rapidly as their parents did. When 10,000 British 11- and 12-year-olds were tested on conservation of volume and weight, their performance was 2 to 3 years behind that of their counterparts 30 years earlier (Shayer, Ginsburg, & Coe, 2007). These results suggest that today's schoolchildren may be getting too much drilling on the three Rs and not enough hands-on experience with the way materials behave.

Checkpoint

Can you . . .

✔ Identify six types of cognitive abilities that emerge or strengthen during middle childhood, and explain how?

✔ Name three principles that help school-aged children understand conservation, and explain why children master different kinds of conservation at different ages?

✔ Give examples of how neurological development can affect ability to perform Piagetian tasks?

Erikson's Approach

Industry Versus Inferiority

It is good to have experiences of success, but we all have limits, and there is a lot of competition. Starting around age 4, children begin comparing themselves to each other, especially those their own age, and many (although not all) develop a sense of competence and achievement. If people have enough success experiences, then they believe in their strength and abilities and assume that, if they just work hard enough, they can do most things they desire to do. This sense of industry—feeling as if they can work to achieve what they want—sets children on their way to being productive members of society. However, with enough failure experiences, children might develop a sense of inferiority, feeling that they don't have the talent or ability to get ahead in life.

industry versus inferiority
Erikson's fourth crisis of
psychosocial development, in which
children must learn the productive
skills their culture requires or else
face feelings of inferiority.

Self-Esteem

According to Erikson (1982), a major determinant of self-esteem is children's view of their capacity for productive work. This fourth stage of psychosocial development focuses on **industry versus inferiority.** Middle childhood is the time when children must learn skills valued in their society. Arapesh boys in New Guinea learn to make bows and arrows and to lay traps for rats; Arapesh girls learn to plant, weed, and harvest. Inuit children of Alaska learn to hunt and fish. Children in industrialized countries learn to read, write, do math, and use computers.

The virtue that follows successful resolution of this stage is *competence,* a view of the self as able to master skills and complete tasks. If children feel inadequate compared with their peers, they may retreat to the protective embrace of the family. If, on the other hand, they become too industrious, they may neglect social relationships and turn into workaholics.

The Child in the Peer Group

Guidepost 3

How do relationships with peers change in middle childhood, and what factors influence popularity and aggressive behavior?

In middle childhood the peer group comes into its own. Groups form naturally among children who live near one another or go to school together and often consist of children of the same racial or ethnic origin and similar socioeconomic status. Children who play together are usually close in age and of the same sex (Hartup, 1992; Pellegrini et al., 2002).

How does the peer group influence children? What determines their acceptance by peers and their ability to make friends?

Positive and Negative Effects of Peer Relations

Children benefit from doing things with peers. They develop skills needed for sociability and intimacy, and they gain a sense of belonging. They are motivated to achieve, and they attain a sense of identity. They learn leadership and communication skills, roles, and rules.

As children begin to move away from parental influence, the peer group opens new perspectives and frees them to make independent judgments. In comparing themselves with others their age, children can gauge their abilities more realistically and gain a clearer sense of self-efficacy. The peer group helps children learn how to get along in society—how to adjust their needs and desires to those of others, when to yield, and when to stand firm. The peer group offers emotional security. It is reassuring for children to find out that they are not alone in harboring thoughts that might offend an adult.

On the negative side, peer groups may reinforce **prejudice:** unfavorable attitudes toward "outsiders," especially members of certain racial or ethnic groups. Children tend to show biases toward children like themselves, but these biases, except for a preference for children of the same sex, diminish with age and cognitive development (Powlishta, Serbin, Doyle, & White, 1994). Prejudice and discrimination can do real damage. In a 5-year longitudinal study of 714 African American 10- to 12-year-olds, those who saw themselves as targets of discrimination tended to show symptoms of depression or conduct problems during the next 5 years (Brody et al., 2006). In a study of 253 English children, prejudice against refugees was reduced by *extended contact:* reading them stories about close friendships between English children and refugee children, followed by group discussions (Cameron, Rutland, Brown, & Douch, 2006).

The peer group also can foster antisocial tendencies. Preadolescent children are especially susceptible to pressure to conform. It is usually in the company of peers that some children shoplift and begin to use drugs (Hartup, 1992). Of course, some degree of conformity to group standards is healthy. It is unhealthy when it becomes destructive or prompts young people to act against their better judgment.

prejudice Unfavorable attitude
toward members of certain groups
outside one's own, especially racial
or ethnic groups.

What's your view ?

• How can parents and schools
reduce racial, religious, and
ethnic prejudice?

Gender Differences in Peer-Group Relationships

Boys' and girls' peer groups engage in different types of activities. Groups of boys more consistently pursue gender-typed activities. They play in large groups with well-defined leadership hierarchies and engage in more competitive and rough-and-tumble play. Girls have more intimate conversations characterized by prosocial interactions and shared confidences (Rose & Rudolph, 2006). Also, girls are more likely than boys to engage in cross-gender activities, such as team sports (McHale, Kim, Whiteman, & Crouter, 2004).

Boys are apt to receive less emotional support from their friends than girls do. Girls tend to seek social connections and are more sensitive to others' distress. They are more likely than boys to worry about their relationships, to express emotions, and to seek emotional support (Rose & Rudolph, 2006).

Why do children segregate themselves by sex and engage in such different activities? One obvious reason is that males and females differ in body size, strength, and energy. Boys need more space and more physical exercise to build physical fitness (Pellegrini & Archer, 2005). Same-sex peer groups help children learn gender-appropriate behaviors and incorporate gender roles into their self-concept. In a 2-year study of 106 ethnically diverse third through seventh graders, a sense of being typical of one's gender and being content with that gender contributed to self-esteem and well-being, whereas feeling pressure—from parents, peers, or oneself—to conform to gender stereotypes lessened well-being (Yunger et al., 2004).

Checkpoint ✔

Can you . . .

✔ Tell what characteristics members of a peer group tend to have in common?

✔ Identify positive and negative effects of peer groups?

✔ Discuss gender differences in peer-group activities and relationships?

Popularity

Popularity becomes more important in middle childhood. Schoolchildren whose peers like them are likely to be well adjusted as adolescents. Those who have trouble getting along with peers are more likely to develop psychological problems, drop out of school, or become delinquent (Hartup, 1992; Kupersmidt & Coie, 1990; Morison & Masten, 1991; Newcomb, Bukowski, & Pattee, 1993). Peer rejection has also been linked to lower levels of classroom participation (Ladd, Herald-Brown & Reiser, 2008).

Popularity can be measured in two ways, and the results may differ. Researchers measure *sociometric popularity* by asking children which peers they like most and least, and use the responses to construct a tally for each child of their positive and negative nominations. Such studies have identified five peer status groups: *popular* (youngsters who receive many positive nominations), *rejected* (those who receive many negative nominations), *neglected* (those who receive few nominations of either kind), *controversial* (those who receive many positive and many negative nominations), and *average* (those who do not receive an unusual number of nominations of either kind). *Perceived popularity* is measured by asking children which children are best liked by their peers.

Sociometrically popular children typically have good cognitive abilities, are high achievers, are good at solving social problems, help other children, and are assertive without being disruptive or aggressive. They are kind, trustworthy, cooperative, loyal, and self-disclosing and provide emotional support. Their superior social skills make others enjoy being with them (Cillessen & Mayeux, 2004; LaFontana & Cillessen, 2002; Masten & Coatsworth, 1998; Newcomb et al., 1993).

Children can be *un*popular (either rejected or neglected) for many reasons. Some unpopular children are aggressive; others are hyperactive, inattentive, or withdrawn (Dodge, Coie, Pettit, & Price, 1990; Masten & Coatsworth, 1998; Newcomb et al., 1993; Pope, Bierman, & Mumma, 1991). Still others act silly and immature or anxious and uncertain. Unpopular children are often insensitive to other children's feelings and do not adapt well to new situations (Bierman, Smoot, & Aumiller, 1993). Some unpopular children expect not to be liked, and this becomes a self-fulfilling prophecy (Rabiner & Coie, 1989).

It is often in the family that children acquire behaviors that affect popularity (Masten & Coatsworth, 1998). Authoritative parents tend to have more popular children than authoritarian parents (Dekovic & Janssens, 1992). Children of authoritarian parents who punish and threaten are likely to threaten or act mean with other children. They are less popular than children whose authoritative parents reason with them and try to help them understand how another person might feel (Hart, Ladd, & Burleson, 1990).

Culture can affect criteria for popularity. One study (Chen, Cen, Li, & He, 2005) points to effects of social change resulting from the radical restructuring of China's economic system, particularly since the late 1990s. During that time China shifted from a completely collectivist system in which the people as a whole, through their

Checkpoint ✔

Can you . . .

✔ Compare two measures of popularity?

✔ Describe characteristics of popular and unpopular children, and tell how they vary?

✔ Identify family and cultural influences on popularity?

government, owned all means of production and distribution, toward a more competitive, technologically advanced, market economy with private ownership and its associated individualist values. Researchers administered sociometric measures and peer assessments of social functioning to three cohorts of third and fourth graders in Shanghai schools in 1990, 1998, and 2002. A striking change emerged with regard to shyness and sensitivity. In the 1990 cohort, shy children were accepted by peers and were high in academic achievement, leadership, and teacher-rated competence. By 2002, the results were just the reverse: Shy children tended to be rejected by peers, to be depressed, and to be rated by teachers as low in competence. In the quasi-capitalist society that China has become, social assertiveness and initiative may be more highly appreciated and encouraged than in the past, and shyness and sensitivity may lead to social and psychological difficulties for children.

Friendship

Children may spend much of their free time in groups, but only as individuals do they form friendships. Popularity is the peer-group's opinion of a child, but friendship is a two-way street.

Children look for friends who are like them in age, sex, and interests. The strongest friendships involve equal commitment and mutual give-and-take. Though children tend to choose friends with similar ethic backgrounds, a recent study of 509 fourth graders showed that cross-racial/ethinic friendships were associated with positive developmental outcomes (Kawabata & Crick, 2008).

Unpopular children can make friends, but tend to have fewer friends than popular children and demonstrate a preference for younger friends, other unpopular children, or children in a different class or a different school (George & Hartmann, 1996; Hartup, 1992, 1996a, 1996b; Newcomb & Bagwell, 1995).

Children learn to communicate and cooperate with their friends. They help each other weather stressful situations, such as starting at a new school or adjusting to parents' divorce. The inevitable quarrels help children learn to resolve conflicts (Furman, 1982; Hartup, 1992, 1996a, 1996b; Hartup & Stevens, 1999; Newcomb & Bagwell, 1995). Friendship seems to help children feel good about themselves, though it's also likely that children who feel good about themselves have an easier time making friends.

Children's concepts of friendship and the ways they act with their friends change with age, reflecting cognitive and emotional growth. Preschool friends play together, but friendship among school-age children is deeper, more reciprocal and more stable. Children cannot be or have true friends until they achieve the cognitive maturity to consider other people's views and needs as well as their own (Hartup, 1992; Hartup & Stevens, 1999; Newcomb & Bagwell, 1995).

On the basis of interviews with more than 250 people between ages 3 and 45, Robert Selman (1980; Selman & Selman, 1979) traced changing conceptions of friendship through five overlapping stages (Table 14-2). He found that most school-age children are in stage 2 (reciprocal friendship based on self-interest), but some older children, ages 9 and up, may be in stage 3 (intimate, mutually shared relationships).

School-age children distinguish among "best friends," "good friends," and "casual friends" on the basis of intimacy and time spent together (Hartup & Stevens, 1999). Children this age typically have three to five "best" friends (Hartup, 1992; Hartup & Stevens, 1999). School-age girls seem to care less about having many friends than about having a few close friends they can rely on. Boys have more friendships, but they tend to be less intimate and affectionate (Furman, 1982; Furman & Buhrmester, 1985; Hartup & Stevens, 1999).

Checkpoint ✔

Can you . . .

✔ Distinguish between popularity and friendship?

✔ List characteristics children look for in friends?

✔ Tell how age and gender affect friendship?

Aggression and Bullying

Aggression declines and changes in form during the early school years. After age 6 or 7, most children become less aggressive as they grow less egocentric, more empathic, more cooperative, and better able to communicate. They can now put themselves in

Table 14-2	Selman's Stages of Friendship	
Stage	**Description**	**Example**
Stage 0: Momentary playmateship (ages 3 to 7)	On this *undifferentiated* level of friendship, children are egocentric and have trouble considering another person's point of view; they tend to think only about what they want from a relationship. Most very young children define their friends in terms of physical closeness and value them for material or physical attributes.	"She lives on my street" or "He has the Power Rangers."
Stage 1: One-way assistance (ages 4 to 9)	On this *unilateral* level, a "good friend" does what the child wants the friend to do.	"She's not my friend anymore because she wouldn't go with me when I wanted her to" or "He's my friend because he always says yes when I want to borrow his eraser."
Stage 2: Two-way fair-weather cooperation (ages 6 to 12)	This *reciprocal* level overlaps stage 1. It involves give-and-take but still serves many separate self-interests, rather than the common interests of the two friends.	"We are friends; we do things for each other" or "A friend is someone who plays with you when you don't have anybody else to play with."
Stage 3: Intimate, mutually shared relationships (ages 9 to 15)	On this *mutual* level, children view a friendship as having a life of its own. It is an ongoing, systematic, committed relationship that incorporates more than doing things for each other. Friends often become possessive and demand exclusivity.	"It takes a long time to make a close friend, so you really feel bad if you find out that your friend is trying to make other friends too."
Stage 4: Autonomous interdependence (beginning at age 12)	In this *interdependent* stage, children respect friends' needs for both dependency and autonomy.	"A good friendship is a real commitment, a risk you have to take; you have to support and trust and give, but you have to be able to let go too."

Source: Selman, 1980; Selman & Selman, 1979.

someone else's place, can understand another person's motives, and can find positive ways of asserting themselves. **Instrumental aggression** (aggression aimed at achieving an objective), the hallmark of the preschool period, becomes much less common (Coie & Dodge, 1998). However, as aggression declines overall, **hostile aggression**—action intended to hurt another person—proportionally increases (Coie & Dodge, 1998), often taking verbal rather than physical form (Pellegrini & Archer, 2005). Boys continue to engage in more *direct aggression*, and girls are increasingly more likely to engage in *social* or *indirect aggression.* A review of 148 studies of child and adolescent aggressive behavior, however, revealed neglible gender differences in levels of social or indirect aggression between boys and girls. These findings contradict the common portrayal of indirect agression as a predominantly female form of aggression (Card, Stucky, Sawalani, & Little, 2008).

A small minority of children do not learn to control physical aggression (Coie & Dodge, 1998). These children tend to have social and psychological problems, but it is not clear whether aggression causes these problems or is a response to them, or both (Crick & Grotpeter, 1995). Direct aggression has been linked to poor peer relations and low prosocial behavior (Card et al., 2008). Highly aggressive children often egg each other on to antisocial acts. Thus school-age boys who are physically aggressive may become juvenile delinquents in adolescence (Broidy et al., 2003).

Although aggressors tend to be personally disliked, physically aggressive boys and some relationally aggressive girls (those who, for example, talk behind another girl's back or exclude her socially) are perceived as among the most popular in the classroom (Cillessen & Mayeux, 2004; Rodkin, Farmer, Pearl, & Van Acker, 2000). In a study of peer-rejected fourth graders, aggressive boys tended to gain in social status by the end of fifth grade, suggesting that behavior shunned by younger children may be seen as cool or glamorous by preadolescents (Sandstrom & Coie, 1999). In a longitudinal study of a

instrumental aggression Aggressive behavior used as a means of achieving a goal.

hostile aggression Aggressive behavior intended to hurt another person.

multiethnic group of 905 urban fifth through ninth graders, physical aggression became less disapproved as children moved into adolescence, and relational aggression was increasingly reinforced by high status among peers (Cillessen & Mayeux, 2004).

Types of Aggression and Social Information Processing

What makes children act aggressively? One answer may lie in the way they process social information: what features of the social environment they pay attention to and how they interpret what they perceive (Crick & Dodge, 1994, 1996).

Instrumental, or *proactive,* aggressors view force and coercion as effective ways to get what they want. They act deliberately, not out of anger. In social learning terms, they are aggressive because they expect to be rewarded; and when they are rewarded, their belief in the effectiveness of aggression is reinforced (Crick & Dodge, 1996). In contrast, a child who is accidentally bumped in line may push back angrily, assuming that the other child bumped her on purpose. This is an example of *hostile,* or *reactive,* aggression. Such children often have a **hostile attribution bias;** they see other children as trying to hurt them, and they strike out in retaliation or self-defense (Crick & Dodge, 1996; de Castro, Veerman, Koops, Bosch, & Monshouwer, 2002; Waldman, 1996).

Children who seek dominance and control may react aggressively to threats to their status, which they may attribute to hostility (de Castro et al., 2002; Erdley et al., 1997). Being a boy, having a reactive temperament, parental separation, early onset of motherhood, and controlling parenting have all been shown to contribute to physical aggression in 6- to 12-year-olds (Joussemet et al., 2008). Rejected children and those exposed to harsh parenting also tend to have a hostile attribution bias (Coie & Dodge, 1998; Masten & Coatsworth, 1998; Weiss et al., 1992). Since people often do become hostile toward someone who acts aggressively toward them, a hostile bias may set in motion a cycle of aggression (de Castro et al., 2002). Hostile attribution bias becomes more common between ages 6 and 12 (Aber, Brown, & Jones, 2003).

Aggressors need to alter the way they process social information so that they do not interpret aggression as either useful or justified. Adults can help children curb aggression by teaching them how to recognize when they are getting angry and how to control their anger. In a New York City school study, children exposed to a conflict resolution curriculum that involved discussions and group role-playing showed less hostile attribution bias, less aggression, fewer behavior problems, and more effective responses to social situations than children who did not participate in the program (Aber et al., 2003).

Does Media Violence Stimulate Aggression?

As television, movies, video games, cell phones and computers take on larger roles in children's daily lives, it is critical to understand the impact mass media has on children's behavior. Children spend more time on entertainment media than on any other activity besides school and sleeping. On average, children spend about 4 hours a day in front of a television or computer screen—some much more than that (Anderson et al., 2003).

Violence is prevalent in U.S. media. About 6 out of 10 television programs portray violence, usually glamorized, glorified, or trivialized (Yokota & Thompson, 2000). In addition the 24-hour news stations provide constant, repetitive coverage of natural disasters and violent acts. Music videos disproportionately feature violence against women and blacks. The motion picture, music, and video game industries aggressively market violent, adult-rated products to children (AAP Committee on Public Education, 2001). In a recent study of U.S. children, 40 movies that were rated R for violence were seen by a median of 12.5 percent of an estimated 22 million children aged 10 to 14. The most popular movie, *Scary Movie,* was seen by over 10 million children (Worth et al., 2008).

Because of the significant amount of time that children spend interacting with media, the images they see can become primary role models and sources of information about how people behave. Evidence from research conducted over the past 50 years on exposure to violence on TV, movies, and video games supports a *causal* relationship between media violence and violent behavior on the viewer's part (Huesmann, 2007).

hostile attribution bias Tendency for individuals to perceive others as trying to hurt them and to strike out in retaliation or self-defense.

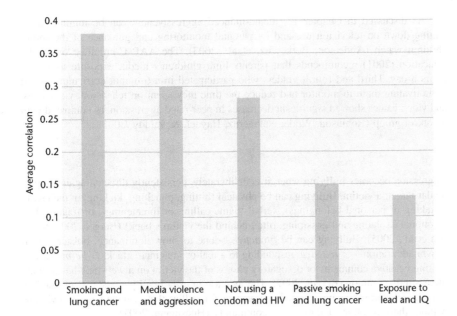

Figure 14-3
The effect of media violence is the same or greater than the effect of many other recognized threats to public health.
Source: Bushman & Huesmann, 2001.

Although the strongest single correlate of violent behavior is previous exposure to violence (AAP Committee on Public Education, 2001; Anderson, Berkowitz, et al., 2003; Anderson, Huston, Schmitt, Linebarger, & Wright, 2001; Huesmann, Moise-Titus, Podolski, & Eron, 2003), the effect of exposure to violence via mass media is significant (Figure 14-3).

How does media violence lead to long-term aggressiveness? Longitudinal studies have demonstrated that children's exposure to violent media increases their risk for long-term effects based on observational learning, desensitization, and enactive learning that occur automatically in human children (Huesmann, 2007). Children's beliefs are influenced by their observation of behavior. Media provides visceral thrills without showing the human cost and leads children to view aggression as acceptable. Children who see characters use violence to achieve their goals are likely to conclude that force is an effective way to resolve conflicts. Repeated exposure can desensitize children. Negative reactions to violent scenes have been shown to decline in intensity with repeated exposure (Huesmann & Kirwil, 2007). The more realistically violence is portrayed, the more likely it is to be accepted (AAP Committee on Public Education, 2001; Anderson, Berkowitz, et al., 2003). Furthermore, each hour that children spend watching violent television reduces time spent with friends. Thus violent TV fare may set off a cycle in which frequent viewers become more aggressive, and their behavior leads to social isolation and, in turn, to viewing more violent television (Bickham & Rich, 2006).

Children are more vulnerable than adults to the influence of televised violence (AAP Committee on Public Education, 2001; Coie & Dodge, 1998). Classic social learning research suggests that children imitate filmed models even more than live ones (Bandura et al., 1963). The influence is stronger if the child believes the violence on the screen is real, identifies with the violent character, finds that character attractive, and watches without parental supervision or intervention (Anderson, Berkowitz, et al., 2003; Coie & Dodge, 1998). Highly aggressive children are more strongly affected by media violence than are less aggressive children (Anderson, Berkowitz, et al., 2003).

Research on effects of video games and the Internet suggest that long-term increases in violent behavior could be even greater for video games than for TV and movies. Players of violent games are active participants who receive positive reinforcment for violent actions (Huesmann, 2007). In experimental studies young video game players have shown decreases in prosocial behavior and increases in aggressive thoughts and violent retaliation to provocation (C. Anderson, 2000).

What's your view ❓

• What can and should be done to reduce children's exposure to violent television programs?

As discussed in Chapter 11, media-induced aggressiveness can be minimized by cutting down on television use and by parental monitoring and guidance of the shows children watch (Anderson, Berkowitz, et al., 2003). The AAP Committee on Public Education (2001) recommends that parents limit children's media exposure to 1 to 2 hours a day. Third and fourth graders who participated in a 6-month curriculum aimed at motivating them to monitor and reduce the time they spent on television, videotapes, and video games showed significant decreases in peer-rated aggression, as compared with a control group (Robinson, Wilde, Navracruz, Haydel, & Varady, 2001).

Bullies and Victims

bullying Aggression deliberately and persistently directed against a particular target, or victim, typically one who is weak, vulnerable, and defenseless.

Aggression becomes **bullying** when it is deliberately, persistently directed against a particular target: a victim. Bullying can be physical (hitting, punching, kicking, or damaging or taking of personal belongings), verbal (name-calling or threatening), or relational or emotional (isolating and gossiping, often behind the victim's back) (Berger, 2007; Veenstra et al., 2005). Bullying can be *proactive*—done to show dominance, bolster power, or win admiration—or *reactive,* responding to a real or imagined attack. *Cyberbullying*—posting negative comments or derogatory photos of the victim on a website—has become increasingly common (Berger, 2007). The increase in use of cell phones, text messaging, e-mail, and chat rooms has opened new venues for bullies that provide access to victims without the protection of family and community (Huesmann, 2007).

Some 24 percent of U.S. primary schools, 42 percent of middle schools, and 21 percent of high schools report student bullying at school at least once a week (Guerino, Hurwitz, Noonan, & Kaffenberger, 2006). Bullying is a problem in other industrialized countries as well (Hara, 2002; Kanetsuna & Smith, 2002; Ruiz & Tanaka, 2001). In a survey of 50,000 children in 34 European countries, almost one-third of the children said they were bullies, victims, or both (Currie et al., 2004). In Japan and Korea, school bullying has been associated with a growing wave of student suicide and suicidal thoughts and behavior (Kim, Koh, & Leventhal, 2005; Rios-Ellis, Bellamy, & Shoji, 2000).

Bullying may reflect a genetic tendency toward aggressiveness combined with environmental influences, such as coercive parents and antisocial friends (Berger, 2007). Most bullies are boys who tend to victimize other boys; female bullies tend to target other girls (Berger, 2007; Pellegrini & Long, 2002; Veenstra et al., 2005). Male bullies tend to use overt, physical aggression; female bullies may use relational aggression (Boulton, 1995; Nansel et al., 2001). Patterns of bullying and victimization may become established as early as kindergarten; as tentative peer groups form, aggressors soon get to know which children make the easiest targets. Physical bullying declines with age, but other forms of bullying increase, especially at ages 11 to 15. Whereas younger children reject an aggressive child, by early adolescence bullies are often dominant, respected, feared, and even liked (Berger, 2007).

Unlike the pattern for bullying, the likelihood of *being* bullied decreases steadily. As children get older, most of them may learn how to discourage bullying, leaving a smaller pool of available victims (Pellegrini & Long, 2002; P. K. Smith & Levan, 1995). Most victims are small, passive, weak, and submissive and may blame themselves for being bullied. Other victims are provocative; they goad their attackers, and they may even attack other children themselves (Berger, 2007; Veenstra et al., 2005).

Risk factors for victimization seem to be similar across cultures (Schwartz, Chang, & Farver, 2001). Victims do not fit in. They tend to be anxious, depressed, cautious, quiet, and submissive and to cry easily, or to be argumentative and provocative (Hodges, Boivin, Vitaro, & Bukowski, 1999; Olweus, 1995; Veenstra et al., 2005). They have few friends and may live in harsh,

Bullying tends to peak in middle grades. Boys are more likely to use overt aggression; girls, relational or social aggression.

punitive family environments (Nansel et al., 2001; Schwartz, Dodge, Pettit, Bates, & Conduct Problems Prevention Research Group, 2000). Victims are apt to have low self-esteem, though it is not clear whether low self-esteem leads to or follows from victimization (Boulton & Smith, 1994; Olweus, 1995). In a study of 5,749 Canadian children, those who were overweight were most likely to become either victims or bullies (Janssen, Craig, Boyce, & Pickett, 2004).

Bullying, especially emotional bullying, is harmful to both bullies and victims—and can even be fatal (Berger, 2007). Bullies are at increased risk of delinquency, crime, or alcohol abuse. In the wave of school shootings since 1994, the perpetrators often had been victims of bullying (Anderson, Kaufman, et al., 2001). Victims of chronic bullying tend to develop behavior problems. They may become more aggressive themselves or may become depressed (Schwartz, McFadyen-Ketchum, Dodge, Pettit, & Bates, 1998; Veenstra et al., 2005). Furthermore, frequent bullying affects the school atmosphere, leading to widespread underachievement, alienation from school, stomachaches and headaches, reluctance to go to school, and frequent absences (Berger, 2007).

The U.S. Department of Health and Human Services has promoted Steps to Respect, a program for grades 3 to 6 that aims to (1) increase staff awareness and responsiveness to bullying, (2) teach students social and emotional skills, and (3) foster socially responsible beliefs. A randomized controlled study of 1,023 third to sixth graders found a reduction in playground bullying and argumentative behavior and an increase in harmonious interactions among children who participated in the program, as well as less bystander incitement to bullying (Frey et al., 2005). However, analysis of research done on a broad variety of these types of intervention programs has indicated that while the programs may enhance students social competence and self-esteem, the impact on actual bullying behavior is minimal (Merrell, Gueldner, Ross, & Isava, 2008).

Checkpoint ✔

Can you . . .

✔ Tell how aggression changes during middle childhood and how social information processing and televised violence can contribute to it?

✔ Discuss gender differences in aggression in school-age children?

✔ Tell how patterns of bullying and victimization become established and change?

✔ List risk factors for bullying and victimization?

Current Perspectives on Bullying

Strategies to Prevent and Heal the Mental Anguish Caused by Cyberbullying

JANET G. FROESCHLE ET AL.

As counselor educators, we are constantly interviewing middle school counselors to ensure current issues are discussed in our courses. During one such interview, a middle school counselor revealed an alarming conversation she had previously had with a student. The student stated, "I'm really scared about the message I got last night on my computer." "If it bothers you that much, just don't log on," I (interviewed counselor) said. "If I don't log on, I won't be able to hang out with my friends," the girl responded. "Little did I (interviewed counselor) know that this young lady would later attempt suicide due to online bullying."

Few middle school educators have escaped the numerous warnings regarding face-to-face school bullying. While this threat is certainly real, the more common danger inflicted via technology, cyberbullying, is relatively unknown to teachers and parents. Cyberbullying has moved bullying behaviors from the schoolyard to a worldwide audience. This exposure ensures that students receive the greatest humiliation possible both during and after school. Not surprisingly, research indicates that victims (who are often also bullies) suffer from mental health problems and lowered academic achievement (Hall, 2006; Reiff, 2006; Willard, 2007). The purpose of this article is to enlighten teachers, school administrators, and school counselors about this new technological danger, describe warning signs to help recognize both victims and perpetrators, and detail school- and home-based strategies for preventing cyberbullying and healing those affected by the phenomenon.

Forms of Technological Victimization

Bullying behavior is not a new phenomenon. Worldwide, children have been known to threaten, harass, and even harm other children perceived as defenseless (Weir, 2001). Nonetheless, new media for victimization have emerged in the form of Internet and cell phone technology.

Cell phone text messaging allows a perpetrator to instantly and constantly harass or threaten the victim. Cell phone cameras offer perpetrators the opportunity to take and spread harmful pictures across the school campus in an instant. Demeaning, humiliating, and slanderous rumors can be spread to large groups using cell phone messages (Paulson, 2003). The aforementioned issues plus new technology that allows cell phone users to access the Internet (Altheide, 2004) mean that what was once shared among a few individuals can now be shared instantly with large groups. Middle school educators must understand this new arena of adolescent communication and find ways to help both victims and bullies handle the emotional scars brought on by these behaviors.

Yet, how do teachers know which students need help? The following information can help educators identify students who may be suffering as a result of cyberbullying.

The Perpetrator

Cyberstalkers and Internet bullies use technology to intimidate and harass in an attempt to gain power over others (Alexy, Burgess, Baker, & Smoyak, 2005; Bocij, 2005). Cyberbullies consist of two types of individuals: social climbers and aggressive harassers. Social climbers use the Internet to expose to denigration those they consider inferior while using bullying as a means to fit in with a particular crowd. Aggressive harassers have been bullied by others and begin to harass other peers as a means of retaliation (Willard, 2006).

Some of the most common media for this deviant behavior include e-mail messages, social networking sites, chat room postings, website postings, text messages to the victim and others, and persistent cell phone calls (Alexy, Burgess, Baker, & Smoyak, 2005; Bocij, 2005; Mann & Sutton, 1998; Paulson, 2003).

Perpetrators use the computer as a tool for harassment for several reasons. Anonymity creates a lowered sense of responsibility for one's actions (Willard, 2006). This decreased feeling of accountability may lead to impulsive behaviors that are heightened by the knowledge that the victim's suffering will be invisible (Bocij, 2005; Willard, 2006). Douglas and McGarry (2001) stated that people lose part of their identity when corresponding over technological media. This may create a loss of perspective leading to a desensitization of the plight of the victim (Alexy, Burgess, Baker, & Smoyak, 2005).

Those who spent much time online (particularly in chat rooms) showed impaired academic performance.

Those who bully over the Internet showed a deficit in emotional bonding and relationships with parents, were more often female than traditional bullies (www.cyberbully.org; Ybarra & Mitchell, 2004), and were typically older than their peers. Further, Internet bullies used cyberspace more often than their peers (Ybarra & Mitchell, 2004). This may be of particular importance to educators, since research by Kubey, Lavin, and Barrows (2001) found that those who spend much time online (particularly in chat rooms) showed impaired academic performance.

The Victim
While more research is needed to describe victims of cyberbullying (Alexy, Burgess, Baker, & Smoyak, 2005), the typical cyberstalking victim is a white female (D'Ovidio & Doyle, 2003) who is harassed primarily through e-mail (although a smaller percentage were contacted through chat rooms, message boards, and websites) (Alexy, Burgess, Baker, & Smoyak, 2005). Nonetheless, Alexy, Burgess, Baker, and Smoyak (2005) and Wolak, Mitchell, and Finkelhor (2002) found that college aged males experienced cyberstalking more often than females and received threats more often than those who were stalked offline. Many believe adolescents and younger children to be future victims, since the phenomenon is rapidly increasing among youth (Alexy, Burgess, Baker, & Smoyak, 2005; D'Ovidio & Doyle, 2003; Wolak, Mitchell, & Finkelor, 2002). As a result, school-based programs are crucial if students are to achieve optimum mental health and academic performance.

Implementing a Collaborative Program
Perpetrators, victims, and schools alike suffer the consequences of technological victimization. Bullying and stalking behaviors cause a sense of isolation, fear, hopelessness, depression, and adjustment problems among victims (Mishna, 2003; Olweus, 1993; Pelligrini, 1998); may increase the risk of delinquent behaviors for perpetrators (Mishna, 2003; Olweus, 1993); and can negatively affect the climate within a school (Espelage, Bosworth, & Simon, 2000). Working collaboratively, classroom teachers, technology teachers, school counselors, law enforcement personnel, and school administrators can implement programs that support the mental health of victims, parents, teachers, and the school as a whole. Following are suggestions for implementation.

1. Monitor student computer use closely within schools and inform parents as to the importance of supervising children at home. First, recognize that filtering software on computers does not ensure these computers cannot be used for harm (Willard, 2007). Even school or library computers can be used as media for cyberbullying, as all websites used by teens cannot be blocked. As a result, educators and parents should place computers in a well trafficked area (both in school and at home). After interviewing many educators, a useful technique that emerged was the installation of mirrors behind each computer. The mirror was placed in a position such that teachers could see each computer screen in the room by simply glancing at the mirror. Many teachers stated that students' improper Internet use was curtailed by simply knowing adults could see everything on the screen at all times.

Other methods used to monitor Internet use include installing firewalls and software to block tunneling sites. For example, a local firewall can be installed on each school and home computer such that specific websites are blocked. In addition, tunneling sites (those that bypass the firewall) can be blocked with the installation of specific software packages. Many of these software packages can block sites containing specific data or words and send an e-mail to parent or teacher addresses when an attempt is made to enter such sites. Specific filtering information and current software packages can be viewed at http://www.kiiitv.com/features/computercorner/6507657.html (Computer Corner, 2007).

2. Inform parents of websites regularly used by teens and the type of communications displayed. Train parents to use technology so that they can effectively monitor their child's communications. For example, parents can be taught to create and monitor pages on websites such as Myspace™ and Facebook™.

3. Integrate a program that teaches social skills and empathy with classroom reading instruction. Hillsberg and Spak (2006), Froeschle (2006), and Salmon (2003) offer specific details or literature lists that aid educators when implementing this strategy. Additional age- and activity-appropriate stories can be found via the California Department of Education's Recommended Literature Search (2001) at http://www.cde.ca.gov/ci/rl/ll/ap/litsearch.asp by searching under the genre "Realistic Fiction." The authors listed above contend that identifying with story characters improves the student's ability to empathize with others (thus decreasing aggressive behaviors) while increasing reading comprehension.

   Based on this premise, we suggest the following activity. First, read a story to students. Next, ask students to identify with the perspectives and feelings of the story's characters. Ask questions such as, "How would you feel if you were this character? How did the way the other characters responded affect this person's actions?" Finally, students can act out opposing roles in the story and discuss the emotions felt by each character. Students may also be asked to put themselves into the shoes of another entity via personifications. Questions such as, "If you were the (inanimate object or animal) in this story, how might you feel? Would this behavior help make friends or enemies?" Such lessons can be enhanced with collaborative efforts between teachers and school counselors.

4. Involve community and law enforcement personnel in educational endeavors. These professionals can teach about the safe use of the Internet and cell phones as well as discuss legal consequences accompanying stalking and other bullying behaviors. Students need to know the difference between public and private information as they often post personal, harmful information on websites and do not realize the dangers involved.

5. Offer emotional support to cyberbullying victims. For example:

   Encourage participation in school groups and extracurricular activities that build friendships and heighten self-esteem (Weir, 2001).

   Assign older empathic students to serve as mentors to victims.

Assign adult volunteers to serve as mentors to victims. Recognize that the victim's fears may occur for years. Do not dismiss these feelings as unnecessary or unreasonable (Alexy, Burgess, Baker, & Smoyak, 2005).

6. Create an environment that does not tolerate bullying in any form and encourages mainstream students to reject bad behaviors. Salmivalli (1999) described a program involving three steps. First, educators create awareness by enlightening all students as to the definition of cyberbullying and the importance of not supporting such behaviors. Revealing that individuals often respond differently as a result of peer pressure is an essential part of this guidance lesson. Discussions of expected and unexpected behaviors reveal discrepancies between the students' behavior and beliefs.

    Next, students are encouraged to self-reflect and commit. Olweus (1991) stated that student-created ideas improve overall commitment to anti-bullying programs. As a result, students are asked to identify their actual behavior when exposed to acts of cyberbullying and to brainstorm ways to stop such harmful behaviors. Salmivalli, Kaukiainen, and Voetenit (2005) have advocated the use of role-plays or drama as part of the brainstorming process and stated the importance of improving not only behaviors specific to bullies but those of bystanders and witnesses as well. Role-plays have been found to offer a safe atmosphere to practice responses intended to dissuade cyberbullying.

7. Provide a safe place for bullies to address underlying issues concerning their behaviors. Adult volunteers can become mentors and role models for bullies who need support to overcome improper behaviors. For example, Balkus (2006) discussed a unique mentoring program designed for at-risk students called TeamMates. Students are matched to community members who offer support and guidance. Rayle (2005) interviewed 22 middle school counselors and found that males, in particular, seek out same sex mentors in an effort to receive guidance on issues such as bullying.

    For seven years (1998–2005), I was fortunate enough to establish a successful mentoring program within a south Texas middle school. During this time, many students known for bullying behaviors were assigned to same sex mentors with similar interests (as pre-screened) for weekly meetings. Mentors met weekly with the school counselor and were given training on child development, bullying behaviors and strategies to prevent all forms of bullying, information and advice-giving strategies, and child abuse and other relevant laws. Mentors met the following requirements: at least 20 years of age, passed a background check, attended all trainings, and met weekly with students for a minimum of one school year. Mentors were recruited and selected by educators and ranged in age from 20 to 76. At the end of each school year, teachers and school administrators reported on the mentees' behaviors. Most students were reported as exhibiting a decrease in aggressive behaviors.

8. Involve school counselors as part of the educational team. These professionals can teach behavioral and emotional intelligence skills (skills that assist in getting along with peers and controlling personal emotions) that avert cyberbullying (Aronson, 2000) as part of a guidance curriculum. School counselors can implement counseling groups and peer support groups that seek to empower victims while offering a safe place to express fear; to teach social behaviors that are needed to get along with others; and to build skills that assist with anger management, appropriate assertiveness (Ross, 1996), self-confidence, and self-esteem. In addition, these professionals can teach conflict resolution techniques that are often alternatives to aggression (Ross, 1996) and make referrals to outside agencies as needed.

9. Assign projects that encourage cooperation in lieu of competition. Aronson (2000) discussed a method of assigning classroom projects found to decrease aggression and bullying behavior. A description of his jigsaw method follows: Divide the classroom into groups of four or five students, with each group assigned to research the same major topic. Break major topics into four or five subtopics (one for each group member). Each student compiles research on their individually assigned subtopic. Next, students compare research with class members who have been assigned the same subtopic. Finally, each original group prepares a cumulative report based on individual members' contributions. This method creates an environment that demands the knowledge, contribution, and cooperation of each student. Further, it builds empathy for others while fostering academic learning.

Harold Wiggs Middle School in El Paso, Texas, implemented the Bilingual Cooperative Integrative Reading and Comprehension Program and Cooperative Integrative Reading and Comprehension Program in 1993 (Calderon, Hertz-Lazarowitz, & Slavin, 1997; Slavin & Fashola, 1998; Stearns, 1999). Students began working together in small groups as opposed to teacher directed individual learning. As the program progressed, compassion and respect learned in the classroom began to infiltrate the entire school and neighborhood. As a result, aggressive behaviors diminished considerably, and test scores improved.

Conclusion

When it comes to technology, adults seem less educated than kids and, therefore, are unaware of many ordinary dangers. Cyberbullies count on an anonymous adult-free environment in which to inflict misery on other students. Working collaboratively, educators, parents, and law enforcement personnel can weaken the control cyberbullies have over victims through education about current technology and victim and bully profiles. Specific programs using reading-empathy instruction, counseling and mentoring programs, peer support programs, and cooperative group assignments are capable of both preventing and counteracting the pain and school failure caused by cyberbullying.

References

Alexy, E. M., Burgess, A. W., Baker, T., & Smoyak, S. A. (2005). Perceptions of cyberstalking among college students. *Brief Treatment and Crisis Intervention, 5,* 279–289.

Altheide, D. L. (2004). The control narrative of the Internet. *Symbolic Interaction, 27,* 223–f235.

Aronson, E. (2000). *Nobody left to hate: Teaching compassion after Columbine.* New York: Worth Publishers.

Balkus, B. (2006). An advocate for every student at Millard Central Middle School. *Middle School Journal, 38*(2), 4–12.

Bocij, P. (2005). Reactive stalking: A new perspective on victimization. *The British Journal of Forensic Practice, 7,* 23–34.

Calderon, M., Hertz-Lazarowitz, R., & Slavin, R. E. (1997). *Effects of Bilingual Cooperative Integrated Reading and Composition (BCIRC) on students transitioning from Spanish to English reading* (Report No. 10). Baltimore: Center for Research on the Education of Students Placed at Risk, Johns Hopkins University.

California Department of Education. (2001). *Recommended literature search.* Retrieved June 23, 2007, from http://www.cde.ca.gov/ci/rl/ll/ap/litsearch.asp

Computer corner: First edition by KIII TV. (2007, March 15). Retrieved June 23, 2007, from http://www.kiiitv.com/features/computercorner/6507657.html

D'Ovidio, R., & Doyle, J. (2003). A study on cyberstalking: Understand investigative hurdles. *FBI Law Enforcement Bulletin, 72*(3), 10–17.

Douglas, K., & McGarry, C. (2001). Identifiability and self-presentation: Computer mediated communication and intergroup interaction. *British Journal of Social Psychology, 40,* 399–416.

Espelage, D. L., Bosworth, K., & Simon, T. R. (2000). Examining the social context of bullying behaviors in early adolescence. *Journal of Counseling and Development, 78,* 326–333.

Froeschle, J. G. (2006). Solution focused empathy training groups for students with fire-setting behaviors. *Journal of School Counseling, 4*(23). Retrieved June 23, 2007, from http://www.jsc.montana.edu/articles/v4n23.pdf

Hall, K. R. (2006). Using problem-based learning with victims of bullying behavior. *Professional School Counseling, 9,* 231–237.

Hillsberg, C., & Spak, H. (2006). Young adult literature as the centerpiece of an anti-bullying program in middle school. *Middle School Journal, 38*(2), 23–28.

Kubey, R. W., Lavin, M. J., & Barrows, J. R. (2001). Internet use and collegiate academic performance decrements: Early findings. *Journal of Communication, 51,* 366–382.

Mann, D., & Sutton, M. (1998). Netcrime: More change in the organization of thieving. *The British Journal of Criminology, 38,* 201–229.

Mishna, F. (2003). Learning disabilities and bullying: Double Jeopardy. *Journal of Learning Disabilities, 36,* 336–346.

Olweus, D. (1991). Bully/victim problems among schoolchildren: Basic facts and effects of a school-based intervention program. In D. Pépier & K. Rubin (Eds.), *The development and treatment of childhood aggression* (pp. 411–448). Hillsdale, NJ: Lawrence Erlbaum.

Olweus, D. (1993). *Bullying in schools: What we know and what we can do.* Oxford, UK: Blackwell Publishers.

Paulson, A. (2003, December 30). Internet bullying. *Christian Science Monitor, 96,* 11.

Pelligrini, A. D. (1998). Bullies and victims in school: A review and call for research. *Journal of Applied Developmental Psychology, 19,* 165–176.

Rayle, A. D. (2005). Cross gender interactions in middle school counselor-student working alliances: Challenges and recommendations. *Professional School Counseling, 9,* 152–155.

Reiff, M. I. (2006). Bullying. *Journal of Developmental & Behavioral Pediatrics, 27,* 77–78.

Ross, D. M. (1996). *Childhood bullying and teasing: What school personnel, other professionals, and parents can do.* Alexandria, VA: American Counseling Association.

Salmivalli, C. (1999). Participant role approach to school bullying: Implications for interventions. *Journal of Adolescence, 22,* 453–459.

Salmivalli, C., Kaukiainen, A., & Voetenit, M. (2005). Anti-bullying interventions: Implementation and Outcome. *British Journal of Educational Psychology, 75,* 465–487.

Salmon, S. (2003). Teaching empathy: The PEACE curriculum. *Reclaiming Children and Youth, 12,* 142–147.

Slavin, R. E., & Fashola, O. S. (1998). *Show me the evidence! Proven promising programs for America's schools.* Thousand Oak, CA: Corwin Press.

Stearns, C. J. (1999). A middle school venture into cooperative learning: Successes and dilemmas. *Theory Into Practice, 38,* 100–104.

Weir, E. (2001). The health impact of bullying. *Canadian Medical Association Journal, 165,* 1249.

Willard, N. (2006). *A briefing for educators: Online social networking communities and youth risk.* Center for Safe and Responsible Internet Use. Retrieved August 7, 2007, from http://www.cyberbully.org/cyberbully/docs/youthriskonlinealert.pdf

Willard, N. (2007). *An educator's guide to cyberbullying and cyberthreats.* Center for Safe and Responsible Internet Use. Retrieved August 7, 2007, http://www.cyberbully.org/cyberbully/docs/cbcteducator.pdf

Wolak, J., Mitchell, K. J., & Finkelhor, D. (2002). Close online relationships in a national sample of adolescents. *Adolescence, 37,* 441–455.

Ybarra, M. L., & Mitchell, K. J. (2004). Youth engaging in online harassment: Associations with caregiver-child relationships, Internet use, and personal characteristics. *Journal of Adolescence, 27,* 319–336.

Janet Froeschle is an assistant professor of education at West Texas A & M University, Amarillo. E-mail: jfroeschle@atamu.edu. **Mary Mayorga** is an assistant professor at the University of Houston–Victoria in Texas. E-mail: mayoram@uhv/edu. **Yvette Castillo** is an assistant professor of education at West Texas A & M University, Amarillo. E-mail: ycastillo@mail.wtamu.edu. **Terry Hargrave** is a professor of education at West Texas A & M University, Amarillo. E-mail: thargrave@mail.wtamu.edu.

Froeschle, J. G., Mayorga, M., Castillo, Y., & Hargrave, T. (2008). Strategies to Prevent and Heal the Mental Anguish Caused by Cyberbullying. *Middle School Journal,* 39(4), pp. 30–35. Reprinted with permission from National Middle School Association.

R U Safe?

Who better to teach young adolescents about online dangers than other adolescents?

JOHANNA MUSTACCHI

It's not just on the bus or during recess anymore. Bullying can happen the minute our students wake up, can creep in during class time, and can continue after the school day ends—and then follow them home, right into their bedrooms.

My generation was safe from the pressures of peer judgment and abuse once we arrived home from school (the class bully would never actually call your house back then). But cyberspace has no boundaries, and students today have only their wits to protect them from teasing, harassment, and threats that can reach them online anytime.

What I call *cyberabuse* is rampant at school, adding to the old-fashioned face-to-face taunting and power plays that take place among students. (I use the term *cyber* rather than *Internet* to include all mobile communication devices.) Such abuse even goes on as we teach. I once confiscated cell phones from two students who were texting each other during another teacher's class. They showed me the conversation, which was full of insults and vulgar language.

According to a series of studies conducted by the *Journal of Adolescent Health,* more than 80 percent of adolescents own at least one form of new media technology, which they use to communicate with one another, present information about themselves, and share new media creations. The studies examined the relationships among bullying, harassment, and aggression among youth and how these issues translated to electronic media. According to one of these studies (Kowalski & Limber, 2007), which surveyed almost 4,000 middle school students, 11 percent had been electronically bullied at least once in the two months preceding the questionnaire, and 7 percent admitted to being both a bully and a victim. Another study (Williams & Guerra, 2007) showed that electronic bullying peaks in middle school and is inflicted most often through instant messaging, although bullying occurs frequently through text messaging, e-mails, chat rooms, and content on websites.

The *Journal of Adolescent Health* research revealed that some state education departments—in Florida, South Carolina, Utah, Oregon, and Washington—have created policies to combat online harassment (David-Ferdon & Hertz, 2007). But many of the authors agreed that stopping adolescents'

use of electronic media in school or installing blocking and filtering software does not adequately address this pervasive problem.

Ideally, we should convince all students to abstain from bullying, and we certainly must try to do so. But it is equally crucial to arm students with the tools they need to protect themselves from bullying, particularly now that bullies take advantage of far-reaching online tools. As a middle school teacher, I've found that a powerful way to arm students against cyberbullying is to have them research some aspect of this phenomenon and then teach others what they have learned—or directly experienced—as they navigate the online world.

Getting Students Talking . . .

During my first year teaching media literacy at the Pierre Van Cortlandt Middle School in Croton-on-Hudson, New York, I developed a unit on social networking sites and cyberbullying. For the culminating project, 8th grade students wrote and performed skits portraying a cyberbullying incident, including the motivation for the incident, the consequences, and any resolution the players came to. "Can we curse?" students asked, amazed that I wanted them to show the real deal. My response: Make it realistic.

On the day students presented their skits to their classmates, I called in some reserves: the school psychologist, guidance counselor, student assistance counselor, and our school's drug abuse resistance education officer (a member of our local law enforcement department). The skits raised important issues that captured every student's interest: body image, "stealing" boyfriends and girlfriends, and threats of violence. They also raised anxious questions. My professional colleagues provided advice for students, and the police officer explained legal consequences and how extensively the police will get involved.

Many parents thanked the school for exposing their children to these issues as part of their education. And when school personnel saw how much students had to say—and ask—about online bullying, the seeds were sown for more comprehensive teaching about cybercitizenship. Principal Barbara Ulm had already received numerous requests for help from parents of students in 5th and 6th grades who had been targeted in cyberspace by other students. She asked me to develop a full-blown Internet safety curriculum for the school's 6th, 7th, and 8th graders.

. . . and Getting Them Teaching

When I began implementing this curriculum the next fall, I noticed how much the 8th graders knew and were eager to impart to one another—with almost desperate urgency. As if riding a rollercoaster, students relayed stories and advice to one another, hitting highs and lows at breakneck speed. They were experts in some aspects of online interaction and risks but complete novices in others. I realized that their knowledge and thirst to exchange information provided a rare opportunity. So I charged my 8th grade students with the job of teaching my 6th graders.

As any middle school teacher knows, there is a vast difference in development between a 6th grader and an 8th grader. The first is a child; the second a young adult. The first wants to emulate the second; 6th graders literally and figuratively look up to their older schoolmates. Most 8th graders realize this and feel a tangible sense of responsibility as role models. These are perfect conditions for motivating older students to present information on a public safety issue—and getting younger students to take it seriously.

One research study showed that electronic bullying peaks in middle school.

Eighth graders first learn *netiquette*—appropriate, courteous online behavior and communication. Students discuss their own definitions of appropriate online behavior. My 8th graders have identified a number of rules, including (1) If you wouldn't say it to the person's face, don't say it online; (2) Be careful with sarcasm—it can be misread; and (3) Be extra careful about what you say online because your audience can't hear tone or see facial expressions.

I then describe certain deviations from appropriate behavior and how to recognize these deviations and safeguard against becoming a victim or perpetrator. I divide 8th graders into groups and make each group responsible for researching one subtopic and creating an engaging 15-minute lesson to deliver to a 6th grade class.[1]

The first year we tried this, students wrote lessons on flaming, phishing, cyberbullying, cyberharassment, cyberbullying or harassment by proxy, and online grooming. They created a list of definitions of these terms followed by succinct advice for coping with each one, which they handed out to 6th graders (see "The Student Guide to Stamping Out Cyberabuse"). Students created PowerPoint presentations, SmartBoard drawings, diagrams, and graphics. They incorporated into their presentations online media they found about cyberbullying, such as videos from TeacherTube.com and the group Netsmartz.org. (One powerful resource they found is a British-made public service announcement video available on YouTube called "Think U Know" that shows a young girl reporting a predatory online groomer.) They shared surveys, bookmarks, and a list of Internet safety tips with their peers.

I also infused the unit with instruction in public speaking, and on the day of the presentations, I assessed each student on his or her presentation, including organization, content knowledge, mechanics, delivery, and the quality of visual aids.

As you might expect, every 8th grade student rose to the occasion, even the most traditionally reluctant participants. Their talks, materials, and activities kept the younger students fully engaged. They asked questions and got their peers to think and reflect, sometimes with creative tactics.

For example, one group burst into the classroom in a friendly manner. They handed out lollipops and asked 6th graders to fill out a questionnaire providing their e-mail passwords, addresses, phone numbers, and parents' and siblings' names, explaining that they needed this information for their presentation. The older students handily made their point about how online groomers befriend victims first to gain their trust.

The "teachers" alerted their students to how seemingly innocuous messages can be precursors to harassment and abuse. In addition to showing realistic examples of bullying and aggressive communiqués, they also informed their younger counterparts about protective tools, like procedures that block certain messages or senders, privacy settings, and logistics for reporting incidents to an Internet service provider. In a clever twist, one group included in their PowerPoint presentation the kinds of questions a groomer might send, leaving the victim's answers blank. They asked 6th graders to write how they would respond to the messages.

Some 8th graders later told me they had been very nervous during their presentations, but it wasn't evident at the time. Students displayed a mature understanding of the seriousness of their responsibility. As Dylan noted in his final reflection,

> Presenting to the 6th graders helped me realize how easily kids will give out their information for a small prize. . . . It's important to always educate kids on Internet safety.

Emily reflected:

> I found it really interesting to hear the 6th graders' responses to our questions and to see their faces as they slowly realized the truth with some parts of the Internet. I was glad to see that they took this seriously, and not as a joke. . . . We wanted to scare them, and we did just that. We wanted to show them that this does happen to people all over, and it could very easily happen to them if they are not careful.

6th Graders Reflect and Respond

Following the 8th graders' cybersafety lessons, I asked my 6th grade students to write an article about the experience for our upcoming class newspaper. This fit in well with my 6th grade

The Student Guide to Stamping out Cyberabuse

The 150 8th grade students at Pierre Van Cortlandt Middle School collaboratively wrote these definitions of aggressive communication practices in cyberspace, as well as tips for handling each one.

Flaming

When someone insults someone else, usually by e-mail, instant message, or text message. To prevent flaming, do not respond, save the messages so you can show a trusted adult, and don't worry if the message is from someone you don't know or recognize; there are ways to track the person down.

Phishing

An attempt to get your personal information by pretending to be a site you are familiar with or trust. Always be sure you know where your e-mails come from. Don't give information over the Internet to sites that don't look valid.

Cyberbullying

A child bullying another child on the Internet. Bullying involves repeated put-downs, insults, and threats, with the emphasis on *repeated*. If you get bullied, tell an adult that you trust. To avoid this situation, do NOT talk to people on the Internet whom you don't know.

Cyberharassment

Harassment through the Internet that involves an adult. An adult can harass a child, a child can harass an adult, and an adult can harass another adult.

Cyberbullying or Harassment by Proxy

(1) When cyberbullies get someone else (or several people) to do their dirty work, or (2) When a bully intentionally provokes a victim to lash back to get the victim in trouble. If this happens to you, don't lash back. Contact your Internet service provider, talk to an adult, or talk to your friends about it.

Online Grooming

When a predator builds an online relationship with a child by giving compliments or a "shoulder to lean on" or sending gifts until the child trusts the predator. Typical "grooming" lines include

- Where is the computer in the house?
- Are your parents around much?
- You can always talk to me.
- I'm always here for you.
- You don't deserve how they treat you.
- You have a great personality.
- You're beautiful. You should be a model.

To protect yourself from a groomer, (1) always know whom you are talking to online, (2) don't give out personal information, (3) don't post seductive or inappropriate pictures of yourself or others online, (4) never meet up in person with anyone you meet online, and (5) talk with your parents if you feel suspicious about something online.

8th Graders' Top Ten Internet Safety Tips

1. Don't give out personal information.
2. Don't talk to anybody you don't know.
3. Use a secure password.
4. Don't give your password to anybody.
5. Be careful about what you post online.
6. Don't put pictures of yourself online.
7. Tell someone if you get cyberbullied.
8. Be honest.
9. Don't click on pop-ups.
10. Only go to sites you know are safe.

media literacy curriculum that year, which focused on print media. It was a perfect opportunity to teach "angle" in journalistic writing. I encouraged students to come at the experience from any vantage point that felt relevant to them and to experiment with different types of articles. They had ample material to draw from because they all took notes during the presentations and received handouts from the 8th grade "teachers."

Students rose to the challenge of choosing varied angles and formats: straight news about the fact that students were teaching students, reviews of the lessons and the 8th graders' teaching skills, an Internet safety advice column, editorials on different subtopics, and informational features on how to protect yourself from online dangers. The pieces they created—such as this excerpt from Rita's article "Staying Safe Online"—show that they took in what their older peers imparted to them:

> The most serious of the online dangers is grooming. Grooming usually happens over instant messaging and e-mail. The 8th graders taught the 6th graders that grooming is when someone tries to create an emotional relationship with another person who is usually younger than them. The reason grooming is so dangerous is because the "groomer" potentially wants to meet the victim in person and abuse or kidnap them.

Another 6th grade student, Sean, wrote,

> With the computer age booming, PCs everywhere are catching fire. But it's not because of unsafe wiring; it's the work of one of the most basic forms of cyberbullying: flaming. Flaming is like an emotional bacteria—small, short

sentences, sometimes casual, sometimes accidental—that make feelings of anger or depression (sometimes both) spread all through the victim's body.

The 6th graders were unanimously grateful for learning about this issue in the safety of the classroom, where all their questions and concerns could be aired. One student wrote, "I am now so much safer and more aware of the Internet and all the dangers. They pop out at me."

The 6th graders were unanimously grateful for learning about this issue in the safety of the classroom.

Another acknowledged the positive effect of being taught by the 8th grade students using digital media:

> With all the PowerPoints [on] Internet safety from the 8th graders, I learned more than I normally would. The pictures and everything really got my attention.

Arming Students to Help One Another

As difficult as it may be for us to accept, our students are potentially threatened with bullying and even predation any time they are online or communicating electronically. In a commentary connected to the *Journal of Adolescent Health*'s study, Maria Worthen (2007) writes that educators owe their students education in media literacy—including training that makes them aware of the dangers of cybercommunication.

We must guide students in how to inform and arm one another.

We must help our students acquire the new literacy skills of recognizing and avoiding aggression in cyberspace. But because this territory is probably more alien to teachers than to students, increasingly students will find *themselves* acting as peer counselors for their friends or fellow students encountering this kind of abuse. We must guide students in how to inform and arm one another. My experience turning 8th graders into peer teachers shows that adolescents are not just up to this task—they will relish it. This new 2.0 world will belong to today's youth. It's our job to help them shape and protect it with courage and wisdom.

Note

1. Many Internet safety organizations offer lesson plans, videos, role-playing games, advice, and even school visits. These include Netsmartz Teens (www.netsmartz.org/netteens.htm), SafeTeens.com (www.safeteens.com), Teen Angels (www.teenangels.org), and Web Wise Kids (www.webwisekids.org).

References

David-Ferdon, C., & Hertz, M. F. (2007). Electronic media, violence, and adolescents: An emerging public health problem. *Journal of Adolescent Health, 41*(6), 1–5.

Kowalski, R., & Limber, S. (2007). Electronic bullying among middle school students. *Journal of Adolescent Health, 41*(6), 22–30.

Williams, K., & Guerra, N. (2007). Prevalence and predictors of Internet bullying. *Journal of Adolescent Health, 41*(6), 14–21.

Worthen, M. (2007). Commentary: Education policy implications from the expert panel on electronic media and youth violence. *Journal of Adolescent Health, 41*(6), 61–63.

Critical Thinking

1. Interview a school psychologist or school counselor at a local middle or high school about issues related to student use of Internet/social media. What do they say about how frequently there are problems among students related to interactions that take place via social networking? What is the school's policy regarding the use of social media and how are situations handled when problems arise beyond the boundaries of the school environment? What are some things the school has implemented to educate students and minimize the risk of incidents related to Internet safety?

2. What were some of the benefits of the activity identified by the sixth- and eighth-grade students?

3. How could this serve as a model for your classroom?

4. Interview three students of different ages (elementary, middle, high school) about Internet and social media use and behaviors. How much similarity was there between the kinds of things your interviewees discussed and the items on the questionnaire used in the study?

Johanna Mustacchi teaches media literacy at Pierre Van Cortlandt Middle School in Croton-on-Hudson, New York; jmustacchi@croton-harmonschools.org.

Tackling a Problematic Behavior Management Issue

Teachers' Intervention in Childhood Bullying Problems

In coping with and addressing a common child behavioral problem, classroom teachers may benefit from viewing bullying as a behavior management issue in the educational setting. The authors offer eight suggestions that specifically address childhood bullying problems in the classroom. Teachers can add these to their toolkit of behavior management strategies.

LAURA M. CROTHERS AND JERED B. KOLBERT

Child disciplinary problems can be stressful for a classroom teacher. Teachers find accommodating behavioral difficulties more challenging and less feasible than making instructional modifications for academic problems (Ritter, 1989). In fact, researchers have suggested the existence of a relationship between disruptive student behavior patterns (e.g., disrespect, poor social skills) and teacher burnout (Hastings & Bham, 2003).

When asked about managing problematic student behavior, teachers often respond in one of two ways: It is not much of a concern, because their classroom management strategies are typically effective in resolving student behavioral concerns, or they feel overwhelmed and impotent to address behavioral difficulties that threaten to disrupt the learning process and subsequent academic achievement of students (Discipline Problems Take a Toll, 2004). Those in the latter group often explain that they were not adequately trained to manage students with behavior problems or they believe that teachers who are effective classroom managers are inherently talented in rectifying disciplinary issues demonstrated by children at school.

The use of such external attributions or excuses can compromise a teacher's ability to successfully take responsibility for student behavior and learning in the classroom. Early intervention is critically important in preventing and reducing children's behavior problems (Dodge, 1993). Interestingly, the primary difference between successful and unsuccessful behavior managers is not the manner in which they handle discipline problems but rather the number of discipline problems they encounter. Effective classroom managers create a structured environment and manage behavior antecedents to diminish the likelihood of behavior problems ever occurring (Duke, 1982; Elliott, Witt, Kratochwill, & Stoiber, 2002).

It is from the vantage of behavior management that childhood bullying problems can be addressed, because such issues often demand a significant portion of teachers' behavior modification efforts. Research has established a normative (i.e., routinely occurring) nature of bully–victim relationships in schools (Smith & Brain, 2000). Further, childhood bullying has increasingly been recognized as one of the most common and widespread forms of school violence occurring not only in the United States but in other countries as well. *Bullying* has been defined as repetitive instrumental aggression that results in an imbalance of power between perpetrator and victim (Smith & Brain, 2000), and it involves approximately 30% of U.S. students during their school careers (Nansel et al., 2001).

Victims of bullying behavior suffer from anxiety, depression, low self-esteem, physical and psychosomatic complaints, posttraumatic stress disorder, and suicidal ideation (Kaltiala-Heino, Rimpela, Marttunen, Rimpela, & Rantenan, 1999; McKenney, Pepler, Craig, & Connolly, 2002; Williams, Chambers, Logan, & Robinson, 1996). Perpetrators of bullying also experience negative effects, including an increased risk of mental health disorders, such as attention-deficit/hyperactivity disorder, depression, oppositional defiant disorder, and conduct disorder (Kumpulainen, Rasanen, & Puura, 2001). Children who bully also exhibit a greater likelihood of engaging in criminal behavior, domestic violence, and substance abuse as adults (Farrington, 1993) and are more likely to struggle with poor academic achievement and poor career performance in adulthood (Carney & Merrell, 2001). Finally, researchers have found that childhood bullies are often severely punitive with their own children, who are subsequently more likely to be aggressive with peers (Eron, Huesmann, Dubow, Romanoff, & Yarmel, 1987; Smokowski & Kopasz, 2005).

Much research has documented the prevalence and negative effects of bullying, yet some literature has also suggested that teachers sometimes contribute to or tolerate the problem. According to Olweus (1991), students often report that teachers do not intervene when a student is being bullied in school, and many times teachers are unaware of occurrences of bullying. This is particularly surprising because students frequently indicate that bullying occurs in the classroom while the teacher is present (Olweus, 1991). Olweus (1993) also explained that when teachers recognize that bullying is occurring, they often do relatively little to put a stop to the behavior and make only limited contact with students involved in the bullying to discuss the problem. This lack of intervention may be particularly dangerous because children who engage in bullying may interpret the resulting adult nonintervention as tacit approval of their behavior.

However, because of the incidence and negative effects on victims and perpetrators, school personnel are increasingly recognizing that bullying is a problem that must be addressed in the educational setting. For purposes of empowerment and a sense of control, it may be helpful for classroom teachers to view the problem of bullying as a behavior management issue, similar to off-task or other non-rule-governed behavior. Also, it may be easier to prevent childhood bullying problems rather than react to them, because responding to incidents of peer victimization can be difficult for such reasons as not directly observing the behavior or not being aware of the extent of the problem due to students not reporting bullying to adults (Crothers & Kolbert, 2004). Eight suggestions are offered to enable teachers to add to their toolkit of behavior management strategies, as well as to specifically address childhood bullying problems in their classrooms.

Assessment

Although teachers measure students' scholastic achievement on a daily basis in their classrooms, they often feel reluctant to use assessment methods to investigate nonacademic problems, believing that such domains are best handled by the training and skills demonstrated by school psychologists and counselors. However, engaging in assessment of bullying behavior is an important first step in addressing the problem. The best news about gathering data regarding childhood bullying is that it can be quite simple. Teachers can compile a list of their students' names and divide the children into three groups: *bullies, victims,* and *bystanders.* Similarly, educators can choose to identify which children match certain behavioral descriptors (e.g., aggressive, assertive, passive). After students have been identified as bullies or victims, they can be targeted for individual intervention efforts.

Some researchers have questioned the accuracy of teacher nomination of bullies and victims, believing that teachers may lack objectivity in identifying bullies and victims and may underestimate the amount of bullying that takes place in school (Smith & Ananiadou, 2003; Smith & Sharp, 1994). Also, teachers may be unable to discern between bullying and horseplay and may have biases regarding their students (Hazler, Carney, Green, Powell, & Jolly, 1997; Pellegrini & Bartini, 2000). However, teachers can minimize such problems by spending long periods of time observing their students in a variety of settings (e.g., classroom, playground, lunchroom) as well as engaging in periodic retraining in conducting accurate observations and reliability checks (e.g., comparing perceptions with another teacher). When possible, information provided through teacher assessment should be compared with students' perceptions of which students are bullying others or are frequently victimized; teachers' and students' shared experiences illuminate the problem (Pellegrini & Bartini, 2000).

Guidance Approaches

Whole-school anti-bullying programs typically use guidance lessons, such as drama (e.g., acting out scenarios), watching videos, and reading books as a means of addressing bullying in the classroom. The primary purpose of such activities can be viewed as sensitization to the problem of bullying. Drama, videos, books, and discussions about bullying can give children the language to identify and talk about the experience of bullying. Teachers of young children can act out bullying scenarios using puppets to play the roles of victim and bully. As children mature into adolescence, teachers can encourage children to develop scripts that depict bullying and use puppets to act out the scenarios.

Videos and books are also a helpful medium for educators to introduce awareness of bullying to their students. Children's literature that addresses bullying behavior, such as *Nobody Knew What to Do: A Story About Bullying* (McCain & Leonardo, 2001), can help children understand that bullying is a common problem by emphasizing the need to seek help from adults (Ralston, 2005). There are also nonfiction selections for students, such as *Bullies to Buddies: How to Turn Your Enemies Into Friends!* (Czarnecki, 2005; Kalman, 2004), which teaches children to avoid being victims of bullying by turning anger into humor, fear into courage, and enemies into friends through the use of verbal interactions and body language.

Videos and DVDs on bullying are also available, such as *Bullies Are a Pain in the Brain* (Comical Sense Company, 2005), in which the main character tries to develop solutions to make a bully leave him alone. Selections for older children, such as *End the Silence: Stop the Bullying* (Sunburst, 2004) are appropriate for Grades 7 through 12 and can model solution strategies for students, such as banding together and refusing to tolerate the behavior, as well as the implementing a whole-school anti-bullying program. Teachers can use these materials and experiences as a catalyst for discussions about bullying in their classrooms.

Classroom Management Techniques

It may be helpful for teachers to consider classroom management as an aspect of instruction, curriculum, and school climate rather than one of control (Duke, 1982; Levin & Nolan, 2004). Effective instruction is probably the most powerful form of classroom management because children who are actively engaged in learning are less likely to have the time and inclination to engage in bullying. Curricula that encourage children to question their own assumptions and engage in critical thinking will reduce boredom and the opportunity to bully for entertainment purposes. Having activities overlap so that students are continuously busy with learning tasks can diminish the opportunity that children have to assert power over one another.

In conjunction with curriculum and effective teaching, consideration should be paid to creating a classroom climate that is inhospitable to bullying. Thus, one of the first strategies in addressing bullying is to establish rules prohibiting it. Teachers can provide students with information that instructs them on how they should handle bullying behavior (Batsche, 1997; Boulton & Underwood, 1992). As a part of a general classroom management strategy, teachers can also implement whole-class incentive systems that encourage children to control their aggressive behavior and concentrate on meeting behavioral goals. Programs such as *The Winning Ticket* (Floyd, 1985) are based on the notion that socially appropriate behaviors are skills that can be learned.

Another means of addressing bullying is teacher vigilance regarding student behavior in the classroom and throughout the school in general. Teachers need to be constantly aware of student conduct and activities, because bullying often occurs in the classroom without the teacher's knowledge. Behavior problems such as bullying are also as likely to occur during unstructured times, such as the transition from one class or activity to the next, in the gym, in the cafeteria, or on the bus. Consequently, adults responsible for supervising children during those times need to be aware of the signs of bullying behavior and be given the authority to intervene when they suspect bullying is occurring.

Cooperative Learning Activities

One way that teachers can increase student familiarity with and acceptance of others is to use cooperative learning activities in the classroom. Researchers have emphasized that such activities have been effective in improving attitudes and relationships among children in ethnically diverse and special education inclusion classrooms (Boulton & Underwood, 1992; Cowie, Smith, Boulton, & Laver, 1994; Johnson & Johnson, 1980). Classroom teachers can develop cooperative learning groups and offer group rewards to facilitate improved social integration that would not ordinarily occur (Hoover & Hazler, 1991; Johnson & Johnson, 1980). Teachers should strive to balance competitive activities, which focus on individual achievement, with cooperative goals that help emphasize group achievement (Hazler, 1996).

Boulton and Underwood (1992) suggested pairing older children with younger children through joint projects in the classroom or through peer tutoring. Cooperative learning activities encourage friendship, identification, and a sense of protectiveness between the older and younger students. Such feelings cause compassion in the children (Pink & Brownlee, 1988) and may help to lessen victimization. This was evidenced in a Japanese study, in which bullies' moral empathic perception and emotion toward victimization were positively related to the reduction of bullying (Honma, 2003).

Teachers should, however, consider power differentials between children when planning for group collaboration work in the classroom. Because bullying is associated with both implicit (i.e., wealth, attractiveness, and athletic competence) and explicit (i.e., physical and relational aggression) forms of power, educators need to make sure that groups are not vastly different in their power status (Vaillancourt, Hymel, & McDougall, 2003). Teachers may be naturally inclined to group bullies and victims together yet may instead consider forming groups with individuals who have only slight differences in social power. Alternately, because bullies tend to have high social status and power, educators can appeal to high-status non-bullies to intervene when victims are being bullied by peers. When assured that a high-status child would be amenable to advocate for another child, a teacher might then feel comfortable assembling these individuals together (Vaillancourt et al., 2003).

Assertiveness, Self-Esteem, and Social Skills Training for Victims of Bullying

Bullying prevention programs often include long-term interventions for victims of bullying to remedy deficits that are commonly found in this population. Social skills development appears to be an essential skill base because researchers have found that social isolation is a major risk factor for victimization (Boulton, Trueman, Chau, Whitehand, & Amataya, 1999), and perpetrators likely recognize the vulnerability of a student whom no peer will assist. Also, the development of friendships provides the unpopular student with a support network to ease the emotional pain of low social status. Teachers can promote victims' self-esteem by helping them identify their personal strengths that might attract peers as potential friends.

Furthermore, teachers can instruct students to replace negative statements about themselves with more positive or realistic ones, which is likely to increase the child's confidence as well as reduce his or her social anxiety. Victimized students are often realistically pessimistic about their chances of success in developing friendships, and research has suggested that the social status of victimized students is both negative and longstanding (Boulton & Smith, 1994; Salmivalli, Lappalainen, & Lagerspetz, 1998). Thus, victimized students often need encouragement to engage in such risk taking in an attempt to establish social connections. One helpful strategy is to encourage the victimized student to focus on his or her effort and performance to make friends, rather than the results of these efforts, which rarely bear immediate fruit.

Another common problem victimized students have as they pursue friendships is the lack of social intelligence, such as failing to understand the social status of other students. As a result, victimized students may attempt to befriend the most popular students, who are unlikely to reciprocate in a mutual desire for friendship. In such cases, the teacher can ask victimized students to think about who seems to want or need a friend, explaining that because popular students have many friends, they may not have enough time for another relationship.

An example of a long-term intervention to assist victimized students is Fox and Boulton's (2003) study of the effects of an eight-session social skills/assertiveness training program in which the curriculum was delivered in a group format to chronically victimized students. The social skills aspect of the program was used to teach students a variety of skills, including listening, having conversations, and asking to join in peer groups. The assertiveness component of the program was used to instruct students in the use of more confident body language, relaxation skills, positive thinking, and verbal strategies for dealing with bullying. Fox and Boulton found that the program led to a significant increase in victims' self-esteem, which was maintained at a 3-month follow-up but noted that the program did not have a significant impact upon victims' number of friends, peer acceptance, depression, or anxiety. Group interventions for victimized students may result in greater success when role-playing is used, with specific behaviors modeled for students and followed by supervised practice with peers.

Constructive Conversations with Victims of Bullying

When asked what teachers do to stop bullying behavior when it occurs, students are likely to report that teachers intervene in bullying scenarios less often than children would prefer (Crothers & Kolbert, 2004). In particular, victims of bullying may feel that bullies are actually receiving more teacher attention than do those who are being harassed by peers. Olweus (1992) has identified characteristics of those who are frequently victimized by bullying:

> Victims of bullying are more anxious and insecure than students in general. They are often cautious, sensitive, and quiet. When attacked by other students, they commonly react by crying (at least in the lower grades) and withdrawal. They have a negative view of themselves and their situation. They often look upon themselves as failures and feel stupid, ashamed, and unattractive. (p. 103)

Furthermore, Olweus (1993) noted that victims are often unpopular among their peers and lack even one identifiable friend. Because victims of bullying tend not to tease or display aggression toward peers, other students may assume that they will not retaliate when harassed.

Assisting the student who is frequently bullied may require both short- and long-term intervention. Short-term interventions address specific incidents of bullying, whereas long-term interventions involve skill building to increase confidence and avoid the probability of future victimization. Victims are unlikely to report bullying incidents because they fear exacerbation of the problem or retribution, so it is essential that teachers attempt to alleviate the anxiety of the victim during an investigation of bullying (Olweus, 1993). Educators should inform the child that whatever he or she decides to reveal will be held in confidence, while simultaneously building rapport and educating the victim in identifying what emotions he or she is likely to be experiencing. In addition, the teacher can instill hope in children by sharing that he or she has had success in dealing with such incidents in the past. Victims often internalize bullying, attributing the unwanted behaviors to characteristics within themselves. Thus, it is important to help the victim realize that he or she has done nothing to provoke the bullying behavior and that his or her anger regarding the experience is normal and justified.

Once information about the bullying behavior has been gathered, it is important to explain to the victim what the teacher will do with the information, which may include talking with witnesses and the alleged perpetrator, assigning a negative consequence to the perpetrator, and informing other teachers of the behavior so that they more closely observe the students who are involved. If the bullying incident is either severe or is indicative of an ongoing pattern, the teacher can gather additional data by interviewing other students who may have witnessed such incidents. Teachers can ask the victim to identify other students (who are not friends of the victim or the perpetrator) who may have observed such events, explaining to the victim that these witnesses will not be informed of how they were recognized as being involved. In many cases, the victimization has been occurring for several months and thus the victim can often readily identify other students who may have observed such events. Furthermore, victims should be encouraged to approach the teacher if bullying incidents reoccur.

Constructive Conversations with Students Who Frequently Bully

Research on students who frequently bully reveals some common characteristics. Perpetrators of bullying behavior tend to lack empathy (Olweus, 1993), misattribute their peers' actions as being the result of hostile intentions, demonstrate impulsivity, perceive aggression as an acceptable way to resolve conflict, and exhibit a high need for dominance (Graham & Juvonen, 1998; Olweus, 1993; Ross, 1996). Whereas students who are frequently victimized are generally unpopular with peers, perpetrators of bullying tend to have above-average popularity in primary grades and declining popularity in junior and senior high school.

When first meeting with a student who has been bullying peers, it is important to use a serious tone to convey an important message. The teacher should immediately indicate that he or she is speaking with the student because of his or her inappropriate behavior. To gain the trust of the bully, it is best to begin the conversation with the identification of the bullying behavior and the consequence for this behavior—a straightforward delivery ensures that the student will not be trapped in a lie by asking for his or her version of events. Thus, it is important that teachers collect evidence from other student witnesses prior to meeting with the perpetrator. The teacher should also inform the bully that other teachers and school staff will be made aware of the incident to prevent such behaviors from occurring in the future.

At this point, the teacher should shift into using more of a concerned and caring tone, as the objective is to enable the perpetrator to nondefensively evaluate whether his or her behavior is meeting his or her goals. A common misperception among adults is that students who bully have low self-esteem and thus are motivated to bully others in an attempt to feel better about themselves (Olweus, 1993). Rather than attempting to increase the self-esteem of the student who frequently bullies, teachers can affirm the student's strengths and popularity. Research has been suggestive of bullies' need for dominance, so a discussion of the student's high social status may be appealing to students who frequently bully (Graham & Juvonen, 1998; Olweus, 1993; Ross, 1996).

Ideally, this tactic will enable the student who frequently bullies to realize that victimizing peers is unnecessary to achieve his or her desire for social status. It also serves to help build the teacher—student relationship, which increases the likelihood that the student will engage in self-evaluative behavior. As the student begins to develop trust in the educator, the teacher can more assertively discuss the value of having concern for others, encouraging the student to consider what the victim was feeling and what restitution may be owed. It may be helpful to engage peer victimizers in middle/junior high school in discussions regarding the potential ramifications of bullying, such as the negative impact upon friendships in later grades, explaining that the popularity of students who use aggression typically decreases when they enter high school.

Parent–Teacher Collaboration

If students continue to bully after several months of intervention, the teacher may want to involve parents, although students who frequently bully are likely to receive parenting with little nurturance, along with discipline that is physical and severe (Olweus, 1993). Moreover, family members of child bullies often demonstrate a high need for power (Bowers, Smith, & Binney, 1994). Parents of children who bully others may not regard the behavior as a concern, possibly because such a strong power differential is demonstrated in their own family system. In other words, such behavior may appear to parents of bullies as normal and effective. Thus, it is important for teachers to recognize that parents of bullies may become emotionally reactive when attention and criticism is paid to their children's victimizing behavior.

A realistic objective in conferencing with the parents of perpetrators is to gain at least enough of their support so that they will not undermine teachers or administrators by directly or indirectly implying to their children that they do not need to adhere to the rules regarding bullying. In conferencing with parents of bullying students, teachers should use a no-nonsense, factual presentation and avoid engaging in questioning, long discussions, or using a tone that invites blame upon the parents of the bully. Similar to student perpetrators of bullying, it is not uncommon for parents for minimize or deny the bullying incident. For such situations, it is best that the school staff be prepared to offer concrete evidence of such behavior. Furthermore, the teacher may explain to the parents of the bully, in a respectful and non-emotional manner, the possible consequences if their child continues such behaviors, which may include further school sanctions and eventually decreased popularity among peers. Another effective technique is for the teacher to share with the parents some of their child's strengths and invite the parents to do so as well. Then ask the parents what they believe their child needs to learn at this point in his or her development.

Victims who require long-term intervention may also benefit from parental involvement. Research has suggested that students who are frequently bullied may be closely connected to their parents (Bowers et al., 1994; Olweus, 1993), which may actually impede the development of appropriate peer relations. Some parents react to knowledge that their child is being bullied through over-protection. For example, they may attempt to become their child's best friend, engaging in many social activities with the youngster that effectively fail to help the child develop positive peer relations. Teachers can help the such parents develop a perspective of their child as competent, able to deal with bullying situations, and able to develop friendships with guided assistance.

Teachers may also encourage parents to think about how they might help to promote their child's social development, such as inviting friends to the home, role playing through social situations, and getting involved in social organizations that relate to their child's strengths. Encouraging non-athletic victimized children to become involved in team sports may lead to further social rejection, so parents of victims can also be encouraged to consider enhancing their child's physical development through supporting participation in individual sports such as karate, bicycling, swimming, and running.

Discussion

One reason that bullying has persisted throughout human history is that it has traditionally been treated as a socially acceptable means of establishing and securing social position as well as cementing power differences between people (Greene, 2003). Calling attention to the problem by encouraging teachers to tackle bullying as a common behavior management issue may help them effectively address peer victimization in the school environment. A variety of strategies have been presented that teachers can use to reduce child bullying. Educators are encouraged to use these techniques in conjunction with one another as researchers have suggested that bullying can be reduced most effectively through a comprehensive effort that addresses both individual incidents of bullying as well as modifying classroom and overall school environments that indirectly support bullying (e.g., Olweus, 1993).

Teachers are also encouraged to carefully consider the timing of implementing these techniques:

1. Assessment would logically precede guidance curricular approaches to both educate children about the nature of the problem and offer solutions for dealing with students who frequently bully.
2. Improving instruction and curriculum, modifying classroom management techniques, and initiating cooperative learning activities should occur alongside guidance lessons.
3. Constructive conversations with perpetrators and students who are frequently victimized should be reserved for when children have been educated about the new norms regarding this form of aggression.
4. Finally, parent–teacher collaboration is best used for the more entrenched cases of bullying problems given the time investment required of this technique.

Teachers have the power and the techniques available to them to make the classroom a socially just environment that is more hospitable to child development and learning. The techniques that have been identified are not complex, but they do require a significant effort on the part of the teacher. Still, such simple but clear efforts on the part of teachers to address the problem are likely to remove some of the tacit support that schools have historically provided to popular students' desire for dominance (Greene, 2003). The potential benefits seem well worth the effort and can be readily justified in the current educational environment given the negative impact bullying has on the social and emotional development and academic achievement of victims.

References

Batsche, G. M. (1997). Bullying. In G. G. Bear, K. M. Minke, & A. Thomas (Eds.), *Children's needs II: Development, problems, and alternatives* (pp. 171–179). Bethesda, MD: National Association of School Psychologists.

Boulton, M. J., & Smith, P. K. (1994). Bully/victim problems in middle school children: Stability, self-perceived competence, peer-perceptions and peer acceptance. *British Journal of Developmental Psychology, 12,* 315–329.

Boulton, M. J., Trueman, M., Chau, C., Whitehand, C., & Amataya, K. (1999). Concurrent and longitudinal links between friendship and peer victimization: Implications for befriending interventions. *Journal of Adolescence, 22,* 461–466.

Boulton, M. J., & Underwood, K. (1992). Bully/victim problems among middle school children. *British Journal of Educational Psychology, 62,* 73–87.

Boulton, L., Smith, P. K., & Binney, V. (1994). Perceived family relationships of bullies, victims, and bully/victims in middle childhood. *Journal of Social and Personal Relationships, 11,* 215–232.

Carney, A. G., & Merrell, K. W. (2001). Bullying in schools: Perspectives on understanding and preventing an international problem. *School Psychology International, 22*(3), 364–382.

The Comical Sense Company (Producer). (2005). *Bullies are a pain in the brain* [Motion picture]. (Available from the Comical Sense Company, http://www.trevorromain.com/Shop/item/?Videos/DVD00)

Cowie, H., Smith, P., Boulton, M., & Laver, R. (1994). *Cooperation in the multi-ethnic classroom.* London: David Fulton.

Crothers, L. M., & Kolbert, J. B. (2004). Comparing middle school teachers' and students' views on bullying and anti-bullying interventions. *Journal of School Violence, 3*(1), 17–32.

Czarnecki, K. (2005). Bullies to buddies: How to turn your enemies into friends! *School Library Journal, 51*(2), 148.

Discipline problems take a toll. (2004). *American Teacher, 89*(1), 7.

Dodge, K. A. (1993). The future of research on the treatment of conduct disorder. *Development and Psychopathology, 5,* 311–319.

Duke, D. L. (1982). *Helping teachers manage classrooms.* Alexandria, VA: Association for Supervision of Curriculum and Instruction.

Elliott, S. N., Witt, J. C., Kratochwill, T. R., & Stoiber, K. C. (2002). Selecting and evaluating classroom interventions. In M. A. Shinn, H. M. Walker, & G. Stoner (Eds.), *Interventions for academic and behavior problems II: Preventive and remedial approaches* (pp. 243–294). Bethesda, MD: National Association of School Psychologists.

Eron, L. D., Huesmann, R. L., Dubow, E., Romanoff, R., & Yarmel, P. W. (1987). Childhood aggression and its correlates over 22 years. In D. Crowell, I. M. Evans, & C. R. O'Donnell (Eds.), *Childhood aggression and violence* (pp. 249–262). New York: Plenum.

Farrington, D. P. (1993). Understanding and preventing bullying. In M. Tonry (Ed.), *Crime and justice: A review of research* (pp. 381–458). Chicago: University of Chicago Press.

Floyd, N. M. (1985). Pick on somebody your own size. *Pointer, 29,* 9–17.

Fox, C. L., & Boulton, M. J. (2003). Evaluating the effectiveness of a social skills training programme for victims of bullying. *Educational Research, 45*(3), 231–247.

Graham, S., & Juvonen, J. (1998). A social cognitive perspective on peer aggression and victimization. *Annals of Child Development, 12,* 21–66.

Greene, M. (2003). Counseling and climate change as treatment modalities for bullying in schools. *International Journal for the Advancement of Counselling, 25*(4), 293–302.

Hastings, R. P., & Bham, M. S. (2003). The relationship between student behavior patterns and teacher burnout. *School Psychology International, 24*(1), 115–127.

Hazler, R. J. (1996). *Breaking the cycle of violence: Interventions for bullying and victimization.* Bristol, PA: Accelerated Development.

Hazler, R. J., Carney, J. V., Green, S., Powell, R., & Jolly, L. S. (1997). Areas of expert agreement on identification of school bullies and victims. *School Psychology International, 18*(1), 5–14.

Honma, T. (2003). Cessation of bullying and intervention with bullies: Junior high school students. *Japanese Journal of Educational Psychology, 51,* 390–400.

Hoover, J. H., & Hazler, R. J. (1991). Bullies and victims. *Elementary School Guidance and Counseling, 25,* 212–219.

Johnson, D. W., & Johnson, R. T. (1980). Integrating handicapped children into the mainstream. *Exceptional Children, 47*(2), 90–98.

Kalman, I. (2004). *Bullies to buddies: How to turn your enemies into friends.* Staten Island, NY: Wisdom Pages.

Kaltiala-Heino, R., Rimpela, M., Marttunen, M., Rimpela, A., & Rantenan, P. (1999). Bullying, depression, and suicidal ideation in Finnish adolescents: School survey. *British Medical Journal, 319*(7206), 348–351.

Kumpulainen, K., Rasanen, E., & Puura, K. (2001). Psychiatric disorders and the use of mental health services among children involved in bullying. *Aggressive Behavior, 27,* 102–110.

Levin, J., & Nolan, J. F. (2004). *Principles of classroom management: A professional decision-making model.* New York: Pearson.

McCain, B. R., & Leonardo, T. (2001). *Nobody knew what to do: A story about bullying.* Morton Grove, IL: Albert Whitman.

McKenney, K. S., Pepler, D. J., Craig, W. M., & Connolly, J. A. (2002). Psychosocial consequences of peer victimization in elementary and high school—An examination of posttraumatic stress disorder symptomatology. In K. A. Kendall-Tackett & S. M. Giacomoni (Eds.), *Child victimization: Maltreatment, bullying and dating violence, prevention and intervention* (pp. 15-1–15-17). Kingston, NJ: Civic Research Institute.

Nansel, T. R., Overpeck, M., Pilla, R. S., Ruan, W. J., Simons-Morton, B., & Scheidt, P. (2001). Bullying behaviors among US youth: Prevalence and association with psychosocial adjustment. *Journal of the American Medical Association, 285,* 2094–2100.

Olweus, D. (1991). Bully/victim problems among school children: Some basic facts and effects of a school-based intervention program. In D. Pepler & K. Rubin (Eds.), *The development and treatment of childhood aggression* (pp. 411–438). Hillsdale, NJ: Lawrence Erlbaum.

Olweus, D. (1992). Bullying among school children: Intervention and prevention. In R. Peters, J. McMahon, & V. I. Quinsley (Eds.), *Aggression and violence throughout the lifespan* (pp. 100–125). Newbury Park, CA: Sage.

Olweus, D. (1993). *Bullying at school: What we know and what we can do.* Cambridge, MA: Blackwell.

Pellegrini, A. D., & Bartini, M. (2000). An empirical comparison of methods of sampling aggression and victimization in school settings. *Journal of Educational Psychology, 92,* 360–366.

Pink, H., & Brownlee, L. (1988, March 4). Playground politics: Pairing off. *Times Educational Supplement,* p. 22a.

Ralston, J. (2005). Nobody knew what to do: A story about bullying. *School Library Journal, 51*(5), 50.

Ritter, D. R. (1989). Teachers' perceptions of problem behavior in general and special education. *Exceptional Children, 55*(6), 559–564.

Ross, D. (1996). *Childhood bullying and teasing.* Alexandria, VA: American Counseling Association.

Salmivalli, C., Lappalainen, M., & Lagerspetz, M. J. (1998). Stability and change of behavior in connection with bullying in schools: A two-year follow-up. *Aggressive Behavior, 24,* 205–218.

Smith, P. K., & Ananiadou, K. (2003). The nature of school bullying and the effectiveness of school-based interventions. *Journal of Applied Psychoanalytic Studies, 5*(2), 189–209.

Smith, P. K., & Brain, P. (2000). Bullying in school: Lessons from two decades of research. *Aggressive Behavior, 26,* 1–9.

Smith, P. K., & Sharp, S. (Eds.). (1994). *School bullying: Insights and perspectives.* London: Routledge.

Smokowski, P. R., & Kopasz, K. H. (2005). Bullying in school: An overview of types, effects, family characteristics, and intervention strategies. *Children and School, 27*(2), 101–110.

Sunburst (Producer). (2004). *End the silence: Stop the bullying* [Motion picture]. (Available from Sunburst, www.sunburstvm.com)

Vaillancourt, T., Hymel, S., & McDougall, P. (2003). Bullying is power: Implications for school-based intervention strategies. *Journal of Applied School Psychology, 19*(2), 157–176.

Williams, K., Chambers, M., Logan, S., & Robinson, D. (1996). Association of common health symptoms with bullying in primary school children. *British Medical Journal, 313,* 17–19.

LAURA M. CROTHERS, DEd, is an assistant professor of school psychology in the Department of Counseling, Psychology, and Special Education at Duquesne University. Her current research interests include bullying of gay, lesbian, bisexual, and transgender children and adolescents and female adolescent relational aggression. JERED B. KOLBERT, PhD, is an associate professor in the Department of Counseling and Development at Slippery Rock University and currently conducts research in bullying and the use of family therapy in responding to adolescent developmental adjustment problems. Address: Laura M. Crothers, Duquesne University, 106 D Canevin Hall, Department of Counseling, Psychology, and Special Education, 600 Forbes Ave., Pittsburgh, PA, 15282; e-mail: crothersl@duq.edu.

Chapter 5
Adolescence

In this chapter we will look at several different facets of the transitional period between childhood and adulthood that we refer to as Adolescence. The first selection gives us a world view of this developmental period, focusing on the impacts of culture and experience. This is done using an excerpt from a textbook written in New Zealand, which offers some unique and interesting perspectives that we in the "western world" might not be as likely to consider. We'll then examine the many physical transformations that take place as well as the cognitive and social changes that are occurring. Next we'll look at how moral reasoning can develop during this time frame and finally four short articles will illustrate the current relevance of these issues.

ADOLESCENCE: A WORLD VIEW

Adolescence usually refers to the period of physiological, personal, psychological and social maturation that occurs in individual humans between the ages of approximately 11 and 18 years. This age is also popularly referred to as the 'teenage' period. In practice, though, there is a definite difference in the experiences of those who are entering adolescence, 'early adolescents', and those who are starting to move through to the end of it, 'youth'. In this chapter, we will look at some of the theoretical ideas that have influenced the ways we think about development at adolescence, and in the next chapter we will consider some of the issues arising for many during this time.

SOME THOUGHTS ABOUT 'ADOLESCENCE'

In the history of humankind, the life stage we call adolescence is relatively new. Of course, puberty (which we will discuss shortly) is not new: what is relatively recent, though, and characteristic of a developmental approach, is the notion of a discrete 'life stage' called adolescence. Much of developmental psychology depends on the idea that developmental stages are both natural and sequential. Like puberty, characteristics of these stages are often seen as an essential aspect of personal growth and development at this time. As social constructionists, we take the position that the biological changes at puberty are a mostly inevitable event in development, but the *meaning* of these bodily changes, and how they are treated and understood are as much a matter of culture as of biology.

We all need to take care with what we take for granted when talking about young people. Many of the expectations of adolescents in the Euro-Western world are produced by cultural and historical processes related to industrial and post-industrial societies, rather than by processes of biological growth. Adolescence is not the same experience everywhere in the world. In many countries, as people increasingly participate in a global culture, it does appear that adolescents may be becoming more similar to each other in different parts of the world. These similarities are more likely to reflect participation in the same global culture, particularly through the influence of the internet, than the bodily experience of puberty meaning the same for everyone. You do not have to agree with us, but it is crucial that you understand our position that all that happens to adolescents is not an inevitable consequence of nature.

Biological approaches to adolescence

Much of the developmental focus on adolescence has been on the biological issues raised by and around puberty. In many instances, it appears to be assumed that biology is destiny: that your biological make-up determines how you will behave—and that you 'can't help it'. Puberty is generally seen as a universal process of maturation. It is sometimes seen as the result of the relentless and mysterious work of hormones, which in turn, are thought to be responsible for multiple effects on the behaviours of young people. Within this point of view, it is sometimes considered that little can be done about the 'raging teens' except to wait for their hormones to settle down.

Various theorists have lent their collective weight to this view over time. US psychologist G. Stanley Hall, published a major work called *Adolescence* in 1904, is often credited with the 'invention' of this new stage of the lifespan. Hall argued that adolescence is a time when children grow into rational adults, and he attributed this to evolutionary and biological rather than social or cognitive processes. Hall also argued that adolescence is a period of inevitable tension and turmoil, naming *conflict with parents*, *mood disruptions* and *risky behavior* as central features—headings which feature strongly still today in discussions of this age group. In the 1930s, the 'Sturm und Drang' (a German phrase usually translated as 'storm and stress') orientation to adolescence was taken further by the psychoanalyst Anna Freud, Sigmund's daughter. Anna Freud declared that '[t]he upholding of a steady equilibrium at adolescence is itself abnormal' (Freud, 1958, p. 275). She thought that the youthful personality was undergoing an internal restructuring during this time, which could account for any real or potential upheaval. This apparent upheaval has been a major focus of theoretical interest in adolescence up until the present day. With this perspective, we see the historical production of the discourse of adolescence, as a developmental stage—and at the same time, we see its production as pathological (a problem), rather than ordinary and healthy. We think this is a narrow view, both of youth and of puberty.

A socio-historical perspective

During the nineteenth century, the process of industrialisation changed places of work so that they were centralised, away from the home base. As a result, families (including children) no longer worked (for their livelihood) together. And as a result of this, childhood became disconnected from the working lives of families, and working lives of adults became separated from the home. As machines took over more and more of the menial jobs, the levels of training required to obtain a job increased, as did the age for leaving compulsory schooling. The period of compulsory schooling has lengthened, as the requirements of industry were deemed to require a more skilled workforce. In the twentieth century in Aotearoa, adolescents were increasingly seen as properly focused on preparation for adulthood (which meant paid work) through participation in education. Thus it is possible to argue that both childhood and adolescence have been produced as developmental life stages by socio-historical factors. After all, children have not always been seen as 'developing' (and, definitely, this is not the case with adolescents!).

The transition to adulthood

'Growing up' is a culturally determined experience that is undergoing significant change around the world. In Aotearoa, consistent with developmental theory, ideas of growing up are linked with getting a job and moving out of home. Yet making this transition is becoming more difficult, and the transition itself is becoming less clear. On the one hand, puberty is occurring before the age of twelve years for up to one in four girls, and children are growing on average into physically larger adults than their parents—so they can appear physically mature earlier than their chronological age would suggest. On the other hand, markers of the transition from childhood to adulthood are confused and confusing: young people can vote at 18, and although they can drink in public at that age in Aotearoa, there is still a lot of nervous discussion in the media and elsewhere about whether this is too young. Such debates suggest to us that the status of adolescents is also uncertain in our society. With certain exceptions, feeding and housing young people who move into tertiary education is seen by government as the responsibility of their parents, at least until young people are 25.

This extension of the age of legal dependency has led some developmental theorists to suggest that we are seeing the creation of another new stage in the lifespan (Arnett, 2000). In this age-and-stage view, adolescence would begin somewhere between 11 and 13, ending around 18, and the new stage, 'youth', would begin around 18 and last until 25. This is the age group of tertiary education students in the USA. Keniston (1970) argued that prolonging of the transition to adulthood is the result of rising prosperity and the increased educational demands of a post-industrial society. In the first decade of the current century, it is difficult to see how this could be the case, as turbulence in the world monetary system is biting into the livelihoods of many families. It would be easier to argue the reverse—that the prolonging of youthful dependency, and the default creation of the stage of youth, is actually about keeping young people occupied, by keeping them in education, mainly, rather like what happened to adolescents after the industrial revolution, because there are no real jobs for them.

What do YOU think?

1. Is there a mismatch between the levels of physical and social maturity of young people in post-industrial societies today? Discuss with another student.
2. Could post-industrial societies do more to offer a useful place for their young people? Explain.
3. Is it inevitable that post-industrial societies will be confused about the place of young people, or could we do better? What would 'better' look like?

A global perspective

In contrast to the assumption that adolescents ought to be in school and shielded from the requirements of the adult world, in some parts of the world children and young people are expected to take what we would see as 'adult' responsibilities, often from a very early age. Of course, in New Zealand, there are young people who take on adult responsibilities, especially for their family—and not only for pocket money. In Pacific societies, it is common for children to take responsibility for their younger siblings from an early age. Although they might have their age in common, young people are not a single homogenous group of people. The many different styles of music that are available to young people give an indication of how diverse young people are. Looking around the world, it is apparent that many families struggle to raise their children past childhood. In many countries, young people must work to bring money and food home for their families; there are young people who know poverty, hardship and starvation, children participating in killing as soldiers, and others killed by adults in warfare. Such experiences are far removed from the picture of a protected, happy, innocent and carefree time that is a dominant discourse affecting the lives of children and young people in New Zealand.

Societies vary in their ideas about when it is appropriate for young people to engage in certain behaviours and life tasks, such as becoming sexually active and having children. Developmental theories might encourage us to believe that the practices of cultures in which young people marry early, for example, are old-fashioned and 'wrong'. This shows the *monocultural* Euro-Western orientation of much developmental theorising. It may be good for Euro-Western adolescents to be shielded from adult responsibilities (a point which you may wish to debate), but is it good for young people in every culture?

Social debates about the status of young people are made all the more poignant because various cultural traditions struggle, each in their different ways, to come to terms with the political and cultural implications of globalisation of capital, and increasing power of world bodies, such as the International Monetary Fund, the World Bank and many multinational companies. The financial crisis that is sweeping the globe as we write, demonstrates how our destinies are increasingly intertwined around the globe. Young people have, to an extent, led the way in using social-networking through internet and other digital forms such as texting, and such developments (particularly the internet) operate across national and geographical boundaries. Access to information has never been easier or more plentiful. These developments must have an impact on the hopes and aspirations of young people, but the focus of concern, from older folk, is often on the risks involved. We think there is plenty of evidence that the lives of young people today are very different from the lives of their parents when they were adolescents. As always, we invite you to think about the impact of current historical and social influences on your life and perhaps discuss these issues with your own family and friends.

If we accept that the world is changing fairly rapidly, this means, among other things, that new generations will meet situations and circumstances that will be unfamiliar to older generations. Thus, young people will inevitably experience social and global developments differently than their parents did at the same age. But we do not wish to imply that young people 'know more' about the future of global development. What it does mean is that the old intergenerational order, where the elders know what it is like to be a certain age, can no longer be counted on. This argument is not a licence for young people to ignore their elders. Equally, older folk ought not to leave young people to meet the conditions of their lives without attempting to understand the impact of newer realities such as social networking and technological changes—and lack of jobs—on the lives of young people. We do think that developmental theorists and others, including parents and grandparents, teachers and policemen, are not helping if we focus on what is pathological, difficult and problematic about young people and their behaviour. At the same time, the shift from a focus on problems and difficulties to issues should not divert attention away from the special developmental considerations at adolescence.

Is there a profound cultural revolution under way, with young people leading a changeover to postmodern society with completely new and more flexible rules for living? Some young people might like to claim so. We think the picture is less clear. One of us authors (Wendy) was part of a movement for environmental change and sustainable living in the early 1970s, while the other (Lise) lived for a year on a communal farm with chickens and vegetables. At the time, there was huge concern about the global reliance on oil and the nature of global development. Sound familiar? Regardless of how the status of young people is viewed, it seems clear that the idea of 'youth' as a single category is not a useful approach to the so-called 'youth question' (Cohen, 1997). Between the ages of about 10 years of age and 30, for example, we can see that major changes occur in people's lives, and it would be wrong to assume that the issues are the same for all young people across this wide age span. We have to be especially wary not to assume that we know what it is like for someone, just because they are of a certain age.

Tutorial suggestions

Ask students to ask their parents, or people of that generation, whether they think the experience of adolescence is different now from what it was when they were young. What are the differences that people talk about? How might we go about studying this question retrospectively? (You could use Chapter 3 to help with this.)

PHYSICAL DEVELOPMENT IN ADOLESCENCE

When Does Puberty Start?

Is the beginning of adolescence marked by any one physiological event? The sequence of bodily changes in puberty is surprisingly constant. This holds true whether puberty starts early or late and regardless of the culture in which the child is reared. Table 12.1 lists the sequences of physiological change.

Hormonal balance   One of the triggering mechanisms of puberty that may be used to indicate the onset of adolescence.

Menarche   Onset of menstruation.

Which of these physical events in the life of the adolescent might we choose as the actual beginning of puberty? Change in **hormonal balance** is first, but its beginning is difficult to pinpoint. Skeletal growth, genital growth, pubic hair, breast development, voice change, growth spurt—are all inconvenient to measure. **Menarche** has been suggested as the major turning point for girls, but many women do not recall menarche as a particularly significant event. Hormonal changes actually precede menarche by about two years, or as early as 8 or 9 years of age. Sometimes the first ejaculation is suggested as the beginning of adolescent puberty for males, but this, too, is often a little-remembered (and possibly repressed) event.

Despite the fact that puberty is primarily thought of as a physical change in an adolescent, the psychological impact can be significant (Dorn & others, 1999; Kosan, 2000). This is especially true with menstruation. Even in these "enlightened" times, too many girls experience menarche without being properly prepared. As a result, an event in a young girl's life that should be remembered as the exciting, positive beginning of the transition to adulthood is instead viewed as a negative, sometimes frightening, experience. When menarche comes early (before 11 years of age), it is more likely to be associated with depression and substance abuse than when it comes later (Beousang & Razor, 2000; Stice, Presenell, & Bearman, 2001). The same is no doubt also the case for a male's first ejaculation. Accurate and accessible information about the changes our bodies undergo benefits adolescents, for whom physical changes often lead to sexual activity (Bingham & Crockett, 1996).

Given our understanding of the physiology of adolescents and differences in individual psychology and culture, we would have to conclude that no single event but, rather, a complex set of events marks the onset of puberty, a process whose effects may be sudden or gradual. Thus, biology alone cannot give us a definition of adolescence; we will need to include psychological and social factors to achieve that.

TABLE 12.1   The Sequence of Physiological Change in Females and Males

FEMALES

- Change in hormonal balance
- The beginning of rapid skeletal growth
- The beginning of breast development
- The appearance of straight, pigmented pubic hair
- The appearance of curly, pigmented pubic hair
- Menarche (first menstruation)
- Maximum growth spurt (when growth is at its fastest rate)
- The appearance of hair on the forearms and underarms

MALES

- Change in hormonal balance
- The beginning of skeletal growth
- The enlargement of the genitals
- The appearance of straight, pigmented pubic hair
- Early voice changes (voice "cracks")
- First ejaculations (wet dreams, nocturnal emissions)
- The appearance of kinky, pigmented pubic hair
- Maximum growth spurt
- The appearance of downy facial hair
- The appearance of hair on the chest and underarms
- Late voice change (the voice deepens)
- Coarse, pigmented facial hair

Note: For more on these physiological changes, see Muuss (1996).

Attitudes Toward Menarche

Menarche can be a confusing experience. Young women learn about menstruation from a number of different sources: their parents (traditionally their mothers) or other relatives, their friends, courses either offered or required in school, or society, including advertising and television shows. However, despite all of these influences, the message that young women learn about this transition has changed very little over the past 40

AN APPLIED VIEW: Dealing with Early or Late Development

Turner, Runtz, and Galambos (1999) found an increased risk of sexual abuse for the early-maturing female. Significantly early to late development has been linked to eating disorders in both boys and girls (Kaltiala-Heino & others, 2001) and to psychological distress and delinquency in boys (Ge, Conger, & Elder, 2001; Williams & Dunlop, 1999), so it is important for practitioners working with adolescents to be aware of the negative reactions to their physical change (or lack of it). If you know a teen who is significantly early or late in body development, be on the lookout for psychological problems. If you find evidence of such problems, make arrangements for the youth to have access to appropriate professional attention.

On the other hand, you should understand that "normal" covers a wide band of developmental time. We should help teens who "hate" their bodies because they are not perfectly average to be more accepting. Finally, if you do feel there is a problem, say nothing to the teen until you have an experienced person's advice on the best course of action.

FIGURE 12.1
This is a picture of typical male and female growth at the turn of last century (King, 1914). What conclusions can you draw from it?

years. According to a study by Beausang and Razor (2000), parents, educators, and the media portray menstruation as mainly a hygienic issue that should be kept a secret from others. Furthermore, they concluded that menstrual education has not changed very much over the past few decades. This is due to a number of factors, including a lack of accurate information on the part of parents and educators, as well as the feelings of embarrassment that people often have when discussing sensitive and personal issues, such as menstruation. However, it is crucial that young women learn the facts about menstruation in a setting where they can feel comfortable to ask questions of an informed individual. This will help them to not only understand their own bodies better, but also to better protect themselves against unplanned sexual activity and pregnancy.

The Secular Trend

Secular trend The phenomenon (in recent centuries) of adolescents puberty sooner and and heavier.

The average teenagers 100 years ago were physically similar in most ways to late maturers of today. This fact is part of the phenomenon called the **secular trend**. The secular trend refers to the decreasing age of the onset of puberty, including a significant drop in the average age at which females in a particular country reach menarche. Earlier puberty affects other developmental factors such as sexual attraction (Alsaker, 1996; McClintock & Herdt, 1996). In Western countries, the average age of menarche has declined about three months per decade over the past hundred years. In the United States, 17 was the average age in the late eighteenth and early nineteenth centuries. By the beginning of the twentieth century, it was 14.5.

Today the average age of menarche is 12.5 years, about the same as it was in 1955. For white girls, the average age is 12.9, for African-Americans, 12.2 (Oberfeld, 1999). Most researchers feel that improved nutrition, sanitation, and health care are responsible for the trend and that we are now at a period of leveling off. There is some evidence that breast development is continuing to occur earlier, however, and that this places even more stress on early maturers. For example, premature development of breasts may make young teens sex objects. Suspected causes for earlier occurrence of these aspects of puberty are

- Lack of exercise—obesity can promote hormone production.
- More fat in diet—same result.
- Presence of hormonelike chemicals in milk and meat (although the evidence for this is scanty (Kaplowitz, 2000).

The findings of the Dorn and associates (1999) study found that girls misreport the onset of menarche by as much as several months. This suggests that girls experience menarche as a series of developmental experiences rather than a single event. Dekovic (1999) found no evidence that childhood conflict influences the timing of puberty. However, Ellis and associates (1999) found that factors of family relationships are associated with starting puberty later. These include fathers' presence in the home, fathers providing more child care,

What are some of the problems that "late maturers" often suffer?

greater supportiveness with the parenting dyad, and more father and mother affection with the daughter. In their study of female athletes, Malina and associates (1998) found that size of family affects menarche. They learned that girls with larger families had later menarche than girls with small families. The delay averaged 2.3 months for each additional sibling in the girls' families. The authors did not offer an explanation for why this should be so. Muscari and associates (1998) found no relationship between the age of menarche of the girls they studied and the age of menarche of their mothers.

Adolescents who experience these changes earlier or later may have no medical problem, but consulting a doctor is probably a good idea. If a glandular imbalance exists, the doctor can usually remedy the problem with little difficulty.

In summary, we may say that the vast majority of human bodies proceed toward maturity in the same way, but that in the last few centuries the timing of the process in females has changed radically. Although timing is affected mainly by biology, psychological and social forces clearly influence it, too.

Three books that provide additional information are (1) Judy Blume's *Are you there, God? It's me, Margaret.* New York: Bradbury. Although written for teens, this book has a wealth of insights into pubertal change, at least for females. (2) R. H. Curtis's *Mind and mood: Understanding and controlling your emotions.* New York: Scribner's. According to Curtis, knowing more about emotions and how they affect the body can help in understanding and controlling them. (3) McCoy and Wibbelsman's *The teenage body book.* Los Angeles, CA: The Body Press. This is an excellent reference book for teenagers and those who work with them.

Guideposts for Study

1. How do adolescents' thinking and use of language differ from younger children's?

2. On what basis do adolescents make moral judgments, and how does prosocial behavior vary?

3. What influences affect adolescents' school success and their educational and vocational planning and preparation?

Aspects of Cognitive Maturation

Adolescents not only look different from younger children, they also think and talk differently. Their speed of information processing continues to increase, though not as dramatically as in middle childhood. Although their thinking may remain immature in some ways, many adolescents are capable of abstract reasoning and sophisticated moral judgments, and they can plan more realistically for the future.

Guidepost 1

How do adolescents' thinking and use of language differ from younger children's?

Piaget's Stage of Formal Operations

Adolescents enter what Piaget called the highest level of cognitive development—**formal operations**—when they develop the capacity for abstract thought. This development, usually around age 11, gives them a new, more flexible way to manipulate information. No longer limited to the here and now, they can understand historical time and extraterrestrial space. They can use symbols for symbols (for example, letting the letter *X* stand for an unknown numeral) and thus can learn algebra and calculus. They can better appreciate metaphor and allegory and thus can find richer meanings in literature. They can think in terms of what *might be,* not just what *is.* They can imagine possibilities and can form and test hypotheses.

People in the stage of formal operations can integrate what they have learned in the past with the challenges of the present and make plans for the future. The ability to think abstractly has emotional implications too. Earlier, a child could love a parent or hate a classmate. Now an adolescent "can love freedom or hate exploitation. . . . The possible and the ideal captivate both mind and feeling" (H. Ginsburg & Opper, 1979, p. 201).

formal operations In Piaget's theory, final stage of cognitive development, characterized by the ability to think abstractly.

Hypothetical-Deductive Reasoning

To appreciate the difference formal reasoning makes, let's follow the progress of a typical child in dealing with a classic Piagetian problem, the pendulum problem.* The child, Adam, is shown the pendulum, an object hanging from a string. He is then shown how he can change any of four factors: the length of the string, the weight of the object, the height from which the object is released, and the amount of force he uses to push the object. He is asked to figure out which factor or combination of factors determines how fast the pendulum swings. (Figure 16-1 depicts this and other Piagetian tasks for assessing the achievement of formal operations.)

When Adam first sees the pendulum, he is not yet 7 years old and is in the preoperational stage. Unable to formulate a plan for attacking the problem, he tries one thing after another in a hit-or-miss manner. First he puts a light weight on a long string and pushes it; then he tries swinging a heavy weight on a short string; then he removes the weight entirely. Not only is his method random, but he also cannot understand or report what has happened.

*This description of age-related differences in the approach to the pendulum problem is adapted from H. Ginsburg and Opper (1979).

(a)

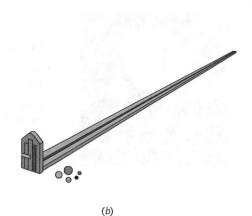

(b)

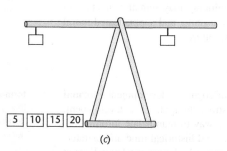

(c)

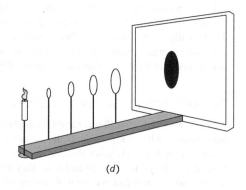

(d)

Figure 16-1

Piagetian tasks for measuring attainment of formal operations.
(a) Pendulum. The pendulum's string can be shortened or lengthened, and weights of varying sizes can be attached to it. The student must determine what variables affect the speed of the pendulum's swing. (b) Motion in a horizontal plane. A spring device launches balls of varying sizes that roll in a horizontal plane. The student must predict their stopping points. (c) Balance beam. A balance scale comes with weights of varying sizes that can be hung at different points along the crossbar. The student must determine what factors affect whether the scale will balance. (d) Shadows. A board containing a row of peg holes is attached perpendicular to the base of a screen. A light source and rings of varying diameters can be placed in the holes, at varying distances from the screen. The student must produce two shadows of the same size, using different-sized rings.

Source: Adapted from Small, Fig. 8-12, 1990.

Adam next encounters the pendulum at age 10, when he is in the stage of concrete operations. This time, he discovers that varying the length of the string and the weight of the object affects the speed of the swing. However, because he varies both factors at the same time, he cannot tell which is critical or whether both are.

Adam is confronted with the pendulum for a third time at age 15, and this time he goes at the problem systematically. He designs an experiment to test all the possible hypotheses, varying one factor at a time—first, the length of the string; next, the weight of the object; then, the height from which it is released; and finally, the amount of force used—each time holding the other three factors constant. In this way, he is able to determine that only one factor—the length of the string—determines how fast the pendulum swings.

Adam's solution of the pendulum problem shows that he has arrived at the stage of formal operations. He is now capable of **hypothetical-deductive reasoning:** He can develop a hypothesis and design an experiment to test it. He considers all the relationships he can imagine and tests them systematically, one by one, to eliminate the false and arrive at the true. Hypothetical-deductive reasoning gives him a tool to solve problems, from fixing the family car to constructing a political theory.

What brings about the shift to formal reasoning? Piaget attributed it chiefly to a combination of brain maturation and expanding environmental opportunities. Both are essential: Even if young people's neurological development has advanced enough to permit formal reasoning, they can attain it only with appropriate environmental stimulation.

As with the development of concrete operations, schooling and culture play a role, as Piaget (1972) ultimately recognized. When adolescents in New Guinea and Rwanda were tested on the pendulum problem, none were able to solve it. On the other hand, Chinese children in Hong Kong, who had been to British schools, did at least as well as U.S. or European children. Schoolchildren in Central Java and New South Wales also showed some formal operational abilities (Gardiner & Kozmitzki, 2005). Apparently, formal reasoning is a learned ability that is not equally necessary or equally valued in all cultures.

Knowing what questions to ask and what strategies work are keys to hypothetical-deductive reasoning. When 30 low-performing urban sixth graders were asked to investigate factors in earthquake risk, those who received a suggestion to focus on one variable at a time made more valid inferences than those who were not given the suggestion (Kuhn & Dean, 2005). This result demonstrates that hypothetical-deductive reasoning can be taught and learned.

Evaluating Piaget's Theory

Although adolescents *do* tend to think more abstractly than younger children, there is debate about the precise age at which this advance occurs (Eccles, Wigfield, & Byrnes, 2003). Piaget's writings provide many examples of children displaying aspects of scientific thinking well before adolescence. At the same time, Piaget seems to have overestimated some older children's abilities. Many late adolescents and adults—perhaps one-third to one-half—seem incapable of abstract thought as Piaget defined it (Gardiner & Kozmitzki, 2005; Kohlberg & Gilligan, 1971; Papalia, 1972), and even those who are capable of abstract thinking do not always use it.

Piaget, in most of his early writings, paid little attention to individual differences, to variations in the same child's performance on different kinds of tasks, or to social and cultural influences. In his later years, Piaget himself "came to view his earlier model of the development of children's thinking, particularly formal operations, as flawed because it failed to capture the essential *role of the situation* in influencing and constraining . . . children's thinking" (Brown, Metz, & Campione, 1996, pp. 152–153). Neo-Piagetian research suggests that children's cognitive processes are closely tied to specific content (what a child is thinking *about*) as well as to the context of a problem and the kinds of information and thought a culture considers important (Case & Okamoto, 1996; Kuhn, 2006).

Furthermore, Piaget's theory does not adequately consider such cognitive advances as gains in information-processing capacity, accumulation of knowledge and expertise in specific fields, and the role of *metacognition,* the awareness and monitoring of one's own mental processes and strategies (Flavell et al., 2002). This ability to "think about what one is thinking about" and, thus, to manage one's mental processes—in other words, enhanced executive function—may be the chief advance of adolescent thought, the result of changes occurring in the adolescent brain (Kuhn, 2006).

hypothetical-deductive reasoning Ability, believed by Piaget to accompany the stage of formal operations, to develop, consider, and test hypotheses.

What's your view **?**

• How can parents and teachers help adolescents improve their reasoning ability?

Checkpoint ✔

Can you . . .

✔ Explain the difference between formal operational and concrete operational thinking, as exemplified by the pendulum problem?

✔ Cite factors influencing adolescents' development of formal reasoning?

✔ Evaluate Piaget's theory of formal operations?

Elkind: Immature Characteristics of Adolescent Thought

We have seen how children develop from egocentric beings to persons capable of solving abstract problems and imagining ideal societies. Yet in some ways adolescents' thinking seems strangely immature. They are often rude to adults, they have trouble making up their minds what to wear each day, and they tend to act as if the whole world revolved around them.

Argumentativeness—usually with parents—is a typical characteristic of adolescent thought, according to David Elkind.

According to the psychologist David Elkind (1984, 1998), such behavior stems from adolescents' inexperienced ventures into formal operational thought. This new way of thinking, which fundamentally transforms the way they look at themselves and their world, is as unfamiliar to them as their reshaped bodies, and they sometimes feel just as awkward in its use. As they try out their new powers, they may sometimes stumble, like an infant learning to walk.

This immaturity of thinking, Elkind suggests, manifests itself in at least six characteristic ways:

1. *Idealism and criticalness:* As adolescents envision an ideal world, they realize how far the real world, for which they hold adults responsible, falls short. They become ultra-conscious of hypocrisy. Convinced that they know better than adults how to run the world, they frequently find fault with their parents and other authority figures.

2. *Argumentativeness:* Adolescents are constantly looking for opportunities to try out their reasoning abilities. They often become argumentative as they build a case for, say, staying out past their curfew.

3. *Indecisiveness:* Adolescents can keep many alternatives in mind at the same time yet may lack effective strategies for choosing among them. They may struggle with simple decisions like whether they should go to the mall with a friend or work on a school assignment.

4. *Apparent hypocrisy:* Young adolescents often do not recognize the difference between expressing an ideal, such as conserving energy, and making the sacrifices necessary to live up to it, such as driving less often.

5. *Self-consciousness:* Adolescents can think about thinking—their own and other people's. However, in their preoccupation with their own mental state, adolescents often assume that everyone else is thinking about the same thing they are thinking about: themselves. Elkind refers to this as the **imaginary audience,** a conceptualized "observer" who is as concerned with a young person's thoughts and behavior as he or she is. The certainty, for example, that everyone is staring at a small pimple all day long is one example of this. The imaginary audience fantasy is especially strong in the early teens but persists to a lesser degree into adult life.

6. *Specialness and invulnerability:* Elkind uses the term **personal fable** to describe a belief by adolescents that they are special, that their experience is unique, and that they are not subject to the rules that govern the rest of the world. This belief might encourage adolescents to believe they can drive fast and recklessly and not get into an accident. According to Elkind, this form of egocentrism underlies much risky, self-destructive behavior. Like the imaginary audience, the personal fable continues into adulthood.

The concepts of the imaginary audience and the personal fable have been widely accepted, but their validity as distinct earmarks of adolescence has little independent research support. In some studies of the personal fable, adolescents were more likely than college students or adults to see themselves as vulnerable to certain risks, such as alcohol and other drug problems, rather than less likely, as the personal fable would predict (Quadrel, Fischoff, & Davis, 1993).

It has been suggested that the imaginary audience and personal fable, rather than constituting universal features of adolescents' cognitive development, may be related to specific social experiences. For example, contrary to the personal fable, in a study of 2,694 urban black adolescents treated at an outpatient clinic in Washington, D.C., about

imaginary audience Elkind's term for observer who exists only in an adolescent's mind and is as concerned with the adolescent's thoughts and actions as the adolescent is.

personal fable Elkind's term for conviction that one is special, unique, and not subject to the rules that govern the rest of the world.

Checkpoint ✔

Can you . . .

✔ Describe Elkind's six proposed aspects of immature adolescent thought, and explain how they may grow out of the transition to formal operational thought?

7 percent of the boys and more than 5 percent of the girls said they believed they would die within the next 2 years. Those who reported taking health risks or being exposed to risky behavior such as weapon carrying were as much as 5.6 times more likely to hold such beliefs than those who had not seen or engaged in such behavior. It is not clear whether these adolescents take risks because, living in dangerous neighborhoods, they expect their lives to be short or whether they expect to die early because of the risks they take (Valadez-Meltzer, Silber, Meltzer, & D'Angelo, 2005).

Guideposts for Study

1. How do adolescents form an identity, and what roles do gender and ethnicity play?

2. What determines sexual orientation, what sexual practices are common among adolescents, and what leads some to engage in risky sexual behavior?

3. How do adolescents relate to parents, siblings, and peers?

4. What causes antisocial behavior, and what can be done to reduce the risk of juvenile delinquency?

5. How do various cultures define what it means to become an adult, and what markers confer adult status?

The Search for Identity

The search for **identity**—according to Erikson, a coherent conception of the self made up of goals, values, and beliefs to which the person is solidly committed—comes into focus during the teenage years. Adolescents' cognitive development now enables them to construct a "theory of the self" (Elkind, 1998). As Erikson (1950) emphasized, the effort to make sense of the self is part of a healthy process that builds on the achievements of earlier stages—on trust, autonomy, initiative, and industry—and lays the groundwork for coping with the challenges of adult life. However, the identity crisis is seldom fully resolved in adolescence; issues concerning identity crop up again and again throughout life.

Erikson: Identity versus Identity Confusion

The chief task of adolescence, said Erikson (1968), is to confront the crisis of **identity versus identity confusion** (or *identity versus role confusion*) so as to become a unique adult with a coherent sense of self and a valued role in society. His concept of the *identity crisis* was based in part on his own life experience. Growing up in Germany as the out-of-wedlock son of a Jewish woman from Denmark who had separated from her first husband, Erikson never knew his biological father. Though adopted at age 9 by his mother's second husband, a German Jewish pediatrician, he felt confusion about who he was. He floundered for some time before settling on his vocation. When he came to the United States, he needed to redefine his identity as an immigrant. All these issues found echoes in the identity crises he observed among disturbed adolescents, soldiers in combat, and members of minority groups (Erikson, 1968, 1973; L. J. Friedman, 1999).

Identity, according to Erikson, forms as young people resolve three major issues: the choice of an *occupation,* the adoption of *values* to live by, and the development of a satisfying *sexual identity.* During middle childhood, children acquire skills needed for success in their culture. As adolescents, they need to find constructive ways to use these skills. When young people have trouble settling on an occupational identity—or when their opportunities are limited—they may engage in behavior with serious negative consequences, such as criminal activity.

Guidepost 1

How do adolescents form an identity, and what roles do gender and ethnicity play?

identity In Erikson's terminology, a coherent conception of the self made up of goals, values, and beliefs to which a person is solidly committed.

identity versus identity confusion Erikson's fifth stage of psychosocial development, in which an adolescent seeks to develop a coherent sense of self, including the role she or he is to play in society. Also called *identity versus role confusion.*

According to Erikson, the *psychosocial moratorium,* the time-out period that adolescence provides, allows young people to search for commitments to which they can be faithful. Adolescents who resolve the identity crisis satisfactorily, according to Erikson, develop the virtue of *fidelity:* sustained loyalty, faith, or a sense of belonging to a loved one or to friends and companions. Fidelity also can mean identification with a set of values, an ideology, a religion, a political movement, a creative pursuit, or an ethnic group (Erikson, 1982).

Fidelity is an extension of trust. In infancy, it is important for trust of others to outweigh mistrust; in adolescence, it becomes important to be trustworthy oneself. Adolescents extend their trust to mentors or loved ones. In sharing thoughts and feelings, an adolescent clarifies a tentative identity by seeing it reflected in the eyes of the beloved. However, these adolescent intimacies differ from mature intimacy, which involves greater commitment, sacrifice, and compromise.

Erikson saw the prime danger of this stage as identity, or role, confusion, which can greatly delay reaching psychological adulthood. (He did not resolve his own identity crisis until his mid-20s.) Some degree of identity confusion is normal, however. According to Erikson, it accounts for the seemingly chaotic nature of much adolescent behavior and for teenagers' painful self-consciousness. Cliquishness and intolerance of differences, both hallmarks of adolescence, are defenses against identity confusion.

Erikson's theory describes male identity development as the norm. According to Erikson, a man is not capable of real intimacy until after he has achieved a stable identity, whereas women define themselves through marriage and motherhood (something that may have been truer when Erikson developed his theory than it is today). Thus, said Erikson, women (unlike men) develop identity *through* intimacy, not before it. As we'll see, this male orientation of Erikson's theory has prompted criticism. Still, Erikson's concept of the identity crisis has inspired much valuable research.

Mastering the challenge of a rope course may help this adolescent boy assess his abilities, interests, and desires. According to Erikson, the process of self-assessment helps adolescents resolve the crisis of identity versus identity confusion.

Marcia: Identity Status—Crisis and Commitment

Caterina, Andrea, Nick, and Mark are all about to graduate from high school. Caterina has considered her interests and her talents and plans to become an engineer. She has narrowed her college choices to three schools that offer good programs in this field.

Andrea knows exactly what she is going to do with her life. Her mother, a union leader at a plastics factory, has arranged for Andrea to enter an apprenticeship program there. Andrea has never considered doing anything else.

Nick is agonizing over his future. Should he attend a community college or join the army? He cannot decide what to do now or what he wants to do eventually.

Mark still has no idea what he wants to do, but he is not worried. He figures he can get some sort of a job and make up his mind about the future when he is ready.

These four young people are involved in identity formation. What accounts for the differences in the way they go about it, and how will these differences affect the outcome? According to research by the psychologist James E. Marcia (1966, 1980), these students are in four different **identity statuses,** states of ego (self) development.

Through 30-minute, semistructured *identity-status interviews* (Kroger, 2003; Table 17-1), Marcia distinguished these four types of identity status: *identity achievement, foreclosure, moratorium,* and *identity diffusion.* The four categories differ according to the presence or absence of **crisis** and **commitment,** the two elements Erikson saw as crucial to forming identity. Marcia defined *crisis* as a period of conscious decision making and *commitment* as a personal investment in an occupation or ideology (system of beliefs). He found relationships between identity status and such characteristics as anxiety, self-esteem, moral reasoning, and patterns of behavior. Building on Marcia's theory, other researchers have identified other personality and family variables related to identity status (Table 17-2). Here is a more detailed sketch of young people in each identity status:

- **Identity achievement** (*crisis leading to commitment*). Caterina has resolved her identity crisis. During the crisis period, she devoted much thought and some emotional struggle to major issues in her life. She has made choices and expresses strong commitment to them. Her parents have encouraged her to make her own

identity statuses Marcia's term for states of ego development that depend on the presence or absence of crisis and commitment.

crisis Marcia's term for a period of conscious decision making related to identity formation.

commitment Marcia's term for personal investment in an occupation or system of beliefs.

identity achievement Identity status, described by Marcia, that is characterized by commitment to choices made following a crisis, a period spent in exploring alternatives.

Table 17-1 Identity-Status Interview

Sample Questions	Typical Answers for the Four Statuses
About occupational commitment: "How willing do you think you'd be to give up going into _____ if something better came along?"	*Identity achievement:* "Well, I might, but I doubt it. I can't see what 'something better' would be for me."
	Foreclosure: "Not very willing. It's what I've always wanted to do. The folks are happy with it and so am I."
	Moratorium: "I guess if I knew for sure, I could answer that better. It would have to be something in the general area—something related . . . "
	Identity diffusion: "Oh, sure. If something better came along, I'd change just like that."
About ideological commitment: "Have you ever had any doubts about your religious beliefs?"	*Identity achievement:* "Yes, I started wondering whether there is a God. I've pretty much resolved that now. The way it seems to me is . . . "
	Foreclosure: "No, not really; our family is pretty much in agreement on these things."
	Moratorium: "Yes, I guess I'm going through that now. I just don't see how there can be a God and still so much evil in the world."
	Identity diffusion: "Oh, I don't know. I guess so. Everyone goes through some sort of stage like that. But it really doesn't bother me much. I figure that one religion is about as good as another!"

Source: Adapted from Marcia, 1966.

Table 17-2 Family and Personality Factors Associated with Adolescents in Four Identity Statuses*

Factor	Identity Achievement	Foreclosure	Moratorium	Identity Diffusion
Family	Parents encourage autonomy and connection with teachers; differences are explored within a context of mutuality.	Parents are overly involved with their children; families avoid expressing differences.	Adolescents are often involved in an ambivalent struggle with parental authority.	Parents are laissez-faire in child-rearing attitudes; are rejecting or not available to children.
Personality	High levels of ego development, moral reasoning, self-certainty, self-esteem, performance under stress, and intimacy.	Highest levels of authoritarianism and stereotypical thinking, obedience to authority, dependent relationships, low level of anxiety.	Most anxious and fearful of success; high levels of ego development, moral reasoning, and self-esteem.	Mixed results, with low levels of ego development, moral reasoning, cognitive complexity, and self-certainty; poor cooperative abilities.

*These associations have emerged from a number of separate studies. Because the studies have all been correlational rather than longitudinal, it is impossible to say that any factor caused placement in any identity status.

Source: Kroger, 1993.

decisions; they have listened to her ideas and given their opinions without pressuring her to adopt them. Research in a number of cultures has found people in this category to be more mature and more socially competent than people in the other three (Marcia, 1993).

- **Foreclosure** (*commitment without crisis*). Andrea has made commitments, not as a result of exploring possible choices, but by accepting someone else's plans for her life. She is happy and self-assured, perhaps even smug and self-satisfied, and she becomes dogmatic when her opinions are questioned. She has close family ties, is obedient, and tends to follow a powerful leader, like her mother, who accepts no disagreement.
- **Moratorium** (*crisis with no commitment yet*). Nick is in crisis, struggling with decisions. He is lively, talkative, self-confident, and scrupulous but also anxious

foreclosure Identity status, described by Marcia, in which a person who has not spent time considering alternatives (that is, has not been in crisis) is committed to other people's plans for his or her life.

moratorium Identity status, described by Marcia, in which a person is considering alternatives (in crisis) and seems headed for commitment.

identity diffusion Identity status, described by Marcia, that is characterized by absence of commitment and lack of serious consideration of alternatives.

What's your view ❓

- Which of Marcia's identity statuses best described you as an adolescent?
- Has your identity status changed since then? If so, how?

and fearful. He is close to his mother but resists her authority. He wants to have a girlfriend but has not yet developed a close relationship. He will probably come out of his crisis eventually with the ability to make commitments and achieve identity.

- **Identity diffusion** (*no commitment, no crisis*). Mark has not seriously considered options and has avoided commitments. He is unsure of himself and tends to be uncooperative. His parents do not discuss his future with him; they say it's up to him. People in this category tend to be unhappy and often lonely.

These categories are not stages; they represent the status of identity development at a particular time, and they are likely to change in any direction as young people continue to develop (Marcia, 1979). When middle-aged people look back on their lives, they most commonly trace a path from foreclosure to moratorium to identity achievement (Kroger & Haslett, 1991). From late adolescence on, as Marcia proposed, more and more people are in moratorium or achievement: seeking or finding their identity. About half of late adolescents remain in foreclosure or diffusion, but when development does occur, it is typically in the direction Marcia described (Kroger, 2003). Furthermore, although people in foreclosure seem to have made final decisions, that is often not so.

Gender Differences in Identity Formation

Much research supports Erikson's view that, for women, identity and intimacy develop together. Rather than view this pattern as a departure from a male norm, however, some researchers see it as pointing to a weakness in Erikson's theory, which, they claim, is based on male-centered Western concepts of individuality, autonomy, and competitiveness. According to Carol Gilligan (1982, 1987a, 1987b; L. M. Brown & Gilligan, 1990), the female sense of self develops not so much through achieving a separate identity as through establishing relationships. Girls and women, says Gilligan, judge themselves on their handling of their responsibilities and on their ability to care for others as well as for themselves.

Some developmental scientists question how different the male and female paths to identity really are—especially today—and suggest that *individual* differences may be more important than gender differences (Archer, 1993; Marcia, 1993). Indeed, Marcia (1993) argues that an ongoing tension between independence and connectedness is at the heart of all of Erikson's psychosocial stages for *both* men and women. In research on Marcia's identity statuses, few gender differences have appeared (Kroger, 2003).

However, the development of self-esteem during adolescence seems to support Gilligan's view. Male self-esteem tends to be linked with striving for individual achievement, whereas female self-esteem depends more on connections with others (Thorne & Michaelieu, 1996).

Some evidence suggests that adolescent girls have lower self-esteem, on average, than adolescent boys, though this finding has been controversial. Several large, recent studies find that self-esteem drops during adolescence, more rapidly for girls than for boys, and then rises gradually into adulthood. These changes may be due in part to body image and other anxieties associated with puberty and with the transitions to junior high or middle school and high school (Robins & Trzesniewski, 2005).

Ethnic Factors in Identity Formation

For many young people in minority groups, race or ethnicity is central to identity formation. Following Marcia's model, some research has identified four ethnic identity statuses (Phinney, 1998):

- *Diffuse:* Juanita has done little or no exploration of her ethnicity and does not clearly understand the issues involved.
- *Foreclosed:* Caleb has done little or no exploration of his ethnicity but has clear feelings about it. These feelings may be positive or negative, depending on the attitudes he absorbed at home.

Identity development can be especially complicated for young people from minority groups. Ethnicity may play a central part in their self-concept.

Table 17-3	Representative Quotations from Each Status of Ethnic Identity Development

Diffusion

"Why do I need to learn about who was the first black woman to do this or that? I'm just not too interested." (African American female)

Foreclosure

"I don't go looking for my culture. I just go by what my parents say and do, and what they tell me to do, the way they are." (Mexican American male)

Moratorium

"There are a lot of non-Japanese people around, and it gets pretty confusing to try and decide who I am." (Asian American male)

Achieved

"People put me down because I'm Mexican, but I don't care anymore. I can accept myself more." (Mexican American female)

Source: Phinney, 1998, Table 2, p. 277.

- *Moratorium:* Cho-san has begun to explore her ethnicity but is confused about what it means to her.
- *Achieved:* Diego has explored his identity and understands and accepts his ethnicity.

Table 17-3 quotes representative statements by minority young people in each status.

A study of 940 African American adolescents, college students, and adults found evidence of all four identity statuses in each age group. Only 27 percent of the adolescents were in the achieved group, as compared with 47 percent of the college students and 56 percent of the adults. Instead, adolescents were more likely to be in moratorium (42 percent), still exploring what it means to be African American. Some 25 percent of the adolescents were in foreclosure, with feelings about African American identity based on their family upbringing. All three of these groups (achieved, moratorium, and foreclosed) reported more positive regard for being African American than the 6 percent of adolescents who were diffused (neither committed nor exploring). Those of any age who were in the achieved status were most likely to view race as central to their identity (Yip, Seaton, & Sellers, 2006).

Another model focuses on three aspects of racial/ethnic identity: *connectedness* to one's own racial/ethnic group, *awareness of racism,* and *embedded achievement,* the belief that academic achievement is a part of group identity. A longitudinal study of low-income minority youth found that all three aspects of identity appear to stabilize and even to increase slightly by midadolescence. Thus racial/ethnic identity may buffer tendencies toward a drop in grades and connection to school during the transition from middle school to high school (Altschul, Oyserman, & Bybee, 2006). On the other hand, perceived discrimination during the transition to adolescence can interfere with positive identity formation and lead to conduct problems or depression. Protective factors are nurturant, involved parenting, prosocial friends, and strong academic performance (Brody et al., 2006).

A 3-year longitudinal study of 420 African American, Latino American, and European American adolescents looked at two dimensions of ethnic identity: *group esteem* (feeling good about one's ethnicity) and *exploration of the meaning of ethnicity* in one's life. Group esteem rose during both early and middle adolescence, especially for African Americans and Latinos, whose group esteem was lower to begin with. Exploration of the meaning of ethnicity increased only in middle adolescence, perhaps reflecting the transition from relatively homogeneous neighborhood elementary or junior high schools into more ethnically diverse high schools. Interactions with members of other ethnic groups may stimulate young people to curiosity about their ethnic identity (French, Seidman, Allen, & Aber, 2006).

Checkpoint ✓

Can you . . .

✔ List the three major issues involved in identity formation, according to Erikson?

✔ Describe four types of identity status found by Marcia?

✔ Discuss how gender and ethnicity affect identity formation?

cultural socialization Parental practices that teach children about their racial/ethnic heritage and promote cultural practices and cultural pride.

Guidepost 2

What determines sexual orientation, what sexual practices are common among adolescents, and what leads some to engage in risky sexual behavior?

The term **cultural socialization** refers to parental practices that teach children about their racial or ethnic heritage, promote cultural customs and traditions, and promote racial/ethnic and cultural pride. Adolescents who have experienced cultural socialization tend to have stronger and more positive ethnic identity than those who have not (Hughes et al., 2006).

Sexuality

Seeing oneself as a sexual being, recognizing one's sexual orientation, coming to terms with sexual stirrings, and forming romantic or sexual attachments all are parts of achieving *sexual identity*. Awareness of sexuality is an important aspect of identity formation, profoundly affecting self-image and relationships. Although this process is biologically driven, its expression is in part culturally defined.

During the 20th century a major change in sexual attitudes and behavior in the United States and other industrialized countries brought more widespread acceptance of premarital sex, homosexuality, and other previously disapproved forms of sexual activity. Recent data indicate that 53 percent of 12th graders report that they are sexually active (Figure 17-1). With widespread access to the Internet, casual sex with fleeting cyber-acquaintances who hook up through online chat rooms or singles' meeting sites has become common. Cell phones, e-mail, and instant messaging make it easy for adolescents to arrange hookups with disembodied strangers, insulated from adult scrutiny. These changes have brought increased concerns about sexual risk-taking. On the other hand, the AIDS epidemic has led many young people to abstain from sexual activity outside of committed relationships or to engage in safer sexual practices.

Sexual Orientation and Identity

sexual orientation Focus of consistent sexual, romantic, and affectionate interest, either heterosexual, homosexual, or bisexual.

Although present in younger children, it is in adolescence that a person's **sexual orientation** generally becomes a pressing issue: whether that person will consistently be sexually attracted to persons of the other sex (*heterosexual*), of the same sex (*homosexual*), or of both sexes (*bisexual*). Heterosexuality predominates in nearly every known culture throughout the world. The prevalence of homosexual orientation varies widely, depending on how it is defined and measured. Depending on whether it is measured by sexual, or romantic, *attraction or arousal* as in the definition we just gave, or by sexual *behavior*, or by sexual *identity*, the rate of homosexuality in the U.S. population ranges from 1 to 21 percent (Savin-Williams, 2006).

Figure 17-1

Percentage of students in grades 9 through 12 who report they are sexually active.

Source: Centers for Disease Control and Prevention, 2008e.

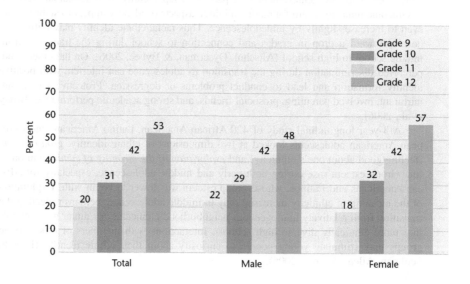

Many young people have one or more homosexual experiences as they are growing up, but isolated experiences or even occasional homosexual attractions or fantasies do not determine sexual orientation. In a national survey, 4.5 percent of 15- to 19-year-old boys and 10.6 percent of 15- to 19-year-old girls reported ever having had same-sex sexual contact, but only 2.4 percent of the boys and 7.7 percent of the girls reported having done so in the past year (Mosher, Chandra, & Jones, 2005). Social stigma may bias such self-reports, underestimating the prevalence of homosexuality and bisexuality.

Origins of Sexual Orientation

Much research on sexual orientation has focused on efforts to explain homosexuality. Although it once was considered a mental illness, several decades of research have found no association between homosexual orientation and emotional or social problems—apart from those apparently caused

Although sexual orientation may be shaped before birth or very early in life, it is in adolescence that it becomes a pressing issue. Here, a Massachusetts high school girl who came out as a lesbian sits in front of a banner for a student support group.

by societal treatment of homosexuals, such as a tendency to depression (American Psychological Association (APA), n. d.; C. J. Patterson, 1992, 1995a, 1995b). These findings led the psychiatric profession in 1973 to stop classifying homosexuality as a mental disorder.

Sexual orientation seems to be at least partly genetic (Diamond & Savin-Williams, 2003). The first full genome-wide scan for male sexual orientation has identified three stretches of DNA on chromosomes 7, 8, and 10 that appear to be involved (Mustanski et al., 2005). However, because identical twins are not perfectly concordant for sexual orientation, nongenetic factors also play a part (Diamond & Savin-Williams, 2003). Among more than 3,800 Swedish same-sex twin pairs, nonshared environmental factors accounted for about 64 percent of individual differences in sexual orientation. Genes explained about 34 percent of the variation in men and 18 percent in women. Shared family influences accounted for about 16 percent of the variation in women but had no effect in men (Långström, Rahman, Carlström, & Lichtenstein, 2008).

The more older biological brothers a man has, the more likely he is to be gay. In an analysis of 905 men and their biological, adoptive, half-, or stepsiblings, each older biological brother increased the chances of homosexuality in a younger brother by 33 percent. The significant factor in sexual orientation was the number of times a man's mother had borne boys. If rearing or social factors influenced the fraternal birth-order effect, then the number of nonbiological older brothers would predict sexual orientation, but they did not. Even when the number of nonbiological older brothers significantly exceeded the number of biological older brothers, and hence the opportunity for an effect via being reared with older male siblings was high, only the number of biological older brothers and not nonbiological older brothers predicted sexual orientation in men. This phenomenon may be a cumulative immunelike response to the presence of successive male fetuses in the womb (Bogaert, 2006).

Imaging studies have found striking similarities of brain structure and function between homosexuals and heterosexuals of the other sex. Brains of gay men and straight women are symmetrical, whereas in lesbians and straight men the right hemisphere is slightly larger. Also, in gays and lesbians, connections in the amygdala, which is involved in emotion, are typical of the other sex (Savic & Lindström, 2008). One researcher reported a difference in the size of the hypothalamus, a brain structure that governs sexual activity, in heterosexual and gay men (LeVay, 1991). In brain imaging studies on pheromones, odors that attract mates, the odor of male sweat activated the hypothalamus in gay men much as it did in heterosexual women. Similarly, lesbian women and straight men reacted more positively to female pheromones than to male ones (Savic, Berglund, & Lindström, 2005; Savic, Berglund, & Lindström, 2006). However, these differences may be an effect of homosexuality, not a cause.

Checkpoint ✔

Can you . . .

✔ Discuss theories and research regarding origins of sexual orientation?

✔ Discuss homosexual identity development?

Homosexual and Bisexual Identity Development

Despite the increased acceptance of homosexuality in the United States, many adolescents who openly identify as gay, lesbian, or bisexual feel isolated in a hostile environment. They may be subject to discrimination and even violence. Others may be reluctant to disclose their sexual orientation, even to their parents, for fear of strong disapproval or a rupture in the family (Hillier, 2002; C. J. Patterson, 1995b). They may find it difficult to meet and identify potential same-sex partners. Thus homosexuals' recognition and expression of their sexual identity are more complex and follow a less defined timetable than heterosexuals' do (Diamond & Savin-Williams, 2003).

There is no single route to the development of gay, lesbian, or bisexual identity and behavior. Because of the lack of socially sanctioned ways to explore their sexuality, many gay and lesbian adolescents experience identity confusion (Sieving, Oliphant, & Blum, 2002). Gay, lesbian, and bisexual youth who are unable to establish peer groups that share their sexual orientation may struggle with the recognition of same-sex attractions (Bouchey & Furman, 2003; Furman & Wehner, 1997).

Conscience and Moral Development

Let a man not do what his own sense of righteousness tells him not to do, and let him not desire what his sense of righteousness tells him not to desire;—to act thus is all he has to do.
     —MENCIUS, *The Book of Mencius*, 7A17

The fruit of conscience is humility, and the fruit of humility is love.
     —THE ETHIOPIAN *Book of the Philosophers* (c. ninth century)

A woman was near death from a rare form of cancer, and there was only one drug that doctors thought could save her. "It was a form of radium that was recently discovered by a druggist in her town. The drug was expensive to make, but the druggist was charging [$2,000] ten times what the drug cost to make . . . The sick woman's husband, Heinz, went to everyone he knew to borrow the money, but he could only get together about $1,000 . . . He told the druggist that his wife was dying, and asked him to sell it cheaper or let him pay later. But the druggist said, 'No, I discovered the drug and I'm going to make money from it.' So Heinz got desperate and began to think about breaking into the man's store and stealing the drug for his wife."

Should Heinz steal the drug?"[1] What would you do in a situation like this? Different people answer this question quite differently.

> Communal life alters the very structure of consciousness by inculcating into it the feeling of respect
>
> —JEAN PIAGET, *The Moral Judgment of Children* (1932), p. 71.

Kohlberg's Stages

Because of the domination of modern psychology by behaviorism—whose corollary in moral philosophy is cultural relativism—Piaget's research on moral development received little attention until relatively recently. In the 1970s, the work of Harvard psychologist Lawrence Kohlberg caught the public's attention. Kohlberg was influenced primarily by Piaget; as well as Socrates, Immanuel Kant, and John Rawls—all philosophers whose works, he believed, exemplified a high stage of moral reasoning.

Kohlberg's ideas about moral development became popular in the wake of the Vietnam War protests and the civil rights movement, both of which gave rise to dissatisfaction with cultural relativism. The analytical movement in moral philosophy had culminated in the theory of emotivism, which disconnects morality from the real world. Kohlberg wanted to return to a synthetic approach in which theory and practical experience came together.

According to Kohlberg, although the specific content of moral codes can vary depending on a person's culture, the difference is only on the surface. The conceptual structures from which these specific codes are formulated are innate and universal (see the selection by Kohlberg below).

> As soon as we talk with children about morality we find that they have many ways of making judgments that are not "internalized" from the outside and that do not come in any direct and obvious way from parents, teachers, or even peers.
>
> —LAWRENCE KOHLBERG, "The Child as Moral Philosopher" (1968)[42]

Kohlberg believed that humans, with the exception of sociopaths and other severely impaired people, have an inherent potential for growth from the lower (earlier) to higher (later) stages of moral development. These stages are transcultural and represent "transformations in the organization of thought, rather than increasing knowledge of cultural values."[43] Each stage, according to him, is distinct and reflects a level of moral judgment that is more complex than that of the preceding stage.[44] Gains that are made in moral judgment tend to be retained. The lower stages are not so much replaced by higher stages as incorporated into them—much like elementary school arithmetic becomes part of our way of understanding calculus.

Kohlberg identified three levels of moral development, each with two distinct stages (Table 6.1). In the preconventional stages, moral duty and moral community are defined primarily in egocentric terms. Young children are preconventional reasoners. The majority of adults in the United States are in the conventional stages of moral reasoning. They are heteronomous moral reasoners who look to outside sources—their peers or cultural norms—for moral guidance. Less than 10 percent of American adults ever reach the postconventional stages of autonomous moral reasoning.

While the so-called higher stages come later than the lower stages in human development, this in itself does not prove that the higher stages are morally better. Kohlberg was well aware that we cannot logically draw a conclusion regarding what *ought* to be from what *is*. Instead, he argued, higher stages are preferable because people at these stages are more satisfied with their moral decisions. People, in general, *prefer* a solution to a moral problem that uses the highest stage of moral reasoning conceptually available to them.[45] People who operate at a higher stage of moral reasoning are less likely to make moral decisions that they will later regret.

Kohlberg also pointed out that *moral philosophers* believe that the principled reasoning that characterizes the higher stages is more desirable than the cultural relativism of the conventional stages or the egoism or ethical subjectivism of the preconventional stages. Most of the world's moral philosophers have long held that autonomous moral reasoning, universality and impartiality, compassion and a concern for justice, and mutual respect are the hallmarks of sound moral reasoning.

Because each new stage of moral development integrates the components of the previous stage, later stages provide us with better tools for resolving crises.

TABLE 6.1   Kohlberg's Stages of Moral Development

STAGE	DESCRIPTION
Preconventional	
1. Punishment and obedience	Avoid punishment; submit to authority. Fear of punishment is the primary motive.
2. Egoist	Satisfy one's own needs; only consider the needs of others if it benefits you: "You scratch my back, I'll scratch yours."
Conventional	
3. Good boy/nice girl	Please and help others; concern for maintaining good relationships and earning others' approval; conformity to peer and group norms.
4. Society maintaining	Respect authority and social rules; maintain the existing social order.
Postconventional	
5. Social contract or legalistic	Obey useful, albeit arbitrary, social rules; appeal to social consensus and majority rule as long as minimal basic rights are safeguarded. The U.S. Constitution is written using this stage of reasoning.
6. Conscience and universal principles	Autonomously recognize universal rules, such as justice and equality, that are rational and logically consistent and reflect a respect for equal human rights and the dignity of each individual.

Based on Barbara Panzi and Timothy McMahon, "Ethical Decision-Making: Developmental Theory and Practice," speech delivered at the National Association of Student Personnel Administrators, Denver, March 1989.

In addition, our concept of the moral community also becomes more inclusive as we mature, going from the self-centered egoism of the young child to universal respect for all beings.

[W]ho says higher stages are better? Subjects do themselves. As people outgrow old ways of thinking—as they see them as too simplistic and inadequate—they still understand them but don't prefer them.

—JAMES REST, *Moral Development in the Professions: Psychology and Applied Ethics* (1994), pp. 16–17

A person will prefer the current stage of moral development until it is, in turn, replaced by a newly comprehended stage. Each stage represents an equilibrium point, so a person will generally remain in that stage until sufficient cognitive or social disequilibrium has occurred. People move beyond their current stage when they encounter a crisis that their current mode of thinking is unable to satisfactorily resolve.

Until the age of forty-three, Aung San Suu Kyi had been leading a quiet life in England as a housewife and academic before she was transformed into a powerful and charismatic leader of the Burmese people. In 1988 she returned to Rangoon to care for her dying mother. While living in England, she had heard about the political unrest and shooting of demonstrators. However, not until Aung San Suu Kyi returned to Burma and came face-to-face with the crisis facing her people was she transformed. "Overnight, Aung San Suu Kyi became the leading representative of the movement for freedom and democracy."[46]

Gains made in moral development affect a person's real-life behavior.[47] Level of moral reasoning is positively correlated with honesty and altruistic behavior—what Piaget called *practical morality*. A study of 86 subjects found that only 9 percent of people at stage 2 (egoist) and 38 percent of people at Kohlberg's stage 4 (society maintaining/cultural relativist) would offer help to someone lying on a sidewalk who appeared to be suffering from drug side effects; yet all of the subjects at stage 6 (conscience and universal moral principles) offered their assistance.[48] Higher stages of moral reasoning are also positively correlated with higher scores on other components of moral behavior and on developmental scales such as ego development, self-esteem, and mental health.

Cross-Cultural Findings

Studies from more than forty Western and non-Western countries support Kohlberg's theory that stages of moral development are universal. Cross-cultural findings also lend support to the claim that some cultures are more prone to promote virtue in their citizens. When matched by age and education, people in the United States score lower in measures of moral development than people from Iceland or Canada but higher than people living in Taiwan.

Subcultures and institutions also influence a person's stage of moral reasoning. One of the greatest frustrations of our current prison system is that criminals often come out in worse shape than when they entered prison. Prisoners interact with the guards primarily in terms of stage 1 behavior—avoiding coercion and punishment. However, with each other, the prisoners are primarily in stage 2, acting out of mutual self-benefit but without any genuine respect for one another. In other words, prison life tends to mold prisoners into a morality that is lower than their "private best."[49]

Colleges and Moral Development

Most high school students and college freshmen use primarily stage 3 moral reasoning; as such, they tend to be very conformist and easily influenced by their peer culture. This phenomenon in college students has been dubbed the "freshman personality."[50] On a more hopeful note, formal education has been found to be an important factor in promoting moral development, probably because it challenges students to analyze their worldviews. When young people leave their family of origin and enter college, they often experience a crisis. Events that conflict with our cherished worldviews—such as encountering people from different backgrounds and learning new ideas—can precipitate disequilibrium.

During the transition from conventional to postconventional moral reasoning, students are often torn between the rejection of moral values as relative and the reluctance to commit to universal moral principles. College students frequently respond, at least initially, to this unsettling experience by becoming more conforming to their peer culture. This conflict can also manifest itself in hedonistic disregard for any moral values—either relative or universal. The movement from conventional to postconventional moral reasoning involves a paradigm shift or change in our worldview. Educator and philosopher Dwight Boyd refers to the condition in which students are struggling with the transition from conventional to principled moral reasoning as "sophomoritis."[51]

Because [college] students generally have not yet internalized the principles necessary to make ethical judgments, they substitute personal and subjective criteria. This makes it appear as though they lack character. A more accurate description is that they are in the process of developing it.

—GREGORY BLIMLING, "Developing Character in College Students" (1990)[52]

Unfortunately, most college students do not complete the transition to postconventional moral reasoning. A college education instead tends to push students into a higher level of *conventional* reasoning. In other words, a traditional college education can make students less reliant on the opinions of their peers; however, the tradeoff is that they conform more to wider societal norms rather than becoming more autonomous in their thinking.

Criticisms of Kohlberg's Stages

Kohlberg has been criticized for inadvertently reflecting the biases of U.S. culture. For example, he did not find much change in level of moral development after the age of twenty-five. However, most of his subjects were students; very few were over the age of forty or fifty, a time of life that is revered in many non-Western cultures for its moral wisdom.

1. The Master said, "At fifteen, I had my mind bent on learning."

2. "At thirty, I stood firm."

3. "At forty, I had no doubts."

4. "At fifty, I knew the decrees of Heaven."

5. "At sixty, my ear was an obedient organ for the reception of truth."

6. "At seventy, I could follow what my heart desired, without transgressing what was right."

—*Confucian Analects*[33]

The adequacy of Kohlberg's description of children's moral reasoning has also been called into question. According to Kohlberg, very young children act morally because of fear of punishment. This claim has not been supported by recent research, however. When children are asked why they share, some will say to avoid punishment or because they want something in return, as Kohlberg predicted they would, but most children share out of a sense of empathy for other people.[54]

Perhaps the most telling criticism of Kohlberg's theory is that, at least when it was initially formulated, it failed to take into account women's moral development. Before the late 1970s, researchers in both medicine and psychology routinely used only male subjects, based on the assumption that men were generic humans and that generalizations about women could legitimately be made from studies done only on men. In keeping with this thinking, the subjects in Kohlberg's initial studies were all male. Adding insult to injury, Kohlberg even drew the conclusion on the basis of his all-male research that men operate at a significantly higher level of moral reasoning than do women.

Carol Gilligan: The Care Perspective

The elusive mystery of women's development lies in its recognition of the continuing importance of attachment in the human life-cycle. Woman's place in man's life-cycle is to protect this recognition while the [masculine] development litany intones the celebration of separation, autonomy, individuation, and natural rights. . . .

—Carol Gilligan, *In a Different Voice* (1982), p. 23

Women and the Care Perspective

The neglect of philosophers and psychologists to take women's perspectives into account has created the false impression that women are morally deficient compared to men. Carol Gilligan, who had studied with Kohlberg, decided it was time to correct this. In her interviews with women and through her study of women in literature, she concluded that women's moral development tends to follow a different path than men's. Men tend to be duty and principle oriented; women are more context oriented and tend to view the world in a more emotional and personal way. Women's moral judgment, Gilligan found, is characterized by a concern for themselves and others, accepting and maintaining responsibility within relationships, attachment, and self-sacrifice. She named this the "care perspective," in contrast to Kohlberg's "justice perspective" (see the selection by Gilligan in this chapter).

In her research with women, Gilligan postulated three stages of moral development (Table 6.2). Although Gilligan and Kohlberg emphasize different aspects of moral development, their stages are roughly parallel. Gender can influence how our moral development unfolds, but the basic paradigms or ground plans that inform our moral development are similar. For example, the preconventional stage in both Gilligan's and Kohlberg's theories includes egoists and ethical subjectivists. Similarly, people at the conventional stage are heteronomous cultural relativists who look to their culture for moral guidance.

The different descriptions of the conventional stage are not surprising, given the different ways in which men and women are socialized in our culture. Men, for the most part, are socialized to be the upholders of law and order and to believe that maleness carries certain privileges. Women, on the other hand, are taught that being a good woman involves self-sacrifice and putting the welfare of others first.

TABLE 6.2 Gilligan's Stages of Moral Reasoning in Women

STAGE	DESCRIPTION	MORAL COMMUNITY
Preconventional	Self-centered	Viewing one's own needs as all that matters
Conventional	Self-sacrificing	Viewing others' needs as more important
Postconventional	Mature care ethics	Able to balance one's own needs and the needs of others

In both Kohlberg's and Gilligan's theories, the postconventional stage is represented by autonomous moral reasoning: The person looks to transcultural values—whether in the form of principles of justice and respect or moral sentiments such as compassion and empathy. The transition to the postconventional stage for women, according to Gilligan, involves realizing that any individual woman has as much moral value as the next person. Kohlberg emphasized cognitive disequilibrium as playing a key role in pushing people into a higher stage of moral development; Gilligan and many other feminist ethicists place more importance on *social disequilibrium* as the "gate" to moral development.[56]

> It is obvious that the values of women differ very often from the values which have been made by the other sex . . . [Yet] it is the masculine values that prevail.
>
> —VIRGINIA WOOLF, *A Room of One's Own* (1929)[57]

Women and Self-Sacrifice

Because of women's inferior social status in most cultures, their socialization generally involves internalizing the message that they should nurture and care for the needs of others. Failure to recognize their own equal worth as humans can be costly for women. In situations of famine, for example, women starve to death at a higher rate than men do. When there is not enough for everyone, women will often engage in deliberate self-deprivation, offering men the best food at the expense of their own nutritional needs.[58]

Placing other's needs before their own can leave women who are at the self-sacrificing stage of moral development vulnerable to the cycle of domination and domestic violence in which abused women discount their own moral worth and remain with or return to their abuser. Younger women are especially at risk. About one-quarter or more of college women have been victims of dating or domestic violence.

In 2009, twenty-year-old singer and pop star Rihanna was brutally assaulted by her boyfriend, singer Chris Brown. A few weeks after her release from the hospital Rihanna dropped the charges against Brown, saying that she still loved him and wanted to marry him. Because of the tendency for victims of domestic violence to drop charges or to refuse to bring charges against their abusers, laws have been passed in several states allowing the state to make the charges. In August 2009 the court found Brown guilty of felony assault and sentenced him to five years probation and 180 hours of community service.

> Put it down in capital letters: SELF-DEVELOPMENT IS A HIGHER DUTY THAN SELF-SACRIFICE. The thing which most retards and militates against women's self-development is self-sacrifice.
>
> —ELIZABETH CADY STANTON to a reporter[59]

The identification of the "good" woman with habitual deference to others' needs and wishes can be destructive not only to women's self-esteem but to their ability to have a genuine caring relationship. In Amy Tan's novel *The Joy Luck Club*, Rose Hsu Jordan, the American-born daughter of An-Mei Hsu, does everything she can to be the perfect wife to her American husband, Ted Jordan.

She sacrifices her own dreams of a career and always defers to her husband's wishes—even when he asks for her opinion—until she is no longer able to make decisions for herself:

> I thought about things, the pros and the cons. But in the end I would be so confused, because I never believed there was ever any one right answer, yet there were many wrong ones. So whenever I said, "You decide," or "I don't care," or "Either way is fine with me," Ted would say in his impatient voice, "No, you decide. You can't have it both ways, none of the responsibility, none of the blame." [60]

Ted, an autonomous moral reasoner, wants a wife who can think for herself. When he asks Rose for a divorce, she is stunned. Her perfect world is shattered, and she experiences social dissonance.

Only by going through the agony of the separation and hearing her mother tell the story of her own mother's marriage in China to an abusive husband does Rose finally come to realize that she does have choices. By learning to say no to her husband and to express her anger at being betrayed, Rose is finally able to make the transition to mature care ethics and, in the end, establish a relationship with Ted that is based on mutual care and respect rather than self-imposed servility.

Synthesizing the Justice and Care Perspectives

Gilligan has been unfairly criticized as trying to drive a wedge between female and male ways of thinking, thereby promoting a type of biological destiny based on gender. However, she does not claim that the care perspective is superior to the justice perspective or even that it is more desirable for women to reason from a care perspective.

Some studies support Gilligan's theory,[61] but others have found gender differences in moral reasoning to be insignificant.[62] In later studies, Gilligan and others found that both the justice and care perspectives are present in most people's thinking, although each of us tends to favor one perspective over the other. Although women are more likely to prefer the care perspective, some women have a strong justice orientation, while some men, including many philosophers, are very empathetic and care oriented. Buddhist ethics likewise emphasizes compassion and community over abstract reason.

The strength inherent in the mature care perspective is that it calls attention to our attachment to each other and to the particular needs and circumstances of individuals. However, by focusing on the individual and on relationships, care ethics also tends to ignore wider issues of equality.

> Reason instructs us in the several tendencies of actions, and humanity (sympathy) makes a distinction in favor of those which are useful and beneficial.
>
> —DAVID HUME, *Enquiry Concerning the Principles of Morality* (1751)

The justice perspective, in contrast, focuses on justice, overcoming oppression, and the ideal of equality for all people. This more detached focus can occur, however, at the expense of attention to individual needs. Gilligan and Kohlberg came to agree in their later work that the most adequate moral orientation takes both the justice and care perspectives into consideration; the two perspectives, rather than being mutually exclusive, complement and enrich each other.[63]

Current Perspectives on Adolescence

The term "adolescence" was coined in 1904 by G. Stanley Hall, one of the world's first psychologists. He saw adolescence as a discrete stage of life that bridges the gap between sexual maturity (puberty) and socioemotional and cognitive maturity. He believed it to be characterized by "storm and stress." At the beginning of the twentieth century, it was typical for young men to begin working in middle childhood (there were no child labor laws), and for young women to work as wives and mothers as soon as they were fertile and/or spoken for. At the turn of the twenty-first century, the beginning of adolescence was marked by the desire to be independent of parental control. The end of adolescence, which once coincided with the age of legal maturity (usually 16 or 18, depending on local laws), has now been extended upwards. Although legal maturity is now 18 (voting, enlisting in the armed services, owning property, marrying without permission), the social norm is to consider persons in their late teens as adolescents, not adults. The years between 18 and 21 are often problematic for youth tethered between adult and not-adult status. They can be married, with children, living in homes of their own, running their own businesses, yet not be able to drive their cars in certain places or at certain times. They can go to college and participate in social activities, but they cannot legally drink. Often the twenty-first birthday is viewed as a rite of passage into adulthood in the United States because it signals the legal right to buy and drink alcoholic beverages. "Maturity" is usually reserved for those who have achieved full economic as well as socioemotional independence as adults.

Erik Erikson, the personality theorist, marked the passage from adolescence to young adulthood by a change in the nuclear conflicts of two life stages: identity versus role confusion and intimacy versus isolation. Adolescents struggle to answer the question, "Who am I?" Young adults struggle to find a place within the existing social order where they can feel intimacy rather than isolation. In the 1960s, Erikson wrote that females resolved both their conflicts of identity and intimacy by living vicariously through their husbands, an unacceptable idea to many females today.

As adolescence has been extended, so too has young adulthood. One hundred years ago, life expectancy did not extend too far beyond menopause for women and retirement for men. Young adulthood began when adolescents finished puberty. Parents of teenagers were middle-aged, between 35 and 55. Later marriages and delayed childbearing have redefined the line between young adulthood and middle age. Many people today consider themselves young adults well into their 40s.

Jean Piaget, the cognitive theorist, marked the end of the development of mental processes with the end of adolescence. Once full physical maturity, including brain maturity, was achieved, one reached the acme of his or her abilities to assimilate, accommodate, organize, and adapt to sensations, perceptions, associations, and discriminations. Piaget did not feel cognitive processing of information ceased with adulthood. He believed, however, that cognitive judgments would not reach a stage higher than the abstract, hypothetical, logical reasoning of formal operations. Today many cognitive theorists believe postformal operations are possible.

© Getty Images/Digital Vision

The first article, "A Peaceful Adolescence," addresses the G. Stanley Hall belief that adolescence was a stage of life marked by "storm and stress." While some teenagers do have conflicts with their parents, new research documents that many teenagers have peaceful passages through adolescence. The authors of this article, Barbara Kantrowitz and Karen Springen, report on what adults do to nurture successful teen years.

The second selection tells a true story about a homosexual adolescent murdered in school because of his sexual orientation. The author, Ramin Setoodeh, questions the role of school personnel in loco parentis (in the role of parent). Should schools have a "don't ask, don't tell" policy? If self-identification as gay, lesbian, or bisexual (GLB) is allowed, should schools assure that the rights of GLB students are protected? What are the parameters of tolerance?

The third article about adolescents deals with video game violence. The authors report conflicting research data about the correlation between heavy, brutal game playing and real-world violence. The United States does not restrict violent video games, as do most other industrialized nations. Future longitudinal studies may be able to demonstrate that violence in games does (or does not) predict more hostile acts in life.

A Peaceful Adolescence

The teen years don't have to be a time of family storm and stress. Most kids do just fine and now psychologists are finding out why that is.

BARBARA KANTROWITZ AND KAREN SPRINGEN

At 17, Amanda Hund is a straight-A student who loves competing in horse shows. The high school junior from Willmar, Minn., belongs to her school's band, orchestra and choir. She regularly volunteers through her church and recently spent a week working in an orphanage in Jamaica. Usually, however, she's closer to home, where her family eats dinner together every night. She also has a weekly breakfast date with her father, a doctor, at a local coffee shop. Amanda credits her parents for her relatively easy ride through adolescence. "My parents didn't sweat the small stuff," she says. "They were always very open. You could ask any question."

Is the Hund family for real? Didn't they get the memo that says teens and their parents are supposed to be at odds until . . . well, until forever? Actually, they're very much for real, and according to scientists who study the transition to adulthood, they represent the average family's experience more accurately than all those scary TV movies about out-of-control teens. "Research shows that most young people go through adolescence having good relationships with their parents, adopting attitudes and values consistent with their parents' and end up getting out of the adolescent period and becoming good citizens," says Richard Lerner, Bergstrom chair of applied developmental science at Tufts University. This shouldn't be news—but it is, largely because of widespread misunderstanding of what happens during the teen years. It's a time of transition, just like the first year of parenthood or menopause. And although there are dramatic hormonal and physical changes during this period, catastrophe is certainly not preordained. A lot depends on youngsters' innate natures combined with the emotional and social support they get from the adults around them. In other words, parents do matter.

The roots of misconceptions about teenagers go back to the way psychologists framed the field of adolescent development a century ago. They were primarily looking for explanations of why things went wrong. Before long, the idea that this phase was a period of storm and stress made its way into the popular consciousness. But in the last 15 years, developmental scientists have begun to re-examine these assumptions. Instead of focusing on kids who battle their way through the teen years, they're studying the dynamics of success.

At the head of the pack are Lerner and his colleagues, who are in the midst of a major project that many other researchers are following closely. It's a six-year longitudinal study of exactly what it takes to turn out OK and what adults can do to nurture those behaviors. "Parents and sometimes kids themselves often talk about positive development as the absence of bad," says Lerner. "What we're trying to do is present a different vision and a different vocabulary for young people and parents."

The first conclusions from the 4-H Study of Positive Youth Development, published in the February issue of *The Journal of Early Adolescence,* show that there are quantifiable personality traits possessed by all adolescents who manage to get to adulthood without major problems. Psychologists have labeled these traits "the 5 Cs": competence, confidence, connection, character and caring. These characteristics theoretically lead to a sixth C, contribution (similar to civic engagement). The nomenclature grows out of observations in recent years by a number of clinicians, Lerner says, but his study is the first time researchers have measured how these characteristics influence successful growth.

The 5 Cs are interconnected, not isolated traits, Lerner says. For example, competence refers not just to academic ability but also to social and vocational skills. Confidence includes self-esteem as well as the belief that you can make a difference in the world. The value of the study, Lerner says, is that when it is completed next year, researchers will have a way to quantify these characteristics and eventually determine what specific social and educational programs foster them.

During these years, parents should stay involved as they help kids move on.

In the meantime, parents can learn a lot from this rethinking of the teen years. Don't automatically assume that your kids become alien beings when they leave middle school. They still care what their parents think and they still need love and guidance—although in a different form. Temple University psychology professor Laurence Steinberg, author of "The Ten Basic Principles of Good Parenting," compares raising kids to building a boat that you eventually launch. Parents have to build a strong underpinning so their kids are equipped to face whatever's ahead. In the teen years, that means staying involved as you slowly let go. "One of the things that's natural in adolescence is that kids are going to pull away from their parents as they become increasingly interested in peers," says Steinberg. "It's important for parents to hang in there, for them not to pull back in response to that."

Communication is critical. "Stay in touch with your kids and make sure they feel valued and appreciated," advises Suniya Luthar, professor of clinical and developmental psychology at Columbia University. Even if they roll their eyes when you try to hug them, they still need direct displays of affection, she says. They also need help figuring out goals and limits. Parents should monitor their kids' activities and get to know their friends. Luthar says parents should still be disciplinarians and set standards such as curfews. Then teens need to know that infractions will be met with consistent consequences.

Adolescents are often critical of their parents but they're also watching them closely for clues on how to function in the outside world. Daniel Perkins, associate professor of family and youth resiliency at Penn State, says he and his wife take their twins to the local Ronald McDonald House and serve dinner to say thank you for time the family spent there when the children had health problems after birth. "What we've done already is set up the notion that we were blessed and need to give back, even if it's in a small way." That kind of example sets a standard youngsters remember, even if it seems like they're not paying attention.

Parents should provide opportunities for kids to explore the world and even find a calling. Teens who have a passion for something are more likely to thrive. "They have a sense of purpose beyond day-to-day teenage life," says David Marcus, author of "What It Takes to Pull Me Through." Often, he says,

kids who were enthusiastic about something in middle school lose enthusiasm in high school because the competition gets tougher and they're not as confident. Parents need to step in and help young people find other outlets. The best way to do that is to regularly spend uninterrupted time with teens (no cell phones). Kids also need to feel connected to other adults they trust and to their communities. Teens who get into trouble are "drifting," he says. "They don't have a web of people watching out for them."

Teens should build support webs of friends and adults.

At some point during these years, teen-agers should also be learning to build their own support networks—a skill that will be even more important when they're on their own. Connie Flanagan, a professor of youth civic development at Penn State, examines how kids look out for one another. "What we're interested in is how they help one another avoid harm," she says. In one of her focus groups, some teenage girls mentioned that they decided none would drink from an open can at a party because they wouldn't know for sure what they were drinking. "Even though you are experimenting, you're essentially doing it in a way that you protect one another," Flanagan says. Kids who don't make those kinds of connections are more likely to get in trouble because there's no one their own age or older to stop them from going too far. Like any other stage of life, adolescence can be tough. But teens and families can get through it—as long as they stick together.

With Julie Scelfo

Young, Gay, and Murdered

Kids are coming out younger, but are schools ready to handle the complex issues of identity and sexuality? For Larry King, the question had tragic implications.

RAMIN SETOODEH

At 15, Lawrence King was small—5 feet 1 inch—but very hard to miss. In January, he started to show up for class at Oxnard, Calif.'s E. O. Green Junior High School decked out in women's accessories. On some days, he would slick up his curly hair in a Prince-like bouffant. Sometimes he'd paint his fingernails hot pink and dab glitter or white foundation on his cheeks. "He wore makeup better than I did," says Marissa Moreno, 13, one of his classmates. He bought a pair of stilettos at Target, and he couldn't have been prouder if he had on a varsity football jersey. He thought nothing of chasing the boys around the school in them, teetering as he ran.

But on the morning of Feb. 12, Larry left his glitter and his heels at home. He came to school dressed like any other boy: tennis shoes, baggy pants, a loose sweater over a collared shirt. He seemed unhappy about something. He hadn't slept much the night before, and he told one school employee that he threw up his breakfast that morning, which he sometimes did because he obsessed over his weight. But this was different. One student noticed that as Larry walked across the quad, he kept looking back nervously over his shoulder before he slipped into his first-period English class. The teacher, Dawn Boldrin, told the students to collect their belongings, and then marched them to a nearby computer lab, so they could type out their papers on World War II. Larry found a seat in the middle of the room. Behind him, Brandon McInerney pulled up a chair.

Brandon, 14, wasn't working on his paper, because he told Mrs. Boldrin he'd finished it. Instead, he opened a history book and started to read. Or at least he pretended to. "He kept looking over at Larry," says a student who was in the class that morning. "He'd look at the book and look at Larry, and look at the book and look at Larry." At 8:30 A.M., a half hour into class, Brandon quietly stood up. Then, without anyone's noticing, he removed a handgun that he had somehow sneaked to school, aimed it at Larry's head, and fired a single shot. Boldrin, who was across the room looking at another student's work, spun around. "Brandon, what the hell are you doing!" she screamed. Brandon fired at Larry a second time, tossed the gun on the ground and calmly walked through the classroom door. Police arrested him within seven minutes, a few blocks from school. Larry was rushed to the hospital, where he died two days later of brain injuries.

Poster Boy: Larry has become a gay-rights icon, but the reason he died isn't as clear-cut as many people think.

The Larry King shooting became the most prominent gay-bias crime since the murder of Matthew Shepard 10 years ago. But despite all the attention and outrage, the reason Larry died isn't as clear-cut as many people think. California's Supreme Court has just legalized gay marriage. There are gay characters on popular TV shows such as "Gossip Girl" and "Ugly Betty," and no one seems to notice. Kids like Larry are so comfortable with the concept of being openly gay that they are coming out younger and younger. One study found that the average age when kids self-identify as gay has tumbled to 13.4; their parents usually find out a year later.

What you might call "the shrinking closet" is arguably a major factor in Larry's death. Even as homosexuality has become more accepted, the prospect of being openly gay in middle school raises a troubling set of issues. Kids may want to express who they are, but they are playing grown-up without fully knowing what that means. At the same time, teachers and parents are often uncomfortable dealing with sexual issues in children so young. Schools are caught in between. How do you protect legitimate, personal expression while preventing inappropriate, sometimes harmful, behavior? Larry King was, admittedly, a problematical test case: he was a troubled child who flaunted his sexuality and wielded it like a weapon—it was often his first line of defense. But his story sheds light on the difficulty of defining the limits of tolerance. As E. O. Green found, finding that balance presents an enormous challenge.

Larry's life was hard from the beginning. His biological mother was a drug user; his father wasn't in the picture. When Greg and Dawn King took him in at age 2, the family was told he wasn't being fed regularly. Early on, a speech impediment made Larry difficult to understand, and he repeated first grade because he had trouble reading. He was a gentle child who loved nature and crocheting, but he also acted out from an early age. "We couldn't take him to the grocery store without him shoplifting," Greg says. "We couldn't get him to clean up his room. We sent him upstairs—he'd get a screwdriver and poke holes in the walls." He was prescribed ADHD medication, and Greg says Larry was diagnosed with reactive attachment disorder, a rare condition in which children never fully bond with their caregivers or parents.

Kids started whispering about Larry when he was in third grade at Hathaway Elementary School. "In a school of 700 students, you'd know Larry," says Sarah Ranjbar, one of Larry's principals. "He was slightly effeminate but very sure of his personality." Finally, his best friend, Averi Laskey, pulled him aside one day at the end of class. "I said, 'Larry, are you gay?' He said, 'Yeah, why?'" He was 10. Averi remembers telling Larry she didn't care either way, but Larry started telling other students, and they did. They called him slurs and avoided him at recess. One Halloween, someone threw a smoke bomb into his house, almost killing the family's Jack Russell terrier. In the sixth grade, a girl started a "Burn Book"—an allusion to a book in the movie "Mean Girls," where bullies scribble nasty rumors about the people they hate—about Larry. The Larry book talked about how he was gay and falsely asserted that he dressed in Goth and drag. And it ended with a threat: "I hate Larry King. I wish he was dead," according to one parent's memory of the book. "The principal called my wife on the phone and she was crying," Greg says. "She found the book, and said we needed to do something to help protect Larry." His parents transferred him to another elementary school, hoping he could get a fresh start before he started junior high.

E. O. Green is a white slab of concrete in a neighborhood of pink and yellow homes. In the afternoons, SUVs roll down the street like gumballs, the sound of hip-hop music thumping. Once the students leave the campus, two blue gates seal it shut, and teachers are told not to return to school after dark, because of gang violence. Outside, there's a worn blue sign that greets visitors: this was a California distinguished school in 1994. The school is under a different administration now.

'Random people would come up to Larry and start laughing,' Moreno says. 'I thought that was very rude.'

E. O. Green was a comfortable place for Larry when he arrived as a seventh grader. He hung out with a group of girls who, unlike in elementary school, didn't judge him. But that didn't mean he was entirely accepted. In gym class, some of his friends say that the boys would shove him around in the locker room. After he started dressing up, he was ridiculed even more. He lost a high heel once and the boys tossed it around at lunch like a football. "Random people would come up to him and start laughing," Moreno says. "I thought that was very rude." One day, in science class, he was singing "Somewhere Over the Rainbow" to himself. Kids nearby taunted him for being gay. "He said to me, 'It's OK'," says Vanessa Castillo, a classmate. "'One day, they'll regret it. One day, I'll be famous'."

Larry's home life wasn't getting any better. At 12, he was put on probation for vandalizing a tractor with a razor blade, and he entered a counseling program, according to his father. One therapist said Larry might be autistic. At 14, Larry told Greg he thought he was bisexual. "It wouldn't matter either way to me," Greg says. "I thought maybe some of the problems would go away if we supported him." But the therapist told Greg he thought that Larry was just trying to get attention and might not understand what it meant to be gay. Larry began telling his teachers that his father was hitting him. Greg says he never harmed Larry; still, the authorities removed Larry from his home in November 2007. He moved to Casa Pacifica, a group home and treatment center in Camarillo, five miles away from Oxnard.

Larry seemed to like Casa Pacifica—"peaceful home" in Spanish. The 23-acre facility—more like a giant campground, with wooden cottages, a basketball court and a swimming pool—has 45 beds for crisis kids who need temporary shelter. Every day a driver would take Larry to school, and some weeks he went to nearby Ventura, where he attended gay youth-group meetings. "I heard this was the happiest time of his life," says Vicki Murphy, the center's director of operations. For Christmas, the home gave Larry a $75 gift card for Target. He spent it on a pair of brown stiletto shoes.

In January, after a few months at Casa Pacifica, Larry decided to dress like a girl. He went to school accessorized to the max, and his already colorful personality got louder. He accused a girl to her face of having breast implants. Another girl told him she didn't like his shoes. "I don't like your necklace," Larry snapped back. Larry called his mom from Casa Pacifica to tell her that he wanted to get a sex-change operation. And he told a teacher that he wanted to be called Leticia, since no one at school knew he was half African-American. The teacher said firmly, "Larry, I'm not calling you Leticia." He dropped the idea without an argument.

The staff at E. O. Green was clearly struggling with the Larry situation—how to balance his right to self-expression while preventing it from disrupting others. Legally, they couldn't stop him from wearing girls' clothes, according to the California Attorney General's Office, because of a state hate-crime law that prevents gender discrimination. Larry, being Larry, pushed his rights as far as he could. During lunch, he'd sidle up to the popular boys' table and say in a high-pitched voice, "Mind if I sit here?" In the locker room, where he was often ridiculed, he got even by telling the boys, "You look hot," while they were changing, according to the mother of a student.

Larry was eventually moved out of the P.E. class, though the school didn't seem to know the extent to which he was clashing with other boys. One teacher describes the gym transfer as more of a "preventative measure," since Larry complained that one student wouldn't stop looking at him. In other classes, teachers were baffled that Larry was allowed to draw so much attention to himself. "All the teachers were complaining, because it was disruptive," says one of them. "Dress code is a huge issue at our school. We fight [over] it every day." Some teachers thought Larry was clearly in violation of the code, which prevents students from wearing articles of clothing considered distracting. When Larry wore lipstick and eyeliner to school for the first time, a teacher told him to wash it off, and he did. But the next day, he was back wearing even more. Larry told the teacher he could wear makeup if he wanted to. He said that Ms. Epstein told him that was his right.

Joy Epstein was one of the school's three assistant principals, and as Larry became less inhibited, Epstein became more a source of some teachers' confusion and anger. Epstein, a calm, brown-haired woman with bifocals, was openly gay to her colleagues, and although she was generally not out to her students, she kept a picture of her partner on her desk that some students saw. While her job was to oversee the seventh graders, she formed a special bond with Larry, who was in the eighth grade. He dropped by her office regularly, either for counseling or just to talk—she won't say exactly. "There was no reason why I specifically started working with Larry," Epstein says. "He came to me." Some teachers believe that she was encouraging Larry's flamboyance, to help further an "agenda," as some put it. One teacher complains that by being openly gay and discussing her girlfriend (presumably, no one would have complained if she had talked about a husband), Epstein brought the subject of sex into school. Epstein won't elaborate on what exactly she said to Larry because she expects to be called to testify at Brandon's trial, but it's certain to become one of the key issues. William Quest, Brandon's public defender, hasn't disclosed his defense strategy, but he has accused the school of failing to intercede as the tension rose between Larry and Brandon. Quest calls Epstein "a lesbian vice principal with a political agenda." Larry's father also blames Epstein. He's hired an attorney and says he is seriously contemplating a wrongful-death lawsuit. "She started to confuse her role as a junior-high principal," Greg King says. "I think that she was asserting her beliefs for gay rights." In a tragedy such as this, the natural impulse is to try to understand why it happened and to look for someone to blame. Epstein won't discuss the case in detail and, until she testifies in court, it's impossible to know what role—if any—she played in the events leading to Larry's death.

Whatever Epstein said to Larry, it's clear that his coming out proved to be a fraught process, as it can often be. For tweens, talking about being gay isn't really about sex. They may be aware of their own sexual attraction by the time they're 10, according to Caitlin Ryan, a researcher at San Francisco State University, but those feelings are too vague and unfamiliar to be their primary motivation. (In fact, Larry told a teacher that he'd never kissed anyone, male or female.) These kids are actually concerned with exploring their identity. "When you're a baby, you cry when you're hungry because you don't know the word for it," says Allan Acevedo, 19, of San Diego, who came out when he was in eighth grade. "Part of the reason why people are coming out earlier is they have the word 'gay,' and they know it explains the feeling." Like older teenagers, tweens tend to tell their friends first, because they think they'll be more accepting. But kids that age often aren't equipped to deal with highly personal information, and middle-school staffs are almost never trained in handling kids who question their sexuality. More than 3,600 high schools sponsor gay-straight alliances designed to foster acceptance of gay students, but only 110 middle schools have them. Often the entire school finds out before either the student or the faculty is prepared for the attention and the backlash. "My name became a punch line very fast," says Grady Keefe, 19, of Branford, Conn., who came out in the eighth grade. "The guidance counselors told me I should not have come out because I was being hurt."

The faculty tried to help Larry as he experimented with his identity, but he liked to talk in a roar.

The staff at E. O. Green tried to help as Larry experimented with his identity, but he liked to talk in a roar. One teacher asked him why he taunted the boys in the halls, and Larry replied, "It's fun to watch them squirm." But Brandon McInerney was different. Larry really liked Brandon. One student remembered that Larry would often walk up close to Brandon and stare at him. Larry had studied Brandon so well, he once knew when he had a scratch on his arm—Larry even claimed that he had given it to Brandon by mistake, when the two were together. Larry told one of his close friends that he and Brandon had dated but had broken up. He also said that he'd threatened to tell the entire school about them, if Brandon wasn't nicer to him. Quest, Brandon's defense attorney, says there was no relationship between Larry and Brandon, and one of Larry's teachers says that Larry was probably lying to get attention.

Like Larry, Brandon had his share of troubles. His parents, Kendra and Bill McInerney, had a difficult, tempestuous relationship. In 1993, Kendra alleged that Bill pointed a .45 handgun at her during a drunken evening and shot her in the arm, according to court records. She and Bill split in 2000, when Brandon was 6. One September morning, a fight broke out after Kendra accused her husband of stealing the ADHD medication prescribed to one of her older sons from her first marriage. Bill "grabbed Kendra by the hair," and "began choking her until she was almost unconscious," according to Kendra's version of the events filed in court documents. He pleaded no contest to corporal injury to a spouse and was sentenced to 10 days in jail. In a December 2001 court filing for a restraining order against Kendra, he claimed that she had turned her home into a "drug house." "I was very functional," Kendra later explained to a local newspaper, in a story about meth addiction. By 2004, she had entered a rehab program, and Brandon went to live with his father. But he spent years caught in the middle of a war.

While his life did seem to become more routine living with his dad, Brandon's troubles resurfaced in the eighth grade. His father was working in a town more than 60 miles away, and he was alone a lot. He began hanging out with a group of misfits on the beach. Although he was smart, he didn't seem to have much interest in school. Except for Hitler—Brandon knew all about the Nuremberg trials and all the names of Hitler's deputies. (When other kids asked him how he knew so much, he replied casually, "Don't you watch the History Channel?" Brandon's father says his son was interested in World War II, but not inappropriately.) By the end of the first semester, as his overall GPA tumbled from a 3.3 to a 1.9, he was kicked out of his English honors class for not doing his work and causing disruptions. He was transferred to Boldrin's English class, where he joined Larry.

Larry's grades were also dropping—he went from having a 1.71 GPA in November to a 1.0 in February, his father says. But he was too busy reveling in the spotlight to care. "He was like Britney Spears," says one teacher who knew Larry. "Everyone wanted to know what's the next thing he's going to do." Girls would take photos of him on their camera phones and discuss him with their friends. "My class was in a frenzy every day with Larry stories," says a humanities teacher who didn't have Larry as one of her students. He wore a Playboy-bunny necklace, which one of his teachers told him to remove because it was offensive to women. But those brown Target stilettos wobbled on.

The commotion over Larry's appearance finally forced the school office to take formal action. On Jan. 29, every teacher received an e-mail with the subject line "Student Rights". It was written by Sue Parsons, the eighth-grade assistant principal. "We have a student on campus who has chosen to express his sexuality by wearing make-up," the e-mail said without mentioning Larry by name. "It is his right to do so. Some kids are finding it amusing, others are bothered by it. As long as it does not cause classroom disruptions he is within his rights. We are asking that you talk to your students about being civil and non-judgmental. They don't have to like it but they need to give him his space. We are also asking you to watch for possible problems. If you wish to talk further about it please see me or Ms. Epstein."

Jerry Dannenberg, the superintendent, says the front office received no complaints about Larry, but according to several faculty members, at least two teachers tried to formally protest what was going on. The first was the same teacher who told Larry to scrub the makeup off his face. She was approached by several boys in her class who said that Larry had started taunting them in the halls—"I know you want me," he'd say—and their friends were calling them gay. The teacher told some of her colleagues that when she went to the office to file a complaint, Epstein said she would take it. "It's about Larry," the teacher said. "There's nothing we can do about that," Epstein replied. (Epstein denies she was ever approached.) A few days later another teacher claims to have gone to the school principal, Joel Lovstedt. The teacher says she told him that she was concerned about Larry and she thought he was a danger to himself—she worried that he might fall in his three-inch stilettos and injure himself. Lovstedt told the teacher that he had directions, though

he wouldn't say from where, that they couldn't intervene with Larry's sexual expression. (Lovstedt denied *Newsweek's* request for an interview.) There was an unusual student complaint, too. Larry's younger brother, Rocky, 12, also attended E. O. Green, and the kids started picking on him the day in January when Larry showed up in hot pink knee-length boots. Rocky says he went to several school officials for help, including Epstein. "I went up to her at lunchtime," he says. "I said, 'Ms. Epstein, can you stop Larry from dressing like a girl? The kids are saying since Larry is gay, I must be gay, too, because I'm his brother'."

As you talk to the teachers, many of them say they tried to support Larry, but they didn't always know how. In blue-collar, immigrant Oxnard, there is no gay community to speak of and generally very little public discussion of gay issues, at least until Larry's murder happened. One teacher was very protective of Larry, his English teacher, Mrs. Boldrin. To help Larry feel better about moving to Casa Pacifica, she brought Larry a present: a green evening dress that once belonged to her own daughter. Before school started, Larry ran to the bathroom to try it on. Then he showed it to some of his friends, telling them that he was going to wear it at graduation.

And then there was Valentine's Day. A day or two before the shooting, the school was buzzing with the story about a game Larry was playing with a group of his girlfriends in the outdoor quad. The idea was, you had to go up to your crush and ask them to be your Valentine. Several girls named boys they liked, then marched off to complete the mission. When it was Larry's turn, he named Brandon, who happened to be playing basketball nearby. Larry walked right on to the court in the middle of the game and asked Brandon to be his Valentine. Brandon's friends were there and started joking that he and Larry were going to make "gay babies" together. At the end of lunch, Brandon passed by one of Larry's friends in the hall. She says he told her to say goodbye to Larry, because she would never see him again.

The friend didn't tell Larry about the threat—she thought Brandon was just kidding. There are many rumors of another confrontation between Larry and Brandon, on Feb. 11, the day before the shooting. Several students and teachers said they had heard about a fight between the two but they hadn't actually witnessed it themselves. The next morning a counselor at Casa Pacifica asked Larry what was wrong, and he said, vaguely, "I've had enough." When he got to school, his friends quizzed him about his noticeably unfabulous appearance. He said that he ran out of makeup and hair gel (which wasn't true) and that he had a blister on his ankle (this was true—he'd just bought a new pair of boots). Larry walked alongside Boldrin to the computer class and sat in front of a computer. A few minutes later, a counselor summoned him to her office. She told him that his grades were so low, he was at risk of not graduating from the eighth grade. He went back to his computer. He had written his name on his paper as Leticia King. Most of the campus heard the gunshots. Some described it like a door slammed shut very hard.

On March 7, the school held a memorial service for Larry. Epstein stood at the podium with students who read from notecards about what they liked best about Larry: he was nice, he was unique, he was brave. The band played "Amazing Grace," and two dozen doves were released into the sky. Averi read a poem about how her friend was like a garden seed that grew, and died; Larry's mom wept in the front row. Deep in the audience, an eighth grader turned to one of Brandon's friends and whispered, "That's so gay."

The obvious question now is whether Larry's death could have been prevented. "Absolutely," says Dannenberg. "Why do we have youngsters that have access to guns? Why don't we have adequate funding to pay for social workers at the school to make sure students have resources? We have societal issues." Many teachers and parents aren't content with that answer. For them, the issue isn't whether Larry was gay or straight—his father still isn't convinced his son was gay—but whether he was allowed to push the boundaries so far that he put himself and others in danger. They're not blaming Larry for his own death—as if anything could justify his murder—but their attitude toward his assailant is not unsympathetic. "We failed Brandon," a teacher says. "We didn't know the bullying was coming from the other side—Larry was pushing as hard as he could, because he liked the attention."

Greg King doesn't feel sympathy for Brandon, but he does believe his son sexually harassed him. He's resentful that the gay community has appropriated his son's murder as part of a larger cause. "I think the gay-rights people want it to be a gay-rights issue, because it makes a poster child out of my son," King says. "That bothered me. I'm not anti-gay. I have a lot of co-workers and friends who are gay." That anger was made worse when he heard this summer that Epstein would be promoted to principal of an elementary school. "This is a slap in the face of my family," Greg says. Many teachers wonder if the district moved her because she had become a lightning rod for criticism after Larry's death. Dannenberg, the superintendent, says that she was the most qualified person for the new principal job.

'If we're going to be sure this isn't going to happen again,' says Elaine Garber, 'this has got to be discussed more.'

The school has conducted its own investigation, though its lawyer won't make it public. But it will likely be brought up when Brandon goes to trial. He is charged with first-degree murder and a hate crime, and is scheduled to be arraigned this week. Hundreds of his classmates have signed a petition asking that he be tried in juvenile court. The district attorney wants him tried as an adult, which could result in a prison sentence of 51 years to life. "Brandon was being terrorized," says Bill, who has set up a public defense fund in his son's name. "He was being stalked almost, to the degree of the school should have never let this happen." What happened to Larry and Brandon was certainly extreme, but it has implications for schools across the country. "If we're going to be absolutely sure this isn't going to happen again," says Elaine Garber, 81, who has served on the school's board for 48 years, "this has got to be discussed some more."

As if anyone has stopped talking—and arguing—about Larry King. He had an entire page devoted to him in the E. O. Green yearbook. On the Internet, he's become a gay martyr, and this year's National Day of Silence, an annual event created to raise awareness of homophobia, was dedicated to Larry. And in Averi Laskey's bedroom, she still keeps a handmade purple get-well card she made for Larry on the day after he was shot. At the time, there was still hope he would pull through. He had survived the night, which the doctors said was a good sign. Averi rounded up dozens of teachers and friends between classes to sign messages of encouragement. "Larry, I miss you. Get better," Boldrin wrote in blue ink. "Keep up your spirit. A lot of people are rooting for you to get better," the principal wrote. Some of Larry's classmates apologized for how he had been treated. A few even left their phone numbers, so he could call them if he ever needed to talk to someone. But when Averi got home that day, she learned that Larry had suffered a fatal stroke. Larry was pronounced brain-dead that afternoon, and the family decided to donate his organs. The following day, Feb. 14, doctors harvested his pancreas, liver, lungs and the most important organ of all, which now beats inside the chest of a 10-year-old girl. On Valentine's Day, Larry King gave away his heart, but not in the way he thought he would.

With Andrew Murr and Jennifer Ordoñez.

Interview with Dr. Craig Anderson
Video Game Violence

Dr. Craig Anderson, a leader in the research on the effects of exposure to violent video games on aggressive behavior, was invited to speak at Nebraska Wesleyan University. A group of Nebraska Wesleyan University students interviewed Dr. Anderson. We explored his interest and experiences in this research area.

SARAH HOWE, JENNIFER STIGGE, AND BROOKE SIXTA

Since 1997, Nebraska Wesleyan University (NE) has held an endowed lecture to honor the 40-year career of Dr. Clifford Fawl. The FAWL Lecture Series brings distinguished psychologists to the Wesleyan campus to present their research and interact with undergraduate psychology students. On March 22, 2007, we welcomed Dr. Craig Anderson as the FAWL lecturer to speak on *Violent Video Games: Theory, Research, and Public Policy.*

Dr. Craig Anderson received his bachelors degree at Butler University (IN) in 1976. He earned a masters degree (1978) and PhD (1980) in psychology at Stanford University (CA). He currently is a distinguished professor of psychology at Iowa State University and is widely regarded as the leader in research on the effects of violent video games and other forms of media violence. He has published widely on depression, loneliness, and shyness; attribution processes; social judgment; and human aggression. He has earned recognition as the second most highly cited scholar in social psychology textbooks. He has testified before the U.S. Senate Committee on Commerce, Science and Transportation's hearing on "The Impact of Interactive Violence on Children" and has served on the Media Violence Expert Panel for the Surgeon General.

Dr. Anderson started his visit by discussing the importance of good methodology to a research methods class. He was then interviewed by a small group of Wesleyan students concerning his work on violence and video games.

Student: What was your motivation for starting research on media violence and video games?

Anderson: It originally had to do with working on the General Aggression Model and learning about the media violence literature. There were literally hundreds of studies, but there were still gaps and unanswered questions. I had some students looking for research topics that were interesting and publishable, and then they identified gaps in the research. That was the initial reason. Later they basically extended the research using video games to test some aspects of the General Aggression Model. Next, my research team looked at priming issues, which prior to our work, had never been used in the context of media violence effects. After talking to some colleagues in cognitive psychology and debating about which method to use, we thought of using some cognitive measures such as a modified Stroop test but we chose a reading reaction time task.

Student: Looking back on many of your articles, we noticed you first did a study on video games in 1987 and another in 1995, but the majority of your studies have been since 1999. Did this more recent increase in research on the effects of video games have anything to do with Columbine and other school shootings?

Anderson: No, it had to do with an internal grant I received about 1996. It funded three graduate students and enabled us to start doing research on the effects of violent video games. I had been writing grant proposals on the topic for some time, but this was the first time I had the opportunity to do some of those studies. Then, Columbine came along.

Student: Were you asked to help with any of the Columbine research?

Anderson: No, although I was asked to testify in the U.S. Senate hearing about violent video games some time after the shooting.

Student: What group of people do you think are the most susceptible to the effects of violent video games, and why?

Anderson: Many researchers in the field of media violence think that people who are high on what you would call trait aggression (especially children and adolescents) are going to be more influenced by exposure to media violence than people who are low on trait aggression. In other words, many scholars believe that highly aggressive people are more susceptible to the harmful effects of media violence than are nonaggressive people. However, I think that the research evidence over the years doesn't bear that out, yet. Some studies show this heightened susceptibility of highly aggressive people, but some studies show the opposite including one of my studies (Anderson, 1997). That study found that people who are lowest on trait aggression showed the biggest effect of a violent movie manipulation. Those data yielded a significant interaction between measures of trait aggression and measures of media violence exposure. The nonaggressive people who watched a violent movie clip displayed more aggressive thoughts than nonaggressive people who saw the nonviolent clip, but highly aggressive people were relatively unaffected by the movie clip manipulation. Other researchers have found the opposite type of interaction. For example, in some studies those who score high on trait aggressiveness and have been exposed to a lot of violent media are the ones who are most likely to have, at some time in their lives, been arrested for assault. Well, is that because the media violence effect only operates on high trait-aggressive people? Perhaps low traitaggressive people are equally affected, but because their general level of aggression is low, media violence can't increase their willingness to aggress enough to rise to the level of assaulting someone.

Student: From where do you recruit your participants?

Anderson: Well, very often, it's a convenience sample. However, the present grant research that my colleagues/students and I have been doing allows us to pay participants. So we are able to pay kids to play video games, which they think is great (laughter). Some try to come in two or three times, and we have to tell them they cannot. In these situations, we have to select samples to fit the particular research question or issue.

Student: In your experimental research, how do you account for the participants who regularly play video games from those who have little to no experience?

Anderson: We usually give the participants questionnaires that tell us how much the individuals have played and what kinds of games they play. Prior experience with video games can then figure into the data analysis. We seldom find any kind of difference in our experimental studies between those participants with a lot of experience and those without. The one difference we do find is that participants with a lot of gaming experience really like being in the violent video game condition. Typically, we do not find much of a statistically reliable effect of gaming experience on aggressive thought processes and behavior.

Student: Do you feel that your research has or will have an impact on the video game industry? If so, what impact do you think it will have?

Anderson: Our research has probably had a bigger impact in countries other than in the United States. Almost every other modern country has legal restrictions on violent media including video games. Many of them ban some of the games outright and most have age-based restrictions. Certainly the research that my students and I have done over the years has been used by child advocacy groups and others in these countries to make sure that these ratings are enforced. The research certainly has increased the awareness of the issue in the United States. However, there are no U.S. laws regarding violent video games. I have never said publicly whether I support a legislative solution, because my political opinion is not relevant to what I regard as my scientific expertise. Even in the court cases with which I have been involved, I say upfront that I will not comment on what I think about the law under judicial review. I will talk about what the science says or what it cannot say. The work and interviews that we've done concerning violence in video games is used to get the word out to parents about the effect of violent video games. Our research has had a big impact on parents, but not as big as it needs to be. There are still people teaching their 2- or 3-year-olds how to shoot a gun in these video games.

Student: What are some of the stronger arguments against your research? How do you counter those arguments?

Anderson: One of the best arguments, until recently, is that there are no longitudinal studies, but we have now published one (Anderson, Gentile, & Buckley, 2007). Previously in my various talks, I had described the lack of longitudinal data on the effects of video games. The paucity of these studies was due to the lack of government support for longitudinal research. The support for the longitudinal study I just mentioned came from non-governmental sources. More recently, we finally got the funding needed to perform a larger, longer-term longitudinal study after being turned down six or seven times. There really aren't any long-term longitudinal studies, such as when you follow the group of individuals and see where these participants end up after several years. Some participants may end up in jail, juvenile detention facilities, or kicked out of school, which makes this an important field of interest. A response to this criticism about the lack of longitudinal studies on violent video games is that such studies have already been done pertaining to television violence, which is the same phenomenon, but some individuals fail to see the similarities between violence on television and violence in video games. People used this lack of a longitudinal study, focusing on violent video games, as a criticism for the evidence found between increased aggression and exposure to violent video games. Of course, they can no longer do this.

Student: Do you have any plans for the future implementation of your research? How should your research be applied to schools, home, everyday life, etc.?

Anderson: We haven't been thinking much about intervention studies, mainly because I don't do intervention studies. There is a group at Iowa State University that does intervention studies, but most of their work focuses on drug use and intervention to reduce kids' use of alcohol, tobacco, and various illegal substances. There have been some TV/video game interventions done in school systems, but intervention as a whole is done by another group of researchers.

Student: Where do you think video game research will go from here?

Anderson: There are two related issues that are going to be big soon. One is the identification of video game addiction or Internet addiction, including text messaging, as a true addiction in need of clinical intervention for some individuals.

The other has to do with attention deficit disorders, executive control, and impulse control. There is potential long-term damage in those brain systems due to extensive viewing of media that flash across the screen and demand constantly shifting attention. Some evidence indicates that extensive use of screening media, whether it is violent or not, leads to attention deficit disorder, especially in very young children who see a lot of TV.

References

Anderson, C. A. (1997). Effects of violent movies and trait irritability on hostile feelings and aggressive thoughts. *Aggressive Behavior, 23,* 161–178.

Anderson, C. A., Gentile, D. A., & Buckley, K. E. (2007). *Violent video game effects on children and adolescents.* New York: Oxford University Press.

SARAH HOWE, a junior at Nebraska Wesleyan University, is a psychology major with a minor in health and human performance. Following graduation, she plans to attend graduate school in counseling. JENNIFER STIGGE, also a junior at Nebraska Wesleyan University, is an industrial-organizational psychology (I/O psychology) major with a business administration minor. She plans to begin graduate school in the fall of 2009 in I/O psychology. BROOKE SIXTA graduated from Nebraska Wesleyan University in December of 2007 with a bachelor's degree in psychology and a minor in business administration. She is currently working; however, plans to also attend I/O psychology graduate school beginning at the fall of 2008.

Author's note—We would like to thank Dr. Anderson for visiting with Nebraska Wesleyan students and faculty, and presenting his research regarding violence and video games. We would also like to give a special thanks to Dr. Marilyn Petro, Dr. Michael Tagler, Allyson Bell, and Amanda Holmgren for their assistance with the process of this interview.

Adolescent Brain Development

From: ACT for Youth Upstate Center of Excellence (Research Facts and Findings: A collaboration of Cornell University, University of Rochester, and the NYS Center for School Safety, May 2002)

Research now supports what parents have *long* suspected-that the teenager's brain is different than the adult brain. Recent research by scientists at the National Institute of Mental Health (NIMH) using magnetic resonance imaging (MRI) has found that the teen brain is not a finished product, but is a work in progress. Until recently most scientists believed that the major "wiring" of the brain was completed by as early as three years of age and that the brain was fully mature by the age of 10 or 12. New findings show that the greatest changes to the parts of the brain that are responsible for functions such as self-control, judgment, emotions, and organization occur between puberty and adulthood. This may help to explain certain teenage behavior that adults can find mystifying, such as poor decision-making, recklessness, and emotional outbursts.

The brain is still developing during the teen years Dr. Jay Giedd of the NIMH has reported that brain "maturation does not stop at age 10, but continues into the teen years and even into the 20's. What is most surprising is that you get a second wave of overproduction of gray matter, something that was thought to happen only in the first 18 months of life (Begley, 2000)." Following the overproduction of gray matter, the brain undergoes a process called "pruning" where connections among neurons in the brain that are not used wither away, while those that are used stay—the "use it or lose it" principle. It is thought that this pruning process makes the brain more efficient by strengthening the connections that are used most often, and eliminating the clutter of those that are not used at all.

What does this mean for teens? According to Dr. Giedd, this is exciting news for teens. "...unlike infants whose brain activity is completely determined by their parents and environment, the teens may actually be able to control how their own brains are wired and sculpted." Kids who "exercise" their brains by learning to order their thoughts, understand abstract concepts, and control their impulses are laying the neural foundations that will serve them for the rest of their lives. "This argues for doing a lot of things as a teenager," says Dr. Giedd. "You are hard-wiring your brain in adolescence. Do you want to hard-wire it for sports and playing music and doing mathematics-or for lying on the couch in front of the television?"

Alcohol use and the developing teen brain Recent research suggests that alcohol use affects adolescents and adults differently, which makes sense given what we now know about the changes going on in the teen brain. While more research needs to be done in this area, Duke University scientists say "the available research suggests that adolescents are more vulnerable than adults to the affects of alcohol on learning and memory (White, 2001). Not only do they react differently to the initial affects of alcohol, studies suggest that teens who repeatedly use alcohol can suffer long-term effects. Preliminary studies using rats have shown that those with repeated alcohol exposure during adolescence are more sensitive to alcohol-induced impairments later in life (White, 2001).

Research on humans by Brown, et al. (2000) has shown the first concrete evidence that heavy, on-going alcohol use by adolescents can impair brain functioning. Brown's research on 15 and 16 year olds showed cognitive impairments in teen alcohol abusers, compared with non-abusing peers, even weeks after they stop drinking. This suggests that abuse of alcohol by teens may have long-term negative effects on the make up of their brains.

Teens and understanding emotions Teens also differ from adults in their ability to read and understand emotions in the faces of others. Recent research shows that teens and adults actually use different regions of the brain in responding to certain tasks. In a study conducted at Boston's McLean Hospital, psychologist Deborah Yurgelun-Todd and colleagues showed pictures of people wearing fearful expressions to teenagers between the ages of 11 and 17 while the teens had their brains scanned using functional magnetic resonance imaging (fMRI). She found that compared to adults the teens' frontal lobes (the seat of goal-oriented rational thinking) are less active and their amygdala (a structure in the temporal lobe that is involved in discriminating fear and other emotions) is more active. The teens often misread facial expressions, with those under the age of 14 more often seeing sadness or anger or confusion instead of fear. Older teenagers answered correctly more often and exhibited a progressive shift of activity from the amygdala to the frontal lobes. The results suggest that "in teens, the judgment, insight and reasoning power of the frontal cortex is not being brought to bear on the task as it is in adults. Teens just process information differently from adults. (Yurgelun-Todd, 2002)"

Brain Regions and Functions

Frontal lobe—self-control, judgment, emotional regulation; restructured in teen years

Corpus callosum—intelligence, consciousness and self-awareness; reaches full maturity in 20's

Parietal lobes—integrate auditory, visual, and tactile signals; immature until age 16

Temporal lobes—emotional maturity; still developing after age 16

Implications It is important to note that experts caution careful interpretation of this new information about adolescent brain development, as it is still very early in the analysis and understanding of what it all means. Yet it is also true that these findings add new dimensions to issues facing young people, as well as their parents and teachers, and they pose a challenge to policy makers (NIH, 2000). If the choices adolescents make about using drugs and alcohol and engaging in or avoiding challenging learning tasks have long-term and irreversible consequences for the development of their brains, then discouraging harmful choices and encouraging healthy ones is all the more urgent. This new research may also provide a compelling explanation for why adolescents often fail to heed adults' warnings about such choices; they may simply not be able to understand and accept arguments that seem logical and decisive to adults. It is also

possible that teens are misperceiving or misunderstanding the emotions of adults, leading to miscommunication both in terms of what the teen thinks the adult is feeling and in terms of the teen's response.

Perhaps most importantly, teenagers are empowered with opportunities to develop their brains through the activities in which they choose to participate.

References

Begley, Sharon. (February 28, 2000). Getting inside a teen brain. Newsweek, 135 (9), 58-59.

Brown, A., Tapert, S., Granholm, E., and Delis, D. (2000). Neurocognitive functioning of adolescents: Effects of protracted alcohol use. *Alcoholism: Clinical and Experimental Research*, 24, 164-171.

Giedd, J., Blumenthal, J., Jeffries, N., Castellanos, F., Liu, H., Zijdenbos, A., Paus, T., Evans, A., and Rapoport, J. (1999). Brain development during childhood and adolescence: A longitudinal MRI study. *Nature Neuroscience*, 2 (10), 861-863.

National Institutes of Health (2000). Adolescent Alcohol Dependence May Damage Brain Function. *NIH News Release*, available on line at www.hih/gov/news/pr/feb2000/niaaa-14.htm

National Institute of Mental Health (2001). Teenage Brain: A work in progress. National Institute of Mental Health publication available on line at www.ninih.nih.gov/publicat/teenbrain.cfm.

White, A. (2001) Alcohol and Adolescent Brain Development. Paper available online at http://www.duke.edu/~amwhite/alc_adol_pf.html.

Yurgelun-Todd, D. (2002) Frontline interview "Inside the Teen Brain" on PBS.org. Full interview available on the web at http://www.pbs.org/wgbh/pages/frontline/shows/teenbrain/interviews/todd.html

Chapter 6
Young Adulthood

Young Adulthood has come to be recognized as a continuation of the transition to adulthood. Adolescence is the beginning of this "conversion" but socially and culturally we often don't think of those in the beginning of this period (18-22 year olds) as "fully adult". We'll look at the many factors that constitute the differences between young, middle and older adulthood in the next few chapters, but for now we'll start with a look at the changes that occur for the "20 and 30 somethings". First we'll examine the physical aspects of change during this period and then consider cognitive, social and ethical issues. We'll finish this chapter with two articles on professional considerations and intimacy, important issues in this time of "emerging" adulthood.

1 The Transition from Adolescence to Adulthood

 LG1 Describe the transition from adolescence to adulthood.

Becoming an Adult

The Transition From High School to College

BECOMING AN ADULT

For most individuals, becoming an adult involves a lengthy transition period. Recently, the transition from adolescence to adulthood has been referred to as **emerging adulthood,** which occurs from approximately 18 to 25 years of age (Arnett, 2006, 2007). Experimentation and exploration characterize the emerging adult. At this point in their development, many individuals are still exploring which career path they want to follow, what they want their identity to be, and which lifestyle they want to adopt (for example, single, cohabiting, or married).

Key Features Jeffrey Arnett (2006) recently concluded that five key features characterize emerging adulthood:

- *Identity exploration, especially in love and work.* Emerging adulthood is the time during which key changes in identity take place for many individuals (Cote, 2009; Kroger, Martinussen, & Marcia, 2010).
- *Instability.* Residential changes peak during early adulthood, a time during which there also is often instability in love, work, and education.
- *Self-focused.* According to Arnett (2006, p. 10), emerging adults "are self-focused in the sense that they have little in the way of social obligations, little in the way of duties and commitments to others, which leaves them with a great deal of autonomy in running their own lives."
- *Feeling in-between.* Many emerging adults don't consider themselves adolescents or full-fledged adults.
- *The age of possibilities, a time when individuals have an opportunity to transform their lives.* Arnett (2006) describes two ways in which emerging adulthood is the age of possibilities: (1) many emerging adults are optimistic about their future; and (2) for emerging adults who have experienced difficult times while growing up, emerging adulthood presents an opportunity to direct their lives in a more positive direction.

emerging adulthood The transition from adolescence to adulthood (approximately 18 to 25 years of age) that involves experimentation and exploration.

Markers of Becoming an Adult In the United States, the most widely recognized marker of entry into adulthood is holding a more or less permanent, full-time job, which usually happens when an individual finishes school—high school for some, college for others, graduate or professional school for still others. However, other criteria are far from clear. Economic independence is one marker of adult status, but achieving it is often a long process. College graduates are increasingly returning to live with their parents as they attempt to establish themselves economically. A longitudinal study found that at age 25 only slightly more than half of the participants were fully financially independent of their family of origin (Cohen & others, 2003). The most dramatic findings in this study, though, involved the extensive variability in the individual trajectories of adult roles across 10 years from 17 to 27 years of age; many of the participants moved back and forth between increasing and decreasing economic dependency.

Other studies show us that taking responsibility for oneself is likely an important marker of adult status for many individuals. In a recent study, both parents and college students agreed that taking responsibility for one's actions and developing emotional control are important aspects of becoming an adult (Nelson & others, 2007).

What we have discussed about the markers of adult status mainly characterize individuals in industrialized societies, especially Americans. Are the criteria for adulthood the same in developing countries as they are in the United States? In developing countries, marriage is more often a significant marker for entry into adulthood, and this usually occurs much earlier than the adulthood markers in the United States (Arnett, 2004).

THE TRANSITION FROM HIGH SCHOOL TO COLLEGE

For many individuals in developed countries, going from high school to college is an important aspect of the transition to adulthood (Bowman, 2010). Just as the transition from elementary school to middle or junior high school involves change and possible stress, so does the transition from high school to college. The two transitions have many parallels. Going from being a senior in high school to being a freshman in college replays the top-dog phenomenon of transferring from the oldest and most powerful group of students to the youngest and least powerful group of students that occurred earlier as adolescence began. For many students, the transition from high school to college involves movement to a larger, more impersonal school structure; interaction with peers from more diverse geographical and sometimes more diverse ethnic backgrounds; and increased focus on achievement and its assessment. And like the transition from elementary to middle or junior high school, the transition from high school to college can involve positive features. Students are more likely to feel grown up, have more subjects from which to select, have more time to spend with peers, have more opportunities to explore different lifestyles and values, enjoy greater independence from parental monitoring, and be challenged intellectually by academic work (Santrock & Halonen, 2010).

Today's college students experience more stress and are more depressed than in the past, according to a national study of more than 200,000 freshmen at more than 400 colleges and universities (Pryor & others, 2009). And a recent national survey conducted by the American College Health Association (2008) of more than 90,000 students on 177 campuses revealed that feeling things are hopeless, feeling overwhelmed with all they have to do, feeling mentally exhausted, feeling sad, and feeling depressed are not uncommon in college students. Figure 13.1 indicates the percentage of students who had these feelings and how many times a year they experienced them.

Most college campuses have a counseling center with access to mental health professionals who can help students learn effective ways to cope with stress. Counselors can provide good information about coping with stress and academic matters.

The transition from high school to college often involves positive as well as negative features. In college, students are likely to feel grown up, be able to spend more time with peers, have more opportunities to explore different lifestyles and values, and enjoy greater freedom from parental monitoring. However, college involves a larger, more impersonal school structure and an increased focus on achievement and its assessment. *What was your transition to college like?*

Mental Health Difficulty	1–4 Times	5–8 Times	9 or More Times
Felt things were hopeless	39	11	13
Felt overwhelmed with all I had to do	32	25	36
Felt mentally exhausted	32	24	35
Felt so depressed it was difficult to function	18	7	10
Seriously contemplated suicide	8	1	1
Attempted suicide	1.2	0.2	0.2

FIGURE **13.1**

COLLEGE STUDENTS' MENTAL HEALTH DIFFICULTIES IN THE PAST YEAR. *Note: Figure shows the percentage of college students who responded to the question: "Within the last school year, how many times have you . . . ?*

As we learn more about healthy lifestyles and how they contribute to a longer life span, emerging and young adults are increasingly interested in learning about physical performance, health, nutrition, exercise, and addiction.

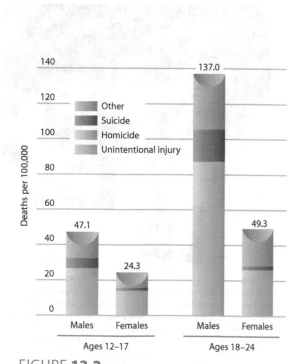

FIGURE **13.2**

MORTALITY RATES OF U.S. ADOLESCENTS AND EMERGING ADULTS

Why might it be easy to develop bad health habits in early adulthood?

PHYSICAL PERFORMANCE AND DEVELOPMENT

Most of us reach our peak physical performance before the age of 30, often between the ages of 19 and 26. This peak of physical performance occurs not only for the average young adult, but for outstanding athletes as well. Different types of athletes, however, reach their peak performances at different ages. Most swimmers and gymnasts peak in their late teens. Golfers and marathon runners tend to peak in their late twenties. In other areas of athletics, peak performance is often in the early to mid-twenties. However, in recent years, some highly conditioned athletes—such as Dana Torres (Olympic swimming), Lance Armstrong (cycling), and Tom Watson (golf)— have stretched the age limit of award-winning performances.

Not only do we reach our peak in physical performance during early adulthood, but it is also during this age period that we begin to decline in physical performance. Muscle tone and strength usually begin to show signs of decline around the age of 30. Sagging chins and protruding abdomens also may begin to appear for the first time. The lessening of physical abilities is a common complaint among the just-turned thirties.

HEALTH

Emerging adults have more than twice the mortality rate of adolescents (Park & others, 2006) (see Figure 13.2). As indicated in Figure 13.2, males are mainly responsible for the higher mortality rate of emerging adults.

Although emerging adults have a higher death rate than adolescents, emerging adults have few chronic health problems, and they have fewer colds and respiratory problems than when they were children (Rimsza & Kirk, 2005). Although most college students know what it takes to prevent illness and promote health, they don't fare very well when it comes to applying this information to themselves (Murphy-Hoefer, Alder, & Higbee, 2004).

A longitudinal study revealed that most bad health habits engaged in during adolescence increased in emerging adulthood (Harris & others, 2006). Inactivity, diet, obesity, substance abuse, reproductive health care, and health care access worsened in emerging adulthood. For example, when they were 12 to 18 years of age, only 5 percent reported no weekly exercise, but when they became 19 to 26 years of age, 46 percent said they did not exercise during a week.

In emerging and early adulthood, few individuals stop to think about how their personal lifestyles will affect their health later in their adult lives. As emerging adults, many of us develop a pattern of not eating breakfast, not eating regular meals, and relying on snacks as our main food source during the day, eating excessively to the point where we exceed the normal weight for our age, smoking moderately or excessively, drinking moderately or excessively, failing to exercise, and getting by with only a few hours of sleep at night (Cousineau, Goldstein, &

Franco, 2005). These lifestyles are associated with poor health, which in turn impacts life satisfaction. In the Berkeley Longitudinal Study—in which individuals were evaluated over a period of 40 years—physical health at age 30 predicted life satisfaction at age 70, more so for men than for women (Mussen, Honzik, & Eichorn, 1982).

A recent study explored links between health behavior and life satisfaction in more than 17,000 individuals 17 to 30 years of age in 21 countries (Grant, Wardle, & Steptoe, 2009). The young adults' life satisfaction was positively related to not smoking, exercising regularly, using sun protection, eating fruit and limiting fat intake, but was not related to consuming alcohol and fiber intake.

The health profile of emerging and young adults can be improved by reducing the incidence of certain health-impairing lifestyles, such as overeating, and by engaging in health-improving lifestyles that include good eating habits, exercising regularly, and not abusing drugs (Teague & others, 2009; Waldron & Dieser, 2010).

EATING AND WEIGHT

Obesity Obesity is a serious and pervasive health problem for many individuals (Howel, 2010; Kruseman & others, 2010). The prevalence of obesity in U.S. adults 20 years of age and older increased from 19 percent in 1997 to 33 percent in 2006 (Centers for Disease Control and Prevention, 2008). In this survey, obesity was defined as having a body mass index (which takes into account height and weight) of 30 or more. The National Health and Nutrition Examination Survey (NHANES) recently projected that 86 percent of Americans will be overweight or obese by 2030 if current weight trends continue (Beydoun & Wang, 2009). And a study of more than 168,000 adults in 63 countries revealed that worldwide 40 percent of the men and 30 percent of the women were overweight and 24 percent of the men and 27 percent of the women were obese (Balkau & others, 2007).

Being overweight or obese are linked to increased risk of hypertension, diabetes, and cardiovascular disease (Granger & others, 2010). Being overweight or obese also are associated with mental health problems. For example, a recent study revealed that overweight women were more likely to be depressed than women who were not overweight (Ball, Burton, & Brown, 2009).

What factors are involved in obesity? The possible culprits include heredity, leptin, set point, and metabolism and environmental factors and gender.

© www.CartoonStock.com

Heredity Until recently, the genetic component of obesity had been underestimated by scientists. Some individuals inherit a tendency to be overweight (Holzapfel & others, 2010). Researchers have documented that animals can be inbred to have a propensity for obesity (Mathes & others, 2010; Osmond & others, 2009). Further, identical human twins have similar weights, even when they are reared apart (Collaku & others, 2004).

Leptin Leptin (from the Greek word *leptos*, which means "thin") is a protein that is involved in satiety (the condition of being full to satisfaction) and released by fat cells, resulting in decreased food intake and increased energy expenditure. Leptin acts as an antiobesity hormone. In humans, leptin concentrations have been linked with weight, percentage of body fat, weight loss in a single diet episode, and cumulative percentage of weight loss (de Luis & others, 2007; Rider & others, 2010). Some scientists are interested in the possibility that leptin might help obese individuals lose weight (Friedman, 2009). Two recent studies found that when obese individuals engaged in regular exercise, they lost weight, which was associated with changes in leptin levels (Nagashima & others, 2010; Rider & others, 2010).

Set Point   The amount of stored fat in your body is an important factor in your *set point*, the weight you maintain when you make no effort to gain or lose weight. Fat is stored in what are called adipose cells. When these cells are filled, you do not get hungry. When people gain weight, the number of their fat cells increases. A normal-weight individual has 30 to 40 billion fat cells. An obese individual has 80 to 120 billion fat cells. Some scientists have proposed that these fat cells can shrink but might not go away.

Environmental Factors   Environmental factors play an important role in obesity (Wardlaw & Smith, 2011). The human genome has not changed markedly in the last century, yet obesity has noticeably increased. The obesity rate has doubled in the United States since 1900. This dramatic increase in obesity likely is due to greater availability of food (especially food high in fat), energy-saving devices, and declining physical activity. One study found that in 2000, U.S. women ate 335 calories more a day and men 168 more a day than they did in the early 1970s (National Center for Health Statistics, 2004).

Sociocultural factors are involved in obesity, which is six times more prevalent among women with low incomes than among women with high incomes. Americans also are more obese than Europeans and people in many other areas of the world (Williams, 2005).

Dieting   Ironically, although obesity is on the rise, dieting has become an obsession with many Americans (Schiff, 2011; Thompson, Manore, & Vaughan, 2011). Although many Americans regularly embark on a diet, few are successful in keeping weight off long term (Saquib & others, 2009). A recent research review of the long-term outcomes of calorie-restricting diets revealed that overall one-third to two-thirds of dieters regain more weight than they lost on their diets (Mann & others, 2007). However, some individuals do lose weight and maintain the loss (Yancy & others, 2009). How often this occurs and whether some diet programs work better than others are still open questions.

What we do know about losing weight is that the most effective programs include exercise (Fahey, Insel, & Roth, 2011; Heitman & others, 2009). A recent research review concluded that adults who engaged in diet-plus-exercise programs lost more weight than diet only programs (Wu & others, 2009). A study of approximately 2,000 U.S. adults found that exercising 30 minutes a day, planning meals, and weighing themselves daily were the main strategies used by successful dieters compared with unsuccessful dieters (Kruger, Blanck, & Gillepse, 2006) (see Figure 13.3). Another recent study also revealed that daily weigh-ins are linked to maintaining weight loss (Wing & others, 2007).

REGULAR EXERCISE

One of the main reasons that health experts want people to exercise is that it helps to prevent diseases, such as heart disease and diabetes (Hales, 2011; Walker & others, 2010). Many health experts recommend that young adults engage in 30 minutes or more of aerobic exercise a day, preferably every day. **Aerobic exercise** is sustained exercise—jogging, swimming, or cycling, for example—that stimulates heart and lung activity. Most health experts recommend that you raise your heart rate to at least 60 percent of your maximum heart rate. Only about one-fifth of adults, however, are active at these recommended levels of physical activity.

Researchers have found that exercise benefits not only physical health, but mental health as well. In particular, exercise improves self-concept and reduces anxiety and depression (Sylvia & others, 2009). Meta-analyses have shown that exercise can be as effective in reducing depression as psychotherapy (Richardson & others, 2005).

Research on the benefits of exercise suggests that both moderate and intense activities produce important physical and psychological gains. The enjoyment and

How effective are diet programs?

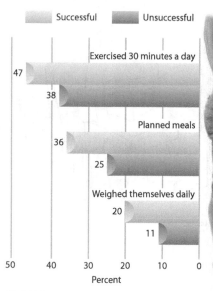

Successful   Unsuccessful

Exercised 30 minutes a day
47
38

Planned meals
36
25

Weighed themselves daily
20
11

50 40 30 20 10 0
Percent

FIGURE **13.3**
COMPARISON OF STRATEGIES IN SUCCESSFUL AND UNSUCCESSFUL DIETERS

pleasure we derive from exercise added to its aerobic benefits make exercise one of life's most important activities (Donatelle, 2011; Shaw, Clark, & Wagenmakers, 2010). Here are some helpful strategies for building exercise into your life:

- *Reduce TV time.* Heavy TV viewing is linked to poor health and obesity (Duvigneaud & others, 2007). Replace some of your TV time with exercise.
- *Chart your progress.* Systematically recording your exercise workouts will help you to chart your progress. This strategy is especially helpful over the long term.
- *Get rid of excuses.* People make up all kinds of excuses for not exercising. A typical excuse is, "I don't have enough time." You likely do have enough time.
- *Imagine the alternative.* Ask yourself whether you are too busy to take care of your own health. What will your life be like if you lose your health?

SUBSTANCE ABUSE

Fortunately, by the time individuals reach their mid-twenties, many have reduced their use of alcohol and drugs. That is the conclusion reached by Jerald Bachman and his colleagues (2002) in a longitudinal analysis of more than 38,000 individuals who were evaluated from the time they were high school seniors through their twenties. As in adolescence, male college students and young adults are more likely to take drugs than their female counterparts (Johnston & others, 2008). A recent study revealed that only 20 percent of college students reported that they abstain from drinking alcohol (Huang & others, 2009).

Let's take a closer look at use of alcohol and nicotine by young adults and at the nature of **addiction,** which is a behavior pattern characterized by an overwhelming involvement with a drug and securing its supply.

Alcohol   Let's examine two problems associated with drinking: binge drinking and alcoholism.

What are some strategies for incorporating exercise into your life?

Binge Drinking   Heavy binge drinking often increases in college, and it can take its toll on students (Kinney, 2009). Chronic binge drinking is more common among college men than women and students living away from home, especially in fraternity houses (Schulenberg & others, 2000).

In a national survey of drinking patterns on 140 campuses, almost half of the binge drinkers reported problems that included (Wechsler & others, 1994) missing classes, physical injuries, troubles with police, and having unprotected sex. For example, binge-drinking college students were 11 times more likely to fall behind in school, 10 times more likely to drive after drinking, and twice as likely to have unprotected sex than college students who did not binge drink.

Drinking alcohol before going out—called *pregaming*—has become common among college students. A recent study revealed that almost two-thirds of students on one campus had pregamed at least once in the last two weeks (DeJong, DeRicco, & Schneider, 2010). Another recent study found that two-thirds of 18- to 24-year-old women on one college pregamed (Read, Merrill, & Bytschkow, 2010). Drinking games, in which the goal is to become intoxicated, also have become common on college campuses (Cameron & others, 2010; Ham & others, 2010; McGuinness, Ahern, & Sole, 2010). Higher levels of alcohol use have been consistently linked to higher

What kinds of problems are associated with binge drinking in college?

rates of sexual risk taking, such as engaging in casual sex, sex without using contraception, and sexual assaults (Lawyer & others, 2010; White & others, 2009).

A special concern is the increase in binge drinking by females during emerging adulthood (Davis & others, 2010; Smith & Berger, 2010). In a national longitudinal study, binge drinking by 19- to 22-year-old women increased from 28 percent in 1995 to 34 percent in 2007 (Johnston & others, 2008).

When does binge drinking peak during development? A longitudinal study revealed that binge drinking peaks at about 21 to 22 years of age and then declines through the remainder of the twenties (Bachman & others, 2002) (see Figure 13.4).

Alcoholism *Alcoholism* is a disorder that involves long-term, repeated, uncontrolled, compulsive, and excessive use of alcoholic beverages and that impairs the drinker's health and social relationships. One in nine individuals who drink continues the path to alcoholism. Those who do are disproportionately related to alcoholics (Hansell & others, 2009). Family studies consistently reveal a high frequency of alcoholism in the first-degree relatives of alcoholics (Kramer & others, 2008). An

aerobic exercise Sustained exercise (such as jogging, swimming, or cycling) that stimulates heart and lung activity.

addiction A pattern of behavior characterized by an overwhelming involvement with using a drug and securing its supply.

FIGURE **13.4**

BINGE DRINKING IN THE ADOLESCENCE—EARLY ADULTHOOD TRANSITION. Note that the percentage of individuals engaging in binge drinking peaked at 21 or 22 years of age and then began to gradually decline through the remainder of the twenties. Binge drinking was defined as having five or more alcoholic drinks in a row in the past two weeks.

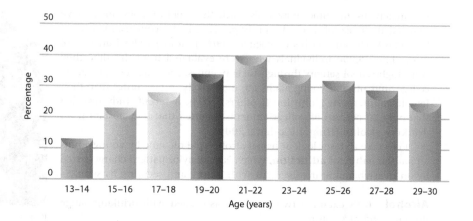

estimated 50 to 60 percent of individuals who become alcoholics are believed to have a genetic predisposition for it.

Although studies reveal a genetic influence on alcoholism, they also show that environmental factors play a role (Bierut & others, 2010; Pautassi & others, 2010). For example, family studies indicate that many individuals who suffer from alcoholism do not have close relatives who are addicted to alcohol (Martin & Sher, 1994). Large cultural variations in alcohol use also underscore the environment's role in alcoholism. For example, Orthodox Jews and Mormons have especially low rates of alcohol use.

About one-third of alcoholics recover whether or not they are ever in a treatment program. This figure was found in a long-term study of 700 individuals over 50 years and has consistently been found by other researchers as well (Vaillant, 1992). There is a "one-third rule" for alcoholism: By age 65, one-third are dead or in terrible shape, one-third are abstinent or drinking socially, and one-third are still trying to beat their addiction. A positive outcome and recovery from alcoholism are predicted by certain factors: (1) a strong negative experience related to drinking, such as a serious medical emergency or condition; (2) finding a substitute dependency to compete with alcohol abuse, such as meditation, exercise, or overeating (which of course has its own negative health consequences); (3) having new social supports (such as a concerned, helpful employer or a new marriage); and (4) joining an inspirational group, such as a religious organization or Alcoholics Anonymous (Vaillant, 1992).

Cigarette Smoking and Nicotine Converging evidence from a number of studies underscores the dangers of smoking or being around those who do (American Cancer Society, 2010). For example, smoking is linked to 30 percent of cancer deaths, 21 percent of heart disease deaths, and 82 percent of chronic pulmonary disease deaths. Secondhand smoke is implicated in as many as 9,000 lung cancer deaths a year. Children of smokers are at special risk for respiratory and middle-ear diseases (Goodwin & Cowles, 2008).

Fewer people smoke today than in the past, and almost half of all living adults who ever smoked have quit. In the United States, the prevalence of smoking in men has dropped from 42 percent in 1965 to 20.6 percent in 2007 (National Center for Health Statistics, 2010a). However, more than 50 million Americans still smoke cigarettes today.

Most adult smokers would like to quit, but their addiction to nicotine often makes quitting a challenge (Travis & Lawrance, 2009). Nicotine, the active drug in cigarettes, is a stimulant that increases the smoker's energy and alertness, a pleasurable and reinforcing experience. Nicotine also stimulates neurotransmitters that have a calming or pain-reducing effect.

"There's no shooting—we just make you keep smoking."
© Michael Shaw/The New Yorker Collection/
www.cartoonbank.com

4 Cognitive Development LG4 Characterize cognitive changes in early adulthood.

> Cognitive Stages

> Creativity

Are there changes in cognitive performance during these years? To explore the nature of cognition in early adulthood, we will focus on issues related to cognitive stages and creative thinking.

COGNITIVE STAGES

Are young adults more advanced in their thinking than adolescents are? Let's examine what Jean Piaget and others have said about this intriguing question.

Piaget's View Piaget concluded that an adolescent and an adult think qualitatively in the same way. That is, Piaget argued that at approximately 11 to 15 years of age, adolescents enter the formal operational stage, which is characterized by more logical, abstract, and idealistic thinking than the concrete operational thinking of 7- to 11-year-olds. Piaget did stress that young adults are more *quantitatively* advanced in their thinking in the sense that they have more knowledge than adolescents. He also reasoned, as do information-processing psychologists, that adults especially increase their knowledge in a specific area, such as a physicist's understanding of physics or a financial analyst's knowledge about finance. According to Piaget, however, formal operational thought is the final stage in cognitive development, and it characterizes adults as well as adolescents.

Some developmentalists theorize it is not until adulthood that many individuals consolidate their formal operational thinking. That is, they may begin to plan and hypothesize about intellectual problems in adolescence, but they become more systematic and sophisticated at this as young adults. Nonetheless, even many adults do not think in formal operational ways (Keating, 2004).

Realistic and Pragmatic Thinking Some developmentalists propose that as young adults move into the world of work, their way of thinking does change. One

What are some ways that young adults might think differently than adolescents?

idea is that as they face the constraints of reality, which work promotes, their idealism decreases (Labouvie-Vief, 1986).

A related change in thinking was proposed that concludes it is unlikely that adults go beyond the powerful methods of scientific thinking characteristic of the formal operational stage (Schaie & Willis, 2000). However, adults do progress beyond adolescents in their use of intellect. For example, in early adulthood individuals often switch from acquiring knowledge to applying knowledge as they pursue success in their work (Schaie & Willis, 2000).

Reflective and Relativistic Thinking   William Perry (1999) also described changes in cognition that take place in early adulthood. He said that adolescents often view the world in terms of polarities—right/wrong, we/they, or good/bad. As youth age into adulthood, they gradually move away from this type of absolutist thinking as they become aware of the diverse opinions and multiple perspectives of others. Thus, in Perry's view, the absolutist, dualistic thinking of adolescence gives way to the reflective, relativistic thinking of adulthood. Other developmentalists also observe that reflective thinking is an important indicator of cognitive change in young adults (Fischer & Bidell, 2006).

Expanding on Perry's view, Gisela Labouvie-Vief (2006) recently proposed that the increasing complexity of cultures in the past century has generated a greater need for more reflective, complex thinking that takes into account the changing nature of knowledge and challenges. She also emphasizes that the key aspects of cognitive development in emerging adulthood include deciding on a particular worldview, recognizing that the worldview is subjective, and understanding that diverse worldviews should be acknowledged. In her perspective, considerable individual variation characterizes the thinking of emerging adults, with the highest level of thinking attained by only some. She argues that the level of education emerging adults achieve especially influences how likely they will maximize their cognitive potential.

Is There a Fifth, Postformal Stage?   Some theorists have pieced together cognitive changes in young adults and proposed a new stage of cognitive development, **postformal thought,** which is qualitatively different from Piaget's formal operational thought (Sinnott, 2003). Postformal thought involves understanding that the correct answer to a problem requires reflective thinking and can vary from one situation to another, and that the search for truth is often an ongoing, never-ending process (Kitchener, King, & Deluca, 2006). Postformal thought also includes the belief that solutions to problems need to be realistic and that emotion and subjective factors can influence thinking.

What is postformal thought like in practice? As young adults engage in more reflective judgment when solving problems, they might think deeply about many aspects of politics, their career and work, relationships, and other areas of life (Labouvie-Vief & Diehl, 1999). They might understand that what might be the best solution to a problem at work (with a coworker or boss) might not be the best solution at home (with a romantic partner). Many young adults also become more skeptical about there being a single truth and often are not willing to accept an answer as final. They also often recognize that thinking can't just be abstract but rather has to be realistic and pragmatic. And many young adults understand that emotions can play a role in thinking—for example, that they are likely to think more clearly when they are in a calm and collected state than when they are angry and highly aroused.

How strong is the evidence for a fifth, postformal stage of cognitive development? Researchers have found that young adults are more likely to engage in this postformal thinking than adolescents are (Commons & Bresette, 2006). But critics

postformal thought A form of thought that is qualitatively different from Piaget's formal operational thought. It involves understanding that the correct answer to a problem can require reflective thinking, that the correct answer can vary from one situation to another, and that the search for truth is often an ongoing, never-ending process. It also involves the belief that solutions to problems need to be realistic and that emotion and subjective factors can influence thinking.

argue that research has yet to document that postformal thought is a qualitatively more advanced stage than formal operational thought.

CREATIVITY

Early adulthood is a time of great creativity for some people. At the age of 30, Thomas Edison invented the phonograph, Hans Christian Andersen wrote his first volume of fairy tales, and Mozart composed *The Marriage of Figaro*. One early study of creativity found that individuals' most creative products were generated in their thirties and that 80 percent of the most important creative contributions were completed by age 50 (Lehman, 1960).

More recently, researchers have found that creativity does peak in adulthood and then decline, but that the peak often occurs in the forties. However, qualifying any conclusion about age and creative accomplishments are (1) the magnitude of the decline in productivity, (2) contrasts across creative domains, and (3) individual differences in lifetime output (Simonton, 1996).

Even though a decline in creative contributions is often found in the fifties and later, the decline is not as great as commonly thought. An impressive array of creative accomplishments occur in late adulthood. One of the most remarkable examples of creative accomplishment in late adulthood can be found in the life of Henri Chevreul. After a distinguished career as a physicist, Chevreul switched fields in his nineties to become a pioneer in gerontological research. He published his last research paper just a year prior to his death at the age of 103!

Any consideration of decline in creativity with age requires consideration of the field of creativity involved. In such fields as philosophy and history, older adults often show as much creativity as when they were in their thirties and forties. By contrast, in such fields as lyric poetry, abstract math, and theoretical physics, the peak of creativity is often reached in the twenties or thirties.

There also is extensive individual variation in the lifetime output of creative individuals. Typically, the most productive creators in any field are far more prolific than their least productive counterparts. The contrast is so extreme that the top 10 percent of creative producers frequently account for 50 percent of the creative output in a particular field. For instance, only 16 composers account for half of the music regularly performed in the classical repertoire.

Intellectual/Ethical Development

Perry (1968a, 1968b, 1981) studied the intellectual/ethical development of several hundred Harvard University students, a group of males ages 17 to 22. These students responded to several checklists on their educational views and were interviewed extensively on the basis of their responses. The results of these studies led Perry to suggest a sequence of intellectual and ethical development that typically occurs during the transition from late adolescence to early adulthood. This sequence consists of nine positions, which indicate progress from belief in the absolute authority of experts to the recognition that one must make commitments and be responsible for one's own beliefs.

Perry's nine stages are divided among three broader categories, as follows:

I. **Dualism** ("Things are either absolutely right or absolutely wrong.")

- *Position 1:* The world is viewed in such polar terms as right versus wrong, we versus they, and good versus bad. If an answer is right, it is absolutely right. We get right answers by going to authorities who have absolute knowledge.

dualism
Perry's initial phase of ethical development, in which "things are either absolutely right or absolutely wrong."

- *Position 2:* The person recognizes that uncertainty exists but ascribes it to poorly qualified authorities. Sometimes individuals can learn the truth for themselves.
- *Position 3:* Diversity and uncertainty are now acceptable but considered temporary because the authorities do not know what the answers are yet. The person becomes puzzled as to what the standards should be in these cases.

relativism
Second phase in Perry's theory; attitude or a philosophy that says anything can be right or wrong depending on the situation; all views are equally right.

II. **Relativism** ("Anything can be right or wrong depending on the situation; all views are equally right.")

- *Position 4a:* The person realizes that uncertainty and diversity of opinion are often extensive and recognizes that this is a legitimate status. Now he or she believes that "anyone has a right to an opinion." It is now possible for two authorities to disagree with each other without either of them being wrong.
- *Position 4b:* Sometimes the authorities (such as college professors) are not talking about right answers. Rather, they want students to think for themselves, supporting their opinions with data.
- *Position 5:* The person recognizes that all knowledge and values (including even those of an authority) exist in some specific context. It is therefore relative to the context. The person also recognizes that simple right and wrong are relatively rare, and even they exist in a specific context.
- *Position 6:* The person apprehends that because we live in a relativistic world, we must make some sort of personal commitment to an idea or a concept, as opposed to looking for an authority to follow.

commitment
Third phase in Perry's theory, in which the individual realizes that certainty is impossible but that commitment to a certain position is necessary, even without certainty.

III. **Commitment** ("Because of available evidence and my understanding of my own values, I have come to new beliefs.")

- *Position 7:* The person begins to choose the commitments that he or she will make in specific areas.
- *Position 8:* Having begun to make commitments, the person experiences the implications of those commitments and explores the various issues of responsibility involved.
- *Position 9:* The person's identity is affirmed through the various commitments made. There is a recognition of the necessity for balancing commitments and the understanding that one can have responsibilities that are expressed through a daily lifestyle. Perry (1981) described this position:

This is how life will be. I will be whole-hearted while tentative, fight for my values yet respect others, believe my deepest values right yet be ready to learn. I see that I shall be retracing this whole journey over and over—but, I hope, more wisely. (p. 276)

Some students move through these stages in a smooth and regular fashion; others, however, are delayed or deflected in one of three ways:

temporizing
Some people remain in one position for a year or more, exploring its implications but hesitating to make any further progress.

- **Temporizing.** Some people remain in one position for a year or more, exploring its implications but hesitating to make any further progress.

escape
Others refuse responsibility for making any commitments because everyone's opinion is "equally right."

- **Escape.** Some people use opportunities for detachment, especially those offered in positions 4 and 5, to refuse responsibility for making any commitments. Because everyone's opinion is "equally right," the person believes that no commitments need be made and, thus, escapes from the dilemma.

retreat
According to Perry's theory of ethical development, when someone retreats to an earlier ethical position.

- **Retreat.** Sometimes, confused by the confrontation and uncertainties of the middle positions, people retreat to earlier positions.

Perry's theory has been criticized because all the subjects of his research were male. However, his work spurred considerable research on females, which we now overview.

"Women's Ways of Knowing"

In a continuing collaborative study, Belenky, Bond, and Weinstock (1997) set out to answer the questions "Do female ways of knowing develop differently than those of males? If so, how do they come to learn and value what they know?" The study was rooted in Perry's work and the work of Carol Gilligan, whose groundbreaking research on the morality of care and responsibility versus the morality of rights and justice was covered in Chapter 9.

Belenky and her associates conducted a series of lengthy and intense interviews with 135 women of diverse socioeconomic backgrounds. The researchers found five general categories of ways in which women know and view the world. Though some of the women interviewed clearly demonstrated a progression from one perspective to the next, the researchers contend that they are unable to discern a progression of clear-cut stages, as did Perry and Gilligan. The five perspectives are silence, received knowledge, subjective knowledge, procedural knowledge, and constructed knowledge.

1. **Silence.** Females in the silence category describe themselves as "deaf and dumb." These women feel passive and dependent. Like players in an authority's game, they feel expected to know rules that don't exist. These women's thinking is characterized by concepts of right and wrong, similar to the men in Perry's first category of dualism. Questions about their growing up revealed family lives filled with violence, abuse, and chaos. The researchers noted that "gaining a voice and developing an awareness of their own minds are the tasks that these women must accomplish if they are to cease being either a perpetrator or victim of family violence" (Belenky et al., 1986, p. 38).

   silence
   Belenky's first phase of women's thinking, characterized by concepts of right and wrong.

2. **Received knowledge.** Women in the received knowledge category see words as central to the knowing process. They learn by listening and assume truths come from authorities. These women are intolerant of ambiguities and paradoxes, always going back to the notion that there are absolute truths. Received knowers seem similar to the men that Perry described as being in the first stage of dualism, but with a difference. The men Perry interviewed felt a great affiliation with the knowing authority. The women of this perspective were awed by the authorities but far less affiliated with them. In contrast to the men of Perry's study, women of received knowledge channel their energies and increased sense of self into the care of others.

   received knowledge
   Belenky's second phase of women's thinking; characterized by being awed by the authorities but far less affiliated with them than in the first phase.

3. **Subjective knowledge.** The researchers noted that women in the subjective knowledge category often had experienced two phenomena that pushed them toward this perspective: some crisis of male authority that sparked a distrust of outside sources of knowledge and some experience that confirmed a trust in themselves. Subjectivists value their "gut," or firsthand, experience as their best source of knowledge and see themselves as "conduits through which truth emerges" (p. 69). The researchers note that subjectivists are similar to males in Perry's second category of relativism in that they embrace the notion of multiple truths.

   subjective knowledge
   Belenky's third phase of women's thinking; characterized by some crisis of male authority that sparked a distrust of outside sources of knowledge and some experience that confirmed a trust in women thinkers themselves.

4. **Procedural knowledge.** The women in the procedural knowledge category have a distrust of both knowledge from authority and their own inner authority, or "gut." The perspective of procedural knowledge is characterized by an interest in form over content (how you say something rather than what you say). Women in this category also have a heightened sense of control. This category is similar to Perry's position 4b, where students learn analytic methods that authorities sanction. But analytic thinking emerges differently in women because they are less likely to affiliate with authorities.

   procedural knowledge
   Belenky's fourth phase of women's thinking; characterized by a distrust of both knowledge from authority and the female thinker's own inner authority, or "gut."

   The researchers describe women as having two kinds of procedural knowledge: separate knowing and connected knowing. These terms are reminiscent of Gilligan's work. Separate knowers are analytical and try to separate the self, to reveal the truth. Connected knowers learn through empathy with others.

constructed knowledge
Belenky's fifth phase of women's thinking; characterized by an integration of the subjective and procedural ways of knowing (Perry's types 3 and 4).

5. **Constructed knowledge.** Those in the constructed knowledge category have integrated the subjective and procedural ways of knowing (Perry's types 3 and 4). Women of this perspective note that "all knowledge is constructed and the knower is an intimate part of the known" (p. 137). They feel responsible for examining and questioning systems of constructing knowledge. Their thinking is characterized by a high tolerance of ambiguity and internal contradiction. Indeed, the women whose ways of knowing are of this perspective often balance many commitments and relationships, as well as ideas.

I think the one lesson I have learned is that there is no substitute for paying attention.

—Diane Sawyer

The work of Perry and Belenky and her associates (as well as that of Piaget, Kohlberg, and Gilligan, discussed earlier in this book) has greatly advanced our knowledge of intellectual and ethical development in the late adolescent and early adult years. It has also produced much controversy. Many questions remain to be answered. For example, does socioeconomic level make any difference? What about cultural background?

Why is intimacy an important aspect of early adulthood?

Intimacy

Self-disclosure and the sharing of private thoughts are hallmarks of intimacy. As we discussed in Chapter 10, adolescents have an increased need for intimacy. At the same time, they are engaged in the essential tasks of developing an identity and establishing their independence from their parents. Juggling the competing demands of intimacy, identity, and independence also becomes a central task of adulthood.

Erikson's Stage: Intimacy Versus Isolation

Recall from our discussion in Chapter 10 that Erik Erikson (1968) argues that identity versus identity confusion—pursuing who we are, what we are all about, and where we are going in life—is the most important issue to be negotiated in adolescence. In early adulthood, according to Erikson, after individuals are well on their way to establishing stable and successful identities, they enter the sixth developmental stage, which is intimacy versus isolation. Erikson describes intimacy as finding oneself while losing oneself in another person, and it requires a commitment to another person. If a person fails to develop an intimate relationship in early adulthood, according to Erikson, isolation results. A longitudinal study revealed that individuals with a higher level of emotional intimacy skills in their early twenties were more likely to have well-adjusted marriages in middle age than their counterparts who had a lower level of intimacy skills in their twenties (Boden, Fischer, & Niehuis, 2010).

An inability to develop meaningful relationships with others can harm an individual's personality. It may lead individuals to repudiate, ignore, or attack those who frustrate them. Such circumstances account for the shallow, almost pathetic attempts of youth to merge themselves with a leader. Many youth want to be apprentices or disciples of leaders and adults who will shelter them from the harm of the "out-group" world. If this fails, and Erikson believes that it must, sooner or later the individuals recoil into a self-search to discover where they went wrong. This introspection sometimes leads to painful depression and isolation. It also may contribute to a mistrust of others.

Intimacy and Independence

Development in early adulthood often involves balancing intimacy and commitment on the one hand, and independence and freedom on the other. At the same time as individuals are trying to establish an identity, they face the challenges of increasing their independence from their parents, developing an intimate relationship with another individual, and continuing their friendship commitments. They also face the task of making decisions for themselves without always relying on what others say or do.

The extent to which young adults develop autonomy has important implications for them. For example, young adults who have not sufficiently moved away from parental ties may have difficulty in both interpersonal relationships and a career.

The balance between intimacy and commitment—and independence and freedom—is delicate (Guerrero, Andersen, & Afifi, 2011). Some individuals are able to experience a healthy independence and freedom along with an intimate relationship. Keep in mind that intimacy and commitment, and independence and freedom, are not just concerns of early adulthood. They are important themes of development that are worked and reworked throughout the adult years.

Friendship

Increasingly, researchers are finding that friendship plays an important role in development throughout the human life span (Rawlins, 2009). Most U.S. men and women have a best friend. Ninety-two percent of women and 88 percent of men

Current Perspectives in Young Adulthood

Finding a Job in the 21st Century

Seek training, be flexible, and get hired in the fast-moving working world of the future.

JOHN A. CHALLENGER

The current recession, expected to be the worst economic crisis since the Great Depression, will surely put to rest those old concerns about looming labor shortages, right? Probably not. In fact, immigration, globalization, outsourcing, and other trends affecting employment and the workplace will evolve over the next five, 10, and 20 years to change the workplace completely, and well-trained and flexible workers will be at a premium.

More than 5 million layoffs have been announced in the United States since the beginning of 2008. Economists are projecting that U.S. unemployment may top out at 10.5% or over 11% by the middle of 2010.

At Challenger, Gray & Christmas, we look at official unemployment, but we also track job-cut announcements. These provide an indication of where the job market is going in the short term.

We observed in April that the rate of layoffs, while still high, was slowing. The global economy was not entering a roaring recovery, but we were hearing faint signals that the worst of the worst was over. On the one hand, manufacturing jobs in the United States continued to vanish. On the other hand, the layoff rate in the financial sector seemed to have stabilized.

At our firm, we talk to human-resources people around the country on a casual, anecdotal basis; the people we're speaking with are taking whatever measures they can to avoid making further layoffs. They don't want to be short-staffed in the event of a turnaround. The current cycle will surely go down in history as the worst in most people's memory. Fortunately, the future of work looks completely different.

Key Piece of Advice for Job Seekers

As unemployment continues to rise, more people are seeking help to improve their employability. My key piece of advice for job seekers is to get a fast start. Don't let your résumé gather dust. If you've been laid off, use contacts as quickly as possible to uncover new positions and opportunities.

The second piece of advice I offer is to consider changing industries. Look outside your normal boundaries, but look within your job function. You'll want to pursue jobs that correspond to your core competency and that let you do what you do best. Your skills are your best asset; they're what you're selling. Be ready to make the potential customer list for those skills as long as possible. What many people don't realize is the variety of jobs in different fields that may be open in a single industry, requiring people with all sorts of talents and abilities.

Let me give an example: Health care is commonly touted as an industry forever in need of workers. Conversely, the personal computer (PC) market in the United States has been weak of late. Our firm counted layoffs in the computer industry up 75% in 2008 from the year before, and analysts expect PC sales to fall an additional 10% by the end of 2009.

For a qualified IT worker or computer programmer seeking employment, one strategy is to wait for the global PC market to recover. Another strategy is to sell your technical skills to a growing industry like health care.

Most of us assume that growth in health care translates into more competition among employers to find qualified nurses and doctors. Surely, the doctor and nurse shortage will continue and favor qualified candidates for those jobs in the future. But in the years ahead, as baby boomers and the United States spend more money on medical care, the industry will need more computer scientists and database technicians to streamline operations and create new systems.

The coming innovation leap that will sweep the health-care field will extend well beyond simply digitizing medical records. If the industry is to meet rising demands for service from an aging population and contain costs, it will become much more reliant on information technology. The industry will need to reach and train qualified workers wherever they may be through e-learning technologies. Health-care providers will want to automate the delivery of health care as much as possible; they'll want to detect symptoms and diagnose patients remotely through advanced sensing technologies.

This is only one example among many. The health-care industry also needs therapists of all types, business managers,

U.S. Employment Ups and Downs, 2006–2016

The Five Largest Employment Increases

Job	Employees, 2006	Employees, 2016	Percentage Change
Network Systems and Data Communications Analyst	262,000	402,000	53.4%
Personal and Home Care Aide	767,000	1.16 million	50.6%
Home Health Aide	787,000	1.17 million	48.7%
Computer Software Engineer	507,000	733,000	44.6%
Veterinary Technologist/ Technician	71,000	100,000	41.0%

The Five Largest Employment Declines

Job	Employees, 2006	Employees, 2016	Percentage Change
Photographic Processing Machine Operator	49,000	25,000	−49.8%
File Clerk	234,000	137,000	−41.3%
Sewing Machine Operator	233,000	170,000	−27.2%
Electrical and Electronic Equipment Assembler	213,000	156,000	−26.8%
Computer Operator	130,000	98,000	−24.7%

Source: "Employment projections: 2006–2016." U.S. Bureau of labor statistics. Website, www.bls.gov.

human resource professionals, and even journalists and communications workers to track new developments and medical breakthroughs and publicize good work or medical research to the public (and to potential hospital donors). The world still needs journalists, but the information gathering and refinement process that is journalism will, more and more, happen at communications offices or niche-specific publications as opposed to regional or local newspapers. Finding opportunity in the future may mean sacrificing the dream of working for a particular cherished employer or even for a particular type of company. Many industrial titans of the twentieth century won't exist five years from now. That doesn't mean skills won't still be in demand.

The Globalized Workforce

Another question I'm asked frequently is, where are the jobs *going?* Many American workers fret about their jobs moving overseas to China and India. Outsourcing and even immigration have become convenient punching bags for pundits looking to blame someone or something for rising unemployment. But the argument that we can protect jobs by "keeping them at home"

or "not hiring immigrant labor" doesn't reflect the realities of globalization or labor in the twenty-first century.

The global labor market is not a zero-sum game. If U.S. firms are going to reach new customers in China and India—and they will have to in order to grow and be relevant in the twentyfirst century—then they will have to hire workers in those countries. More people in these countries finding work will create bigger markets for U.S. goods. China will continue to build factories and operations in order to put its large population to work; India will grow as a mathematics and engineering center. In the Philippines, a great accounting and health-care center exists; in South Korea, a manufacturing base is flourishing and will continue to do so.

All of these countries will experience employment growth, and yes, some of the growth will be from American firms hiring in those countries partly to better secure access to the Chinese and Indian consumers. There's no getting around it: U.S. companies need to be able to compete in these international markets if they are to expand in the United States.

However, companies from around the world will also have plenty of reasons to hire in the United States, which has a highly skilled labor force and the most diverse population of

Careers for "Re-Careering"

"Retirement years" may be a great time to take up a new line of work. According to a recent study, older workers tend to be more satisfied with their jobs, less stressed, and enjoy more flexible hours.

"Many older workers are ready to give up the long-time grind and look for stimulating jobs with flexible schedules as they begin the process toward retirement," says Susan Reinhard, senior vice president of the AARP's Public Policy Institute. AARP is the official name of the former American Association of Retired Persons.

The study surveyed 1,750 workers ages 55 and older over a period of 14 years. An overwhelming 91% say that they enjoy their current jobs, compared with 79% who said they liked the jobs they had held previously.

There are some tradeoffs, though. Most of the older workers who switched jobs took pay cuts, lost pension or health-care benefits, and forfeited some managerial duties.

Older workers who switch jobs tend to have lower wages than they earned in their previous jobs: $11 per hour versus $17 (36% difference). Older workers also lose pension coverage when they take up a new job, and they are less likely to have health coverage as an employment benefit. Still, Reinhard is optimistic.

"The current downturn presents a real bump in the road," She adds, "but, for the future, the findings are a welcome signal that workers 50 and over can really enjoy themselves while remaining productive in a vibrant economy."

AARP's website lists these as some of the most promising lines of work for adults over 55 to pursue:

- **Nursing.** As populations of elderly adults increase, so will the need for specialists in treating long-term health conditions.
- **Health-care technician.** Workers with training in laboratory operations, radiology, physical therapy, and nursing assistance will be in high demand.
- **Teacher and teaching assistant.** Society needs good teachers, especially given high teacher turnover and retirement rates.
- **Home health aide.** Specialists who can offer personalized care in the comfort of one's home will be in great demand.
- **Massage and yoga practitioner.** Most businesses expect to lose customers when economic times get tough, but not massage therapists or yoga practitioners. Many have seen their customer base expand due to stressed-out adults who need relief.
- **Car service technician.** Consumers are learning to be more frugal. That means maintaining the cars they have instead of buying new ones. Mechanics who can keep cars running are wanted.
- **Shoe worker and repairer.** Frugality applies to apparel as well. Customers are finding that fixing a good pair of shoes that wear out is much more economical than replacing them.
- **Office and administrative assistant.** Staffing agencies can steer skilled retirees to temporary, part-time, and temporary-to-hire administrative and office positions.
- **Health-care administration (nonmedical).** Medical facilities and insurance companies will need employees with general education and skills to handle administrative, clerical, and management responsibilities.
- **General merchandise.** Retirees with management experience may come in handy at department stores in any community.

—Rick Docksai

Source: AARP, www.aarp.org.

---

any country. The United States is uniquely suited to reach out to a global population.

The strength of the U.S. economy lies in its ability to capture global growth and to collaborate with economies around the planet. In the years ahead, the way that growth occurs will be very different from the past. From the middle of the twentieth century onward, U.S. companies began expanding aggressively into other countries; the pursuit of global growth translated into large U.S. firms cajoling foreign officials for special treatment or special contracts to set up shop. For U.S. employees overseas, a corporate expansion meant higher salaries and more money to live apart from the local community. I call this the colonial corporate expansion model.

IBM is one of the first big companies to transition out of that mode of overseas expansion and into a more community-focused strategy. In February 2009, IBM gave 4,000 laid-off workers the opportunity to move to other countries where the company had positions open (India and Brazil, for example)

through a program called Project Match. IBM was willing to pay for the move and help with visa procurement. The catch? The company told the employees that they would be paid local wages; the employees would live among the population.

Naturally, not every IBMer took to the idea. As originally reported in *Information Week,* one employee group called the Alliance@IBM was furious, complaining that the company was asking employees to "offshore themselves." They had a point; wages in India even for highly skilled IT workers are often a quarter of what they are in the United States.

But many of the employees—those with fewer commitments, who didn't have to worry about paying down a mortgage because they were young and just starting out, or who were looking to do something other than play shuffleboard in retirement— were intrigued by the idea and took the company up on the offer. Arrangements like Project Match may be a wave of the future, exciting and increasingly *de rigueur.* It reminds me of something I heard Larry Summers remark at a Harvard alumni event not long ago. When he was a student, he said, the final requirement to graduate was to swim a lap around the pool. In the future, it will be having spent a semester overseas.

Mobility, Flexibility, and the Workforce of the Future

IBM's Perfect Match program showcases one of the biggest trends to affect the future of work: increased mobility and flexibility. The information-technology revolution, which began with widespread adoption of PCs in the workplace in the 1980s, has changed virtually every aspect of doing business. In the next decade, that trend will accelerate and obliterate many long-held notions of work.

For many, the office of the future will not be an office at all. The mobile workforce will carry their office in their pocket; they'll work when it's most convenient for them or for the client. The U.S. Bureau of Labor Statistics reports that the number of Americans who worked from home or remotely at least one day per month for their employer rose from 12.4 million in 2006 to 17.2 million in 2008. (The trend may slow slightly in 2009.) Telecommuting is an easy way for employers facing tight budgets to give employees something that more and more of them say they want: time. Enhanced mobile flexibility will be a boon to the employers that take advantage of it as well. This will better enable smart companies to place employees where they can be most useful—namely, where customers and clients are located.

Contrary to a lot of popular opinion, face time is still important, but it may be less important within companies than between companies and customers.

Imagine, for instance, a customer walking into a car dealership and being greeted not by a salesperson but by an actual car designer, available to answer any and every technical query a consumer might have, or even design specifications on the spot (for a premium, of course). Many Ferrari buyers already get something like this royal treatment when they buy a new car directly from the factory in Maranello, Italy. For about $3.1 million, wealthy car enthusiasts can, in essence, design their own F430, 612 Scaglietti, or Enzo. What does the famously hobbled U.S. car industry look like when Chevrolet buyers can have the same personalized car-buying experience as someone buying a Ferrari Enzo?

Getting to that future from where we are now doesn't require a tremendous amount of technical IT innovation. What's needed is a little imagination and, again, flexibility. The twenty-somethings will lead this change. Today's younger workers will be the ones who help U.S. companies succeed abroad in the new era of globalization and mobility.

Hopefully, we'll continue to see more examples of the Project Match phenomenon playing with more people from more countries, coming to the United States to work as elements of the economy and to take advantage of U.S. educational opportunities. America's ability to attract these people is one of its key assets.

The U.S. economy will need these highly skilled workers desperately, a fact that underscores why immigration reform is so vital to the future of U.S. business. If the United States cannot remain an attractive destination for talented and well-trained workers from around the world, the country won't grow economically as it did in the past. Also, the U.S. government must find ways to support lifelong education. As new fields grow, education must become a permanent part of every worker's career. Immigration reform and lifelong learning are critical if the United States is to overcome the looming talent shortage. In the years ahead, it will pay dividends not just economically, but also in terms of more-effective foreign policy.

The more people from more places who feel they have a connection to America—either because someone they know has gone to America on a work or student visa or because they had a positive experience with a U.S. worker locally—the more effective the U.S. government will be in marketing its policies abroad. My hope is that people from around the world still want to take part in the U.S. educational experience. But American educational institutions will also expand as global brands with campuses in China, India, Europe, Africa, and Latin America.

The opportunities of the future will go to the best-trained, most-flexible candidates, and they will be spread globally. But opportunity exists and will increase; of that you can be certain.

JOHN A. CHALLENGER, chief executive officer of Challenger, Gray & Christmas, is one of the most quoted labor and employment experts in America. He's become a regular fixture on CNN, CBS, and a host of other networks and is a featured speaker at World-Future 2009, the annual conference of the World Future Society. Website www.challengergray.com.

Originally published in the September/October 2009, vol. 43, no.5, pp. 29–33 issue of *The Futurist*. Copyright © No.5 by World Future Society, 7910 Woodmont Avenue, Suite 450, Bethesda, MD 20814. Telephone: 301/656-8274; Fax: 301/951-0394; http://www.wfs.org. Used with permission from the World Future Society.

Hold Me Tight

Love demands the reassurance of a touch most fights are really protests over emotional disconnection. Underneath the distress, partners are desperate to know: Are you there for me?

SUE JOHNSON

I grew up in my parents' pub in England, where there was always a lot of drama. And all the drama—fights, flirting, tears, tantrums—revolved around love. I also watched my parents destroy their own love for each other. Since that time I've been on a mission to figure out exactly what love is. My mother described it as "a funny five minutes." It's also been called a mysterious mix of sentiment and sex. Or a combination of infatuation and companionship. Well, it's more than that.

My personal insights, gleaned from researching and counseling more than a thousand couples over 35 years, have now merged with a growing body of scientific studies, to the point where I can now say with confidence that we know what love is. It's intuitive and yet not necessarily obvious: It's the continual search for a basic, secure connection with someone else. Through this bond, partners in love become emotionally dependent on each other for nurturing, soothing, and protection.

We have a wired-in need for emotional contact and responsiveness from significant others. It's a survival response, the driving force of the bond of security a baby seeks with its mother. This observation is at the heart of attachment theory. A great deal of evidence indicates that the need for secure attachment never disappears; it evolves into the adult need for a secure emotional bond with a partner. Think of how a mother lovingly gazes at her baby, just as two lovers stare into each other's eyes.

Although our culture has framed dependency as a bad thing, a weakness, it is not. Being attached to someone provides our greatest sense of security and safety. It means depending on a partner to respond when you call, to know that you matter to him or her, that you are cherished, and that he will respond to your emotional needs.

The most basic tenet of attachment theory is that isolation—not just physical isolation but emotional isolation—is traumatizing for human beings. The brain actually codes it as

danger. Gloria Steinem once said a woman needs a man like a fish needs a bicycle. That's nonsense.

The drama of love that I saw played out at the bar each night as a child is all about the human hunger for safe emotional connection, a survival imperative we experience from the cradle to the grave. Once we do feel safely linked with our partner, we can tolerate the hurts they will—inevitably—inflict upon us in the course of daily life.

Broken Connections

We start out intensely connected to and responsive to our partners. But our level of attentiveness tends to drop off over time. We then experience moments of disconnection, times when we don't express our needs clearly. He is upset and really wants to be comforted, but she leaves him alone, thinking that he wants solitude. These moments are actually inescapable in a relationship. If you're going to dance with someone, you're going to step on each other's feet once in a while.

Losing the connection with a loved one, however, jeopardizes our sense of security. We experience a primal feeling of panic. It sets off an alarm in the brain's amygdala, our fear center, where we are highly attuned to threats of all kinds. Once the amygdala sends out an alarm, we don't think—we act. The threat can come from the outside world or from our own inner cosmos. It's our perception that counts, not the reality. If we feel abandoned at a moment of need, we are set up to enter a state of panic.

It's what we do next, after those moments of disconnection, that has a huge impact on the shape of our relationship. Can you turn around and reconnect? If not, you'll start engaging in fights that follow a clear pattern. I call these "demon dialogues." If they gain momentum, they start to take over and induce a terrible sense of emotional aloneness. Your relationship feels less and less like a safe place, and it starts to unravel. You start to doubt that your partner is there for you, that he values you. Or that she will put you first.

Consider a couple with their firstborn child. Having a baby is a stressful, sleep-depriving experience. But it's also a time when people's attachment fears and needs are particularly strong. The man might think something like, "I know it's wrong, and I know it's pathetic, but I feel like I've lost my wife to my kid." And the woman might say, "When I had the baby I felt so fragile. I was taking care of this little being, and I just needed extra comfort and caring myself, but he was out working all the time." Their intentions are good—she cares for the infant, he works hard to support his new family—but they fail to give each other what they really need.

Or think of a man who is doing just fine in his job while his wife flies high in a new career. She's spending long hours on exciting projects while he is deprived of affection, attention, and sex. Lying in bed alone each night, waiting for her, he feels like a fool for needing her so much—and also angry that she can't see how deeply her absence affects him.

But we don't talk about these conflicts in terms of deeply rooted attachment needs. We talk about the surface emotions, the ire or indifference, and blame the other. "He's so angry; I feel so attacked," or "She's so cold. I don't think she cares at all!" Each person retreats into a corner, making it harder and harder for the two to express their fundamental attachment needs, foreclosing the ability to gain reassurance from each other.

Women are often more sensitive to the first signs of connection breakdown than men, and their response is often to begin what I call the dance of disconnection. Almost ritualistically they will pursue their partners in a futile attempt to get a comforting response. But they do it in a way that almost guarantees their basic need will not be met—they blame their partner for failing in some essential way.

Men, on the other hand, have been taught to suppress emotional responses and needs, which inclines them to withdraw from the conflict. But her rage and his withdrawal both mask what lies below the surface—an underlying vulnerability and need for connection, now compounded by sadness, shame, and, most of all, fear.

Too often, what couples do not see is that most fights are really protests over emotional disconnection. Underneath all the distress, partners are desperate to know: Are you there for me? Do you need me? Do you rely on me?

Repairing Bonds

For years, therapists have viewed these demon dialogues as power struggles. They've attempted to resolve couples' fights by teaching them problem-solving skills. But this is a little like offering Kleenex as the cure for viral pneumonia. It ignores the attachment issues that underlie the pattern. Rather than conflict or control, the issue, from an attachment perspective, is emotional distance.

And what's frustrating to people is not knowing how to bridge that emotional distance. In my office, men sometimes tell me, "I do all kinds of things to show I care. I mow the lawn, bring in a good salary, solve problems, and I don't play around. Why is it that in the end, these things don't seem to matter, and all that counts with my wife is that we talk about emotional stuff and cuddle?" I tell them, "Because that's just the way we are made. We need someone to pay real attention to us, to hold us tight. Have you forgotten that you need that, too?"

When we fight with our partners, we tend to follow the ball as it goes over the net, paying attention to the last barb lobbed at us—and not whether we even want to be in the game at all. It's possible to break out of the demon dialogues, but the first step is to be aware of the game itself, not just the play-by-play. Once you realize you are latched onto your pattern of arguing, you can agree to put the whole game on hold.

Disappointments are always part of relationships. But you can always choose how you handle them. Will you react defensively, out of fear, or in the spirit of understanding? Let's say your partner says, "I don't feel like having sex tonight." You can take a deep breath and think about how much she loves you, and say, "Gee, that's too bad, I was really looking forward to that." Or you can spit out a sarcastic, "Right! Well, we never make love anymore, do we?"

Of course, you may not feel you really have a choice if your panic button has been pushed and your emotions are boiling over. But just being aware that it has been pushed can help calm you down. You can think to yourself, "What is happening here? I'm yelling. But inside, I'm feeling really small." Then you can tell your partner, "I got really scared there—I'm feeling hurt."

If you take that leap of faith and respond with such a bid for reconnection, you have to hope your partner will, too, instead of saying something hurtful like, "Well, you're being asinine and difficult." That's the tricky part about relationships: To change the dance, both people have to change their steps.

Simply accepting your attachment needs instead of feeling ashamed of them is a big and necessary first step, and it applies to single people as well as to those in relationships. A single person might say, "I'm depressed because I'm lonely, and I know I shouldn't be lonely; I know I should be independent." Well, *of course* you're depressed if you're feeling lonely and then you turn around and beat yourself up for it! When you're ashamed, you tend to hide from others, setting off a vicious cycle that nearly ensures you won't find the social connection you need.

Healing Touches

A man will often say to me, "Even if I do think that she really needs me or is feeling scared, I don't know what to do!" He'll end up making his wife a cup of tea, which is very nice—but it's not what is called for. Had he put his hand on her shoulder and pulled her towards him, however, his bid for connection would have been much more successful.

Men often say they don't know what to do. Yet men do know how to soothe—they do it with their children, tucking them in at night and whispering gently to them. The difference is, they see their children's vulnerability, and respond to it, but when they look at their wives, they see only someone who is judging them. But she feels vulnerable, too.

Touch is the most basic way of connecting. Taking your partner's hand when she is nervous can instantly defuse anxiety and anger.

Touch is the most basic way of connecting with another human being. Taking your partner's hand when she is nervous or touching his shoulder in the middle of an argument can instantly defuse anxiety and anger.

The world of therapy has been obsessed with maintaining boundaries in recent years. I say our problem is just the opposite—we're all cut off from each other.

If you watch two people in love, they touch each other all the time. If you watch two people finding their way back into a love relationship, after falling into demon dialogues, they touch each other more, too. They literally reach for each other; it's a tangible sign of their desire for connection.

Secure (and Saucy) Sex

A big myth about love is that it's got a "best before" date, that passion is a burning fever that must subside. That's pretty silly. I don't see any scientific or human reason why people can't have happy long-term love relationships.

Among people who do have affairs, they don't do so because their sex lives are boring. I've never had anyone come to my office and tell me that they had an affair because they were bored in bed. They have affairs because they're lonely, because they can't emotionally connect with their partner. Then somebody else smiles at them and makes them feel special and valued—and suddenly, they're in this strange situation where they're committed to one person but find themselves responding to another.

Sex is boring if it's cut off from emotional connection. But if you're emotionally involved, sex is play and passion with a hundred dimensions.

Passion is like everything else: It ebbs and flows. But sex is always going to be boring if it's one-dimensional, cut off from emotional connection. On the other hand, if you're

emotionally involved, sex has a hundred dimensions to it, and is as much play as passion.

I call this kind of secure sex "synchrony sex," where emotional openness and responsiveness, tender touch, and erotic exploration all come together. When partners have a secure emotional connection, physical intimacy can retain all of its initial ardor and creativity and then some. Lovers can be tender and playful one moment, fiery and erotic another. Securely attached partners can more openly express their needs and preferences and are more willing to experiment sexually with their lovers.

Excitement comes from the risk involved in staying open in the here and now experience of physical and emotional connection.

In a secure relationship, excitement comes not from trying to resurrect the novel moments of infatuated passion but from the risk involved in staying open in the moment-to-moment, here-and-now experience of physical and emotional connection. With this openness comes the sense that lovemaking with your partner is always a new adventure.

Lasting Love

Once you're reconnected with your partner, and both of you are getting your attachment needs filled, you have to keep working at being emotionally responsive to one another. You can do that by helping each other identify the attachment issues that tend to come up in your recurring arguments.

If, for example, you always erupt over your girlfriend's risky mountain climbingtrips, talk to her about how your anger is born out of a fear of losing her. Figure out how she can take more precautions. Or, if you often feel abandoned when left with the brunt of childcare duties, plan out how you and your husband can be better parents together, so that you won't call him a deadbeat in a moment of pent-up frustration.

You should also celebrate positive moments together, both big and small. Regularly and deliberately hold, hug, and kiss each other when you wake up, leave the house, return, and go to sleep. Recognize special days, anniversaries, and birthdays in very personal ways. These rituals keep your relationship safe in a distracting and chaotic world.

Stories shape our lives, and the stories we tell about our lives shape us in turn. Create a future love story for you and your partner that outlines what your life together will look like five or ten years down the road. It will prime you to keep your bond strong.

Arms Wide Open

Because attachment is a universal need, the attachment view of love can also help parents understand conflicts with their children. I was recently in a café with my teenage son, yelling at him over the roar of the latte machine, while he sulked and huffed. Then suddenly he said, "Mom, we're doing that thing, where I feel like you are criticizing me, and you feel like I don't care what you have to say." We both started laughing and my anger melted away.

Now that we know what love is really about, we know how to sustain it. It's up to us to use that knowledge to nurture it with our partners and families. And then, with the empathy and courage it teaches us, we can search for ways to take it out into the world and make a difference.

SUE JOHNSON is a clinical psychologist and author of *Hold Me Tight*. She lives in Ottawa, Canada, and has been happily married for 20 years. Learn more at www.holdmetight.net.

From *Psychology Today*, January/February 2009, vol. 42, no. 1, pp. 74–75, 78–79. Copyright © by Sussex Publishers, LLC. Reprinted by permission.

Chapter 7
Middle Adulthood

Not so long ago, Middle Adulthood (40-65) was characterized in much the same way we now talk about Older Adulthood (65 on). This shift is due to an ever increasing life expectancy as a result of medical/technological advancements and a better understanding of how diet and exercise affect our health and longevity. This new view is also reflective of a shift in social expectations – baby boomers don't want to be thought of as "old" and many have given public voice to this sentiment by saying "60 is the new 40" and it has changed the way we collectively view this time of life. We'll start off with a discussion of physical changes and then look at cognitive, emotional and social considerations for this "new" life stage, including the introduction of a new life stage model that focuses on the "second half" of life by Robert Peck.

The Nature of Middle Adulthood

Is midlife experienced the same way today as it was 100 years ago? How can middle adulthood be defined, and what are some of its main characteristics?

Changing Midlife

Many of today's 50-year-olds are in better shape, more alert, and more productive than their 40-year-old counterparts from a generation or two earlier. As more people lead healthier lifestyles and medical discoveries help to stave off the aging process, the boundaries of middle age are being pushed upward. It looks like middle age is starting later and lasting longer for increasing numbers of active, healthy, and productive people. A current saying is "60 is the new 40," implying that many 60-year-olds today are living a life that is as active, productive, and healthy as earlier generations did in their forties.

Questions such as, "To which age group do you belong?" and "How old do you feel?" reflect the concept of *age identity*. A consistent finding is that as adults become older their age identity is younger than their chronological age (Setterson & Trauten, 2009; Westerhof, 2009). One study found that almost half of the individuals 65 to 69 years of age considered themselves middle-aged (National Council on Aging, 2000), and another study found a similar pattern: Half of the 60- to 75-year-olds viewed themselves as being middle-aged (Lachman, Maier, & Budner, 2000). Also, some individuals consider the upper boundary of midlife as the age at which they make the transition from work to retirement.

When Carl Jung studied midlife transitions early in the 20th century, he referred to midlife as "the afternoon of life" (Jung, 1933). Midlife serves as an important preparation for late adulthood, "the evening of life" (Lachman, 2004, p. 306). But "midlife" came much earlier in Jung's time. In 1900 the average life expectancy was only 47 years of age; only 3 percent of the population lived past 65. Today, the average life expectancy is 78, and 12 percent of the U.S. population is older than 65. As a much greater percentage of the population lives to an older age, the midpoint of life and what constitutes middle age or middle adulthood are getting harder to pin down. Statistically, the middle of life today is about 39 years of age, but most 39-year-olds don't want to be called "middle-aged." What we think of as middle age comes later—anywhere from 40 or 45 to about 60 or 65 years of age. And as more people live longer, the 60 to 65 years upper boundary will likely be nudged upward.

How is midlife changing?

Compared to previous decades and centuries, an increasing percentage of the population is made up of middle-aged and older adults. In the past, the age structure of the population could be represented by a pyramid, with the largest percentage of the population in the childhood years. Today, the percentages of people at different ages in the life span are more similar, creating what is called the "rectangularization" of the age distribution (a vertical rectangle) (Himes, 2009a).

Although middle adulthood has been a relatively neglected period of the human life span (except for pop psychology portrayals of the midlife crisis), life-span developmentalists are beginning to give more attention to this age period (Schaie, 2011; Willis & Martin, 2005). One reason for the increased attention is that the largest cohort in U.S. history is currently moving through the middle-age years. From 1990 to 2015, the middle-aged U.S. population is projected to increase from 47 million to 80 million, a 72 percent increase. Because of the size of the baby-boom cohort (recall from Chapter 1 that a *cohort* is a group of people born in a particular year or time period), the median age of the U.S. population will increase from 33 years in 1990 to 42 years in 2050. The baby boomers, born from 1946 to 1964, are of interest to developmentalists not only because of their increased numbers but also because they are the best-educated and most affluent cohort in history to pass through middle age (Willis & Martin 2005).

> middle adulthood The developmental period beginning at approximately 40 years of age and extending to about 60 to 65 years of age.

Defining Middle Adulthood

Though the age boundaries are not set in stone, we will consider **middle adulthood** as the developmental period that begins at approximately 40 years of age and extends to about 60 to 65 years of age. For many people, middle adulthood is a time of declining physical skills and expanding responsibility; a period in which people become more conscious of the young-old polarity and the shrinking amount of time left in life; a point when individuals seek to transmit something meaningful to the next generation; and a time when people reach and maintain satisfaction in their careers. In sum, middle adulthood involves "balancing work and relationship responsibilities in the midst of the physical and psychological changes associated with aging" (Lachman, 2004, p. 305).

In midlife, as in other age periods, individuals make choices, selecting what to do, how to invest time and resources, and evaluating what aspects of their lives they need to change. In midlife, "a serious accident, loss, or illness" may be a "wake-up call" and produce "a major restructuring of time and a reassessment" of life's priorities (Lachman, 2004, p. 310).

As we mentioned earlier, for many increasingly healthy adults, middle age is lasting longer. Indeed, an increasing

What are the main characteristics of middle adulthood? What differentiates early and late midlife?

number of experts on middle adulthood describe the age period of 55 to 65 as *late midlife* (Deeg, 2005). Compared to earlier midlife, late midlife is more likely to be characterized by the death of a parent, the last child leaving the parental home, becoming a grandparent, the preparation for retirement, and in most cases actual retirement. Many people in this age range experience their first confrontation with health problems. Overall, then, although gains and losses may balance each other in early midlife, losses may begin to dominate gains for many individuals in late midlife (Baltes, Lindenberger, & Staudinger, 2006).

Keep in mind, though, that midlife is characterized by individual variations (Perrig-Chiello & Perren, 2005). As life-span expert Gilbert Brim (1992) commented, middle adulthood is full of changes, twists, and turns; the path is not fixed. People move in and out of states of success and failure.

Physical Development

What physical changes accompany the change to middle adulthood? How healthy are middle-aged adults? How sexually active are middle-aged adults?

How Would You...?
As a human development and family studies professional, how would you characterize the impact of the media in shaping middle-aged adults' expectations about their changing physical appearance?

Physical Changes

Although everyone experiences some physical change due to aging in the middle adulthood years, the rates of this aging vary considerably from one individual to another. Genetic makeup and lifestyle factors play important roles in whether chronic disease will appear and when (Kaplan, Gurven, & Winking, 2009). Middle age is a window through which we can glimpse later life while there is still time to engage in prevention and to influence some of the course of aging (Lachman, 2004).

Visible Signs

One of the most visible signs of physical changes in middle adulthood is physical appearance. The first outwardly noticeable signs of aging usually are apparent by the forties or fifties. The skin begins to wrinkle and sag because of a loss of fat and collagen in underlying tissues (Datta & others, 2010). Small, localized areas of pigmentation in the skin produce aging spots, especially in areas that are exposed to sunlight, such as the hands and face. For most people, their hair becomes thinner and grayer. Fingernails and toenails develop ridges and become thicker and more brittle.

Since a youthful appearance is stressed in our culture, many individuals whose hair is graying, whose skin is wrinkling, whose bodies are sagging, and whose teeth are yellowing strive to make themselves look younger. Undergoing cosmetic surgery, dyeing hair, wearing wigs, enrolling in weight-reduction programs, participating in exercise regimens, and taking heavy doses of vitamins are common in middle age. Many baby boomers have shown a strong interest in plastic surgery and Botox, which may reflect their desire to take control of the aging process (Ascher & others, 2010; Wu, 2010).

Height and Weight

Individuals lose height in middle age. On average, from 30 to 50 years of age, men lose about 1/2 inch in height, then may lose another 3/4 inch from 50 to 70 years of age (Hoyer & Roodin, 2009). The height loss for women can be as much as 2 inches over a 50-year span from 25 to 75 years of age. Note that there are large variations in the extent to which individuals become shorter with aging. The decrease in height is due to bone loss in the vertebrae.

Actor Sean Connery as a young adult in his twenties (*top*) and as a middle-aged adult in his fifties (*bottom*). *What are some of the most outwardly noticeable signs of aging in the middle adulthood years?*

Although people in middle age may lose height, many gain weight. On average, body fat accounts for about 10 percent of body weight in adolescence; it makes up 20 percent or more in middle age. In a national survey, 29 percent of U.S. adults 40 to 59 years of age were classified as obese (Centers for Disease Control and Prevention, 2006). In Chapter 11, we saw that in this survey 22 percent of U.S. adults 20 to 39 years of age were classified as obese. Being overweight is a critical health problem in middle adulthood (Himes, 2009b; Wyn & Peckham, 2010). For example, obesity increases the probability that an individual will suffer a number of other ailments, among them hypertension (abnormally high blood pressure), diabetes, and digestive disorders (Bazzano & others, 2010; Bloomgarden, 2010). A large-scale study found that being overweight or obese in middle age increases an individual's risk of dying earlier (Adams & others, 2006).

How Would You...?
As a social worker, how would you apply the statistics on weight and health to promote healthier lifestyles for middle-aged adults?

Strength, Joints, and Bones

As we saw in Chapter 11, maximum physical strength often is attained in the twenties. The term *sarcopenia* is given to age-related loss of muscle mass and strength (Doran & others, 2009; Narici & Maffulli, 2010). The rate of muscle loss with age occurs at a rate of approximately 1 to 2 percent per year past the age of 50 (Marcell, 2003). A loss of strength especially occurs in the back and legs. Exercise can reduce the decline involved in sarcopenia (Park & others, 2010).

Peak functioning of the body's joints also usually occurs in the twenties. The cartilage that cushions the movement of bones and other connective tissues, such as tendons and ligaments, become less efficient in the middle-adult years, a time when many individuals experience joint stiffness and more difficulty in movement.

Maximum bone density occurs by the mid- to late thirties, from which point there is a progressive loss of bone. The rate of this bone loss begins slowly but accelerates in the fifties (Ryan & Elahi, 2007). Women experience about twice the rate of bone loss as men. By the end of midlife, bones break more easily and heal more slowly (Neer & SWAN Investigators, 2010; Ritchie, 2010).

Vision and Hearing

Accommodation of the eye—the ability to focus and maintain an image on the retina—experiences its sharpest decline between 40 and 59 years of age. In particular, middle-aged individuals begin to have difficulty viewing close objects, which means that many individuals have to wear glasses with bifocal lenses, lenses with two sections to see items at different distances (Scheiber, 2006). Also, there is some evidence that the retina becomes less sensitive to low levels of illumination.

Hearing also can start to decline by the age of 40 (Roring, Hines, & Charness, 2007). Sensitivity to high pitches usually declines first. The ability to hear low-pitched sounds does not seem to decline much in middle adulthood, though. Men usually lose their sensitivity to high-pitched sounds sooner than women do. However, this gender difference might be due to men's greater exposure to noise in occupations such as mining, automobile work, and so on (Scialfa & Kline, 2007).

Cardiovascular System

Midlife is the time when high blood pressure and high cholesterol take many individuals by surprise (Lachman, 2004). The level of cholesterol in the blood increases through the adult years and in midlife begins to accumulate on the artery walls, increasing the risk of cardiovascular disease (Khera & Rader, 2010; Yetukuri & others, 2010). Blood pressure (hypertension), too, usually rises in the forties and fifties. At menopause, a woman's blood pressure rises sharply and usually remains above that of a man through life's later years (Taler, 2009).

Members of the Masai tribe in Kenya, Africa, can stay on a treadmill for a long time because of their active lives. Heart disease is extremely low in the Masai tribe, which also can be attributed to their energetic lifestyle.

Exercise, weight control, and a diet rich in fruits, vegetables, and whole grains can often help to stave off many cardiovascular problems in middle age (Natali & others, 2009; O'Donovan & others, 2010). For example, though heredity influences cholesterol levels, LDL (the bad cholesterol) can be reduced and HDL (the good cholesterol) increased by eating food that is very low in saturated fat and cholesterol and by exercising regularly (Kawano & others, 2009). A recent study of postmenopausal women found that 12 weeks of aerobic exercise training improved their cardiovascular functioning (O'Donnell, Kirwan, & Goodman, 2009).

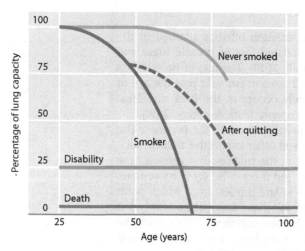

Figure 13.1 The Relation of Lung Capacity to Age and Cigarette Smoking

Lung capacity shows little change through middle age for individuals who have not smoked. However, smoking is linked with reduced lung capacity in middle-aged and older adults. When individuals stop smoking their lung capacity becomes greater than those who continue to smoke, but not as great as the lung capacity of individuals who have never smoked.

An increasing problem in middle age is *metabolic syndrome*, a condition characterized by hypertension, obesity, and insulin resistance. Metabolic syndrome often leads to the development of diabetes and cardiovascular disease (Cheung, 2010). A recent meta-analysis revealed that metabolic syndrome was an important risk factor for all-cause mortality (Hui, Liu, & Ho, 2010).

Lungs

There is little change in lung capacity through most of middle adulthood. However, at about the age of 55, the proteins in lung tissue become less elastic. This change, combined with a gradual stiffening of connective tissues in the chest wall, decreases the lungs' capacity to shuttle oxygen from the air people breathe to the blood in their veins. As shown in Figure 13.1, the lung capacity of individuals who are smokers drops precipitously in middle age, but if the individuals quit smoking their lung capacity improves, although not to the level of individuals who have never smoked.

Sleep

Some aspects of sleep become more problematic in middle age (McCrae & Dubyak, 2009). The total number of hours slept usually remains the same as in early adulthood, but beginning in the forties, wakeful periods are more frequent and there is less of the deepest type of sleep (stage 4). The amount of time spent lying awake in bed at night begins to increase in middle age, and this can produce a feeling of being less rested in the morning (Abbott, 2003). Sleep problems in middle-aged adults are more common in individuals who use a higher number of prescription and nonprescription drugs, are obese, have cardiovascular disease, or are depressed (Kaleth & others, 2007; Lopenen & others, 2010).

Health and Disease

In middle adulthood, the frequency of accidents declines, and individuals are less susceptible to colds and allergies than in childhood, adolescence, or early adulthood. Indeed, many individuals live through middle adulthood without having a disease or persistent health problem. For others, however, disease and persistent health problems become more common in middle adulthood than in earlier life stages.

Stress is increasingly being found to be a factor in disease (Kahana, Kahana, & Hammel, 2009). The cumulative effect of stress often takes a toll on the health of individuals by the time they reach middle age. Stress is linked to disease through both the immune system and cardiovascular disease (Bauer, Jeckel, & Luz, 2009; Ho & others, 2010).

Mortality Rates

Infectious disease was the main cause of death until the middle of the 20th century. As infectious disease rates declined and more individuals lived through middle age, chronic disorders increased. These are characterized by a slow onset and a long duration (Kelley-Moore, 2009).

In middle age, many deaths are caused by a single, readily identifiable condition, whereas in old age, death is more likely to result from the combined effects of several chronic conditions. For many years heart disease was the leading cause of death in middle adulthood, followed by cancer; however, in 2005 more individuals 45 to 64 years old in the United States died of cancer, followed by cardiovascular disease (National Center for Health Statistics, 2008). The gap between cancer as the leading cause of death widens as individuals age from 45 to 54 and 55 to 64 years of age (National Center for Health Statistics, 2008). Men have higher mortality rates than women for all the leading causes of death.

> **climacteric** The midlife transition in which fertility declines.
>
> **menopause** The complete cessation of a woman's menstruation, which usually occurs in the late forties or early fifties.

Sexuality

What kinds of changes characterize the sexuality of women and men as they go through middle age? **Climacteric** is a term that is used to describe the midlife transition in which fertility declines. Let's explore the substantial differences in the climacteric of women and men during middle adulthood.

Menopause

Menopause is the time in middle age, usually in the late forties or early fifties, when a woman's menstrual periods completely cease. The average age at which women have their last period is 51 (Wise, 2006). However, there is large variation in the age at which menopause occurs—from 39 to 59 years of age. Later menopause is linked with increased risk of breast cancer (Mishra & others, 2009).

In menopause, production of estrogen by the ovaries declines dramatically, and this decline produces uncomfortable symptoms in some women—"hot flashes," nausea, fatigue, and rapid heartbeat, for example. Cross-cultural studies also reveal wide variations in the menopause experience (Anderson & Yoshizawa, 2007; Lerner-Geva & others, 2010). For example, hot flashes are uncommon in Mayan women (Beyene, 1986). Asian women report fewer hot flashes than women in Western societies (Payer, 1991). It is difficult to determine the extent to which these cross-cultural variations are due to genetic, dietary, reproductive, or cultural factors.

Menopause overall is not the negative experience for most women it was once thought to be (Weissmiller, 2009). Most women do not have severe physical or psychological problems related to menopause. However, the loss of fertility is an important marker for women—it means that they have to make final decisions about having children. Women in their thirties who have never had children sometimes speak about being "up against the biological clock" because they cannot postpone choices about having children much longer.

Researchers have found that almost 50 percent of Canadian and American women have occasional hot flashes, but only 1 in 7 Japanese women do (Lock, 1998). *What factors might account for these variations?*

How Would You...? As a human development and family studies professional, how would you counsel middle-aged women who voice the belief that hormone replacement therapy is necessary to "stay young"?

Until recently, hormone replacement therapy was often prescribed as treatment for unpleasant side effects of menopause. *Hormone replacement therapy (HRT)* augments the declining levels of reproductive hormone production by the ovaries (Nappi & Polatti, 2009; Studd, 2010). HRT can consist of various forms of estrogen, and usually a progestin. A study of HRT's effects was halted as evidence emerged that participants who were receiving HRT faced an increased risk of stroke (National Institutes of Health, 2004). Recent analyses also confirmed that combined estrogen and progestin hormone therapy poses an increased risk of cardiovascular disease (Toh & others, 2010). Studies have also revealed that coinciding with the decreased use of HRT is a related decline in the incidence of breast cancer (Dobson, 2009; Parkin, 2009).

The National Institutes of Health recommends that women with a uterus who are currently taking hormones should consult with their doctor to determine whether they should continue the treatment. If they are taking HRT for short-term relief of symptoms, the benefits may outweigh the risks. However, the evidence of risks associated with HRT suggests that long-term hormone therapy should be seriously reevaluated (Warren, 2007). Consequently, many middle-aged women are seeking alternatives to HRT such as regular exercise, dietary supplements, herbal remedies, relaxation therapy, acupuncture, and nonsteroidal medications (Holloway, 2010).

Hormonal Changes in Middle-Aged Men

Do men go through anything like the menopause that women experience? That is, is there a male menopause? During middle adulthood, most men do not lose their capacity to father children, although there usually is a modest decline in their sexual hormone level and activity. They experience hormonal changes in their fifties and sixties, but nothing like the dramatic drop in estrogen that women experience. Testosterone production begins to decline about 1 percent a year during middle adulthood, and sperm count usually shows a slow decline, but men do not lose their fertility in middle age. What has been referred to as "male menopause," then, probably has less to do with hormonal change than with the psychological adjustment men must make when they are faced with declining physical energy and with family and work pressures. Testosterone therapy has not been found to relieve such symptoms, suggesting that they are not induced by hormonal change.

The gradual decline in men's testosterone levels in middle age can reduce their sexual drive (Goel & others, 2009). Their erections are less full and less frequent, and men require more stimulation to achieve them. Researchers once attributed these changes to psychological factors, but increasingly they find that as many as 75 percent of the erectile dysfunctions in middle-aged men stem from physiological problems. Smoking, diabetes, hypertension, and elevated cholesterol levels are at fault in many erectile problems in middle-aged men (Corona & others, 2009; Heidelbaugh, 2010).

Treatment for men with erectile dysfunction has focused on the drug Viagra and on similar drugs, such as Levitra and Cialis (Althof & others, 2010; Sperling & others, 2010). Viagra works by allowing increased blood flow into the penis, which produces an erection. Its success rate is in the 60 to 85 percent range (Claes & others, 2010).

Sexual Attitudes and Behavior

Although the ability of men and women to function sexually shows little biological decline in middle adulthood, sexual activity usually occurs on a less frequent basis than in early adulthood (Burgess, 2004). Career interests, family matters, energy level, and routine may contribute to this decline (Avis & others, 2009).

In the Sex in America survey (described initially in Chapter 11), the frequency of having sex was greatest for individuals 25 to 29 years old (47 percent had sex twice a week or more) and dropped off for individuals in their fifties (23 percent of 50- to 59-year-old males said they had sex twice a week or more, while only 14 percent of the females in this age group reported this frequency) (Michael & others, 1994). Note, though, that the Sex in America survey may underestimate the frequency of sexual activity of middle-aged adults because the data were collected prior to the widespread use of erectile dysfunction drugs such as Viagra.

Living with a spouse or partner makes all the difference in whether people engage in sexual activity, especially for women over 40 years of age. In one study conducted by the MacArthur Foundation, 95 percent of women in their forties with partners said that they have been sexually active in the last six months, compared with only 53 percent of those without partners (Brim, 1999). By their fifties, 88 percent of women living with a partner have been sexually active in the last six months, but only 37 percent of those who are neither married nor living with someone say they have had sex in the last six months.

How does the pattern of sexual activity change when individuals become middle-aged?

A recent large-scale study of U.S. adults 40 to 80 years of age found that early ejaculation (26 percent) and erectile difficulties (22 percent) were the most common sexual problems of older men (Laumann & others, 2009). In this study, the most common sexual problems of women were lack of sexual interest (33 percent) and lubrication difficulties (21 percent).

How Would You...? As a psychologist, how would you counsel a couple about the ways that the transition to middle adulthood might affect their sexual relationship?

crystallized intelligence Accumulated information and verbal skills, which increase in middle age, according to Horn.

fluid intelligence The ability to reason abstractly, which steadily declines from middle adulthood on, according to Horn.

Cognitive Development

We have seen that middle-aged adults may not see as well, run as fast, or be as healthy as they were in their twenties and thirties. We've also seen a decline in their sexual activity. What about their cognitive skills? Do they decline as we enter and move through middle adulthood? To answer this question we explore the possibility of cognitive changes in intelligence and information processing.

Intelligence

Our exploration of possible changes in intelligence in middle adulthood focuses on the concepts of fluid and crystallized intelligence, cohort effects, and the Seattle Longitudinal Study.

Fluid and Crystallized Intelligence

John Horn argues that some abilities begin to decline in middle age, whereas others increase (Horn & Donaldson, 1980). He argues that **crystallized intelligence**, an individual's accumulated information and verbal skills, continues to increase in middle adulthood, whereas **fluid intelligence**, one's ability to reason abstractly, begins to decline in the middle adulthood years (see Figure 13.2).

Horn's data were collected in a cross-sectional manner. Remember from Chapter 1 that a cross-sectional study assesses individuals of different ages at the same point in time. For example, a cross-sectional study might assess the intelligence of different groups of 40-, 50-, and 60-year-olds in a single evaluation, such as in 1980. The 40-year-olds in the study would have been born in 1940 and the 60-year-olds in 1920—different eras that offered different economic and educational opportunities. The 60-year-olds likely had fewer educational opportunities as they grew up. Thus, if we find differences between 40- and 60-year-olds on intelligence tests when they are assessed cross-sectionally, these differences might be due to cohort effects related to educational differences rather than to age.

By contrast, remember from Chapter 1 that in a longitudinal study, the same individuals are studied over a period of time. Thus, a longitudinal study of intelligence in middle adulthood might consist of giving the same intelligence test to the same individuals when they are 40, then 50, and then 60 years of age. As we see next, whether data on intelligence are collected cross-sectionally or longitudinally can make a difference in what is found about changes in crystallized and fluid intelligence and about intellectual decline.

How Would You...?
As an educator, how would you explain how changes in fluid and crystallized intelligence might influence the way middle-aged adults learn?

The Seattle Longitudinal Study

K. Warner Schaie (1996, 2005, 2010, 2011) is conducting an extensive study of intellectual abilities in the adulthood years. Five hundred individuals initially were tested in 1956. New waves of participants are added periodically. The main focus in the Seattle Longitudinal Study has been on individual change and stability in intelligence. The

Figure 13.2 Fluid and Crystallized Intellectual Development Across the Life Span
According to Horn, crystallized intelligence (based on cumulative learning experiences) increases throughout the life span, but fluid intelligence (the ability to perceive and manipulate information) steadily declines from middle adulthood.

Intellectual development

Crystallized intelligence

Fluid intelligence

Infancy   Early adulthood   Late adulthood
Childhood   Middle adulthood

Figure 13.3
**Longitudinal
Changes in Six
Intellectual Abilities from Age 25
to Age 88**

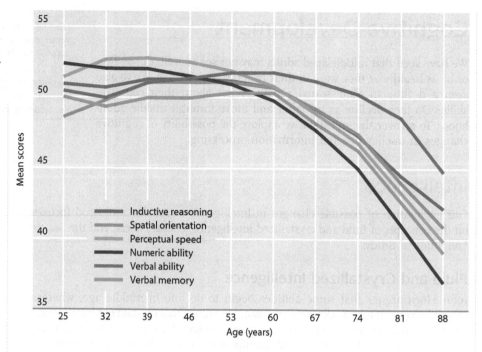

main mental abilities tested are *verbal ability* (ability to understand ideas expressed in words); *verbal memory* (ability to encode and recall meaningful language units, such as a list of words); *numeric ability* (ability to perform simple mathematical computations such as addition, subtraction, and multiplication); *spatial orientation* (ability to visualize and mentally rotate stimuli in two- and three-dimensional space); *inductive reasoning* (ability to recognize and understand patterns and relationships in a problem and use this understanding to solve other instances of the problem); and *perceptual speed* (ability to quickly and accurately make simple discriminations in visual stimuli).

The highest level of functioning for four of the six intellectual abilities occurred in the middle adulthood years (Willis & Schaie, 2005) (see Figure 13.3). For both women and men, peak performance on verbal ability, verbal memory, inductive reasoning, and spatial orientation was attained in middle age. Only two of the six abilities—numeric ability and perceptual speed—showed a decline in middle age. Perceptual speed showed the earliest decline, actually beginning in early adulthood. Interestingly, in terms of John Horn's ideas that were discussed earlier, for the participants in the Seattle Longitudinal Study, middle age was a time of peak performance for some aspects of both crystallized intelligence (verbal ability) and fluid-intelligence (spatial orientation and inductive reasoning).

Notice in Figure 13.3 that decline in functioning for most cognitive abilities began in the sixties, although the decline in verbal ability did not drop until the mid-seventies. From the mid-seventies through the late eighties, all cognitive abilities showed considerable decline.

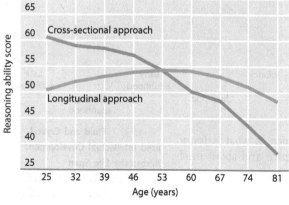

Figure 13.4 **Cross-Sectional and Longitudinal Comparisons of Intellectual Change in Middle Adulthood**

Why do you think reasoning ability peaks during middle adulthood?

When Schaie (1994) assessed intellectual abilities both cross-sectionally and longitudinally, he found decline more likely in the cross-sectional than in the longitudinal assessments. For example, as shown in Figure 13.4, when assessed cross-sectionally, inductive reasoning showed a consistent decline in the middle adulthood years. In contrast, when assessed longitudinally, inductive reasoning increased until toward the end of middle adulthood, when it began to show a slight decline. In Schaie's (2009, 2010, 2011) view, it is in middle adulthood, not early adulthood, that people reach a peak in their cognitive functioning for many intellectual skills.

> **working memory** Closely related to short-term memory but places more emphasis on mental work. Working memory is like a mental "workbench" where individuals can manipulate and assemble information when making decisions, solving problems, and comprehending written and spoken language.

Personality Theories and Development

What is the best way to conceptualize middle age? Is it a stage or a crisis? How extensively is middle age influenced by life events? Do middle-aged adults experience stress differently than young and older adults? Is personality linked with contexts such as the point in history in which individuals go through midlife, their culture, and their gender?

Stages of Adulthood

Adult stage theories have been plentiful, and they have contributed to the view that midlife brings a crisis in development. Two prominent theories that define stages of adult development are Erik Erikson's life-span view and Daniel Levinson's seasons of a man's life.

Erikson's Stage of Generativity Versus Stagnation

Erikson (1968) proposed that middle-aged adults face a significant issue—*generativity versus stagnation*, which is the name Erikson gave to the seventh stage in his life-span theory. **Generativity** encompasses adults' desire to leave legacies of themselves to the next generation. Through these legacies adults achieve a kind of immortality. By contrast, **stagnation** (sometimes called "self-absorption") develops when individuals sense that they have done little or nothing for the next generation.

Generative adults commit themselves to the continuation and improvement of society as a whole through their connection to the next generation. Generative adults develop a positive legacy of the self and then offer it as a gift to the next generation. Middle-aged adults can develop generativity in a number of ways (Kotre, 1984). Through biological generativity, adults have offspring. Through parental generativity, adults nurture and guide children. Through work generativity, adults develop skills that are passed down to others. And through cultural generativity, adults create, renovate, or conserve some aspect of culture that ultimately survives.

Through generativity, adults promote and guide the next generation by parenting, teaching, leading, and doing things that benefit the community (Pratt & others, 2008). One of the participants in a study of aging said: "From twenty to thirty I learned how to get along with my wife. From thirty to forty I learned

How Would You...? As an educator, how would you describe ways in which the profession of teaching might establish generativity for someone in middle adulthood?

Era of late adulthood:
60 to ?

Late adult transition: Age 60 to 65

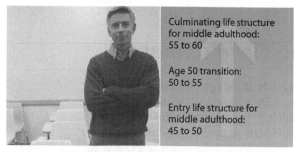

Culminating life structure
for middle adulthood:
55 to 60

Age 50 transition:
50 to 55

Entry life structure for
middle adulthood:
45 to 50

Middle adult transition: Age 40 to 45

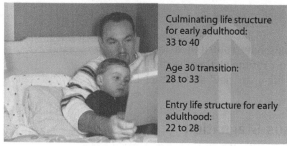

Culminating life structure
for early adulthood:
33 to 40

Age 30 transition:
28 to 33

Entry life structure for early
adulthood:
22 to 28

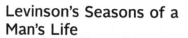

Early adult transition: Age 17 to 22

Figure 14.1 Levinson's Periods of Adult Development
According to Levinson, adulthood for men has three main stages, which are surrounded by transition periods. Specific tasks and challenges are associated with each stage.

how to be a success at my job, and at forty to fifty I worried less about myself and more about the children" (Vaillant, 2002, p. 114).

Does research support Erikson's theory that generativity is an important dimension of middle age? Yes, it does (McAdams, 2009; Pratt & others, 2008). In one study, Carol Ryff (1984) examined the views of women and men at different ages and found that middle-aged adults especially were concerned about generativity. In a longitudinal study of Smith College women, the desire for generativity increased as the participants aged from their thirties to their fifties (Stewart, Ostrove, & Helson, 2001). And in a recent study, generativity was strongly linked to middle-aged adults, positive social engagement in such contexts as family life and community activities (Cox & others, 2010).

Levinson's Seasons of a Man's Life

In *The Seasons of a Man's Life* (1978), clinical psychologist Daniel Levinson reported the results of extensive interviews with 40 middle-aged men. The interviews were conducted with hourly workers, business executives, academic biologists, and novelists. Levinson bolstered his conclusions with information from the biographies of famous men and the development of memorable characters in literature. Although Levinson's major interest focused on midlife change in men, he described a number of stages and transitions during the period from 17 to 65 years of age, as shown in Figure 14.1. Levinson emphasizes that developmental tasks must be mastered at each stage.

At the end of one's teens, according to Levinson, a transition from dependence to independence should occur. This transition is marked by the formation of a dream—an image of the kind of life the youth wants to have, especially in terms of a career and marriage. Levinson sees the twenties as a *novice phase* of adult development. It is a time of reasonably free experimentation and of testing the dream in the real world. In early adulthood, the two major tasks to be mastered are exploring the possibilities for adult living and developing a stable life structure.

From about the ages of 28 to 33, the man goes through a transition period in which he must face the more serious question of determining his goals. During the thirties, he usually focuses on family and career development. In the later years of this period, he enters a phase of *Becoming One's Own Man* (or BOOM, as Levinson calls it). By age 40, he has reached a stable location in his career, has outgrown his earlier, more tenuous attempts at learning to become an adult, and now must look forward to the kind of life he will lead as a middle-aged adult.

According to Levinson, the transition to middle adulthood lasts about five years (ages 40 to 45) and requires the adult male to come to grips with four major conflicts that have existed in his life since adolescence: (1) being young versus being old, (2) being destructive versus being constructive, (3) being masculine versus being feminine, and (4) being attached to others versus being separated

How Would You...?
As a human development and family studies professional, how would you advise a middle-aged woman who never had children and now fears she has little opportunity to leave a legacy to the next generation?

from them. Seventy to 80 percent of the men Levinson interviewed found the midlife transition tumultuous and psychologically painful, as many aspects of their lives came into question. According to Levinson, the success of the midlife transition rests on how effectively the individual reduces the polarities and accepts each of them as an integral part of his being.

Because Levinson interviewed middle-aged males, we can consider the data about middle adulthood more valid than the data about early adulthood. When individuals are asked to remember information about earlier parts of their lives, they may distort and forget things. The original Levinson data included no females, although Levinson (1996) reported that his stages, transitions, and the crisis of middle age hold for females as well as males. Levinson's work included no statistical analysis. However, the quality and quantity of the Levinson biographies make them outstanding examples of the clinical tradition.

> **contemporary life-events approach** An approach that emphasizes that how a life event influences the individual's development depends not only on the life event, but also on mediating factors, the individual's adaptation to the life event, the life-stage context, and the sociohistorical context.

How Pervasive Are Midlife Crises?

Levinson (1978) views midlife as a crisis, believing that the middle-aged adult is suspended between the past and the future, trying to cope with this gap that threatens life's continuity. George Vaillant (1977) has a different view. Vaillant's study—called the "Grant Study"—involved men who were in their early thirties and in their late forties who initially had been interviewed as undergraduates at Harvard University. He concludes that just as adolescence is a time for detecting parental flaws and discovering the truth about childhood, the forties are a decade of reassessing and recording the truth about the adolescent and adulthood years. However, whereas Levinson sees midlife as a crisis, Vaillant maintains that only a minority of adults experience a midlife crisis.

Today, adult development experts are virtually unanimous in their belief that midlife crises have been exaggerated (Brim, Ryff, & Kessler, 2004; Lachman & Krantz, 2010). In sum, the stage theories place too much emphasis on crises in development, especially midlife crises. Also, there often is considerable individual variation in the way people experience the stages, a topic that we turn to next.

The Life-Events Approach

Age-related stages represent one major way to examine adult personality development. A second major way to conceptualize adult personality development is to focus on life events. In the early version of the life-events approach, life events were viewed as taxing circumstances for individuals, forcing them to change their personality (Holmes & Rahe, 1967). Such events as the death of a spouse, divorce, marriage, and so on were believed to involve varying degrees of stress, and therefore likely to influence the individual's development.

Today's life-events approach is more sophisticated. The **contemporary life-events approach** emphasizes that how life events influence the individual's development depends not only on the life event itself but also on mediating factors (physical health, family supports, for example), the individual's adaptation to the life event (appraisal of the threat, coping strategies, for example), the life-stage context, and the sociohistorical context (see Figure 14.2). For example, if individuals are in poor health and have little family support, life events are likely to be more stressful. Whatever the context or mediating variables, however, one individual may perceive a life event as highly stressful, whereas another individual may perceive the same event as a challenge.

Though the life-events approach is a valuable addition to understanding adult development, like other approaches to adult development, it has its drawbacks. One significant drawback is that the life-events approach places too much emphasis on

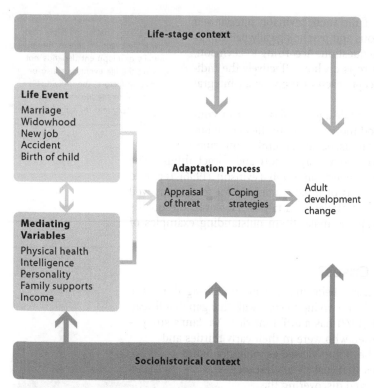

Figure 14.2 A Contemporary Life-Events Framework for Interpreting Adult Developmental Change

According to the contemporary life-events approach, the influence of a life event depends on the event itself, on mediating variables, on the life-stage and sociohistorical context, and on the individual's appraisal of the event and coping strategies.

change. Another drawback is that it may not be life's major events that are the primary sources of stress, but our daily experiences (O'Connor & others, 2009). Enduring a boring but tense job, staying in an unsatisfying marriage, or living in poverty do not show up on scales of major life events. Yet the everyday pounding we take from these living conditions can add up to a highly stressful life and eventually illness (McIntosh, Gillanders, & Rodgers, 2010).

Stress and Personal Control in Midlife

As we have seen, there is conclusive evidence that midlife is not a time when a majority of adults experience a tumultuous crisis, and when they do experience a midlife crisis, it is often linked to stressful life events. Do middle-aged adults experience stress differently than young adults and older adults? One study using daily diaries over a one-week period found that both young and middle-aged adults had more stressful days than older adults (Almeida & Horn, 2004). In this study, although young adults experienced daily stressors more frequently than middle-aged adults, middle-aged adults experienced more "overload" stressors that involved juggling too many activities at once.

To what extent do middle-aged adults perceive that they can control what happens to them? Researchers have found some aspects of personal control increase with age while others decrease (Lachman, 2006; Lachman & others, 2011). For example, middle-aged adults feel they have a greater sense of control over their finances, work, and marriage than younger adults but less control over their sex life and their children (Lachman & Firth, 2004; Lachman & Weaver, 1998).

Contexts of Midlife Development

The contemporary life-events approach (like Bronfenbrenner's theory, discussed in Chapter 1) highlights the importance of the complex setting of our lives—of everything from our income and family supports to our sociohistorical circumstances. Let's examine how two aspects of the contexts of life influence development during middle adulthood: historical contexts (cohort effects) and culture.

Historical Contexts (Cohort Effects)

Bernice Neugarten (1964) has been emphasizing the power of age group or cohort since the 1960s. Our values, attitudes, expectations, and behaviors are influenced by the period in which we live. For example, the group of individuals born during the difficult times of the Great Depression may have a different outlook on life than the group born during the optimistic 1950s, says Neugarten.

How Would You...?
As a health-care professional, how would you convince a company that it should sponsor a stress-reduction program for its middle-aged employees?

Neugarten (1986) argues that the social environment of a particular age group can alter its **social clock**—the timetable according to which individuals are expected to accomplish life's tasks, such as getting married, having children, or establishing themselves in a career. Social clocks provide guides for our lives; individuals whose lives are not synchronized with these social clocks find life to be more stressful than those who are on schedule, says Neugarten. She argues that today there is much less agreement than in the past on the right age or sequence for the occurrence of major life events such as having children or retiring.

Trying to tease out universal truths and patterns about adult development from one birth cohort is complicated because the findings may not apply to another birth cohort (Schaie, 2010, 2011). Most of the individuals studied by Levinson and Vaillant, for example, were born before and during the Great Depression. What was true for these individuals may not be true for today's 50-year-olds, born in the optimistic aftermath of World War II, or for the post-baby-boom generation as they approach the midlife transition. The midlife men in Levinson's and Vaillant's studies might have been burned out at a premature age rather than being representatives of a normal adult developmental pattern (Rossi, 1989).

social clock The timetable according to which individuals are expected to accomplish life's tasks, such as getting married, having children, or establishing a career.

Cultural Contexts

In many cultures, especially nonindustrialized cultures, the concept of middle age is not very clear or, in some cases, is absent. It is common in nonindustrialized societies to describe individuals as young or old, but not as middle-aged (Grambs, 1989). Some cultures have no words for "adolescent," "young adult," or "middle-aged adult," but they do have other categories they use.

What is middle age like for women in other cultures? It depends on the modernity of the culture and the culture's view of gender roles. Some anthropologists believe that when women become middle-aged in nonindustrialized societies they may experience certain advantages (Brown, 1985). First, they are often freed from cumbersome restrictions that were placed on them when they were younger. For example, in middle age they enjoy greater geographical mobility. Child care has ceased or can be delegated, and domestic chores are reduced. They may venture forth from the village for commercial opportunities, visit relatives living at a distance, and attend religious events. Second, with middle age a woman has the right to exercise authority over specified younger kin. Middle-aged women can extract labor from younger family members. The work of middle-aged women tends to be administrative, delegating tasks and making assignments to younger women. Middle-aged women also make important decisions for certain members of the younger generation: what a grandchild is to be named, who is ready to be initiated into adulthood, and who is eligible to marry whom. Third, middle-aged women may become eligible for special statuses, which may provide recognition beyond the household. These statuses include the vocations of midwife, curer, holy woman, and matchmaker.

Gusii dancers perform on World Habitat Day in Nairobi, Kenya. Movement from one status to another in the Gusii culture is due primarily to life events, not age. The Gusii do not have a clearly labeled midlife transition.

Close Relationships

There is a consensus among middle-aged Americans that a major component of well-being involves positive relationships with others, especially parents, spouse, and offspring (Lachman, 2004). To begin our examination of midlife relationships, let's explore love and marriage in middle-aged adults.

Love and Marriage at Midlife

Remember from Chapter 12 that two major forms of love are romantic love and affectionate love. The fires of romantic love are strong in early adulthood. Affectionate, or companionate, love increases during middle adulthood. That is, physical attraction, romance, and passion are more important in new relationships, especially those begun in early adulthood. Security, loyalty, and mutual emotional interest become more important as relationships mature, especially in middle adulthood.

A recent study revealed that marital satisfaction increased in middle age (Gorchoff, John, & Helson, 2008). Even some marriages that were difficult and rocky during early adulthood turn out to be better adjusted during middle adulthood. Although the partners may have lived through a great deal of turmoil, they eventually discover a deep and solid foundation on which to anchor their relationship. In middle adulthood, the partners may have fewer financial worries, less housework and chores, and more time with each other. Middle-aged partners are more likely to view their marriage as positive if they engage in mutual activities.

> **empty nest syndrome** A term used to indicate a decrease in marital satisfaction after children leave home.

Most individuals in midlife who are married voice considerable satisfaction with being married. In a large-scale study of individuals in middle adulthood, 72 percent of those who were married said their marriage was either "excellent" or "very good" (Brim, 1999). Possibly by middle age, many of the worst marriages already have dissolved. However, a recent study revealed that married and partnered middle-aged adults were more likely to rate their relationships as more ambivalent or indifferent than their late adulthood counterparts (Windsor & Butterworth, 2010).

Divorce in middle adulthood may be more positive in some ways, more negative in others, than divorce in early adulthood (Pudrovska, 2009). On the one hand, for mature individuals, the perils of divorce can be fewer and less intense than for younger individuals. They have more resources, and they can use this time as an opportunity to simplify their lives by disposing of possessions, such as a large home, which they no longer need. Their children are adults and may be able to cope with their parents' divorce more effectively. The partners may have gained a better understanding of themselves and may be searching for changes that could include the end to an unhappy marriage.

On the other hand, the emotional and time commitment to marriage that has existed for so many years may not be lightly given up. Many midlife individuals perceive a divorce as failing in the best years of their lives. The divorcer might see the situation as an escape from an untenable relationship, but the divorced partner usually sees it as betrayal, the ending of a relationship that had been built up over many years and that involved a great deal of commitment and trust.

A survey by AARP (2004) of 1,148 40- to 79-year-olds who were divorced at least once in their forties, fifties, or sixties found that staying married because of their children was by far the main reason many people took so long to become divorced. Despite the worry and stress involved in going through a divorce, three in four of the divorcees said they had made the right decision to dissolve their

What characterizes marriage in middle adulthood?

marriage and reported a positive outlook on life. Sixty-six percent of the divorced women said they initiated the divorce compared with only 41 percent of the divorced men. The divorced women were much more afraid of having financial problems (44 percent) than the divorced men (11 percent).

Following are the main reasons the middle-aged and older adults cited for their divorce:

How Would You...?

As a social worker, how would you describe the different reasons for divorce between young and middle-aged adults?

Main Causes for Women	Main Causes for Men
1. Verbal, physical, or emotional abuse (23 percent)	1. No obvious problems, just fell out of love (17 percent)
2. Alcohol or drug abuse (18 percent)	2. Cheating (14 percent)
3. Cheating (17 percent)	3. Different values, lifestyles (14 percent)

The Empty Nest and Its Refilling

An important event in a family is the launching of a child into adult life. Parents face new adjustments as a result of the child's absence. Students usually think that their parents suffer from their absence. In fact, parents who live vicariously through their children might experience the **empty nest syndrome**, which includes a decline in marital satisfaction after children leave the home. For most parents, however, marital satisfaction does not decline after children have left home. Rather, for most parents marital satisfaction increases during the years after child rearing (Fingerman & Baker, 2006). With their children gone, marital partners have time to pursue careers and other interests and more time for each other. A recent study

Doonesbury　　　　　　　　　　　　　BY GARRY TRUDEAU

DOONESBURY © 1991 G. B. Trudeau. Reprinted with permission of Universal Uclick. All Rights Reserved.

revealed that the transition to an empty nest increased marital satisfaction and this increase was linked to an increase in the quality of time—but not the quantity of time—spent with partners (Gorchoff, John, & Helson, 2008).

In today's uncertain economic climate, the refilling of the empty nest is becoming a common occurrence as adult children return to live at home after several years of college, after graduating from college, or to save money after taking a full-time job (Merrill, 2009). Young adults also may move back in with their parents after an unsuccessful career or a divorce. And some individuals don't leave home at all until their middle to late twenties because they cannot financially support themselves. Numerous labels have been applied to these young adults who return to their parents' homes to live, including "boomerang kids" and "B2B" (or Back-to-Bedroom) (Furman, 2005).

The middle generation has always provided support for the younger generation, even after the nest is bare. Through loans and monetary gifts for education, and through emotional support, the middle generation has helped the younger generation. Adult children appreciate the financial and emotional support their parents provide them at a time when they often feel considerable stress about their career, work, and lifestyle. And parents feel good that they can provide this support.

However, as with most family living arrangements, there are both pluses and minuses when adult children return to live at home. One of the most common complaints voiced by both adult children and their parents is a loss of privacy. The adult children complain that their parents restrict their independence, cramp their sex lives, reduce their rock music listening, and treat them as children rather than adults. Parents often complain that their quiet home has become noisy, that they stay up late worrying when their adult children will come home, that meals are difficult to plan because of conflicting schedules, that their relationship as a married couple has been invaded, and that they have to shoulder too much responsibility for their adult children. In sum, when adult children return home to live, a disequilibrium in family life is created, which requires considerable adaptation on the part of parents and their adult children.

What are some strategies that can help parents and their young adult children get along better?

When adult children ask to return home to live, parents and their adult children should agree on the conditions and expectations beforehand. For example, they might discuss and agree on whether young adults will pay rent, wash their own clothes, cook their own meals, do any household chores, pay their phone bills, come and go as they please, be sexually active or drink alcohol at home, and so on. If these conditions aren't negotiated at the beginning, conflict often results because the expectations of parents and young adult children will likely be violated.

How Would You...? As a psychologist, how would you counsel parents of adult children who return to live at home for a few years following their college?

Sibling Relationships and Friendships

Sibling relationships persist over the entire life span for most adults (Dunn, 2007). Eighty-five percent of today's adults have at least one living sibling. Sibling relationships in adulthood may be extremely close, apathetic, or highly rivalrous (Bedford, 2009). The majority of sibling relationships in adulthood are close (Cicirelli, 2009). Those siblings who are psychologically close to each other in adulthood tended to be that way in childhood. It is rare for sibling closeness to develop for the first time in adulthood (Dunn, 1984). A recent study revealed that adult siblings often provide practical and emotional support to each other (Voorpostel & Blieszner, 2008). Another study revealed that men who had poor sibling relationships in childhood were more likely to develop depression by age 50 than men who had more positive sibling relationships as children (Waldinger, Vaillant, & Orav, 2007).

Friendships continue to be important in middle adulthood just as they were in early adulthood (Antonucci, 1989). It takes time to develop intimate friendships, so friendships that have endured over the adult years are often deeper than those that have just been formed in middle adulthood.

Grandparenting

The increase in longevity is influencing the nature of grandparenting (Szinovacz, 2009). In 1900 only 4 percent of 10-year-old children had four living grandparents, but in 2000 that figure had risen to more than 40 percent. And in 1990 only about 20 percent of children at 30 years of age had living grandparents, a figure that is projected to increase to 80 percent in 2020 (Hagestad & Uhlenberg, 2007). Further increases in longevity are likely to support this trend in the future, although the current trend in delaying childbearing is likely to undermine it (Szinovacz, 2009).

Grandparent Roles

Grandparents play important roles in the lives of many grandchildren (Oberlander, Black, & Starr, 2007). Many adults become grandparents for the first time during middle age. Researchers have consistently found that grandmothers have more contact with grandchildren than do grandfathers (Watson, Randolph, & Lyons, 2005). Perhaps women tend to define their role as grandmothers as part of their responsibility for maintaining ties between family members across generations. Men may have fewer expectations about the grandfather role and see it as more voluntary.

What are some grandparents' roles and styles?

Three prominent meanings are attached to being a grandparent (Neugarten & Weinstein, 1964). For some older adults, being a grandparent is a source of biological reward and continuity. For others, being a grandparent is a source of emotional self-fulfillment, generating feelings of companionship and satisfaction that may have been missing in earlier adult-child relationships. And for yet others, being a grandparent is a remote role.

The grandparent role may have different functions in different families, in different ethnic groups and cultures, and in different situations (Szinovacz, 2009). For example, in one study of White, African American, and Mexican American grandparents and grandchildren, the Mexican American grandparents saw their grandchildren more frequently, provided more support for the grandchildren and their parents, and had more satisfying relationships with their grandchildren (Bengtson, 1985). And in a study of three generations of families in Chicago, grandmothers had closer relationships with their children and grandchildren and gave more personal advice than grandfathers did (Hagestad, 1985).

The Changing Profile of Grandparents

An increasing number of U.S. grandchildren live with their grandparents (Silverstein, 2009). In 1980, 2.3 million grandchildren lived with their grandparents, but in 2005 that figure had reached 6.1 million (U.S. Census Bureau, 2006). Divorce, adolescent pregnancies, and drug use by parents are the main reasons that grandparents are thrust back into the "parenting" role they thought they had shed. A recent study revealed that grandparent involvement was linked with better adjustment when it occurred in single-parent and stepparent families than in two-parent biological families (Attar-Schwartz & others, 2009).

Grandparents who are full-time caregivers for grandchildren are at elevated risk for health problems, depression, and stress (Silverstein, 2009). Caring for grandchildren is linked with these problems in part because full-time grandparent caregivers are often characterized by low-income, minority status and by not being married (Minkler & Fuller-Thompson, 2005). Grandparents who are part-time caregivers are less likely to have the negative health portrait that full-time grandparent caregivers have. In a recent study of part-time grandparent caregivers, few negative effects on grandparents were found (Hughes & others, 2007).

As divorce and remarriage have become more common, a special concern of grandparents is visitation privileges with their grandchildren. In the last 10 to 15 years, more states have passed laws giving grandparents the right to petition a court for visitation privileges with their grandchildren, even if a parent objects. Whether

How Would You...?
As a human development and family studies professional, how would you educate parents about the mutual benefits of having grandparents actively involved in their children's lives?

such forced visitation rights for grandparents are in the child's best interest is still being debated.

Intergenerational Relationships

Family is important to most people. When 21,000 adults aged 40 to 79 in 21 countries were asked, "When you think of who you are, you think mainly of _____," 63 percent said "family," 9 percent said "religion," and 8 percent said "work" (HSBC Insurance, 2007). In this study, in all 21 countries, middle-aged and older adults expressed a strong feeling of responsibility between generations in their family, with the strongest intergenerational ties indicated in Saudi Arabia, India, and Turkey. More than 80 percent of the middle-aged and older adults reported that adults have a duty to care for their parents (and parents-in-law) in time of need later in life.

Adults in midlife play important roles in the lives of the young and the old (Birditt & others, 2010; Martini & Busseri, 2010). Middle-aged adults share their experience and transmit values to the younger generation. They may be launching children and experiencing the empty nest, adjusting to having grown children return home, or becoming grandparents. They also may be giving or receiving financial assistance, caring for a widowed or sick parent, or adapting to being the oldest generation after both parents have died.

Middle-aged and older adults around the world show a strong sense of family responsibility. A recent study of middle-aged and older adults in 21 countries revealed the strongest intergenerational ties in Saudi Arabia.

Middle-aged adults have been described as the "sandwich," "squeezed," or "overload" generation because of the responsibilities they have for their adolescent and young adult children on the one hand and their aging parents on the other (Etaugh & Bridges, 2010; Pudrovska, 2009). These simultaneous pressures from adolescents or young adult children and aging parents may contribute to stress in middle adulthood. Many middle-aged adults experience considerable stress when their parents become very ill and die. One survey found that when adults enter midlife, 41 percent have both parents alive but that 77 percent leave midlife with no parents alive (Bumpass & Aquilino, 1994). A recent study revealed that middle-aged parents are more likely to provide support to their grown children than to their parents (Fingerman & others, 2010). When middle-aged adults' parents have a disability, their support for their aging parents increases.

A valuable service that adult children can perform is to coordinate and monitor services for an aging parent who becomes disabled. This might involve locating a nursing home and monitoring its quality, procuring medical services, arranging public service assistance, and handling finances. In some cases, adult children provide direct assistance with

What is the nature of intergenerational relationships?

daily living, including such activities as eating, bathing, and dressing. Even less severely impaired older adults may need help with shopping, housework, transportation, home maintenance, and bill paying.

In most cases researchers have found that relationships between aging parents and their children are usually characterized by ambivalence (Birditt, Fingerman, & Zarit, 2010; Davey & others, 2009; Fingerman & others, 2008). Perceptions include love, reciprocal help, and shared values on the positive side and isolation, family conflicts and problems, abuse, neglect, and caregiver stress on the negative side.

With each new generation, personality characteristics, attitudes, and values are replicated or changed. As older family members die, their biological, intellectual, emotional, and personal legacies are carried on in the next generation. Their children become the oldest generation and their grandchildren the second generation. As adult children become middle-aged, they often develop more positive perceptions of their parents (Field, 1999). Both similarity and dissimilarity across generations are found. For example, similarity between parents and an adult child is most noticeable in religion and politics, least in gender roles, lifestyle, and work orientation.

The following studies provide further evidence of the importance of intergenerational relationships in development:

- The motivation of adult children to provide social support to their older parents was linked with earlier family experiences (Silverstein & others, 2002). Children who spent more time in shared activities with their parents and were given more financial support by them earlier in their lives provided more support to their parents when they became older.

- Adult children of divorce who were classified as securely attached were less likely to divorce in the early years of their marriage than their insecurely attached counterparts (Crowell, Treboux, & Brockmeyer, 2009).

- Parents who smoked early and often, and persisted in becoming regular smokers, were more likely to have adolescents who became smokers (Chassin & others, 2008).

Gender differences also characterize intergenerational relationships (Etaugh & Bridges, 2010) Women have an especially important role in connecting family relationships across generations. Women's relationships across generations are typically closer than other family bonds (Merrill, 2009). In one study, mothers and their daughters had much closer relationships during their adult years than mothers and sons, fathers and daughters, and fathers and sons (Rossi, 1989). Also in this study, married men were more involved with their wives' kin than with their own. And maternal grandmothers and maternal aunts were cited twice as often as their counterparts on the paternal side of the family as the most important or loved relative. Also, a recent study revealed that mothers' intergenerational ties were more influential for grandparent-grandchild relationships than fathers' (Monserud, 2008).

How Would You...?
As a health-care professional, how would you advise a family contemplating the potential challenges of having a middle-aged family member take on primary responsibility for the daily care of a chronically ill parent?

Psychological Developments in the Second Half of Life

Robert C. Peck

Stages in Psychological Development in the Second Half of Life

Erikson, like Freud before him, conceived his "stages" of early life by considering the psychological problems that must be universally met and mastered at specific developmental (age) periods. Thus, his first four Stages are defined as 44 psychic developmental tasks" which must be faced in infancy and childhood. The fifth, Identity, seems to be defined as it is because adolescence (at least, in our society) uniquely poses the problem of developing a new kind and sense of identity. That is, this problem does not ordinarily arise acutely during middle childhood; and it can not be perfectly resolved if deferred to the adult years. The sixth and seventh stages are denned and located as they are, it seems, because they describe tasks which are uniquely crucial issues in young adulthood. That is, they do not arise until adolescent problems are behind, and they probably can not be successfully deferred much beyond the age of thirty.

Erikson's eighth stage, however, Ego-Integrity vs. Despair, seems to be intended to represent in a global, nonspecific way all of the psychological crises and crisis-solutions of 'the last forty or fifty years of life. Clearly, his phrasing of it states a major issue of life after thirty. A closer look at the second half of life, however, suggests that it might be accurate and useful to divide it into several quite different kinds of psychological learnings and adjustments, at different stages in the latter half of life. If this is true, these stages and the tasks they present may be as worthy of distinct definition and study as Erikson has devoted to the stages of early fife. For reasons which will be discussed later, the chief chronological division which seems sound is between a Middle Age period and an Old Age period. Within these periods, the stages may occur in different time sequence, for different individuals.

Adapted from *Psychological Aspects of Aging*, Proceedings of a Conference on Planning Research, Bethesda, Maryland, April 24-27, 1955, ed. John E. Anderson (Washington, D.C.: American Psychological Association, 1956), pp. 44-49. Reproduced by permission.

Middle Age

1. *Valuing Wisdom vs. Valuing Physical Powers*—One of the inescapable consequences of aging, after the late twenties, is a decrease in physical strength, stamina, and attractiveness (if, as in America, "attractiveness" is usually defined as "young-looking"). On the other hand, the sheer experience which longer living brings can, if it is used, make the middle aged person able to accomplish a good deal more than younger people, *though by a different means.*

"Wisdom" seems to be a widely used word which may sum up this increment in judgmental powers that aging makes possible.

Wisdom is to be distinguished from intellectual capacity. It might be defined as the ability to make the most effective choices among the alternatives which intellectual perception and imagination present for one's decision. Such choice-making is affected by one's emotional stability, and one's unconflicted or conflicted motivation-set, as well as by intellectual ability. Sheer life experience seems to be essential in giving one a chance to encounter a wide range of emotional relationships, as a corrective to the over-generalized perceptual-attitudinal set derived from one's necessarily limited experience in one family, and one subculture, during childhood and adolescence.

Judging from personality analysis of some thousands of business people in the middle range of life—mostly men—it is my impression that most reach a critical transition point somewhere between the late thirties and the late forties. Some people cling to physical powers, both as their chief "tool" for coping with life, and as the most important element in their value-hierarchy, especially in their I self-definition. Since physical powers inevitably decline, such people tend to grow increasingly depressed, bitter, or otherwise unhappy as they grow older. Moreover, they may become increasingly ineffective in their work roles and social roles, if they try to rely on physical powers which they no longer possess. (This appears to be a major etiological element in the "middle age depression," particularly in men.)

Conversely, it has been my impression that those people who age most "successfully" in this stage, with little psychic discomfort and with no less effectiveness, are those who calmly invert their previous value hierarchy, now putting the use of their "heads" above the use of their "hands," both as their standard for self-evaluation and as their chief resource for solving life problems.

Thus, it might be conceived that the optimum course for people who reach this first stage of physical decline is to switch from physique-based values to wisdom-based- or mental-based-values, in their self-definition and in their behavior.

2. *Socializing vs. Sexualizing in Human Relationships*—Allied to general physical decline, but partially separate from it, is the sexual climacteric. The opportunity the climacteric presents might be this: that people can take on a new kind of value for one—or to a much more dominant degree—as individual personalities, rather than primarily as sex-objects.

If a person takes positive action at this point, redefining men and women as individuals and as companions, with the sexual element decreasingly significant, it would at least be understandable that interpersonal living *could* take on a depth of understanding which the earlier, perhaps inevitably more egocentric, sex-drive would have tended to prevent to some degree.

3. *Cathectic Flexibility vs. Cathectic Impoverishment*— The phenomenon for which this label is intended might equally well be described as "emotional flexibility": the capacity to shift emotional investments from one person to another, and from one activity to another. In some ways, this cross-cuts any and all adjustive shifts that are made throughout life. The reason for considering it as a distinct function, perhaps more crucial in middle age than at earlier ages, rests in the fact that this is the period, for most people, when their parents die, their children grow up and leave home, and their circle of friends and relatives of similar age begins to be broken by death.

On the other hand, for many people this is the time of life when they have the greatest range of potential cathexis-objects. They have the widest circle of acquaintances in their community and vocational worlds. They have achieved informal and formal status as "mature" or "experienced" people, to whom others actively turn. In' fact, this may give them contacts with people over the widest age-range, from young to old, which they will ever encounter. Further, by contrast with younger ages, it may be that experience with a greater variety of people, of roles, of relationships, can lead to a more complex set of more varied, differentiated relationships than is possible at younger ages.

Some people suffer an increasingly impoverished emotional life through the years, because as their cathexis-objects disappear they are unable to reinvest their emotions in other people, other pursuits, or other life settings. Hence this too looks like a crisis-stage where positive adaptation

requires new learning—not only of specific new cathexis, but of a generalized set toward *making* new cathexes (or redefining, existing cathectic relationships, as in the case of grown-up children).

4. *Mental Flexibility vs. Mental Rigidity*—One of the major issues in human growth and living seems to be the question, which will dictate one's life—oneself, or the events and experiences one undergoes? Some people learn to master their experiences, achieve a degree of detached perspective on them, and make use of them as *provisional* guides to the solution of new issues. There are other people who seem to become dominated by their experiences. They take the patterns of events and actions which they happen to have encountered, as a set of fixed inflexible rules which almost automatically govern their subsequent behavior.

In any case, there appears to be a widespread feeling by a great many people that "too many" tend to grow increasingly set in their ways, inflexible in their opinions and actions, and closed-minded to new ideas, as they go through the Middle years. This is often said of elderly people; but it seems that the *first* time when it becomes a critical issue for most people may well be during middle age, when they have peak status, have worked out a set of "answers" to life, and may be tempted to forego further Mental effort to envision new or different "answers."

Like Cathectic Flexibility, this function cross-cuts all adaptive learning behavior. It is no doubt particularly related to stage one, Wisdom vs. Physique; but insofar as it may be a generalized phenomenon, including that first choice-point as a special case, it may be worthy of separate study.

Old Age

1. *Ego Differentiation vs. Work-Role Preoccupation*— The specific issue, here, particularly for most men in our society, is created by the impact of vocational retirement, usually in the sixties. What this phrase is intended to represent is a general, crucial shift in the value system by which the retiring individual can reappraise and redefine his worth, and can take satisfaction in a broader range of role activities than just his long-time specific work role. The chief issue might be put this way: "Am I a worthwhile person only insofar as I can do a full time job; or can I be worthwhile in other, different ways—as a performer of several other roles, and also because of the kind of person I am?"

The process of ego-differentiation into a complex, varied set of self-identifications begins in early childhood. There are reasons, however, for considering it a centrally important issue at the time of vocational retirement. For most men, the ability to find a sense of self-worth in activities beyond the "job" seems to make the most difference between a despairing loss of meaning in life, and a continued, vital interest in living. (For many women, this stage may arrive when their "vocational" role as mother is removed by the departure of the grown children. In that case, this crisis-stage might well come in middle age, for many women.)

Thus, one critical requisite for successful adaptation to old age may be the establishment of a varied set of valued activities and valued self-attributes, so that any one of several alternatives can be pursued with a sense of satisfaction and worthwhileness. This, at any rate, is what the term ego-differentiation is here intended to represent.

2. *Body Transcendence vs. Body Preoccupation*— Old age brings to almost everyone a marked decline in resistance to illness, a decline in recuperative powers, and increasing experience with bodily aches and pains. For people to whom pleasure and comfort mean predominantly physical well-being, this may be the gravest, most mortal of insults. There are many such people whose elder years seem to move in a decreasing spiral, centered around their growing preoccupation with the state of their bodies.

There are other people, however, who suffer just as painful physical unease, yet who enjoy life greatly. It may be that these are people who have learned to define "happiness" and "comfort" more in terms of satisfying human relationships,

or creative activities of a mental nature, which only sheer physical destruction could seriously interfere with. In their value system, social and mental sources of pleasure and self-respect may transcend physical comfort, alone.

This is the hypothesis underlying the selection of this issue as a critical decision-point of old age. While such an orientation must almost certainly be developed in its initial form by early adulthood, if it is to be achieved at all, old age may bring the most critical test of whether this kind of value system has been achieved. In the form in which this issue occurs in late life, it may thus be viewed as one of the goals of human development. It recognizes that physical decline occurs, but it also takes account of mental and social powers which may actually increase with age, for many people.

3. *Ego Transcendence vs. Ego Preoccupation*—One of the new and crucial facts of old age is the appearance of the certain prospect of personal death. In earlier years death comes unexpectedly, as it were; but elderly people know it must come. Chinese and Hindu philosophers, as well as Western thinkers, have suggested that a positive adaptation is possible even to this most unwelcome of prospects. The constructive way of living the late years might be defined in this way: To live so generously and

unselfishly that the prospect of personal death—the night of the ego, it might be called—looks and feels less important than the secure knowledge that one has built for a broader, longer future than any one ego ever could encompass. Through children, through contributions to the culture, through friendships—these are ways in which human beings can achieve enduring significance for their actions which goes beyond the limit of their own skins and their own lives. It may, indeed, be the only *knowable* kind of self-perpetuation after death.

Such an adaptation would not be a stage of passive resignation or of ego-denial. On the contrary, it requires deep, active effort to make life more secure, more meaningful, or happier for the people who will go on after one dies. Since death is the one absolute certainty for all people, this kind of adaptation to its prospect may well be the most crucial achievement of the elder years. Success in this respect would probably be measurable, both in terms of the individual's inner state of contentment or stress, and in terms of his constructive or stress-inducing impact on those around him. It seems reasonable to suppose that one could find objective evidence that there are destructive effects from a narrowly ego-centered clinging to one's private, separate identity, at the expense of contributing to others' welfare or happiness. The "successful ager" at this final stage would be the person who is purposefully active as an ego-transcending perpetuation of that culture which, more than anything else, differentiates human living from animal living. Such a person would be experiencing a vital, gratifying absorption in the future. He would be doing 'all he could to make it a good world for his familial or cultural descendants. While in a sense, this might be considered a vicarious source of satisfaction, actually as long as one lives this is a direct, active, emotionally significant involvement in the daily life around one. It might almost be seen as the most complete kind of ego-realization, even while it is focused on people and on issues which go far beyond immediate self-gratification in the narrow sense.

Use of Developmental Criteria Rather Than Age Criteria for Studying Stages in Later Life

If stages in later life are to be defined, certain special problems must be faced which do not pertain, or not as much, to the study of early life. For one thing, there is far greater variability in the chronological age at which a given psychic crisis arises in later life, than is true of the crisis-points of youth. For instance, one critical test of Cathectic Vitality occurs when one's children grow up and leave home for good. In one family, this may occur in the parents' late thirties. In another family, the parents may be close to sixty before this happens. Thus, if one practical criterion of mastery of a later-life psychological task is the person's handling of certain critical experiences, then older people who are equated for the *stage* they are "working on" may differ very widely in chronological *age*.

An even more complex situation exists, moreover. In studying children who are at the pre-pubertal stage, we can almost take it for granted that they are almost all working on the same *total set* of developmental tasks. With adults, the pattern of developmental tasks can vary more greatly, from one individual to another. For example, the man whose children are grown when he is forty, may not yet have experienced the male climacteric; he may still be working "uphill" to master his vocational role; and he may just be entering a widened circle of social, political or other activities, and a widened circle of friends. This makes "the departure of children" a much different thing for this man, than for a man of sixty whose youngest child is just leaving home; who is nearing vocational retirement; whose family and friendship circle has been broken by several deaths; and whose interest or po-

tency in sexual activity may be markedly less than in his earlier years.

One practical conclusion might be drawn from such reflections, with regard to the conceptualizing of stages in later life: they may have to be much more divorced from chronological age than is true of the childhood stages. There probably are still certain broadly delimitable periods, such as "middle age" and "old age" but these are apt to be statistical artifacts, describing "the average person" of 40-60, or some such span. There are bound to be some people of 65 who act, think and feel like the "middle age" group, while other 65-year-olds act, think and feel very elderly. At least, observation indicates that this is likely to be found.

This leads to one conclusion about the design of future researches on aging: it may be that the best way to get samples which are homogeneous with respect to their "stage in life," will be to use some "stage" criterion and disregard chronological age, except as it proves to be similar for the members of a sample which is defined by a nonchronological criterion.

The Research World

Box 16-1 *Fowler's Stages of Faith*

Can spiritual belief be studied from a developmental perspective? Yes, according to James Fowler (1981, 1989). Fowler defined faith as a way of seeing or knowing the world. To find out how people arrive at this way of seeing or knowing, Fowler and his students at Harvard Divinity School interviewed more than 400 people of all ages with various ethnic, educational, and socioeconomic backgrounds and various religious or secular identifications and affiliations.

Faith, according to Fowler, can be religious or nonreligious. People may have faith in a god, in science, in humanity, or in a cause to which they attach ultimate worth and that gives meaning to their lives. Faith develops, said Fowler, as do other aspects of cognition, through interaction between the maturing person and the environment. Fowler's stages correspond roughly to those described by Piaget, Kohlberg, and Erikson. New experiences—crises, problems, or revelations—that challenge or upset a person's equilibrium may prompt a leap from one stage to the next. The ages at which these transitions occur are variable, and some people never leave a particular stage; but the first three stages normally occur during childhood and adolescence.

- *Stage 1: Primal,* or *intuitive-projective, faith* (ages 18–24 months to 7 years). The beginnings of faith, says Fowler, arise after toddlers become self-aware, begin to use language and symbolic thought, and have developed *basic trust:* the sense that their needs will be met by powerful others. As young children struggle to understand the forces that control their world, they form powerful, imaginative, often terrifying images of God, heaven, and hell, drawn from the stories adults tell. These images are often irrational; preoperational children tend to be confused about cause and effect and about the difference between reality and fantasy. Still egocentric, they may identify God's point of view with their own or their parents'. They think of God mainly in terms of obedience and punishment.
- *Stage 2: Mythic-literal faith* (ages 7 to 12 years). Children capable of concrete operations begin to develop a more coherent view of the universe. As they adopt their family's and community's beliefs and observances, they tend to take religious stories and symbols literally. They can now see God as having a perspective, beyond their own, that takes into account people's effort and intent. They believe that God is fair and that people get what they deserve.
- *Stage 3: Synthetic-conventional faith* (adolescence or beyond). Adolescents capable of abstract thought form belief systems and commitments to ideals. As they search for identity, they seek a more personal relationship with God but look to others, usually peers, for moral authority. Their faith is unquestioning and conforms to community standards. This stage is typical of followers of organized

religion; about 50 percent of adults may never move beyond it to Fowler's more advanced stages: critically examined faith and, finally, universalized faith.

- *Stage 4: Individuative-reflective faith* (early to middle 20s or beyond). Adults who reach this stage examine their faith critically and think out their own beliefs, independent of external authority and group norms.
- *Stage 5: Conjunctive faith* (midlife or beyond). Middle-aged people may become more aware of the limits of reason. They recognize life's paradoxes and contradictions, and they often struggle with conflicts between fulfilling their own needs and sacrificing for others. As they begin to anticipate death, they may achieve a deeper understanding and acceptance through faith.
- *Stage 6: Universalizing faith* (late life). In this rare category Fowler placed such moral and spiritual leaders as Mahatma Gandhi, Martin Luther King Jr., and Mother Teresa, whose vision or commitment profoundly inspires others. Because they threaten the established order, they may become martyrs; and though they love life, they do not cling to it. This stage parallels Kohlberg's proposed seventh stage of moral development.

As one of the first researchers to study faith systematically, Fowler has had great impact but has been criticized on several counts (Koenig, 1994). Critics say Fowler's concept of faith is at odds with conventional definitions. They challenge his emphasis on cognitive knowledge and claim that he underestimates the maturity of a simple, solid, unquestioning faith. Critics also question whether faith develops in universal stages or in those Fowler identified. Fowler's sample was not randomly selected; it consisted of paid participants who lived in or near North American cities with major colleges or universities. Thus the findings may be more representative of people with above-average intelligence and education, and they are not representative of non-Western cultures.

Some investigators have looked more narrowly at children's understanding of prayer, one aspect of religious activity, and have come up with stages somewhat different from Fowler's. One early study using Piaget-style questioning (Goldman, 1964) noted a progression from a magical stage before age 9, in which children believe that prayers come true as if by magic, toward rational and, finally, faith-based stages.

What's your view ?

- From your experience and observation, can faith be nonreligious?
- Can you recall having gone through any of Fowler's stages of faith? At which stage would you say you are now?

Current Perspectives in Middle Adulthood

Joseph Campbell, a twentieth-century sage, said that the privilege of a lifetime is being who you are. This ego-confidence often arrives during middle and late adulthood, even as physical confidence declines. There is a gradual slowing of the rate of mitosis of cells of all the organ systems with age. This gradual slowing of mitosis translates into a slowed rate of repair of cells of all organs. By the 40s, signs of aging can be seen in skin, skeleton, vision, hearing, smell, taste, balance, coordination, heart, blood vessels, lungs, liver, kidneys, digestive tract, immune response, endocrine functioning, and ability to reproduce. To some extent, moderate use of any body part (as opposed to disuse or misuse) helps retain its strength, stamina, and repairability. However, by middle and late adulthood persons become increasingly aware of the effects of aging organ systems on their total physical fitness. A loss of height occurs as spinal disks and connective tissues diminish and settle. Demineralization, especially loss of calcium, causes weakening of bones. Muscles atrophy, and the slowing of cardiovascular and respiratory responses creates a loss of stamina for exercise. All of this may seem cruel, but it occurs very gradually and need not adversely affect a person's enjoyment of life.

Healthful aging, at least in part, seems to be genetically pre-programmed. The females of many species, including humans, outlive the males. The sex hormones of females may protect them from some early aging effects. Males, in particular, experience earlier declines in their cardiovascular system. Diet and exercise can ward off many of the deleterious effects of aging. A reduction in saturated fat (low density lipid) intake coupled with regular aerobic exercise contributes to less bone demineralization, less plaque in the arteries, stronger muscles (including heart and lung muscles), and a general increase in stamina and vitality. An adequate intake of complex carbohydrates, fibrous foods, fresh fruits, fresh vegetables, unsaturated fats (high density lipids), and water also enhances good health.

Cognitive abilities do not appreciably decline with age in healthy adults. Research suggests that the speed with which the brain carries out problems involving abstract (fluid) reasoning may slow but not cease. Complex problems may simply require more time to solve with age. On the other hand, research suggests that the memory banks of older people may have more crystallized (accumulated and stored) knowledge and more insight. Creativity also frequently spurts after age 50. One's ken (range of knowledge) and practical skills (common sense) grow with age and experience. Older human beings also become expert at the cognitive tasks they frequently do. Many cultures celebrate these abilities as the "wisdom of age."

© Getty Images/Digital Vision

"Fifty Reasons to Love Being 50+" is a collection of anecdotes from older adults (including B. B. King, Judge Judy, and Martina Navratilova) explaining the joys of seniority. Old age for these respondents represents wisdom, veneration, and autonomy, coupled with new creative outlets and the love of friends and family.

"Are You Ready for Act II?," by Paula Ketter, discusses steps which adults can take before they make a decision about retirement. Planning ahead helps people make more realistic choices about pursuing work they enjoy and in which they find more pleasure. Recommendations include networking, volunteering, and phasing out of one's active working occupation.

50 Reasons to Love Being 50+

1 Because you can spoil the grandkids with sweets

It's all about the shamelessness of lots of butter and sugar and eggs. It's about quantity and variety and having things coming warm from the oven when my kids' kids tumble through my kitchen door. It's about gingersnaps and chocolate chips and short-bread. It's about my grandson Ralphie saying, "I want go Nana cookie house."

Twenty-four years ago my first grandchild spackled his mouth with my corn muffins—and two years later, his little brother, when I was showing him a single apple on a tree, held out both hands and said gleefully, "Whole bunch!" I have 12 grandchildren now. They don't all come at the same time, although the two sets of twins born three years ago often show up on the same weekend. Good thing I love to bake.

Living alone, I don't dare bake without kids around. I would never get the cookies into a tin, nor would anything delicious wind up carefully wrapped in the freezer. I'd eat it all. So when the kids come, it is reason for celebration. It's about eating more than is good for you, once in a while.

I was allowed three desserts in a row at my grandmother's house. I like tradition, and I'm passing it on.

ABIGAIL THOMAS writes in *Woodstock,* New York.

2 Gray stripes
(Anthony Bourdain, Edward James Olmos, Jay Leno)

3 Wavy gray
(Emmylou Harris, Linda Evans, Cloris Leachman)

4 Gray beards
(Kofi Annan, Willie Nelson, Sean Connery)

5 Gray bangs
(Olympia Dukakis, Paula Deen, Ruby Dee)

6 Solid gray
(Richard Gere, James Earl Jones, Ted Danson)

7 Faux gray
(Santa Claus, Gandalf, Statler and Waldorf)

8 Because sex gets better with age

Too much of a good thing, Mae West told us, can be wonderful, even at this age. Our hormones aren't as abundant as they used to be, but with a little help from our friends—Viagra, Estrace cream, Astroglide—we can still be as bad as we wanna be. When the spirit is willing but the body isn't, we improvise. We're self-confident enough to say what we want, content enough to swap calisthenics for intimacy. More tenderness and less testosterone can be very sexy indeed.

A female friend of mine says her husband used to want sex so often, she felt "dispensable." These days it feels more like a choice. It's different for men, too. "I'm more concerned with making the other person happy," says a male friend. His wife is happy, too: "Who knew we'd be having so much fun?"

ELIZABETH BENEDICT is a novelist who writes frequently about sex (www.elizabethbenedict.com).

9 Because you're more compassionate

You've always been the rightest person in the room—so why did your boss just fire you? You were certain your parents made terrible mistakes raising you—now your own kids say you made the same errors (and they're forwarding their therapy bills to you). You've led a charmed life—but suddenly you know what it's like to live with depression . . . or cancer . . . or losing a spouse . . . or a sudden turn in fortune that's left you wondering how to pay the bills.

By the time we pass the half-century mark, we've all withstood our share of slights, indignities, or outright suffering. Watched our self-image go up in flames. Played a starring role in our own TV version of *When Bad Things Happen to Good People.*

And maybe it's lucky. Lucky because we've seen enough, felt enough, been self-aware enough to learn from our experiences. What we've learned is that all of us are inherently flawed and very, very vulnerable; that this, in part, is what it means to be human; and that—most important—we really are all in this together. It's the reason we treat our fellow humans with a heavy dose of compassion and respect. Okay, so it's taken a handful of decades and some life upheavals to figure this all out. That still puts us in the catbird seat, compared with people who have never learned it at all.

NANCY WARTIK is a writer based in New York City.

10 Because men can use "midlife crisis" as an excuse for any embarrassing, highly questionable activity

Including body piercings, bad toupees, love-handle surgery, leather pants (or any wardrobe addition that makes you look like David Hasselhoff), and the purchase of a sports car more expensive than your first house.

11 Because you have the guts to change careers

I look up from a phonics lesson to hear screaming in my classroom. Emmanuel, a sad-eyed first grader who joined our class three days earlier, is hurling books, punching any kids who come near. At least ten children are sobbing and hurt. I call the main office: "I need help in 221—*now!*" Emmanuel hits more children in the seconds I'm on the phone. Another teacher runs into the room and ushers him out. I am the lone adult with 24 traumatized children. Now I do the only thing I can think of to calm everyone down: we sing the class favorite, "If I Had a Hammer."

I had brought in some CDs a few weeks earlier, hoping that deciphering song lyrics would improve my students' ability to listen. After a 20-year career as a magazine editor, I'm teaching at-risk first graders in one of the country's poorest neighborhoods. A large percentage of students at this South Bronx school are borderline autistic, have ADD, or suffer from an array of developmental disorders. Some, like Emmanuel, are shuffled from one foster home to another. Many others have parents who are absent, jailed, unemployed, addicted to drugs, or abusive.

Emmanuel returns after a few days' suspension and mumbles "Sorry" after a brief discussion of the earlier events. Juan, a helpful child who loves Spider-Man and sharks, has a suggestion, "Why don't we make Emmanuel the Student of the Day so we can get to know him better?"

I marvel at Juan's maturity. Maybe his live-in-the-moment attitude, however naive, is the best way to cope. I realize how much I can learn from these kids about forgiveness, and the value of starting anew.

EILEEN GARRED

12 Because you get better at crossword puzzles

It's simple. We know words our kids don't. Studies show that 50-plus folks have larger vocabularies than people in their 20s or 30s do, partly because of the younger generation's more video-obsessed lives, but also because we know more obsolete terms (mimeograph, phonograph . . .). What matters is we can kick serious bahookey—an eight-letter word for *buttocks*—at crossword puzzles. Here's a test. Ask your under-30 family members to define these words: **larder, eight-track, analog, Instamatic.** When they can't answer, just smile and return to your puzzle.

13 Because you know money can buy some happiness

Our dog's name is Lucky. The twins named him. They were seven years old and weren't listening when I said naming anything Lucky is tempting fate. I was perfectly willing to go to the shelter for a cute terrier mix named Peanut, but the hypoallergenic hype on Labradoodles—they don't shed!—and the puppy pictures online won the day. The breeder got $900, and we got Lucky.

There were other costs. To fit him into our life, we bought a minivan, slightly used. Of course Lucky needed schooling—a bargain at $10 a week—and I'm sure it helped give him the discipline to chew up just one household object per day for his first two years. From an early age Lucky showed us how to get along with less.

Then there are the four vacuum cleaners, each stronger than the last. I can't fault Lucky for taking after his Labrador mother, but, yes, he does shed, prodigiously. At some point I toted up Lucky-related costs and started calling him our $30,000 dog.

One of my jobs at this magazine is encouraging AARP members to be careful with their money. Really, folks, put away whatever you can. Spend only on necessities. But what is a necessity? Last fall Lucky bolted across the street toward a friend and was hit by a speeding SUV. In 12 days we spent $20,000 to save him.

Yes, there went a semester at college, or a new car, or years off the mortgage. There went the emergency fund. But I have no regrets. We could find the money. In good conscience we couldn't not spend it. Love made that a necessity, just as love prompted family to send unsolicited checks.

And now that Lucky is back to rolling in rabbit poop and eating, let's just say, very widely, he's become my daily reminder of what we really can and can't do without.

GEORGE BLOOSTON

14 Because if Keith Richards can make it into his 60s, there's hope for all of us

1965 Knocked out by electric shock onstage after whacking microphone with guitar

1969 Wrecks his 19-foot Nazi staff car, gets it repaired, then wrecks it down embankment

1973 (Or maybe it was '74 . . .) Falls asleep and crashes into speaker, breaking nose

1974 Falls asleep mid-sentence during live television interview

1980 Declares in interview, "I've been drunk for 27 years"

1981 Doesn't recognize title of new Stones album: "What's this Tattoo You?"

1998 While reaching for book in home library, gets pummeled by avalanche of texts. Suffers three broken ribs and punctured lung

2006 Falls out of coconut tree in Fiji

2007 Claims he snorted Dad's ashes (later denies snorting Dad's ashes)

2008 Gives key to his longevity: "I'm doomed to live"
—Alex Kizer

Because You're Free to Do What You Want!

When we asked readers what they like best about being 50-plus, one answer popped up more than others: freedom.

15 "I do things simply because I want. I can go to a movie or a restaurant alone and not worry whether someone thinks I'm a loser."

GAIL PAUL, Los Angeles, California

16 "No one is shocked if I decide the refrigerator looks nice in the living room."

KAREN EDGAR, Olive Branch, Mississippi

17 "I don't give a flip what other people think. I sing at the top of my lungs in the car with the windows down, even at traffic lights."

BARBARA KEETON, Taylors, South Carolina

18 Because our music rocks!

> *AARP The Magazine's* music critic, Richard Gehr, picks five songs music lovers will still be listening to in 100 years.
>
> Angel-voiced Carl Wilson seeks romantic guidance from above in this gorgeous track from brother Brian's 1966 pop masterpiece, *Pet Sounds*. This one will still be on iPods (or implants) in 2108.
>
> The Queen of Soul unforgettably blends stirring gospel and soaring R&B in her first hit single, written by Ronnie Shannon. She'd soon have bigger hits, but this one gives you chills.
>
> Among the world's most memorable riffs—"Sunshine of Your Love," "Smoke on the Water"—this could be the catchiest, courtesy of the instrumental group that launched a thousand Stax R&B hits.
>
> *Motherhood, freight trains, prison, and church.* Merle Haggard's autobiographical hit sums up the domestic consolations and outlaw impulses of great American country music. It's an underrated classic.
>
> A cool psychedelic breeze blows through John Lennon's nostalgic memories of his Liverpool childhood. The Beatles rarely sounded more revolutionary than on this dreamy slice of genius.
>
> . . . So tell us your picks for the best songs ever. Go to www.aarpmagazine.org/people.

19 Because you've been embarrassed so much, you're all out of chagrin

When I was in second grade I wet my pants.

It was at a rehearsal of the school play, just before I spoke my lines—well, line. But an important line. For, in our version of *Little Red Riding Hood*, the Big Bad Wolf (yours truly) was transformed from predator ("*Grrr*") to protector ("Leave her alone! *Grrr*").

I didn't grasp that symbolism. I just knew the other parts had gone to sixth graders and that I was one of the few Negro children in the school. Motivated by pride, I spent hours practicing my snarling. But the script called for the Big Bad Wolf to appear in nearly every scene, and as rehearsals grew longer, eventually, almost inevitably, I experienced . . . a release of dramatic tension.

In the boys' room, waiting for my mother to fetch fresh pants, I *grr*ed at my own stupidity. Big Bad Wolf? Big, bad disgrace. I cringed recalling how, before exiting, dripping, stage left, I'd actually delivered my line. But the next day the director said that showed "stage presence" and told me not to worry; this was not the most embarrassing thing I'd ever do.

Too right. There was that solo I began as a boy soprano and ended sounding like a bullfrog. There was that jump shot at the buzzer that swished through the wrong net. And after I left home in rural Pennsylvania for college, there were all those city customs I never got right.

I practiced public obtuseness, ignoring astonished looks when my savoir fell behind my faire. But privately I was haunted by echoes of my inanities ("A friend of Bill who?" "Aren't you going to cook that?")

As the years passed, I learned to check my facts, and also my fly—better to be caught at that than with my zipper down. But recently, listening to an old friend introduce me with an exaggerated account of one of my Greatest Misses, it struck me, now that I'm fiftysomething, that the most embarrassing thing I'd ever do was probably something I'd already done.

So I checked my fly and I stepped onstage in a state of grace beyond disgrace, beyond chagrin.

DAVID BRADLEY, author of *The Chaneysville Incident,* teaches creative writing at the University of Oregon.

20 Because you *experienced* the Beatles

I was 13 years old when my best friend, Margo, won tickets to see the Beatles in San Francisco in '65. We'd seen girls scream for the Fab Four on television and vowed we would never act so silly. But when the Beatles arrived onstage, we were swept away by the hysteria. We screamed, we jumped, we cried, we shook—we even tried climbing the chainlink fence that surrounded the stage. We were gasping for breath the entire show, slightly lightheaded, tears streaming down our faces. I've been to other concerts, but none were ever like this.

LIBBY GUTHRIE is an AARP member in Redwood Valley, California.

21 Because we know how to fight—literally

In March 2008, Saoul Mamby, age 60, became the oldest boxer to compete in a pro bout, going ten rounds with 32-year-old fighter Anthony Osborne. Okay, Mamby didn't win. So what. The guy is doing what he loves: punching other guys in the face until they drool. Since turning pro in 1969, the Bronx-born fighter has held the World Boxing Council (WBC) junior-welterweight title, amassed 56 wins (plus 11 grandchildren), and fought on the same card as Muhammad Ali. Now he's training in hopes of another bout. "To be successful at boxing—at anything—it has to become a part of you," says Mamby. "You get out of it what you put in—and I put in 100 percent."

NICK KOLAKOWSKI

22 Because love grows deeper over time

In the early days it was all about him. His favorite foods, favorite color, favorite flavor of ice cream, and whether he liked my hair up or down. I loved to make him laugh, and worked hard not to cry in front of him. I cleaned my house before he came over, always wore mascara, always had champagne in the fridge.

Marriage changes that, of course. Artifice goes, as it should. Love deepens, maybe even relaxes a little. And anyway, who has time to set a scene or arrange the canapés when somebody has to be picked up at soccer practice, or the boss has a fit, or the creek rises (literally) into the cellar an hour before the in-laws are to arrive for Easter brunch? When the dog is throwing up, or your mother breaks her hip, who among us can be bothered to murmur, "Darling, I've always loved that color of blue on you."

We've seen each other at our worst, and that's not an exaggeration. Physically ill, emotionally grief-stunned, job-panicked, or angry enough to throw crockery at the wall (and then do it again). Red-faced, blotchy, hoarse from yelling. Our parents grow old, and ill, or nutty; our children make mistakes that drop us to our knees. Through it all, how on earth can he love me, given what a flawed, messy, moody person I am? The artifice is long gone; he sees me. As my oldest friend said when we were girls, "If Prince Charming loves me, he's probably not really Prince Charming."

Well, as it turns out, maybe he is. Okay, so we won't make love on the kitchen table again (there's not enough ibuprofen and, besides, that's why God invented pillow-top mattresses). But lately, when he puts his arm around me in the movie line, or takes my hand as we cross the street, my heart jumps as it did in the beginning. I'm happy to see him in the morning and blessed to sleep beside him at night; there are even days, in a certain light, that he makes me feel all swoony. He *does* see me, which is why he's still here. And I see him, far more clearly than I did—burnished, like my grandmother's sterling silver, and as grounded as the white oak in our front yard. I couldn't have known that's how it would be, back when I was putting on a show.

LARKIN WARREN lives in Connecticut. She is working on her first novel.

23 Because B. B. King proves the pursuit of perfection never ends

I play "The Thrill Is Gone" every night. But I never do exactly what I did last night or the night before. I tell my band to play it as they feel it each night. I like that. It keeps it fresh.

I have a motto: Always do your best. When I was in grade school there was a poem a teacher used to tell us. It went something like "Be the labor great or small, do it well or not at all." I do the best I can each night. Even though a lot of nights my best is nothing as good as I'd like it to be.

Every day I learn something. I have a computer that's my professor. If I don't learn something every day, it's a day lost.

As told to Richard Gehr. B.B. King's new album is *One Kind Favor.*

Because We Can Live Alone and Not Be Lonely

When I used to get home from work, I'd pull up in the driveway and the front door would fly open and out would shoot my three kids, two dogs, and my husband, Vince. They'd all start talking at once as the dogs barked their welcome. "Just let me get in the house," I'd plead. "Then you can tell me what's going on." Flash forward 25 years. Now I come home to an almost empty house. I say almost because my two cats—a fat tabby named Penny Lane and spunky Jenny Jones—are waiting at the front door. No, it's not the same. But those of us who live alone have come to appreciate some simple truths:

24 You can finally hear yourself think

I remember when I'd long for a quiet house. Even after my divorce, there was always someone around. And there was noise. It was the sound-track of my life. Then one day it stopped and my emptying nest was completely empty. And the quiet was almost deafening. It took a long while before I valued hearing my own thoughts. But I never really got used to the silence. To this day I switch on the stereo when I walk in the house.

25 Good neighbors are a godsend

I never realized how true that was until I had to move cross-country for my work. I knew no one. I bought a great house, but even more important, I got a great bunch of neighbors. Over the years they have helped me when I was sick, watched my house, and invited me to their parties. Because of them, I'm never really alone.

26 Single friends are protective friends

I have many friends. But my closest ones are women like me, who live alone. We have an almost natural tendency to look out for one another. Shortly after I moved, a single neighbor came over with a bottle of wine and a welcome. She introduced me to her women friends. We laugh, we cry, we share our deepest secrets. But most important, we understand one another.

27 You cherish new opportunities

I savor being on my own, doing what I want, when I want. But I wouldn't enjoy this freedom half as much if I hadn't experienced a noisy home full of loved ones. Yes, I'm used to living alone, but my door is always open to future possibilities.

KAREN REYES

28 Because . . . Paul Newman

Back in 1961, I was dumb enough to think *The Hustler* was a Jackie Gleason movie. But then came this upstart pool shark with cobalt-blue eyes (yes, *The Hustler* was in black and white, but somehow the blue still showed). He got into The Great One's face and bragged, "I'm the best you ever seen," and there was no arguing the point.

By the time he turned 50 in 1975, Paul Newman could have coasted. But the actor rewrote his career with one breakaway role after another: there he is barreling across the ice in *Slap*

Shot (1977). Then he solemnly offers a summation to the jury in *The Verdict* (1982). Later there's his Oscar-winning return to the role of *The Hustler*'s Fast Eddie Felson in *The Color of Money* (1986).

A new generation knows Newman more as a racecar driver, or as the voice of an old sedan in the animated *Cars,* or as the face on McDonald's salad dressing packets, than for his turn as Butch Cassidy. But for those who grew up with Paul Newman, he's more than a brand, a voice, or a set of blazing peepers. He's proof you can keep chasing that checkered flag even after you've entered the winner's circle.

Read Bill Newcott's Movies for Grownups® reviews at www.aarpmagazine.org.

29 Because your spiritual side grows stronger

The older I get, the more I realize I don't know everything. And that makes me spirituality sensitive to others. I'm less dogmatic, more open to other people's experience of the divine. As we age, we experience things that aren't easily explained—tragedies, failing health—and we become more reflective. There is so much more to learn about the mystery that is the divine, and I've got this thimbleful of knowledge, and I want more. Earlier, a thimbleful was all I could handle. Not anymore. Our spiritual life has a chance to be richer now, with so many more life experiences to reflect upon.

As told to Lynne Meredith Schreiber. Brent Bill is a Quaker minister in Mooresville, Indiana, and the author of *Sacred Compass: The Way of Spiritual Discernment* (Paraclete Press, 2008).

Because We Are Powerful

30
41 percent of American adults are over 50, the highest percentage in U.S. history.

31
80 percent of Congress is over 50.

32
Half of the Americans who voted in the 2006 elections were 50+.

33
People over 55 own 77 percent of all financial assets in the United States.

34
50+ adults account for 45 percent of U.S. consumer spending, or $2.1 trillion per year.

35
By 2011 the American 50+ population will surpass the 100 million mark.

36 Because we're living longer than ever before

Let's get the distressing stats out of the way first: Citizens in 41 countries have longer average life spans than we Americans

do. In some parts of the United States—portions of the Deep South, the Midwest—life expectancy has actually declined (the big reasons are smoking, obesity, and high blood pressure). The upbeat stats? If you are 50 today, on average you'll live to be 80.5. If you're 65, you'll live to 83.4. In fact, if you go back to our one-celled ancestors, we're doing way better than humans at any point in history.

Average Years of Life for . . .
Americans today: 78
Americans in 1900: 47.3
Europeans in the Middle Ages: 31.3
Ancient Greeks: 28
Cro-Magnons: 25
Amoebas: 2 to 3 days, tops

37 "When you get older, hopefully you've developed the smarts to know that if you wake up in the morning and you're vertical and your kids are healthy, that's 90 percent of being happy. That's it!"

JUDGE JUDY

38 Because you're secure enough to take as much advice as you dish out

If it's true we are judged by the company we keep, the evidence in my favor is compelling: a bevy of strong, self-sufficient, passionate young women, 30—and more—years younger than I am. Being this far past 50 frees me to wallow in their youthful exuberance without competition or regret. I am both their patient sage and their eager student.

Each appeared at different points in my life and from various spots on the globe, and though we are sometimes separated by months, years, even continents, our links are so elastic that we never lose touch. They are dream catchers, all: the brilliant, book-loving hell-raiser, who at 16 was as skilled with her fists as she was with a pen when we met 18 years ago; the enchanting poet/actress; the fierce lawyer; the self-assured entrepreneur.

Early on, each of them evoked an intense whisper in me—"I know her"—and I recognized they were parts of that girl I used to be. We are "like" attracting "like"—as intensely loyal as we are truthful. So, when I confess to feeling fat, the actress dares me to shut up and flaunt it. In the middle of my tiresome ranting, the businesswoman shames me—lovingly—into clearing my space of ancient hurts and weary narratives. If I am weak, the lawyer argues me back to warrior-woman status. When I get stuck, the hell-raiser—now the college student/wife/mother—leads me out.

I admire all the things they are that I will never be, but because I'm older, my instructions to them rarely change: Trust your gut. Get angry. If it scares you, do it. Don't go with the flow unless you started it. Eat dessert first.

My young friends revel in my steady assurances, even as they rescue me from the tedium of old certainties and instruct me in the protocol of cool. Watching them—and listening—is pure joy and wonder.

BERNESTINE SINGLEY (www.BernestineSingley.com) is a writer and lawyer based in Dallas.

39 Because you've seen the world change in inconceivable ways

At 57 years of age, I am nervous about the future—the economy, the environment, to say nothing of those deepening crow's-feet. But the long view sustains me. My grandfather was born in the 1880s to former slaves. I hung on to the stories he told—about a life before cars, plastics, the Wright brothers, the Panama Canal, even before Jim Crow laws.

My father was born in 1915. Despite five strokes, he is still vibrant and funny. He was a technical editor back in the days of computer mainframes, back when FORTRAN and COBOL were the lingua franca of techno-nerds. He regales my son with tales of automobiles that had to be cranked. He recalls lynchings when he was growing up. The integration of the Army. The battle of Anzio. The etymology of the word *smog*.

My father still types letters on an old sticky-keyed Smith Corona. As I craft my own words on a brand-new MacBook Air, I am grateful for the strength that intergenerational engagement brings. I am a black female law professor, something my grandfather could never have imagined. And I am about to e-mail these words through an invisible cushion of whooshing cyberspace, something my father worked to create but still can't entirely grasp.

Across the table my son is writing a school paper about the oil crisis and looks up with a glint of panic. "How," he asks me, "will humanity continue?"

I am not so fearful. Like my son, I worry about the crossroads at which we stand. But I am old enough to appreciate how quickly the course of events can change—for the worse, to be sure, but also for the better, if only the will is there. If my father can remember the very first U.S. smog alert, then my son might live to see the haze subside and the heavens reemerge. The human spirit is amazingly, unexpectedly resilient. Anything can happen.

PATRICIA WILLIAMS is the James L. Dohr Professor of Law at Columbia University and a columnist for *The Nation*.

40 Because you actually enjoy going to high-school reunions

For the first few decades, high-school reunions are like updated versions of an old cartoon show: the hairstyles and voices are a little different, but, really, Archie and Jughead haven't changed that much. Reunions after age 50 are more like *Return to Mayberry*, where Opie's gone bald and Aunt Bee is dead. This is not a bad thing, because while everyone else looks like a jack-o'-lantern left on the porch too long, you haven't changed a bit. You know this is true, because everybody tells you so. (You tell everybody the same thing, but that's just because you're so nice.) And yet these later reunions are somehow more pleasant than those in years past. The smoldering one-up-manship has

pretty much quenched itself; you've filed away a lot of the old jealousies and insecurities that dogged your younger years. At last you're free to enjoy those fleeting connections with your youth. And if you aren't, that old classmate who's now a psychiatrist will gladly give you his card.

BILL NEWCOTT

Because Older Brains Have New Strengths

41 You're a better judge of character

The proof: In tests at North Carolina State University, older folks outperformed younger participants in determining whether people were honest and intelligent.

42 Your brain is more efficient

The proof: Duke University researchers discovered that older individuals use the brain's right and left hemispheres at the same time (typically the brain uses the left for some tasks, and the right for others). "In effect, the mature brain creates a synergy that helps it think outside the box," says Gene Cohen, MD, PhD, author of *The Mature Mind* (Basic Books, 2005).

43 You're less neurotic than you used to be

The proof: Australian scientists found that neuroticism was less prevalent in subjects ages 50 to 79. Brain scans also revealed a more controlled response to fear. The experts' theory: A growing awareness of mortality and a desire for meaning mellows the mind.

MELISSA GOTTHARDT

44 Because you don't tolerate bad service

For years I went to a hairstylist whose end result never quite worked. A nice person, and so proud of owning her own salon—it was fun to spend time with her every couple of months. The friendship was swell—we went through joy, grief, and menopause together—but the hairdo? Not so much. Yet I couldn't leave her; I didn't want her to feel bad. Then I saw the mother-of-the-groom pictures from my son's wedding. Bad hair. Very bad hair. Anyone with a heart would've handed me a baseball cap.

And so, with shaking hands and a sinking stomach, I took my leave. She cried, I cried, and I soon found someone else, who is better than good; sometimes she's great. Yay me. But, wow, how many hundreds of dollars did I spend over the years for bad hair? What is it that holds us to doctors, mechanics, or electricians who don't or won't do what we need? Why do we cling to friendships that take more than they give, or relationships that drag on our hearts like boat anchors? Is it my mother's fault, for tamping down my big teenage mouth with "Be polite; don't make a scene"? Is it my father's, for instructing me to appreciate other people's efforts? "She's doing the best she can," he said about the piano teacher whose breath melted paint. So I dutifully played my scales, never told a waitress that I'd wanted milk, not orange juice, and grew up to gnash my teeth in my sleep.

Finally, the freedom of a fully flowered adulthood dropped the hammer on this Go Along to Get Along baloney. Bad hairstylist? Gone. The plumber who didn't fix the mess under the kitchen sink and charged me anyway? Gone. The old friend who in a three-week period canceled a lunch date four times, then scolded me for arriving ten minutes late? Well, not gone, exactly, but definitely on my pay-no-mind list. The car dealer who tried to muscle me 20 minutes into our first conversation? Summarily exchanged for the nice, slow-moving guy at the dealership down the road. From him, we'll buy two.

No matter how many birthdays we get, the salient lesson remains the same: Life is short. There's never enough time for the people and activities we love, so why allot time (or sleepless nights, or money) to those we don't? Being nice doesn't equal suffering fools; being compassionate does not translate as "take a hosing, write the check, and feel like a sucker." I don't want to waste my time anymore; I don't want to waste yours. Can we make a deal that will make us both happy? Otherwise (and I say this with deep respect for how good you are, how hard you work, and how long we've known each other), you're fired.

LARKIN WARREN

45 Because you realize that trauma can lead to enlightenment

When I used to tell friends, half jokingly, that a potentially fatal disease had actually saved my life, they rarely understood what I meant. I wasn't claiming I was glad to have it. I wasn't pretending to be overjoyed by the prospect of an early departure. I was simply confessing an odd bit of truth. Without the threat of mortal loss, I would never have had the fuel to find my way through terrible dread to something stronger than my fear.

Hardship can render us bitter, selfish, defensive, and miserable. It can also be used as the artery of interconnection, a bridge to other people in pain, as blood in the muscles that push us forward. Crisis takes us to the brink of our limits and forces us to keep moving. When people in extremis call it a blessing, this is the paradox they are describing. It's why men sometimes blossom in wartime and why women are changed by childbirth—they come alive as never before on that knife-blade danger and pain. There's vitality in facing life's extremes, including our own extinction.

Adapted from Mark Matousek's new book, *When You're Falling, Dive: Lessons in the Art of Living* (Bloomsbury USA).

46 Because you grew up in an age before video games

When we were kids, we played outside. Our bodies were hard-breathing little rainbows of energy and earth—red cheeks from running, brown hands from mud, green-grass streaks on our pants. We dreamed of grandiose forts that never got built, had sword fights with sticks while riding our bikes (okay, that was more of a boy thing). But we lived, baby. We lived! Unlike so many kids today, whose every micromanaged, remote-control moment is seemingly spent indoors. Oh, how the play times have changed:

Then	Now
Eating wild berries in the woods	Eating Lunchables on a play date
Climbing trees	Allergy tests
Walking with pals along train tracks	Walking with parents on a leash
Stickball	Xbox
"Be home by dark"	"Answer your cell phone when I call"
Summer camp	Fat camp
Doing cannonballs off the high dive	Wearing floaties in the shallow end
Skinned knees	Carpal tunnel
Jumping on a trampoline	What's a trampoline?

47 Because we can be as fit now as we were at 20 (Just ask Martina)

Tennis legend Martina Navratilova is 52, and she has a message: age is no excuse for being flabby. Too often, she says, 50-plus folks are inactive for so long, they think: Why bother? But Martina isn't buying it. "Age is not part of the equation," she says. "Exercise at your own level. Take a walk. Anything. Once I saw a woman with one leg running on crutches. Another time I saw a man with no legs in a wheelchair playing hockey. So, what is your excuse? A headache? You're too tired? Look in the mirror."

Yeah, yeah—like the eternally buff Martina has any idea what it's like to fight fat. Turns out she does. When she first came to the United States in 1973, she began a love affair with pancakes and eggs, and her rock-hard tennis bod became . . . pudgy. In 1981, despite Martina's having dropped down to a svelte 145 pounds, a friend told her she wasn't in great shape and was wasting her talent.

Thus was born a lifelong commitment to fitness. But you don't have to be as fanatical as Martina. "Start with a ten-minute walk," she says. "Then do more. Go gradually, not too intense. You'll feel better each day. It doesn't have to be painful."

PAT JORDAN

48 "Happiness no longer seems like an unobtainable goal—it can reside in a superb cup of coffee."

MAGGIE FRIEDE, Quincy, Massachusetts

49 "Before I turned 50, I was always pushing to do more. Now I'm able to step back mentally and just look around. Was all this beauty here all along?"

JAN LUFF, Milford, Delaware

50 Because you know who your friends are

It's no mystery at this point. Your old friends are the ones who don't desert you, who share a beer or a tear when life is dark, who make you laugh. (Your new friends do the same; they just haven't been on the job as long.) Harvard professor Daniel Gilbert, PhD, who studies happiness, says we tend to tighten our circle of friends as we age—to focus on those who make us happy now. Yet the squabbling Simon and Garfunkel model of friendship—my "partner in arguments," Simon once called his musical other half—should not be tossed aside like Oscar flinging dirty socks at an exasperated Felix. We need the people who fight with us but will also fight for us. Friendship is like shares in a growing company: the investment isn't easy, but the dividends enrich our lives.

KEN BUDD

Are You Ready for Act II?

Learning professionals nearing retirement age need to start thinking about what they want to do in the next phase of their lives.

PAULA KETTER

The definition of retirement is outdated. The word retirement used to mean "withdrawal from one's occupation or from active working life," but it now has a multitude of meanings, including leaving your current job for entrepreneurship, entering a new phase of life and work, or finding meaning as a volunteer or part-time worker.

Regardless of how you define this term or at what age you begin this new career, you need to ensure that you are ready to leave your current job and start afresh.

"The biggest piece of advice I can give to anyone thinking about retiring is to plan ahead," says Kiki Weingarten, cofounder and coach of Daily Life Consulting. "The time to be laying the groundwork is while you are still working. You need to be in a place psychologically, financially, and emotionally where you can think clearly about the future and your place in it.

"The corporate setting has a tremendous amount of structure, and as much as we complain about it, that structure helps us get up in the morning and plan our day," she adds.

As a workplace learning and performance professional, your skills and competencies can take you far, long after life in your current work is complete. It won't be an end of work for you, just a career transition that could include continuing to work in a reduced role, returning to school for additional training, changing careers, becoming an entrepreneur, volunteering in your community, writing a book, or traveling.

Retirement is a time to be very honest about who you are, what you want to do, and what you do best. If you decide to become a consultant or start a small business for example, you need to ensure that you are ready to work on your own.

"Know clearly what your skills and competencies are and what you don't do well," says Judy Estrin, president of Partners in Enterprise. "Also, you need to answer these questions: Do have what it takes to be by yourself? Do you have the discipline to work by yourself? Are you easily distracted? You need to answer these questions before you decide to be a consultant."

It is critical to know what you do best because as a consultant, you are taking on a substantial risk. You will be doing everything yourself, from faxing and mailing, to doing your own IT support.

Candice Phelan, former director of learning systems at Lockheed Martin, retired recently and relocated to Florida to be near her mother. Her plan was to do some consulting work and stay abreast of what was going on in the field, but she wasn't prepared for the lack of technical support.

"I don't have an IT help desk I can call," she says. "I consider myself computer savvy, but I just didn't have the support of an IT infrastructure."

Ed Betof, former vice president of talent management and chief learning officer at BD, left the corporate world for the academic, as a senior fellow at the University of Pennsylvania. He admits that he wasn't completely prepared for his career change.

"I'm finding that even though I'm engaged in a really rich program at Penn, I'm experiencing the challenge of not having my foot on the gas pedal all the time," he explains. "This career change is also a lifestyle change. Like so many other situations, you need to have a really clear awareness of your personality style, your personal values, and what you want to do because this is a huge change. It's a life-planning situation."

Create a Strategy

Whatever you decide to pursue in this new phase of your life, you need to start planning for it now, before you leave the workplace. Knowing what you want to do is only part of the plan.

"How much time are you going to work? What are your boundaries surrounding work hours and leisure time? You need to have a plan and really stick to it," Weingarten says.

Geoff Bellman, who retired from the corporate world in the late 1970s to become a consultant and then scaled back his "second career" about a decade ago, advises people who are nearing retirement to start preparing for it four years before they leave their current jobs.

"You certainly don't want to go back to work once you've left because you haven't found any place to go or something to do," Bellman says. "If you can use the skills that you liked using in the corporate world, the transition will be a lot easier."

Before you retire, there are several things you need to do to prepare for the challenges ahead.

Decide What You Want to Do

This sounds simple, but many people walk away from their jobs without knowing what they want to do with the next 20 or 30 years of their lives. In search of the answer, ask yourself these questions:

- Do I want to do work that is fun, meaningful, or both?
- How many hours do I want to work?
- Do I want to work a few hours every day for six months and then take six months off, or full time with a few weeks for vacation?
- With what kind of organizational cultures do I want to work?
- Do I want to do volunteer work?

Write a Letter of Introduction for Yourself

Write a letter of introduction as though you are five years into the future, or write a paragraph about what you have been doing for the last five years. "This will give you an idea of where you are today," Weingarten explains. "The best time to do this is while you are still at your old job because you have a certain confidence to sell yourself that will disappear when you leave the workplace."

Start Networking Now

Put the word out to everyone you know that you are starting a new "career." Ask them to pass the information along to people they know. "Networking is so much harder when you are out on your own," says Weingarten. "While you are still working, you can pick up the phone and talk to the people you know. It's easier to get through when you have that corporate identity."

Networking can be one of the most difficult things to do, depending on your personality, your experience doing it, or your future needs. If you don't feel comfortable talking with others or selling yourself, you may want of find a coach to help you prepare for these situations.

Networking can be one of the most difficult things to do, depending on your personality, your experience doing it, or your future needs. If you don't feel comfortable talking with others or selling yourself, you may want to find a coach to help you prepare for these situations. It's critical that you create business cards, practice your pitch, and make eye contact. Don't forget to sign up for profiles on LinkedIn, MySpace, Plaxo, or other social networking forums. These are great ways to meet other people with similar interests.

Fast Facts about the New Retirement Ideal

- There were 34.9 million women aged 55 and above in the United States in 2004. Of those women, 10.7 million were in the workforce (either working or looking for work).
  Source: U.S. Department of labor

- Between 1995 and 2000, the estimated age of retirement for women was 61.4 years.
  Source: U.S. Department of labor

- Nearly four in 10 workers between the ages of 50 and 64 plan to continue to work beyond retirement age. Thirty-one percent of respondents who planned to retire at 65 would reconsider if their employers allowed them to work flexibly.
  Source: Chartered Institute of Personnel and Development survey

- Forty-two percent of men say they definitely want to work beyond 65, compared to 34 percent of women.
  Source: Chartered Institute of Personnel and Development survey

- More than 75 percent of baby boomers have no intention of seeking a traditional retirement.
  Source: The Merrill lynch New Retirement Study

- The ideal retirement for 71 percent of adults surveyed is to work in some capacity. Half of that 71 percent do not plan to ever stop working.
  Source: The Merrill lynch New Retirement Study

To expand your network of contacts, consider joining clubs or professional associations. "Sometimes a great way to get your name out there is to sit on a panel or give a workshop for free or minimal cost," Weingarten says. "Make sure you attend meetings, workshops, and conferences. That is one of the best ways to sell yourself and expand your network."

Estrin agrees, adding that joining clubs and associations can give you a sense of belonging and helps you stay active professionally. "What I discovered about three years into my new life was that I got lonely," she says. "I missed the affiliation of being corporate, but I didn't want to be affiliated, so I found a consortium of other consultants that I met with every four to six weeks just to chit chat.

"I also subscribe to association publications in my field because if I don't, the jargon gets away from me," Estrin adds.

Volunteer Opportunities

A recent Merrill Lynch study finds that boomers want to give back and prefer to pursue "retirement careers" where they can share or pass on knowledge to others through training and teaching. Volunteering ranks high on lists of things boomers want to do in retirement.

You've spent the majority of your life in a rigid corporate structure, so whatever you decide to do, do something you love—whether that's working in a new career or volunteering with a not-for-profit that shares your beliefs and values.

"Volunteering is a great way to keep your skills up if you can afford to do it financially," Estrin says. "There are plenty of places to apply your training skills. Explore the Small Business Economic Development Council in your community, or contact the chamber of commerce in your city."

Weingarten agrees, adding, "Be a mentor, or an advisor, or give talks to kids—there are hundreds of things that you can do every day. Check out message boards and blogs, or visit idealist .org for a list of not-for-profits. There are a lot of things that you can do that don't come naturally to others, so you just have to do a little research."

Planned Phase Out

Part of your work as a workplace learning and performance professional includes creating a succession plan for positions within your company. But, what happens when you decide to retire?

"I worked with the senior vice president of HR to create a current role description for my position," Betof explains. "That description emphasized the mission-critical competencies for the role."

As with any position, keeping your immediate supervisor aware of your plans can make the transition easier for you and the company.

"You can certainly help engineer a replacement using a succession plan," says Phelan. "But another is to ask, 'Is there a better way for this position to be organized?' When I made the decision to leave, I was able to make the case to move my functions to different departments instead of replacing me."

Before you walk out the door, you need to expect that you will be helping with transitioning your successor into your previous role, Betof says. "That will help minimize the risk of that successor."

Once you've told your supervisor of your plans to leave, you need to start thinking about how to transfer the knowledge you have to others in the company. "If there is a bad relationship with the company, tacit knowledge transfer may never happen," Betof explains. "The really important thing is to let the company know what your plans are as soon as possible. If there is a degree of trust between you and your immediate supervisor, it is going to make things a lot easier."

Retiring from corporate life is not as easy as setting a date or deciding on a new "career."

"Be prepared for change," Weingarten says. "In the beginning, there is a big psychological shift. Don't be blindsided."

PAULA KETTER is editor of *T+D;* pketter@astd.org.

Chapter 8
Later Adulthood

In this chapter we will examine the many issues related to Later Adulthood. Some of these topics are the same as earlier developmental periods, but some are quite unique, like a discussion of cognitive development as "wisdom". We will look again at the alternative cultural perspective on this time of life, given by the New Zealand authors we introduced in Adolescence. Much new research is currently taking place around this important time of life that is giving us new insights into what it means to "live life to the fullest".

Eighty-five-year-old Sadie Halperin engaging in her exercise routine.

adulthood raises some truly fascinating questions about life-span development, which we explore in this chapter. They include: Why do we age, and what, if anything, can we do to delay the aging process? What chance do you have of living to be 100? How does the body change in old age? How well do older adults function cognitively? What roles do work and retirement play in older adults' lives?

life span The upper boundary of life, the maximum number of years an individual can live. The maximum life span of human beings is about 120 to 125 years of age.

life expectancy The number of years that will probably be lived by the average person born in a particular year.

Longevity, Biological Aging, and Physical Development

What do we really know about longevity? What are the current biological theories about why we age? How does our brain change during this part of our life span? What happens to us physically? Does our sexuality change?

Longevity

The United States is no longer a youthful society. As more individuals are living past age 65, the proportion of individuals at different ages has become increasingly similar. Indeed, the concept of a period called "late adulthood," beginning in the sixties or seventies and lasting until death, is a recent one. Before the 20th century, most individuals died before they reached 65.

Life Span and Life Expectancy

Since the beginning of recorded history, **life span,** the maximum number of years an individual can live, has remained at approximately 120 to 125 years of age. But since 1900 improvements in medicine, nutrition, exercise, and lifestyle have increased our life expectancy an average of 31 additional years.

Recall from Chapter 1 that **life expectancy** is the number of years that the average person born in a particular year will probably live. Sixty-five-year-olds in the United States today can expect to live an average of 18 more years (20 for females, 16 for males). The average life expectancy of individuals born today in the United States is 78 years (National Center for Health Statistics, 2009).

Differences in Life Expectancy

How does the United States fare in life expectancy, compared with other countries around the world? We do considerably better than some, a little worse than some others (Powell, 2009). Japan has the highest life expectancy at birth today (82 years) (Guillot, 2009).

Today, the overall life expectancy for females is 80.7 years of age, for males 75.4 years of age (National Center for Health Statistics, 2009). Beginning in the mid-thirties, females outnumber males; this gap widens during the remainder of the adult years. By the time adults are 75 years of age, more than 61 percent of the population is female; for those 85 and over, the figure is almost 70 percent female. Why can women expect to live longer than men? Social factors such as health attitudes, habits, lifestyles, and occupation are probably important (Saint Onge, 2009). In fact, men are more likely than women to die from the leading causes of death in the United States, such as cancer of the respiratory system, evolutionary theory of aging The view that natural selection has not eliminated many harmful conditions and nonadaptive characteristics in older adults.

cellular clock theory Leonard Hayflick's theory that the maximum number of times that human cells can divide is about 75 to 80. As we age, our cells become increasingly less capable of dividing.

motor vehicle accidents, cirrhosis of the liver, emphysema, and coronary heart disease (Yoshida & others, 2006). These causes of death are associated with lifestyle. For example, the sex difference in deaths due to lung cancer and emphysema occurs because men are heavier smokers than women.

The sex difference in longevity also is influenced by biological factors (Guillot, 2009; Oksuzyan & others, 2008). In virtually all species, females outlive males. Women have more resistance to infections and degenerative diseases (Candore & others, 2006). For example, the female's estrogen production helps to protect her from arteriosclerosis (hardening of the arteries). And the additional X chromosome that women carry in comparison to men may be associated with the production of more antibodies to fight off disease.

Centenarians

In the United States, there were only 15,000 centenarians in 1980, a number that had risen to 55,000 in 2008. It is projected that this number will reach more than 800,000 by 2050. Many people expect that "the older you get, the sicker you get." However, researchers are finding that is not true for some centenarians (Kutner, 2009). A study of 93 centenarians revealed that despite some physical limitations, they had a low rate of age-associated diseases and most had good mental health (Selim & others, 2005).

What chance do you have of living to be 100? Genes play an important role in surviving to an extreme old age (Bostock, Solza, & Whalley, 2009). As we saw in Chapter 2, the search for longevity genes has recently intensified (Hinks & others, 2009). But there are also other factors at work such as family history, health (weight, diet, smoking, and exercise), education, personality, and lifestyle (Barbieri & others, 2009).

Biological Theories of Aging

Even if we stay remarkably healthy, we begin to age at some point. Four biological theories provide intriguing explanations of why we age: evolutionary, cellular clock, free-radical, and hormonal stress.

Evolutionary Theory

In the **evolutionary theory of aging**, natural selection has not eliminated many harmful conditions and nonadaptive characteristics in older adults (Austad, 2009; Kittas, 2010). Why? Because natural selection is linked to reproductive fitness, which only is present in the earlier part of adulthood. For example, consider Alzheimer disease, an irreversible brain disorder, which does not appear until the late middle adulthood or late adulthood years. In evolutionary theory, possibly if Alzheimer disease occurred earlier in development, it may have been eliminated many centuries ago.

Cellular Clock Theory

Cellular clock theory is Leonard Hayflick's (1977) theory that cells can divide a maximum of about 75 to 80 times and that, as we age, our cells become less capable of dividing. Hayflick found that cells extracted from adults in their fifties to seventies divided fewer than 75 to 80 times. Based on the ways cells divide, Hayflick places the upper limit of the human life-span potential at about 120 to 125 years of age.

In the last decade, scientists have tried to fill in a gap in cellular clock theory (Sahin & Daphino, 2010; Zou & others, 2009). Hayflick did not know why cells die. The answer may lie at the tips of chromosomes, at *telomeres,* which are DNA sequences that cap chromosomes (Davoli, Denchi, & de Lange, 2010; Osterhage & Friedman, 2009). Each time a cell divides, the telomeres become shorter and shorter (see Figure 15.1). After about 70 or 80 replications, the telomeres are dramatically reduced, and the cell no longer can reproduce. A recent study revealed that healthy centenarians had longer telomeres than unhealthy centenarians (Terry & others, 2008).

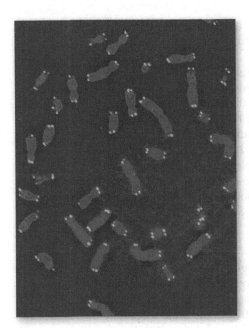

Figure 15.1 Telomeres and Aging
The photograph shows actual telomeres lighting up the tips of chromosomes. Each time a cell divides, the telomeres become shorter and shorter, until eventually they can no longer reproduce.

Injecting the enzyme *telomerase* into human cells grown in the laboratory can substantially extend the life of the cells beyond the approximately 70 to 80 normal cell divisions (Aubert & Lansdorp, 2008). However, telomerase is present in approximately 85 percent of cancerous cells and thus may not produce healthy life extension of cells (Fakhoury, Nimmo, & Autexier, 2007). To capitalize on the high presence of telomerase in cancerous cells, researchers currently are investigating gene therapies that inhibit telomerase and lead to the death of cancerous cells while keeping healthy cells alive (Effros, 2009).

Free-Radical Theory

A third theory of aging is **free-radical theory**, which states that people age because when cells metabolize energy, the by-products include unstable oxygen molecules known as *free radicals*. The free radicals ricochet around the cells, damaging DNA and other cellular structures (Afanas'ev, 2009). The damage can lead to a range of disorders, including cancer and arthritis (Farooqui & Farooqui, 2009).

free-radical theory A theory of aging that states that people age because inside their cells normal metabolism produces unstable oxygen molecules known as free radicals. These molecules ricochet around inside cells, damaging DNA and other cellular structures.

hormonal stress theory The theory that aging in the body's hormonal system can lower resilience to stress and increase the likelihood of disease.

Hormonal Stress Theory

Cellular clock and free radical theories attempt to explain aging at the cellular level. In contrast, **hormonal stress theory** argues that aging in the body's hormonal system can lower resistance to stress and increase the likelihood of disease. Normally, when people experience stressors, the body responds by releasing certain hormones. As people age, the hormones stimulated by stress remain at elevated levels longer than when people were younger (Simm & others, 2008). These prolonged, elevated levels of stress-related hormones are associated with increased risks for many diseases, including cardiovascular disease, cancer, diabetes, and hypertension (Epel, 2009; Wolkowitz & others, 2010).

Recently, a variation of hormonal stress theory has emphasized the contribution of a decline in immune system functioning with aging (Walston & others, 2009). Aging contributes to immune system deficits that give rise to infectious diseases in older adults (Bauer, Jeckel, & Luz, 2009). The extended duration of stress and diminished restorative processes in older adults may accelerate the effects of aging on immunity.

Which of these biological theories best explains aging? That question has not yet been answered. It might turn out that more than one or all of these biological processes contribute to aging.

The Aging Brain

How does the brain change during late adulthood? Does it retain plasticity? Here we examine how the brain shrinks and slows but still has considerable adaptive ability.

The Shrinking, Slowing Brain

On average, the brain loses 5 to 10 percent of its weight between the ages of 20 and 90. Brain volume also decreases (Bondare, 2007). One study found that the volume of the brain was 15 percent less in older adults than younger adults (Shan & others, 2005). Scientists are not sure why these changes occur but think that they might result from a decrease in dendritic connections or damage to the myelin sheath that covers axons. For decades they also concluded that brain cells died though the current consensus is that under normal conditions adults are unlikely to lose brain cells per se (Nelson, 2008).

Some brain areas shrink more than others with aging (Raz & others, 2010). The prefrontal cortex is one area that shrinks, and recent research has linked this shrinkage with a decrease in working memory and other cognitive activities in older adults (Pardo & others, 2007; Sakatini, Tanida, & Katsuyama, 2010).

A general slowing of function in the brain and spinal cord begins in middle adulthood and accelerates in late adulthood (Birren, 2002). Both physical coordination and intellectual performance are affected. For example, after age 70 many adults no longer show a knee-jerk reflex, and by age 90 most reflexes are much slower (Spence, 1989). Slowing of the brain can impair the performance of older adults on intelligence tests, especially timed tests (Birren, Woods, & Williams, 1980).

The Adaptive Brain

If the brain were a computer, this description of the aging brain might lead you to think that it could not do much of anything. However, unlike a computer, the brain has remarkable repair capability (Jessberger & Gage, 2009; Prakash, Snook, & Kramer, 2010; Zelazo & Lee, 2010). Even in late adulthood, the brain loses only a portion of its ability to function, and the activities older adults engage in can still influence the brain's development. For example, in a recent fMRI study, higher levels of aerobic fitness were linked with greater volume in the hippocampus, which translates into better memory (Erickson & others, 2009).

Can adults, even aging adults, generate new neurons? Researchers have found that *neurogenesis*, the generation of new neurons, does occur in lower mammalian species, such as mice (Marlatt & others, 2010; Zhu & others, 2009). Also, research indicates that exercise and an enriched, complex environment can generate new brain cells in rats and mice, and that stress reduces their survival rate (Segovia, Arco, & Mora, 2009). Researchers recently have discovered that if rats are cognitively challenged to learn something, new brain cells survive longer (Shors, 2009).

It also is now accepted that neurogenesis can occur in human adults (Hagg, 2009). However, researchers have documented neurogenesis in only two brain regions: the hippocampus, which is involved in memory, and the olfactory bulb, which is involved in smell (Arenkiel, 2010; Zou & others, 2010). It also is not known what functions these new brain cells perform, and at this point researchers have documented that they last for only several weeks (Nelson, 2008). Researchers currently are studying factors that might inhibit and promote neurogenesis, including various drugs, stress, and exercise (Gil-Mohapel & others, 2010; van Praag, 2009). They also are examining how the grafting of neural stem cells to various regions of the brain, such as the hippocampus, might increase neurogenesis (Farin & others, 2009; Szulwach & others, 2010).

Dendritic growth can occur in human adults, possibly even in older adults (Eliasieh, Liets, & Chalupa, 2007). Recall from Chapter 3 that dendrites are the receiving portion of the neuron. One study compared the brains of adults at various ages (Coleman, 1986). From the forties through the seventies, the growth of dendrites increased. However, in people in their nineties, dendritic growth no longer occurred.

Changes in lateralization may provide one type of adaptation in aging adults (Angel & others, 2009; Zhu, Zacks, & Slade, 2010). Recall that lateralization is the specialization of function in one hemisphere of the brain or the other. Using neuroimaging techniques, researchers found that brain activity in the prefrontal cortex is lateralized less in older adults than in younger adults when they are engaging in cognitive tasks (Cabeza, 2002). For example, Figure 15.2

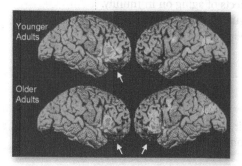

Figure 15.2 The Decrease in Brain Lateralization in Older Adults

Younger adults primarily used the right prefrontal region of the brain (*top left photo*) during a recall memory task, whereas older adults used both the left and right prefrontal regions (*bottom two photos*).

How Would You...?
As an educator, how would you use a biological perspective to explain changes in learning as people age?

shows that when younger adults are given the task of recognizing words they have previously seen, they process the information primarily in the right hemisphere; older adults are more likely to use both hemispheres (Madden & others, 1999). The decrease in lateralization in older adults might play a compensatory role in the aging brain. That is, using both hemispheres may improve the cognitive functioning of older adults.

The Nun Study

The Nun Study, directed by David Snowdon, is an intriguing ongoing investigation of aging in 678 nuns, many of whom are from a convent named the Sisters of Notre Dame in Mankato, Minnesota (Snowdon, 2003; Tyas & others, 2007). They lead an intellectually challenging life, and brain researchers conclude that this contributes to their quality of life as older adults and possibly to their longevity. Each of the 678 nuns agreed to participate in annual assessments of their cognitive and physical functioning. They also agreed to donate their brains for scientific research when they die, and they are the largest group of brain donors in the world. Examination of the nuns' donated brains, as well as others', has led neuroscientists to believe that the brain has a remarkable capacity to change and grow, even in old age.

In one study of the nuns, idea density, a measure of linguistic ability assessed early in the adult years (age 22), was linked with higher brain weight, fewer incidences of mild cognitive impairment, and fewer characteristics of Alzheimer disease in 75- to 95-year-old nuns (Riley & others, 2005). In another study, sisters who had taught for most of their lives showed more moderate declines in intellectual skills than those who had spent most of their lives in service-based tasks, which supports the notion that stimulating the brain with intellectual activity keeps neurons healthy and alive (Snowdon, 2002).

This and other research provide hope that scientists will discover ways to tap into the brain's capacity to adapt in order to prevent and treat brain diseases. For example, scientists might learn more effective ways to help older adults recover from strokes (Carter & others, 2010; Saur & others, 2010). Even when areas of the brain are permanently damaged by stroke, new message routes can be created to get around the blockage or to resume the function of that area, indicating that the brain does adapt.

Physical Development

Physical decline is inevitable if we manage to live to an old age, but the timing of physical problems related to aging is not uniform. Let's examine some physical changes that occur as we age, including in physical appearance and movement, with some of the senses, and in our circulation and lungs.

Physical Appearance and Movement

In late adulthood, the changes in physical appearance that began occurring during middle age (as discussed in Chapter 13) become more pronounced. Wrinkles and age spots are the most noticeable changes. We also get

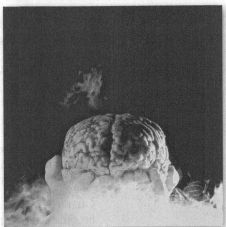

Top: Sister Marcella Zachman (*left*) finally stopped teaching at age 97. Now, at 99, she helps ailing nuns exercise their brains by quizzing them on vocabulary or playing a card game called Skip–Bo, at which she deliberately loses. Sister Mary Esther Boor (*right*), also 99 years of age, is a former teacher who stays alert by doing puzzles and volunteering to work the front desk. *Below:* A technician holds the brain of a deceased Mankato nun. The nuns donate their brains for research that explores the effects of stimulation on brain growth.

cataracts Involve a thickening of the lens of the eye that causes vision to become cloudy, opaque, and distorted.

glaucoma Damage to the optic nerve because of the pressure created by a buildup of fluid in the eye.

macular degeneration A disease that involves deterioration of the macula of the retina, which corresponds to the focal center of the visual field.

shorter when we get older. As we saw in Chapter 13, both men and women become shorter in late adulthood because of bone loss in their vertebrae (Hoyer & Roodin, 2009).

Our weight usually drops after we reach 60 years of age. This likely occurs because we lose muscle, which also gives our bodies a "sagging" look (Evans, 2010).

Older adults move slower than young adults, and this slowing occurs for many types of movement with a wide range of difficulty (Sakuma & Yamaguchi, 2010). A recent study revealed that obesity was linked to mobility limitation in older adults (Houston & others, 2009).

Exercise and appropriate weight lifting can help to reduce the decrease in muscle mass and improve the older person's body appearance (Peterson & others, 2009; Venturelli & others, 2010). And a recent study revealed that it's not just physical exercise that is linked to preserving older adults' motor functions; in this study, engaging in social activities protected against loss of motor abilities (Buchman & others, 2009).

Sensory Development

Seeing, hearing, and other aspects of sensory functioning are linked with our ability to perform everyday activities, and they decline in older adults (Cimarolli, 2009; Wood & others, 2010).

Vision In late adulthood, the decline in vision that began for most adults in early or middle adulthood becomes more pronounced (Dillon & others, 2010; Sharts-Hopko, 2009). The eye does not adapt as quickly when moving from a well-lighted place to one of semidarkness. The tolerance for glare also diminishes. The area of the visual field becomes smaller, and it's possible that events that occur away from the center of the visual field might not be detected (Scialfa & Kline, 2007). All these changes may make night driving especially difficult (Babizhayev, Minasyan, & Richer, 2009; Wood & others, 2010).

Recent research has shown that sensory decline in older adults is linked to a decline in cognitive functioning. One study of individuals in their seventies revealed that visual decline was related to slower speed of processing information, which in turn was associated with greater cognitive decline (Clay & others, 2009).

Color vision also may decline as a result of the yellowing of the lens of the eye (Scheiber, 2006). As a result, older adults may have trouble accurately matching closely related colors such as navy socks and black socks.

Depth perception typically declines in late adulthood, which can make it difficult for the older adult to determine how close or far away or how high or low something is (Bian & Anderson, 2009). A decline in depth perception can make steps or street curbs difficult to manage.

Three diseases that can impair the vision of older adults are cataracts, glaucoma, and macular degeneration:

- **Cataracts** involve a thickening of the lens of the eye that causes vision to become cloudy, opaque, and distorted. By age 70, approximately 30 percent of individuals experience a partial loss of vision due to cataracts. Initially, cataracts can be treated by glasses; if they worsen, a simple surgical procedure can remove them (Chung & others, 2009).

- **Glaucoma** involves damage to the optic nerve because of the pressure created by a buildup of fluid in the eye (Fechtner & others, 2010). Approximately 1 percent of individuals in their seventies and 10 percent of those in their nineties have glaucoma, which can be treated with eyedrops. If left untreated, glaucoma can ultimately destroy a person's vision (Musch & others, 2009).

- **Macular degeneration** is a disease that involves deterioration of the *macula* of the retina, which corresponds to the focal center of the visual field. Individuals with macular degeneration may have relatively normal peripheral vision but be unable to see clearly what is right in front of them (Ghosh & others,

Exercise, Nutrition, and Weight

Although we may be in the evening of our lives in late adulthood, we are not meant to live out our remaining years passively. Everything we know about older adults suggests they are healthier and happier the more active they are. Can regular exercise lead to a healthier late adulthood and increase longevity? How does eating a calorie-restricted diet and controlling weight also contribute?

Exercise

In one study, exercise literally meant a difference in life or death for middle-aged and older adults (Blair, 1990). More than 10,000 men and women were divided into categories of low fitness, medium fitness, and high fitness (Blair & others, 1989). Then they were studied over a period of eight years. As shown in Figure 15.4, sedentary participants (low fitness) were more than twice as likely to die during the eight-year time span of the study than those who were moderately fit and more than three times as likely to die as those who were highly fit. The positive effects of being physically fit occurred for both men and women in this study. Also, a recent study of more than 11,000 women found that low cardiorespiratory fitness was a significant predictor of all-cause mortality (Farrell & others, 2010).

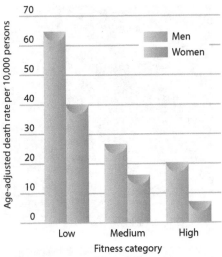

Figure 15.4 Physical Fitness and Mortality
In this study of middle-aged and older adults, being moderately fit or highly fit meant that individuals were less likely to die over a period of eight years than their less fit (sedentary) counterparts (Blair & others, 1989).

Gerontologists increasingly recommend strength training in addition to aerobic activity and stretching for older adults. Resistance exercise can preserve and possibly increase muscle mass in older adults (Williamson & others, 2010). A recent meta-analysis revealed that resistance training—especially high intensity training—was effective in improving older adults' strength and is a viable strategy for reducing muscular weakness associated with aging (Peterson & others, 2010).

Exercise is an excellent way to maintain health, and researchers continue to document its positive effects in older adults (Desai, Grossberg, & Chibnall, 2010; Erickson & others, 2009). Exercise helps people to live independent lives with dignity in late adulthood. At age 80, 90, and even 100, exercise can help prevent older adults from falling down or even being institutionalized (Maimoun & others, 2010; Peterson & others, 2009). And exercise increases the information processing skills of older adults (Marks, Katz, & Smith, 2009; Williamson & others, 2009).

Exercise is linked to increased longevity. A recent study also revealed that systolic blood pressure during exercise was linked to an increase in long-term survival of 75-year-olds (Hedberg & others, 2009). Energy expenditure during exercise of at least 1,000 kcal/week reduces mortality by about 30 percent, while 2,000 kcal/week reduces mortality by about 50 percent (Lee & Skerrett, 2001).

Nutrition and Weight

Scientists have accumulated considerable evidence that caloric restriction (CR) in laboratory animals (in most cases rats) can increase the animals' life span (Minor & others, 2010). Animals fed diets restricted in calories, although adequate in protein, vitamins, and minerals, live as much as 40 percent longer than animals given unlimited access to food (Jolly, 2005). And chronic problems such as kidney disease appear at a later age (Fernandez, 2008). CR also delays biochemical alterations such as the age-related rise in cholesterol and triglycerides observed in both humans and animals (Fontana, 2009). And recent

Figure 15.5 Calorie Restriction in Monkeys
Shown here are two monkeys at the Wisconsin Primate Research Center. Both are 24 years old. The monkey in the top photograph was raised on a calorie-restricted diet, while the monkey in the bottom photograph was raised on a normal diet. Notice that the monkey on the calorie-restricted diet looks younger; he also has lower glucose and insulin levels. The monkey raised on a normal diet has higher triglycerides and more oxidative damage to his cells.

How Would You...?
As a psychologist, how would you structure the environment of a nursing home to produce maximum health and psychological benefits for the residents?

research indicates that CR may provide neuroprotection for an aging central nervous system (Contestabile, 2009; Opalach & others, 2010) (see Figure 15.5). For example, a recent study revealed that following CR for three months, the verbal memory of older adults improved (Witte & others, 2009).

No one knows for certain how CR works to increase the life span of animals. Some scientists say that CR might lower the level of free radicals and reduce oxidative stress in cells. Others argue that CR might trigger a state of emergency called "survival mode" in which the body eliminates all unnecessary functions to focus only on staying alive.

Whether similar very low calorie diets can stretch the human life span is not known (Blagosklonny, 2010). In some instances the animals in these studies ate 40 percent less than normal. In humans, a typical level of calorie restriction involves a 30 percent decrease, which translates into about 1,120 calories a day for the average woman and 1,540 for the average man.

Leaner adults, especially women, do live longer, healthier lives (Wandell, Carlsson, & Theobold, 2009). In one study of 19,297 Harvard alumni, those weighing the least were less likely to die over the three decades studied.

Health Treatment

About 3 percent of adults age 65 and older in the United States reside in a nursing home at some point in time. As older adults age, however, their probability of being in a nursing home or other extended-care facility increases. Twenty-three percent of adults aged 85 and older live in nursing homes or other extended-care facilities.

The quality of nursing homes and other extended-care facilities for older adults varies enormously and is a source of continuing national concern (Eskildsen & Price, 2009). More than one-third are seriously deficient. They fail federally mandated inspections because they do not meet the minimum standards for physicians, pharmacists, and various rehabilitation specialists (occupational and physical therapists). Further concerns focus on the patient's right to privacy, access to medical information, safety, and lifestyle freedom within the individual's range of mental and physical capabilities.

Because of the inadequate quality and the escalating costs of many nursing homes, many specialists in the health problems of the aged stress that home health care, elder-care centers, and preventive medicine clinics are good alternatives (Katz & others, 2009). They are potentially less expensive than hospitals and nursing homes. They also are less likely to engender the feelings of depersonalization and dependency that occur so often in residents of institutions. Currently, there is an increased demand for but shortage of home care workers because of the increase in population of older adults and their preference to stay out of nursing homes (Moos, 2007).

In a classic study, Judith Rodin and Ellen Langer (1977) found that an important factor related to health, and even survival, in a nursing home is the patient's feelings of control and self-determination. One group was encouraged to make more day-to-day choices and thus feel they had more responsibility for control over their lives. They began to decide such matters as what they ate, when their visitors could come, what movies they saw, and who could come to their rooms. Another group in the same nursing home was told by the administrator how caring the nursing home was and how much the staff wanted to help, but these residents were given no added responsibility over their lives. Eighteen months later, the residents given extra responsibility were healthier, happier, and more alert and active than the residents who did not receive added responsibility. Even more important was the finding that after 18 months only half as many nursing home residents in the "responsibility" group had died as in the "dependent" group (see Figure 15.6). Perceived control over one's environment, then, can literally be a matter of life or death.

Geriatric nurses can be especially helpful in creating a better quality of health treatment. To read about the work of one geriatric nurse, see "Careers in Life-Span Development."

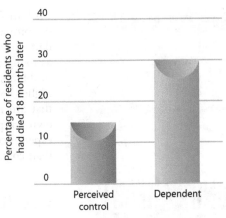

Figure 15.6 Perceived Control and Mortality
In the study by Rodin and Langer (1977), nursing home residents who were encouraged to feel more in control of their lives were more likely to be alive 18 months later than those who were treated to feel more dependent on the nursing home staff.

Wisdom

Does wisdom, like good wine, improve with age? What is this thing we call "wisdom"? **Wisdom** is expert knowledge about the practical aspects of life that permits excellent judgment about important matters. This practical knowledge involves exceptional insight into human development and life matters, good judgment, and an understanding of how to cope with difficult life problems. Thus, wisdom, more than standard conceptions of intelligence, focuses on life's pragmatic concerns and human conditions (Bluck & Barron, 2009; Karelitz, Jarvin, & Sternberg, 2011). A recent study revealed that older adults engaged in superior reasoning about social conflicts than young or middle-aged adults (Grossman & others, 2010). Older adults' superior reasoning included taking multiple perspectives, allowing for compromise, and recognizing the limits of their knowledge.

In regard to wisdom, Paul Baltes and his colleagues (2006) have found the following. (1) High levels of wisdom are rare. Few people, including older adults, attain a high level of wisdom. That only a small percentage of adults show

Older adults might not be as quick with their thoughts or behavior as younger people, but wisdom may be an entirely different matter. This older man shares the wisdom of his experience with a classroom of children. *How is wisdom described by life-span developmentalists?*

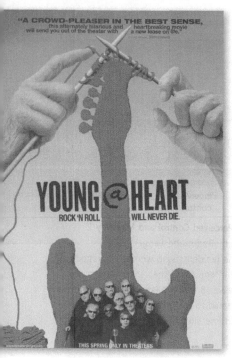

The Young@Heart chorus—whose average age is 80. Young@Heart became a hit documentary in 2008. The documentary displays the singing talents, energy, and optimism of a remarkable group of older adults, who clearly are on the "use it" side of "use it or lose it."

wisdom supports the contention that it requires experience, practice, or complex skills. (2) Factors other than age are critical for wisdom to develop to a high level. For example, certain life experiences, such as being trained and working in a field concerned with difficult life problems and having wisdom-enhancing mentors, contribute to higher levels of wisdom. Also, people higher in wisdom have values that are more likely to consider the welfare of others than their own happiness. (3) Personality-related factors, such as openness to experience, generativity, and creativity, are better predictors of wisdom than cognitive factors such as intelligence.

Use It or Lose It

Changes in cognitive activity patterns might result in disuse and consequent atrophy of cognitive skills (Hughes, 2010). This concept is captured in the concept of "Use it or lose it." The mental activities that likely benefit the maintenance of cognitive skills in older adults are activities such as reading books, doing crossword puzzles, and going to lectures and concerts (La Rue, 2010; Park & Reuter-Lorenz, 2009). A recent study revealed that reading daily was linked to reduced mortality in men in their seventies (Jacobs & others, 2008). In another recent study, 75- to 85-year-olds were assessed for an average of five years (Hall & others, 2009). At the beginning of the research, the older adults indicated how often they participated in these six activities on a daily basis: reading, writing, doing crossword puzzles, playing card or board games, having group discussions, and playing music. For each additional activity the older adult engaged in, the onset of rapid memory loss was delayed by .18 year. For older adults who participated in 11 activities per week compared to their counterparts who engaged in only 4 activities per week, the point at which accelerated memory decline occurred was delayed by 1.29 years.

Training Cognitive Skills

If older adults are losing cognitive skills, can they be retrained? An increasing number of research studies indicate that they can to a degree (Baker & others, 2010; Kramer & Morrow, 2010; Reuter-Lorenz & Park, 2010). Two key conclusions can be derived from research in this area: (1) Training can improve the cognitive skills of many older adults, but (2) there is some loss in plasticity in late adulthood, especially in the oldest group of old, age 85 and older (Baltes, Lindenberger, & Staudinger, 2006). A recent research review concluded that providing structured experience in situations requiring higher-level cognitive coordination of skills—such as playing complex video games, switching tasks, and dividing attention—can improve older adults' cognitive skills (Hertzog & others, 2009).

Evidence of plasticity and the effectiveness of cognitive training comes from the research of Sherry Willis and K. Warner Schaie (1986), who studied approximately 400 adults, most of whom were older adults. Using individualized training, they improved the spatial orientation and reasoning skills of two-thirds of the adults. Nearly 40 percent of those whose abilities had declined returned to a level they had reached 14 years earlier. Further, the effects of training on reasoning lasted up to seven years after training. Other research supports the finding that cognitive training interventions can improve the mental functioning and daily functioning of older adults (Boron, Willis, & Schaie, 2007; Levine & others, 2007). And as we discussed earlier in the chapter, researchers are also finding that improving the physical fitness of older adults can improve their cognitive functioning (Erickson & others, 2009).

How Would You...?
As a psychologist, how would you design activities and interventions to elicit and maintain cognitive vitality in older adults?

Work and Retirement

What percentage of older adults continue to work? How productive are they? Who adjusts best to retirement? These are some of the questions we now examine.

Work

In the beginning of the 21st century, the percentage of men over age 65 who continue to work full-time is less than at the beginning of the 20th century. The decline from 1900 to the beginning of the 21st century has been as much as 70 percent. An important change in older adults' work patterns is the increase in part-time work after retirement (Hardy, 2006). The percentage of older adults who work part-time postretirement has steadily increased since the 1960s. Some individuals maintain their productivity throughout their lives. Some of these older workers work as many or more hours than younger workers. In the National Longitudinal Survey of Older Men, good health, a strong psychological commitment to work, and a distaste for retirement were the most important characteristics related to continued employment into old age (seventies and eighties) (Parnes & Sommers, 1994). The probability of employment also was positively correlated with educational attainment and being married to a working wife.

Especially important to think about is the large cohort of baby boomers—78 million people—who began to reach traditional retirement age in 2010. Because this cohort is so large, and these are difficult economic times, we are likely to see increasing numbers of older adults continue to work (Hart, 2007). The aging of the U.S. workforce will continue at least until 2034 when the largest number of the baby boom cohorts reaches 70 (Manton & others, 2007).

Older workers have lower rates of absenteeism, fewer accidents, and increased job satisfaction, compared with their younger counterparts (Warr, 2004). This means that the older worker can be of considerable value to a company, above and beyond the older worker's cognitive competence. Changes in federal law now allow individuals over the age of 65 to continue working (Shore & Goldberg, 2005).

Ruby Johnson, 93, wraps heat-resistant tape around coils to insulate an electrical terminal at the company where she works in Menomonee Falls, Wisconsin. *What are some variations in work and retirement in older adults?*

An increasing number of middle-aged and older adults are embarking on a second or a third career (Feldman, 2007). In some cases, this is an entirely different type of work or a continuation of previous work but at a reduced level. Many older adults also participate in unpaid work—as volunteers or as active participants in a voluntary association. These options afford older adults opportunities for productive activity, social interaction, and a positive identity.

Adjustment to Retirement

In the past, when most people reached an accepted retirement age, such as some point in their sixties, retirement meant a one-way exit from full-time work to full-time leisure (Higo & Williamson, 2009). Leading expert Phyllis Moen (2007) described how today, when people reach their sixties, the life path they follow is less clear: (1) some individuals don't retire, continuing in their career jobs, (2) some retire from their career work and then take up a new and different job, (3) some retire from career jobs but do volunteer work, (4) some retire from a post-retirement job and go on to yet another job, (5) some move in and out of the workforce, so they never really have a "career" job from which they retire, (6) some individuals who are in poor health move to a disability status and eventually into retirement, and (7) some who are laid off define it as "retirement."

Older adults who adjust best to retirement are healthy, have adequate income, are active, are educated, have an extended social network including both friends and family, and usually were satisfied with their lives before they retired (Jokela & others, 2010; Moen & Spencer, 2006). Older adults with inadequate income and poor health, and who must adjust to other stress that occurs at the same time as retirement, such as the death of a spouse, have the most difficult time adjusting to retirement (Reichstadt & others, 2007). One study also found that individuals who had difficulty in adjusting to retirement had a strong attachment to work, including full-time jobs and a long work history, lack of control over the transition to retirement, and low self-efficacy (van Solinge & Henkens, 2005).

How Would You...? As a psychologist, how would you assist older adults in making appropriate adjustments and preparations for a psychologically satisfying retirement?

major depression A mood disorder in which the individual is deeply unhappy, demoralized, self-derogatory, and bored. The person does not feel well, loses stamina easily, has poor appetite, and is listless and unmotivated. Major depression is so widespread that it has been called the "common cold" of psychological disorders.

dementia A global term for any neurological disorder in which the primary symptoms involve a deterioration of mental functioning.

Mental Health

Although a substantial portion of the population can now look forward to a longer life, that life may unfortunately be hampered by a psychological disorder in old age. This prospect is both troubling to individuals and their families, and costly to society. Psychological disorders make individuals increasingly dependent on the help and care of others. The cost of psychological disorders in older adults is estimated at more than $40 billion per year in the United States. More important than the loss in dollars, though, is the loss of human potential and the suffering. Although psychological disorders in older adults are a major concern, older adults do not have a higher incidence of psychological disorders than younger adults do (Busse & Blazer, 1996).

Depression

What characterizes depression in older adults?

Major depression is a mood disorder in which the individual is deeply unhappy, demoralized, self-derogatory, and bored. The person does not feel well, loses stamina easily, has a poor appetite, and is listless and unmotivated. Major depression has been called the "common cold" of mental disorders. However, a recent review concluded that depression is less common among older adults than younger adults (Fiske, Wetherell, & Gatz, 2009). More than half of the cases of depression in older adults represents the first time these individuals have developed depression in their life (Fiske, Wetherell, & Gatz, 2009).

Among the most common predictors of depression in older adults are earlier depressive symptoms, poor health, disability, loss events such as the death of a spouse, and low social support (Lee & Park, 2008). Insomnia is often overlooked as a risk factor for depression in older adults (Fiske, Wetherell, & Gatz, 2009). Curtailment of daily activities is a common pathway to late-life

How Would You...?
As a psychologist, how would you advise families who are dealing with an aging parent suffering from depression?

depression (Fiske, Wetherell, & Gatz, 2009). Often accompanying this curtailment of activity is an increase in self-critical thinking that exacerbates depression.

Depression is a treatable condition, not only in young adults but in older adults as well (Asghar-Ali & Braun, 2009; Nolen-Hoeksema, 2011). Unfortunately, as many as 80 percent of older adults with depressive symptoms receive no treatment at all. Combinations of medications and psychotherapy produce significant improvement in almost four out of five older adults with depression (Koenig & Blazer, 1996). Also, engagement in valued activities and religious/spiritual involvement can reduce depressive symptoms (Fiske, Wetherell, & Gatz, 2009). Life review/reminiscence therapy, which we will further discuss in Chapter 16, is underutilized in the treatment of depression in older adults (Fiske, Wetherell, & Gatz, 2009).

Dementia, Alzheimer Disease, and Parkinson Disease

Among the most debilitating of mental disorders in older adults are the dementias. In recent years, extensive attention has been focused on the most common dementia, Alzheimer disease. Other afflictions common in older adults are multi-infarct dementia and Parkinson disease.

Dementia

Dementia is a global term for any neurological disorder in which the primary symptoms involve a deterioration of mental functioning. Individuals with dementia often lose the ability to care for themselves and can lose the ability to recognize familiar surroundings and people—including family members (Travers, Martin-Kahn, & Lie, 2010). It is estimated that 23 percent of women and 17 percent of men 85 years and older are at risk for developing dementia (Alzheimer's Association, 2010). However, these estimates may be high because of the Alzheimer's Association's lobbying efforts to increase funding for research and treatment facilities. Dementia is a broad category and it is important that every effort is made to narrow the older adult's disorder and determine a specific cause of the deteriorating mental functioning.

Alzheimer disease A progressive, irreversible brain disorder characterized by a gradual deterioration of memory, reasoning, language, and eventually physical function.

How Would You...?
As a health-care professional, how would you respond to an older adult who is concerned that their declining short-term memory is an early symptom of dementia?

Alzheimer Disease

One form of dementia is **Alzheimer disease**—a progressive, irreversible brain disorder that is characterized by a gradual deterioration of memory, reasoning, language, and eventually, physical function. In 2009, an estimated 5.3 million adults in the United States had Alzheimer disease, and it is projected that 10 million baby boomers will develop Alzheimer disease in their lifetime (Alzheimer's Association, 2010). Figure 15.7 shows the estimated risks for developing Alzheimer disease at different ages for women and men (Alzheimer's Association, 2010). Women are likely to develop Alzheimer disease because they live longer than men and their longer life expectancy increases the number of years during which they can develop it. It is estimated that Alzheimer disease triples the health-care costs of Americans 65 years of age and older (Alzheimer's Association, 2010). Because of the increasing prevalence of Alzheimer disease, researchers have stepped up their efforts to discover the causes of the disease and find more effective ways to treat it (O'Bryant & others, 2009; Reiman, Langbaum, & Tariot, 2010).

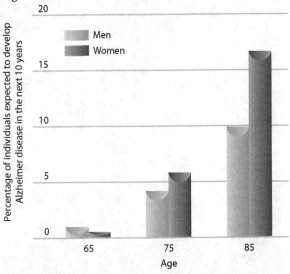

Figure 15.7 Estimated Risks for Developing Alzheimer Disease at Different Ages for Women and Men

Source: Alzheimer's Association (2010). 2010 Alzheimer's facts and figures. *Alzheimer's & Dementia, 6,* 158–194.

Causes and Risk Factors Once destruction of brain tissue occurs from Alzheimer disease, it is unlikely that treatment of the disease will reverse the damage, at least based on the current state of research and the foreseeable future. Thus, an important agenda for Alzheimer disease researchers is to focus on the disease's biological and environmental risk factors, the development of preventive strategies to reduce the likelihood that brain tissue damage will occur, and the maintenance of cognitive reserves in middle adulthood.

Alzheimer disease involves a deficiency in the important brain messenger chemical acetylcholine, which plays an important role in memory (Alcaro & others, 2010). Also, as Alzheimer disease progresses, the brain shrinks and deteriorates (see Figure 15.8). This deterioration is characterized by the formation of *amyloid plaques* (dense deposits of protein that accumulate in the blood vessels) and *neurofibrillary tangles* (twisted fibers that build up in neurons) (Galimberti & Scarpini, 2010). Researchers are seeking ways to interrupt the progress of such plaques and tangles in Alzheimer patients (Miura & others, 2007).

There is also increasing interest in the role that oxidative stress might play in Alzheimer disease (Bonda & others, 2010; Di Bona & others, 2010; Galasko & others, 2010). Oxidative stress occurs when the body fails in defending against free-radical attacks and oxidation. Recall from earlier in the chapter that free-radical theory is a major theory of aging.

Although scientists are not certain what causes Alzheimer disease, age is an important risk factor and genes also likely play an important role (Bettens, Sleegers, & Van Broeckhoven, 2010). The number of individuals with Alzheimer disease doubles every five years after the age of 65. A gene called *apolipoprotein E (apoE)*, which is linked to increasing presence of plaques and tangles in the brain, could play a role in as many as one-third of the cases of Alzheimer disease (Lane & He, 2009; Vemuri & others, 2010). In one study of almost 12,000 pairs of twins in Sweden, identical twins were both more likely to develop Alzheimer disease than fraternal twins, suggesting a genetic influence on the disease (Gatz & others, 2006).

Although individuals with a family history of Alzheimer disease are at greater risk, the disease is complex and likely caused by a number of factors, including lifestyles. For many years, scientists have known that a healthy diet, exercise, and weight control can lower the risk of cardiovascular disease. Now, they are finding that these healthy lifestyle factors may also lower the risk of Alzheimer disease. Researchers have revealed that older adults with Alzheimer disease are more likely also to have cardiovascular disease than are individuals who do not have Alzheimer disease (Helzner & others, 2009). Autopsies show that brains with the telltale signs of tangles and plaques of Alzheimer patients are three times more common in individuals with cardiovascular disease (Sparks & others, 1990). Recently, more cardiac risk factors have been implicated in Alzheimer disease—obesity, smoking, atherosclerosis, high cholesterol, and lipids (Abellan & others, 2009; Florent-Bechard & others, 2009).

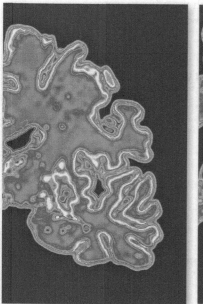 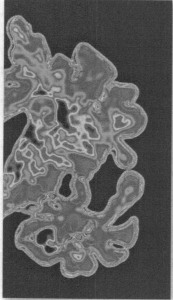

Figure 15.8 Two Brains: Normal Aging and Alzheimer Disease
The left computer graphic shows a slice of a normal aging brain, the right photograph a slice of a brain ravaged by Alzheimer disease. Notice the deterioration and shrinking in the Alzheimer disease brain.

Mild Cognitive Impairment *Mild cognitive impairment (MCI)* represents a transitional state between the cognitive changes of normal aging and very early Alzheimer disease and other dementias. MCI is increasingly recognized as a risk factor for Alzheimer disease. Estimates indicate that as many as 10 to 20 percent of individuals age 65 and older have MCI (Alzheimer's Association, 2010). Some individuals with MCI do not go on to develop Alzheimer disease, but MCI is a risk factor for Alzheimer disease.

Distinguishing between individuals who merely have age-associated declines in memory and those with MCI is difficult, as is predicting which individuals with MCI will subsequently develop Alzheimer disease (Vellas & Aisen, 2010). One effort in this regard is to have individuals with MCI undergo an fMRI (functional magnetic resonance imaging) brain scan (Pihlajamaki, Jauhiainen, & Soininen, 2009). If the scan shows that certain brain regions involved in memory are smaller than those of individuals without memory impairments, the individual is more likely to progress to Alzheimer disease (Alzheimer's Association, 2010). A recent research review concluded that fMRI measurement of neuron loss in the medial temporal lobe is a predictor of memory loss and eventually dementia (Vellas & Aisen, 2010).

Drug Treatment of Alzheimer Disease Several drugs called cholinerase inhibitors have been approved by the U.S. Food and Drug Administration to treat Alzheimer disease. They are designed to improve memory and other cognitive functions by increasing levels of acetylcholine in the brain (Emre & others, 2010; Howland, 2010). Keep in mind, though, that the drugs used to treat Alzheimer disease only slow the downward progression of the disease; they do not treat its cause (Rafii & Aisen, 2009). These drugs slow the worsening of Alzheimer symptoms for approximately 6 to 12 months for about 50 percent of the individuals who take them (Alzheimer's Association, 2009). Also, no drugs have yet been approved by the Federal Drug Administration for the treatment of MCI (Alzheimer's Association, 2009).

> **Parkinson disease** A chronic, progressive disease characterized by muscle tremors, slowing of movement, and partial facial paralysis.

Caring for Individuals With Alzheimer Disease A special concern is caring for Alzheimer patients (Kelsey & others, 2010; Silverstein, Wong, & Brueck, 2010). Health-care professionals believe that the family can be an important support system for the Alzheimer patient, but this support can have costs for the family, who can become emotionally and physically drained by the extensive care required for a person with Alzheimer disease (Elliott, Burgio, & Decoster, 2010).

Respite care (services that provide temporary relief for those who are caring for individuals with disabilities, illnesses, or the elderly) has been developed to help people who have to meet the day-to-day needs of Alzheimer patients. This type of care provides an important break away from the burden of providing chronic care (Tompkins & Bell, 2009).

Parkinson Disease

Another type of dementia is **Parkinson disease**, a chronic, progressive disease characterized by muscle tremors, slowing of movement, and partial facial paralysis. Parkinson disease is triggered by degeneration of dopamine-producing neurons in the brain (Swanson, Sesso, & Emborg, 2009). Dopamine is a neurotransmitter that is necessary for normal brain functioning. Why these neurons degenerate is not known.

The main treatment for Parkinson disease involves administering drugs that enhance the effect of dopamine (dopamine agonists) in the disease's earlier stages and later administering the drug L-dopa, which is converted by the brain into dopamine (Pahwa & Lyons, 2010; Wood, 2010). However, it is difficult to determine the correct level of dosage of L-dopa and it loses its efficacy over time (Nomoto & others, 2009). Another treatment for advanced Parkinson disease is deep brain stimulation (DBS), which involves implantation of electrodes within the brain (Kim & others, 2010). The electrodes are then stimulated by a pacemaker-like device (Troster, 2009). Recent research also indicates that certain types of dance, such as the tango, can improve the movement skills of individuals with Parkinson disease (Hackney & Earhart, 2010a, b). Stem cell transplantation and gene therapy offer hope for the future in treating Parkinson disease (Fricker-Gates & Gates, 2010; Lindvall & Kokaia, 2010).

Summary

Longevity, Biological Aging, and Physical Development

- Life expectancy has increased dramatically; life span has not. In the United States, the number of people living to age 100 or older is increasing.
- Four biological theories of aging are evolutionary, cellular clock theory, free-radical theory, and hormonal stress theory.

- The aging brain retains considerable plasticity and adaptability.
- Among physical changes that accompany aging are slower movement and the appearance of wrinkled skin and age spots on the skin. There are also declines in perceptual abilities, cardiovascular functioning, and lung capacity.

integrity versus despair Erikson's eighth and final stage of development, which individuals experience in late adulthood. This involves reflecting on the past and either piecing together a positive review or concluding that one's life has not been well spent.

life satisfaction, adapting to changing skills, and the positive role of close relationships with friends and family in an emotionally fulfilling life.

Our coverage of socioemotional development in late adulthood describes a number of theories of the socioemotional lives of older adults; the older adult's personality and roles in society; the importance of family ties and social relationships; the social contexts of ethnicity, gender, and culture; and the increasing trend of focusing on successful aging.

Bob Cousy, as a Boston Celtics star when he was a young adult (*left*) and as an older adult (*right*). *What are some changes he has made in his life as an older adult?*

Theories of Socioemotional Development

In this section, we explore four main theories of socioemotional development that focus on late adulthood: Erikson's theory, activity theory, socioemotional selectivity theory, and selective optimization with compensation theory.

Erikson's Theory

We initially described Erik Erikson's (1968) eight stages of the human life span in Chapter 1, and as we explored different periods of development in this book we examined the stages in more detail. Here we discuss his final stage.

Integrity versus despair is Erikson's eighth and final stage of development, which individuals experience during late adulthood. This stage involves reflecting on the past and either piecing together a positive review or concluding that one's life has not been well spent. Through many different routes, the older adult may have developed a positive outlook in each of the preceding periods. If so, retrospective glances and reminiscences will reveal a picture of a life well spent, and the older adult will be satisfied (integrity). But if the older adult resolved one or more of the earlier stages in a negative way (being socially isolated in early adulthood or stagnated in middle adulthood, for example), retrospective glances about the total worth of his or her life might be negative (despair).

Life review is prominent in Erikson's final stage of integrity versus despair. Life review involves looking back at one's life experiences, evaluating them, interpreting them, and often reinterpreting them (George, 2010; Robitaille & others, 2010). Distinguished aging researcher Robert Butler (2007) argues that the life review is set in motion by looking forward to death. Sometimes the life review proceeds quietly; at other times it is intense, requiring considerable work to achieve some sense of personality integration. The life review may be observed initially in stray and insignificant thoughts about oneself and one's life history. These thoughts may continue to emerge in brief intermittent spurts or become essentially continuous.

When older adults engage in a life review, they may reevaluate previous experiences and their meaning, often with revision or expanded understanding taking place. This reorganization of the past may provide a more valid picture for the individual, providing new and significant meaning to one's life (Stinson & Kirk, 2006).

activity theory The theory that the more active and involved older adults are, the more likely they are to be satisfied with their lives.

socioemotional selectivity theory The theory that older adults become more selective about their social networks. Because they place a high value on emotional satisfaction, older adults often spend more time with familiar individuals with whom they have had rewarding relationships.

One aspect of life review involves identifying and reflecting not only on the positive aspects of one's life but also on regrets as part of developing a mature wisdom and self-understanding (Choi & Jun, 2009). The hope is that by examining not only the positive aspects of one's life, but also what an individual has regretted doing, a ate vision of the complexity of one's life and possibly increased life satisfaction will be attained (King & Hicks,

What characterizes a life review in late adulthood?

2007). A recent study revealed that for low-income older adults, regrets about education, careers, and marriage were common, but the intensity of regrets was greater for finance/money, family conflict and children's problems, loss and grief, and health (Choi & Jun, 2009). Common indications of pride involved children and parenting, careers, volunteering/informal caregiving, having a long/strong marriage, and personal growth.

Some clinicians use *reminiscence therapy* with their older clients. Reminiscence therapy involves discussing past activities and experiences with another individual or group. The therapy may include the use of photographs, familiar items, and video/audio recordings (Peng & others, 2009). Researchers have found that reminiscence therapy improves the mood of older adults (Fiske, Wetherell, & Gatz, 2009). For example, a recent study of institutionalized older adults found that

How Would You...?
As a psychologist, how would you explain to an older adult the benefits of engaging in a life review?

reminiscence therapy increased their life satisfaction and decreased their depression and loneliness (Chiang & others, 2010). Also, a recent study revealed that a life-review course, "Looking for Meaning," reduced the depressive symptoms of middle-aged and older adults (Pot & others, 2010).

Activity Theory

Activity theory states that the more active and involved older adults are, the more likely they are to be satisfied with their lives. Researchers have found strong support for activity theory, beginning in the 1960s and continuing into the 21st century (Neugarten, Havighurst, & Tobin, 1968; Riebe & others, 2005). These researchers have found that when older adults are active, energetic, and productive, they age more successfully and are happier than if they disengage from society.

Activity theory suggests that many individuals will achieve greater life satisfaction if they continue their middle-adulthood roles into late adulthood. If these roles are stripped from them (as in early retirement), it is important for them to find substitute roles that keep them active and involved.

Socioemotional Selectivity Theory

Socioemotional selectivity theory states that older adults become more selective about their social networks. Because they place a high value on emotional satisfaction, older adults spend more time with familiar individuals with whom they have had rewarding relationships. Developed by Laura Carstensen (1998, 2006, 2008), this theory argues that older adults deliberately withdraw from social contact with individuals peripheral to their lives while they maintain or increase contact with close friends and family members with whom they have had enjoyable relationships. This selective narrowing of social interaction maximizes positive emotional experiences and minimizes emotional risks as individuals become older.

Affect and outlook on life are also linked to mortality in older adults (Chida & Steptoe, 2008). Older adults characterized by negative affect don't live as long as those who display more positive affect, and optimistic older adults who have a positive outlook on life live longer than their counterparts who are more pessimistic and have a negative outlook on life (Levy & others, 2002).

ageism Prejudice against other people because of their age, especially prejudice against older adults.

Older Adults in Society

Does society negatively stereotype older adults? What are some social policy issues in an aging society? What role does technology play in the lives of older adults?

Stereotyping of Older Adults

Social participation by older adults is often discouraged by **ageism**, which is prejudice against others because of their age, especially prejudice against older adults (Leifheit-Limson & Levy, 2009). They are often perceived as incapable of thinking clearly, learning new things, enjoying sex, contributing to the community, or holding responsible jobs. Many older adults face painful discrimination and might be too polite and timid to attack it (Cunningham, 2004). Because of their age, older adults might not be hired for new jobs or might be eased out of old ones; they might be shunned socially; and they might be edged out of their family life.

Ageism is widespread (Anderson & Harwood, 2009). One study found that men were more likely to negatively stereotype older adults than were women (Rupp, Vodanovich, & Crede, 2005). Research indicates that the most frequent form is disrespect for older adults, followed by assumptions about ailments or

How Would You...?
As a human development and family studies professional, how would you design a public awareness campaign to reduce ageism?

frailty caused by age (Palmore, 2004). However, the increased number of adults living to an older age has led to active efforts to improve society's image of older adults, obtain better living conditions for older adults, and gain political clout.

Policy Issues in an Aging Society

The aging society and older persons' status in this society raise policy issues about the well-being of older adults (Street & D'Amuro, 2009). These include the status of the economy and income, provision of health care, and eldercare, each of which we consider in turn.

Status of the Economy and Income An important issue involving the economy and aging is the concern that our economy cannot bear the burden of so many older persons, who by reason of their age alone are usually consumers rather than producers. Especially troublesome is the low rate of savings of U.S. adults, which further exacerbated the financial status of older adults in the recent economic downturn (Keister & Destro, 2009).

Of special concern are older adults who are poor. Researchers have found that poverty in late adulthood is linked to an increase in physical and mental health problems (Wight & others, 2009). And a recent study revealed that low SES increases the risk of earlier death in older adults (Krueger & Chang, 2008).

Census data suggest that the overall number of older people living in poverty has declined since the 1960s, but in 2008, 9.7 percent of older adults in the U.S. still were living in poverty (U.S. Census Bureau, 2010). In 2008, almost twice as many U.S. women 65 years and older (11.9 percent) lived in poverty than did their male counterparts (U.S. Census Bureau, 2010).

Health Care An aging society also brings with it various problems involving health care (Aldwin, Yancura, & Boeninger, 2011; Bashir & Holroyd, 2010). Escalating health-care costs are currently causing considerable concern (Alzheimer's Association, 2010; Seidler & others, 2010). Approximately one-third of the total health bill of the United States is for the care of adults 65 and over, who comprise only 12 percent of the population. The health-care needs of older adults are reflected in Medicare, the program that provides health-care insurance to adults over 65 under the Social Security system (Fu & others, 2010).

A special concern is that while many of the health problems of older adults are chronic rather than acute, the medical system is still based on a "cure" rather than a "care" model. Chronic illness is long-term, often lifelong, and requires long-term, if not life-term, management (Harris, Pan, & Mukhtar, 2010).

Eldercare Eldercare is the physical and emotional caretaking of older members of the family, whether that care is day-to-day physical assistance or responsibility for arranging and overseeing such care. An important issue involving eldercare is how it can best be provided (Beverly & others, 2010; Nabe-Nielsen & others, 2009). Before so many women entered the workforce, they often served as caretakers for the elderly. Now with so many women working outside the home, there is a question of who will replace them as caregivers. An added problem is that many caregivers are in their sixties, and many of them are ill themselves. They may find it especially stressful to be responsible for the care of relatives who are in their eighties or nineties.

eldercare Physical and emotional caretaking for older members of the family, whether by giving day-to-day physical assistance or by being responsible for overseeing such care.

How Would You...?
As a health-care professional, how would you recommend addressing the medical community's emphasis on "cure" rather than "care" when treating chronic illness in older adults?

Technology

The Internet plays an increasingly important role in access to information and communication for adults as well as youth (Cresci, Yarandi, & Morrell, 2010; Rosenberg & others, 2009). How well are older adults keeping up with changes in technology? Older adults are less likely to have a computer in their home and less likely to use the Internet than younger adults, but older adults are the fastest-growing segment of Internet users (Czaja & others, 2006). Older adults log more time on the Internet (an average of 8.3 hours per week), visit more Web sites, and spend

Are older adults keeping up with changes in technology?

more money on the Internet than their younger adult counterparts. They are especially interested in learning to use e-mail and going online for health information (Westlake & others, 2007). Increasing numbers of older adults use e-mail to communicate with relatives. And a recent study found that frequent computer use was linked to higher performance on cognitive tasks in older adults (Tun & Lachman, 2010). As with children and younger adults, cautions about the accuracy of information—in areas such as health care—on the Internet need to always be kept in mind (Cutler, 2009).

Families and Social Relationships

Are the close relationships of older adults different from those of younger adults? What are the lifestyles of older adults like? What characterizes the relationships of older adult parents and their adult children? What do friendships and social networks contribute to the lives of older adults? How might older adults' altruism and volunteerism contribute to positive outcomes?

Lifestyle Diversity

The lifestyles of older adults are changing (Blieszner & Bedford, 2011; Carr & Moorman, 2011). Formerly, the later years of life were likely to consist of marriage for men and widowhood for women. With demographic shifts toward marital dissolution characterized by divorce, one-third of adults can now expect to marry, divorce, and remarry during their lifetime. Let's now explore some of the diverse lifestyles of older adults, beginning with those who are married or partnered.

What are some characteristics of marriage in late adulthood?

Married Older Adults

In 2009, 56 percent of U.S. adults over 65 years of age were married (U.S. Census Bureau, 2010). Individuals who are in a marriage or a partnership in late adulthood are usually happier, are less distressed, and live longer than those who are single (Peek, 2009). One study found that older adults were more satisfied with their marriages than were young and middle-aged adults (Bookwala & Jacobs, 2004). Indeed, the majority of older adults evaluate their marriages as happy or very happy (Huyck, 1995). A recent study of octogenerians revealed that marital satisfaction helped to protect their happiness from daily fluctuations in perceived health (Waldinger & Schulz, 2010). Also, a longitudinal study of adults 75 years of age and older revealed that individuals who were married were less likely to die across a span of seven years (Rasulo, Christensen, & Tomassini, 2005).

Divorced and Remarried Older Adults

How Would You...?
As a psychologist, how would you assist older adults in coping with the unique challenges faced by divorcées at this age?

In 2008, 13 percent of women and 10 percent of men 65 years and older in the United States were divorced or separated (U.S. Census Bureau, 2010). Many of these individuals were divorced or separated before they entered late adulthood (Carr & Pudrovska, 2011). The majority of divorced older adults are women, due to their greater longevity, and men are more likely to remarry, thus removing themselves from the pool of divorced older adults (Peek, 2009). Divorce is far less common in older adults than younger adults likely reflecting cohort effects rather than age effects since divorce was somewhat rare when current cohorts of older adults were young (Peek, 2009).

There are social, financial, and physical consequences of divorce for older adults (Carr & Pudrovska, 2011). Divorce can weaken kinship ties when it occurs in later life, especially in the case of older men. Divorced older women are less likely to have adequate financial resources than married older women, and as earlier in adulthood, divorce is linked to more health problems in older adults (Bennett, 2006).

Rising divorce rates, increased longevity, and better health have led to an increase in remarriage by older adults (Ganong & Coleman, 2006). What happens when an older adult wants to remarry or does remarry? Researchers have found that some older adults perceive negative social pressure about their decision to remarry (McKain, 1972). These negative sanctions range from raised eyebrows to rejection by adult children (Ganong & Coleman, 2006). However, the majority of adult children support the decision of their older adult parents to remarry.

Adult children can be personally impacted by remarriage between older adults. Researchers have found that remarried parents and stepparents provide less support to adult stepchildren than parents in first marriages (White, 1994).

Cohabiting Older Adults

An increasing number of older adults cohabit. In the middle of the 20th century, hardly any older adults cohabited. Today, approximately 3 percent of older adults cohabit, but that percentage is expected to increase as baby boomers with their less traditional values about love, sex, and relationships enter late adulthood. In many cases, the cohabiting is more for companionship than for love. In other cases, for example, when one partner faces the potential for expensive care, a couple may decide to maintain their assets separately and thus not marry. One study found that older adults who cohabited had a more positive, stable relationship than younger adults who cohabited, although cohabiting older adults were less likely to have plans to marry their partner than younger ones (King & Scott, 2005). Other research also has revealed that middle-aged and older adult cohabiting men and women reported higher levels of depression than their married counterparts (Brown, Bulanda, & Lee, 2005).

Older Adult Parents and Their Adult Children

Approximately 80 percent of older adults have living children, many of whom are middle-aged. About 10 percent of older adults have children who are 65 years or older. Adult children are an important part of the aging parent's social network. Researchers have found that older adults with children have more contacts with relatives than those without children (Johnson & Troll, 1992).

Increasingly, diversity characterizes older adult parents and their adult children. Divorce, cohabitation, and nonmarital childbearing are more common in the history of older adults today than in the past (Carr & Pudrovska, 2011).

Gender plays an important role in relationships involving older adult parents and their children (Ward-Griffin & others, 2007). Adult daughters rather than adult sons are more likely to be involved in the lives of aging parents. For example, adult daughters are three times more likely than are adult sons to give parents assistance with daily living activities (Dwyer & Coward, 1991).

A valuable task that adult children can perform is to coordinate and monitor services for an aging parent (or relative) who becomes disabled (Silverstein, 2009). This might involve locating a nursing home and monitoring its quality, procuring medical services, arranging public service assistance, and handling finances. In some cases, adult children provide direct assistance with daily living, including such activities as eating, bathing, and dressing. Even less severely impaired older adults may need help with shopping, housework, transportation, home maintenance, and bill paying.

Friendship

How Would You...?
As a human development and family studies professional, how would you characterize the importance of friendships for older adults?

In early adulthood, friendship networks expand as new social connections are made away from home. In late adulthood, new friendships are less likely to be forged, although some adults do seek out new friendships, especially following the death of a spouse (Zettel-Watson & Rook, 2009).

Aging expert Laura Carstensen (2006) concluded that people choose close friends over new friends as they grow older. And as long as they have several close people in their network, they seem content, says Carstensen.

In one study of 128 married older adults, women were more depressed than men if they did not have a best friend, and women who did have a friend reported lower levels of depression (Antonucci, Lansford, & Akiyama, 2001). Similarly, women who did not have a best friend were less satisfied with life than women who did have a best friend. And a longitudinal study of adults 75 years of age and older revealed that individuals with close ties with friends were less likely to die across a seven-year age span (Rasulo, Christensen, & Tomassini, 2005). The findings were stronger for women than men.

Social Support and Social Integration

Social support and social integration play important roles in the physical and mental health of older adults (Antonucci & others, 2011). In the *social convoy* model of social relations, individuals go through life embedded in a personal network of individuals to whom they give, and from whom they receive, social support (Antonucci, Birditt, & Kalinauskas, 2009; Antonucci & others, 2011). Social support can help individuals of all ages cope more effectively (Griffiths & others, 2007). For older adults, social support is related to their physical and mental health (Cheng, Lee, & Chow, 2010). It is linked with a reduction in symptoms of disease, with the ability to meet one's own health-care needs, and mortality (Rook & others, 2007). Social support also decreases

What role does social support play in the health of older adults?

the probability that an older adult will be institutionalized and is associated with a lower incidence of depression (Cacioppo & others, 2006).

Social integration also plays an important role in the lives of many older adults (Antonucci & others, 2011). Remember from our earlier discussion of socioemotional selectivity theory that many older adults choose to have fewer peripheral social contacts and more emotionally positive contacts with friends and family (Charles & Carstensen, 2010). Thus, a decrease in the overall social activity of many older adults may reflect their greater interest in spending more time in the small circle of friends and families where they are less likely to have negative emotional experiences. A low level of social integration is linked with poorer health and earlier death in older adults (Koropeckyj-Cox, 2009). A recent study found that loneliness predicted increased blood pressure four years later in middle-aged and older adults (Hawkley & others, 2010).

Researchers have found that older adults tend to report being less lonely than younger adults and less lonely than would be expected based on their circumstances (Schnittker, 2007). Their reports of feeling less lonely than younger adults likely reflect their more selective social networks and greater acceptance of loneliness in their lives (Koropeckyj-Cox, 2009).

Altruism and Volunteerism

A common perception is that older adults need to be given help rather than give help themselves. However, a recent study found that older adults perceived their well-being as better when they provided social support to others than when they received, except when received from a spouse or sibling (Thomas, 2010). And a 12-year longitudinal study revealed that older adults who had persistently low or declining feelings of usefulness to others had an increased risk of earlier death (Gruenewald & others, 2009). Further, researchers recently have found that when older adults engage in altruistic behavior and volunteering, they benefit from these activities (Morrow-Howell, 2010). For example, one study revealed that volunteering, was linked to less frailty in older adults (Jung & others, 2010). A recent analysis concluded that rates of volunteering do not decline significantly until the mid-seventies, and older adults commit more hours than younger volunteers (Morrow-Howell, 2010). Older adults are also more likely than any other age group to volunteer more than 100 hours annually (Burr, 2009).

Researchers also have found that volunteering as an older adult is associated with a number of positive outcomes (Burr, 2009). For example, a study of 2,000 older adults in Japan revealed that those who gave more assistance to others had better physical health than their elderly counterparts who gave less assistance (Krause & others, 1999). Among the reasons for the positive outcomes of volunteering are its provision of constructive activities and productive roles, social integration, and enhanced meaningfulness (Tan & others, 2007).

How Would You...?
As an educator, how would you persuade the school board to sponsor a volunteer program to bring older adults into the school system to work with elementary students?

Ninety-eight-year-old volunteer Iva Broadus plays cards with 10-year-old DeAngela Williams in Dallas, Texas. Iva recently was recognized as the oldest volunteer in the Big Sister program in the United States. Iva says that card-playing helps to keep her memory and thinking skills good and can help DeAngela's as well.

AGEISM AND DISCOURSES OF LATE ADULTHOOD

Older people go through stages just as younger people do

As we have noted often in this book, being a particular chronological age is never a good indicator of developmental stage. In the last chapter, you saw that the period that is often called 'mid-life' used to be seen as a bridge between youth and age. As such, it has often been treated as a time when the middle-aged person was confronted with their mortality and supposed to resolve the problem of growing old gracefully. As we mentioned in the previous chapter, with the increasing length of the lifespan, there is a need to rethink both our personal and our theoretical approaches to the entire span of adulthood. We should no longer see mid-life as a period of transition between youth and age, or later adulthood as a time of simply coming to terms with or being defined by the ageing process. For many people reaching the middle of their lives now, expectations about the quality of their current and future lives are very different from those of their parents at the same age. The lengthening period of later life offers opportunities as well as challenges for 'the ageing process'.

It is important to acknowledge that we all eventually get older, and that this chronological fact will have both personal and social effects on such things as where we live, whom we interact with and what kind of work we do. Some people simply avoid thinking about what they will be like in 'old age'. Perhaps this is a resistance to the negative way ageing has been viewed in Euro-Western cultures, rather than 'denial'. Some people assume that they will somehow become the mythical 'kind old lady' or 'kindly old gent'. Others may expect to be a 'feisty older woman' or 'grumpy older man'. Does the ageing process inevitably produce benign or difficult personalities? Or, is it just that cumulative life experiences, in a sense, entitle us to become more (or less) cynical, more (or less) knowledgable about ourselves and others, or more (or less) resigned to the possibilities of changing the world?

Old people are 'all the same'

There may be a negative discourse that operates in society that lumps all older people together as a group characterised only by physical decline. But as it happens, among people who have lived a long time, there is an even greater diversity than among any other age group. People become more distinct as they age, not more alike, for a logical reason. If you think about the unusual life experiences that you have had so far, think about how many more you might have in the next few decades—and all the time you have your own family, culture and background that makes these events specific to your life experience. By the time you are much older, all these experiences will

add up to make you increasingly unique as you get older. Just being the same age may be the only thing that older people have in common! This is quite a different perspective from the stereotypes of older people that are often presented in advertising and elsewhere. Part of this diversity is reflected in the way developmental writers have tried to carve out phases of later adulthood.

Ageism

Negative stereotypes about older people abound, which probably reflects the focus on youth in contemporary Western societies. This is connected with the idea (termed 'modernism') that dominated scientific and development work in the twentieth century, that the latest, newest, fastest (most modern) things are the best (see for example Morss, 1990). In contrast, things that are 'old fashioned' have a negative connotation. But, there are other discourses in everyday life that are completely contradictory to the youth-focused view. For example, while there may be the cliché that 'you can't teach an old dog new tricks', there are also contradictory popular sayings such as, 'good things take time' or 'you're only as old as you feel'. There are positive connotations of words like 'vintage' and 'classical'.

Ageism is a prejudice about people, based on age alone. It is possible to have ageist attitudes towards young people (and there is some evidence that many people do hold such attitudes), but most people think about stereotypes of 'old age' when they talk about ageism. The stereotypical picture of the older person seems to be someone who is losing their faculties, who lives alone, is typically ill and very, very needy. Although studies show that generally older people do not feel ill and isolated, this is the picture many people have of the last part of life. Simply living as an older person in a society where ageist attitudes are rife is a psychological challenge in itself. However, coming to terms with the many likely changes in the way daily life is structured, such as the role of work in life and our relationships with others, requires major psychological adjustment.

In fact, evidence from a survey of New Zealand employers found differing ageist stereotypes. Older workers were described positively as loyal workers with a good work ethic and interpersonal skills, but were described as less creative and adaptable than younger workers (Sparrow, 1999, in Davey, 2007). This sounds like a predictable stereotype, based on the discourse of ageism we just discussed. A review of research on the productivity of workers by the New Zealand Human Rights Commission (1998, cited in Davey, 2007) found that older workers were no less productive than their younger counterparts. Of course, older workers themselves can be influenced by the pervading ageist discourse, not valuing just how innovative and productive they are (Davey, 2007). We could call this internalised ageism. This is not just a 'bad attitude' that is easily put to rights with cheerful thoughts; we argue that there is a pervasive social atmosphere with many low expectations of older people, one that we are all caught up in. We hope that by studying this topic, and reflecting more on our lives and those of others around us, we can help to unsettle this discourse.

What do YOU think?

1. What images come to mind when you see the words 'ageing' or 'elderly'? Do you think of grey hair and wrinkles, or a relaxed life of retirees on a cruise ship?
2. What do you expect to be doing when you turn 55? If you are already 55, do you think you would have guessed what you are doing now back when you were 25?
3. Do you think you will retire some day? If so, when will that be?

People seem to use certain characteristics such as looks, posture and physical mobility as strong cues for relating to people on the basis of age (Ng & Salmond, 1998). Research on social cognition shows that these kinds of images 'filter' the ways people are perceived, and the behaviour towards them (Brewer, 1988). There is some anecdotal evidence that ageist expectations are changing (especially among Baby Boomers as they move past 50). However, other anecdotes, such as the problems some older people experience when getting into new relationships or waiting for service in shops, suggest that ageist attitudes are alive and well in New Zealand (Ng, Weatherall, Liu & Loong, 1998).

Ageing as loss

As people get older, it is common to count the loss of some physical abilities such as conventional ideas about youthful beauty. However, much more damaging is the ageism that is part of a larger discourse that constructs getting older as losing out: on health, appearance and options for living. The discourse goes beyond stereotyping because it is more than attitudes: it is a pervasive set of language, social organisation and social habits that help to create stereotypes that keep popping up in new forms. The view of ageing as loss is linked to a dominant political and economic belief about efficiency, as measured by speed and volume of output. Because older people are thought to be slower than younger people, they are also thought to be less efficient. It is true that many people slow down as they age, and their bodies will not work as quickly as they did at the height of their youth. But, this does not mean that older people should be regarded as no longer able to contribute as efficiently as they once did, as you will see later in the section on work. A variety of studies have shown that older workers surpass younger workers in speed of output as well as accuracy. Length of service is linked with greater competence, and this can compensate for any slowing down. Older workers tend to have fewer days off, and be generally more reliable. Therefore, as far as efficiency is concerned, experience can more than compensate for age. In the technology-driven race of the twenty-first century, it may sometimes seem hard to maintain respect for the accrued value of experience, and the slower, more considered approach that is more typical of 'old age'.

FROM MID-LIFE TO LATER LIFE: EVIDENCE FROM LONGITUDINAL NEW ZEALAND RESEARCH *FIONA ALPASS*

Due to increases in life expectancy and rapid improvements in medical care, older adults may now spend a significantly greater length of time in retirement compared to previous generations. Although there is a popular discourse around the continued social agency of 'third agers' (see Gilleard & Higgs, 2002; Laslett, 1989), and the potential for self-actualisation through increased travel and leisure activities, the reality is that social inequalities are readily apparent in this cohort. Access to health and financial resources differ significantly suggesting that, overall, an ageing population will increase demands for health care and income support.

There are a number of possible policy responses to this projected demand on resources. One is to encourage people to postpone retirement and prolong their economic activity. Another is to ensure that those in retirement can remain healthy and independent. Two of the main determinants of whether older adults remain in the workforce *and* maintain independence post-retirement are health status and health changes (Alavinia & Burdorf, 2008; Davey & Cornwall, 2003; Disney, Emmerson & Wakefield, 2006; Hansson, DeKoekkoek, Neece, & Patterson, 1997).

Although it is well documented that normal ageing involves changes in physical and mental health (Crimmins, 2004; Masoro & Austad, 2001), the antecedents of many health conditions, such as cardiovascular illness, are present in early midlife (e.g. Ilmarinen, 1994) and it is increasingly understood that such health deficits are not necessarily the result of ageing itself (Chandola, Ferrie, Sacker & Marmot, 2007; Rueda, Artazcoz & Navarro, 2008). The Health Work and Retirement study (HWR: Alpass, Towers, Stephens, Davey, Fitzgerald & Stevenson, 2007) was designed to identify the influences on health and wellbeing in later midlife that lay the basis for continued participation and health in later life. Specifically, this research follows the choices and life circumstances of midlife New Zealand adults to determine the factors that predict positive health outcomes in old age. The initial 3-year project collected information on physical and mental health, work and retirement factors, and socioeconomic and demographic status over time as older individuals (55 to 70 years) made the transition from work to retirement.

Analyses from the first wave data collection found that most of our participants were in paid employment. The proportion of retirees increased in the mid- to late sixties, but there were still a significant number of 65 to 70 year olds (34.9 per cent) in some form of paid employment. In addition, nearly three-quarters of our working respondents expressed a desire to continue in some form of part-time paid employment after their intended retirement age (Alpass, 2008). This is in line with the increasing workforce participation of older New Zealanders with the most recent census data showing 43 per cent of men and 25 per cent of women aged 65–69 years in the workforce—a 134 per cent and 400 per cent increase respectively over a twenty-year period (Statistics New Zealand, 2009b). Although these figures are an encouraging sign of the continued workforce participation and economic contribution of our older citizens, the recent economic crisis may mean that older workers are more vulnerable to the increasing probability of unemployment, redundancy and downsizing (Statistics New Zealand, 2009b).

Looking at the health of our participants in relation to their workforce participation, physical health declined across all age groups for all participants irrespective of their work or retirement status (Stephens & Noone, 2008). The relationship between poor health and employment status is well documented (Marmot & Wilkinson, 2006) and likely to be more salient as workers age. In contrast, mental health scores for our participants *increased* with age for workers but *decreased* with age for those in retirement. Although those with poorer mental health are likely to retire at a younger age, the trend for mental health to improve with age has been consistently found elsewhere (Chandola et al., 2007). Our initial cross-sectional data limits the extent to which causal inferences can be made, however these findings suggest a possible protective benefit for the work role on mental health in later life and provide a baseline snapshot of the current work and retirement experiences of our participants. With our longitudinal design (wave two of the HWR study and the subsequent New Zealand Longitudinal Study of Ageing), we will be able to track changes in individuals' work and retirement situations and the relationship of these changes to health and wellbeing. Further waves of data will help to distinguish between age and cohort effects and provide evidence for the causal links between midlife choices and subsequent health in older age.

About the author: **Fiona Alpass** *is an Associate Professor in the School of Psychology at Massey University. Fiona's research interests are focused on health-related topics with an emphasis on the older adult, with particular emphasis on the transition to retirement. Dr Alpass is a principal investigator on the New Zealand Longitudinal Study of Ageing funded by the Foundation for Research, Science and Technology.*

Let's face it: you have been ageing since before you were born. The biological process of ageing is simply the changes that occur as the organism gets older, a process which affects every living being, whether foetus or 50 year old. Socially, we count the 'milestones', such as the first word, first step, first birthday (not necessarily in that order), going to school, high school, leaving school. This list goes on to include settling down and starting a family, but then what? Is youth truly the best time of life, after which there is little more than a downhill slide into 'old age'?

Ageism is not a problem that can be solved by older people somehow 'getting their act together'. One of the ways in which this problem can be tackled is by reducing the social distance between old and young. However, a study by Ng and colleagues found considerable barriers to communication between old and young people who are not in the same family (Ng, Liu, Weatherall & Loong, 1997). Joan Cumming argued that relationships with children are crucial to the wellbeing of older adults, and that older adults can enhance the lives of children (Cumming, 1998). Not independence, but interdependence, was Joan's goal. The organisation Age Concern (www.ageconcern.org.nz) has run successful programs that encourage schools to invite older people in to talk with students, and there is increasing interest in these intergenerational relationships in early childhood education. Fortunately, there are going to be more older people around for the young ones to consult, for the foreseeable future.

Restrictive attitudes to ageing, such as not including older people in conversation, or setting up pensioner housing well away from busy centres, constitute negative stereotypes, and do not help either older people themselves or younger people who hold such attitudes. One of the main disadvantages of ageism is that these attitudes will turn against you if you live long enough! Many people feel shock and dismay when they see their first grey hair, and it can be very difficult to come to terms with such things as the 'chicken flesh' that appears on the neck as the skin begins to show the signs of ageing. Looking in the mirror to see an 'old' face looking back can be quite challenging, especially if you feel just like you did at a much younger age (most ageing faces have a young person behind them). Given some of the negative images of the older body, it is amazing that most older people come to terms with the new challenges that later life presents. The later years do not need to be a time to dread, but living longer does require some planning and adapting.

Ageing as gain

There is an opposing discourse about getting older, one that is much more positive than one that emphasises ageing as loss. Instead, there are many indications that the Euro-Western world is returning to more positive spaces for its older people. It seems timely, in a post-industrial society, to embrace the idea that adulthood is a time for renewal, and for finally getting the things right that we attempted when we were younger and less worldly-wise.

Getting older can be seen as the ongoing process of reflecting on and improving one's life: getting older and bolder. Our views of our ageing process are undoubtedly influenced by cultural ideas about the importance of older people. If we see mid-life as the top of the hill, with old age on the downhill side, we are in a very different place from those who see their experiences, to date as resources pointing to the incredible opportunities awaiting them in this latter portion of their lives. We expect that the way older people view themselves, and how they are treated by others, will continue to change with the ongoing shifts in the age structure of the population in the next 50 years, in New Zealand and elsewhere. Organisations such as Grey Power (www.greypower.co.nz) are advocacy groups that focus on acknowledging and expanding the rights of older people.

There are already systematic efforts under way, both globally and locally, to challenge ageist attitudes and to move beyond these to new positive frameworks. The United Nations International Year of Older Persons was part of an International Plan of Action on Ageing, set up in 1982. One of the main objectives of this UN Year was to raise awareness of the growing numbers of older people around the world, and to change attitudes so that societies become more consciously inclusive of all citizens, regardless of age. In New Zealand, the Prime Ministerial Task Force on Positive Ageing (1997) was set up 'to consider how our society can ensure that people move through their lives towards a healthy, independent, safe, secure and dignified old age; one in which they can participate in and contribute to society to the extent of their abilities and wishes' (p. 2). Although economic issues were clearly a motivating factor, a major goal of the Task Force was to achieve a social change in attitudes towards ageing in New Zealand. The Task Force noted the prevalence of age discrimination in the workplace, and the need to examine media portrayals of older people as two areas where attitude change to reduce ageism could be effected. These points have been incorporated into the New Zealand Government's *Positive Ageing Strategy* (Ministry of Social Policy, 2001). Age Concern has continued to run a variety of successful campaigns aimed at raising awareness about, and understanding issues for older people. But there is still a long way to go.

Why do some societies place great value on their old people? In Aotearoa, we have the example of Māori society, where, as Angus Macfarlane (2004c) explained, people are expected gradually to take up the positions of kaumātua (elders) as they get older. With their greater age and accumulated wisdom, they are accorded the mana (prestige) which a long life, well lived, deserves. These kaumātua are acknowledged as the repositories of cultural history; they are the kaitiaki (guardians) of the sacred knowledge and deep cultural values which find their expression in rituals and ceremony; they are the authorities from whom the health and wellbeing of the culture springs. There is no expectation of 'retirement' for kaumātua, who become busier as they get older (Parker, 1982).

According to Ng and his colleagues, the Confucian teaching of *xiao* (or filial piety), suggests that Chinese elders, too, are expected to continue in productive activities, to guide and support the young, and to take responsibility for bonding households together. Ng et al.'s (1998) careful study of intergenerational relationships in Chinese families in New Zealand shows how this teaching has survived as the Chinese community has become acculturated to life in a new country. At the same time, younger and mid-life Chinese adults interviewed had both positive ('well-travelled', family-oriented') and negative (e.g. 'stubborn', 'slow thinking') stereotypes of elders. However, another study, of views of intergenerational communication between elders from young students in a number of Pacific Rim countries, had diverse findings. Cynthia Gallois (1998) found that students from English-speaking countries were more likely than those from Asian and Pacific countries to say that they would act respectfully to accommodate an elder. She wondered if the anonymity of the questionnaire format meant that students from Asian cultures were able to 'complain' about elders in a way that would not be acceptable to say out loud in their cultures. Questionnaires can only measure what people say that they believe or do, which may not be as accurate as an observation of behaviour. In any case, it is clear that cultural and social values have a great deal to do with the extent to which older people, as a group, are respected. And this, in turn, affects the quality of their lives.

A very different discourse of ageing views it as a rich process of differentiation in which the human individual may be seen as becoming more exceptional and more interesting, increasing in their potential usefulness to succeeding generations. This is a discourse of age as a resource that dominates in Māori society. The experience that older people bring to decision making is an important resource which is often overlooked. We expect that the ageist attitudes that abound in Aotearoa will increasingly be challenged as the balance of the population shifts to favour older people. Older people today are healthier, better educated than their predecessors and more politically active (Ng & Salmond, 1998). Like any other group, when older people are seen to be in control of resources available to them, they will undoubtedly be given more respect, whereas it seems easy to dismiss someone who has little power over resources, is not youthful in appearance, doesn't shout over others and may not be dressed in the height of youthful fashion!

PERSONALITY DEVELOPMENT IN LATER ADULTHOOD

Erikson thought that towards the end of life the older person would spend some time reflecting on their life. He suggested that the crisis of integrity versus despair is the issue for the last stage of adult life. The positive outcome of this challenge to personal development would be a sense of satisfaction with what had been achieved over the person's lifetime. The negative outcome for the person would be to feel a sense of despair that they had not done what they may have hoped to do in their life. While it is likely that people reflect on these issues as they move into and through later adulthood, integrity and despair may not be issues just for older adults. Also, there may be many other issues that concern older adults, such as financial concerns about personal circumstances as well as about the next generation.

It is important for people who are approaching later life to think ahead, with an awareness of the diverse ways that people manage their later years. It is common to admire people who can 'still' do the things younger people do, or who 'still' look young. This shows the greater social value placed on youth rather than on the elderly. However, we all get old, and there seems to be little point denying the inevitable effects of ageing.

This is why it is important to consider the psychological debates about disengagement and the possibilities for generative reflection before cognitive development in later life.

Generative reflection

During the period of later life, it is common for older people to engage in generative reflection. The older person entering this period may undertake a life review, looking back on their life to examine and evaluate it. For many people, of course there is both pleasure and regret in looking back. Many films use 'deathbed' scenes to organise the portrayal of a person's life, showing the way that a person might look back on their lives with hope for change, through disclosing secrets or with regret about past mistakes; for example, the blind, bandaged traveller in the film *The English Patient* (dir. Minghella, 1997). There may be unresolved conflicts to face, or there may be new insights. Life review is different from simple reminiscence. At its best, generative reflection can enable a person to reflect purposefully on their life and achieve a sense of its integrity, and considerable satisfaction, as a result (Millar, 2001). For this reason, it can be a useful strategy for those experiencing difficulty in adjusting to the challenges of ill health (in particular) in old age. In recognition of the value of this form of life review, many rest homes now offer a service where someone will sit with the older person, listening to their life stories, and then write their biography.

Disengagement

One of the most influential theories of psychosocial ageing was the proposal by Cumming and Henry (1961) that people gradually withdraw from society as they age, and society reciprocally withdraws from them. These theorists suggested that this was a psychological process that perhaps offered older people the opportunity to reflect and come to terms with their lives in relative solitude. This theory had a huge influence on how older people were treated in the latter part of the twentieth century. While many older people would refute this theory, from their own experience, it is only relatively recently that it has been challenged through research. In a 12-year longitudinal study with adults aged over 65, Bassuk, Glass and Berkman (1999) showed that there is a relationship between social engagement and cognitive decline. You will not be surprised that they found that older people retain better health when they are involved in social activities in an ongoing way. Being part of a network of close interpersonal ties, and feeling wanted and useful, are, no doubt, aspects of a healthy life at any age. It seems strange that anyone ever thought that getting older could change people so markedly that they would not need or want good social contacts! As you will see in the section below, contrary to the picture of loneliness and neglect, older people have complex family and wider social networks.

COGNITIVE DEVELOPMENT IN LATER ADULTHOOD

One stereotype about older adults is that we 'lose our memories' as we age. Many studies have been done to investigate whether learning capabilities decline as people get older, and the news is good: many cognitive skills can be maintained or improved with age. Given the variety of individual experiences with ageing, it is not surprising that there are wide differences in people's adaptability in later life. Those with serious health problems may have difficulties in coping with the motivation or attention needed for certain activities, but this problem is not specific to later adulthood.

Early research on cognitive capacities in later life seemed to suggest that the intellectual skills of older adults tend to decline with age. It is now well accepted that such research relied too heavily on cross-sectional studies, where they were comparing the performances of people who had been born early in the twentieth century, with people who had been born much later. Of course, older people tended to have had very different educational experiences (Baltes & Schaie, 1974; Schaie, 1990). Such results are a prime example of the way researchers have tended to focus on negative ageing (Ng & Salmond, 1998). Older adults may be slightly less efficient in more mechanical cognitive skills, such as recalling lists of names, but on the other hand they are likely to be more widely informed than those of previous generations. Older adults have more memories and more to consider. Therefore, they can seem to be slower to respond in testing, or exam situations.

Research on older adults shows ways that people can grow in wisdom over the lifespan (Holliday & Chandler, 1986; Sternberg, 1990). Knowledge based on understanding of one's culture and history can be an enormous resource in managing the stresses of life. A lifetime of experience, and the work of nurturing the next generation, adds up to greater knowledge and understanding on the part of older adults.

PEOPLE CONNECTIONS

Changes in couple and friend relationships

In 2001, New Zealand-born women over age 65 were about as likely to live alone (40 per cent) as with a partner (38 per cent), but men of that age were much more likely to be in a couple (66 per cent versus 19 per cent alone: Callister, 2006). There is evidence that older people who are in a relationship with a partner have somewhat better health and less likelihood of physical difficulty or reported disability than those who are single or widowed (Statistics New Zealand, 2004). For people who remain in a couple relationship in their later years, perhaps the biggest adjustment one or the other will face is the death of their partner. In most partnerships, it is women who take care of their partner if they become frail, and women who are left to make a new life and face the extra years alone—and who therefore are more likely to require external support later in life. The older woman has often made some 'anticipatory' psychological preparations for the impact of widowhood, especially if she has seen the deaths of her other friends' partners, or cared for her own partner through declining health or terminal illness. This process of anticipatory psychological adjustment is less likely to have occurred for younger partners. Thus, the death of a partner at a young age can have a more powerful effect, as the one left behind may have no economic or social 'backup' plans for such an eventuality (Marshall & Levy, 1990). Maintaining friendships, family connections and other intergenerational relationships are strategies that enable successful adjustment at such times.

Some older people will be very involved with their extended family, perhaps doing some of the caregiving for younger children. Others may find that, because they do not live near relatives, most social contact is with friends, neighbours and people in their local community. Losses of friends can be hard: the grandmother of one of the authors felt much grief about losing most of her peer group, by outliving both her husband and her close women friends. Even though there was a big extended family nearby, her grandmother missed talking to others who had 'been there alongside her' in earlier times.

Gender still has an important part to play in the differing lives of older people. Women over age 65 are more likely to socialise with friends and family outside the home (55 per cent versus 44 per cent of men) and to participate in voluntary work for the community (until about age 80 for the latter). Men are more likely to continue to provide financial support to family members in later life (11 per cent versus 7 per cent of women) and to carry out unpaid chores for others outside their own home (all from Statistics New Zealand, 2004).

Grandparenting

Grandparenting has become a much more important phase of family life. Children born in 1900 had little chance of having any grandparents surviving by the time they reached adulthood. Now, however, with the increasing life expectancy, there is a chance that children will have living great-grandparents into their young adulthood. This creates possibilities for a very special time in the lifespan as the position of grandparent receives more acknowledgment and appreciation, and offers unique experiences:

> the roles of grandparent and grandchild can each span a period of up to 40 years in terms of potential intergenerational links. Someone who becomes a grandparent at age 50 is likely to experience many ways of being a grandparent over the ensuing 40 years, and will possibly live to experience their own children becoming grandparents (Keeling, Glasgow & Morris, 2008, p. 7).

Parents of 100 years ago were unlikely to be able to imagine ever seeing their great-grandchildren. There is also greater diversity in ages of parents and grandparents, as we saw in Chapter 2. Lise, one of the authors of this book, was fortunate to have her great-grandmother in her life till she was 21. There are still adults having children when they are in their late teens and early twenties, who may be grandparents in their forties. The trend towards later childbearing means that there are also a great many adults having children much later, who will then be grandparents later in life.

There is probably a discourse about grandparenting that constructs stereotyped images of the 'apple-cheeked', grey-haired Nana sitting in a rocking chair knitting, or the Granddad who takes the grandchildren off fishing. Such images of the grandparent, found in popular media, like magazines and television programs, tend to portray people in their sixties or seventies, but you could in fact be a grandparent anytime between your late thirties and the end of your life. Younger grandparents could feel that they do not fit the 'expected' age for this role, based on those media stereotypes, but, in fact, grandparents are a very diverse group of people who are mostly active adults. Many grandparents are in full-time work and/or may be taking responsibility for important family, community, economic or health development initiatives.

There is also great diversity in the intergenerational connections that grandparents have within families. Some grandchildren, whose parents are under extreme pressure in some way, spend a lot of time with their grandparents. The grandparents may have volunteered for regular child-minding duties, or the children may actually live with their grandparents—with or without their parents. Some parents at mid-life find that they become de facto grandparents, as their children meet and settle with partners who have children from previous relationships. Some grandparents find that they lose touch with their grandchildren, by a reverse process after their son's or daughter's relationship ends.

The type of grandparent you can become may be influenced by a variety of things, not all of which will be within your control. There is also the desire of many older people to move back to their homeplace, or simply to move to a favourite place to retire, perhaps near the sea. Geographical distance between grandparents and grandchildren can work against the development of close intergenerational relationships. This is particularly difficult for immigrants from other countries, as we noted in the last chapter. On the other hand, grandparenting can be a most wonderful and fulfilling experience, free of the nervous concerns of parenting, and we think it is heartening how many people maintain regular contact with extended family in later life.

One study of grandparenthood proposed three different styles of grandparenting (Cherlin & Furstenburg, 1986): **remote, companionate** or **involved**. Grandparents may be remote if they see their grandchildren infrequently, and at the same time do not try to build a particularly warm or close relationship with them. Companionate grandparents, on the other hand, may be those who want to be friends with their mokopuna and enjoy them, but tend not to discipline or criticise them. Finally, involved grandparents might take a role very similar to that of a parent, correcting the grandchildren, giving them advice, discussing the child's problems and helping them with schoolwork. Of course, any such categorisation tends to oversimplify the complexities of grandparenting.

There are likely to be many more styles of interacting and many more nuances within each of these special relationships. In times gone by, when families were larger and households were often multi-generational, grandparents were likely to have a significant role in supporting the parents and caring for the grandchildren. In such situations, grandparents and parents may have worked together to care for the children, and grandparents might have stood in place of parents, in much the same way many Māori families do today. A similar style of involved grandparenting may occur if grandparents take on major responsibilities for an infant born to a a young daughter living at home. In other situations, there may be young parents who live with their own parents or in-laws as a way to save money; though in our experience these adults will often be motivated to move out as soon as this is possible. Nowadays, there is usually a longer gap between the time young people leave home and the time they might have a first baby. This means that prospective grandparents also have a period when the children have left home and they are 'free' to develop a lifestyle not unlike that of their offspring without children. The onset of grandparenting might even be something of a shock for this group, if they have become involved in activities without children (e.g. going to clubs or other evening entertainment).

We should emphasise here that there are bound to be diverse experiences of grandparenting depending on place and culture. Recent research in Aotearoa has looked at experiences of grandparents in rural South Island communities. Keeling et al. (2008) looked at views of 11- to 13-year-old students about people they considered to be grandparents, whether living or not. It was interesting that, though the majority of children lived in nuclear family homes without extended family, half lived within 90 minutes' drive of a grandparent, and nearly 40 per cent had daily or weekly contact with a grandparent. These findings indicate that many grandparents in these rural areas led lives closely interwoven with their children and grandchildren.

Some commentators suggest that grandparents can become important at times of family stress, such as separation and divorce (Millar, 2001; Troll, 1983). Moreover, Millar boldly states that 'grandparents are an undervalued asset in an increasingly materialistic society' (Millar, 2001, p. 57). She suggests that changes in society have impacted on grandparents more than on any previous generation. For this reason, and given changes we have discussed regarding Māori and immigrant families, we think it is likely that the generation known as grandparents may have much in common across different cultures compared with other generations.

Work

Using Census data for her analyses, Davey (2007) noted that in the past 25 years there has been an increase in the number of men working after age 65, so that now more than 1 in 5 men of this age are in paid work. In the past decade, there have been more men working after age 55, and this is expected to continue to increase (Dunstan & Thomson, 2006). There has also been an increase over time for women in paid work in this age-group, though fewer women are involved (only about 1 in

14 in paid work: Davey, 2007). This is a higher rate of workforce participation than found for older people in Canada, Australia and the UK, but lower than rates for Japan and the USA (Dunstan & Thomson, 2006).

At a personal level, there are likely to be many changes in the place of work in one's life, especially during the later years. One thing to notice about 'retirement' is its name. Exactly what is it that one is supposed to be retiring from? Another thing to notice is that the idea of retirement is linked to age, as if older people cannot be expected to engage in paid work. However, as we suggested above, the once dominant idea of thinking of the life cycle in three sequential stages, namely, preparation for paid work, paid work and well-earned leisure, is fading as work patterns shift and change. More and more adults are finding themselves out of work when they least expected to be. Such experiences challenge the idea that retirement occurs at a particular age, and underline the fact that retiring from the world of paid work is something that can happen at any age. Such retirement can be temporary, or it can be permanent.

Preparing for retirement

Whether you retire from paid work forcibly or by choice, and when you decide not to seek further work, it may be difficult to change the centrality of work in your life. It may have structured your days, weeks and years for a long time. It certainly structures the way many, if not most other people in our society think of their daily life—just think of how most people view weekends (and how cheated you feel if you have to work). 'Retirees' need to find new ways to use time, and to take advantage of the new opportunities this opens up. It is possible to think ahead, and perhaps develop new interests that can be enjoyed for a long time before reaching this milestone. For example, if you have been a runner, you might move to becoming a tramper during mid-life, and it may be possible to continue this interest for some time post-retirement. However, there will come a time when you may find it more comfortable—and just as enjoyable—to simply go walking with friends on a regular basis. These examples are not everyone's ideal occupations, but the point is that you can deliberately manage your interests and preoccupations to accord with your capacities as you age. This is the same principle as adapting to new conditions at any time of life, which you will already have done many times. Another, perhaps greater, challenge on retirement can be the loss of status that goes with having a paid job in Aotearoa.

On the day after her retirement from a busy teaching career, New Zealander Joan Cumming felt 'devastated'. It seemed that older people, such as she suddenly was, were not welcome in places she wanted to be. Eventually, she began a new career as an age activist, working mainly with Age Concern. Asked about her philosophy of ageing, she said, 'If you don't want to die a slow, boring death, you have to get involved in community—and not just your way. You have to be aware of what young people are having to learn now, not just what you want to learn'. One of the high points of her career was her eightieth birthday party, which included champagne, a trip around Raglan harbour on a boat, 'octogenarian games' and a banquet on a wild beach with her grandchildren, family and a few close friends. The contribution by Bruce McMillan in this chapter gives a more detailed look at the diversity of lives for people who have retired.

THE EXPERIENCE OF RETIREMENT *BRUCE McMILLAN*

There is no alarm jarring us into alertness, but we wake as usual around 7 am There is no 'work' ahead of us, so no rushing to get anywhere on time. Instead, our regular routine applies: get up, dressed, set out the breakfast, collect the morning paper from the gate, and sit together to eat, read the newspaper, have the first of two mandatory coffees for the morning, and talk to each other.

Some time after breakfast, I check email and the computer calendar. We will already have noted if there is a meeting, or some other commitment one or both of us may have. Usually there is not, so the day really is our own. Perhaps it is a good day for a long walk, or a bike ride. Or we realise a grandchild or friend has a birthday next week, so arrange to buy a card or present, and check what other shopping might be necessary.

Despite both being retired, we are busy people: 'busy' in having more than enough tasks and activities to fill our day, but not pressured by the number of commitments we used to try to fit around full-time work. We've been there, and enjoyed our professional roles. But now we are glad we can choose what we wish to be busy at.

We are able to make such choices that were only dreamed of when we were young adults with family, community, and work commitments necessarily limiting our freedom. What we actually experience is very different from the myths or common misrepresentations about older people (for example, those addressed by the American Psychological Association (undated): we are not alone and lonely; we are not sick, frail or dependent on others; we are not cognitively impaired (though our offspring may wonder at times)). There are, of course, a few to whom such descriptions apply. But the research and census data on older people shows that retired people typically are in fact healthy, contented and engage in a variety of activities.

But facts alone do not represent the human face of retirement. Our personal experience provides some illustrations.

- Many of us retired people still work, but at times and to the extent we choose. I teach a university Summer School class, and undertake some other university tasks.
- Many have community responsibilities. That is nothing new, as we have both been involved in many different groups over the years. These days regular commitments include being on the committee of our local U3A (providing learning experiences for seniors) where my university contacts are a valuable resource in course planning, and we both attend all the courses. We are also involved with other groups, including music commitments, garden group or occasional ones such as organising a fiftieth reunion of a professional group.
- The family becomes even more important. Our adult 'children' are all busy in their own work and family commitments, so understanding (but not imposing our solutions on) the little dramas that occupy them means keeping in touch with them in order to know what each is doing. Since some are overseas, we are grateful for cheaper communication compared to the past.
- It seems our grandchildren are growing quickly. It is no time at all before this one is beginning school, or that one leaving school to continue at university, and each of them appreciates time with us to explain the excitement and novelty of the choices they are making—as if we had never heard of the options they confront.
- We have friends! At our age, many of our friends drop by or are able to visit from afar. Or we contact them by email, letter mail, phone calls or the occasional trip away from home to see them. (We never go overseas as tourists, but do go occasionally to visit family and friends.)

Keeping in touch with friends is more important than ever, and sometimes that involves going to the funeral of one of them ... where we inevitably meet many of our other friends, too.

It is important for us retired folk to have projects for the future. One we planned for 2008 was to cycle the Otago Central Rail Trail over 5 days. It was a wonderful physical activity. It was also a social event, and deeply personal: we both have life-long links to the area and remember travelling it by train. So for us it was a time of reminiscence and rediscovery of the past. We also discovered we were not alone in being retired and enjoying the experience: we heard from those operating trail support businesses that the most common age for biking the trail is age 60 to 70; the next most common is 70 to 80. We enjoyed meeting and talking with many of them.

We cannot deny the inevitability of death. It has been close to us. We each married early (as was common in the 1960s) but each has experienced the early death of our marriage partners: one from cardiac arrest at age 45, the other from cancer at age 50. But we had all been friends for many years, and enjoy having known each other's partner and being part of each other's families. We are sharply aware of the importance of continuing to attend to those of our age group or older, especially those who are perhaps not able to be as active as we are.

We are enjoying this third age of our lives. We know where we have come from in our developmental pathway, and we know it will come to an end. Till then, we will remain busy, socially active, thinking and reasonably energetic senior citizens. We know that what we do and have done with our lives did not achieve fame, but is sufficiently valued by our families and by others. Life is good.

*About the author: Over 40 years ago, in his first year as a student, **Bruce McMillan** chose a paper in Human Development at Otago, though it was not required for his chosen professional path. The paper appealed because it was of practical value in dealing with real human beings. He eventually completed postgraduate study and was appointed to the School of Education at the University of Otago. Now retired, he still enjoys teaching that paper in Summer School: it gives a focus to his continued reading of interesting new research in the field, and is relevant to understanding his own development and his growing three-generational family life, which in turn continues to challenge his understanding of families, society and culture.*

What do YOU think?

1. What is your own experience of participation in paid work?
2. Have you thought about retirement for yourself? How do you see your life during a time of retirement?
3. Do you think there are advantages of planning for retirement from an early age? What kinds of things might you consider?

LIFESTYLES IN LATER LIFE

Where to live

The idea that older people mostly live in rest homes is a myth. According to statistical projections, women aged 65 in 2001 are likely to live another 20 years, of which only the last 8.5 years might be in supported living situations; while men of this age might live about 16.5 more years, of which 7 years might be in assisted settings (Statistics New Zealand, 2004). Of course, these figures are averages, and there is huge diversity in the lives of older people. About one in three older people lives alone, and most older people live in their own home (Statistics New Zealand, 2004). At the 1996 census, only 4.9 per cent of the population over 65 were living in rest homes, and almost half of these were 85 years or older (Statistics New Zealand, 1998d). The 2006 New Zealand Disability Survey showed that only 5 per cent of persons with a disability live in residential facilities: the highest proportion of these are persons with a physical disability, aged over 65 years (Statistics New Zealand, 2007c). This reflects again the fact that disability, rather than age, is a major factor determining the lifestyle of older people. For those who can afford it, there is an increasingly creative variety of lifestyle options on offer for older people. These include the development of whole complexes that incorporate living arrangements for people with different levels of dependency, and insurance options that enable a person to buy into schemes that will guarantee an income for as long as they live, in return for signing over some or all of their assets.

Studies overseas reveal that older people tend to stay in regular touch with their families and their communities, and this finding was supported by a report commissioned by Age Concern (Colmar Brunton, 1990). Indeed, it is quite clear that one of the central concerns for people at mid-life is keeping in touch with ageing parents. These results suggest that the stereotype of the lonely, isolated older person is not the norm. Nevertheless, work by Ng and his colleagues suggests that while intergenerational communication between family members may be more frequent, there remain barriers to communication between non-family members (Ng et al., 1997). One of the issues here is that, in Aotearoa, people tend to look for friends among their own age group. This strategy can of course become problematic as one gets older. Joining a 'retirement village' might provide just such a peer group.

Keeping physically active

One of the important 'facts' about ageing is encapsulated in the adage 'use it or lose it'. This is as true of your intellect as it is of your physical capacities, including your sex life. Yet such have been the expectations of the later years—that older people 'can't'—that many older people really do lose their capacities simply because they have not set themselves the goal of maintaining an active life. In this way, physical losses with ageing can become a self-fulfilling prophecy. The relatively quick advances in life expectancies have perhaps found us generally unprepared for the extension of our own later years. But pictures of the retired person lying back on their couch, or travelling round in their camper van, or lying about at home, resting after the struggles of their 'active' life, do not help us to adapt either. There are many good reasons for rethinking this picture of rest at retirement, and for giving some serious thought to how you personally want to spend the last one-fifth of your life.

In a piece called 'On your marks, get set, slow down', Bevan Grant (2004) suggested that older people have very divergent ideas about what constitutes successful ageing. He pointed out that people aged 70 or more today grew up at a time when physical activity for their ageing parents was actually discouraged, in the belief that the body should not be too stressed as it ages (Grant, 2001). Grant (2004) also noted that cultures differ in the amount of exercise that is considered usual for older people. We live in such a youth-oriented culture that seeing an older person in running gear or working out at a gym may be so unusual that the person feels conspicuous and even embarrassed. Yet, keeping active and exercising are important for continuing health in later years. Lise, one of the authors of this book, has a relative who organised a jogging class for people in a retirement home, a class that had one keen 90 year old participant. Other kinds of movement can provide exercise that keeps us more flexible and stable as we get older. For example, there are classes for people over 60 in some swimming pools that focus on aerobic exercise in the low-impact environment of a warm pool. China has given people around the world a martial art that can be done by people of any age: tai chi is unusual in its emphasis on slow movement and balance, and is popular with older people in this country. Computer fitness games with a large muscle component (e.g. virtual tennis) provide exercise to older people who have difficulty getting outside. Weight-bearing exercise is also important for continued bone health, even if weights are 200 gram tins rather than 3 kilogram free weights. If you currently exercise or play sport regularly, is your form of exercise one that you are likely to maintain for the next 10, 20 or 40 years? Finding exercise we enjoy as our bodies change requires some creativity and willingness to try new things.

Interdependence and support

At the time of planning for the International Year of Older Persons in 1999, the United Nations (1998) put out a statement of Principles for Older Persons. This was done in acknowledgement of changes in the world demographic towards a greater proportion of older people, and the incredible resource represented by our elders for all levels of contemporary culture, including the spiritual, economic and possibilities for peace across the world. The principles were divided into five main areas. The first was an emphasis on the *independence* of older people, to ensure that elders would have the sustenance and support to live good lives. The second set of principles was created to ensure that elders are entitled to full *participation* as integrated members of their communities. The third set focused on the level of *care* and protection to which older people should have a right. There was attention paid to the older person's right to *self-fulfillment* through a wide range of opportunities in their culture and *dignity* as human beings, in the last two sets of principles.

THE FRAIL OLDER ADULT

The period of late older adulthood lasts until the person's death. For some people, age or ill-health may catch up, and eventually it may dictate that they need support in order to live comfortably. Most old older adults prefer to live in their own home, only leaving it when poor health or disability demands otherwise. If this happens, and they need to make longer term changes in order to cope with a health problem, they may move into a supported living situation. In a few circumstances, this may mean full hospital facilities or, alternatively, it may be in a retirement complex with facilities set up for the supportive care of the old.

At some point in life, all of us who die from an illness or just general deterioration (rather than a sudden event like an accident) are likely to experience a period of frailty. It would be irresponsible to deny that the physical tendency of ageing is towards becoming more frail. However, most older people feel that they are in fairly good health. One acquaintance of 82 remarked that getting older is 'the art of the possible': he regrets that he is unable to do many of the things he used to do, but he is nevertheless able to do many other things which he enjoys to the full.

It is crucial to realise that a time could come when you must recognise that you are not caring for yourself properly, and you must decide to allow others to help you care for yourself. In this situation, the body may be failing, but this does not necessarily imply that the spirit is failing also, and many older people find this decision very difficult because it can feel like losing control of one's life. But not recognising, and not talking about, our declining strength may make it harder, especially if others are forced to make a life-changing decision on our behalf. While independence is a well-articulated goal of Euro-Western maturity, this 'independent streak' can be the downfall of an older person: it can prevent them from accepting appropriate care. Frail older people, like frail people of any age, need support to live comfortably. When people become frail—and this can happen at any age—it is incumbent on the rest of society to care for and support them in ways that do not take away their dignity. Valuing independence does not mean that everyone else is absolved from offering appropriate support!

Physiological changes in later life

One of the myths of ageing is that all older people are sick. This is quite simply not true. 'Old age' is not an illness, and ageing is not a medical condition. An older adult who is ill deserves the same quality of care that is due to anyone who becomes ill, regardless of age. Nevertheless, it is true that the older the body gets, the more vulnerable it becomes to disease, first because the immune system may not work so well, and also because, for various reasons, the processes of self-healing may not work as effectively either. Various small deleterious changes, such as the loss of **collagen** that helps the body tissue to remain supple, gradually add up, and the body begins to find it harder to adapt to new challenges. Loss of **adaptive capacity** may be responsible for greater susceptibility to diseases such as arthritis in later life, but it is important to note that ageing per se is not a cause. As the body gets older various systems may lose efficiency. For example, an older body tends to lose the ability to detect up to 9-degree differences in temperature, making it difficult to know when one may be getting too cold and leaving the oldest people more vulnerable to hypothermia.

Cognitive difficulties in later life

A major 'epidemic' affecting large numbers of people in the Euro-Western world over the age of 85 is dementia, which refers to a significant loss of mental powers, such as memory and reasoning. Dementia can also be associated with changes in behaviour and personality. In New Zealand, the incidence of all kinds of dementias was estimated to be 5 per cent up to age 80, and at least 20 per cent thereafter (Richmond, Baskett, Bonita & Melding, 1995). This is consistent with similar estimates in the Euro-Western world. Dementia presents strong challenges to families, such as the demands of in-family care, problems of finding suitable alternative and respite care and the (living) loss of the person who was once so dear (see Opie, 1991, 1992, 1995; Richmond et al., 1995, for further discussion).

Dementias take several forms, but the most common is Alzheimer's Disease. This is a progressive, degenerative condition of the brain, for which there is as yet no known cure, though there are medications that appear to be successful in slowing some of its effects. A recent Report (Alzheimer's New Zealand, 2008) estimated that dementia affects over 40 000 or 1 per cent of the population of Aotearoa, 60 per cent of whom are female. The Report suggests that this figure is likely to climb to almost double in the next 20 years. Dementia creates havoc in the brain, particularly in the way neurons connect from one part of the brain to another: the smooth transmission of information that underlies many ordinary tasks is disrupted. As a result, our short-term memory gradually wears away, and with it goes the organisation that enables the brain to link ideas and behaviours together so that these make sense. As time goes on, the behaviour of the person with Alzheimer's becomes more erratic, and hence much harder for those around the person to cope with.

The future of ageing

The increasing number of older people around the world is a huge global shift that was called the 'agequake' at a UN World Assembly on Ageing in Madrid in 2002 (Boston & Davey, 2006). The negative discourses about ageing create a social atmosphere of some negativity around this change, with doom and gloom predictions about economies suffering from the increase in frail older people. We would like to remind you here of more positive discourses about ageing that construct a gain for all our cultures in future, as older people move towards longer lives of more activity and social connection. People may pursue education much later in life, have a greater variety of partner relationships and accrue the economic benefits of an age-diversified workforce (Boston & Davey, 2006). We think 'on the ground' there is bound to be greater diversity among older people, with an increasing gap between older people who are affluent, or who are more impoverished. Whether this is accompanied by greater respect for what elders in society have to offer, or increasing distrust between generations, will be up to us.

Current Perspectives in Later Adulthood

There are a wide range of beliefs regarding the social position and status of the aged in American society today. Some people believe that the best way to understand the problems of the elderly is to regard them as a minority group, faced with difficulties similar to those of other minority groups. Discrimination against older people, like racial discrimination, is believed to be based on a bias against visible physical traits. Since the aging process is viewed negatively, it is natural that the elderly try to appear and act younger. Some spend a tremendous amount of money trying to make themselves look and feel younger.

The theory that old people are a minority group is weak because too many circumstances prove otherwise. The U.S. Congress, for example, favors its senior members, and delegates power to them by bestowing considerable prestige. The leadership roles in most religious organizations are held by older persons. Many older Americans are in good health, have comfortable incomes, and are treated with respect by friends and associates.

Perhaps the most realistic way to view the aged is as a status group, like other status groups in society. Every society has some method of "age grading," by which it groups together individuals of roughly similar age. ("Preteens" and "senior citizens" are some of the age-grade labels in American society.)

Because it is a labeling process, age grading causes members of the age group, as well as others, to perceive them in terms of the connotations of the label. Unfortunately, the tag "old age" often has negative connotations in American society.

The readings included in this section illustrate the wide range of stereotypical attitudes toward older Americans. Many of society's typical assumptions about the limitations of old age have been refuted. A major force behind this reassessment of the elderly is that there are so many people living longer and healthier lives, and in consequence, playing more of a role in all aspects of our society. Older people can remain productive members of society for many more years than has been traditionally assumed.

Such standard stereotypes of the elderly as frail, senile, childish, and sexually inactive are topics discussed in this section. Mary Pipher, in "Society Fears the Aging Process," contends that young people often avoid interacting with older persons because it reminds them that someday they too will get old and die. She further argues that the media most often portray a negative and stereotypical view of the elderly.

© Royalty-Free/CORBIS

In "Research: Oldest Americans Happiest," Lindsey Tanner points out that the stereotype view of the older Americans being lonely, isolated, and unhappy was not proven to be the reality that was found in a number of different studies on this subject.

"Lost and Found," deals with people with Alzheimer's disease. The author, Barbara Basler, describes new therapeutic methods devised by Cameron Camp, the head of the Myers Research Institute in Ohio. Dr. Camp's methods, deemed valid and reliable by researchers, help draw patients out of their confusion and recapture some of their basic skills and knowledge.

Society Fears the Aging Process

Americans fear the processes of aging and dying, Mary Pipher contends in the following viewpoint. She claims that younger and healthier adults often avoid spending time around the aging because they want to avoid the issues of mortality and loss of independence. In addition, she contends that negative views of the aging process are portrayed in the media and expressed through the use of pejorative words to describe the elderly. Pipher is a psychologist and author of several books, including *Another Country: Navigating the Emotional Terrain of Our Elders,* the book from which this viewpoint was excerpted.

MARY PIPHER

We segregate the old for many reasons—prejudice, ignorance, a lack of good alternatives, and a youth-worshiping culture without guidelines on how to care for the old. The old are different from us, and that makes us nervous. Xenophobia means fear of people from another country. In America we are xenophobic toward our old people.

How Greeting Cards Reflect Culture

An anthropologist could learn about us by examining our greeting cards. As with all aspects of popular culture, greeting cards both mirror and shape our realities. Cards reflect what we feel about people in different roles, and they also teach us what to feel. I visited my favorite local drugstore and took a look.

There are really two sets of cards that relate to aging. One is the grandparent/grandchild set that is all about connection. Even a very dim-witted anthropologist would sense the love and respect that exist between these two generations in our culture. Young children's cards to their grandparents say, "I wish I could hop on your lap," or, "You're so much fun." Grandparents' cards to children are filled with pride and love.

There is another section of cards on birthdays. These compare human aging to wine aging, or point out compensations. "With age comes wisdom, of course that doesn't make up for what you lose." We joke the most about that which makes us anxious. "Have you picked out your bench at the mall yet?" There are jokes about hearing loss, incontinence, and losing sexual abilities and interest. There are cards on saggy behinds, gray hair, and wrinkles, and cards about preferring chocolate or

sleep to sex. "You know you're getting old when someone asks if you're getting enough and you think about sleep."

Fears of Aging and Dying

Poking fun at aging isn't all bad. It's better to laugh than to cry, especially at what cannot be prevented. However, these jokes reflect our fears about aging in a youth-oriented culture. We younger, healthier people sometimes avoid the old to avoid our own fears of aging. If we aren't around dying people, we don't have to think about dying.

We baby boomers have been a futureless generation, raised in the eternal present of TV and advertising. We have allowed ourselves to be persuaded by ads that teach that if we take good care of ourselves, we will stay healthy. Sick people, hospitals, and funerals destroy our illusions of invulnerability. They force us to think of the future.

Carolyn Heilbrun said, "It is only past the meridian of fifty that one can believe that the universal sentence of death applies to oneself." Before that time, if we are healthy, we are likely to be in deep denial about death, to feel as if we have plenty of time, that we have an endless vista ahead. But in hospitals and at funerals, we remember that we all will die in the last act. And we don't necessarily appreciate being reminded.

When I first visited rest homes, I had to force myself to stay. What made me most upset was the thought of myself in a place like that. I didn't want to go there, literally or figuratively. Recently I sat in an eye doctor's office surrounded by old people with white canes. Being in this room gave me intimations of mortality. I thought of Bob Dylan's line: "It's not dark yet, but it's getting there."

We know the old-old will die soon. The more we care and the more involved we are with the old, the more pain we feel at their suffering. Death is easier to bear in the abstract, far away and clinical. It's much harder to watch someone we love fade before our eyes. It's hard to visit an uncle in a rest home and realize he no longer knows who we are or even who he is. It's hard to see a grandmother in pain or drugged up on morphine. Sometimes it's so hard that we stay away from the people who need us the most.

Our culture reinforces our individual fears. To call something old is to insult, as in *old hat* or *old ideas.* To call something young is to compliment, as in *young thinking* or *young acting.* It's considered rude even to ask an old person's age. When we meet an adult we haven't seen in a long time, we compliment her by saying, "You haven't aged at all." The taboos against acknowledging age tell us that aging is shameful.

Many of the people I interviewed were uncomfortable talking about age and were unhappy to be labeled old. They said, "I don't feel old." What they meant was, "I don't act and feel like the person who the stereotypes suggest I am." Also, they were trying to avoid being put in a socially undesirable class. In this country, it is unpleasant to be called old, just as it is unpleasant to be called fat or poor. The old naturally try to avoid being identified with an unappreciated group. . . .

The Elderly Are Treated Poorly

Nothing in our culture guides us in a positive way toward the old. Our media, music, and advertising industries all glorify the young. Stereotypes suggest that older people keep younger people from fun, work, and excitement. They take time (valuable time) and patience (in very short supply in the 1990s). We are very body-oriented, and old bodies fail. We are appearance-oriented, and youthful attractiveness fades. We are not taught that old spirits often shimmer with beauty.

Language is a problem. Old people are referred to in pejorative terms, such as *biddy, codger,* or *geezer,* or with cutesy words, such as *oldster, chronologically challenged,* or *senior citizen.* People describe themselves as "eighty years young." Even *retirement* is an ugly word that implies passivity, uselessness, and withdrawal from the social and working world. Many of the old are offended by ageist stereotypes and jokes. Some internalize these beliefs and feel badly about themselves. They stay with their own kind in order to avoid the harsh appraisals of the young.

Some people do not have good manners with the old. I've seen the elderly bossed around, treated like children or simpletons, and simply ignored. Once in a cafe, I heard a woman order her mother to take a pill and saw the mother wince in embarrassment. My mother-in-law says she sees young people but they don't see her. Her age makes her invisible.

In our culture the old are held to an odd standard. They are admired for not being a bother, for being chronically cheerful. They are expected to be interested in others, bland in their opinions, optimistic, and emotionally generous. But the young certainly don't hold themselves to these standards.

Accidents that old drivers have are blamed on age. After a ninety-year-old friend had his first car accident, he was terrified that he would lose his license. "If I were young, this accident would be perceived as just one of those things," he pointed out. "But because I am old, it will be attributed to my age." Now, of course, some old people are bad drivers. But so are some young people. To say "He did that because he's old" is often as narrow as to say, "He did that because he's black" or "Japanese." Young people burn countertops with hot pans, forget appointments, and write overdrafts on their checking accounts. But when the old do these same things, they experience double jeopardy. Their mistakes are not viewed as accidents but rather as loss of functioning. Such mistakes have implications for their freedom.

Media Stereotypes

As in so many other areas, the media hurts rather than helps with our social misunderstandings. George Gerbner reported on the curious absence of media images of people older than sixty-five. Every once in a while a romantic movie plot might involve an older man, but almost never an older woman. In general, the old have been cast as silly, stubborn, and eccentric. He also found that on children's programs, older women bear a disproportionate burden of negative characteristics. In our culture, the old get lumped together into a few stereotyped images: the sweet old lady, the lecherous old man, or the irascible but softhearted grandfather. Almost no ads and billboards feature the old. Every now and then an ad will show a grandparent figure, but then the grandparent is invariably youthful and healthy.

In *Fountain of Age,* Betty Friedan noted that the old are portrayed as sexless, demented, incontinent, toothless, and childish. Old women are portrayed as sentimental, naive, and silly gossips, and as troublemakers. A common movie plot is the portrayal of the old trying to be young—showing them on motorbikes, talking hip or dirty, or liking rock and roll. Of course there are exceptions, such as *Nobody's Fool, On Golden Pond, Mr. and Mrs. Bridge, Driving Miss Daisy, Mrs. Brown,* and *Twilight.* But we need more movies in which old people are portrayed in all their diversity and complexity.

The media is only part of much larger cultural problems. We aren't organized to accommodate this developmental stage. For example, being old-old costs a lot of money. Assisted-living housing, medical care, and all the other services the old need are expensive. And yet, most old people can't earn money. It's true that some of our elders are wealthy, but many live on small incomes. Visiting the old, I heard tragic stories involving money. I met Arlene, who, while dying of cancer, had to fear losing her house because of high property taxes. I met Shirley, who lived on noodles and white rice so that she could buy food for her cat and small gifts for her grandchildren. I met people who had to choose between pills and food or heat.

The American Obsession with Independence

Another thing that makes old age a difficult stage to navigate is our American belief that adults need no one. We think of independence as the ideal state for adults. We associate independence with heroes and cultural icons such as the Marlboro man and the Virginia Slims woman, and we associate dependence with toxic families, enmeshment, and weakness. To our post-modern, educated ears, a psychologically healthy but dependent adult sounds oxymoronic.

We all learn when we are very young to make our own personal declarations of independence. In our culture, *adult* means "self-sufficient." Autonomy is our highest virtue. We want relationships that have no strings attached instead of understanding, as one lady told me, "Honey, life ain't nothing but strings."

These American ideas about independence hurt families with teens. Just when children most need guidance from parents, they turn away from them and toward peers and media. They are socialized to believe that to be an adult, they must break away from parents. Our ideas about independence also hurt families with aging relatives. As people move from the young-old stage into the old-old stage, they need more help. Yet in our culture we provide almost no graceful ways for adults to ask for help. We make it almost impossible to be dependent yet dignified, respected, and in control.

As people age, they may need help with everything from their finances to their driving. They may need help getting out of bed, feeding themselves, and bathing. Many would rather pay strangers, do without help, or even die than be dependent on those they love. They don't want to be a burden, the greatest of American crimes. The old-old often feel ashamed of what is a natural stage of the life cycle. In fact, the greatest challenge for many elders is learning to accept vulnerability and to ask for help.

If we view life as a time line, we realize that all of us are sometimes more and sometimes less dependent on others. At certain stages we are caretakers, and at other stages we are cared for. Neither stage is superior to the other. Neither implies pathology or weakness. Both are just the results of life having seasons and circumstances. In fact, good mental health is not a matter of being dependent or independent, but of being able to accept the stage one is in with grace and dignity. It's an awareness of being, over the course of one's lifetime, continually interdependent.

Rethinking Dependency

In our culture the old fear their deaths will go badly, slowly, and painfully, and will cost lots of money. Nobody wants to die alone, yet nobody wants to put their families through too much stress. Families are uneasy as they negotiate this rocky terrain. The trick for the younger members is to help without feeling trapped and overwhelmed. The trick for older members is to accept help while preserving dignity and control. Caregivers can say, "You have nurtured us, why wouldn't we want to nurture you?" The old must learn to say, "I am grateful for your help and I am still a person worthy of respect."

As our times and circumstances change, we need new language. We need the elderly to become elders. We need a word for the neediness of the old-old, a word with less negative connotations than *dependency,* a word that connotes wisdom, connection, and dignity. *Dependency* could become mutuality or

interdependency. We can say to the old: "You need us now, but we needed you and we will need our children. We need each other."

However, the issues are much larger than simply which words to use or social skills to employ. We need to completely rethink our ideas about caring for the elderly. Like the Lakota, we need to see it as an honor and an opportunity to learn. It is our chance to repay our parents for the love they gave us, and it is our last chance to become grown-ups. We help them to help ourselves.

We need to make the old understand that they can be helped without being infantilized, that the help comes from respect and gratitude rather than from pity or a sense of obligation. In our society of disposables and planned obsolescence, the old are phased out. Usually they fade away graciously. They want to be kind and strong, and, in America, they learn that to do so means they should ask little of others and not bother young people.

Perhaps we need to help them redefine kindness and courage. For the old, to be kind ought to mean welcoming younger relatives' help, and to be brave ought to mean accepting the dependency that old-old age will bring. We can reassure the old that by showing their children how to cope, they will teach them and their children how well this last stage can be managed. This information is not peripheral but rather something everyone will need to know.

Further Readings

Henry J. Aaron and Robert D. Reischauer. *Countdown to Reform: The Great Social Security Debate.* New York: Century Foundation Press, 2001.

Claude Amarnick. *Don't Put Me in a Nursing Home.* Deerfield Beach, FL: Garrett, 1996.

Dean Baker and Mark Weisbrot. *Social Security: The Phony Crisis.* Chicago: University of Chicago Press, 1999.

Margret M. Baltes. *The Many Faces of Dependency in Old Age.* Cambridge, England: Cambridge University Press, 1996.

Sam Beard. *Restoring Hope in America: The Social Security Solution.* San Francisco: Institute for Contemporary Studies, 1996.

Robert H. Binstock, Leighton E. Cluff, and Otto von Mering, eds. *The Future of Long-Term Care: Social and Policy Issues.* Baltimore: Johns Hopkins University Press, 1996.

Robert H. Binstock and Linda K. George, eds. *Handbook of Aging and the Social Sciences.* San Diego: Academic Press, 1996.

Jimmy Carter. *The Virtues of Aging.* New York: Ballantine, 1998.

Marshall N. Carter and William G. Shipman. *Promises to Keep: Saving Social Security's Dream.* Washington, DC: Regnery, 1996.

Martin Cetron and Owen Davies. *Cheating Death: The Promise and the Future Impact of Trying to Live Forever.* New York: St. Martin's Press, 1998.

William C. Cockerham. *This Aging Society.* Upper Saddle River, NJ: Prentice-Hall, 1997.

Peter A. Diamond, David C. Lindeman, and Howard Young, eds. *Social Security: What Role for the Future?* Washington, DC: National Academy of Social Insurance, 1996.

Ursula Adler Falk and Gerhard Falk. *Ageism, the Aged and Aging in America: On Being Old in an Alienated Society.* Springfield, IL: Charles C. Thomas, 1997.

Peter J. Ferrara and Michael Tanner. *A New Deal for Social Security.* Washington, DC: Cato Institute, 1998.

Arthur D. Fisk and Wendy A. Rogers, eds. *Handbook of Human Factors and the Older Adult.* San Diego: Academic Press, 1997.

Muriel R. Gillick. *Lifelines: Living Longer: Growing Frail, Taking Heart.* New York: W. W. Norton, 2000.

Margaret Morganroth Gullette. *Declining to Decline: Cultural Combat and the Politics of the Midlife.* Charlottesville: University Press of Virginia, 1997.

Charles B. Inlander and Michael A. Donio. *Medicare Made Easy.* Allentown, PA: People's Medical Society, 1999.

Donald H. Kausler and Barry C. Kausler. *The Graying of America: An Encyclopedia of Aging, Health, Mind, and Behavior.* Urbana: University of Illinois Press, 2001.

Eric R. Kingson and James H. Schulz, eds. *Social Security in the Twenty-First Century.* New York: Oxford University Press, 1997.

Thelma J. Lofquist. *Frail Elders and the Wounded Caregiver.* Portland, OR: Binford and Mort, 2001.

Joseph L. Matthews. *Social Security, Medicare, and Pensions.* Berkeley, CA: Nolo, 1999.

E. J. Myers. *Let's Get Rid of Social Security: How Americans Can Take Charge of Their Own Future.* Amherst, NY: Prometheus Books, 1996.

Evelyn M. O'Reilly. *Decoding the Cultural Stereotypes About Aging: New Perspectives on Aging Talk and Aging Issues.* New York: Garland, 1997.

S. Jay Olshansky and Bruce A. Carnes. *The Quest for Immortality: Science at the Frontiers of Aging.* New York: W. W. Norton, 2001.

Fred C. Pampel. *Aging, Social Inequality, and Public Policy.* Thousand Oaks, CA: Pine Forge Press, 1998.

Peter G. Peterson. *Gray Dawn: How the Coming Age Wave Will Transform America—And the World.* New York: Times Books, 1999.

Peter G. Peterson. *Will America Grow Up Before It Grows Old?: How the Coming Social Security Crisis Threatens You, Your Family, and Your Country.* New York: Random House, 1996.

John W. Rowe and Robert L. Kahn. *Successful Aging.* New York: Pantheon Books, 1998.

Sylvester J. Schieber and John B. Shoven. *The Real Deal: The History and Future of Social Security.* New Haven, CT: Yale University Press, 1999.

Ken Skala. *American Guidance for Seniors—And Their Caregivers.* Falls Church, VA: K. Skala, 1996.

Max J. Skidmore. *Social Security and Its Enemies: The Case for America's Most Efficient Insurance Program.* Boulder, CO: Westview Press, 1999.

Richard D. Thau and Jay S. Heflin, eds. *Generations Apart: Xers vs. Boomers vs. the Elderly.* Amherst, NY: Prometheus Books, 1997.

Dale Van Atta. *Trust Betrayed: Inside the AARP.* Washington, DC: Regnery, 1998.

James W. Walters, ed. *Choosing Who's to Live: Ethics and Aging.* Urbana: University of Illinois Press, 1996.

David A. Wise, ed. *Facing the Age Wave.* Stanford, CA: Hoover Institutional Press, Stanford University, 1997.

Periodicals

W. Andrew Achenbaum. "Perceptions of Aging in America," *National Forum,* Spring 1998. Available from the Honor Society of Phi Kappa Phi, Box 16000, Louisiana State University, Baton Rouge, LA 70893.

America. "Keep an Eye on the Third Age," May 16, 1998.

Robert Butler. "The Longevity Revolution," *UNESCO Courier,* January 1999.

Issues and Controversies on File. "Age Discrimination," May 21, 1999. Available from Facts on File News Services, 11 Penn Plaza, New York, NY 10001-2006.

Margot Jefferys. "A New Way of Seeing Old Age Is Needed," *World Health,* September/October 1996.

Ann Monroe. "Getting Rid of the Gray: Will Age Discrimination Be the Downfall of Downsizing?" *Mother Jones,* July/August 1996.

Bernadette Puijalon and Jacqueline Trincaz. "Sage or Spoilsport?" *UNESCO Courier,* January 1999.

Jody Robinson. "The Baby Boomers' Final Revolt," *Wall Street Journal,* July 31, 1998.

Dan Seligman. "The Case for Age Discrimination," *Forbes,* December 13, 1999.

Ruth Simon. "Too Damn Old," *Money,* July 1996.

John C. Weicher. "Life in a Gray America," *American Outlook,* Fall 1998. Available from 5395 Emerson Way, Indianapolis, IN 46226.

Ron Winslow. "The Age of Man," *Wall Street Journal,* October 18, 1999.

Research: Oldest Americans Happiest

LINDSEY TANNER

I t turns out the golden years really are golden.

Eye-opening new research finds the happiest Americans are the oldest, and older adults are more socially active than the stereotype of the lonely senior suggests. The two go hand-in-hand: Being social can help keep away the blues.

"The good news is that with age comes happiness," said study author Yang Yang, a University of Chicago sociologist. "Life gets better in one's perception as one ages."

A certain amount of distress in old age is inevitable, including aches and pains and the deaths of loved ones and friends. But older people generally have learned to be more content with what they have than younger adults, Yang said.

This is partly because older people have learned to lower their expectations and accept their achievements, said Duke University aging expert Linda George. An older person may realize "it's fine that I was a school-teacher and not a Nobel prize winner."

George, who was not involved in the new study, believes the research is important because people tend to think that "late life is far from the best stage of life, and they don't look forward to it."

Yang's findings are based on periodic face-to-face interviews with a nationally representative sample of Americans from 1972 to 2004. About 28,000 people ages 18 to 88 took part.

There were ups and downs in overall happiness levels during the study, generally corresponding with good and bad economic times. But at every stage, older Americans were the happiest.

While younger blacks and poor people tended to be less happy than whites and wealthier people, those differences faded as people aged.

In general, the odds of being happy increased 5 percent with every 10 years of age.

Overall, about 33 percent of Americans reported being very happy at age 88, versus about 24 percent of those age 18 to their early 20s. And throughout the study years, most Americans reported being very happy or pretty happy. Less than 20 percent said they were not too happy.

A separate University of Chicago study found that about 75 percent of people aged 57 to 85 engage in one or more social activities at least every week. Those include socializing with neighbors, attending religious services, volunteering or going to group meetings.

Those in their 80s were twice as likely as those in their 50s to do at least one of these activities.

Both studies appear in April's *American Sociological Review.*

"People's social circles do tend to shrink a little as they age—that is mainly where that stereotype comes from, but that image of the isolated elderly really falls apart when we broaden our definition of what social connection is," said study co-author Benjamin Cornwell, also a University of Chicago researcher.

The New Face of Health Care

PATRICIA BARRY

A s the Obama administration and Congress rev up for the Herculean task of reforming the health care system, one major goal is spelled out in a phrase the president and others often use: "to improve the quality of American health care while lowering its cost." The idea seems a contradiction. How do we get more for less? Doesn't "better" always cost more?

Not in health, it seems. The United States spends about $8,000 per person a year on health care—more than twice as much as Western countries that have universal health coverage and better medical results. The money spent "does not appear to buy us outstanding health," Paul Ginsburg, president of the nonprofit Center for Studying Health System Change, told the Senate last year. "By almost any measure, ranging from infant mortality to preventable deaths, the United States does not measure up well against other developed nations."

How to reverse that damning report has pre-occupied health policy brains for years. But increasingly eyes have turned to a few medical centers around the country as possible models for national reform. These centers—among them the Mayo Clinic, the Cleveland Clinic and the Geisinger Health System in rural Pennsylvania—have developed systems that change the way care is delivered and paid for.

What they have is a new way of doing business that rewards doctors and hospitals for taking better care of patients—instead of paying them for the number of patients they see and the individual services they use, as the widespread fee-for-service system does. Results suggest that improving quality may actually be the best way of reducing costs.

"That's the key, in my opinion, to getting the clinicians [onboard]," says Len Nichols, director of health policy at the New America Foundation, a Washington think tank. "If it's just about cost, there's no way they'll buy into it. But if it's also about improving patient care, then you can motivate them, because that's why they went to med school."

So how do these incentives work? To find out, the *AARP Bulletin* visited the award-winning, nonprofit Geisinger Health System, which has 750 physicians serving 2.6 million patients across 43 counties in Pennsylvania. Its flagship medical center—which began as a 70-bed hospital in 1915—dominates the small town of Danville in the Susquehanna River Valley.

Geisinger has developed several strategies to integrate its operations into a system that offers better care at lower cost: a coordinated approach to primary care; hospital surgery that comes with a warranty; electronic health records; and engaging patients in their own care. Obama's proposals for health care reform also advance these principles.

Best practices pay off "Some researchers believe that health care costs could be reduced by a stunning 30 percent—or about $700 billion a year—without harming quality if we moved as a nation toward the proven and successful practices adopted by the lower-cost areas and hospitals."

—President Obama, in his budget proposal for 2009

Coordinated Primary Care

A model known as the "patient-centered medical home" helps patients manage the complexities of their care in one setting, typically a family practice or clinic. "It's focused on putting patients and their families at the center of care, instead of doing what's convenient for the provider," says Janet Tomcavage, a registered nurse and vice president of medical operations in Geisinger's own insurance plan.

A team of doctors, nurses, technicians and a case manager who coordinates all care constantly monitors patients' needs, especially those with chronic conditions like heart failure, diabetes and lung disease. The team also helps patients navigate transitions into and out of the hospital or nursing home and puts them in contact with community social services.

The system has features unheard of in regular primary care. High-risk patients, for example, can call their case manager's cellphone anytime. Those with incipient heart failure are given scales that electronically transmit their daily weight directly from home to the clinic. If there's a spike indicating retention of fluid, the team is alerted and can take quick action to prevent a hospital emergency. "We're seeing a 12 to 13 percent reduction in heart failure admissions," Tomcavage says, not all due to the scales, but they help.

At a Geisinger medical home in Bloomsburg, one team is headed by a doctor, Karl Luxardo, and Maureen Conner, a registered nurse who's the case manager. Both say the system introduces "another layer of care" that allows them to help patients avoid medical complications—by rigorous monitoring and training them to better manage their own conditions.

"Maureen is another set of eyes and ears for me," Luxardo says. "She's making phone calls and spending the extra time on patients' questions and concerns that I might not have been able to address during the visit or that the patient may have forgotten to ask."

Conner says getting patients involved in their own care is a cornerstone of the medical home concept. "It's a big process," she says. "You have to gain their trust and get a relationship going."

Joaquin Mathew of Millville, a 71-year-old former paratrooper, has lupus, rheumatoid arthritis and heart problems. He calls Conner "my guardian angel" and "my lifeline." He looks after himself carefully, "but as soon as I sense anything is wrong, I call Maureen." It's that availability between scheduled appointments, Mathew says, that he appreciates most. "I try not to bother them with insignificant items, but it's good to know they're there," he says. "The connection's always maintained." He adds, "I get the feeling I'm special."

But why does this system, which requires major investment, save money? One reason is that Geisinger has changed the financial incentives for primary care doctors who work for its insurance plan. They get back half of any savings they've achieved in their medical home practices—through, for example, fewer hospital admissions and unnecessary tests—as compared with conventional practices. But they get the money only if they've also met a checklist of quality measures for preventive care, chronic disease management and so on, says Ronald Paulus, M.D., Geisinger's chief technology and innovation officer. "If they've saved $100,000, and have achieved 100 percent of the quality goals, they'd earn $50,000. If they've achieved 25 percent, they'd earn one-fourth of that amount [$12,500]."

So, Paulus says, the primary care practice is rewarded for efficiency but without sacrificing quality. "We didn't want the doctors and nurses to skimp on care to save in the short run but not have the patient do the best in the long run."

The other half of the savings goes to the Geisinger health plan to pay for extra services offered in medical homes. The incentives have paid off, Paulus says. In a region where patients are older, poorer and sicker than the national average, "the health plan earned 2.5 times its investment back in the very first year."

Surgery with a Warranty

Nationally, Medicare patients who are admitted to the hospital have an 18 percent chance of returning within 30 days. Typically, the surgeon does another operation and sends in a second bill, which the insurer or Medicare pays without question (except in the case of some preventable medical errors).

"You'd never do that with your car," says Alfred S. Casale, M.D., director of cardiothoracic surgery at Geisinger. "If you brought your car in, told them to rebuild the transmission and a week later the reverse gear was slipping, you'd demand they fix it because you paid them good money to fix it the first time."

In 2006 Geisinger embarked on a bold gamble to improve the situation. Starting with elective coronary bypass surgery, Casale and others drew up a 40-point checklist of best surgical practices developed by the American College of Cardiology and the American Heart Association. Each point on the list has to be checked off before a procedure begins, or it's canceled. Then Geisinger offered insurers what is in effect a warranty: Pay a flat price for each operation, and any further treatment arising from complications that put the patient back in the hospital within 90 days is free.

This system has so far succeeded in lowering the readmission rate by 44 percent and raised net hospital revenue by 7.8 percent.

Electronic Health Records

A vast room filled with black consoles humming away is the hub of Geisinger's electronic record system in Danville. Paulus says it allows "every one of our 750 doctors, whether they're spread across 20,000 square miles or right down the hall from one another, to use the same health record with all the information about a patient available at the click of a mouse."

Many patients are sold on it, too. About 119,000 have so far signed up to access their own records through personal por-monitor their own progress, schedule appointments and e-mail their doctors—and can do so from anywhere.

Hariteeny Fritz, 79, a retired banker from Bloomsburg, recalls the time she was in Bar Harbor, Maine, and developed double vision. Taken to a clinic there, she told the staff to use her password so they could access her entire medical record online. "There was this kind of disbelief," she says. "But it saved them a good deal of time."

Patients don't see everything in their records that the doctor does. "One of the things we don't share is physician's notes," e-health manager Jodi Norman says. Lab test results are posted quickly, but must be released by the doctor first. Sensitive results, such as HIV tests or just bad news, are withheld so that the doctor can discuss them in person with the patient.

Patient Involvement

"Where costs can really come down is in more engaged patients doing more preventive care for themselves," says Paulus. But lifestyle changes—like losing weight—are a tall order for many.

Yet with help from the medical home staff, patients can learn the value of their own efforts—quite often with the subtle prod of seeing a cool graphic in their e-health record showing their progress.

In another innovation, patients facing hip and knee replacement surgery are offered a two-hour class in which the whole team—surgeon, anesthetist, pharmacist, physical therapist and social worker—demonstrate what's in store and how they can improve the outcome.

Registered nurse Linda McGrail, who organizes the classes, says patients who take them are often ready to leave the hospital earlier and are less likely to be readmitted. That's because individually tailored plans for coping after patients leave the hospital, and the exercises they've begun even before surgery, make them "more confident and better able to bounce back."

Reprinted from *AARP Bulletin*, April 2009, by Patricia Berry. Copyright © 2009 by American Association for Retired Persons (AARP). Reprinted by permission.

Lost and Found

Promising therapy for Alzheimer's draws out the person inside the patient.

BARBARA BASLER

The woman wore a plain housedress and a big apron, its pockets stuffed with plastic checkers. Head down, eyes blank, she shuffled aimlessly around the activity room. Cameron Camp, a research psychologist who was visiting this assisted living home in Kentucky, watched the 70-year-old woman for a moment. Then, he recalls, "I went up to her and gave her one of our books—the one on Gene Kelly, the dancer—and asked her to please read a page."

He pauses, remembering the woman and the skeptical staff—and the very next moment.

"She took the book and read aloud—clear as a bell," Camp says with a smile. "A shocked staffer turned to me and said, 'I didn't even know she could speak. That's a miracle.'"

Camp heads the Myers Research Institute in Beachwood, Ohio, and his cutting-edge work with patients in all stages of Alzheimer's has left him improbably upbeat—because he sees miracles like this day after day.

His research is part of a sea of change in the care of Alzheimer's patients who are in the later stages of the disease: "Ten to 15 years ago these people were institutionalized, and their care involved physical or chemical restraints," says Kathleen O'Brien, vice president of program and community services for the Chicago-based Alzheimer's Association, which, with the National Institutes of Health, has helped fund Camp's work.

> **Psychologist Cameron Camp says patients live in the moment. "Our job is to give them as many good moments as we can."**

"Today," she says, "more than 70 percent of those with Alzheimer's are cared for in the family home, and we talk about controlling the disease and enhancing daily life for those who have it."

Alzheimer's, the most common form of dementia in people over the age of 65, affects 4.5 million Americans. An irreversible brain disorder, the disease robs people of their memory and eventually impairs most of their mental and physical functions.

While research typically focuses on preventing Alzheimer's or delaying its progress in the early stages, some medical specialists and long-term care professionals are investigating activities that will help patients in the later stages.

"We can't stop cell death from Alzheimer's," Camp explains. "But at any stage of dementia there is a range of capability. If you give people a reason to get out of bed, activities that engage them and allow them to feel successful, they will be at the top of their game, whatever it is."

Camp, 53, began his research 10 years ago when he looked at the activities developed for young children by the educator Maria Montessori, whose "method" is followed today in Montessori schools around the world. There, children learn by manipulating everyday objects like balls, seashells and measuring spoons in highly structured activities that engage children but rarely allow them to fail.

Camp adapted these kinds of exercises for older people with dementia, tailoring them to the individual's background and interests, and found he could draw out the person inside the patient.

"Suddenly, they just wake up, come alive for the moment," he says.

That happened to Mary Anne Duffy's husband when they took part in Camp's research. James Duffy, 77, has Parkinson's disease and dementia and is confined to a wheelchair in a nursing home in Mentor, Ohio.

"James loved woodworking," Duffy says, "and he liked fixing things, so the researcher brought him a small box to paint, nuts and bolts to put together, puzzles." Before her husband began the activities, she says, he "just sat there, nodding off."

But when he was working a puzzle or painting a box, "James actually smiled—something I hadn't seen for a long time," Duffy says. "And he would talk. That was amazing."

People with Alzheimer's "live in the moment, and our job is to give them as many good moments as we can," Camp says. "We need to be thinking about these people in a new way. Instead of focusing on their problems and deficits, we need to ask what strengths and abilities remain."

People had assumed, for instance, that the woman with the checkers in her apron pockets was too impaired to read. But studies have found that reading is one of the very last skills to fade away. "It's automatic, almost a reflex," Camp says.

"If the print is right," he says as he flips through one of his specially designed books with big, bold letters, many Alzheimer's patients can read.

One goal of Camp's work has been to turn his research into practical how-to guides for professional and family caregivers. Published by the Myers Research Institute, the guides have been translated into Chinese, Japanese and Spanish.

While long-term care residences may have some activities for dementia patients—like coloring in a picture or listening to a story—often they don't have activities "that are meaningful, that call on an adult's past," Camp says. "And even people with Alzheimer's are bored if an activity isn't challenging or interesting."

Much of Camp's research is with residents at Menorah Park Center for Senior Living in Beachwood, which is affiliated with Myers Research. After Alzheimer's patients were given the large-print books that he and his colleagues developed, many could read aloud and discuss the books.

A brief biography of Leonardo da Vinci, for instance, talks about some of his wildly imaginative inventions, like a machine that would let soldiers breathe underwater so they could march underneath enemy ships, drill holes in their hulls and sink them.

"It's a wonderful, wacky idea," Camp says. "Dementia patients react to it just as we do. They love it. They laugh, they shake their heads. They talk about it."

Education Director Lisa P. Gwyther of the Bryan Alzheimer's Disease Research Center at Duke University Medical Center recalls visiting a facility where she saw Alzheimer's patients themselves teaching some of the simple activities they had learned to preschool children. "I was so impressed with the dignity and the purpose and the fun that was observable between the older person and younger child," she says. Camp's work has been rigorously studied in a number of small pilot projects, she adds, "which means this is a reliable, valid method."

At Menorah Park, Camp and his team look at what basic skills remain in those with dementia: Can the person read, sort, categorize, manipulate objects? Then they customize activities for those skills.

"We had one man who loved baseball," Camp says. "We had him sort pictures of baseball players into American and National leagues. Another man who loved opera sorted titles into operas by Puccini and operas by Verdi."

The activities help patients maintain the motor skills needed to feed themselves or button buttons. They also trigger memories, then conversations that connect the patient and the caregiver.

People with dementia won't consciously remember the activity from one session to the next. But, Camp says, "some part of them does remember, and eventually they will get bored. So you can't have them match the same pictures each time."

It doesn't matter if patients make mistakes, Camp adds. "What's important is that they enjoy the process."

Mike Skrajner, a project manager for Myers Research who monitored an Alzheimer's reading group at Menorah Park, recalls one morning when the group was reading a biography of Gene Kelly and came to the part where Kelly tells his father he is quitting law school—to take ballet lessons. "They stopped right there and had a great conversation about how they would react to that news," he says. "It was a wonderful session, and at the end they all wound up singing 'Singin' in the Rain.'"

Manipulating everyday objects helps patients maintain skills for feeding themselves or brushing their teeth.

Camp's research shows that people who engage in such activities tend to exhibit fewer signs of agitation, depression and anxiety.

George Niederehe, acting chief of the geriatrics research branch of the National Institute of Mental Health, which is funding some of Camp's work, says a large study of patients in long-term care facilities is needed for definitive proof of the effectiveness of Camp's approach. But his method could be as helpful to caregivers as it is to people with Alzheimer's, he says, because it would improve "staff morale, knowing they can do something useful for these patients." And that, he adds, would enhance the overall environment for staff and residents alike.

One vital part of Camp's theory—like Montessori's—is that residents need activities that give them a social role, whether it's contributing at a book club or stirring lemonade for a party.

The Menorah Park staff worked with one patient, a former mailman, who loved folding pieces of paper stamped with "Have a Nice Day!" He stuffed the notes into envelopes and delivered them to other residents.

"What we try to do," Camp says, "is let the person you remember shine through the disease, even if it's only a few moments a day."

To Learn More

- To download samples of Cameron Camp's activities for dementia patients, go to www.aarp/bulletin/longterm.
- The caregiver's manual "A Different Visit" costs $39.95 plus shipping, and the special large-print books for Alzheimer's patients cost $5.95 each (or six copies for the price of five) plus shipping. To order, go to www.myersresearch.org, or write Myers Research Institute, 27100 Cedar Road, Beachwood, OH 44122.
- For general information, go to the Alzheimer's Association website at www.alz.org.

For nine simple habits you can adopt that may delay dementia, see the September-October issue of *AARP The Magazine*.

Chapter 9
Death and Dying

There are many "end of life" issues worth discussing and here we focus on attitudes toward death, ways of coping with death and dying and the different perspectives on how to approach this final stage of life. We start with the New Zealand perspectives and include a short discussion of the Kubler-Ross' stages. We end with an article on terminal care considerations in an attempt to present some ideas for discussion about this last, but important time of life.

Length of life

Since the time of early human history there has been a myth about a fountain of youth, where people go to find the elixir that will keep them alive forever. Life expectancy increasing, everywhere in the world (outside Africa), providing many new and different possibilities for living. The figures that give average years for longevity (length of lifespan) are based on averages, calculated from large samples of people. As you know, the figures include everyone, whether it is the infant that lives only a few days, the child who dies of an illness, the young person killed in a road crash, the adult who dies from a stroke at a young age or the older person who passes away peacefully of multiple organ failure. If the average number of years which a girl born in New Zealand in 2010 will live is over 82 years, that still means that perhaps a third of people will live longer than this, and also that a third of people will live a shorter time.

The extension of the human lifespan is one of the greatest changes affecting contemporary life around the globe. As we saw in the last chapter, the numbers of people aged over 80 is the fastest growing age group in this country. Contrary to some dire predictions, we do not see this as heralding an era of hospitalisation and illness. Rather than years being added to the end of life, it seems to us that years have been added into the middle—perhaps into the end of the middle.

Tutorial suggestions

1. Talk informally with someone who is aged over 70 about their recollections of their own parents and grandparents. Make some notes.
2. In small groups, discuss your findings and see if they support the authors' suggestion that the 'young old' seem to live in ways that reflect much younger lives than people the same age two generations ago.

Thinking about death

Few healthy people in our society spend time in daily contemplation of their own death, but in some of the world's greatest belief systems, such as Islam, Christianity and Buddhism, the inevitability of death is thought to give meaning to life. Beliefs and advice, about the progression from this world to the next, or from this form of life to the next, are a kind of developmental philosophy encompassed by these and other major belief systems. When they come into contact with death, many people also confront, perhaps in a small way, how death invites us to think about living well in every moment. The fact of death (particularly—but not only—our own) seems to require a special quality of consideration. And yet, in industrialised societies at least, death is often seen as something to be avoided at all costs. We put enormous amounts of medical skill into keeping people alive, sometimes even when they themselves would prefer to die.

Euro-Western attitudes towards death are, we believe, strongly influenced by what has been called the 'Project of Modernity' (Habermas, 1987). Modernity is a movement that began several centuries ago in Europe, when human beings began to believe that human endeavour, and especially scientific work, was the key to improving the human condition. Modernity is a period of human history characterised by hopefulness, a belief in the unlimited power of humans to improve the lot of the entire race (human development), the successful use of technology and scientific successes of many kinds. According to Habermas, the Project of Modernity contains the hope that humankind is moving always towards better times, times when there will be more equality, more democracy, a better distribution of the benefits of human development: that the overarching trend of history is onwards and upwards. The sixteenth and seventeenth centuries were a time when the influence of the Christian Church in Europe began to be replaced by new scientific ideas.

An important distinction that developed around this time—sometimes referred to as the 'Enlightenment'—was between the physical or material world and the spiritual and mental worlds. Science was thought to be more about the former, while religion was more about the latter.

Late in the nineteenth century, psychology defined itself as an experimental science by creating quantitative, measurable tests of mental phenomena such as memory. This turn towards science and rationality provided the background for the absence of 'spirituality' in many developmental theories today. One of the most stunning successes of modernity has been the lengthening of the lifespan. Much of the gain in years in the human lifespan are due to public health programs that have reduced the numbers of early deaths due to such things as poor sanitation and (in some places) inadequate nutrition. The current campaign to get New Zealanders to drive more carefully is another such campaign, though the figures for deaths on the road suggest that we need to target the driving of young people aged 15 to 24 more directly.

At the same time, **thanatology**, the scientific study of death, is attracting more interest from researchers. One of the reasons for this is that as medical science develops, questions are being raised about the nature and even the definition of death. Advances in medical practice and its related disciplines raise important ethical questions about how long to keep someone alive when they have little or no hope of recovery from serious trauma. There are questions, too, about whether people should be able to choose the time of their own death, or when death might be desirable for others who are unable to take responsibility for such a decision. In lifespan developmental terms, dying may present a special opportunity for reflection and review, leading to new understandings of our life and its importance to those around us. One of the tasks of human development must surely be to accept and reflect on the certainty of death.

Physiological considerations

What causes death? Major causes of death are, in order, cancer, heart disease, cerebro-vascular disease and diabetes. Most deaths occur in the older age groups. Among younger people aged 15 to 24 years, the major causes of death are unintended injury (such as motor vehicle accidents), suicide, and cancer (Ministry of Health, 2009a). Some theories of physiological ageing are not about ageing so much as about why our bodies don't live forever. We are well used to the notion that wear and tear will eventually account for loss of function. One theory about why the human body dies is that our bodies become debilitated through the 'wear and tear' of ageing. Another theory proposes that over time, the 'mistakes' made in cell reproduction (all cells occasionally reproduce incorrectly) eventually accumulate so that there are too many incorrect copies of cells. This last theory is the so-called 'error catastrophe' theory. These 'catastrophes' are thought to mount up so that the body cannot function, and the result is death.

People of any age who have a terminal illness may face a gradual deterioration in their body's ability to function; however, one does not have to have a particular illness to experience the onset of increasing physical frailty. Frailty is associated with general muscular weakness, exhaustion and an inability to maintain social roles, and is usually distinguished from any specific illness (see Chapter 11). This condition may be reversible through increasing the quality of nutrition and exercise. Those caring for older people who seem to be deteriorating in the absence of disease should check that their nutritional requirements are being met adequately. Ultimately though, in spite of the efforts of many wise people (and others) over many centuries, there is no 'elixir of youth'. We cannot avoid our own death.

The death of a young person

Death is not something that only occurs after a certain age, yet the death of someone who is not 'old' can be experienced as extremely shocking. The death of a child or young person may be seen as more devastating than that of an older person—most likely because there is no social expectation that a young person will die 'before their time'. For parents, losing a child is completely contrary to the 'normal' course of events. Similarly, children do not expect to lose a parent until they are grown, and couples do not expect to have to think about losing their partner until late in life. In 2006, Wendy Drewery's son Mark died of a brain tumour at the age of 28. She reflects on Mark's life in her contribution (case study) later in this chapter.

Bev Gatenby (1998) collected the stories of many families in New Zealand who have lost a child, teenager or young adult. These families must come to grips with losing someone who had their own special place in the family. They will no longer be able to be with their child day by day and see their child grow up. And yet, it is important to remind ourselves that any life, however short, has made a contribution to those left behind.

There tended to be a focus on the triumphant march of modern life which is supposed to get better and better (see Morss, 1996; we discuss modernism again shortly). Now, we hope there is more willingness to see that the lifespan looks different in different cultures, and in different parts of the world. As well, we think that the successes of science and technology, such as the motor car, mobile phone and the computer (not to mention nuclear energy) are mixed blessings. It is not clear to us that humankind will ever be able to control nature, for example. And while the study of the human lifespan can help in the consideration of optimal conditions for development, it is unlikely to force people to behave well.

Another issue that this march to the future obscures is that lives are meaningful no matter how long or short they may be. Not every child survives to adulthood, but that does not mean that life is wasted. As John Winslade (2004, p. 353) wrote: each child's life is worthwhile and important, an interlinked part of their family and community. For those who survive childhood, the idea of lifespan development holds out a kind of psychological hope which makes it attractive because it allows people to think they can still improve the quality of their life, even if they have 'grown up'. Many students have the experience of doing badly at school and assuming that they 'are no good at' a certain subject. Later, they may find that they do very well in tertiary study. These experiences challenge ideas, such as that one's skills and competencies are fixed from or in childhood, or given at birth. In fact, many capacities are nurtured, or not, by the complexities of the environment in which people find themselves. When conditions change, people may find out new 'facts' about themselves. That can make the journey of life an exciting one, as well as one with sometimes mind-boggling challenges and unforeseen outcomes.

Preparing for death

The experience of caring for someone who has a major illness is one that a growing number of people are becoming familiar with. This experience is giving rise to a growing interest in the preparation for death, both by the person who is dying, and those who love them. Since the 1960s, much of this interest has centred around the progression of grief proposed by Elisabeth Kübler-Ross (1969, 1981). From her work with dying people, Kübler-Ross observed five stages in coming to terms with dying (see Figure 12.2). It is now widely accepted that losses of various kinds, including bereavement, may follow a similar pattern.

1. **Denial:** rejection of the reality of impending death, refusal to talk about it.
2. **Anger:** rage at others who are not affected, at God, envy and jealousy of healthy people.
3. **Bargaining:** attempt to arrange a temporary reprieve in return for some concessions.
4. **Depression:** nothing has worked, and the problem is still there.
5. **Acceptance:** quiet acknowledgment, and giving up of the struggle.

FIGURE 12.2 **Kübler-Ross' five stages of dying**

The ability to anticipate a particular event in the life course is called **anticipatory socialisation** because we have the chance to think about such possibilities in our social lives ahead of time. If the person can anticipate the loss of a loved one ahead of time, there is a developmental suggestion that it may be easier to adjust to the event itself. Conversely, when sudden death occurs, or when a death is 'out of time', it can be experienced as particularly shocking.

There is also a new awareness among those who work with the dying and the grieving that these ideas about 'stages' (in terms of dealing with the loss of a loved one) can be too constraining.

The notion of coming to terms with loss appears to suggest that one should 'get over it'. Yet, some bereaved parents, for example, never want to forget their dead child (Gatenby, 1998). Such parents may have some difficulty in responding to questions about how many children they have, because it is a relatively common assumption that once you have 'dealt with' grief issues they cease to be an issue in your life. Saying that you have a child who has died can invoke suspicion that you 'haven't got over it yet'.

Lorraine Hedtke and John Winslade (2004) made another major contribution to our understanding of grief and loss, with their notion of 're-membering' conversations. They propose that relationships with loved ones do not necessarily end with their death, because their influence on our lives continues forever. Following the work of some other narrative therapists (e.g. Myerhoff, 1978, 1982, 1986; White, 1989), they suggest that the significant others in our lives can be thought of as members of the 'club of (our) life', and that the club of each person's life has a changing membership over their lifetime and beyond. Hedtke and Winslade suggest that:

> ... the idea that a relationship ends and that the bereaved need to cease to recognise a dead loved one as a member of their club of life is a mistake. It assumes too great an identification of personhood with corporeal existence and of relationship with continuous physical presence. (Hedtke & Winslade, 2004, p. 8)

They argue that personhood continues on after a person dies and, similarly, our relationships with them can be deliberately continued by means of conversations whose task is to maintain their membership of our club of life—thus the term 're-membering' conversations. As Hedtke explains in her case study in this chapter, these conversations can begin even before the person dies, for example by talking with them about how they want to continue to be included in the lives of their loved ones, after they have died. This work raises some interesting questions about the notion of anticipatory grief, and even makes us reconsider the idea of loss.

THE PRACTICE OF RE-MEMBERING *LORRAINE HEDTKE*

The advent of 're-membering conversations' produces ways of speaking with people who are dying that invite forward stories of hope, strength, love and resilience, even in the face of great hardship and sometimes tragic circumstance. Unlike a modernist approach to death and grief that focuses on an individual's inner experience, re-membering highlights a relational approach which is a distinction from how death and grief has been thought of in recent times. Re-membering conversations act, in one regard, as a map for people who are dying and also for people who are living with grief, but the map is one of their own creation. Re-membering conversations can be contrasted with the 'correct' prescriptions for conversations with the dying which encourage stories of completion, leave taking and the saying of good-bye. The experience of grief may actually be worsened by formulaic practices—both for the dying and the bereaved.

Michael White (1989) introduced 're-membering' in his seminal article, 'Saying Hullo again: the incorporation of the lost relationship in the resolution of grief'. 'Saying hullo' embraced a new metaphor through which a person could be reintroduced in new ways following death, rather than being forgotten by those whom he or she loves. I routinely support conversations in which people can select which aspects of their life they wish to be kept alive and in which ways they would be interested in being posthumously authored.

In order to create re-membering conversations, I assume that relationships can live on past the physical death of a person. I consistently enquire of people who are dying how they want to be remembered as an entry point into this form of conversation. I might ask, 'What kind of things do you want people saying in the future about who you are and about the life you have lived?' Embedded in these questions is always a notion of the other; that is, who will be hearing these stories in the future and what does the dying person hope the story might offer their audience.

I will broach conversations, too, about how dying persons would continue to be part of their families' or friends' lives if they were not here physically. I am not suggesting that relationship is continued in the same manner as it once was, or to carry it forward in a way that necessitates certain spiritual beliefs. Rather, I am suggesting that relationship can continue to live on in storied form and the inception of this can be granted to the person who is dying. For example, we might ask a person who is facing death questions to build a legend for a future map that their loved ones will need to draw—a treasure map, if you will, that restores the connection to a place of resourcefulness. The legend might include the keys to where the deceased can be 'found' in storied form. One gentleman told me that if his loved ones wanted to find him after his death and to have a pleasant recollection of him, they only had to go as far as their garden which housed hundreds of plants he had carefully nurtured.

To build a good legend for a map, I might include questions about various actions that might be taken, rather than passively suffering the experience of grief. For example I might ask, 'What kind of activities would you suggest that your loved ones do if they were missing you?' 'What words would you offer them to help them handle challenges in their lives?' 'Are there rituals you would like to see continued in your family around birthdays or holidays?' The legend could be made more detailed still by asking the dying person to speak to the caliber of the connection. Questions could be asked such as, 'What would you hope others might say about what you have meant to them during your life?' 'What difference would it make to you now if you knew they were to remember these things about you?'

These kinds of questions offer the dying person a chance to know that they will continue to feature in the lives of those they love, even if they are not able to be there physically. I ask these questions so that they can build the legend in a way that gives them a say in the formation of ongoing stories and connections. This purpose lies at the heart of re-membering conversations. Imagine if you are dying how this might be comforting and hopeful—to know that your loved ones will continue to value you and think about you long after your death. The treasure ready to be found by those who succeed you lies in the legacy of stories that you carefully left for them to discover in your physical absence.

About the author: **Lorraine Hedtke,** *MSW, ACSW, LCSW specialises in working with people who are dying and with families after a loved one has died. She is employed by VITAS Innovative Hospice Care for the Inland Empire in California. She teaches nationally and internationally about death, dying and bereavement and narrative therapy. She is the author, along with John Winslade, of the book,* Re-membering Lives: Conversations with the dying and the bereaved *(Baywood Publishing, 2004). Her children's book,* My Grandmother is Always With Me, *is co-authored with her daughter, Addison.*

Ethical issues

Advances in medical technology are currently changing the approach of western societies to the ethics of death and dying. It is now possible, for example, to keep a woman who is 'brain dead' alive while the foetus she is carrying grows to maturity. It is also possible to keep a baby born with severe disabilities (perhaps as a result of being born too early) alive, and bring it to a point where the baby can go home, even when the predicted quality of life (and, perhaps, that of its parents) may be relatively low. For doctors and nurses, whose professional lives are devoted to keeping patients alive, the death of a patient can feel like failure. These ethical dilemmas are increasingly common. At the other end of the lifespan, the growing incidence of forms of dementia, especially in the over-85 age group, is causing many older people to think about how they would prefer to end their life.

Euthanasia is the deliberate shortening of a life, in order to end suffering or allow people who are ill to die with dignity. Voluntary euthanasia refers to the idea that the person chooses this course of action. The right to die with dignity, at a time and using a method of one's own choice (sometimes also called 'assisted suicide') is a contested topic, and is likely to become more so as the population continues to age. Dr Jack Kevorkian, nicknamed 'Doctor Death', was tried in the USA and served 8 years in prison for his part in helping a terminally ill patient die. A New Zealand woman, Lesley Martin, was found guilty of attempted murder while caring for her dying mother. She served time in prison for helping her mother to die (Martin, 2002, 2006). In the Netherlands, voluntary euthanasia and physician-assisted suicide have been legal since April 2002, but tolerated for a lot longer. In Australia, there have been several (so far unsuccessful) attempts to establish new laws that would allow assisted suicide to take place.

Another perspective, on the same theme, is the idea that older people have a 'duty to die'. As medical technology advances, people can be kept alive long after they would have died in earlier times (Kissell, 2000). One of the concerns here is whether older people have a right to be kept alive at an increasing cost and a diminishing quality of life. Clearly the traditional Euro-Western ethic concerning the sanctity of all human life, irrespective of its nature or its quality, is breaking down (Singer, 1994). We are likely to see a lot more debate on these issues in the next few years.

Dying well

Most older people remain in their own homes until within weeks or days of their death. There is a general trend towards both public and professional awareness of the need to preserve the dignity of the dying—to infuse their last days with peace and compassion (Sogyal Rinpoche, 1992). Nevertheless, these ideas about dying can sometimes be undermined by intrusive medical intervention. 'Advances' in the technological capacity to keep people alive mean it is becoming crucial that each of us thinks ahead to a time when others may have to decide for us, whether to resuscitate us after a stroke, or to keep us on life support, for example. Living wills are documents that allow you to set out your wishes about your final days.

An Enduring Power of Attorney (EPA) over your money and property is a legal authority that is given by you to someone who will look after your affairs if you lose your capacity to make decisions and communicate. It is also wise to make out an EPA over your personal care and welfare, appointing someone who you trust to make difficult decisions for you, when you are still alive but unable to act on your own behalf. We anticipate that the current Baby Boomers will be aware of their own health condition and will make sensible provision for themselves as they age. It is helpful (to you, in the event, and to others who care for you) if you discuss your wishes—regarding your care if you become incapacitated, and your funeral—with someone you trust, well before the end of your life is imminent. The EPA is a legal document that can help set out these plans.

The hospice movement is dedicated to ensuring that terminally ill people die in comfort, offering both physical and emotional support for the dying and their families. Here the aim is not so much to prolong life as to die well. Provisions for hospice care vary around the country, with some respite day care in centralised hostels. However, the main focus is on providing expert help in palliative (rather than curative) care, thus enabling the dying to remain in comfort at home. Comfort for the dying should include the opportunity to say goodbye to loved ones. It also could include the opportunity to use one's death as a point of transition. Facing death is a time when the conflicts and problems of one's individual life can not only be left behind but transcended, when the significance of the life now ending can be appreciated in all its raw complexity. It is at such times that one realises that the manner in which we live our everyday lives truly matters. While it is sad to think of dying ourselves, or that we might lose loved ones, the very reality of death speaks to us of living, and alerts us, above all, to the importance of living well, now, while we have the chance.

Navigating Practical Dilemmas in Terminal Care

Helen Sorenson, MA, RRT, FAARC

Introduction

It has been stated that one-fourth of a person's life is spent growing up and three-fourths growing old. The aging process is universal, progressive, irreversible and eventually decremental.[1] Cellular death is one marker of aging. When cells are not replaced or replicated at a rate constant enough to maintain tissue or organ function, the eventual result is death of the organism.

Although not an unexpected endpoint for any human being, death unfortunately is often fraught with turmoil and dilemmas. Patients, family, friends, caregivers and health care professionals often get caught up in conflicting opinions regarding how terminal care should be approached. For the patient, the result often is suboptimal symptom management, an increased likelihood of being subjected to painful and often futile therapy and the unnecessary prolonging of death. For the family and friends of the patient, the psychosocial consequences can be devastating. Conflict at the bedside of a dying loved one can result in long-lasting and sometimes permanent rifts in family relationships.

There are some complicated issues surrounding terminal care, such as fear, lack of trust, lack of understanding, lack of communication, and stubbornness on the part of both the physicians and family members. There are moral, ethical, economic, cultural and religious issues that must be considered. Some of the dilemmas in terminal care come up more frequently than others. This paper will discuss some of the more commonly encountered ones. And possible interventions and/or alternate ways of coming to concordance regarding end-of-life care will be presented for consideration by the reader.

Fear/Death Anxiety

A degree of fear is the natural response of most individuals to the unknown. Despite many attempts at conceptualization and rationalization, preparing for death involves coming to terms with a condition unknown in past or present experience. Fear of death has been referred to in the literature as death anxiety. Research indicates that younger people have a higher level of death anxiety than older people.[2] The reasons are not difficult to understand. Younger adults in our society are often shielded from death. Many young adults may not have had close contact with individuals dying from a terminal or chronic disease. When younger people confront death, it is most likely that of a grandparent, a parent, a sibling or a friend. Death is commonly from an acute cause. Grief is intense, with many unanswered questions and psychological ramifications.

Older adults have had more experience with death, from having lost a spouse, colleagues, a friend or relatives over the years. They undoubtedly will have experienced grief and worked through loss at some time in their life. Older adults may be more apt to express the fear of dying alone.

When facing a terminal diagnosis and impending death older adults are more likely to be concerned with "mending fences" and seeking forgiveness for perceived wrongdoing. There is a need on the part of many adults to put their affairs in order and resolve any outstanding financial matters. Some interesting research on death anxiety and religiosity conducted by Thorson & Powell[3] revealed that persons higher in religiosity were lower in death anxiety.

How can the potential dilemma caused by fear be circumscribed? Possibly allowing patients to discuss the issue may ease death anxiety, but patients may be advised not to talk about funeral arrangements, since "they're not going to die." While well intended, the statement may not be helpful. Instead of preventing the patient from discussing "depressing thoughts," encouraging frank discussions about end-of-life issues may ease death anxiety. Asking the patient to verbalize his or her fears may lead to understanding the fears and alleviate the anxiety they cause.

It is important to guard against treating dying patients as though they are no longer human. For example, asking if a person would like to talk to a minister, priest or rabbi does not impinge the religious belief of the patient—it simply allows another avenue to reduce death anxiety.

Issues of Trust

Patients who have been under the care of a personal physician for an extended period of time generally exhibit a high level of trust in the diagnosis, even when the diagnosis is that of a terminal disease. Good end-of-life care requires a measure of continuity among caregivers. The patient who has had the same physician from the onset of a serious illness to the terminal stages of the disease has a substantial advantage.[4]

Planning, family support and social services, coordinated to meet the patient's needs, can be more easily arranged if there is an atmosphere of trust and confidence.

Health care today however, has become increasingly fragmented. A physician unknown to the family and/or patient may be assigned to a case. It is difficult for very sick patients to develop new relationships and establish trust with an on-going stream of care providers.[5] When circumstances are of an immediate and critical nature, issues of trust become paramount. Lack of trust in the physician and/or the health care system can erode into a lack of confidence in a diagnosis, which